EYES ON THE PRIZE, the fourteen-part television series and related educational materials, was created and produced by Blackside, Inc., 486 Shawmut Avenue, Boston, Massachusetts 02118.

This book is one of several publications produced in conjunction with the television series, which is available for rental by institutions from PBS Video (1-800-344-3337). For information on other publications, see pages 727–728.

For information on the college telecourse, of which this book is the text, contact PBS Adult Learning Service, 1320 Braddock Place, Alexandria, Virginia 22314 (1-800-ALS-ALS8).

This book is a revision of, and replaces, *Eyes on the Prize: America's Civil Rights Years, A Reader and Guide* (general editors: Clayborne Carson, David J. Garrow, Vincent Harding, and Darlene Clark Hine), published by Penguin Books in 1987.

Special thanks to the Charles H. Revson Foundation for its support of this book and the *Eyes on the Prize* telecourse.

THE EYES ON THE PRIZE

CIVIL RIGHTS READER

DOCUMENTS, SPEECHES, AND
FIRSTHAND ACCOUNTS FROM
THE BLACK FREEDOM STRUGGLE,
1954–1990

General Editors

Clayborne Carson
David J. Garrow
Gerald Gill
Vincent Harding
Darlene Clark Hine

PENGUIN BOOKS

PENGUIN BOOKS
Published by the Penguin Group
Penguin Books USA Inc.,
375 Hudson Street, New York, New York 10014, U.S.A.
Penguin Books Ltd, 27 Wrights Lane,
London W8 5TZ, England
Penguin Books Australia Ltd, Ringwood,
Victoria, Australia
Penguin Books Canada Ltd, 10 Alcorn Avenue,
Toronto, Ontario, Canada M4V 3B2
Penguin Books (N.Z.) Ltd, 182–190 Wairau Road,
Auckland 10, New Zealand

Penguin Books Ltd, Registered Offices:
Harmondsworth, Middlesex, England

First published in simultaneous hardcover and paperback editions by
Viking Penguin, a division of Penguin Books USA Inc., 1991

15 17 19 20 18 16

An earlier, different edition of this anthology was published as *Eyes on the Prize:
A Reader and Guide* by Penguin Books. Copyright © Blackside, Inc., 1987.

Acknowledgments for permission to reprint copyrighted material appear on
pages 729–741.

LIBRARY OF CONGRESS CATALOGING IN PUBLICATION DATA
The Eyes on the prize civil rights reader/ general editors,
Clayborne Carson . . . [et al.].
p. cm.
Includes bibliographical references and index.
ISBN 0 14 01.5403 5
1. Afro-Americans—Civil rights. 2. United States—Race
relations. 3. Civil rights movements—United States—History—20th
century. I. Carson, Clayborne, 1944– . II. Eyes on the prize.
E185.615.E95 1991
973′.0496073—dc20 91–9507

Printed in the United States of America

Set in Baskerville
DESIGNED BY MARY WIRTH

The only chain that a man can stand
Is the chain of hand in hand.
Keep your eyes on the prize,
Hold on, hold on.

We're gonna board that old Greyhound,
Carrying love from town to town.
Keep your eyes on the prize,
Hold on, hold on

The only thing we did wrong,
Stayed in the wilderness a day too long.
Keep your eyes on the prize,
Hold on, hold on.

But the one thing we did right
Was the day we started to fight.
Keep your eyes on the prize,
Hold on, hold on.

From the traditional freedom song
"KEEP YOUR EYES ON THE PRIZE"

CONTENTS

PROLOGUE
**WE THE PEOPLE: THE LONG JOURNEY TOWARD A MORE
PERFECT UNION**   1
by Vincent Harding

CHAPTER ONE
AWAKENINGS (1954–1956)   35
Introduction by Vincent Harding
Articles on the Emmett Till Case   37
"Coming of Age in Mississippi," by Anne Moody   41
A Letter from the Women's Political Council to the Mayor of   44
    Montgomery, Alabama
Interview with Rosa Parks   45
"The Movement Gathers Momentum," by Martin Luther King,   47
    Jr.
Speech by Martin Luther King, Jr., at Holt Street Baptist   48
    Church
"At Holt Street Baptist Church," by Joe Azbell   51
Resolution of the Citizens' Mass Meeting, December 5, 1955   54
"The Violence of Desperate Men," by Martin Luther King, Jr.   56
"Desegregation at Last," by Martin Luther King, Jr.   57

CHAPTER TWO

FIGHTING BACK (1957–1962)   **61**
Introduction by Darlene Clark Hine
Brown et al. v. *Board of Education of Topeka et al.*   64
"How Children Learn About Race," by Kenneth B. Clark   74
"The Atlanta Declaration," by the National Association for the   82
    Advancement of Colored People
"Black Monday: Segregation or Amalgamation . . . America   83
    Has Its Choice," by Tom P. Brady
Brown v. *Board of Education*—The Implementation Decision   95
"The Long Shadow of Little Rock," by Daisy Bates   97
A Roundtable Discussion   103

CHAPTER THREE

AIN'T SCARED OF YOUR JAILS (1960–1961)   **107**
Introduction by Clayborne Carson
"Is Violence Necessary to Combat Injustice? For the Positive: 110
    Williams Says 'We Must Fight Back,' " by Robert F.
    Williams
"The Social Organization of Non-Violence," by Martin Luther   112
    King, Jr.
Interview with Franklin McCain   114
"An Appeal for Human Rights"   117
"Student Nonviolent Coordinating Committee Statement of   119
    Purpose"
"Bigger than a Hamburger," by Ella J. Baker   120
"A Conference on the Sit-Ins," by Ted Dienstfrey   122
"In Pursuit of Freedom," by William Mahoney   124
Interview with Robert Zellner   127
"Eve of Nonviolent Revolution?," by James M. Lawson, Jr.   130

CHAPTER FOUR

NO EASY WALK (1961–1963)   **133**
Introduction by David J. Garrow
Organizing in Albany, Georgia, by Charles Sherrod   138
Letter from the Albany Movement to the Albany City   140
    Commission, January 23, 1962
Interview with Bernice Reagon   143
Letter from Albany Merchant Leonard Gilberg to Albany   146
    Police Chief Laurie Pritchett, July 23, 1962

"Birmingham: People in Motion," by the Alabama Christian   147
   Movement for Human Rights
Wiretap Transcript of Phone Conversation Between Martin   151
   Luther King, Jr., and Coretta Scott King, April 15, 1963
"Letter from Birmingham City Jail," by Martin Luther King,   153
   Jr.
The Birmingham Truce Agreement, May 10, 1963   159
President John F. Kennedy's Nationally Televised Speech,   160
   June 11, 1963
Original Text of Speech to Be Delivered at the Lincoln   163
   Memorial, by John Lewis

CHAPTER FIVE

MISSISSIPPI: IS THIS AMERICA? (1962–1964)   **166**
Introduction by Clayborne Carson
"Mississippi: 1961–1962," by Robert Moses   170
"To Praise Our Bridges," by Fannie Lou Hamer   176
"Interim Report of the United States Commission on Civil   179
   Rights, April 16, 1963"
"Freedom Summer," by Sally Belfrage   180
"Mississippi at Atlantic City," by Charles M. Sherrod   186
Student Nonviolent Coordinating Committee Brief Report on   190
   Guinea, by James Forman
"The Trip," by John Lewis and Donald Harris   195
"To Mississippi Youth," by Malcolm X   200
"From Protest to Politics: The Future of the Civil Rights   201
   Movement," by Bayard Rustin

CHAPTER SIX

BRIDGE TO FREEDOM (1965)   **204**
Introduction by David J. Garrow
"Early Attempts at Betterment," by Amelia Platts Boynton   208
"Selma, Alabama," by Bernard Lafayette   209
"A Letter from a Selma, Alabama, Jail," by Martin Luther   211
   King, Jr.
"Midnight Plane to Alabama: Journey of Conscience," by   213
   George B. Leonard
SNCC–SCLC Relations, by James Forman   217
Personal Letter from Muriel and Art Lewis to Her Mother,   221
   Selma, Alabama, March 19, 1965
"Our God Is Marching On!" by Martin Luther King, Jr.   224

INTERLUDE
WE THE PEOPLE: THE STRUGGLE CONTINUES   **228**
by Vincent Harding

CHAPTER SEVEN
THE TIME HAS COME (1964–1966)   **244**
Introduction by Clayborne Carson
"Message to the Grass Roots," by Malcolm X   248
"Malcolm," by Sonia Sanchez   261
"Black Belt Election: New Day A'Coming," by Stokely   262
    Carmichael and Charles V. Hamilton
Lowndes County Freedom Organization Pamphlet   269
"How the Black Panther Party Was Organized," by John   273
    Hulett
"From Black Consciousness to Black Power," by Cleveland   279
    Sellers with Robert Terrell
"What We Want," by Stokely Carmichael   282
"Black Power: A Voice Within," by Ruth Turner Perot   286

CHAPTER EIGHT
TWO SOCIETIES (1965–1968)   **288**
Introduction by Darlene Clark Hine
"A Proposal by the Southern Christian Leadership Conference   291
    for the Development of a Nonviolent Action Movement
    for the Greater Chicago Area"
Demands Placed on the Door of Chicago City Hall by Martin   300
    Luther King, Jr., July 10, 1966
"Agreement of the Subcommittee to the Conference on Fair   303
    Housing Convened by the Chicago Conference on
    Religion and Race"
Interview with Linda Bryant Hall   310
"Profiles of Disorder . . . Detroit"   316
"A Man's Life," by Roger Wilkins   323

CHAPTER NINE
POWER! (1966–1968)   **333**
Introduction by Gerald Gill
"Taking Over," by Carl B. Stokes   338
Interview with Thompson J. "Mike" Gaines   341
Interview with Geraldine Williams   343

"The Founding of the Black Panther Party" and "Patrolling,"   345
     by Huey P. Newton
"Seize the Time," by Bobby Seale   348
Interview with Dolores Torres   361
"A JHS 271 Teacher Tell It Like He Sees It," by Charles S.   362
     Isaacs
Interview with Karriema Jordan   376
"Anti-Semitism?—A Statement by the Teachers of Ocean Hill-   377
     Brownsville to the People of New York"

CHAPTER TEN
THE PROMISED LAND (1967–1968)   **383**
Introduction by David J. Garrow
"A Time to Break Silence," by Martin Luther King, Jr.   387
"Conversation with Martin Luther King"   393
"I See the Promised Land," by Martin Luther King, Jr.   409
"My Last Letter to Martin," by Ralph David Abernathy   419
"On the Case in Resurrection City," by Charlayne A. Hunter   426

CHAPTER ELEVEN
AIN'T GONNA SHUFFLE NO MORE (1964–1972)   **439**
Introduction by Gerald Gill
". . . 'I'm the Greatest,' a poem by Cassius Clay"   443
"The Greatest," by Muhammad Ali with Richard Durham   444
"Muhammad Ali—The Measure of a Man," from *Freedomways*   458
Interview with Paula Giddings   460
An Open Letter Sent to Howard President James M. Nabrit   462
Interview with Tony Gittens   465
"The Nature and Needs of the Black University," by Gerald   470
     McWorter
"It's Nation Time," by Amiri Baraka   480
"We Must Pave the Way: An Independent Black Political   482
     Thrust," by Richard Hatcher
"National Black Political Agenda. The Gary Declaration: Black   493
     Politics at the Crossroads"

CHAPTER TWELVE
A NATION OF LAW? (1968–1971)   **500**
Introduction by Gerald Gill
"Fred Speaks"   504
Interview with Akua Njere (Deborah Johnson)   509
"Search and Destroy: A Report by the Commission of Inquiry   517
    into the Black Panthers and the Police," Roy Wilkins and
    Ramsey Clark, Chairmen
"The FBI's Efforts to Disrupt and Neutralize the Black Panther   529
    Party"
"Angela Davis: An Autobiography"   539
Letter from George Jackson   548
Attica Prisoners' Demands   557
"Negotiations and Failure," by Herman Badillo and Milton   560
    Haynes
"The Brothers of Attica," by Richard X. Clark   586

CHAPTER THIRTEEN
THE KEYS TO THE KINGDOM (1974–1980)   **591**
Introduction by Gerald Gill
Statement to the Boston School Committee, June 11, 1963   596
"Death at an Early Age," by Jonathan Kozol   603
Tallulah Morgan et al. v. *James W. Hennigan* et al.   609
Commencement Address at Howard University   611
    by Lyndon B. Johnson
Inaugural Address by Mayor Maynard Jackson   614
"Can Atlanta Succeed Where America Has Failed? An   618
    Exclusive *Atlanta* Magazine Interview with Mayor Maynard
    Jackson as He Completes His First 500 Days in Office"
Amicus Curiae Brief in *Regents of University of California* v.   625
    Allan Bakke
Regents of University of California v. *Allan Bakke* (The Supreme   631
    Court Judgment), June 28, 1978
Regents of University of California v. *Allan Bakke* (Justice   634
    Marshall's Dissent), June 28, 1978
"Whites Say I Must Be on Easy Street," by Nell Irvin Painter   651

CHAPTER FOURTEEN
BACK TO THE MOVEMENT (1979–mid-1980s)   **656**
Introduction by Vincent Harding
"A Historic Look at Our Neighborhoods," by the Black   663
    Archives, History and Research Foundation of South
    Florida
"Death Watch," by Marvin Dunn   666
"Confronting Racial Isolation in Miami," by the U.S.   682
    Commission on Civil Rights
Interview with Edward Gardner   687
Harold Washington's Announcement of Candidacy for the   691
    Democratic Nomination for Mayor of Chicago
"Harold Washington: Uniting Chicago for *All* People"   694
Harold Washington's Inaugural Speech   698
"Of Harold Washington," by Gwendolyn Brooks   702
"Address by the Reverend Jesse Jackson," Democratic National 705
    Convention, San Francisco, July 17, 1984
Interview with Unita Blackwell   710
"Platform Presentation by Mayor Henry G. Cisneros,"   711
    Democratic National Convention, San Francisco, July 17,
    1984
Address to the National College and University Student   712
    Conference, Shen Tong
Address by Nelson Mandela   718

ABOUT THE GENERAL EDITORS   723

The Eyes on the Prize Civil Rights Reader   725
    PUBLISHING PROJECT STAFF
Eyes on the Prize: THE FILM AND PUBLISHING PROJECT   727

NOTES ON SOURCES   729

INDEX   743

THE
EYES
ON THE
PRIZE

WE THE PEOPLE: THE LONG JOURNEY TOWARD A MORE PERFECT UNION

By Vincent Harding

Constitution of the United States

PREAMBLE

We the people of the United States, in order to form a more perfect union, establish justice, insure domestic tranquility, provide for the common defense, promote the general welfare, and secure the blessings of liberty to ourselves and our posterity, do ordain and establish this Constitution for the United States of America.

T*he images strike us, sometimes touching home at levels deeper than we dare acknowledge. Images: Men and women, many of them still alive in our own time, there on the screen, standing firm, unarmed, facing gun-wielding, menacing police and state troopers, standing their ground, refusing to give in to fears, discovering powerful weapons, old and new, at the center of their lives. Men and women, possessed by new power, determined to be counted as full citizens of this nation, committed to transform this grand and needy country, in search of "a more perfect union."*

Images: Women, men, and children, standing, sometimes being smashed down to the ground, paying the price for wanting justice, for believing in a more perfect union. Broken bones, bleeding heads, but spirits undaunted, returning from beds and hospitals and jails to stand and struggle again— for justice, for freedom, for the right to vote, for equal access, for a "domestic tranquility" that we have not yet experienced, for a new society for us all.

Images: Young people, often children, full of life and play and seriousness. Marching, facing dogs and fire hoses, singing freedom songs on the way to jail, rocking the paddy wagons with "Ain't afraid of your jail, 'cause I want my freedom now." Young people, walking the gauntlets of hate, ignorance, and fear, listening to the less-than-human shrieks, just to go to school—really to redefine "the general welfare," to educate America and the world to the meaning of "the blessings of liberty." Teenagers, children, not purposelessly wandering through the fantasy worlds of consumer malls, but sitting in jails, singing in jails, determined to create a land of justice, committed to move with new dignity and hope in their lives.

Images: Black and white women and men, braving the storms of violence and hatred together, marching with King and Fannie Lou Hamer together, taking on the hard, explosive rock of Mississippi together, murdered and hidden underground together, rising as great inspirations and new hope together. Black and white, discovering their common ancestry, their common pain, and their common hope. Unashamed to cry together. Swaying, singing together: "We shall overcome." Singing, "We'll never turn back/Until we've all been freed . . ." Living, arguing, sharing together, "to secure the blessings of liberty to ourselves and our posterity . . ."

Who are these people? Where did they come from, especially these black people, who seemed—at least for a time—to offer direction, purpose, and hope to an entire generation of Americans of every racial, social, and religious background? What did they mean then when they spoke of "redeeming the soul of America"? What do they mean now? For us, for African-American us, for Hispanic-American us, for Asian-American us, for Euro-American us, for the Natives of this land? What do they mean for our personal, collective, and national prospects, for our "posterity"?

The images and questions insinuate themselves into our beings and raise fundamental issues about our nation's past and future. They present us with many surprises, not only about the historical similarities between our land and South Africa, but more importantly they surprise us about humans, ordinary humans like us, whose names we have never learned, whose faces are both familiar and unknown. Ordinary human beings at times acting with extraordinary courage, vision, and hope (at other times stumbling and falling into all the internal and external traps we know so well). Who are they? How are we related to them . . . we the people?

It is often this way: Women and men who look carefully, persistently into the face of history are often rewarded with breathtaking surprises—and a host of questions. Of course, in our own time, after the furnaces of Auschwitz and Hiroshima, after the gulags and the "disappeared," in the midst of South Africa abroad and the human-created epidemics of joblessness, homelessness, and drug addiction at home, some things—unfortunately—do not surprise us. We no longer consider it noteworthy to be confronted with our stunning human capacities for harsh, ruthless, and inhuman oppression. But considerable evidence shows us that we are yet capable of being amazed by unexpected revelations of the great, still largely untapped human potential for resistance and hope, for compassion and grandeur, for courage and visionary self-transcendence—even when pressed against all the walls that oppression has created.

In the annals of our own young nation, no greater repository of such unexpected testimonies to the re-creative powers of the human spirit exists than the history of the black struggle for freedom, equality, and social transformation. In the public television series *Eyes on the Prize—America's Civil Rights Years,* we are drawn into just one generation's experience of that struggle, especially as it developed after World War II. But no human history is rootless, and we see the fullest meaning of the post-1945 events only as we dig deeper.

Such probing work could take us back to the coast of Africa, to the earliest liberation struggles there and on the prison slave ships, and could open up the long, unbroken history of black resistance to slavery and the concomitant movement toward freedom in this country. Digging deep, we might explore the period of great hope and profound betrayal after the Civil War, examining the unpredictable ways in which a people who had been largely defined as humanly inferior, ignorant chattel slaves, came bursting out of the furnaces of the Civil War, bearing the traditions of resistance and hope, to create their own powerful and impressive postwar testimonies to the meaning of freedom, democracy, and justice in America.

Indeed, if we looked closely we would discover that the commitment of these former slaves to the transformation of their own lives and the life of the nation was often so great that it could not be borne by the majority of white America. For this majority was not prepared for fundamental changes toward justice, especially if the changes involved redistribution of landed wealth in the South and the abandonment of white supremacy everywhere, in exchange for a truly shared community, a more perfect union. So we would also need to see the ways in which the postwar black communities and the relatively small band of white allies who offered themselves as full participants in the political, economic, and social/spiritual process to re-create the nation, were effectively, often brutally, driven back from the footholds they had begun to gain. We would see this especially in the political institutions of the postwar South, the region that was home to more than 90 percent of Black Americans.

To probe that deeply would bring us to a history of antiblack repression that had possessed the entire South (and too many northern outposts) by the end of the 1870s. We would witness lynchings, ritual burnings, and mutilations, the rise of the Ku Klux Klan (KKK) and other paramilitary organizations, all implicitly or explicitly approved by much southern white leadership, with increasing acquiescence from the northern keepers of power. To dig so deep would reveal to us harsh economic intimidation in the development of a kind of peonage, often called sharecropping. It would recount through much of the 1870s and 1880s the misuses of political, legal, and social systems in a ruthless attempt to deny, subvert, and destroy the power of blackness that had briefly appeared in the land during Reconstruction. In other words, we would see the ways in which a nation—led by southern white elites, and often in cooperation with the federal government—sought to create an ersatz "domestic tranquility," by repressing the voices, subverting the power, and destroying the lives of those black people who insisted they were part of "we the people," who dared dream of a just society. For this African-American minority the "manifest destiny" of the United States was something much richer and deeper than "winning the West," destroying the Natives of the land, and acquiring material wealth anywhere, and by any means necessary.

Then in 1895, Frederick Douglass died. The great black symbol of the movement from slavery to freedom had not been very active for several years, but he represented something powerful. He bore within himself a history of protest and challenge, a tradition of black determination to claim all the rights and responsibilities of a renewed American citizenship. So it seemed like an even greater loss when, in the same year, the nation's attention was called to Booker T. Washington, head of Tuskegee Institute. Coming to national prominence after more than a dozen years of building an important black educational institution in the heart of Alabama's dangerous white supremacy, Washington's voice carried a different message which seemed to discourage bold, direct, open challenges to white power on behalf of the beleaguered black communities.

It was a hard time, and for many black persons, it seemed as if all the broken promises of Reconstruction were finally, ironically epitomized in the actions of the Supreme Court of the United States. Ever since the 1870s, the Court had been eviscerating the congressional legislation and constitutional amendments which had been established at the height of Reconstruction to protect some of the basic citizenship rights of black people. In 1883, reversing the intentions of the Reconstruction congresses, it had claimed that the Reconstruction-bred Civil Rights Acts did not guarantee black people the same unhampered access to public accommodations that was due to all citizens. Finally, in 1896, the court brought to a climax its trashing of the hopes of Reconstruction, and essentially gave its blessing to a status of second-class citizenship for African-Americans. The infamous *Plessy* v. *Ferguson* decision ruled that state laws mandating separate facilities for black citizens did not violate the equal protection clause of the Fourteenth Amendment to the Constitution, if the separated facilities were "substantially equal."

With that action, separate-but-equal became both the law of the land and the symbol of the fundamental schizophrenia at the heart of American democracy. But there was more: From that moment on the decision also became the target of a steadily rising, unrelenting black-led attack against the fundamental injustice of the court's action, against its betrayal of the most humane understandings of "we the people of the United States." So *Plessy* v.

Ferguson became a stimulus to struggle and defiance, a signal to resistance. It was not surprising, then, that in the same year that the words of the Supreme Court were hurled against black (and white) freedom, it was possible to hear the voices of resistance.

During the 1890s, Nashville, Tennessee (source of much leadership for the continuing freedom movement) was the base of John Hope, a professor at the city's Roger Williams University. Speaking in 1896 to a gathering of black people, immersing himself in the tradition of Douglass, preparing the way for the coming times, Hope urged his audience to resist all temptations to acquiesce and despair. He said,

> Rise, Brothers! Come let us possess this land. Never say "Let well enough alone." Cease to console yourself with adages that numb the moral sense. Be discontented. Be dissatisfied. . . . Be restless as the tempestuous billows on the boundless sea. Let your dissatisfaction break mountain-high against the walls of prejudice and swamp it to the very foundation. Then we shall not have to plead for justice nor on bended knee crave mercy; for we shall be men. Then and not until then will liberty in its highest sense be the boast of our Republic.

This was a response to oppression, but it was more. Just thirty years after the official end of slavery, here was the articulation of a free people's fierce determination "to possess this land" that had enslaved them, to claim a land they had worked so hard to create. It was an amazing statement of faith in the best possibilities of our republic, and therefore an expression of profound belief in their own capacities—and those of their fellow citizens—to create a more perfect union.

Such a complex, powerful, and explosive cluster of human intentions was at the heart of almost all the struggles for justice, survival, defense, and transformation which were carried on by black people as one century ended and another began. This claiming of the land, this determination to speak the black-envisioned truth and create a new American reality—all these are part of the roots of the struggle that became impossible to hold back.

All these were present in a crusader like Ida B. Wells-Barnett, who was born into the last years of slavery in Mississippi and became another of the living bridges between the black freedom struggles of the nineteenth and twentieth centuries. By the time she was in her late twenties, the articulate and courageous Wells-Barnett had been teacher, newspaper publisher, unrelenting public scourge of injustice, fugitive from southern mob action, and preeminent international lecturer and organizer in the antilynching campaigns of the turning centuries. She spoke and acted in defense of black rights and life, but she always knew that her campaign was for the future of democracy in the United States. That is why, in one of her major speeches (which included a report on her exile from Memphis, Tennessee, because of her bold newspaper attacks on white mob rule) she could say to the nation:

> In one section, at least of our common country, a government of the people, by the people, and for the people means a government by the mob; where the land of the free and the home of the brave means a land of lawlessness, murder, and outrage and where liberty of speech means the license of might to destroy the business and drive from home those who exercise this privilege contrary to the will of the mob.

Although she was describing her own situation and the fate of other outspoken black heralds, the nature of Wells's language made it clear that she was also reaching beyond the personal. For her, as for many others, this truth-telling tradition, this protest against injustice, this unrelenting demand for the maturing of American democracy was a part of the larger commitment to possess the land. For them, a necessary part of that process was the action of forcing white America to recognize the degradation of democracy that accompanied all attempts to throttle the voices of black discontent. So the children of the slaves became the major carriers of the dream of freedom, the quintessential visionaries of a more perfect union.

But there was always a tension in the heart of black America, a tension that continues yet, one expressed with typical eloquence by the man who was already becoming the nation's preeminent Afro-American scholar-activist, W. E. B. Du Bois. For Du Bois, as the nineteenth century ended, black people could not possess this land unless at the same moment they claimed, nurtured, and possessed their own souls, their African-American heritage, their history, their culture. Du Bois, child of the diaspora by birth and by choice, born in the North, educated at Fisk and Harvard, as well as in Berlin, felt this tension at the center of his being.

Later he would speak of it as an "eternal twoness," this life of blackness and of Americanness. But in 1897 he described it less as a tension than as a calling, and he proclaimed, "For the development of Negro genius, of Negro literature and art, of Negro spirit, only Negroes bound and welded together, Negroes inspired by one vast ideal, can work out in its fullness the great message we have for humanity." This audacious young intellectual said he saw black people as "the advanced guard of Negro people" of the world. So he urged his people to see their calling and to recognize that "if they are to take their just place in the vanguard of Pan-Negroism, then their destiny is not absorption by the white Americans . . . not a servile imitation of Anglo-Saxon culture, but a stalwart originality which shall unswervingly serve Negro ideals."

For Du Bois, the vision was worldwide. While he agreed on the need for Afro-Americans to lay full claim to the U.S.A., he cautioned against being possessed by America and its worst values. Du Bois was setting forth a large, messianic, freedom-fighting, freedom-shaping task for Afro-Americans. So his statement put the community of former slaves in its fullest light, declaring that they "must be inspired with the Divine faith of our black mothers, that out of the blood and dust of battle will march a victorious host, a mighty nation, a peculiar people, to speak to the nations of the earth a Divine truth that shall make them free."

(As his language constantly indicated, while Du Bois conscientiously avoided any commitment to conventional religious creeds, he was—like most of his contemporary black colleagues—steeped in the language, literature, and imagery of the Bible. The Afro-American freedom movement cannot be fully apprehended without that context.)

One of the most fascinating elements of the post-Reconstruction black movement toward new freedom and extended equality was the continuing work of creating independent and semi-independent black institutions. Without them the black community would have been lost. In addition to the central institution of the family, they included schools at every level, churches and other religious institutions, newspapers and other journals, fraternal and sororal organizations, mutual aid societies, women's clubs, banks, insurance companies, unions, farmers' alliances, and emancipation societies.

These were only a portion of the internal, self-claiming, self-defining work that was constantly re-creating the black community. Sometimes the institutions were a necessary response to the legal and extralegal exclusion of black people from most white-dominated American institutions. Just as often, they were expressions of the Du Boisian search "for the development of Negro genius." Often they were both. For many wise men and women clearly understood the paradoxical necessity of developing institutions which would be the grounds for creating and training generations of younger people who would eventually venture out to let their "discontent break mountain-high against the walls of prejudice and swamp it to the very foundation."

At the turn of the century, black people who were committed to challenging the fundamental injustice of the nation's institutions knew that they must always deal with yet another paradox. In a country almost 90 percent white, in a society permeated by conscious and unconscious white supremacist beliefs and social Darwinist assumptions, black people needed dedicated white allies in the struggle for justice. Hope, Wells-Barnett, and Du Bois knew this, as did black miners, farmers, forest workers, and many others. As a result, the struggle for, with, and against white allies was then, as it has always been since then, a crucial element in the black freedom movement.

By the beginning of the twentieth century, those battles were carried on in many an arena, among them the Republican party, labor unions, farmers' alliances, populist movements, Christian churches, the world of white philanthropy, and temperance and women's suffrage movements. Almost without exception, the critical issues—sometimes issues of life and death—centered on the willingness of white people to treat black women and men as allies and equals, rather than as wards, pawns, or tools; the willingness of whites occasionally to accept direction and leadership from black people; the readiness of white allies to stand as firmly for the advancement of black-centered concerns as they were asking blacks to stand for other issues; and the determination of whites to pay the psychological, economic, and political costs of black-white solidarity in the midst of an American white supremacy that often turned murderous in its methods. Perhaps all of this was really the willingness of black and white justice-seekers to recognize their own need to become new people in order to create a new society.

To create a new society, a more perfect union. How new? How much more perfect? Afro-Americans, whether in their own organizations and institutions or banding together with allies, were never monolithic or dogmatic in response to such questions. The largest agreement among them was that the newness must minimally mean the breaking down of all the nation's legal barriers to full black participation in the life of the society. No truly perfect union could even begin to come into being without that—a reality many "progressive" white reformers never recognized.

But then there were the details: Did a new society mean that black farmers or miners should band together with those of their white counterparts who wanted more than a larger income, who envisioned a new social, economic, and political order as the only sound foundation for a society which would accord justice to all its workers? Did it mean creating more truly democratic alternatives to both the Republican and Democratic parties, especially in the light of their different but similar betrayals of black hopes? Did the search for a new society mean that black fathers and sons would no longer have to kill the regularly and variously identified enemies of the American government in order to prove themselves worthy of being men, in order to merit recognition as citizens of a more perfect union? What of those black people who uncritically accepted the nation's destruction of the Natives of the land, or entered into the spirit of manifest destiny as it suppressed the revolutions of colored peoples in Cuba and the Philippines? Would they have to take seriously the words of a black socialist who said, "The American Negro cannot become the ally of imperialism without enslaving his own race"? And one of the hardest questions of all, which occasionally surfaced in black debates: Did the creation of a new society require the loss of racial distinctiveness, the disbanding of racially identified institutions, the erosion and deracination of a people's cultural base?

For many persons, of course, these were premature questions. Simply surviving in the midst of a hostile majority was a major focus. For these people, freedom is represented by a name that became almost legendary for a time in part of the black community: Robert Charles. This was the man Ida B. Wells-Barnett called in 1900 "the hero of New Orleans."

Robert Charles was one of those people to improvise their lives while pressed against the wall, compelled to define in time of personal crisis what will be necessary for the possession of one's soul. Quiet, intense, in his twenties, a worker at odd jobs, a native of Mississippi, Charles was an agent of an emigration society, a reader of the materials of Bishop Henry McNeal Turner, the brilliant, caustic promoter of African emigration in the black communities of America. Charles apparently did some writing of his own. He also had collected a small arsenal.

Then on a night in July 1900, he is sitting quietly on a front stoop, talking with a male friend. It is near midnight when the almost mythic, tragic encounter begins. Three white policemen appear. The arrogance of race and power is in the air, concretized in the drawn, menacing pistols, the flailing billy clubs, and the unprovoked announcement of arrest. Charles draws a pistol, shoots one of the officers, and runs, wounded, from the scene. But he refuses to keep running. He reaches his cache of arms, chooses at least one rifle, and moving from one hiding place to another, kills at least five policemen and wounds a dozen more from the scores who are on his trail. A mob of more than a thousand white men offer their welcome assistance to the police force, periodically, randomly pouring their fury and their ammunition into the black community. Finally Charles is burned out, cut down in a hail of bullets, and badly mutilated in death.

But that was not the end. Wells-Barnett almost immediately investigated the incident, and at the end of her report she said, "The white people of this country may charge that he was a desperado, but to the people of his own race Robert Charles will always be regarded as 'the hero of New Orleans.' " This tradition of improvised, life-sacrificing courage, with or without the gun, goes deep into the history of the black struggle to establish justice, to assure domestic tranquility, to possess lives, to claim the land.

Finally, the emergence of the twentieth century freedom struggle is not set in proper perspective without remembering what Robert Charles was studying—black emigration. Afro-Americans everywhere, but especially in the South, were always conscious of that option, the possibility of return to Africa. They were stirred by the vision of possessing themselves through reclaiming the motherland, building a new society by returning to the old. Between the crushing of Reconstruction's best hopes and the beginning of the twentieth century, thousands of black people returned to Africa. It was so much of a movement and an obsession that it was often called "Africa fever." Indeed, it is likely that tens of thousands more might have tried to go if there had been ships to take them, and if land on which to settle had been available—if European countries had not divided up the African continent among themselves. But the option, at least the dream, was always alive in the heart of Black Americans, and in those post-Reconstruction years, thousands of persons were able to follow the dream of possession and renewal at least as far as Kansas and Oklahoma. Others, like their foreparents, the fugitive slaves, were satisfied to create new beginnings in the cities of the North and South.

Now we see. In the roiling, blood-red years of the closing and opening of the centuries, the deeper roots of the 1950s and 1960s were manifest. Many black people had determined that it was not enough for their slavery to be officially ended, and they refused to leave the future definitions of their freedom—and the shaping of this nation—in the hands of white Americans. Rather, by the close of the nineteenth century, it was clear that some of the most prescient black leaders and seers had declared that it was absolutely necessary for black people to take the initiative. Not only would they defend themselves against the onslaughts of those days, but they would move forward to extend the internal and external limits of their human freedom—and their participation in the re-creation of America—as far as was possible, whatever the costs might be.

Often, as the new century began, it seemed that the costs were more than men and women could bear. All the psychosocial anesthesia of white avoidance and denial, joined with a crippling array of legalized injustice at local, state, and national levels, backed by every cruel variety of physical force (represented by, but not limited to, the KKK) were brought to bear in the struggle against all serious black definitions of a more perfect union. Meanwhile, in almost every public forum, from the halls of Congress to the smallest white churches and newspapers, black people were subjected to a never-ending torrent of racial epithets and public insults attacking their intelligence, the authenticity of their humanity, and their capacities for moral development. But in the midst of all this, the amazingly resilient black thrust toward freedom and justice in America was never destroyed.

Of course, it is constantly necessary to remind ourselves that there were always some whites (and many black people) who understood that the deep issues of the freedom struggle had to do with more than rights for Afro-Americans. They realized that the integrity and future of American democracy were also at stake. In other words, the prize of freedom, justice, and equality for Africa's children in the United States was ultimately a gift for the entire nation. As a result, the central tasks of the twentieth century black freedom movement were defined at their best not only as the achievement of rights and justice, but also as transformation of the spirit, consciousness, and heart of a people who had been developed and nurtured on the poisons of white supremacist politics, social philosophy, theology, and history. As Martin Luther King, Jr., would one day put it, achieving the "prize" meant "redeeming the soul of America."

By the beginning of the twentieth century many of the essential characteristics of the life of the next period of freedom struggle had already been suggested. Perhaps if we were steeped in Chinese methodology we might summarize them as The Six Claims:

1. Claiming the right to the land, to full unhindered participation in the life of the nation and in the reshaping of that life
2. Claiming the right and responsibility to speak the truth from black perspectives and to insist that those truths become part of a new American reality

3. Claiming the right to possess themselves, their heritage, their Africanness, their souls
4. Claiming the necessity of building black institutions, as ends in themselves, and as bases for the creation of the women and men who would eventually join others to develop a more perfect union in America
5. Claiming the right of self-defense against the intrusive and arrogantly destructive forces of white power
6. Claiming the same right of principled emigration to Africa or elsewhere that brought the pilgrims and subsequent generations of immigrants to these shores

Now, as we move fully into the twentieth century and explore some of the more directly connected predecessors of the movements of the 1950s and 1960s, we can trace their root sources to the soil of Afro-American life and struggles. Among the many possible pre-1954 developments, perhaps a dozen briefly sketched, but deeply etched, images will suffice. They help prepare the way. They illuminate the transformations that took us from the time when constitutionally sanctioned segregation and widespread, life-threatening antiblack violence seemed ascendant in the nation to the years when the long, black-led movement toward justice and "a more perfect union" burst to the surface with unparalleled force and creative power.

In 1905 many of the lines of force which moved from the past toward the future were gathered in one place when W. E. B. Du Bois sent out a letter to sixty black middle-class professionals, declaring, "The time seems more than ripe for organized, determined, and aggressive action on the part of men who believe in Negro freedom and growth." Standing with Du Bois (not always comfortably) was William Monroe Trotter, the outspoken, anti–Booker T. Washington editor of the Boston *Guardian,* like Du Bois, a Harvard graduate. Their letter and organizing action led to the formation of the Niagara Movement, a black leadership group. Its first meeting, drawing twenty-nine participants, took place on the Canadian side of Niagara Falls because no unsegregated facilities existed for the meeting in the U.S.A. Niagara's essential focus (apart from its continuing critique of Washington's nonconfrontative leadership and his attempts at censorship and control) was probably best summed up in the words which appeared in the second annual declaration: "We will not be satisfied to take one jot or tittle less than our full manhood rights. . . . Until we get these rights we will never cease to protest and assail the ears of America."

The Niagara men were responding to the ever-expanding network of legal repression, especially the outpouring of state laws that denied more and more black people access to the vote. They were looking for ways to check the spread of antiblack riots, to call the nation to take a stand against the crime of lynching. They were rebelling against what they considered the dangerous, misleading attempts at sabotage and subversion by Washington. But the Niagara men (and their women's auxiliary, which was the style of the time) had very little money and were not equipped to raise the sums that would match their plans. They did not have the resources to maintain their ground against Washington's divisive and well-financed machinations or to spread their word of protest. In addition, they did not move far enough beyond middle-class protest positions to take on the issue of economic exploitation of the rural majority of the black population, nor did they know how to manage their internal divisions, especially Du Bois and Trotter. Within five years after its first meeting at Fort Erie, Niagara had essentially disbanded. But seeds had been sown, a model proposed. The possibility of a twentieth century black protest organization undominated by Booker T. Washington was established.

Meanwhile, the scourges of lynchings and antiblack riots continued. At that point in America's history, race riots essentially meant white mobs, on one pretense or another, surging through black communities, battering, burning, killing, raping, and looting, often unhindered by the official forces of the law until it was too late. Black people, hindered by the law (and perhaps by inclination) from organizing local, armed self-defense units, and lacking experience in the development of trained, unarmed corps of protectors, fought back as best they could. In 1908, the black community of Springfield, Illinois, was visited with such a burst of armed white hatred. It was Abraham Lincoln's hometown, and some members of the mob on their errands of death were heard to shout: "Lincoln freed you—well, we'll show you where you belong." Faced with this bestial denial of their own basic humanity, the small group of Niagara leaders publicly urged black people everywhere to prepare to defend themselves with guns against white mobs.

And yet they knew, as others knew, that defensive action alone was never sufficient. Thus Du Bois and some other members of the deteriorating Niagara organization were soon faced with a hard choice, one familiar to the black freedom movement. In 1909, a group of men and women based largely in the white abolitionist tradition was stirred by the Springfield terrorism to call a national "conference on the Negro." It was a white initiative, and the black demand for a larger role in the conference and then in the organization which was created out of it led to harsh debates and crushed feelings.

So when the National Association for the Advancement of Colored People (NAACP) came into existence in 1910 it was immediately heir to much of the ambivalent heritage of such black-white alliances. Du Bois was the only black person in a senior staff position when the new organization opened its offices in downtown Manhattan. Stalwarts, like Wells-Barnett and Trotter, believing that they had been shut out of any real power in the organization by a paternalistic, politically moderate-to-liberal white leadership, essentially went their own ways.

Over the next four decades, the conflicts and ambiguities regarding race and power would persist, often with Du Bois, founding editor of the NAACP's influential journal, *The Crisis*, at the center of the storm. He and others recognized the elements of a harsh dilemma: In an overwhelmingly white, often murderously supremacist society, it was critical to have relatively friendly white voices raised on behalf of black freedom. It was crucial to have white fund-raisers to gain the trust of white philanthropists. As the NAACP focused on its legal attacks against discrimination, segregation, and white terrorism, it was often necessary to have white allies who had access to the centers of power.

But these were the galling necessities, for black women and men never stopped asking themselves whether it was possible to possess the land if they could not possess themselves and take leadership in the struggle for justice in their own hands. Gradually, this bellwether organization came increasingly under black executive leadership, expanding its unique (but underutilized) membership structure ever more widely throughout the black communities of America, but with white men still in crucial roles on its governing board and in its fund-raising tasks. Meanwhile, the "N double A" developed crucial skills in the tasks of public truth-telling, lobbying for antidiscriminatory and antiterrorist legislation, and carrying on the continuing, judicially based assault on the legal structures of separate-but-equal.

Black leaders like Trotter and Wells-Barnett tried to handle the dilemmas represented by the NAACP in several personal and organizational ways. One was to form new, largely local and regional black organizations for social services and protest actions, centered on their own strong, courageous, but sometimes divisive personalities.

At the same time, other alternatives were constantly being developed out of the desperate creativity of the black community's pre–World War I existence. For instance, Timothy Drew, who had migrated from North Carolina to New Jersey in that period, emerged from his meditations and preaching in the back lots and tenement basements of Newark's black wards to declare his possession of a new name: Noble Drew Ali. Indeed, his vision of possession was for all black people, who he now declared to be Moors in America, a lost-found people whose ancestors, "descendants of the ancient Moabites," had come originally from the area of Morocco. He taught black people that the repossession of their true identity would provide new power for their lives, power eventually to overcome the worst afflictions of this doomed and evil white society.

But neither a relative handful of Moors, a courageous contingent of middle-class leaders, nor a fledgling white-dominated association for their "advancement" could affect the emerging black freedom movement of the twentieth century in the way that it was cataclysmically moved by the guns of August 1914 and the onset of "the great war."

Some black folk in the United States knew instinctively—as well as through serious study and discussion—that the war was more than a European conflagration. For Europe was much more than a small geographical appendage on the Asian land mass. Ever since the fifteenth century, its imperial tentacles had gradually reached all over the world of nonwhite peoples, and members of the major body of nonwhite peoples in the U.S.A. sensed that the war—whatever its other issues—was a struggle for international power, for a greater share of the goods of the colonized colored peoples of the globe. Thus the war heightened an international consciousness that had already evolved out of the nineteenth century, out of "Africa fever," perhaps out of deeply embedded, often unconscious, longings for "home." So when Hubert Harrison, the brilliant black socialist streetcorner lecturer, spoke of his vision of the war on the avenues of Harlem, the crowds cheered, for he was articulating their sense of reality when he said, "As representatives of one of the races constituting the colored majority of the world, we deplore the agony and bloodshed [of the war]; but we find consolation in the hope that when the white world shall have been washed clean by its baptism of blood, the white race will be less able to thrust the strong hand of its sovereign will down the throats of other races."

Based on that set of hopes and assumptions, the self-taught black intellectual declared that as a result of the war he looked for "a free India and an independent Egypt; for nationalities in Africa flying their own flags and dictating their own internal and foreign policies."

Though relatively few persons could know it at the time, this was a prophetic statement; for the "great war" did begin to shake the foundations of Europe's hold on the nonwhite world. But black people in America, even the most internationally conscious ones, soon saw other, more immediate issues rising out of the fields of war. As with all wars in which the nation became involved, this one served to heighten the already vivid consciousness of Afro-Americans concerning the tragic contradictions endemic to their own native, alien land. Indeed, nothing could have expressed the contradictions more sharply than the April 1917 speech in which a staunchly segregationist president, Woodrow Wilson, called upon a joint session of Congress to enter the war and was interrupted by a Mississippi legislator who led the thunderous applause when Wilson urged them to send American troops "to make the world safe for democracy."

Most African-American leaders and spokespersons acceded to the conventional wisdom: It was necessary to go, necessary to send sons, fathers, and husbands to fight overseas for "democracy" in segregated, humiliated military units in order to "prove" to white Americans their worthiness to possess the full rights of first-class citizenship. Of course, according to the conventional wisdom, it was also necessary to go to avoid jail.

Eventually, some four hundred thousand black men were drafted and served in the war, in spite of the sentiments of A. Philip Randolph, a young black socialist editor, who wrote that those black leaders who supported military participation should "volunteer to go to France, if they are so eager to make the world safe for democracy." As for Randolph and his radical colleagues, he said, "We would rather fight to make Georgia safe for the Negro."

Of course Randolph was essentially right, and every black and every honest white person knew it. And they rediscovered it at excruciatingly deep levels when the word came from East St. Louis, Illinois, less than three months after the declaration of the war for democracy, less than a week before the Fourth of July. They knew it when the screams arose and the fires burned, sending signals to the world that another white mob was on the rampage, burning, raping, destroying black women, infants, and old people, as well as armed and unarmed men who were determined to possess their souls. It was one of the most brutal pogroms the nation had known, just when the segregated black servicemen were training to go make the world safe.

The black troops in Houston, Texas, knew Randolph was right when in August 1917, perhaps with the stench and the screams of East St. Louis still filling their being, they made their choice. Goaded by continuous and cruel white civilian attacks and provocations, finding no support from their military superiors, they used their democracy-defending weapons to strike out against those who chose to be their tormentors rather than their fellow Americans. White civilians were killed in a nighttime engagement. The soldiers were imprisoned, secretly tried, and secretly executed. But when the word broke loose, they were applauded by their people as heroes of the long and costly war to make America safe for its black citizens, safe for democracy and justice, safe for its posterity of every color. These were the brothers of Robert Charles.

Of course, the "great war" brought more than consciousness,

contradictions, and home-front deaths to the struggle for black freedom. It also burst dams and opened up outpourings of human life so vast and roiling that they deeply affected every aspect of the nation's existence, especially its internal struggle to possess its own identity. Within the decade of 1910–1920 a half million black people flooded into the north, breaking like a great tide during the years of the war. For the chaos created by the European-based conflict, and the dangers presented by German submarines operating in the Atlantic Ocean, practically shut down the decades-long surge of European immigrants, just as America's burgeoning wartime industries were expanding in massive proportions. Workers were needed.

The war and the need for workers came at a time of economic depression in the South. It was affected by a disastrous boll weevil epidemic among the cotton crops, along with seasons of devastating floods. Combined with the traditional southern versions of the scourges of lynchings and riots, this concatenation of local, national, and international events unleashed a great black (and white) migration out of the South to the North, out of the rural areas to the cities. Black people began to emerge out of their southernness, their ruralness, their relative hiddenness. They appeared in urban centers all across the country. They showed up at factory gates, in hiring lines for the mines and mills. By their very presence they were placing unprecedented pressure on white America to face critical questions: Who are "we the people of the United States"? Whose country is this? Who are its jobs for? Who are its neighborhoods, its parks, its beaches for? Who are meant to be the creators and benefactors of its justice, its democracy, its future?

Large numbers of white people responded to the expanded black presence and to its insistent questions with fear and rage and great resistance. So the KKK leaped in its membership numbers, and black-white struggles over jobs, over living space, over recreation areas exploded in the North. Then in 1919, shortly after the long and bloody war to make the world safe for democracy had ended, warfare seemed to be erupting on the streets of the United States. In places as apparently disparate as Charleston, South Carolina; Washington, D.C.; Longview, Texas; and Chicago,

Illinois, white mobs attempted many of their familiar tactics of brutal, pogromlike attacks, often with the assistance of the police forces. But in that Red Summer, as it was called, there was more open, organized, armed black resistance than ever before, and the Afro-American veterans of the "great war" were usually in the forefront of the action. After the Red Summer of 1919 the murderous white civilian-led forays into black communities did not entirely cease, but they clearly became less and less a regular feature of American life.

Many black veterans of World War I were at the core of Marcus Garvey's Universal Negro Improvement Association (UNIA), the largest centralized organization ever created by African-Americans. Arriving here in 1916 from his native Jamaica and from travels throughout the Caribbean, Latin America, and England, Garvey stepped into the maelstrom of Afro-American history and attracted major public attention in 1919, the year the war came home.

Sensitive to the pulse of his people, unparalleled in his magnificent capacities to give words to their deepest-felt hurts and their great aspirations, Garvey stood firmly in a rich black tradition. Essentially it was the one that Du Bois (his archenemy) had articulated two decades before, a tradition that constantly called for "Negroes bound and welded together, Negroes inspired by one vast ideal [to] work out in its fullness the great message we have for humanity."

Making history, made by history, Garvey came to an aroused people already passing through the travail and transformation of the twentieth century. His great gifts of vision, expression, and organization caught the movement of what Du Bois had called "the advance guard of Negro People" and urged it forward. Garvey's familiar clarion call became, "UP, up you mighty race! You can accomplish what you will!" And for Garvey there seemed at first to be only one accomplishment worthy of a self-possessed black people, and that was the redemption of Africa from European control.

So in the midst of the struggle in America, Garvey focused the people on a task beyond America. In the heat of that Red Summer of 1919 he dared to announce before cheering black audiences:

> Every American Negro and every West Indian Negro must understand that there is but one fatherland for the Negro, and that is Africa . . . as the Irishman is struggling and fighting for the fatherland of Ireland, so must the new Negro of the world fight for the fatherland of Africa.

Then becoming—or at least it seemed so—much more specific, Garvey hurled out this challenge: "We say to the white man who now dominates Africa, that it is to his interest to clear out of Africa now, because we are coming . . . 400,000,000 strong; and we mean to retake every square inch of the 12,000,000 square miles of African territory that belong to us by right Divine."

In the tradition of self-possession, no one had ever spoken like Garvey. It was an intoxicating vision, this promise of bringing all the scattered and gathered children of Africa into one mighty force. (That was the meaning of Garvey's figure of 400,000,000.) It was not calling for the return of all black people to Africa, but for the focus of all black energies to be on the struggle to "redeem" Africa. Connected to the bold talk was a vibrant national and international organization, with new chapters developing in many parts of the country and throughout the African diaspora. Its initial focus was on black people possessing themselves, expressing themselves through a variety of commercial enterprises, self-help organizations, religious institutions, publications, including a major newspaper—eventually through the much-heralded, hope-filled Black Star Line, a deeply flawed experiment in developing a pan-African shipping enterprise.

But for those men and women who were committed to redefining the nature of "we the people of the United States," something was amiss—even for those who held great admiration for Garvey (and that was not a universal sentiment in the black freedom-seeking organizations). For Garvey had essentially agreed with white supremacists of this nation, had conceded this to be "a white man's country," and called upon black people to gear themselves toward the redemption of Africa. Only then, he said, could there be any hope of respect and justice here.

As is generally known, the central story did not end well. In spite of tremendous accomplishments, especially where the building of black morale was concerned, in spite of great organizational beginnings, Garvey's summons to African-Americans to possess themselves in order to possess Africa had no clear strategic future. And because he conceded this country to its white racist majority, there was no real future here, either.

In a sense, the dilemma was epitomized in his own life. As an alien who had not sought American citizenship, who did not choose to be part of "we the people of the United States," he was dangerously vulnerable to deportation actions. The U.S. government held the threat of deportation over Garvey's head. It infiltrated his organization. It connived with his enemies in the black community. It finally brought trumped-up charges against him. Then when it ganged up on him and closed off his channels to African contacts and harassed him into a prison sentence, Garvey seemed unprepared to mobilize his followers for any serious resistance. In 1925 he was sent to the federal prison in Atlanta, Georgia. Two years later he was deported to Jamaica.

Garveyism still lives in many forms and places, especially among black men and women who choose its orientation for the absolutely necessary possession of their souls, the affirmation of their Africanness. It lives on in a consciousness, sometimes more or less political, concerning the Afro-American connections to the still beleaguered homeland communities. Through Garvey it was possible to see the dangers inherent in a position where the tradition of profound black self-possession is not connected to a struggle to claim and possess the land that the Americans of African descent have helped to create and fertilize with their blood, spirit, and skills. On the other hand, in their experience with the Communist party in the United States, black people were able to apprehend some of the greatest strengths and weaknesses of black-white alliances in the struggle for justice.

At their best, the white members of the Communist movement in the U.S.A. were among the most courageous and committed of allies. Many risked their lives organizing with and for black people, often exposing themselves to the terrors of the Deep South by insisting on interracial organizing and living in Birmingham, in Atlanta, in the rural areas of Alabama, and in the small textile towns of North Carolina—in the 1930s! They offered new visions of hope to black men and women like Angelo Herndon, the young southern organizer who became a hero; Richard Wright, who discovered the party in Chicago after a harsh pilgrimage from Mississippi; and Louise Thompson, the well-educated, articulate Harlem social worker and organizer. With a great mixture of motivations the white-dominated party helped to save the lives of a group of southern black teenagers who were headed for a relatively quiet, legal lynching, when they put the Scottsboro Boys into the limelight of the world.

During the depression years the Communists seemed to be one of the few political forces who knew where they were going and were organized to do what they wanted to do. In those years they offered tremendous hope that the black struggle for freedom in the U.S.A. could become part of the forever imminent worldwide revolution of the working classes, and thousands of black people found great resonance with that vision. As a legal party in those days, it became the first significant American political party to nominate a black man—James W. Ford—for vice president.

But the ambiguities of black-white relationships were still present, intensified by a special problem peculiar to the Communist party. Not only did many party members still have hard battles to wage against their paternalism and racism, but they were a predominantly white party and their whiteness and their radicalism made it very difficult for them to have large organizing successes in a black community where the spirit of Marcus Garvey never died. Ultimately, though, what broke the heart of the alliance was the fact that the Communist party, with its black and white members and its ever-widening circle of influence, was not an independent force. It was far too submissive to the strong will of the international center of power in Moscow, a center that was ultimately devoted to the protection of "the mother country" of world communism at any cost.

By the late 1930s, those costs included Russia's selling essential material goods to Italy while it was engaged in its imperialistic war against Ethiopia, a nation considered "the mother country" of the African diaspora. Finally, when Hitler broke a fragile treaty with Stalin and attacked Russia, the word was given throughout the Communist International that all activities which internally challenged the allied, capitalist nations, including the U.S.A., needed to be curtailed. They were now allies of mother Russia in her desperate war against Hitler, and the black vision that demanded an incessant attempt to "swamp . . . the very foundations" of American racism and injustice was no longer convenient. So the black freedom movement was betrayed, as the party withdrew from the front lines of black challenges to America.

Another high hope was lost, another set of white allies found wanting. But women and men who had seen new visions of a world transformed by the actions of common people, who had caught a glimpse of the possibilities of a more perfect union in which poverty and exploitation would also be overcome, could never be quite the same again. Indeed, it was toward the end of this period of great expectations and soaring vision that Langston Hughes, who was closely allied with the Communist forces in the 1930s, wrote one of his most prophetic poems, "Let America Be America Again," closing it with a series of announcements, perhaps predictions:

O, yes,
I say it plain,
America never was America to me,
And yet I swear this oath—
America will be!
An ever-living seed,
Its dream
Lies deep in the heart of me.
We, the people, must redeem
Our land, the mines, the plants, the rivers,
The mountains and the endless plains—
All, all the stretch of these great green states—
And make America again.

Visions were needed in those days. For the realities of separate-but-equal (better known as Jim Crow) were harsh and often seemed immovable. Wherever black people traveled or lived in the South, and in too many parts of the North, they were faced with the humiliation of seeing doors that were open to white citizens legally closed to them: restaurant and motel doors, movie house doors, skilled employment doors, Marine Corps and Air Force doors, the large doors to public parks, pools, beaches, entire neighborhoods, the doors to public service were all closed. Or they would find two sets of doors, two kinds of facilities, from ticket lines to water fountains, from waiting rooms to public schools. One white, one colored, one reasonably clean, well cared for, well supplied, the other usually broken, neglected by the white authorities, shamefully unequal.

And often in the North, the trouble was that there were too many times when you couldn't tell which doors were which before being shocked by the cruel humiliation of rejection or bodily harm. Of course, it was especially cruel to have to explain these visible and invisible doors, signs and dangers, to young black children who tugged innocently at hands and hearts, eager to be taken in. Only men and women of vision were ready to break the barriers and open the way for the children.

Yes, in the 1930s visions were certainly needed, not only to break open the brutal circle of Jim Crow, but for more as well. The nation was in the grip of the most extended and grueling economic depression it had ever known, one that was being experienced in many parts of the industrialized world. As usual, black people were feeling it in an especially acute way; and, as usual, there were a variety of creative responses to the crisis, many of them based in the religious genius of African-Americans.

It was the time when Father Divine rose out of southern black obscurity to great prominence in the communities of black America. Here was a phenomenon to challenge every deeply held American belief. According to Father and his followers of the Peace Mission, here was God, manifesting himself among humans as a short, ebulient, balding black man. Here was his Kingdom, scattered in Peace Mission centers across the country, populated with black and white "angels" with new names (like Precious Faith, Heavenly Joy, and Patient Bliss), many of whom had contributed all of their earthly goods to the new Kingdom of Peace. Here was a divine being who provided ample feasts, adequate shelter, and a joyful community of singing and spiritual dancing—and celibacy—for all who wanted to share their lives. Here was a religious leader who forbade his followers to resort to violence and who taught them to refuse to take up arms against other humans and to work for justice in the land.

For those who did not choose the way of Father Divine, the dynamic young associate pastor of Harlem's massive Abyssinian Baptist Church provided another alternative. Adam Clayton Powell, Jr., worked with other organizations to struggle for jobs, for government services, for justice. Through effective organizing, he and his coworkers put picket lines on the streets, demanded that white-owned stores in Harlem hire black employees, and offered active, confrontative ways for women and men to carry on a daily struggle to challenge the authorities, to redefine justice, and to possess the land, or at least some part of it. Here again, leadership developed and honed by the black church was moving out of the pulpits into the streets on behalf of a just society. It was an old tradition, and even with the charismatic, academically trained Powell, its fullest moment had not yet arrived.

Meanwhile, in those depression years, other forms of black religion were also creating amazing new and old possibilities out of the caldron of suffering. In Detroit, the children of Noble Drew Ali and the children of Garvey were melding. Elijah Poole, who had been a part of the Garvey movement, had also known the forces of Ali. But in 1930 he met a man who appeared to be an itinerant peddler of clothes, but who announced, "My name is W. D. Fard, and I come from the Holy City of Mecca." Later there would be disagreement about whether Mr. Fard was a messenger of Allah or a human manifestation of the divine; however, there was no essential disagreement about what he taught and what it meant for black people. One testimony was that Fard taught that "the black men in North America are not Negroes, but members of the lost tribe of Shebazz, stolen by traders from the Holy city of Mecca 379 years ago. The prophet came to America to find and to bring life to his long-lost brethren, from whom the Caucasians had taken away their language, their nation, and their religion."

So the process of repossession involved regaining the religion of Islam, the Arabic language, and "their culture, which is astronomy and higher mathematics, especially calculus." Through strict dietary and moral laws, the lost and found black people were told they must "clean themselves up—both their bodies and their houses," to be prepared for their deliverance by Allah, who would return them to Mecca.

This, too, was black religion, providing a path for the repossession of a people. Eventually, when Mr. Fard mysteriously disappeared, Elijah Poole, whom Mr. Fard had renamed Elijah

Kerriem, became the Honorable Elijah Muhammad. Under his guidance the Temple people emerged, soon to be known as the Nation of Islam, the Black Muslims, carrying new names, new histories, new creation myths and cosmologies, attempting to create a new people to serve Allah in the wilderness of North America.

Ever since their first enchained contacts with the terrifying and beautiful land, the children of Africa in America had understood how crucial it was to possess—and repossess—their souls, to define and redefine their own identity, to create—and re-create—their own purpose and direction. So all through slavery and the postslavery decades they fought to protect, maintain, and reshape their basic institutions, especially the family, the centers of worship and spiritual renewal, and the schools. Whether faced toward redemption of Africa or committed to the humanizing transformation of the United States of America—or both—the people knew that they needed solid ground, protected space, to create the soul-full men, women, and children who would catch the vision and do the work, immediate work, generational work.

As the depression years produced their havoc and their many creative responses, nowhere did the potential creative power of black institutions become more evident than in the rather inelegant collection of buildings and often brilliant collection of men and women called Howard University in Washington, D.C. Established in the post–Civil War years by benevolent and often committed white and black educators, Howard had finally found its first black president, the Reverend Mordecai Johnson, in 1926. The dynamic, authoritarian leader breathed new life and fire into the federally funded institution, demanding and receiving more funds and respect than it had ever had before.

Howard's faculty included some of the best minds in America, among them Ralph Bunche, E. Franklin Frazier, Abram Harris, and John Hope. Kenneth Clark, the eminent psychologist who would play a central role in the *Brown* v. *Board of Education of Topeka* decision, at one point reminisced concerning his student days at Howard in the 1930s. He said "there was a great ferment" at the university in those days. Everyone, Clark said, felt the "enormous drive and purpose" of preparing themselves to participate in a movement toward a society of justice and opportunity.

Perhaps the place where this was most evident was at the

university's small law school. In 1929 Johnson had convinced Charles Hamilton Houston, a native Washingtonian and graduate of Harvard Law School, to come and transform the mediocre institution. In the course of six years, this brilliant, unyielding, and magnificently obsessed black man had created a law school whose central, relentless purpose was to develop the highly trained cadre of lawyers who would lead the next great assault against the legal foundations which supported America's structures of racial injustice. Led by Thurgood Marshall, the most famous graduate of Houston's training ground, they seemed to hear again John Hope's call from 1896: "Let your discontent break mountain-high against the wall of prejudice and swamp it to the very foundation."

Using the laws and the courts of the land, working largely within the structures of the NAACP, undergirded by a generation of unsung and courageous black plaintiffs, they headed toward the foundation. In the midst of the depression, they decided to take on the segregated public school systems as the central support of the entire structure of legalized injustice. Within twenty years, *Plessy* v. *Ferguson* was undone. Using the base of their own institutions, the grandchildren of slaves were creating a more perfect order, redefining the general welfare.

It was only two decades after the armistice which halted "the war to end all wars" that World War II began. Viewed from the perspective of the black struggle for freedom and justice in the United States, much of the wartime drama seemed like déjà vu, a reenactment of all the tendencies of "the war to make the world safe for democracy," with many elements now intensified and magnified.

Before December 7, 1941, the debates over black participation were sharp and the issue of color had been heightened by Japan's involvement. After Pearl Harbor, holding a position against black participation became much more difficult. Still, the old contradictions were present. For instance, when the nation's leaders began to mobilize public opinion against the "racism" of Hitler's "Aryan" forces, or when Franklin Roosevelt stood with leaders of the French and English imperialist nations and invited African-Americans into the struggle for freedom, the contradictions were sharp.

Meanwhile, black soldiers were again segregated, harassed, sometimes killed, even before a half million of them left the United States for the official war zones. Black newspapers in this country were so vociferous in their protests against the contradictions inherent in the situation that they were threatened with censorship and with the loss of access to rationed newsprint. Aside from the newspapers, black people were organizing, threatening to march on Washington (under A. Philip Randolph's eloquent leadership) unless a presidential order forced the defense industries to end their shameful discrimination against black workers, unless black soldiers could find safety and justice in their own country. The liberal president finally relented under the pressures of possible international embarrassment and internal discord. He made a move toward breaking down the discriminatory defense industry hiring, but little was done to improve the conditions of black men and women in the military.

All the old ironies were present. In response to another massive, wartime migration of black people out of the South into the coastal cities of the West and Southwest, into the heartland of industrial centers, white violence was explosive. In 1943, black and white warfare broke out in Detroit. By the time the war ended in 1945, it was clear to some sensitive observers that nothing at home or overseas would ever be quite the same again where the black struggle for freedom and justice was concerned. The momentum that had been building in the courts, on the streets, in churches, temples and mosques, in the minds and hearts of marching men and women, on battlegrounds at home and overseas, could not be denied.

Besides, the war had helped to transform the world itself, even beyond all the blood and death and terrible grieving. For the colonial foundations which World War I had shaken were now being irredeemably torn asunder. The earlier Harlem vision of Hubert Harrison was now being realized. In India, China, all over Africa, Southeast Asia, and the Caribbean, the power of European domination was being challenged and undermined by the rising revolutionary forces of the colonized colored people who were determined to be free, to repossess themselves.

Nothing would ever be the same again, neither within the Afro-American movement for freedom and transformation, nor in the far-scattered confrontations between Europe (and Euro-Americans) and the colonized peoples, confrontations in which many Black Americans somehow felt themselves a part. So some black people looked closely at Gandhi's nonviolent revolutionary movement in India and, while recognizing important differences, saw a possible source of hope. Others were encouraged by China's great movement away from its feudal and European-dominated past. Most Black Americans caught the quickening sounds of rebellion rising beneath the surface of Africa and recognized a message there. Nothing would ever be the same again.

Adam Clayton Powell, Jr., knew this. In 1945 he published *Marching Blacks*, an account of the awakening in the postdepression black community, a statement of the domestic meaning of the new international situation. Closing the work, he quoted at length from a statement by one of the black movement's most highly prized white allies, Edwin Embree. In the last year of the war, Embree said,

> The white man of the western world is offered his last chance for equal status in world society. If he accepts equality, he can hold a self-respecting place—maybe a leading place in the new order. And he may continue to contribute much in science, in industry, and in political maturity. But if the western white man persists in trying to run the show, in exploiting the whole earth, in treating the hundreds of millions of his neighbors as inferiors, then the fresh might of the billion and a half nonwhite, non-western people may in a surging rebellion smash him to nonentity.

Powell agreed and said, "[White] America is not ready for the postwar world," but concluded that "the black man" was. According to Powell, "The black man . . . plods wearily no longer—he is striding Freedom Road. . . . He is ready to throw himself into the struggle to make the dream of America become flesh and blood, bread and butter, freedom and equality." This was the dream of John Hope in 1896 and of his enslaved foreparents before him. It was Langston Hughes's dream, and in Powell's own lifetime the dream would burst forth again into powerful reality, as the great-grandchildren of the slaves kept their eyes on the prize.

After World War II, it was somewhat easier to see what was happening in the United States. From 1941, when Roosevelt was pressured into his executive order on fair employment, there was no single year that did not produce at least one new positive reaction to the black movement from the executive or judicial branches. For instance, in the years from 1944 to 1950, white primaries were struck down in the courts, President Truman formed the first presidential civil rights commission, segregation in interstate bus travel was legally denied, segregation in the army was attacked, literacy tests for voting were declared unconstitutional, and the border states began token desegregation of the graduate schools of their universities.

Then, in 1950, as the international power struggle involving Russia, China, and the United States developed into its first major armed conflict in Korea, the courts seemed to open like a bursting dam. In separate decisions, cases involving five state universities were decided in favor of token black petitioners. Railroad dining car segregation was struck down. Finally, with a group of courageous black families as plaintiffs, the NAACP decided to make a frontal attack on the basic principle of separate-but-equal education. With their eyes on the prize, Houston's cadre was striking home.

Why did it happen with such momentum in those years? Part of the answer surely rests with the veterans who came home from the war, determined to create freedom in America, veterans like Amzie Moore and Medgar Evers of Mississippi, like Harry Briggs of Clarendon County, South Carolina, and Oliver Brown of Topeka, Kansas.

Why?

Part of the reason may have been the moral passion and tough, loving courage of the men like Bayard Rustin and Bill Sutherland, who had been conscientious objectors during the war and who had fought disciplined, costly battles against the racism of the federal prisons. Part of it was the women, like Ella Baker and Grace Boggs, who developed their skills to high levels during the wartime years, working with old campaigners like A. Philip Randolph in the March on Washington movement and with C. L. R. James, the great black Trotskyite organizer-intellectual. Of course, much of the answer is wrapped up in the history of the NAACP, continuing to keep the faith, finally zeroing in on the heart of the system of segregation, challenging the idea of the existence of any true equality when forced segregation exists.

Why did it happen with such momentum in those years? Because there were black churches, often built in the hard, post-Reconstruction days, where rallies, mobilizing, and planning could now take place. Because black (and a few white) ministers were willing to stand firm on the front lines against the moral evil of segregation and call their people to do the same, regardless of the cost.

It happened because white American leaders knew the cold war–conscious world was watching a nation that dared call itself "the leader of the free world" to see how it would deal with its own citizens who had so long clamored for freedom.

It happened because the post–World War II generation of men and women were the first African-Americans who grew to their maturity in a world where the power, hegemony, and wisdom of the European world were everywhere being publicly questioned, rejected, and attacked. They knew a new time had come, was coming, all over the nonwhite world, and that they were related to it all. At great personal risk and cost, Du Bois, Paul Robeson, Lena Horne, and others kept reminding black people of their relationship to this vaster world of men and women struggling for transformation.

It happened because the great migrations out of the South had continued and had thrust new millions of black voters into the precincts of urban politics all over the North, many of them into the company of the Democratic party. Their strength could not be ignored. The party could no longer allow its southern white racist firebrands to shape its racial policies. The black presence and its insistent questions about "we the people of the United States" were part of the reason for the momentum.

It happened because the Nation of Islam was quietly rising, gaining power, calling attention to the hypocrisy of white America. It happened because some white people really decided that they must have a more perfect union, must secure the blessing of liberty for themselves and their posterity. And they finally understood that such things were impossible without the establishment of justice for black people. It happened because some white people and their children were ready to pay the price for freedom.

Of course, no one knows all the answers to such a question as why. That's one of the surprises of history—how little we know about so much.

But one thing is clear. It happened with such momentum because a people had kept their eyes on the prize, had persisted in a vision of a more perfect union, had waded through rivers of blood to keep promises to their fore-parents and to their children. Such unyielding commitment and action eventually builds its own momentum, creates new, surprising realities, beginning deep within individual lives, opening up to the re-creation of a society.

CHAPTER ONE

AWAKENINGS (1954–1956)

Introduction by Vincent Harding

"Another man done gone" was the painfully ambiguous, often bitter cry that was so familiar to the black community of the United States in the 1950s. Thus, many persons would not have been surprised if the inhuman, atavistic (but terribly recognizable) murder of a young Chicago-based teenager in Mississippi, and the predictable legal exoneration of his murderers, had led to nothing more than tears, burning, bottled-up rage, and a great outpouring of indignant words from the relatively safe North.

But 1955 was a new time, and more than tears and words were needed. Now, even though the newness of the time was only dimly perceived in that brutally familiar summer, some things were known. Just about everyone who was black and alive at the time realized that the long, hard struggles, led by the National Association for the Advancement of Colored People (NAACP), its often brilliant and courageous lawyers, and its lengthening line of risk-taking black plaintiffs, had forced the Supreme Court to take a major stand on the side of justice in the *Brown* v. *Board of Education of Topeka* decision. A young black man who had been in the Marine Corps at the time of the Court's decision spoke for many black people when he later remembered how he felt when he heard about the 1954 decision:

My inner emotions must have been approximate to the Negro slaves' when they first heard about the Emancipation Proclamation. Elation took hold of me so strongly that I found it very difficult to refrain from yielding to an urge of jubilation. . . . On this momentous night of May 17, 1954, I felt that at last the government was willing to assert itself on behalf of first-class citizenship, even for Negroes. I experienced a sense of loyalty that I had never felt before. I was sure that this was the beginning of a new era of American democracy.

Robert Williams, who shared those memories, in *Negroes with Guns* (Marzani Munsall, 1962), soon after became a fugitive from America's justice.

Yes, it seemed clear that 1955 was different. By then a rising tide of the nonwhite peoples of the globe had gathered at Bandung, Indonesia, to demand that the Western world hear their determined pronouncements that the old white-dominated colonial order was a dying way of life. And many Afro-Americans understood that they were somehow part of this reemerging contingent of the world's most ancient peoples. They felt a fundamental agreement with Adam Clayton Powell, Jr., the audacious preacher-politician from Harlem who came back from Bandung to announce that the revolutions of the nonwhite world had brought us all to a new point in history with new responsibilities for justice and freedom. Of course, a similarity existed between Powell's sentiments and those of the thousands of black veterans of World War II who had returned home determined to carry on the struggle for democracy. It was they, too, who helped to make it a different time.

In 1955 the nation was deeply involved in what it chose to call a "cold war" with a Russian-led, anticapitalist network of nations. The United States was proclaiming itself "the leader of the free world," and many of its white leaders especially wanted to demonstrate to the raw materials–rich nations of the nonwhite world that the U.S.A. did not deserve their acerbic taunts concerning the apparently unfree condition of this nation's own major nonwhite community. In a variety of ways, the new international situation put the black community in the United States in its best bargaining position since the end of the Civil War.

Finally, if anyone had any doubts that 1955 was a new time, they needed only to pay close attention to what was developing in Montgomery, Alabama, by the end of the year. There, in the old capital of the Confederacy, inspired by one woman's courage; mobilized and organized by scores of grassroots leaders in churches, community organizations, and political clubs; called to new visions of their best possibilities by a young black preacher named Martin Luther King, Jr., a people was reawakening to its destiny.

By the end of the following year, after a long, hard, and dangerous struggle, it was clear that the events that transpired in Montgomery, Alabama, marked a unique, mass-based new beginning in a struggle that had been going on in this land since the first slave ships denied the colonists' claims to be democratic, since the first enslaved Africans demanded through their words and their deeds that this new nation be faithful to its own best vision. Montgomery was the newest manifestation of the embattled black dream, the latest coming of the vision-based people determined to create a new reality for themselves and all Americans, beginning with a chance to sit in peace and dignity on a Montgomery city bus.

1. Articles on the Emmett Till Case

In August 1955, fourteen-year-old Emmett Till traveled from his home in Chicago to visit relatives in Mississippi. He was brutally murdered there for purportedly whistling at—or speaking disrespectfully to—a white woman. His gruesome death and the subsequent trial of two white men accused of the kidnap-slaying received extensive coverage in the nation's black newspapers. These are excerpts from articles in the **Chicago Defender** *(October 1, 1955).*

The mother of Emmett Louis Till has accused Tallahatchie County Sheriff H. C. Strider of hiding two key witnesses who possibly would have given explosive testimony in the trial of two white men cleared by an all-white [jury of the] slaying of her 14-year-old son.

———

Meanwhile, Mrs. Bradley announced through her attorney, William Henry Huff of Chicago, that she will file suits totaling at least $200,000 on civil charges with malice counts against persons involved in the kidnap-slaying of her son. Huff said the suits will be filed in U.S. District Court in Mississippi.

Congressman Charles Diggs, Jr., of Detroit, joined Mrs. Bradley in blasting Sheriff Strider, charging that two "very important witnesses" are being held in the Charleston, Miss., jail. Diggs flew to Sumner last week to observe the trial.

The prisoners in question were identified as LeRoy (Too Tight) Collins and Henry Lee Loggins, both in their late teens, who reportedly worked as truck drivers on the Leslie Milam farm. Leslie is a half-brother of J. W. Milam [a defendant].

Sheriff Strider reportedly denied that either boy was being held and claimed he couldn't find them to serve trial subpoenas.

The youths are said to have washed blood from Milam's truck shortly after Till was kidnapped from his uncle's farm the night of August 28. Milam was quoted as saying the blood was from a deer he had shot. (Deer hunting season is closed in Mississippi.)

Congressman Diggs flew to Chicago early Saturday from Mississippi. With him was Willie Reed, 18, of Drew, Miss., one of the prosecution's surprise witnesses. Reed is believed to be the last person, not involved in the brutal slaying, to see Emmett Till alive. . . .

A second surprise witness, Mrs. Mary (Amanda) Bradley, has also arrived in Chicago, where she will reside.

———

During a brief stop-over enroute to Detroit, Diggs said, "I am disappointed. I went to Sumner with the hope that the Till trial would result in a conviction." When asked if he planned to propose any legislation as a result of what he observed at the trial, the Congressman replied: "I have some legislation already to give the Justice Department the right to intervene in Civil Rights Cases and from this new experience I hope to strengthen our case for legislation that would have more than the presently casual regard for Negroes trying to participate in the elections."

He continued: "I am interested in something that would assure the right to vote to all citizens. The basis of the selection of the jury is the voter [rolls] and the public officials are elected by the voters. An anti-lynch bill and legislation to eliminate the poll tax are the basic solutions I believe for this. I still have hope that the people will wake up to the international significance of this."

WHAT YOU CAN DO ABOUT THE DISGRACE IN SUMNER [AN EDITORIAL]

How long must we wait for the Federal Government to act? Whenever a crisis arises involving our lives or our rights we look to Washington hopefully for help. It seldom comes.

For too long it has been the device, as it was in the Till case, for the President to refer such matters to the Department of Justice.

And usually, the Department of Justice seems more devoted to exploring its lawbooks for reasons why it can't offer protection of a Negro's life or rights.

In the current case, the Department of Justice hastily issued a statement declaring that it was making a thorough investigation to determine if young Till's civil rights had been violated.

The Department evidently concluded that the kidnapping and lynching of a Negro boy in Mississippi are not violations of his rights.

This sounds just like both the defense and the prosecution as they concluded their arguments by urging the jury to "uphold our way of life."

The trial is over, and this miscarriage of justice must not be left unavenged. The Defender will continue its investigations, which helped uncover new witnesses in the case, to find other Negroes who actually witnessed the lynching, before they too are found in the Tallahatchie river.

At this point we can only conclude that the administration and the justice department have decided to uphold the way of life of

Mississippi and the South. Not only have they been inactive on the Till case, but they have yet to take positive action in the kidnapping of Mutt Jones in Alabama, who was taken across the state line into Mississippi and brutally beaten. And as yet the recent lynchings of Rev. [George] Lee and LaMarr Smith in Mississippi have gone unchallenged by our government.

The citizens councils, the interstate conspiracy to whip the Negro in line with economic reins, open defiance to the Supreme Court's school decision—none of these seem to be violations of rights that concern the federal government.

And congress isn't concerned either. There has never been a congressional investigation of lynching, or of any of the other abuses and humiliations suffered by Negroes.

And the inactivity of congress is all the more pointed when we consider that there are three Negroes in congress, any one of whom could at least propose such.

The President has steadfastly considered any effort to protect the Negro in the United States from those who would ignore him as a citizen as "extraneous."

The appointment of a Morrow, Wilkins, a Davis or a Mahoney [black Eisenhower administration appointees] is significant and is rightfully applauded, but it means little to the millions of Mose Wrights [Wright, Till's granduncle, testified against Milam and Bryant at the Sumner trial] throughout the South.

For the Mose Wrights are born with low ceilings over their heads. They're denied an education, they're denied a fair return for their labor; they're denied the right to participate in their government; they're denied a chance to walk in the sun and frequently denied the right to live until they're sixty-five, as Milam reminded Mose Wright.

In the midst of this frustration, it appears that the Negro in the South as well as the North, has but one way to go. That is to the ballot box.

One of the most important factors accounting for the difference between the Negro in Chicago and the Negro in Money, Miss., is that the Negro in Chicago can and does vote.

And the Negro in Money can and must register and vote. And the federal government, starting with the White House that has been so negligent in the past in these matters, must be prodded

into making it possible for the Negro to exercise this one right—
the right to vote.

Yes, the Till trial is over, but the Till case cannot be closed until
Negroes are voting in Tallahatchie and Leflore counties and
throughout the South.

2. "Coming of Age in Mississippi"
Anne Moody

*The murder of Emmett Till, and the justice-mocking trial afterward,
made a dramatic impact on an entire generation of African-Americans.
Anne Moody was fourteen years old when Till was killed. This excerpt
is from her 1968 autobiography,* Coming of Age in Mississippi.

. . . I was now working for one of the meanest white women in
town, and a week before school started Emmett Till was killed.

Up until his death, I had heard of Negroes found floating in a
river or dead somewhere with their bodies riddled with bullets.
But I didn't know the mystery behind these killings then.

That evening when I stopped off at the house on my way to Mrs.
Burke's, Mama was singing. . . . I wondered if she knew about
Emmett Till. The way she was singing she had something on her
mind and it wasn't pleasant either.

Ralph, the baby, started crying, and she went in the bedroom to
give him his bottle. I got up and followed her.

"Mama, did you hear about that fourteen-year-old Negro boy
who was killed a little over a week ago by some white men?" I
asked her.

"Where did you hear that?" she said angrily.

"Boy, everybody really thinks I am dumb or deaf or something.
I heard Eddie them talking about it this evening coming from
school."

"Eddie them better watch how they go around here talking.

These white folks git a hold of it they gonna be in trouble," she said.

"What are they gonna be in trouble about, Mama? People got a right to talk, ain't they?"

"You go on to work before you is late. And don't you let on like you know nothing about that boy being killed before Miss Burke them. Just do your work like you don't know nothing," she said. "That boy's a lot better off in heaven than he is here," she continued and then started singing again.

On my way to Mrs. Burke's that evening, Mama's words kept running through my mind. "Just do your work like you don't know nothing." "Why is Mama acting so scared?" I thought. "And what if Mrs. Burke knew we knew? Why must I pretend I don't know? Why are these people killing Negroes? What did Emmett Till do besides whistle at that woman?"

By the time I got to work, I had worked up my nerves some. I was shaking as I walked up on the porch. "Do your work like you don't know nothing." But once I got inside, I couldn't have acted normal if Mrs. Burke were paying me to be myself.

———

When they had finished [dinner] and gone into the living room as usual to watch TV, Mrs. Burke called me to eat. I took a clean plate out of the cabinet and sat down. Just as I was putting the first forkful of food in my mouth, Mrs. Burke entered the kitchen.

"Essie, did you hear about that fourteen-year-old boy who was killed in Greenwood?" she asked me, sitting down in one of the chairs opposite me.

"No, I didn't hear that," I answered, almost choking on the food.

"Do you know why he was killed?" she asked and I didn't answer.

"He was killed because he got out of his place with a white woman. A boy from Mississippi would have known better than that. This boy was from Chicago. Negroes up North have no respect for people. They think they can get away with anything. He just came to Mississippi and put a whole lot of notions in the boys' heads here and stirred up a lot of trouble," she said passionately.

"How old are you, Essie?" she asked me after a pause.

"Fourteen, I will soon be fifteen though," I said.

"See, that boy was just fourteen too. It's a shame he had to die so soon." She was red in the face, she looked as if she was on fire.

When she left the kitchen I sat there with my mouth open and my food untouched. I couldn't have eaten now if I were starving. "Just do your work like you don't know nothing" ran through my mind again and I began washing the dishes.

I went home shaking like a leaf on a tree. For the first time out of all her trying, Mrs. Burke had made me feel like rotten garbage. Many times she had tried to instill fear within me and subdue me and had given up. But when she talked about Emmett Till there was something in her voice that sent chills and fear all over me.

Before Emmett Till's murder, I had known the fear of hunger, hell, and the Devil. But now there was a new fear known to me— the fear of being killed just because I was black. This was the worst of my fears. I knew once I got food, the fear of starving to death would leave. I also was told that if I were a good girl, I wouldn't have to fear the Devil or hell. But I didn't know what one had to do or not do as a Negro not to be killed. Probably just being a Negro period was enough, I thought.

———————

I was fifteen years old when I began to hate people. I hated the white men who murdered Emmett Till and I hated all the other whites who were responsible for the countless murders Mrs. Rice [my homeroom teacher] had told me about and those I vaguely remembered from childhood. But I also hated Negroes. I hated them for not standing up and doing something about the murders. In fact, I think I had a stronger resentment toward Negroes for letting the whites kill them than toward the whites. Anyway, it was at this stage in my life that I began to look upon Negro men as cowards. I could not respect them for smiling in a white man's face, addressing him as Mr. So-and-So, saying yessuh and nossuh when after they were home behind closed doors that same white man was a son of a bitch, a bastard, or any other name more suitable than mister.

3. A Letter from the Women's Political Council to the Mayor of Montgomery, Alabama

The Montgomery bus boycott of 1955–1956 marks a watershed in the modern era of America's civil rights years. For twelve and a half months, black residents of Alabama's state capital walked, carpooled, and rode in taxis and hearses temporarily converted into buses rather than ride in the back of segregated "Jim Crow" buses. Jo Ann Robinson's May 21, 1954, letter (written on behalf of the Women's Political Council, of which she was president) to the mayor of Montgomery presaged the great non-violent boycott by eighteen months.

Dear Sir:

The Women's Political Council is very grateful to you and the City Commissioners for the hearing you allowed our representatives during the month of March, 1954, when the "city-bus-fare-increase case" was being reviewed. There were several things the Council asked for:

1. A city law that would make it possible for Negroes to sit from back toward front, and whites from front toward back until all the seats are taken;
2. That Negroes not be asked or forced to pay fare at front and go to the rear of the bus to enter;
3. That busses stop at every corner in residential sections occupied by Negroes as they do in communities where whites reside.

We are happy to report that busses have been stopping at more corners now in some sections where Negroes live than previously. However, the same practices in seating and boarding the bus continue.

Mayor [W. A.] Gayle, three-fourths of the riders of these public conveyances are Negroes. If Negroes did not patronize them, they could not possibly operate.

More and more of our people are already arranging with neighbors and friends to ride to keep from being insulted and humiliated by bus drivers.

There has been talk from twenty-five or more local organizations of planning a city-wide boycott of busses. We, sir, do not feel that forceful measures are necessary in bargaining for a convenience which is right for all bus passengers. We, the Council, believe that when this matter has been put before you and the Commissioners, that agreeable terms can be met in a quiet and unostensible manner to the satisfaction of all concerned.

Many of our Southern cities in neighboring states have practiced the policies we seek without incident whatsoever. Atlanta, Macon and Savannah in Georgia have done this for years. Even Mobile, in our own state, does this and all the passengers are satisfied.

Please consider this plea, and if possible, act favorably upon it, for even now plans are being made to ride less, or not at all, on our busses. We do not want this.

> Respectfully yours,
> The Women's Political Council
> Jo Ann Robinson, President

4. Interview with Rosa Parks

On December 1, 1955, Rosa Parks, an NAACP organizer and a seamstress in Montgomery, refused to give up her seat to a white man who had boarded the bus after her. Her determined refusal was the spark that ignited the boycott. This is an excerpt from an interview with Rosa L. Parks in My Soul Is Rested: Movement Days in the Deep South Remembered, *by Howell Raines (1977).*

I had left my work at the men's alteration shop, a tailor shop in the Montgomery Fair department store, and as I left work, I crossed the street to a drugstore to pick up a few items instead of trying to go directly to the bus stop. And when I had finished this, I came across the street and looked for a Cleveland Avenue bus that apparently had some seats on it. At that time it was a little hard to get a seat on the bus. But when I did get to the entrance of the bus, I got in line with a number of other people who were getting on the same bus.

As I got up on the bus and walked to the seat I saw there was only one vacancy that was just back of where it was considered the white section. So this was the seat that I took, next to the aisle, and a man was sitting next to me. Across the aisle there were two women, and there were a few seats at this point in the very front of the bus that was called the white section. I went on to one stop and I didn't particularly notice who was getting on the bus, didn't particularly notice the other people getting on. And on the third stop there were some people getting on, and at this point all of the front seats were taken. Now in the beginning, at the very first stop I had got on the bus, the back of the bus was filled up with people standing in the aisle and I don't know why this one vacancy that I took was left, because there were quite a few people already standing toward the back of the bus. The third stop is when all the front seats were taken, and this one man was standing and when the driver looked around and saw he was standing, he asked the four of us, the man in the seat with me and the two women across the aisle, to let him have those front seats.

At his first request, didn't any of us move. Then he spoke again and said, "You'd better make it light on yourselves and let me have those seats." At this point, of course, the passenger who would have taken the seat hadn't said anything. In fact, he never did speak to my knowledge. When the three people, the man who was in the seat with me and the two women, stood up and moved into the aisle, I remained where I was. When the driver saw that I was still sitting there, he asked if I was going to stand up. I told him, no, I wasn't. He said, "Well, if you don't stand up, I'm going to have you arrested." I told him to go on and have me arrested.

He got off the bus and came back shortly. A few minutes later, two policemen got on the bus, and they approached me and asked if the driver had asked me to stand up, and I said yes, and they wanted to know why I didn't. I told them I didn't think I should have to stand up. . . . They placed me under arrest then and had me to get in the police car, and I was taken to jail and booked on suspicion, I believe. . . . They had to determine whether or not the driver wanted to press charges or swear out a warrant, which he did. Then they took me to jail and I was placed in a cell. In a little while I was taken from the cell, and my picture was made and fingerprints taken. I went back to the cell then, and a few minutes later I was called back again, and when this happened I found out that Mr. E. D. Nixon and Attorney and Mrs. Clifford Durr had come to make bond for me.

5. "The Movement Gathers Momentum"
Martin Luther King, Jr.

The newest minister in Montgomery was twenty-six-year-old Martin Luther King, Jr. He had recently completed his doctoral course work at Boston University and the Dexter Avenue Baptist Church was his first ministerial assignment. On December 5, 1955, King was elected president of the newly formed Montgomery Improvement Association. He had but a few hours to prepare a speech for the boycott's first mass meeting, held that evening at the Holt Street Baptist Church. This is an excerpt from King's first book, Stride Toward Freedom: The Montgomery Story *(1958).*

Within five blocks of the church I noticed a traffic jam. Cars were lined up as far as I could see on both sides of the street. It was a moment before it occurred to me that all of these cars were headed for the mass meeting. I had to park at least four blocks from the church, and as I started walking I noticed that hundreds of people were standing outside. In the dark night, police cars circled slowly around the area, surveying the orderly, patient, and good-humored crowd. The three or four thousand people who could not get into the church were to stand cheerfully throughout the evening listening to the proceedings on the loudspeakers that had been set up outside for their benefit. And when, near the end of the meeting, these speakers were silenced at the request of white people in surrounding neighborhoods, the crowd would still remain quietly, content simply to be present.

It took fully fifteen minutes to push my way through to the pastor's study, where Dr. Wilson told me that the church had been packed since five o'clock. By now my doubts concerning the success of our venture were dispelled. The question of calling off the protest was now academic. The enthusiasm of these thousands of people swept everything along like an onrushing tidal wave.

It was some time before the remaining speakers could push their way to the rostrum through the tightly packed church. When the meeting began it was almost half an hour late. The opening hymn was the old familiar "Onward Christian Soldiers," and when that mammoth audience stood to sing, the voices outside swelling the chorus in the church, there was a mighty ring like the glad echo of heaven itself.

Rev. W. F. Alford, minister of the Beulah Baptist Church, led the congregation in prayer, followed by a reading of the Scripture by Rev. U. J. Fields, minister of the Bell Street Baptist Church. Then the chairman introduced me. As the audience applauded, I rose and stood before the pulpit. Television cameras began to shoot from all sides. The crowd grew quiet.

6. Speech by Martin Luther King, Jr., at Holt Street Baptist Church

This is a substantial portion of the speech delivered by Martin Luther King, Jr., on the evening of December 5, 1955, at Holt Street Baptist Church, Montgomery, Alabama.

We are here this evening for serious business. We are here in a general sense because first and foremost we are American citizens, and we are determined to apply our citizenship to the fullness of its means. We are here because of our love for democracy, because of our deep-seated belief that democracy transformed from thin paper to thick action is the greatest form of government on earth. But we are here in a specific sense, because of the bus situation in Montgomery. We are here because we are determined to get the situation corrected.

This situation is not at all new. The problem has existed over endless years. For many years now Negroes in Montgomery and so many other areas have been inflicted with the paralysis of crippling fear on buses in our community. On so many occasions,

Negroes have been intimidated and humiliated and oppressed because of the sheer fact that they were Negroes. I don't have time this evening to go into the history of these numerous cases. . . . But at least one stands before us now with glaring dimensions. Just the other day, just last Thursday to be exact, one of the finest citizens in Montgomery—not one of the finest Negro citizens but one of the finest citizens in Montgomery—was taken from a bus and carried to jail and arrested because she refused to get up to give her seat to a white person. . . . Mrs. Rosa Parks is a fine person. And since it had to happen I'm happy it happened to a person like Mrs. Parks, for nobody can doubt the boundless outreach of her integrity. Nobody can doubt the height of her character, nobody can doubt the depth of her Christian commitment and devotion to the teachings of Jesus. . . .

And just because she refused to get up, she was arrested. . . . You know my friends there comes a time when people get tired of being trampled over by the iron feet of oppression. There comes a time my friends when people get tired of being flung across the abyss of humiliation where they experience the bleakness of nagging despair. There comes a time when people get tired of being pushed out of the glittering sunlight of life's July and left standing amidst the piercing chill of an Alpine November.

We are here, we are here this evening because we're tired now. Now let us say that we are not here advocating violence. We have overcome that. I want it to be known throughout Montgomery and throughout this nation that we are Christian people. We believe in the Christian religion. We believe in the teachings of Jesus. The only weapon that we have in our hands this evening is the weapon of protest. And secondly, this is the glory of America, with all of its faults. This is the glory of our democracy. If we were incarcerated behind the iron curtains of a Communistic nation we couldn't do this. If we were trapped in the dungeon of a totalitarian regime we couldn't do this. But the great glory of American democracy is the right to protest for right.

My friends, don't let anybody make us feel that we ought to be compared in our actions with the Ku Klux Klan or with the White Citizens' Councils. There will be no crosses burned at any bus stops in Montgomery. There will be no white persons pulled out of their homes and taken out to some distant road and murdered.

There will be nobody among us who will stand up and defy the Constitution of this nation. We only assemble here because of our desire to see right exist.

My friends, I want it to be known that we're going to work with grim and firm determination to gain justice on the buses in this city. And we are not wrong, we are not wrong in what we are doing. If we are wrong, then the Supreme Court of this Nation is wrong. If we are wrong, the Constitution of the United States is wrong. If we are wrong, God Almighty is wrong. If we are wrong, Jesus of Nazareth was merely a utopian dreamer and never came down to earth. If we are wrong, justice is a lie. And we are determined here in Montgomery to work and fight until justice runs down like water and righteousness like a mighty stream.

I want to say that with all of our actions we must stick together. Unity is the great need of the hour. And if we are united, we can get many of the things that we not only desire but which we justly deserve. And don't let anybody frighten you. We are not afraid of what we are doing, because we are doing it within the law. There is never a time in our American democracy that we must ever think we're wrong when we protest. We reserve that right. . . .

We, the disinherited of this land, we who have been oppressed so long are tired of going through the long night of captivity. And we are reaching out for the daybreak of freedom and justice and equality. . . . In all of our doings, in all of our deliberations . . . whatever we do, we must keep God in the forefront. Let us be Christian in all of our action. And I want to tell you this evening that it is not enough for us to talk about love. Love is one of the pinnacle parts of the Christian faith. There is another side called justice. And justice is really love in [application]. Justice is love correcting that which would work against love. . . . Standing beside love is always justice. And we are only using the tools of justice. Not only are we using the tools of persuasion but we've got to use the tools of coercion. Not only is this thing a process of education but it is also a process of legislation.

And as we stand and sit here this evening, and as we prepare ourselves for what lies ahead, let us go out with a grim and bold determination that we are going to stick together. We are going to work together. Right here in Montgomery when the history books are written in the future, somebody will have to say "There lived a race of people, black people, fleecy locks and black complexion, of people who had the moral courage to stand up for their rights." And thereby they injected a new meaning into the veins of history and of civilization. And we're gonna do that. God grant that we will do it before it's too late.

7. "At Holt Street Baptist Church"
Joe Azbell

The white daily newspaper in Montgomery was **The Advertiser.** *Joe Azbell, city editor of the paper, covered the December 5 mass meeting. This is an excerpt from his December 7 article titled "At Holt Street Baptist Church, Deeply Stirred Throng of Colored Citizens Protests Bus Segregation."*

As I drove along Cleveland Avenue en route to the Holt Street Baptist Church Monday night, I could see Negroes by the dozens forming a file, almost soldierly, on the sidewalk. They were going to the Rosa Parks protest meeting at the church.

They were silent people, bundled in overcoats, performing what appeared to be a ritual. I parked my automobile a block from the church and noticed the time was 6:45. Already cars were strung out for six or seven blocks in each direction. In fact, the area around the church looked like Cramton Bowl at an Alabama State–Tuskegee football game. Except for one thing: these people were stony silent.

The Negroes eyed me and one inquired if I was a policeman. He turned to his three companions: "He says he ain't the law." I walked up to the steps of the church and two Negro policemen were standing there chatting. Both were courteous when I introduced myself and one went inside and found out about the seating arrangement for the press. Chairs were placed down front for the reporters. The TV cameraman from WSFA-TV and the United Press reporter later took these seats. I stood in the rear of the church during the meeting while Reporter Steve Lesher anchored himself in a chair near the church's pulpit.

I went inside the church and stood at the front for a few minutes. The two rear doors were jammed with people and a long aisle was crammed with human forms like a frozen food package. I went to the rear of the church and it was the same. The Negro policemen pleaded with the Negroes to keep the aisles free so people could get out. In the end the policemen gave up in despair of correcting the safety hazard. Bodies at the front were packed one against the other. It required five minutes for a photographer to move eight feet among these people. . . .

The purpose of this meeting was to give "further instructions" on the boycott of city buses which had been started as a protest of the Negroes against the arrest, trial and conviction of Rosa Parks, 42-year-old seamstress, on a charge of violating segregation laws. . . .

There were four white reporters or photographers at the meeting. Only one other white person attended. He appeared to be a young college student or airman and he came with a Negro and left with a Negro. He sat in the group of Negroes in the balcony.

The meeting was started in a most unusual fashion. A Negro speaker—apparently a minister—came to the microphone. He did not introduce himself but apparently most of the Negroes knew him. He said there were microphones on the outside and in the basement, and there were three times as many people outside as on the inside. There was an anonymity throughout the meeting of the speakers. None of the white reporters could identify the speakers. Most of the Negroes did. . . .

The passion that fired the meeting was seen as the thousands of voices joined in singing. . . . The voices thundered through the church.

Then there followed a prayer by a minister. It was prayer interrupted a hundred times by "yeas" and "uh-huhs" and "that's right." The minister spoke of God as the Master and the brotherhood of man. He repeated in a different way that God would protect the righteous.

As the other speakers came on the platform urging "freedom and equality" for Negroes "who are Americans and proud of this democracy," the frenzy of the audience mounted. There was a volume of clapping that seemed to boom through the walls. Outside the loudspeakers were blaring the message for blocks. White people stopped blocks away and listened to the loudspeakers' messages.

The newspapers were criticized for quoting police authorities on reports of intimidation of Negroes who attempted to ride buses and for comparing the Negro boycott with the economic reprisals of White Citizens groups.

The remark which drew the most applause was: "We will not retreat one inch in our fight to secure and hold our American citizenship." Second was a statement: "And the history book will write of us as a race of people who in Montgomery County, State of Alabama, Country of the United States, stood up for and fought for their rights as American citizens, as citizens of democracy."

Outside the audience listened as more and more cars continued to arrive. Streets became Dexter traffic snarls. There was hymn singing between speeches. In the end there was the passing of the hats and Negroes dropped in dollar bills, $5 bills and $10 bills. It was not passive giving but active giving. Negroes called to the hat passers outside—"Here, let me give."

When the resolution on continuing the boycott of the bus was read, there came a wild whoop of delight. Many said they would never ride the bus again. Negroes turned to each other and compared past incidents on the buses.

At several points there was an emotionalism that the ministers on the platform recognized could get out of control and at various intervals they repeated again and again what "we are seeking is by peaceful means."

"There will be no violence or intimidation. We are seeking things in a democratic way and we are using the weapon of protest," the speakers declared.

The meeting was much like an old-fashioned revival with loud applause added. It proved beyond any doubt that there was a discipline among Negroes that many whites had doubted. It was almost a military discipline combined with emotion.

8. Resolution of the Citizens' Mass Meeting
December 5, 1955

The official business of the December 5 mass meeting at Holt Street Baptist Church was the approval of a series of resolutions relating to the continuation of the bus boycott. Their text was carried in the December 13, 1955, issue of the **Birmingham World,** *the major regional black weekly newspaper.*

WHEREAS, there are thousands of Negroes in the city and county of Montgomery who ride busses owned and operated by the Montgomery City Lines, Incorporated, and

WHEREAS, said citizens have been riding busses owned and operated by said company over a number of years, and

WHEREAS, said citizens, over a number of years, and on many occasions have been insulted, embarrassed and have been made to suffer great fear of bodily harm by drivers of busses owned and operated by said bus company, and

WHEREAS, the drivers of said busses have never requested a white passenger riding on any of its busses to relinquish his seat and stand so that a Negro may take his seat; however, said drivers have on many occasions too numerous to mention requested Negro passengers on said busses to relinquish their seats and stand so that white passengers may take their seats, and

WHEREAS, said citizens of Montgomery city and county pay their fares just as all other persons who are passengers on said busses, and are entitled to fair and equal treatment, and

WHEREAS, there has been any number of arrests of Negroes caused by drivers of said busses and they are constantly put in jail for refusing to give white passengers their seats and stand.

WHEREAS, in March of 1955, a committee of citizens did have a conference with one of the officials of said bus line; at which time said official arranged a meeting between attorneys representing the Negro citizens of this city and attorneys representing the Montgomery City Lines, Incorporated and the city of Montgomery, and

WHEREAS, the official of the bus line promised that as a result of the meeting between said attorneys, he would issue a statement of policy clarifying the law with reference to the seating of Negro passengers on the bus, and

WHEREAS, said attorneys did have a meeting and did discuss the matter of clarifying the law, however, the official said bus lines did not make public statements as to its policy with reference to the seating of passengers on its busses, and

WHEREAS, since that time, at least two ladies have been arrested for an alleged violation of the city segregation law with reference to bus travel, and

WHEREAS, said citizens of Montgomery city and county believe that they have been grossly mistreated as passengers on the busses owned and operated by said bus company in spite of the fact that they are in the majority with reference to the number of passengers riding on said busses.

Be It Resolved As Follows:

1. That the citizens of Montgomery are requesting that every citizen in Montgomery, regardless of race, color or creed, to refrain from riding busses owned and operated in the city of Montgomery by the Montgomery City Lines, Incorporated until some arrangement has been worked out between said citizens and the Montgomery City Lines, Incorporated.
2. That every person owning or who has access to automobiles use their automobiles in assisting other persons to get to work without charge.
3. That the employers of persons whose employees live a . . . distance from them, as much as possible afford transportation to your own employees.
4. That the Negro citizens of Montgomery are ready and willing to send a delegation of citizens to the Montgomery City Lines to discuss their grievances and to work out a solution for the same.

Be it further resolved that we have not, are not, and have no intentions of using an unlawful means or any intimidation to persuade persons not to ride the Montgomery City Lines' busses.

However, we call upon your consciences, both moral and spiritual, to give your whole-hearted support to this undertaking. We believe we have [a just] complaint and we are willing to discuss this matter with the proper officials.

9. "The Violence of Desperate Men"
Martin Luther King, Jr.

Seven weeks into the boycott, Martin Luther King, Jr., experienced how seriously his commitment to nonviolence would be tested. This is an excerpt from **Stride Toward Freedom.**

. . . On January 30, [1956] I left home a little before seven to attend our Monday evening mass meeting at the First Baptist Church. A member of my congregation, Mrs. Mary Lucy Williams, had come to the parsonage to keep my wife company in my absence. After putting the baby to bed, Coretta and Mrs. Williams went to the living room to look at television. About nine-thirty they heard a noise in front that sounded as though someone had thrown a brick. In a matter of seconds an explosion rocked the house. A bomb had gone off on the porch.

———————

I interrupted the collection and asked all present to give me their undivided attention. After telling them why I had to leave, I urged each person to go straight home after the meeting and adhere strictly to our philosophy of nonviolence. . . .

I was immediately driven home. As we neared the scene I noticed hundreds of people with angry faces in front of the house. The policemen were trying, in their usual rough manner, to clear the streets, but they were ignored by the crowd. One Negro was saying to a policeman, who was attempting to push him aside: "I ain't gonna move nowhere. That's the trouble now; you white folks is always pushin' us around. Now you got your .38 and I got mine; so let's battle it out." As I walked toward the front of the porch I realized that many people were armed. Nonviolent resistance was on the verge of being transformed into violence.

In this atmosphere I walked out to the porch and asked the crowd to come to order. In less than a moment there was complete silence. Quietly I told them that I was all right and that my wife and baby were all right. "Now let's not become panicky," I continued. "If you have weapons, take them home; if you do not have them, please do not seek to get them. We cannot solve this problem through retaliatory violence. We must meet violence with nonviolence. Remember the words of Jesus: 'He who lives by the sword will perish by the sword.' " I then urged them to leave peacefully. "We must love our white brothers," I said, "no matter what they do to us. We must make them know that we love them. Jesus still cries out in words that echo across the centuries: 'Love your enemies; bless them that curse you; pray for them that despitefully use you.' This is what we must live by. We must meet hate with love. Remember," I ended, "if I am stopped, this movement will not stop, because God is with the movement. Go home with this glowing faith and this radiant assurance."

10. "Desegregation at Last"
Martin Luther King, Jr.

After a prolonged legal battle while the boycott continued, the Supreme Court ruled on November 13, 1956, that segregation on Montgomery's buses was unconstitutional. But the ruling would not take effect until December 21. Like the previous selection, this is an excerpt from Stride Toward Freedom.

Meanwhile, we went to work to prepare the people for integrated buses. In mass meeting after mass meeting we stressed nonviolence. The prevailing theme was that "we must not take this as a victory over the white man, but as a victory for justice and democracy." We hammered away at the point that "we must not go back on the buses and push people around unnecessarily boasting of our rights. We must simply sit where there is a vacant seat."

In several meetings we ran teaching sessions to school the people in nonviolent techniques. We lined up chairs in front of the altar to resemble a bus, with a driver's seat out front. From the audience we selected a dozen or so "actors" and assigned each one a role in a hypothetical situation. One man was driver and the others were white and Negro passengers. Both groups contained some hostile and some courteous characters. As the audience watched, the actors played out a scene of insult or violence. At the end of each scene the actors returned to the audience and another group took their place; and at the end of each session a general discussion followed.

Sometimes the person playing a white man put so much zeal into his performance that he had to be gently reproved from the sidelines. Often a Negro forgot his nonviolent role and struck back with vigor; whenever this happened we worked to rechannel his words and deeds in a nonviolent direction.

As the day for the mandate drew near, several MIA [Montgomery Improvement Association] leaders went into the schools and urged the high school and college students to adhere to the way of nonviolence. We also distributed throughout the city a mimeographed list of "Suggestions for Integrating Buses." In preparing this text we had the assistance of the Rev. Glenn Smiley, a Southern-born white minister of the Fellowship of Reconciliation who was in Montgomery at the time.

INTEGRATED BUS SUGGESTIONS

This is a historic week because segregation on buses has now been declared unconstitutional. Within a few days the Supreme Court Mandate will reach Montgomery and you will be re-boarding *integrated* buses. This places upon us all a tremendous responsibility of maintaining, in face of what could be some unpleasantness, a calm and loving dignity befitting good citizens and members of our race. If there is violence in word or deed it must not be our people who commit it.

For your help and convenience the following suggestions are

made. Will you read, study and memorize them so that our nonviolent determination may not be endangered. First, some general suggestions:

1. Not all white people are opposed to integrated buses. Accept goodwill on the part of many.
2. The *whole* bus is now for the use of *all* people. Take a vacant seat.
3. Pray for guidance and commit yourself to complete nonviolence in word and action as you enter the bus.
4. Demonstrate the calm dignity of our Montgomery people in your actions.
5. In all things observe ordinary rules of courtesy and good behavior.
6. Remember that this is not a victory for Negroes alone, but for all Montgomery and the South. Do not boast! Do not brag!
7. Be quiet but friendly; proud, but not arrogant; joyous, but not boisterous.
8. Be loving enough to absorb evil and understanding enough to turn an enemy into a friend.

Now for some specific suggestions:

1. The bus driver is in charge of the bus and has been instructed to obey the law. Assume that he will cooperate in helping you occupy any vacant seat.
2. Do not deliberately sit by a white person, unless there is no other seat.
3. In sitting down by a person, white or colored, say "May I" or "Pardon me" as you sit. This is a common courtesy.
4. If cursed, do not curse back. If pushed, do not push back. If struck, do not strike back, but evidence love and goodwill at all times.
5. In case of an incident, talk as little as possible, and always in a quiet tone. Do not get up from your seat! Report all serious incidents to the bus driver.
6. For the first few days try to get on the bus with a friend in

se nonviolence you have confidence. You can uphold one another by a glance or a prayer.

7. If another person is being molested, do not arise to go to his defense, but pray for the oppressor and use moral and spiritual force to carry on the struggle for justice.

8. According to your own ability and personality, do not be afraid to experiment with new and creative techniques for achieving reconciliation and social change.

9. If you feel you cannot take it, walk for another week or two. We have confidence in our people. GOD BLESS YOU ALL.

In spite of all of our efforts to prepare the Negroes for integrated buses, not a single white group would take the responsibility of preparing the white community. We tried to get the white ministerial alliance to make a simple statement calling for courtesy and Christian brotherhood, but in spite of the favorable response of a few ministers, Robert Graetz reported that the majority "dared not get involved in such a controversial issue." This was a deep disappointment. Although the white ministers as a group had been appallingly silent throughout the protest, I had still maintained the hope that they would take a stand once the decision was rendered. Yes, there were always a few; but they were far too rare.

CHAPTER TWO

FIGHTING BACK
(1957–1962)

Introduction by Darlene Clark Hine

"Fighting back" is the general theme unifying the disparate documents in this chapter. The phrase has a double-edged meaning, signifying both black protest against segregation and inequality, and the massive resistance of white southerners determined to preserve a distinct way of life grounded in the ideology of white supremacy. Indeed, so entrenched were beliefs in the efficacy of black subordination that many southern whites viewed their racial hierarchy as natural, even ordained, order. Black and white southerners used governmental structures in their "fighting back" strategies. Both sides wrote books and pamphlets, and made speeches, to win adherence.

Certainly the work of the National Association for the Advancement of Colored People (NAACP) represents the most sustained assault against the edifice of racial segregation. During the 1930s the NAACP charted a legal strategy designed to end segregation in graduate and professional schools. Charles H. Houston, the NAACP's chief legal counsel, believed that the battle against segregation had to begin at the highest academic level in order to lessen fear of race mixing that could create even greater hostility and reluctance on the part of white judges. After establishing a series of favorable legal precedents in higher education, NAACP attorneys planned an all-out attack against the separate-but-equal doctrine in primary and secondary schools.

With the landmark 1954 *Brown* v. *Board of Education* U.S. Supreme Court decision the NAACP achieved its most impressive victory. The Court's declaration that a classification based solely on race violated the Fourteenth Amendment to the U.S. Constitution reversed the 1896 *Plessy* v. *Ferguson* ruling, which had established the separate-but-equal doctrine. *Brown,* more than any other case, launched the "equalitarian revolution" in American jurisprudence and signaled the emerging primacy of equality as a guide to constitutional decisions. Soon, however, the limitations of the decision became apparent. Indeed, the second *Brown* decision, known as *Brown II,* delivered a year later, restricted the impact of the 1954 case by providing southern states with the opportunity to delay the implementation of desegregation.

The *Brown* decision relied heavily on the research findings of social scientists. Among the seven scholarly works cited in the opinion were the studies completed by social psychologist Kenneth B. Clark on the adverse effects of prejudice and discrimination on personality development. In a society that valued whiteness and denigrated blackness, young African-American children early exhibited self-rejection and self-denial. If black children were to develop positive identities, then segregated education had to end.

Black Americans had celebrated *Brown,* equating it with the Emancipation Proclamation, but white southerners almost universally denounced the ruling and even questioned the right of the Supreme Court to deliver such a devastating blow. While black local and national leaders organized and orchestrated the legal struggles, and students joined in freedom rides and sit-ins, another equally important dimension of the rights quest took shape: the battle between federal and state authority and the evolution of federalism. To "fight back," white southerners engaged in massive resistance and embraced the doctrine of interposition.

Massive resistance to racial integration assumed many forms. In hundreds of communities local businessmen and social and political leaders organized white Citizens' Councils. These leaders employed economic sanctions, held rallies, and used intimidating rhetoric to thwart the black freedom struggle. Of the many proponents of massive resistance, none remained more intransigent than Tom P. Brady, a circuit judge from Brookhaven, Mississippi. Brady delivered the extremely vitriolic speech that the white Citizens' Councils published as a pamphlet, *Black Monday: Segregation or Amalgamation . . . America Has Its Choice.* Brady attacked the *Brown* decision, intermarriage, and black intelligence. Further, he charged that a number of black rights organizations were nothing more than a part of an international Communist conspiracy to destroy white supremacy.

The intervention of the federal government and the deployment of the National Guard in the 1954 Little Rock crisis, and again in 1963 when the enrollment of James Meredith desegregated the University of Mississippi, highlights the role of federal power in promoting social change during this era. President Dwight D. Eisenhower's use of federal troops in Little Rock, and President John F. Kennedy's deployment of the same forces in Oxford, represented a departure from the reluctance of earlier presidents to display federal power in the South, especially to protect the lives of black citizens.

Interposition holds that a state may reject a federal mandate it considers to be an encroachment upon the state's rights. An array of southern governors, such as Orval Faubus of Arkansas, Ross Barnett of Mississippi, and George Wallace of Alabama, acquired national notoriety in their bold display of defiance to court-ordered desegregation of secondary schools and state universities. Their stubborn challenges and adherence to the doctrine of interposition helped to provoke the confrontation between state and federal authority. But this is only half of the explanation of how the confrontations originated, especially in the Meredith episode. The other half involves the protracted delays, and considerable vacillation, of the Kennedy administration before it finally acted decisively to protect Meredith's life and his right to attend "Ole Miss."

A little-considered dimension of these dramatic events involves the transformative impact of school integration on white and black students in Little Rock, Arkansas. As shown in one of the documents in this chapter, a group of white and black students at Central High School discovered that through frank discussion of the fears that divided them these fears dwindled to insignificance. This candid roundtable discussion reveals the deep-seated anxiety and suspicion among whites that school integration was but a harbinger of racial intermarriage. The students concluded that freedom and democracy are color-blind concepts, and that as long as black rights receive scant protection and are denied, then the rights of all American citizens stand imperiled.

1. *Brown et al.* v. *Board of Education of Topeka et al.*

This is the text of the U.S. Supreme Court's decision in the group of cases decided on May 17, 1954, that became known as **Brown** *v.* **Board of Education of Topeka.**

NO. 1. APPEAL FROM THE UNITED STATES DISTRICT COURT FOR THE DISTRICT OF KANSAS*

Argued December 9, 1952—Reargued December 8, 1953— Decided May 17, 1954.

OPINION OF THE COURT
  MR. CHIEF JUSTICE WARREN delivered the opinion of the Court.
  These cases come to us from the States of Kansas, South Carolina, Virginia, and Delaware. They are premised on different

---

  * Together with No. 2, *Briggs et al.* v. *Elliott et al.*, on appeal from the United States District Court for the Eastern District of South Carolina, argued December 9–10, 1952, reargued December 7–8, 1953; No. 4, *Davis et al.* v. *County School Board of Prince Edward County, Virginia, et al.*, on appeal from the United States District Court for the Eastern District of Virginia, argued December 10, 1952, reargued December 7–8, 1953; and No. 10, *Gebhart et al.* v. *Belton et al.*, on certiorari to the Supreme Court of Delaware, argued December 11, 1952, reargued December 9, 1953.

facts and different local conditions, but a common legal question justifies their consideration together in this consolidated opinion.[1]

---

1. In the Kansas case, *Brown* v. *Board of Education,* the plaintiffs are Negro children of elementary school age residing in Topeka. They brought this action in the United States District Court for the District of Kansas to enjoin enforcement of a Kansas statute which permits, but does not require, cities of more than 15,000 population to maintain separate school facilities for Negro and white students. Kan. Gen. Stat. § 72-1724 (1949). Pursuant to that authority, the Topeka Board of Education elected to establish segregated elementary schools. Other public schools in the community, however, are operated on a nonsegregated basis. The three-judge District Court, convened under 28 U. S. C. §§ 2281 and 2284, found that segregation in public education has a detrimental effect upon Negro children, but denied relief on the ground that the Negro and white schools were substantially equal with respect to buildings, transportation, curricula, and educational qualifications of teachers. 98 F. Supp. 797. The case is here on direct appeal under 28 U. S. C. § 1253.

In the South Carolina case, *Briggs* v. *Elliott,* the plaintiffs are Negro children of both elementary and high school age residing in Clarendon County. They brought this action in the United States District Court for the Eastern District of South Carolina to enjoin enforcement of provisions in the state constitution and statutory code which require the segregation of Negroes and whites in public schools. S. C. Const., Art. XI, § 7; S. C. Code § 5377 (1942). The three-judge District Court, convened under 28 U. S. C. §§ 2281 and 2284, denied the requested relief. The court found that the Negro schools were inferior to the white schools and ordered the defendants to begin immediately to equalize the facilities. But the court sustained the validity of the contested provisions and denied the plaintiffs admission to the white schools during the equalization program. 98 F. Supp. 529. This Court vacated the District Court's judgment and remanded the case for the purpose of obtaining the court's views on a report filed by the defendants concerning the progress made in the equalization program. 324 U. S. 350. On remand, the District Court found that substantial equality had been achieved except for buildings and that the defendants were proceeding to rectify this inequality as well. 103 F. Supp. 920. The case is again here on direct appeal under 28 U. S. C. § 1253.

In the Virginia case, *Davis* v. *County School Board,* the plaintiffs are Negro children of high school age residing in Prince Edward County. They brought this action in the United States District Court for the Eastern District of Virginia to enjoin enforcement of provisions in the state constitution and statutory code which require the segregation of

In each of the cases, minors of the Negro race, through their legal representatives, seek the aid of the courts in obtaining admission to the public schools of their community on a nonsegregated basis. In each instance, they had been denied admission to schools attended by white children under laws requiring or permitting segregation according to race. This segregation was alleged to deprive the plaintiffs of the equal protection of the laws under the Fourteenth Amendment. In each of these cases other

---

Negroes and whites in public schools. Va. Const., § 140; Va. Code § 22-221 (1950). The three-judge District Court, convened under 28 U. S. C. §§ 2281 and 2284, denied the requested relief. The court found the Negro school inferior in physical plant, curricula, and transportation, and ordered the defendants forthwith to provide substantially equal curricula and transportation and to "proceed with all reasonable diligence and dispatch to remove" the inequality in physical plant. But, as in the South Carolina case, the court sustained the validity of the contested provisions and denied the plaintiffs admission to the white schools during the equalization program. 103 F. Supp. 337. The case is here on direct appeal under 28 U. S. C. § 1253.

In the Delaware case, *Gebhart* v. *Belton,* the plaintiffs are Negro children of both elementary and high school age residing in New Castle County. They brought this action in the Delaware Court of Chancery to enjoin enforcement of provisions in the state constitution and statutory code which require the segregation of Negroes and whites in public schools. Del. Const., Art. X, § 2; Del. Rev. Code § 2631 (1935). The Chancellor gave judgment for the plaintiffs and ordered their immediate admission to schools previously attended only by white children, on the ground that the Negro schools were inferior with respect to teacher training, pupil-teacher ratio, extracurricular activities, physical plant, and time and distance involved in travel. 87 A. 2d 862. The Chancellor also found that segregation itself results in an inferior education for Negro children (see note 10, *infra*), but did not rest his decision on that ground. *Id.,* at 865. The Chancellor's decree was affirmed by the Supreme Court of Delaware, which intimated, however, that the defendants might be able to obtain a modification of the decree after equalization of the Negro and white schools had been accomplished. 91 A. 2d 137, 152. The defendants, contending only that the Delaware courts had erred in ordering the immediate admission of the Negro plaintiffs to the white schools, applied to this Court for certiorari. The writ was granted, 344 U. S. 891. The plaintiffs, who were successful below, did not submit a cross-petition.

than the Delaware case, a three-judge federal district court denied relief to the plaintiffs on the so-called "separate but equal" doctrine announced by this Court in *Plessy* v. *Ferguson,* 163 U.S. 537. Under that doctrine, equality of treatment is accorded when the races are provided substantially equal facilities, even though these facilities be separate. In the Delaware case, the Supreme Court of Delaware adhered to that doctrine, but ordered that the plaintiffs be admitted to the white schools because of their superiority to the Negro schools.

The plaintiffs contend that segregated public schools are not "equal" and cannot be made "equal," and that hence they are deprived of the equal protection of the laws. Because of the obvious importance of the question presented, the Court took jurisdiction.[2] Argument was heard in the 1952 Term, and reargument was heard this Term on certain questions propounded by the Court.[3]

Reargument was largely devoted to the circumstances surrounding the adoption of the Fourteenth Amendment in 1868. It covered exhaustively consideration of the Amendment in Congress, ratification by the states, then existing practices in racial segregation, and the views of proponents and opponents of the Amendment. This discussion and our own investigation convince us that, although these sources cast some light, it is not enough to resolve the problem with which we are faced. At best, they are inconclusive. The most avid proponents of the post-War Amendments undoubtedly intended them to remove all legal distinctions among "all persons born or naturalized in the United States." Their opponents, just as certainly, were antagonistic to both the letter and the spirit of the Amendments and wished them to have the most limited effect. What others in Congress and the state legislatures had in mind cannot be determined with any degree of certainty.

An additional reason for the inconclusive nature of the Amend-

---

2. 344 U. S. 1, 141, 891.

3. 345 U. S. 972. The Attorney General of the United States participated both Terms as *amicus curiae.*

ment's history, with respect to segregated schools, is the status of public education at that time.[4] In the South, the movement toward free common schools, supported by general taxation, had not yet taken hold. Education of white children was largely in the hands of private groups. Education of Negroes was almost nonexistent, and practically all of the race were illiterate. In fact, any education of Negroes was forbidden by law in some states. Today, in contrast, many Negroes have achieved outstanding success in the arts and sciences as well as in the business and professional world. It is true that public school education at the time of the Amendment had advanced further in the North, but the effect of the Amendment on Northern States was generally ignored in the congressional debates. Even in the North, the conditions of public education did not approximate those existing today. The curriculum was usually rudimentary; ungraded schools were common in rural areas; the school term was but three months a year in

---

4. For a general study of the development of public education prior to the Amendment, see Butts and Cremin, A History of Education in American Culture (1953), Pts. I, II; Cubberley, Public Education in the United States (1934 ed.), cc. II-XII. School practices current at the time of the adoption of the Fourteenth Amendment are described in Butts and Cremin, *supra,* at 269–275; Cubberley, *supra,* at 288–339, 408–431; Knight, Public Education in the South (1922), cc. VIII, IX. See also H. Ex. Doc. No. 315, 41st Cong., 2d Sess. (1871). Although the demand for free public schools followed substantially in the same pattern in both the North and the South, the development in the South did not begin to gain momentum until about 1850, some twenty years after that in the North. The reasons for the somewhat slower development in the South (*e.g.,* the rural character of the South and the different regional attitudes toward state assistance) are well explained in Cubberley, *supra,* at 408–423. In the country as a whole, but particularly in the South, the War virtually stopped all progress in public education. *Id.,* at 427–428. The low status of Negro education in all sections of the country, both before and immediately after the War, is described in Beale, A History of Freedom of Teaching in American Schools (1941), 112–132, 175–195. Compulsory school attendance laws were not generally adopted until after the ratification of the Fourteenth Amendment, and it was not until 1918 that such laws were in force in all the states. Cubberley, *supra,* at 563–565.

many states; and compulsory school attendance was virtually unknown. As a consequence, it is not surprising that there should be so little in the history of the Fourteenth Amendment relating to its intended effect on public education.

In the first cases in this Court construing the Fourteenth Amendment, decided shortly after its adoption, the Court interpreted it as proscribing all state-imposed discriminations against the Negro race.[5] The doctrine "separate but equal" did not make its appearance in this Court until 1896 in the case of *Plessy* v. *Ferguson, supra,* involving not education but transportation.[6] American courts have since labored with the doctrine for over half a century. In this Court, there have been six cases involving the "separate but equal" doctrine in the field of public education.[7] In

---

5. *Slaughter-House Cases,* 16 Wall. 36, 67–72 (1873); *Strauder* v. *West Virginia,* 100 U. S. 303, 307–308 (1880): "It ordains that no State shall deprive any person of life, liberty, or property, without due process of law, or deny to any person within its jurisdiction the equal protection of the laws. What is this but declaring that the law in the States shall be the same for the black as for the white; that all persons, whether colored or white, shall stand equal before the laws of the States, and, in regard to the colored race, for whose protection the amendment was primarily designed, that no discrimination shall be made against them by law because of their color? The words of the amendment, it is true, are prohibitory, but they contain a necessary implication of a positive immunity, or right, most valuable to the colored race,—the right to exemption from unfriendly legislation against them distinctively as colored,—exemption from legal discriminations, implying inferiority in civil society, lessening the security of their enjoyment of the rights which others enjoy, and discriminations which are steps towards reducing them to the condition of a subject race." See also *Virginia* v. *Rives,* 100 U. S. 313, 318 (1880); *Ex parte Virginia,* 100 U. S. 339, 344–345 (1880).

6. The doctrine apparently originated in *Roberts* v. *City of Boston,* 59 Mass. 198, 206 (1850), upholding school segregation against attack as being violative of a state constitutional guarantee of equality. Segregation in Boston public schools was eliminated in 1855. Mass. Acts 1855, c. 256. But elsewhere in the North segregation in public education has persisted in some communities until recent years. It is apparent that such segregation has long been a nationwide problem, not merely one of sectional concern.

7. See also *Berea College* v. *Kentucky,* 211 U. S. 45 (1908).

Cumming v. *County Board of Education,* 175 U.S. 528, and *Gong Lum* v. *Rice,* 275 U.S. 78, the validity of the doctrine itself was not challenged.[8] In more recent cases, all on the graduate school level, inequality was found in that specific benefits enjoyed by white students were denied to Negro students of the same educational qualifications. *Missouri ex rel. Gaines* v. *Canada,* 305 U.S. 337; *Sipuel* v. *Oklahoma,* 332 U.S. 631; *Sweatt* v. *Painter,* 339 U.S. 629; *McLaurin* v. *Oklahoma State Regents,* 339 U.S. 637. In none of these cases was it necessary to re-examine the doctrine to grant relief to the Negro plaintiff. And in *Sweatt* v. *Painter, supra,* the Court expressly reserved decision on the question whether *Plessy* v. *Ferguson* should be held inapplicable to public education.

In the instant cases, that question is directly presented. Here, unlike *Sweatt* v. *Painter,* there are findings below that the Negro and white schools involved have been equalized, or are being equalized, with respect to buildings, curricula, qualifications and salaries of teachers, and other "tangible" factors.[9] Our decision, therefore, cannot turn on merely a comparison of these tangible factors in the Negro and white schools involved in each of the cases. We must look instead to the effect of segregation itself on public education.

In approaching this problem, we cannot turn the clock back to

---

8. In the *Cumming* case, Negro taxpayers sought an injunction requiring the defendant school board to discontinue the operation of a high school for white children until the board resumed operation of a high school for Negro children. Similarly, in the *Gong Lum* case, the plaintiff, a child of Chinese descent, contended only that state authorities had misapplied the doctrine by classifying him with Negro children and requiring him to attend a Negro school.

9. In the Kansas case, the court below found substantial equality as to all such factors. 98 F. Supp. 797, 798. In the South Carolina case, the court below found that the defendants were proceeding "promptly and in good faith to comply with the court's decree." 103 F. Supp. 920, 921. In the Virginia case, the court below noted that the equalization program was already "afoot and progressing" (103 F. Supp. 337, 341); since then, we have been advised, in the Virginia Attorney General's brief on reargument, that the program has now been completed. In the Delaware case, the court below similarly noted that the state's equalization program was well under way. 91 A. 2d 137, 149.

1868 when the Amendment was adopted, or even to 1896 when *Plessy* v. *Ferguson* was written. We must consider public education in the full light of its full development and its present place in American life throughout the Nation. Only in this way can it be determined if segregation in public schools deprives these plaintiffs of the equal protection of the laws.

Today, education is perhaps the most important function of state and local governments. Compulsory school attendance laws and the great expenditures for education both demonstrate our recognition of the importance of education to our democratic society. It is required in the performance of our most basic public responsibilities, even service in the armed forces. It is the very foundation of good citizenship. Today it is a principal instrument in awakening the child to cultural values, in preparing him for later professional training, and in helping him to adjust normally to his environment. In these days, it is doubtful that any child may reasonably be expected to succeed in life if he is denied the opportunity of an education. Such an opportunity, where the state has undertaken to provide it, is a right which must be made available to all on equal terms.

We come then to the question presented: Does segregation of children in public schools solely on the basis of race, even though the physical facilities and other "tangible" factors may be equal, deprive the children of the minority group of equal educational opportunities? We believe that it does.

In *Sweatt* v. *Painter, supra,* in finding that a segregated law school for Negroes could not provide them equal educational opportunities, this Court relied in large part on "those qualities which are incapable of objective measurement but which make for greatness in a law school." In *McLaurin* v. *Oklahoma State Regents, supra,* the Court, in requiring that a Negro admitted to a white graduate school be treated like all other students, again resorted to intangible considerations: ". . . his ability to study, to engage in discussions and exchange views with other students, and, in general, to learn his profession." Such considerations apply with added force to children in grade and high schools. To separate them from others of similar age and qualifications solely because of their race generates a feeling of inferiority as to their status in the community that may affect their hearts and minds in a way unlikely ever to be undone. The effect of this separation on their educational opportunities was well stated by a finding in the Kansas case by a court which nevertheless felt compelled to rule against the Negro plaintiffs:

> Segregation of white and colored children in public schools has a detrimental effect upon the colored children. The impact is greater when it has the sanction of the law; for the policy of separating the races is usually interpreted as denoting the inferiority of the negro group. A sense of inferiority affects the motivation of a child to learn. Segregation with the sanction of law, therefore, has a tendency to [retard] the educational and mental development of negro children and to deprive them of some of the benefits they would receive in a racial[ly] integrated school system.[10]

Whatever may have been the extent of psychological knowledge at the time of *Plessy* v. *Ferguson,* this finding is amply supported by modern authority.[11] Any language in *Plessy* v. *Ferguson* contrary to this finding is rejected.

We conclude that in the field of public education the doctrine of "separate but equal" has no place. Separate educational facilities are inherently unequal. Therefore, we hold that the plaintiffs and

---

10. A similar finding was made in the Delaware case: "I conclude from the testimony that in our Delaware society, State-imposed segregation in education itself results in the Negro children, as a class, receiving educational opportunities which are substantially inferior to those available to white children otherwise similarly situated." 87 A. 2d 862, 865.

11. K. B. Clark, Effect of Prejudice and Discrimination on Personality Development (Midcentury White House Conference on Children and Youth, 1950); Witmer and Kotinsky, Personality in the Making (1952), c. VI; Deutscher and Chein, The Psychological Effects of Enforced Segregation: A Survey of Social Science Opinion, 26 J. Psychol. 259 (1948); Chein, What are the Psychological Effects of Segregation Under Conditions of Equal Facilities?, 3 Int. J. Opinion and Attitude Res. 229 (1949); Brameld, Educational Costs, in Discrimination and National Welfare (MacIver, ed., 1949), 44-48; Frazier, The Negro in the United States (1949), 674-681. And see generally Myrdal, An American Dilemma (1944).

others similarly situated for whom the actions have been brought are, by reason of the segregation complained of, deprived of the equal protection of the laws guaranteed by the Fourteenth Amendment. This disposition makes unnecessary any discussion whether such segregation also violates the Due Process Clause of the Fourteenth Amendment.[12]

Because these are class actions, because of the wide applicability of this decision, and because of the great variety of local conditions, the formulation of decrees in these cases presents problems of considerable complexity. On reargument, the consideration of appropriate relief was necessarily subordinated to the primary question—the constitutionality of segregation in public education. We have now announced that such segregation is a denial of the equal protection of the laws. In order that we may have the full assistance of the parties in formulating decrees, the cases will be restored to the docket, and the parties are requested to present further argument on Questions 4 and 5 previously propounded by the Court for the reargument this Term.[13] The Attorney

---

12. See *Bolling* v. *Sharpe, post,* p. 497, concerning the Due Process Clause of the Fifth Amendment.

13. "4. Assuming it is decided that segregation in public schools violates the Fifth Amendment

"(a) would a decree necessarily follow providing that, within the limits set by normal geographic school districting, Negro children should forthwith be admitted to schools of their choice, or

"(b) may this Court, in the exercise of its equity powers, permit an effective gradual adjustment to be brought about from existing segregated systems to a system not based on color distinctions?

"5. On the assumption on which questions 4 (a) and (b) are based, and assuming further that this Court will exercise its equity powers to the end described in question 4 (b),

"(a) should this Court formulate detailed decrees in these cases;

"(b) if so, what specific issues should the decrees reach;

"(c) should this Court appoint a special master to hear evidence with a view to recommending specific terms for such decrees;

"(d) should this Court remand to the courts of the first instance with directions to frame decrees in these cases, and if so what general directions should the decrees of this Court include and what procedures should the courts of first instance follow in arriving at the specific terms of more detailed decrees?"

General of the United States is again invited to participate. The Attorneys General of the states requiring or permitting segregation in public education will also be permitted to appear as *amici curiae* upon request to do so by September 15, 1954, and submission of briefs by October 1, 1954.[14]

It is so ordered.

2. "How Children Learn About Race"
Kenneth B. Clark

The Supreme Court's unanimous decision in the **Brown** *case relied quite heavily on the research findings of social scientists. Among the seven scholarly works cited in footnote 11 of the opinion was the report entitled* **Effect of Prejudice and Discrimination on Personality Development** *prepared for the 1950 Midcentury White House Conference on Children and Youth by psychologist Kenneth Clark. The report was later revised and expanded and published for the general public as* **Prejudice and Your Child** *(1955).*

Are children born with racial feelings? Or do they have to learn, first, what color they are and, second, what color is "best"?

Less than fifty years ago, some social theorists maintained that racial and religious prejudices are inborn—that they are inherent and instinctive. These theorists believed that children do not have to *learn* to dislike people who differ from them in physical characteristics; it was considered natural to dislike those different from oneself and to like those similar to oneself.

However, research over the past thirty years has refuted these earlier theories. Social scientists are now convinced that children learn social, racial, and religious prejudices in the course of observing, and being influenced by, the existence of patterns in the culture in which they live. Students of the problem are now facing these questions:

---

14. See Rule 42, Revised Rules of this Court (effective July 1, 1954).

1. How and when do children learn to identify themselves with some people and to differentiate themselves from others?
2. How and when do children acquire racial attitudes and begin to express these attitudes in their behavior?
3. What conditions in the environment foster the development of these racial attitudes and behavior?
4. What can be done to prevent the development and expression of destructive racial prejudices in children?

Until quite recently, there were differences in opinion concerning the age at which children develop and express racial prejudices. Some observers (in the tradition of those who believed that prejudices are inborn) said that even infants express racial preferences and that therefore such preferences play little or no role in the life of the child until the early teens. They pointed out that children of different races have been observed playing together and sometimes developing close friendships; this fact, they thought, showed that young children are unaware of racial or religious differences.

Within the past two decades, social scientists have made a series of studies of this problem.[1] They indicate, on the one hand, that there is no evidence that racial prejudices are inborn; and, on the other hand, that it is equally false to assume that the child remains unaffected by racial considerations until his teens or pre-teens.

Racial attitudes appear early in the life of children and affect the ideas and behavior of children in the first grades of school. Such attitudes—which appear to be almost inevitable in children in our society—develop gradually.

According to one recent study, white kindergarten children in New York City show a clear preference for whites and a clear

---

1. A pioneer work in this field is *Race Attitudes in Children* by Bruno Lasker. Since its publication in 1935, a number of psychologists and other social scientists have studied aspects of racial attitudes in children by more precise methods. Eugene Horowitz set the pattern for empirical investigations of this problem in his study of the development of racial attitudes in children. His results have been supported and extended by the findings of Ruth Horowitz; Kenneth and Mamie Clark; Radke, Trager, and Davis; and Mary Ellen Goodman. . . .

rejection of Negroes. Other studies show that Negro children in the kindergarten and early elementary grades of a New England town, in New York City, in Philadelphia, and in two urban communities in Arkansas know the difference between Negroes and whites; realize they are Negro or white; and are aware of the social meaning and evaluation of racial differences.

The development of racial awareness and racial preferences in Negro children has been studied by the author and his wife. To determine the extent of consciousness of skin color in these children between three and seven years old, we showed the children four dolls all from the same mold and dressed alike; the only difference in the dolls was that two were brown and two were white. We asked the children to choose among the dolls in answer to certain requests:

1. "Give me the white doll."
2. "Give me the colored doll."
3. "Give me the Negro doll."

These children reacted with strong awareness of skin color. Among three-year-old Negro children in both northern and southern communities, more than 75 per cent showed that they were conscious of the difference between "white" and "colored." Among older children, an increasingly greater number made the correct choices.

These findings clearly support the conclusion that racial awareness is present in Negro children as young as three years old. Furthermore, this knowledge develops in stability and clarity from year to year, and by the age of seven it is a part of the knowledge of all Negro children. Other investigators[2] have shown that the same is true of white children.

Some children whose skin color is indistinguishable from that of white people, but who are nonetheless classified as Negroes by the society, have difficulty in making a correct racial identification of themselves at an age when other children do so. Soon, how-

---

2. Ruth Horowitz; Mary Ellen Goodman; Radke, Trager, and Davis.

ever—by the age of five or six—the majority of these children also begin to accept the social definition of themselves, even though this differs from their observance of their own skin color.

There is now no doubt that children learn the prevailing social ideas about racial differences early in their lives. Not only are they aware of race in terms of physical characteristics such as skin color, but also they are generally able to identify themselves in terms of race.

The problem of the development and awareness of religious ideas and identification in children involves more subtle and complex distinctions which understandably require a longer period of time before they are clearly understood.

It is much more difficult for children to know if they are Catholic, Protestant, or Jewish than it is to know if they are white or Negro. In one study (Radke, Trager, and Davis), children were shown pictures of a church with a cross, and of a building clearly marked as a synagogue. The investigators asked the children their reactions to these pictures. Only a minority of children between the ages of five and eight made stable and accurate identification of themselves in terms of religion. Less than half the Jewish children in this age group identified themselves as Jews, while only 30 per cent of the Catholic children and less than 27 per cent of the white Protestant children made correct religious identifications. The relatively high percentage of Jewish children who identified themselves as Jews indicates that for these children there is an earlier awareness of religious identification and probably of minority status.

In these tests, no Negro child identified himself in religious terms. This fact probably indicates that for the Negro child at these ages the dominant factor in self-identification is skin color. The impact of their minority status as determined by skin color is so great that it precludes more abstract bases for self-identification.

A study of seven- and eight-year-old Jewish boys (by Hartley, Rosenbaum, and Schwartz) found that these boys had a generalized preference for all things "Jewish." The children responded to all questions concerning self-identification and preference with such

comments as: "Because I am Jewish." "Because I like Jewish."
"Because they are Jewish like me." "Because I like to play with
Jewish people."

This undifferentiated preference for Jewishness was found by
Radke to be appreciably less among Jewish children of ten and
eleven, and even less in thirteen- and fourteen-year-olds. It is
possible that as these children mature their increased contact with
the larger culture results in a decreased interest in Jewishness as
such. It is also possible that this tendency reflects an increase in
rejection of Jewishness—indicating the children's growing awareness of the minority status of Jews in America.

The same social scientists have studied small groups of Jewish,
Catholic, Negro, and white Protestant children in New York City.
These children were asked to respond to the simple question,
"What are you?" Jewish children on all age levels answered by the
term "Jewish," rarely identifying themselves in terms of nationality
or color. On the other hand, a considerable proportion of the
non-Jewish children identified themselves in terms of nationality
rather than religion.

Non-Jewish children between the ages of $3\frac{1}{2}$ and $4\frac{1}{2}$ were usually
not certain what religion they belonged to. Some non-Jewish white
children in this age group said that they were Jewish; the fact that
they were enrolled in a Jewish neighborhood center may have
accounted for their mistaken belief that they were Jewish. At this
stage of development, a non-Jewish child in a Jewish setting may
conceive of himself as Jewish, and vice versa. These results suggest
that the problem of religious identification involves a level of
abstract thinking of which pre-school children are generally
incapable.

These investigators also studied the meaning of such terms as
"Jewish" and "Catholic" for children between the ages of four and
ten. They found that at these ages the concepts are understood
in terms of concrete activities. Jewish children mentioned "Going
to shul," "Not eating bacon," or "Talking Jewish." Catholic children
mentioned "Going to church," "Making communion," or "To
speak as a Catholic."

Certain conclusions arise from the many independent investigations of the development of racial awareness and identification

in children. By the age of four, Negro and white children are generally aware of differences in skin color and can identify themselves correctly in terms of such differences. Jewish children are not consistently aware of their Jewishness until around the age of five. The average Catholic or Protestant child does not begin to identify himself in religious terms until around seven or eight. Thus it appears that the concrete and perceptible fact of skin color provides a basis for earlier self-identification and preferences in American children than the more abstract factor of the family religion.

A child gradually learns what status the society accords to his group. The tendency of older Jewish children to show less preference for Jewishness than younger Jewish children suggests that they have learned that Jews do not have a preferred status in the larger society, and that these children have accordingly modified their self-appraisal. This effect of the awareness of the status of one's own group is even more clearly apparent in the case of Negro children.

In addition to Negro children's awareness of differences in skin color, the author and his wife studied the ability of these children to identify themselves in racial terms. We asked the children to point out the doll "which is most like you." Approximately two-thirds of all the children answered correctly. Correct answers were more frequent among the older ones. (Only 37 per cent of the three-year-olds but 87 per cent of the seven-year-olds responded accurately.) Negro children of light skin color had more difficulty in choosing the brown doll than Negro children of medium-brown or dark-brown skin color. This was true for older as well as younger children.

Many personal and emotional factors probably affected the ability of these Negro children to select the brown doll. In an effort to determine their racial preferences, we asked the children the following four questions:

1. "Give me the doll that you like to play with" or "the doll you like best."
2. "Give me the doll that is the nice doll."

3. "Give me the doll that looks bad."
4. "Give me the doll that is a nice color."

The majority of these Negro children at each age indicated an unmistakable preference for the white doll and a rejection of the brown doll.[3]

Studies of the development of racial awareness, racial identification, and racial preference in both Negro and white children thus present a consistent pattern. Learning about races and racial differences, learning one's own racial identity, learning which race is to be preferred and which rejected—all these are assimilated by the child as part of the total pattern of ideas he acquires about himself and the society in which he lives. These acquired patterns of social and racial ideas are interrelated both in development and in function. The child's first awareness of racial differences is found to be associated with some rudimentary evaluation of these differences. Furthermore, as the average child learns to evaluate these differences according to the standards of the society, he is at the same time required to identify himself with one or another group. This identification necessarily involves a knowledge of the status assigned to the group with which he identifies himself, in relation to the status of other groups. The child therefore cannot learn what racial group he belongs to without being involved in a larger pattern of emotions, conflict, and desires which are part of his growing knowledge of what society thinks about his race.

Many independent studies enable us to begin to understand how children learn about race, how they identify themselves and others in terms of racial, religious, or nationality differences, and what meaning these differences have for the growing child. Racial and religious identification involves the ability of the child to

---

3. Even at three years the majority preferred the white doll and rejected the brown doll. The children of six or seven showed some indication of an increased preference for the brown doll; even at this age, however, the majority of the Negro children still preferred the doll with the white skin color.

identify himself with others of similar characteristics, and to distinguish himself from those who appear to be dissimilar.

The fact that young Negro children would prefer to be white reflects their knowledge that society prefers white people. White children are generally found to prefer their white skin—an indication that they too know that society likes whites better. It is clear, therefore, that the self-acceptance or self-rejection found so early in a child's developing complex of racial ideas reflects the awareness and acceptance of the prevailing racial attitudes in his community.

Some children as young as three years of age begin to express racial and religious attitudes similar to those held by adults in their society. The racial and religious attitudes of sixth-graders are more definite than the attitudes of pre-school children, and hardly distinguishable from the attitudes of high-school students. Thereafter there is an increase in the intensity and complexity of these attitudes, until they become similar (at least, as far as words go) to the prevailing attitudes held by the average adult American.

The racial ideas of children are less rigid, more easily changed, than the racial ideas of adults. It is probable, too, that racial attitudes and behavior are more directly related among adults. The racial and religious attitudes of a young child may become more positive or more negative as he matures. The direction these attitudes will take, their intensity and form of expression, will be determined by the type of experiences that the child is permitted to have. One student of this problem says that, although children tend to become more tolerant in their general social attitudes as they grow older, they become less tolerant in their attitudes toward the Negro. This may reflect the fact that the things children are taught about the Negro and the experiences they are permitted to have usually result in the development of racial intolerance.

3. "The Atlanta Declaration"

National Association for the Advancement of Colored People

Two days after the Brown *decision was handed down, an NAACP conference was held in Atlanta, Georgia, during which the organization expressed complete confidence in rapid compliance with Court-ordered desegregation. This selection is excerpted from a press release from that conference.*

All Americans are now relieved to have the law of the land declare in the clearest language: ". . . in the field of public education the doctrine of 'separate but equal' has no place. Separate educational facilities are inherently unequal." Segregation in public education is now not only unlawful; it is un-American. True Americans are grateful for this decision. Now that the law is made clear, we look to the future. Having canvassed the situation in each of our states, we approach the future with the utmost confidence. . . .

We stand ready to work with other law abiding citizens who are anxious to translate this decision into a program of action to eradicate racial segregation in public education as speedily as possible. . . .

While we recognize that school officials will have certain administrative problems in transferring from a segregated to a nonsegregated system, we will resist the use of any tactics contrived for the sole purpose of delaying desegregation. . . .

We insist that there should be integration at all levels, including the assignment of teacher-personnel on a nondiscriminatory basis. . . .

We look upon this memorable decision not as a victory for Negroes alone, but for the whole American people and as a vindication of America's leadership of the free world.

Lest there be any misunderstanding of our position, we here rededicate ourselves to the removal of all racial segregation in public education and reiterate our determination to achieve this goal without compromise of principle.

4. "Black Monday: Segregation or Amalgamation . . . America Has Its Choice"

Tom P. Brady

Judge Tom P. Brady of Brookhaven, Mississippi, has been called the "intellectual leader" of the Citizens' Council movement. His speech "Black Monday" was first delivered to the Sons of the American Revolution in Greenwood, Mississippi, and subsequently repeated before the Citizens' Council of nearby Indianola. Brady then expanded the speech into a ninety-two-page booklet, of which excerpts are here reprinted. Widely disseminated throughout the South at $1 per copy, it was published by the Association of Citizens' Councils, Winona, Mississippi, in 1955.

FOREWORD

"Black Monday" is the name coined by Representative John Bell Williams of Mississippi to designate Monday, May 17th, 1954, a date long to be remembered throughout this nation. This is the date upon which the Supreme Court of the United States handed down its socialistic decision in the Segregation cases on appeal from the States of Kansas, South Carolina, Virginia and Delaware. "Black Monday" is indeed symbolic of the date. Black denoting darkness and terror. Black signifying the absence of light and wisdom. Black embodying grief, destruction and death. Should Representative Williams accomplish nothing more during his membership in Congress he has more than justified his years in office by the creating of this epithet, the originating of this watchword, the shouting of this battle cry.

Black Monday ranks in importance with July 4th, 1776, the date upon which our Declaration of Independence was signed. May 17th, 1954, is the date upon which the declaration of socialistic doctrine was officially proclaimed throughout this nation. It was on Black Monday that the judicial branch of our government usurped the sacred privilege and right of the respective states of this union to educate their youth. This usurpation constitutes the greatest travesty of the American Constitution and jurisprudence in the history of this nation.

Denunciation and abuse are the favorite weapons of the clumsy, frustrated and uncontrolled. I shall strive to proceed without them, but impartial frankness and truth should not be confused with bitter criticism and reproach.

"Black Monday" is not written primarily in behalf of the white people of the seventeen States affected by the Segregation decision, though it is hoped it will be beneficial to them. It is, however, written with the fervent desire that it will be of material benefit to both the white and colored people of this country, wheresoever situated. It is written to alert and encourage every American, irrespective of race, who loves our Constitution, our Government and our God-given American way of life. It is composed for the average American who firmly believes that the legislative, judicial and executive branches of our Federal Government should remain separate and distinct; who maintains that the Federal Government was constructed by the States for the benefit of the States, and that the States were not created for the establishment and advancement of a paternalistic or totalitarian Government. It is dedicated to those who firmly believe that socialism and communism are lethal messes of porridge for which our sacred birthright shall not be sold.

AMERICA COMES OF AGE

The years from 1620 to 1936 were miraculous. The whole gamut of American experience can be found in this interim. Thirteen pathetically weak colonies oppose the greatest military power on earth, Great Britain. They were not without assistance, and after almost seven trying, bloody years, victory is won at Yorktown, and a nation is born. Certain figures stand out from the crowd: Washington, Jefferson, Franklin, Patrick Henry, Wayne, Randolph, Paine, Adams, Greene, Morgan and Hamilton. It is ridiculous to assume that the American negro played any part in this struggle, though he had been in this country approximately one hundred and fifty years. He made no contribution whatsoever.

After 1782, when peace was signed with England, the colonies began to recuperate from the devastating experience. Expansion took place and commerce came into being. The trek southward had begun and the cry of "Westward Ho!" was first being faintly heard. England, smarting under her previous defeat and irked by the Yankee merchant ships which were importing and exporting goods from all over the world, precipitated the War of 1812. Again certain men are conspicuous—John Marshall, who had already given us his inestimable genius; Stephen Decatur, Paul Jones, Lawrence, Hull, Bainbridge, Francis Scott Key and Andrew Jackson. Like the war of 1776, the War of 1812 was a just war, and the United States emerged victorious. It is ridiculous to assume that the American negro played any part in this struggle, though he had been in this country almost two hundred years.

The Louisiana purchase and then the conquering of the West began. The "Forty Niners"—the Indian wars, the liberation of Texas. No American negroes were massacred with Custer, or died in the sacred Alamo. In the struggle for development, in the expansion and growth which was taking place—in the laying of the solid foundation of our nation, it is ridiculous to assume that the American negro played any part except as a body servant or hostler.

Then came the bloodiest of all wars—the most destructive to the white genius and ability of this country—the Civil War. The negro was the fundamental cause of this war—never forget this fact—and it is ridiculous to assume that he played any part in it except as a servant to those unable to fight. And then the saddest and most terrible of all American dramas was enacted—the Reconstruction period—the pious greed of the New England slave trader had brought the negro to our shores and now his insatiable hatred and envy was to be placated. Military governments were established, the face of the Southern white soldier who had survived the war was ground in the dust by the foot of his conqueror with the aid of the carpetbagger from the North—the scalawag of the South, and the negro. Yes, you are correct in assuming a small segment of the negro race played a part in this rapine. It was as thorough as Sherman's "March to the Sea." In truth, the South has not yet fully recovered from this scorched earth policy, pillage and the bitter hatred which blazed and still smolders against it. Let us briefly review a few significant events of this tragic era.

The true and succinct words of Charles Wallace Collins, found in his remarkable book, "Whither Solid South," best outlines the situation and problem:

"**Immediately after the Civil War, Amendments 13 and 15, which prohibited slavery and provided that the power to vote should not be denied on account of race or color,** [here as elsewhere, emphasis in original] were submitted to the States for ratification. They attracted little attention. **But when the 14th Amendment came along it was filled with dynamite.** The Radical Republicans were in control of Congress and they intended to enact legislation under this Amendment which would weaken the States and set up a strong central Government in Washington which would take over jurisdiction of the civil rights of individuals and thereby dominate the South through carpetbagger-negro rule.

"**On June 16, 1866, Congress submitted the Fourteenth Amendment** to the States for ratification. This required the approval of **three-fourths of the States.** Each of the former Confederate States, except Tennessee, voted to reject the Amendment, and ratification was thereby defeated. **The Amendment had been lawfully submitted and the rejection was lawful under the procedure provided by the Constitution. That should have been the end of the matter. But Congress became infuriated at the failure of the Amendment to be ratified and from thenceforth adopted high-handed measures. It took over the Southern States by military occupation, disfranchised the white people and put the ballot into the hands of the negro—coached by the carpetbaggers.**"

Now hear this, oh, High Priests of Washington:
"**In 1868 the Fourteenth Amendment was resubmitted to the States for ratification, and this time it was ratified almost unanimously by the Southern States. The United States Army attended to the details. This last ratification was unlawful and in violation of the Constitution.** That is why, in so far as the negro is concerned,

the Fourteenth Amendment has never been of any moral force in the South." (See Chapter VI of "Whither Solid South.")

Congress next proceeded to enact legislation to enforce the Amendment. There went to the statute books at this time **the Enforcement Act of 1870, the Ku Klux Act of 1871 and the Civil Rights Act of 1875. The first case to reach the Supreme Court in a test of these Acts was U.S. vs. Cruikshank.** This case arose in Louisiana. Cruikshank and a number of other white men broke up by violent means a negro political meeting. Cruikshank and other whites were arrested, tried in the Federal Court and convicted of the violation of the Enforcement Act of 1870.

The case reached the Supreme Court of the United States in 1876 on appeal. **The Court held that Congress of itself had no power, and derived no power from the Fourteenth Amendment to legislate in respect to the acts of individual persons; that the restrictions of the Amendment ran only against action by the State.** In this case the State of Louisiana had taken no action. It held that whatever crime which may have been committed could only be a violation of the law of the State, in respect to which the State courts were open. The Court said:

"The very highest duty of the States, when they entered into the Union under the Constitution, was to protect all persons within their boundaries in the enjoyment of these inalienable rights."

The Cruikshank case saved the South and, furthermore, **saved our Republican form of Government.** It was strongly and completely confirmed by the **Supreme Court in 1883 in the Civil Rights Case,** which held that Congress gained 'no countenance of authority' from the Fourteenth Amendment to enact laws governing the civil rights of individuals.

From the time of these decisions until 1936—a period of sixty years—there was peace in the South between the two races. However, during the latter part of this period, large numbers of negroes moved north to such cities as Chicago, Detroit, Philadelphia and New York. Here they gradually developed political power under the simple qualification of the age of manhood for voting. They developed local leadership. **The National Association for the Advancement of the Colored People was organized in New York.** It became a nationwide organization, with chapters all over the country, including the South. It entered politics. The Association and all of its subsidiaries and affiliates went over to the Democratic Party in 1936, and there, with the support of Northern Democrats, successfully—although indirectly—challenged the South. **The Convention's two-thirds rule was abolished, the South thereby losing its traditional veto over the nomination.** The South was thereafter unable to make any show of strength to recover its former position.

As a result of this development, the negro leaders began to agitate for a reversal of the Supreme Court's position on civil rights. They planned to ask for new civil rights legislation by Congress with a view to having it confirmed by the Supreme Court. The core of this movement was the Truman Civil Rights Program, which has now been reintroduced in the 83rd Congress as a somewhat obverse side to the segregation cases.

It is interesting to note that the Attorney General in his appearance for the Eisenhower Administration in the segregation cases, in effect, refused to support these civil rights bills. **He advised the Court against legislation by Congress in this field. He warned that great confusion would be caused if the long line of precedents stemming from the Cruikshank case were to be reversed.**

[Attorney General Herbert] Brownell advised the Court **that it had the judicial power in itself to decree that segregation in the public school violates the Fourteenth Amendment by the State concerned.** The question then arises: by what means could the Court enforce its decree? The Federal judiciary in the South has no equipment, personnel or any sort of organization to enforce such a decree in the face of a solid adverse public opinion, against one-third of the population of the United States.

Such decree has been promulgated, and when the States refuse to abolish segregation and the doctrine in the Cruikshank case remains inviolate, the decree will be frustrated.

The Supreme Court does not possess the legislative power. When a case comes before the Court, as does a case before any court, the issue is joined, arguments are made and a decision rendered. That decision binds the parties to that particular case. The legislative power of the Federal Government is vested in the Congress of the United States. **The Supreme Court has no power**

to make a decree which could have the effect of an Act of Congress. The Supreme Court can, of course, exceed its powers and violate the Constitution and invade the province of Congress and that of the state legislatures—as has frequently been the case. Has the Supreme Court the power to establish by decree a national segregation policy which would bind all of the forty-eight states—a power which Congress itself does not possess?

This is the true question which "Black Monday" actually decided.

Repeated Warnings

. . . It appears that the NAACP used excellent judgment in selecting the cases, the forums, the time and the attorneys in presenting the questions involved and the proponents of the States' Rights principle of segregation have, at best, had but a poor day in court, which is, of course, of no concern to the United States Supreme Court.

The Supreme Court should be accorded all the deference and respect possible because of the nature of the office. It should be given at least the esteem accorded Pontius Pilate. It should, however, be borne in mind that it is not infallible, and it is not clothed with "the divinity which doth hedge a king." To blindly submit to an erroneous decision which breaks all long established rules of law, violates the principle of **stare decisis,** and adopts sociological assertions instead of laws as its guide is not loyalty or patriotism. It is simple folly or ignorance. Since when has a fallacious opinion of the Supreme Court been above review or censure? There are those who confuse freedom of thought and criticism with subversiveness. Each decision stands on its own legs and if it is unsound, is not based on solid rules of law which have been in force and effect it should be so classified. If the result of the decision will be harmful to the bulk of the people of this country, will be calculated to foster those forces which seek this country's destruction, then to fail to resist the decision is morally wrong and the man who fails to condemn it and do all that he can to see that it is reversed is not a patriotic American.

This is, moreover, not a case of turning the other cheek as the tinkling cymbals in some of our churches and educational institutions would have us believe, but one of driving the money changers out of the temple. Yes, the Supreme Court should receive all the honor possible, in spite of the fact, as in the case of Brother Lawrence in the Spanish cloister, if odium and disrespect could have killed it, its obituary would have been written long ago.

The ruling laid down in Plessey vs. Ferguson, which has been in full force and effect for fifty-eight years, is now but a scrap of paper. In destroying this ruling, the Supreme Court likewise had to void the principle that State laws providing for racial segregation in the public schools did not conflict with the Fourteenth Amendment which was laid down in five cases heretofore decided by the Supreme Court. These cases are: Gong Lum vs. Rice, 275 U.S. 78 (1927). See Mo. ex rel. Gaines vs. Canada, 305 U.S. 337, 344 (1938); Cumming vs. Richmond County Board of Education, 175 U.S. 528, 545 (1899); Plessey vs. Ferguson, 163 U.S. 537, 544 (1896); Hall vs. Decuir, 95 U.S. 485, 504 (concurring opinion, Clifford, J.) (1877).

In addition to overruling these former Supreme Court decisions, they likewise overruled thirty-five decisions of the lower Federal Courts, including the Circuit Courts of Appeal. It should be noted in passing that in the Gong Lum vs. Rice case, the Supreme Court, which at that time was composed of Chief Justice Taft and Associate Justices Holmes, Van Devanter, Brandeis, Stone, McReynolds, Butler and Sanford, Mr. Justice Sullivan being absent on account of illness, held that the doctrine in the Plessey vs. Ferguson case applied—that is, the separate but equal rule was applicable. Of course the legal ability, the character and the experience of the present Supreme Court far exceeds that of the Supreme Court which handed down the decision in the Gong Lum case. Then, too, Attorney Marshall, Secretary White and the NAACP did not have the $75,000 contributed by the CIO as fees and expenses in the handling of that case. . . .

It can scarcely be hoped that the observations and admonitions of Booker T. Washington, whose wisdom the Secretary of the NAACP considers dull and effete, could make an impression on the adamantine Supreme Court. Booker T. Washington was the first great American negro this country has produced. His wisdom transcended his time. He did more for his people than all who have come since his passing. He delivered the opening address at the Atlanta Exposition on September 18, 1895, and among other statements said, "No race can prosper till it learns that there is as much dignity in tilling a field as in writing a poem. It is at the bottom of life we must begin, and not at the top. Nor should we permit our grievances to overshadow our opportunities. . . . In all things that are purely social we can be as separate as the fingers, yet one as the hand in all things essential to mutual progress. . . . The wisest among my race understand that the agitation of questions of social equality is the extreme folly and that progress in the enjoyment of all the privileges that will come to us must be the result of severe and constant struggle rather than of artificial forcing. No race that has anything to contribute to the markets of the world is long in any degree ostracized. It is important and right that all privileges of the law be ours, but it is vastly more important that we be prepared for the exercise of these privileges. The opportunity to earn a dollar in a factory just now is worth infinitely more than the opportunity to spend a dollar in an opera house."

SUBSEQUENT TO DECISION, WARNINGS REPEATED

Subsequent to the decision, the outstanding editors in the South have candidly and fearlessly repudiated the action and warned the Court of the ultimate results. Major Frederick Sullens, editor of the Jackson Daily News, Jackson, Mississippi, on May 18th, the next day after Black Monday, came out with his candid editorial, "Bloodstains on White Marble Steps":

> "Members of the Nation's highest tribunal may be learned in the law, but they were utterly lacking in common sense when they rendered Monday's decision, common sense of the kind that should have told them about the tragedy that will inevitably follow. When the courts toss common sense

out the window and substitute specious reasoning, shallow subterfuge, silly sophistry and sordid politics, then our nation is in a deplorable plight! . . ."

"Human blood may stain Southern soil in many places because of this decision, but the dark red stains of that blood will be on the marble steps of the United States Supreme Court building."

This courageous editor has the benefit of almost half a century of association with and observation of the negro of the South. He has forgotten more about interracial problems than the Supreme Court will ever know. The poignant truth of the conditional potential which he stated is what is so terrifying.

Senator Richard Russell of Georgia, on the same day, sacrificed gladly any presidential possibilities he may have had in denouncing and bemoaning on the floor of the United States Senate the creation of this Frankenstein monster by the Supreme Court's decision.

On May 19th, 1954, Representative Williams in the House of Representatives boldly spoke out against the propriety and wisdom of the decision—**branding May 17th as "Black Monday."**

On May 27th Senator James O. Eastland delivered, on the floor of the United States Senate, the tersest, the clearest and the most accurate analysis of the segregation problem yet propounded. This speech should go into the homes of every white and negro family in the South. It will do much to extinguish the widely scattered, smoldering fires of racial hate the decision has rekindled. It is fitting that a portion of that illustrious speech be quoted:

"The southern institution of racial segregation or racial separation was the correct, self-evident truth which arose from the chaos and confusion of the reconstruction period. Separation promotes racial harmony. It permits each race to follow its own pursuits, and its own civilization. Segregation is not discrimination. Segregation is not a badge of racial inferiority, and that it is not is recognized by both races in the Southern States. In fact, segregation is desired and supported by the vast majority of the members of both races in the South, who dwell side by side under harmonious conditions.

"The negro has made a great contribution to the South. We take pride in the constant advance he has made. It is where social questions are involved that Southern people draw the line. It is these social institutions with which Southern people, in my judgment, will not permit the Supreme Court to tamper.

"Let me make this clear, Mr. President: There is no racial hatred in the South. The negro race is not an oppressed race. A great Senator from the State of Idaho, Senator William E. Borah, a few years ago said on the floor of the Senate: 'Let us admit that the South is dealing with this question as best it can, admit that the men and women of the South are just as patriotic as we are, just as devoted to the principles of the Constitution as we are, just as willing to sacrifice for the success of their communities as we are. Let us give them credit as American citizens, and cooperate with them, sympathize with them, and help them in the solution of their problem, instead of condemning them. We are one people, one nation, and they are entitled to be treated upon this basis.'

"Mr. President, it is the law of nature, it is the law of God, that every race has both the right and the duty to perpetuate itself. All free men have the right to associate exclusively with members of their own race, free from governmental interference, if they so desire. Free men have the right to send their children to schools of their own choosing, free from governmental interference and to build up their own culture, free from governmental interference. These rights are inherent in the Constitution of the United States and in the American system of government, both state and national, to promote and protect this right."

Although these "lockings of the stable occurred subsequent to the stealing of the horse"—they should help deter future similar tyrannical acts. Communism disguised as "new democracy" is still communism, and tyranny masquerading as liberalism is still tyranny. **The resistance of communism and tyranny, irrespective of whatever guise they may adopt, is not treason. It is the prerequisite of freedom, the very essence of liberty.**

Is it out of order to assume that the members of the new

Sociological Supreme Court should have at least a working knowledge of anthropology, ethnology, biology, social evolution, and the science of society as well as the Constitution and decisions thereunder?

Is it expecting too much to anticipate that the United States Supreme Court, when deciding socio-legal questions, which profoundly affect the destiny of this nation, will take into consideration the great truths which these scientific studies have established, and what inestimable destruction the violation by it of these basic laws, which lie beyond its petty jurisdiction, will produce. Perhaps the United States Supreme Court is unconcerned with the ultimate destructive results of this tragic decision since "there are none so blind as those who will not see."

In conclusion of this analysis of **the decision,** let us remember the reargument was largely devoted to the circumstances surrounding the adoption of the Fourteenth Amendment in 1886. Is it possible that the Supreme Court feels that President Lincoln did not understand what was and what was not to be done for the negro in this country? Does this Supreme Court believe that Mr. Lincoln's ideas were not considered and endorsed by Congress or that his conception of the ultimate goal for the negro was erroneous? There has never been a man who understood the negro problem as did Mr. Lincoln. There has never been another man who has done so much for the negro. This Supreme Court counts for naught the statement made by Mr. Lincoln at Charleston, Illinois, on September 18th, 1858:

> "I am not, nor never have been, in favor of bringing about in any way the social and political equality of the white and black races. I am not, nor never have been, in favor of making voters or jurors of negroes, nor of qualifying them to hold office, nor to intermarry with white people, and I will say, in addition to this, that there is a physical difference between the white and black races which I believe **will forever forbid the two races living together on terms of social and political equality.**"

The Standard Bearer for the emancipation of the negro, according to the present Supreme Court, knew nothing about the problem or was sadly mistaken.

5. *Brown* v. *Board of Education—* The Implementation Decision

In its 1954 opinion, the Supreme Court invited the attorney generals of the states involved in the **Brown** *cases to prepare arguments concerning implementation methods for desegregation. After considering the various suggestions and plans, the Court handed down a supplementary ruling on May 31, 1955, establishing guidelines for the lower courts to follow. The* **Brown II** *decision, as it came to be known, with its "deliberate speed" formula, asked blacks to defer the exercise of a constitutional right and gave southern states time to hold fast to the practice and doctrine of segregation.*

Mr. Chief Justice Warren delivered the opinion of the Court.

These cases were decided on May 17, 1954. The opinions of that date, declaring the fundamental principle that racial discrimination in public education is unconstitutional, are incorporated herein by reference. All provisions of federal, state, or local law requiring or permitting such discrimination must yield to this principle. There remains for consideration the manner in which relief is to be accorded. . . .

Full implementation of these constitutional principles may require solution of varied local school problems. School authorities have the primary responsibility for elucidating, assessing, and solving these problems; courts will have to consider whether the action of school authorities constitutes good faith implementation of the governing constitutional principles. Because of their proximity to local conditions and the possible need for further hearings, the courts which originally heard these cases can best perform this judicial appraisal. Accordingly, we believe it appropriate to remand the cases to those courts.

In fashioning and effectuating the decrees, the courts will be guided by equitable principles. Traditionally, equity has been characterized by a practical flexibility in shaping its remedies and by a facility for adjusting and reconciling public and private needs. These cases call for the exercise of these traditional attributes of equity power. At stake is the personal interest of the plaintiffs in admission to public schools as soon as practicable on a nondiscriminatory basis. To effectuate this interest may call for elimination of a variety of obstacles in making the transition to school systems operated in accordance with the constitutional principles set forth in our May 17, 1954, decision. Courts of equity may properly take into account the public interest in the elimination of such obstacles in a systematic and effective manner. But it should go without saying that the vitality of these constitutional principles cannot be allowed to yield simply because of disagreement with them.

While giving weight to these public and private considerations, the courts will require that the defendants make a prompt and reasonable start toward full compliance with our May 17, 1954, ruling. Once such a start has been made, the courts may find that additional time is necessary to carry out the ruling in an effective manner. The burden rests upon the defendants to establish that such time is necessary in the public interest and is consistent with good faith compliance at the earliest practicable date. To that end, the courts may consider problems related to administration, arising from the physical condition of the school plant, the school transportation system, personnel, revision of school districts and attendance areas into compact units to achieve a system of determining admission to the public schools on a nonracial basis, and revision of local laws and regulations which may be necessary in solving the foregoing problems. They will also consider the adequacy of any plans the defendants may propose to meet these problems and to effectuate a transition to a racially nondiscriminatory school system. During this period of transition, the courts will retain jurisdiction of these cases. The . . . [cases, except Delaware, are remanded to the lower courts] to take such proceedings and enter such orders and decrees consistent with this opinion as are necessary and proper to admit to public schools on a racially nondiscriminatory basis with all deliberate speed the parties to these cases. . . .

6. "The Long Shadow of Little Rock"

Daisy Bates

The first serious confrontation between federal authority and southern resistance to school desegregation occurred in Little Rock, Arkansas, in the fall of 1957. In this selection from her 1962 book, **The Long Shadow of Little Rock,** *Daisy Bates, president of the Arkansas NAACP and editor-in-chief of the black newspaper the* **Arkansas State Press,** *describes her role in the efforts to integrate Central High School in spite of the concerted opposition of Governor Orval Faubus.*

It was Labor Day, September 2, 1957. The nine pupils who had been selected by the school authorities to enter Central High School—Carlotta Walls, Jefferson Thomas, Elizabeth Eckford, Thelma Mothershed, Melba Pattillo, Ernest Green, Terrance Roberts, Gloria Ray, and Minnijean Brown—were enjoying the last day of their summer vacation. . . . About mid-afternoon young Jefferson Thomas was on his way home from the pool and stopped at my house for a brief visit. While Jeff was raiding the refrigerator, a news flash came over the radio that the Governor would address the citizens of Arkansas that night.

"I wonder what he's going to talk about," said Jeff. The youngster then turned to me and asked, "Is there anything they can do—now that they lost in court? Is there any way they can stop us from entering Central tomorrow morning?"

"I don't think so," I said.

About seven o'clock that night a local newspaper reporter rang my doorbell. "Mrs. Bates, do you know that national guardsmen are surrounding Central High?"

L.C. [Bates] and I stared at him incredulously for a moment. A friend who was visiting us volunteered to guard the house while we drove out to Central. L.C. gave him the shotgun. We jumped into our car and drove to Central High. . . . Men in full battle dress—helmets, boots, and bayonets—were piling out of the trucks and lining up in front of the school.

As we watched, L.C. switched on the car radio. A newscaster

was saying, "National guardsmen are surrounding Central High School. No one is certain what this means. Governor Faubus will speak later this evening."

————

I don't recall all the details of what Governor Faubus said that night. But his words electrified Little Rock. By morning they shocked the United States. By noon the next day his message horrified the world.

Faubus' alleged reason for calling out the troops was that he had received information that caravans of automobiles filled with white supremacists were heading toward Little Rock from all over the state. He therefore declared Central High School off limits to Negroes. For some inexplicable reason he added that Horace Mann, a Negro high school, would be off limits to whites.

Then, from the chair of the highest office of the State of Arkansas, Governor Orval Eugene Faubus delivered the infamous words, "blood will run in the streets" if Negro pupils should attempt to enter Central High School.

In a half dozen ill-chosen words, Faubus made his contribution to the mass hysteria that was to grip the city of Little Rock for several months.

The citizens of Little Rock gathered on September 3 to gaze upon the incredible spectacle of an empty school building surrounded by 250 National Guard troops. At about eight fifteen in the morning, Central students started passing through the line of national guardsmen—all but the nine Negro students.

I had been in touch with their parents throughout the day. They were confused, and they were frightened. As the parents voiced their fears, they kept repeating Governor Faubus' words that "blood would run in the streets of Little Rock" should their teen-age children try to attend Central—the school to which they had been assigned by the school board.

————

On the afternoon of the same day, September 3, when the school was scheduled to open, Superintendent [Virgil] Blossom called a meeting of leading Negro citizens and the parents of the nine children . . . [and] instructed the parents *not* to accompany their children the next morning when they were scheduled to enter Central. "If violence breaks out," the Superintendent told them, "it will be easier to protect the children if the adults aren't there."

During the conference Superintendent Blossom had given us little assurance that the children would be adequately protected. As we left the building, I was aware of how deeply worried the parents were, although they did not voice their fears.

About ten o'clock that night I was alone in the downstairs recreation room.

I sat huddled in my chair, dazed, trying to think, yet not knowing what to do. I don't recall how much time went by . . . before some neighbors entered. One of them was the Reverend J. C. Crenshaw, President of the Little Rock branch of the NAACP.

"Maybe," I said, "maybe we could round up a few ministers to go with the children tomorrow. Maybe then the mob wouldn't attack them. Maybe with the ministers by their side—"

I called a white minister, Rev. Dunbar Ogden, Jr., President of the Interracial Ministerial Alliance. I did not know Mr. Ogden. I explained the situation, then asked if he thought he could get some ministers to go with the children to school the next morning.

Tensely I waited for his return call. When it came, he sounded apologetic. The white ministers he had talked to had questioned whether it was the thing to do. Some of the Negro ministers had pointed out that the Superintendent of Schools had asked that no Negro adults go with the children, and that in view of this they felt they shouldn't go. Then he added gently, "I'll keep trying— and, God willing, I'll be there."

Next I called the city police. I explained to the officer in charge that we were concerned about the safety of the children and that we were trying to get ministers to accompany them to school the next morning. I said that the children would assemble at eight thirty at Twelfth Street and Park Avenue. I asked whether a police car could be stationed there to protect the children until the ministers arrived.

The police officer promised to have a squad car there at eight o'clock. "But you realize," he warned, "that our men cannot go any closer than that to the school. The school is off limits to the city police while it's 'occupied' by the Arkansas National Guardsmen."

By now it was two thirty in the morning. Still, the parents had to be called about the change in plan. At three o'clock I completed my last call, explaining to the parents where the children were to assemble and the plan about the ministers. Suddenly I remembered Elizabeth Eckford. Her family had no telephone. Should I go to the Union Station and search for her father? Someone had once told me that he had a night job there. Tired in mind and body, I decided to handle the matter early in the morning. I stumbled into bed.

A few hours later, at about eight fifteen in the morning, L.C. and I started driving to Twelfth Street and Park Avenue. On the way I checked out in my mind the possibilities that awaited us. . . .

The bulletin over the car radio interrupted. The voice announced: "A Negro girl is being mobbed at Central High. . . ."

"Oh, my God!" I cried. "It must be Elizabeth! I forgot to notify her where to meet us!"

L.C. jumped out of the car and rushed to find her. I drove on to Twelfth Street. There were the ministers—two white—Mr. Ogden and Rev. Will Campbell, of the National Council of Churches, Nashville, Tennessee—and two colored—the Reverend Z. Z. Driver, of the African Methodist Episcopal Church, and the Reverend Harry Bass, of the Methodist Church. With them also was Mr. Ogden's twenty-one-year-old son, David. The children were already there. And, yes, the police had come as promised. All of the children were there—all except Elizabeth.

Elizabeth, whose dignity and control in the face of jeering mobsters had been filmed by television cameras and recorded in pictures flashed to newspapers over the world, had overnight become a national heroine. . . . The first day that her parents agreed she might come out of seclusion, she came to my house, where the reporters awaited her. Elizabeth was very quiet, speaking only when spoken to. I took her to my bedroom to talk before I let the reporters see her. I asked her how she felt now. Suddenly all her pent-up emotion flared.

"Why am I here?" she said, turning blazing eyes on me. "Why are you so interested in my welfare now? You didn't care enough to notify me of the change of plans—"

Little by little Elizabeth came out of her shell. Up to now she had never talked about what happened to her at Central. Once when we were alone in the downstairs recreation room of my house, I asked her simply, "Elizabeth, do you think you can talk about it now?"

She remained quiet for a long time. Then she began to speak.

"You remember the day before we were to go in, we met Superintendent Blossom at the school board office. He told us what the mob might say and do but he never told us we wouldn't have any protection. He told our parents not to come because he wouldn't be able to protect the children if they did.

"That night I was so excited I couldn't sleep. The next morning I was about the first one up. While I was pressing my black-and-white dress—I had made it to wear on the first day of school—my little brother turned on the TV set. They started telling about a large crowd gathered at the school. The man on TV said he wondered if we were going to show up that morning.

"Before I left home Mother called us into the living room. She said we should have a word of prayer. Then I caught the bus and got off a block from the school. I saw a large crowd of people standing across the street from the soldiers guarding Central. As I walked on, the crowd suddenly got quiet. Superintendent Blossom had told us to enter by the front door. I looked at all the people and thought, 'Maybe I will be safer if I walk down the block to the front entrance behind the guards.'

"At the corner I tried to pass through the long line of guards around the school so as to enter the grounds behind them. One of the guards pointed across the street. So I pointed in the same direction and asked whether he meant for me to cross the street and walk down. He nodded 'yes.' So, I walked across the street conscious of the crowd that stood there, but they moved away from me.

"For a moment all I could hear was the shuffling of their feet. Then someone shouted, 'Here she comes, get ready!' I moved away from the crowd on the sidewalk and into the street. If the mob came at me I could then cross back over so the guards could protect me.

"The crowd moved in closer and then began to follow me, calling me names. I still wasn't afraid. Just a little bit nervous. Then my knees started to shake all of a sudden and I wondered whether I could make it to the center entrance a block away. It was the longest block I ever walked in my whole life.

"Even so, I still wasn't too scared because all the time I kept thinking that the guards would protect me.

"When I got in front of the school, I went up to a guard again. But this time he just looked straight ahead and didn't move to let me pass him. I didn't know what to do. Then I looked and saw the path leading to the front entrance was a little further ahead. So I walked until I was right in front of the path to the front door.

"I stood looking at the school—it looked so big! Just then the guards let some white students through.

"The crowd was quiet. I guess they were waiting to see what was going to happen. When I was able to steady my knees, I walked up to the guard who had let the white students in. He too didn't move. When I tried to squeeze past him, he raised his bayonet and then the other guards moved in and they raised their bayonets.

"They glared at me with a mean look and I was very frightened and didn't know what to do. I turned around and the crowd came toward me.

"They moved closer and closer. Somebody started yelling, 'Lynch her! Lynch her!'

"I tried to see a friendly face somewhere in the mob—someone who maybe would help. I looked into the face of an old woman and it seemed a kind face, but when I looked at her again, she spat on me.

"They came closer, shouting, 'No nigger bitch is going to get in our school. Get out of here!'

"I turned back to the guards but their faces told me I wouldn't get any help from them. Then I looked down the block and saw a bench at the bus stop. I thought, 'If I can only get there I will be safe.' I don't know why the bench seemed a safe place to me, but I started walking toward it. I tried to close my mind to what they were shouting, and kept saying to myself, 'If I can only make it to the bench I will be safe.'

"When I finally got there, I don't think I could have gone another step. I sat down and the mob crowded up and began shouting all over again. Someone hollered, 'Drag her over to this tree! Let's take care of that nigger.' Just then a white man sat down beside me, put his arm around me and patted my shoulder. He raised my chin and said, 'Don't let them see you cry.'

"Then, a white lady—she was very nice—she came over to me on the bench. She spoke to me but I don't remember what she said. She put me on the bus and sat next to me. She asked my name and tried to talk to me but I don't think I answered. I can't remember much about the bus ride, but the next thing I remember I was standing in front of the School for the Blind, where Mother works."

7. A Roundtable Discussion

Before the Little Rock Nine had been in school for a month, NBC set up a roundtable discussion moderated by Mrs. Jorunn Ricketts. Four of the participants were white students—Sammy Dean Parker, Kay Bacon, Robin Woods, and Joseph Fox—and two were black—Ernest Green and Minniejean Brown. Minniejean did not finish the school year in Little Rock; after getting into a fight with some white students, she was suspended and finished the year at an independent school in New York City.

MRS. RICKETTS: Do you think it is possible to start working this out on a more sensible basis than violent demonstration?

SAMMY: No, I don't because the South has always been against racial mixing and I think they will fight this thing to the end. . . . We fight for our freedom—that's one thing. And we don't have any freedom any more.

ERNEST: Sammy, you said that you don't have any freedom. I wonder what do you mean by it—that you don't have any freedom? You are guaranteed your freedom in the Bill of Rights and your Constitution. You have the freedom of speech—I noticed that has been exercised a whole lot in Little Rock. The freedom of petition, the freedom of religion and the other freedoms are guaranteed to you. As far as freedom, I think that if anybody should kick about freedoms, it should be us. Because I think we have been given a pretty bad side on this thing as far as freedom.

SAMMY: Do you call those troops freedom? I don't. And I also do not call free when you are being escorted into the school every morning.

ERNEST: You say why did the troops come here? It is because our government—our state government—went against the federal law. . . . Our country is set up so that we have forty-eight states and no one state has the ability to overrule our nation's government. I thought that was what our country was built around. I mean, that is why we fight. We fought in World War II together— the fellows that I know died in World War II, they died in the Korean War. I mean, why should my friends get out there and die for a cause called "democracy" when I can't exercise my rights—tell me that.

ROBIN: I agree with Ernest.

JOE: Well, Sammy, I don't know what freedom has been taken away from you because the truth there—I know as a senior myself—the troops haven't kept me from going to my classes or participating in any school activity. I mean, they're there just to keep order in case—I might use the term "hotheads"—get riled up. But I think as long as—if parents would just stay out of it and let the children of the school at Central High figure it out for themselves, I think it would be a whole lot better. I think the students are mature enough to figure it out for themselves. . . . As far as I'm concerned, I'll lay the whole blame of this trouble in Governor Faubus's lap.

SAMMY: I think we knew before this ever started that some day we were going to have to integrate the schools. And I think that our Governor was trying to protect all of us when he called out the National Guard—and he was trying to prepare us, I think.

ERNEST: . . . Well, I have to disagree. . . . I know a student that's over there with us, Elizabeth, and that young lady, she walked two blocks, I guess—as you all know—and the mob was behind her. Did the troops break up the mob?

ROBIN: . . . And when Elizabeth had to walk down in front of the school I was there and I saw that. And may I say, I was very ashamed—I felt like crying—because she was so brave when she did that. And we just weren't behaving ourselves—just jeering her. I think if we had had any sort of decency, we wouldn't have acted that way. But I think if everybody would just obey the Golden Rule—do unto others as you would have others do unto you—might be the solution. How would you like to have to . . . walk down the street with everybody yelling behind you like they yelled behind Elizabeth?

MRS. RICKETTS: Sammy, why do these children not want to go to school with Negroes?

SAMMY: Well, I think it is mostly race mixing.

MRS. RICKETTS: Race mixing? What do you mean?

SAMMY: Well, marrying each other.

MINNIEJEAN: Hold your hand up. I'm brown, you are white. What's the difference? We are all of the same thoughts. You're thinking about your boy—he's going to the Navy. I'm thinking about mine—he's in the Air Force. We think about the same thing.

SAMMY: I'll have to agree with you.

ERNEST: Well, getting back to this intermarriage and all that. I don't know [where] people get all that. Why do I want to go to school? To marry with someone? I mean, school's not a marriage bureau. . . . I'm going there for an education. Really, if I'm going there to socialize, I don't need to be going to school. I can stand out on the corner and socialize, as far as that.

MINNIEJEAN: Kay, Joe and Robin—do you know anything about me, or is it just that your mother has told you about Negroes?

MRS. RICKETTS: . . . Have you ever really made an effort to try to find out what they're like?

KAY: Not until today.

SAMMY: Not until today.

TTS: And what do you think about it after today?

., you know that my parents and a lot of the other ᵤdents and their parents think that the Negroes aren't equal to us. But—I don't know. It seems like they are, to me.

SAMMY: These people are—we'll have to admit that.

ERNEST: I think, like we're doing today, discussing our different views . . . if the people of Little Rock . . . would get together I believe they would find out a different story—and try to discuss the thing instead of getting out in the street and kicking people around and calling names—and all that sort of thing. If . . . people got together it would be smoothed over.

KAY: I think that if . . . our friends had been getting in this discussion today, I think that maybe some of them—not all of them—in time, they would change their mind. But probably some of them would change their mind today.

SAMMY: I know now that it isn't as bad as I thought it was—after we got together and discussed it.

KAY: We [Sammy and I] both came down here today with our mind set on it [that] we weren't going to change our mind that we were fully against integration. But I know now that we're going to change our mind.

MRS. RICKETTS: What do your parents say to that?

KAY: I think I'm going to have a long talk with my parents.

CHAPTER THREE

AIN'T SCARED OF YOUR JAILS (1960–1961)

Introduction by Clayborne Carson

The years 1960 and 1961 were a time of profound change, growth, and development in the civil rights movement. Although the Supreme Court's *Brown* v. *Board of Education* decision had outlawed school segregation in 1954, few changes in discriminatory practices had occurred. But there was a restlessness that was slowly building in the black community. The 1959 controversy over Robert F. Williams's advocacy of armed self-defense for blacks was an early sign that some blacks were moving away from the NAACP's cautious reform strategy. Even more than the example of Williams, however, memories of Emmett Till's brutal killing in 1955 and of Elizabeth Eckford walking alone to Little Rock's Central High School profoundly influenced young blacks. It was out of this festering discontent and an awareness of earlier isolated protests that the sit-ins of 1960 were born. Though few realized it when the sit-ins began, they would eventually attract national media attention and federal intervention in the South. Student activism galvanized established organizations, brought about the creation of new ones, and generated mass support for the civil rights movement among all segments of the black populace.

The first sit-in occurred in Greensboro, North Carolina, on February 1, 1960. The four North Carolina Agricultural and Technical College students who initiated this wave of protests had acted on their own, although they were members of an NAACP youth chapter. The sit-ins would spread rapidly throughout the South, with over seventy thousand participants and three thousand arrests by August 1961. The sit-ins provided an important model for protest and showed students that they could affect the political process. They also encouraged liberal white students to work together with blacks for social change. The increasing confidence of the student activists was evident in a new organization, the Student Nonviolent Coordinating Committee (SNCC), and in a new wave of protests called Freedom Rides.

The formation of SNCC followed the sit-ins by only a few months and not only solidified student involvement in the movement but placed students in leadership roles. SNCC was established at the Southwide Student Leadership Conference held at Shaw University in Raleigh, North Carolina, on April 15–17, 1960. The conference was called by Ella J. Baker of the Southern Christian Leadership Conference (SCLC), who became an important advisor to the students. Influenced by James Lawson, a divinity student at Vanderbilt University with a philosophical commitment to nonviolent direct action, the students began to develop an organization that would channel their concerns and energy. What emerged was a coordinating committee that operated independently of other established civil rights organizations and relied on strong local leadership. The formation of SNCC helped transform the student movement from one that emphasized small-scale protests to a sustained force that would challenge racism throughout American society.

The growth, spread, and intensity of movement activities had a major effect on the presidential election contest of 1960 between John F. Kennedy and Richard M. Nixon. The tactic of mass, nonviolent sit-ins brought the civil rights agenda to national prominence and caused both candidates to pay at least lip service to the movement. John F. Kennedy's phone call to Coretta Scott King in October 1960 following Martin Luther King, Jr.'s arrest at an Atlanta sit-in had a dramatic impact on the 1960 presidential campaign. While his actions were politically motivated, Kennedy's pressure to help secure King's release was appreciated in the black community and prompted a large black voter turnout. Kennedy won the election by the narrowest of margins and the black vote was acknowledged as an important factor in his victory. In spite of this, however, Kennedy ruled out adopting a major civil rights legislative agenda, opting for a less controversial plan that focused on investigating voting rights violations. Only later, after numerous movement activities, would his administration push for the strengthening of federal civil rights laws.

Of all the tactics utilized during this period, the one that most galvanized national attention was the Freedom Rides. When they were announced by the Congress of Racial Equality (CORE) in 1961, the goal was to challenge segregation on interstate buses and in terminals. When the Freedom Riders were brutally attacked in Alabama, however, it initiated a new phase of the movement. As CORE was preparing to call off the rides because of the fear of violence, the original group of Freedom Riders flew to New Orleans. Diane Nash, a sit-in leader in Nashville, called James Farmer, the executive director of CORE, to insist that the rides not be stopped. She announced that volunteers from Nashville would continue the rides. The ensuing confrontation in Mississippi forced the federal government to take action to protect the Freedom Riders, thus supporting desegregation. The Freedom Rides also solidified support for CORE, marked the emergence of SNCC, and caused the nation to focus on the civil rights movement.

In summary, the development of nonviolent tactics, intergenerational conflicts between students, parents, and established organizations, and an increasing involvement of young white activists in the civil rights struggle all helped take the movement to a new level. More importantly, the expansion of protest activity caused youth and elders alike to think about the realities of the prevailing American value system and what it would take to achieve the type of society they wanted to live in.

1. "Is Violence Necessary to Combat Injustice? For the Positive: Williams Says 'We Must Fight Back' "

Robert F. Williams

Robert F. Williams of Monroe, North Carolina, was one of the few civil rights activists who openly challenged the idea that blacks should rely on nonviolent tactics. In 1959 Williams's position had prompted the national office of the NAACP to suspend him as head of its Monroe chapter. This selection originally appeared in Liberation *magazine (September 1959).*

In 1954, I was an enlisted man in the United States Marine Corps. I shall never forget the evening we (heard) the historic Supreme Court decision that segregation in the public schools is unconstitutional.

At last I felt that I was a part of America and that I belonged. That was what I had always wanted, even as a child.

I returned to civilian life in 1955 and the hope I had for Negro liberation faltered. Acts of violence and words and deeds of hate and spite rose from every quarter. There is open defiance to law and order throughout the South today. I have become disillusioned.

Laws serve to deter crime and protect the weak from the strong in civilized society. Where there is a breakdown of law, where is the force of deterrent? Only highly civilized and moral individuals respect the rights of others. The Southern brute respects only force. Nonviolence is a very potent weapon when the opponent is civilized, but nonviolence is no repellent for a sadist.

I have great respect for the pacifist, that is for the pure pacifist. I am not a pacifist and I am sure I may safely say most of my people are not. Passive resistance is a powerful weapon in gaining concessions from oppressors, but I venture to say that if Mack Parker [a black man lynched in 1959] had had an automatic shotgun at his disposal, he could have served as a great deterrent against lynching.

In 1957 the Klan moved into Monroe and Union County (N.C.). Their numbers steadily increased to the point wherein the local press reported 7500 at one rally. They became so brazen that mile-long motorcades started invading the Negro community.

These hooded thugs fired pistols from car windows. On one occasion they caught a Negro woman on the street and tried to force her to dance for them at gun point. Drivers of cars tried to run Negroes down. Lawlessness was rampant. Instead of cowing, we organized an armed guard. On one occasion, we had to exchange gunfire with the Klan.

Each time the Klan came on a raid they were led by police cars. We appealed to the President of the United States to have the Justice Department investigate the police. We appealed to Governor Luther Hodges. All our appeals to constituted law were in vain.

A group of nonviolent ministers met the City Board of Aldermen and pleaded with them to restrict the Klan from the colored community. The city fathers advised these cringing, begging Negro ministers that the Klan had constitutional rights to meet and organize the same way as the NAACP.

Not having been infected by turn-the-other-cheekism, a group of Negroes who showed a willingness to fight caused the city officials to deprive the Klan of its constitutional rights after local papers told of dangerous incidents between Klansmen and armed Negroes. Klan motorcades have been legally banned from the City of Monroe.

On May 5, 1959, while president of the Union County branch of the NAACP, I made a statement to the United Press International after a trial wherein a white man was supposed to have been tried for kicking a Negro maid down a flight of stairs in a local white hotel. In spite of the fact that there was an eyewitness, the defendant failed to show up for his trial, and was completely exonerated.

Another case in the same court involved a white man who had come to a pregnant Negro mother's home and attempted to rape her. In recorder's court the only defense offered for the defendant was that "he's not guilty. He was just drunk and having a little fun." A white woman neighbor testified that the woman had come to her house excited, her clothes torn, her feet bare and begging her for assistance; the court was unmoved.

This great miscarriage of justice left me sick inside, and I said then what I say now. I believe Negroes must be willing to defend themselves, their women, their children and their homes. They must be willing to die and to kill in repelling their assailants. Negroes *must* protect themselves, it is obvious that the federal government will not put an end to lynching; therefore it becomes necessary for us to stop lynching with violence.

Some Negroes leaders have cautioned me that if Negroes fight back, the racist will have cause to exterminate the race.

This government is in no position to allow mass violence to erupt, let alone allow twenty million Negroes to be exterminated.

It is instilled at an early age that men who violently and swiftly rise to oppose tyranny are virtuous examples to emulate. I have been taught by my government to fight. Nowhere in the annals of history does the record show a people delivered from bondage by patience alone.

2. "The Social Organization of Non-Violence"
Martin Luther King, Jr.

The article from which this selection is excerpted originally appeared in the issue of Liberation *magazine (October 1959), following the one in which Robert F. Williams's article was published. King was by now a national figure and president of the Southern Christian Leadership Conference, an organization he and other activist ministers had formed early in 1957 in the wake of the Montgomery bus boycott.*

Here one must be clear that there are three different views on the subject of violence. One is the approach of pure nonviolence, which cannot readily or easily attract large masses, for it requires extraordinary discipline and courage. The second is violence exercised in self-defense, which all societies, from the most primitive to the most cultured and civilized, accept as moral and legal.

The principle of self-defense, even involving weapons and blood-shed, has never been condemned, even by Gandhi, who sanctioned it for those unable to master pure nonviolence. The third is the advocacy of violence as a tool of advancement, organized as in warfare, deliberately and consciously. To this tendency many Negroes are being tempted today. There are incalculable perils in this approach. It is not the danger or sacrifice of physical being which is primary, though it cannot be contemplated without a sense of deep concern for human life. The greatest danger is that it will fail to attract Negroes to a real collective struggle, and will confuse the large uncommitted middle group, which as yet has not supported either side. Further, it will mislead Negroes into the belief that this is the only path and place them as a minority in a position where they confront a far larger adversary than it is possible to defeat in this form of combat. When the Negro uses force in self-defense he does not forfeit support—he may even win it, by the courage and self-respect it reflects. When he seeks to initiate violence he provokes questions about the necessity for it, and inevitably is blamed for its consequences. It is unfortunately true that however the Negro acts, his struggle will not be free of violence initiated by his enemies, and he will need ample courage and willingness to sacrifice to defeat this manifestation of violence. But if he seeks it and organizes it, he cannot win. . . .

The Negro people can organize socially to initiate many forms of struggle which can drive their enemies back without resort to futile and harmful violence. In the history of the movement, . . . many creative forms have been developed—the mass boycott, sitdown protests and strikes, sit-ins—refusal to pay fines and bail for unjust arrests—mass marches—mass meetings—prayer pilgrimages, etc.

There is more power in socially organized masses on the march than there is in guns in the hands of a few desperate men. Our enemies would prefer to deal with a small armed group rather than with a huge, unarmed but resolute mass of people. However, it is necessary that the mass-action method be persistent and unyielding. Gandhi said the Indian people must "never let them rest," referring to the British. He urged them to keep protesting daily and weekly, in a variety of ways. This method inspired and organized the Indian masses and disorganized and demobilized the British. It educates its myriad participants, socially and morally. All history teaches us that like a turbulent ocean beating great cliffs into fragments of rock, the determined movement of people incessantly demanding their rights always disintegrates the old order.

3. Interview with Franklin McCain

On February 1, 1960, in Greensboro, North Carolina, Franklin McCain, David Richmond, Joseph McNeil, and Ezell Blair, Jr., all students at North Carolina A&T, launched a wave of lunch counter sit-ins across the South when they sat at the Woolworth's lunch counter and asked to be served. It was not the first desegregation sit-in, but it had special significance because it was initiated by black college students and would serve as a model for discontented black students in other southern black colleges. Though all four had been affiliated with NAACP youth chapters, they planned their protest on their own during extended discussion sessions in their dormitory rooms. This is an excerpt from an interview with Franklin McCain in My Soul Is Rested: Movement Days in the Deep South Remembered, *by Howell Raines (1977).*

The planning process was on a Sunday night, I remember it quite well. I think it was Joseph who said, "It's time that we take some action now. We've been getting together, and we've been, up to this point, still like most people we've talked about for the past few weeks or so—that is, people who talk a lot but, in fact, make very little action." After selecting the technique, then we said, "Let's go down and just ask for service." It certainly wasn't titled a "sit-in" or "sit-down" at that time. "Let's just go down to Woolworth's tomorrow and ask for service, and the tactic is going to be simply this: we'll just stay there." We never anticipated being served, certainly, the first day anyway. "We'll stay until we get served." And I think Ezell said, "Well, you know that might be weeks, that might be months, that might be never." And I think it was the consensus of the group, we said, "Well, that's just the chance we'll have to take."

Once getting there . . . we did make purchases of school supplies and took the patience and time to get receipts for our purchases, and Joseph and myself went over to the counter and
asked to be served coffee and doughnuts. As anticipated, the reply
was, "I'm sorry, we don't serve you here." And of course we said,
"We just beg to disagree with you. We've in fact already been
served." . . . The attendant or waitress was a little bit dumbfounded,
just didn't know what to say under circumstances like that. And
we said, "We wonder why you'd invite us in to serve us at one
counter and deny service at another. If this is a private club or
private concern, then we believe you ought to sell membership
cards." . . . That didn't go over too well, simply because I don't
really think she understood what we were talking about, and for
the second reason, she had no logical response to a statement like
that. . . .

At that point there was a policeman who had walked in off the
street, who was pacing the aisle . . . behind us, where we were
seated, with his club in his hand, just sort of knocking it in his
hand, and just looking mean and red and a little bit upset and a
little bit disgusted. And you had the feeling that he didn't know
what the hell to do. You had the feeling that this is the first time
that this big bad man with the gun and the club has been pushed
in a corner, and he's got absolutely no defense, and the thing
that's killing him more than anything else—he doesn't know what
he can or what he cannot do. He's defenseless. Usually his defense
is offense, and we've provoked him, yes, but we haven't provoked
him outwardly enough for him to resort to violence. And I think
this is just killing him; you can see it all over him.

If it's possible to know what it means to have your soul cleansed—
I felt pretty clean at that time. I probably felt better on that day
than I've ever felt in my life. Seems like a lot of feelings of guilt
or what-have-you suddenly left me, and I felt as though I had
gained my manhood, so to speak, and not only gained it, but had
developed quite a lot of respect for it. Not Franklin McCain only
as an individual, but I felt as though the manhood of a number
of other black persons had been restored and had gotten some
respect from just that one day.

The movement started out as a movement of nonviolence and as a Christian movement, and we wanted to make that very clear to everybody, that it was a movement that was seeking justice more than anything else and not a movement to start a war. . . . We knew that probably the most powerful and potent weapon that people have literally no defense for is love, kindness. That is, whip the enemy with something that he doesn't understand.

. . . The individual who had probably the most influence on us was Gandhi, more than any single individual. During the time that the Montgomery Bus Boycott was in effect, we were tots for the most part, and we barely heard of Martin Luther King. Yes, Martin Luther King's name was well-known when the sit-in movement was in effect, but to pick out Martin Luther King as a hero . . . I don't want you to misunderstand what I'm about to say: Yes, Martin Luther King was a hero. . . . No, he was not the individual that we had upmost in mind when we started the sit-in movement.

Credit for the initiation of the sit-in movement has been granted to one or two ministers, the NAACP, Ralph Johns, CORE, at least a dozen people, and it's rather amusing when you do read some of these articles. I think it's a game. The same type tactic that has been used over and over and over by the white news media and the white press to discredit blacks with particular types of achievement.

Remember, too, you had four guys who were pretty strong-willed, pretty bull-headed, and who were keenly aware that people would rush in and try to take over the Movement, so to speak. And we were quite aware of that, and we felt—not felt—*were* very independent. . . . As a matter of fact, we were criticized on several occasions for being too damned independent. But I still don't regret it.

4. "An Appeal for Human Rights"

In each city where sit-ins occurred student protest groups produced leaders with unique qualities and distinct long-range goals. The Nashville student leaders were noted for their firm commitment to the philosophy of nonviolent direct action. Student leaders elsewhere, however, were more likely to view nonviolence as an appropriate strategy, but not as a philosophy of life. Some students had a narrow conception of their goals; others believed that the lunch counter sit-ins were only the first stage of a struggle to bring about far-reaching reforms. The Atlanta Committee on Appeal for Human Rights launched that city's sit-in movement with a statement printed as a paid advertisement in the March 9, 1960, **Atlanta Constitution.** *It expressed the broad range of social concerns that produced black student discontent.*

We, the students of the six affiliated institutions forming the Atlanta University Center—Clark, Morehouse, Morris Brown, and Spelman Colleges, Atlanta University, and the Interdenominational Theological Center—have joined our hearts, minds, and bodies in the cause of gaining those rights which are inherently ours as members of the human race and as citizens of these United States.

We want to state clearly and unequivocally that we cannot tolerate, in a nation professing democracy and among people professing Christianity, the discriminatory conditions under which the Negro is living today in Atlanta, Georgia—supposedly one of the most progressive cities in the South.

Among the inequalities and injustices in Atlanta and in Georgia against which we protest, the following are outstanding examples:

1. Education: In the Public School System, facilities for Negroes and whites are separate and unequal. Double sessions continue in about half of the Negro Public Schools, and many Negro children travel ten miles a day in order to reach a school that will admit them.

2. Jobs: Negroes are denied employment in the majority of city, state, and federal governmental jobs, except in the most menial capacities.
3. Housing: While Negroes constitute 32% of the population of Atlanta, they are forced to live within 16% of the area of the city.

4. Voting: Contrary to statements made in Congress recently by several Southern Senators, we know that in many counties in Georgia and other Southern states, Negro college graduates are declared unqualified to vote and are not permitted to register.
5. Hospitals: Compared with facilities for other people in Atlanta and Georgia, those for Negroes are unequal and totally inadequate.

6. Movies, Concerts, Restaurants: Negroes are barred from most downtown movies and segregated in the rest. Negroes must even sit in a segregated section of the Municipal Auditorium. If a Negro is hungry, his hunger must wait until he comes to a "colored" restaurant, and even his thirst must await its quenching at a "colored" water fountain.
7. Law Enforcement: There are grave inequalities in the area of law enforcement. Too often, Negroes are maltreated by officers of the law. An insufficient number of Negroes is employed in the law-enforcing agencies. They are seldom, if ever promoted. Of 830 policemen in Atlanta only 35 are Negroes.

5. "Student Nonviolent Coordinating Committee Statement of Purpose"

On the weekend of April 15, 1960, student leaders of the southern sit-in movement met at Shaw University in Raleigh, North Carolina. The meeting, held at the initiative of Ella Baker, acting executive director of the SCLC, attracted 126 student delegates from fifty-six colleges in twelve southern states. In addition, nineteen northern schools were represented, along with thirteen organizations and fifty-seven students and observers. A temporary coordinating body was formed during the meeting; this body eventually became the Student Nonviolent Coordinating Committee.

SCLC's president, Martin Luther King, Jr., spoke to the gathering, but many accounts suggest that the students were more strongly influenced by the speech given by Reverend James Lawson, who had been expelled from Vanderbilt University Divinity School because of his refusal to withdraw from the protest movement. Lawson drafted this document, dated May 14, 1960, for the Temporary Student Nonviolent Coordinating Committee.

Carrying out the mandate of the Raleigh Conference to write a statement of purpose for the movement, the Temporary Student Nonviolent Coordinating Committee submits for careful consideration the following draft. We urge all local, state or regional groups to examine it closely. Each member of our movement must work diligently to understand the depths of nonviolence.

We affirm the philosophical or religious ideal of nonviolence as the foundation of our purpose, the pre-supposition of our faith, and the manner of our action. Nonviolence as it grows from Judaic-Christian traditions seeks a social order of justice permeated by love. Integration of human endeavor represents the crucial first step towards such a society.

Through nonviolence, courage displaces fear; love transforms hate. Acceptance dissipates prejudice; hope ends despair. Peace dominates war; faith reconciles doubt. Mutual regard cancels enmity. Justice for all overthrows injustice. The redemptive community supersedes systems of gross social immorality.

Love is the central motif of nonviolence. Love is the force by which God binds man to himself and man to man. Such love goes to the extreme; it remains loving and forgiving even in the midst of hostility. It matches the capacity of evil to inflict suffering with an even more enduring capacity to absorb evil, all the while persisting in love.

By appealing to conscience and standing on the moral nature of human existence, nonviolence nurtures the atmosphere in which reconciliation and justice become actual possibilities.

6. "Bigger than a Hamburger"
Ella J. Baker

Ella Baker had graduated from Shaw University in the 1920s and spent many years as an activist in movements to bring about social change. Active during the 1930s in Harlem's Young Negroes' Cooperative League and later a member of the NAACP's field staff, she would leave her post as director of SCLC's headquarters to accept a job with the YWCA shortly after the April conference at Shaw. Her growing disenchantment with the cautiousness of the established civil rights groups led her to encourage black students to form their own independent organization rather than affiliate with the SCLC. After SNCC's founding, she continued to advise its staff. This June 1960 article by Miss Baker originally appeared in the Southern Conference Educational Fund's newspaper, **The Southern Patriot.**

RALEIGH, N.C.—The Student Leadership Conference made it crystal clear that current sit-ins and other demonstrations are concerned with something much bigger than a hamburger or even a giant-sized Coke.

Whatever may be the difference in approach to their goal, the Negro and white students, North and South, are seeking to rid America of the scourge of racial segregation and discrimination— not only at lunch counters, but in every aspect of life.

In reports, casual conversations, discussion groups, and speeches, the sense and the spirit of the following statement that appeared in the initial newsletter of the students at Barber-Scotia College, Concord, N.C., were re-echoed time and again:

> We want the world to know that we no longer accept the inferior position of second-class citizenship. We are willing to go to jail, be ridiculed, spat upon and even suffer physical violence to obtain First Class Citizenship.

By and large, this feeling that they have a destined date with freedom, was not limited to a drive for personal freedom, or even freedom for the Negro in the South. Repeatedly it was emphasized that the movement was concerned with the moral implications of racial discrimination for the "whole world" and the "Human Race."

This universality of approach was linked with a perceptive recognition that "it is important to keep the movement democratic and to avoid struggles for personal leadership."

It was further evident that desire for supportive cooperation from adult leaders and the adult community was also tempered by apprehension that adults might try to "capture" the student movement. The students showed willingness to be met on the basis of equality, but were intolerant of anything that smacked of manipulation or domination.

This inclination toward *group-centered leadership,* rather than toward a *leader-centered group pattern of organization,* was refreshing indeed to those of the older group who bear the scars of the battle, the frustrations and the disillusionment that come when the prophetic leader turns out to have heavy feet of clay.

However hopeful might be the signs in the direction of group-centeredness, the fact that many schools and communities, especially in the South, have not provided adequate experience for young Negroes to assume initiative and think and act independently accentuated the need for guarding the student movement against well-meaning, but nevertheless unhealthy, over-protectiveness.

Here is an opportunity for adult and youth to work together and provide genuine leadership—the development of the individual to his highest potential for the benefit of the group.

Many adults and youth characterized the Raleigh meeting as the greatest or most significant conference of our period.

Whether it lives up to this high evaluation or not will, in a large measure, be determined by the extent to which there is more effective training in and understanding of non-violent principles and practices, in group dynamics, and in the re-direction into creative channels of the normal frustrations and hostilities that result from second-class citizenship.

7. "A Conference on the Sit-Ins"
Ted Dienstfrey

Ted Dienstfrey, a white student at the University of Chicago, attended the conference at Shaw University as one of the representatives from northern schools. His article from which these excerpts were taken appeared in Commentary *magazine in June 1960.*

It is with a desire to do *something* that many Northern white college students look at the sit-in movement of their Southern Negro counterparts. . . . That the Northern response has been almost unanimously favorable is no surprise: of all the current social and political issues—the cold war, disarmament, the draft, planned obsolescence, the double standard—integration is the only one which does not have to be discussed. We all agree that segregation must end; we only disagree on when it will end, on what will end it, and who is responsible for ending it.

We have had our student government pass resolutions decrying the present situation, and we have sent many telegrams stating our position. Several times we have tried unsuccessfully to pressure the University into enforcing desegregation on its off-campus real estate holdings. We have circulated and signed petitions addressed to city, state, and national legislatures and executives asking them to pass and *enforce* various anti-segregation ordinances and laws.

In April 1959, we participated enthusiastically along with 25,000 other students in the Youth March for Integration. (Reverend Martin Luther King, Jr., in the May *Progressive,* claims that there were 40,000 in the march; 25,000 was the figure the police reported.) With the backing of the NAACP, labor unions, Reverend King, and various other notables, the students of the country were to demonstrate in Washington—to Congress, to the people, and to ourselves—that the youth wanted segregation to end *now*. But when we went to Washington, we found ourselves walking down four back streets to the rear of the Washington Monument, and listening there to an endless number of self-righteous speeches by labor leaders and Congressmen who told us what we already knew—that integration was better than segregation. The newspapers gave us only minimal coverage, and many of us—the white Northerners, I mean—felt very little enthusiasm over attending another such event, and giving our energy and support to what seemed a kind of betrayal.

Yet in February 1960 we began hearing about the Southern sit-in demonstrations, and by March we had set up sympathetic picket lines in front of Chicago's Woolworth stores. Our reasons for picketing were, as usual, mixed. We were picketing to demonstrate sympathetic support, to arouse Northern interest, to pressure Woolworth, to be part of the movement. Few of us thought we would go to jail. (One of my friends brought his schoolbooks to the picket line just in case.) But mixed as they were, our feelings must have been duplicated throughout the North. The spread of similar picket lines to other cities was in no way coordinated, and they seem to have been as spontaneous as the sit-ins themselves.

The only heated discussion of the entire meeting came on Sunday: were Northerners to be represented on the temporary planning committee of the not yet established organization? Lawson and the other leaders felt that whatever ideology and/or momentum the group now had would be dissipated by Northern intervention. But to the Northerners and to many Southern participants, such "second class membership" was unacceptable. A compromise set up a de facto all-Southern planning committee which Northerners could *earn* the right to join by participating in non-violent demonstrations against segregation in the North. Sympathetic Woolworth picketing did not count as such a demonstration.

What did the weekend mean? That with or without the help of Northern students, the South is changing. Soon Negroes will be able to eat at most restaurants, and their friends will not have to pack big lunches for traveling. And schools will be integrated, and the Negro will vote. All this will change, but—and this is what no one at the Southern conference wanted to discuss—very much in American society will not change.

8. "In Pursuit of Freedom"
William Mahoney

William Mahoney, a student at Howard University, was one of hundreds of student activists who continued the Freedom Rides after the initial CORE-sponsored group was attacked by segregationists at Anniston, Birmingham, and Montgomery, Alabama. Mahoney and other students were arrested on breach of peace charges soon after their arrival in Jackson, Mississippi, and imprisoned in Parchman Penitentiary. He wrote about his Freedom Ride experiences for Liberation *magazine.*

In early May I heard from fellow Howard University students that the Congress of Racial Equality was looking for volunteers to ride from Washington, D.C., to New Orleans by bus to determine whether bus station facilities were integrated in compliance with Supreme Court rulings. I was sympathetic to the idea, but approaching final examinations. . . .

I forgot about the CORE-sponsored trip, known as the Freedom Ride, until Monday, May 15th, when the morning papers were delivered to the dormitory desk at which I was working and I saw pictures of a fellow Howard student with whom I had participated the past year and a half in the Non-Violent Action Group (N.A.G.) of Washington, leaving a flaming bus on the outskirts of Anniston, Alabama. The caption said that the student . . . had been struck on the head as he left the bus. I was infuriated.

———

At 11 P.M. on Friday, May 26th . . . I boarded a Greyhound bus in Washington with tickets for Montgomery. . . .

At our first stop in Virginia . . . I [was] confronted with what the Southern white has called "separate but equal." A modern rest station with gleaming counters and picture windows was labelled "White," and a small wooden shack beside it was tagged "Colored." The colored waiting room was filthy, in need of repair, and overcrowded. When we entered the white waiting room Frank [Hunt] was promptly but courteously, in the Southern manner, asked to leave. Because I am a fair-skinned Negro I was waited upon. I walked back to the bus through the cool night trembling and perspiring. . . .

The Montgomery bus station was surrounded by Army jeeps, trucks, and the National Guard in battle gear. . . . We found the people from the Christian Leadership Council who had been sent to meet us and drove away cautiously, realizing that the least traffic violation would be an excuse for our arrest.

———————

Once across the [Mississippi] state line we passed a couple of police cars, which began to follow us. At our first stop the station was cordoned off a block in every direction. A police officer jumped on the bus and forbade anyone to move. One woman, who was a regular passenger, frantically tried to convince the police that she was not involved with us. After checking her ticket the police let her get off.

As we rolled toward Jackson, every blocked-off street, every back road taken, every change in speed caused our hearts to leap. Our arrival and speedy arrest in the white bus station in Jackson, when we refused to obey a policeman's order to move on, was a relief.

———————

At 2 P.M. on May 29th, after spending the night in a barracks-like room of which I can only remember, with trepidation, a one-foot-high sign written on the wall in blood, "I love Sylvia," our group joined nine other Freedom Riders in court. . . .

We were charged with a breach of the peace and then the tall, wiry state prosecutor examined Police Chief Wray, the only witness called to the stand. Chief Wray said that we had been orderly but had refused to move on when ordered to do so by his men.

———————

The thirty or more of us occupied five cells and a dining hall on the top floor. At night we slept on lumpy bags of cotton and were locked in small, dirty, blood-spattered, roach-infested cells. Days were passed in the hot, overcrowded dining room playing cards, reading, praying and, as was almost inevitable, fighting among ourselves over the most petty things. . . .

Time crawled painfully, 15 days becoming 45 meals, 360 hours, 100 card games or 3 letters from home. The killing of a roach or the taking of a shower became major events, the subjects of lengthy debate. But morale remained high; insults and brutality became the subject of jokes and skits. The jailers' initial hostility was broken down by responding to it with respect and with good humor.

The jails began to bulge as even Mississippi Negroes, who according to Southern whites are happy, began to join in the protest. To relieve the crowding, about fifty of us were piled into trucks at 2 A.M. June 15th and sped off into the night. It was rumored that in spite of a law against putting persons convicted of misdemeanors into a penitentiary, we were going to the state penitentiary.

Questions have been raised as to the character of the people who willingly withstand such punishment. . . .

In cell 14 was a middle-aged art dealer from Minneapolis who had three dollars to his name and had come . . . "because it is one way of fighting a system which not only hurts the Negro but is a threat to world peace and prosperity." . . .

My cellmate, a Negro worker, came because he had been chased home by white toughs once too often, because his sister was determined to come, and because a friend of his, William Barbee, had been almost killed by a mob while on a Freedom Ride. He admits that his behavior is not ordinarily disciplined, but he readily accepted any restrictions required of him by the movement. . . .

On my right, in cell 12, was the son of a well-to-do business man who had come because it was his moral duty. His aim was to "change the hearts of my persecutors through the sympathy and understanding to be gained by non-violent resistance." He spoke proudly of his father who had fought hard and "made it," and was constantly defending North America's economic and political system from the attacks made upon it by myself and the art dealer. We never changed each other's views but the arguments passed time and gave us mental exercise.

These three philosophies—political, emotional, and moralist—represent the three major viewpoints I found while spending forty days in various Mississippi prisons.

9. Interview with Robert Zellner

The protest movement led by southern black students had a dramatic impact on white college students, for it offered them new and appealing models for political activism. Robert Zellner, a white native southerner who joined the movement, was one of a number of white students who played significant roles in SNCC. This is an excerpt from a 1978 interview with Zellner by Clayborne Carson.

My father's father was a Klansman and my father's father's father might have been a Klansman . . . but I do know my grandfather was a Klansman, and he was in Birmingham, Alabama. So my father grew up in Birmingham, which . . . is [a] very rough kind of town [with] a terrorist conservative tradition. . . . He went to Bob Jones College . . . [a] very reactionary fundamentalist institution . . . I think, and my mother also graduated from Bob Jones College. . . . But dad was also a thinking person and [a] real dedicated Christian and as he got older he just could not . . . make his Klanism and his Christianity jive. . . .

One of the reasons . . . I was a little bit different from my peers [is] we were poor. Now, my mother was a schoolteacher and my father was a preacher and there were five boys in the family. [But] my daddy never was a first church minister. He was always the circuit rider preacher with six, seven, sometimes twelve churches, mostly in the country and always in small towns.

When I was in tenth grade we moved to Mobile [Alabama], where I got my first taste of big city life and I graduated high school there in '57 and went to Huntington College in Montgomery, Alabama. It was while I was in college in Montgomery that I first got involved in the civil rights movement.

In my senior year, which was '60 and '61, in a sociology class, I was assigned . . . to study the racial problem and write a paper presenting my ideas of solutions to the problem. Now, this was in Montgomery, Alabama—the heart of the Confederacy, heart of Dixie—but it was an academic thing, and you are supposed to have enough sense to know that you looked in the books and stuff like that, and I did all that. And then some of the students went to the Klan headquarters, and they came back with literally wheelbarrows full of Klan literature. So I said okay, we'll do that, too. So we went and got our Klan literature, too, and the Citizens' Council's. We said, "Well what about the Montgomery Improvement Association?" That was the other side of the question. Being good academicians, we figured [we] should check that out, too.

Anyway, to make a long story short, we did go to the Montgomery Improvement Association and we went to a federal court hearing in Montgomery where Dr. King, Reverend [Ralph] Abernathy, and Reverend [Solomon] Seay, and many other local and national leaders, had been charged with libel of the Montgomery city commissioners and the county commissioners and so forth. . . . Four or five of us from campus went there and in the process we met Dr. King and Reverend Abernathy and . . . we asked them if it was possible for us to maybe meet with some students from Alabama State, which was a black campus near our campus. In the back of our minds this was in keeping with our assignment. They gave us the names of students and we just went over there and met with them. By this time the police got interested, and they were following us; it became sort of an adventure thing. Eventually it wound up that a nonviolence workshop was to be held at the . . . Baptist Church.

So right after the workshop . . . we told Rev. Abernathy and the other ministers that we wanted to come to the meetings and they said, "Well, we'd like you to come, too, but you will be arrested if you come."

We said, "Oh, we don't believe it. We have a right to come. We know the Constitution and everything." They said, "Well, we want you to come, but we want you to know what's going to happen."

We'd come to the meetings after they started, and the people would take us to the balcony, or they would hide us out at the corner somewhere because state investigators were in the meetings. . . . By the end of the week they knew who we all were and after the Saturday workshop the whole church was surrounded by police. There were five of us in the church—five white students— and the Rev. Abernathy told us that the police were going to arrest us when we left and that the police told him that we would be placed under arrest. So we said, "Well, you know we're willing to be arrested," but we said that it's important to make an attempt to escape. . . . This seemed important at the time. It's ridiculous now. We went to the back door. All the police were up in the front. Sure enough we got back to campus and after we were on campus for about an hour the administration came and collected all of us and said, "The police think you are still trapped in the . . . church." So there was a big meeting with the administration, and we were asked to resign from the school on the grounds [that] what we were doing [was illegal].

So out of the five guys involved in that particular incident, I was the only person out of the five that graduated. One attempted suicide. [The others] got tremendous pressure from their families. Mine was the only family that backed me up in the whole thing. In a sense . . . they gave no white southerner of that period any choice. If you backed the system at all you had two choices: you either capitulated absolutely and completely, or you became a rebel, a complete outlaw, and that's the way I went because I was contrary enough and had backing from my family, which was very important.

———————

[In the] early spring of '61, SNCC was looking for someone to do white campus traveling. I had already met some of the SNCC people at the nonviolence workshop and SNCC already had a name and an image before it was even basically an organization. One thing that had gotten me involved in this whole thing was the whole p.r. thing of the sit-ins [in] the spring of '60, actually the end of my junior year in college. So here were all these students. They all wore trench coats and suits and ties. They never went to a sit-in without their books. . . . I know they're studying biology and sociology and psychology and everything like I'm studying and . . . going out and going up against this authority. That was exciting to me, because I was in an authoritarian state, and I was in an authoritarian college. And here these guys sit down and say, "If you don't feed me I'm going to tie up your place of business. And if you're going to haul me to jail, then let's go on to jail, and we'll sing and everything." That was really inspiring.

. . . Spring of '61 was the end of my senior year in college. Here I am in Montgomery, and the buses are coming. They leave Atlanta. They come to Anniston. And the mob bust them up and burned the bus and everything. They go to Birmingham. It looks like it's all over. You know the Klan has won, and then a new shipment of blood comes from Nashville, and the guys say they are going on. Here they are. I am in Montgomery. I'm in the direct path of all this and still I'm a civilian. The Freedom Rides are coming through. They eventually get to Montgomery, and here is a riot going on in my own city, and people are getting stoned. I'm here. I'm seeing this. I'm hearing it on the radio so I go down to the city to see if I could put my body between some Klansmen and some Freedom Rider. And cars are being burned up, and churches are being torn and everything. How could you fail to get involved?

10. "Eve of Nonviolent Revolution?"
James M. Lawson, Jr.

Although the proponents of nonviolent direct action were often described in press reports as less militant than such self-defense advocates as Robert F. Williams, they often saw themselves as the true revolutionaries of the black struggle. James Lawson, for example, insisted that violent revolution was "counterfeit," because it sought only to destroy an evil regime without creating anything better in its place. In the article from which these excerpts are taken (which originally appeared in The Southern Patriot *in November 1961), he outlines his plan for a nonviolent campaign to bring about a "total" revolution that would question all existing social institutions.*

Nonviolent revolution is always a real, serious revolution. It seeks to transform human life in both private and public forms . . .

involves the whole man in his whole existence . . . maintains balance between tearing down and building up, destroying and planting.

———————

It is interesting to notice that while we recognize segregation as harmful to the whole nation and the South, we rarely blame this on the system and the structure of our institutions. Most of us work simply for concessions from the system, not for transforming the system.

But if after over 300 years, segregation (slavery) is still a basic pattern rather than a peripheral custom, should we not question the American way of life which allows segregation so much structural support?

Does not our political system encourage segregation? Is it not just the lack of Negro voting, but the failure of systems to provide real choices for voters?

———————

We must recognize that we are merely in the prelude to revolution, the beginning, not the end, not even the middle. . . . I do not wish to minimize the gains we have made thus far. . . . But it would be well to recognize that we have been receiving concessions, not real changes. The sit-ins won concessions, not structural changes; the Freedom Rides won great concessions, but not real change.

There will be no revolution until we see Negro faces in all positions that help to mold public opinion, help to shape policy for America. . . .

One federal judge in Mississippi will do more to bring revolution than sending 600 marshals to Alabama. We must never allow the President to substitute marshals for putting people into positions where they can affect public policy. . . .

Remember that the way to get this revolution off the ground is to forge the moral, spiritual and political pressure which the President, the nation and the world cannot ignore. . . .

How can we do this? I propose a very concrete way. The only way is through a nonviolent army. Let SCLC, in concert with other groups committed to nonviolence begin to plan, recruit, organize and discipline a nonviolent corps. . . . Let us call for from 2000 to 7 or 8 thousand nonviolent volunteers.

Let us work out with them a private discipline, reconciliation in personal life. Let us establish work camps for training, study, reading, meditation and constructive work in voting, repairing neighborhood slums, community centers.

Let us prepare these people for mass nonviolent action in the Deep South. Let us recruit people who will be willing to go at a given moment and stay in jail indefinitely; the Freedom Rides were a start at this, but they involved too many people for a court test and too few for a jail-in.

Imagine, if you can, what would happen in the next 12 months if we had such an army ready. The whole nation would know that we meant serious business. The Deep South would begin to realize that . . . the moment of truth is not far off.

A campaign with such an army would cause world-wide crisis, on a scale unknown in the western world except for actual war; not even a Berlin crisis could be used as an excuse for America to escape its cancer at home. . . .

We would lay this issue on the soul of the nation and perhaps cause the nation . . . to adjust to the world by beginning a revolutionary change at home. . . . The womb of revolution is the nonviolent movement. . . .

CHAPTER FOUR

No Easy Walk
(1961–1963)

Introduction by David J. Garrow

In August 1961, the Student Nonviolent Coordinating Committee (SNCC), the group of young college student activists who had emerged from the 1960 sit-ins as the new shock troops of the black freedom struggle in the South, made a decision that represented a crucial turning point in the civil rights movement. A number of SNCC activists decided that rather than return to college that fall, they would move into rural areas of the Deep South and become full-time organizers, seeking to stimulate new black initiatives in thoroughly segregated and often Klan-dominated local communities.

One group of young SNCC workers went into the small city of McComb in southwest Mississippi and persevered in its efforts despite heavy white harassment. Another youthful SNCC activist, Charles Sherrod, later to be joined by Cordell Reagon and Charles Jones, made initial contacts in and around the city of Albany—*All-benny,* residents pronounced it—in southwest Georgia.

In both towns the SNCC workers found some black adults, often middle-class professional men who had served abroad in the U.S. military, who already were trying to pursue modest, local-level civil rights initiatives despite white opposition and hostility. Over time, the local civil rights movements that emerged in towns like McComb and Albany owed their strength and resilience to the combination of both the SNCC workers' outside organizational ties and the long-term commitment and dedication of local activists whose names often have gone largely unrecorded.

Although McComb and southwest Mississippi became an intense civil rights battleground in the fall of 1961, it was Albany that emerged as America's first nationally covered civil rights struggle since the Freedom Rides crisis in May 1961. Like the Freedom Rides, the initial focus was transportation. While the Interstate Commerce Commission (ICC) order, stemming from the Freedom Rides, mandated the desegregation of all interstate transportation facilities—such as train stations and bus terminals—on November 1, 1961, Albany was one city where local officials had no interest in complying with that ruling. When both SNCC and Albany's branch of the National Association for the Advancement of Colored People (NAACP) organized "tests" of those facilities, Albany Police Chief Laurie Pritchett had the participants, often young black students recruited by SNCC workers from Albany State College or local high schools, arrested for attempting to desegregate the terminals. Those arrests mobilized the local black community into peaceful mass prayer marches that resulted in hundreds of further arrests. The local black adult leadership, which had banded together into the Albany Movement to give direction to the new civil rights efforts, called Dr. Martin Luther King, Jr., in Atlanta to seek his assistance and involvement.

The arrival of King and several aides from the Southern Christian Leadership Conference (SCLC) gave a boost to the mass demonstrations but further intensified the organizational tension and conflict between the representatives of SNCC, the NAACP, the Albany Movement, and the SCLC, all of which wanted at least a degree of primacy in the daily news stories about Albany's demonstrations that now were being featured on network television news and the front pages of major national newspapers.

On December 18, the protests ended when the Albany Movement leadership reached what they believed was a negotiated desegregation accord with representatives of the city government. King left town, but over the next few weeks it became increasingly clear that the whites would not make good on their promises, which they had voiced simply to end the demonstrations and remove Albany from the national headlines. When Albany Movement representatives appeared before the City Commission on January 23, 1962, to ask that the city not renege on its promises, white officials curtly dismissed them and asserted that no binding agreement had ever taken place.

Throughout the spring and early summer of 1962 the Albany Movement and the small band of SNCC workers kept up their efforts, focusing much energy on an economic boycott of white Albany businesses. Many white business leaders were angered when the City Commission allowed the city bus company to go out of business rather than permit the company to desegregate bus seating as the Movement had demanded and the company had agreed. The business leaders lobbied without success for the city officials to place Albany's economic well-being ahead of a hard-line defense of rigid segregation. The commission held its ground, and when protests resumed in mid-July, the city fathers instructed Police Chief Pritchett to continue with a policy of mass arrests rather than give in to King's and the Albany Movement's request that the city sanction some desegregation efforts and open official biracial discussions with its own black citizens.

Laurie Pritchett's peaceful defense of segregation led not to national criticism but to widespread news media praise of his professionalism and strategic sagacity. Without any incidents of mass violence akin to the attacks on the Freedom Riders, neither the American public nor the Kennedy administration paid much heed to Albany's successful repression of the black demonstrations. By the end of August both the Albany Movement and King's SCLC had concluded that any further protests and arrests served no strategic purpose. Albany activists shifted their efforts to voter registration and attempted to rebut press claims that Albany had been a civil rights "failure" and "defeat." SNCC turned its attention to the rural counties around Albany, and King and his SCLC colleagues pondered how a more successful mass protest campaign might be launched in some other southern city.

That next city would be Birmingham, Alabama, where King's longtime SCLC colleague, Rev. Fred Shuttlesworth, had headed up an aggressive local civil rights organization, the Alabama Christian Movement for Human Rights (ACMHR), ever since state authorities had forced the NAACP out of business in Alabama in 1956. Shuttlesworth was eager for King and the SCLC to help him mount a full-scale protest campaign against Birmingham's rigid segregation and the man who aggressively led its defense, infamous Public Safety Commissioner Eugene "Bull" Connor. Although some Birmingham merchants, much like Albany's businessmen, had told Shuttlesworth they would rather desegregate than pay the economic price that would result from mass demonstrations, they refused to act in the face of Connor's forceful championing of total segregation. King and the SCLC weighed a number of factors including the ACMHR's commitment, the economic vulnerability of the white merchants, Connor's quick-tempered penchant for violent responses to black activism, and the 1961–1962 lesson that the Kennedys would respond to violent civil rights repression with direct federal intervention while largely ignoring Pritchett-style repression. They decided that Connor and Birmingham might well be just the tonic that the southern movement needed after the disappointments and frustrations of Albany.

The SCLC and the ACMHR launched their Birmingham demonstrations in April 1963. After a slow start, King intentionally chose to submit to arrest, hoping his incarceration might spark the campaign into greater action and win it more national—and federal—attention. When Connor's jailers placed King in solitary confinement, King's friends and aides became deeply concerned and persuaded his wife, Coretta Scott King, to phone the Kennedy White House to seek federal reassurance of her husband's safety. Both Attorney General Robert Kennedy and President John Kennedy responded with personal calls to Mrs. King, and King's jailing did help spark an intensification of the movement's Birmingham protests. "Bull" Connor employed both snarling police attack dogs and high-powered fire hoses to drive back black demonstrators who sought to march into downtown Birmingham. National and international outrage resulted as graphic photos and television footage of the police violence were printed and shown across the country and around the world. The Kennedy administration sprang into action and successfully lobbied Birmingham's economic leadership into reaching a desegregation accord with King and Shuttlesworth before the police violence and resulting black anger got totally out of hand.

Coverage of the Birmingham protests made Americans more profoundly aware of the obstacles and opposition facing the southern black freedom struggle than any events from preceding years. Several weeks later, as smaller demonstrations spread across the South and Alabama governor George C. Wallace sought unsuccessfully to block the court-ordered integration of the University of Alabama, President Kennedy went on television to declare, in words far stronger than he or any previous president had ever used, that racial discrimination and injustice was a serious and profound moral evil that American society had to confront and strive to eliminate. For the first time in his presidency, Kennedy committed himself to aggressively championing federal legislation that would mandate public desegregation and racial nondiscrimination in many facets of American life.

Although Kennedy's declaration of support for far-reaching civil rights legislation was greeted enthusiastically by civil rights proponents, Kennedy and his administration at first openly opposed black leaders' announcement of a late-August March on Washington which would seek to highlight the economic disadvantages experienced by black America as well as call upon the Congress to pass Kennedy's civil rights bill. The longtime dean of black American leaders, A. Philip Randolph, president of the Brotherhood of Sleeping Car Porters (BSCP) and the Negro American Labor Council (NALC), was the major proponent of the march and its economic focus. The Kennedys, plus some civil rights supporters, feared that any such mass demonstration might harm rather than help the congressional prospects of the civil rights bill. Only after some hesitation did NAACP executive secretary Roy Wilkins and National Urban League (NUL) chief Whitney Young endorse and join in the march.

Throughout the weeks leading up to the August 28 March on Washington, Kennedy administration officials and such civil rights leaders as Wilkins did all they could to ensure that the tone of the march and the content of its leaders' speeches at the climactic Lincoln Memorial rally would do everything possible to aid Kennedy's legislation. In the process, Randolph's original economic focus became largely invisible, and administration loyalists became extremely concerned when the advance text of SNCC chairman John Lewis's speech called the Kennedy bill "too little, and too late." Under great pressure that continued up until just a few moments before the rally itself got under way, Lewis, a veteran of both the sit-ins and the Freedom Rides, finally was convinced to delete the language that the Kennedys and some of their civil rights allies found offensive.

Notwithstanding the serious private controversy over Lewis's text, the March on Washington, which drew over two hundred thousand participants and climaxed with Martin Luther King, Jr.'s famous "I Have A Dream" oration, represented a new high-water mark for the black freedom struggle. Even more so than in the wake of the Birmingham protests, America seemed to manifest a new and greater level of support for fundamental improvements in the lives of black citizens. Nonetheless, the march was only a one-day event, and when it concluded, as Martin Luther King, Jr., stated that afternoon, "it was time once again for the movement to 'return to the valley' "—the harshly segregated valley of the American South, exemplified best—or worst—by Mississippi and the deadly obstacles that movement workers continued to encounter in that most southern of southern states.

1. Organizing in Albany, Georgia
Charles Sherrod

SNCC worker Charles Sherrod was twenty-two when he became the first "outside agitator" for civil rights to go into Albany and southwest Georgia in 1961. In this excerpt from an untitled and undated account of his work that Sherrod wrote just a year or two later, he recounts the experiences that he and his first SNCC partner, Cordell Reagon, encountered in Albany.

Cordell Reagon of Nashville, and Charles Sherrod of Petersburg, Virginia, arrived in Albany by bus in early October, after having been "railroaded" out of McComb, Mississippi, where we had been engaged in a voter-registration campaign that erupted into a significant move on the part of the populace which has won the attention of the nation.

The population of Albany was, in the first days of our stay here, very apprehensive. We had told many that our intention was to organize a voter-registration campaign, the first step of which was to establish an office. At the same time, it was known that we had little or no money. Further, there was doubt in the minds of many people as to who we really were.

The first obstacle to remove was the mental block in the minds of those who wanted to move but were unable for fear that we were not who we said we were. But when people began to hear us in churches, social meetings, on the streets, in the pool halls, lunchrooms, nightclubs, and other places where people gather, they began to open up a bit. We would tell them of how it feels to be in prison, what it means to be behind bars, in jail for the cause. We explained to them that we had stopped school because we felt compelled to do so since so many of us were in chains. We explained further that there were worse chains than jail and prison. We referred to the system that imprisons men's minds and robs them of creativity. We mocked the system that teaches men to be good Negroes instead of good men. We gave an account of the many resistances [to] injustice in the courts, in employment, registration, and voting. The people knew that such evils existed but when we pointed them out time and time again and emphasized the need for concerted action against them, the people began to think. At this point, we started to illustrate what had happened in Montgomery, Macon, Nashville, Charlotte, Atlanta, Savannah, Richmond, Petersburg, and many other cities where people came together and protested against an evil system.

This placed us near November first, the date when the Interstate Commerce Commission had issued its ultimatum for all interstate facilities to be desegregated. . . .

2. Letter from the Albany Movement to the Albany City Commission
January 23, 1962

Despite the fact that city officials reneged on an oral agreement that had brought the mass demonstrations of December 1961 to a halt, Albany Movement leaders continued to hope, up until their January 23, 1962, appearance before the Albany City Commission, that the city would live up to its promises. This document was presented to the commission that evening. The city officials rejected the statement out of hand, and Albany experienced a renewed round of mass civil rights protests that summer.

Gentlemen:

The Albany Movement came into being as a result of repeated denials of redress for inadequacies and wrongs, and finally, for the refusal to even consider petitions which have been presented to your group from as far back as 1957.

The first request was for sewage and paving relief in the Lincoln Heights area—nothing done. Next, the stoning of Negro ministers' houses, following an inflammatory editorial in the local press, caused a request to be sent by registered mail to the Mayor that a joint group try to stop the worsening conditions—no official acknowledgement of this request has ever been received by us. Again, a request that segregated polling places, which we felt were used to counteract the effect of our vote, was made from the top to the bottom—the refusal to attempt any kind of redress necessitated a successful suit to be waged in the Federal Court by us. Finally, it was the refusal of Albany officials, through its police department, to comply with the ICC regulation which became effective last November 1, that made the creation of this body a necessity. Test rides were conducted throughout the entire state of Georgia. Atlanta, Savannah, Augusta, Macon, Columbus, Valdosta and Waycross all complied. Only Albany resisted.

Accordingly we staged further tests on November 22, which resulted in the initial arrests, trials, convictions and appeals. The cases were headed for higher courts and things would have proceeded in an orderly fashion to its conclusion, but for the arrests of the so-called "Freedom Riders."

This testing of the railroad's compliance with another ICC directive has been laid at our doors. Actually, we had absolutely nothing to do with this. It was the elaborately staged "infraction" and arrests of those people that caused us to rush to their defense. They were fighting for the same purpose as we and we could not abandon them to the wolves.

The mockery of fair play and justice which followed, in turn, caused the first planned "Marching Protest." The harsh, repressive measures employed caused further protests and further arrests. By now, the whole country, and the world for that matter, were aware of the unyielding, cruelly repressive measures used to combat our use of that First Amendment to the United States Constitution, "Freedom of Speech" through peaceful protest.

When an agreement was reached on December 18, one of the cardinal points was the privilege of substituting signature bonds in lieu of cash bonds. This agreement has not been kept by the city of Albany. Another agreement was that the police department would not interfere with the compliance of the bus company to the ICC order. This agreement has been only partly kept by the city of Albany.

The Albany Movement wishes to go on record, without reservation, of requesting the city of Albany to keep the faith by honoring its commitments.

We the members of the Albany Movement, with the realization that ultimately the people of Albany, Negro and white, will have to solve our difficulties; realizing full well that racial hostility can be the downfall of our city; realizing that what happens in Albany, as well as what does *NOT* happen in Albany, affects the whole free world, call upon you tonight to hear our position.

It is our belief that discrimination based on race, color or religion is fundamentally wrong and contrary to the letter and intent of the Constitution of the United States. It is our aim in the Albany Movement to seek means of ending discriminatory practices in public facilities, both in employment and in use. Further, it is our aim to encourage private businesses to offer equal opportunity for all persons in employment and in service.

Some of these ideals which are inherent in the Constitution of the United States of America are:

1. Equal opportunity to improve one's self by good education.
2. Equal opportunity to exercise freedom and responsibility through the vote and participation in governmental processes.
3. Equal opportunity to work and advance economically.
4. Equal protection under the law.
5. The creation of a climate in which the talents and abilities of the entire community may be used for the good of all, unfettered by considerations of race or class.

Before going into plans for implementation of these goals, we wish to ask of you, gentlemen, tonight to reaffirm in writing your oral agreement of December 18, 1961, that, (1) the bus and train station will be open at all times without interference from the police; (2) the cash bonds will be refunded in exchange for security bonds, at an early date, the date to be set tonight.

We submit as the next step the creation of a biracial planning committee . . . [to] be composed of 6 members, 3 of which shall be appointed by the Albany Movement and 3 by the City Commission. Because of the tremendous responsibilities that will be invested in this committee, we pledge ourselves, as we also urge the commission, to choose men of the highest integrity, good will and sincerity.

It is our hope that through negotiations and arbitrations, through listening and learning from each other, that we can achieve the purposes that will benefit the total community.

The problem of human rights belongs to us all, therefore, let us not falter in seizing the opportunity which almighty God has given to create a new order of freedom and human dignity. What is your pleasure, gentlemen, in proceeding with the negotiations?

Respectfully Submitted,
For The Albany Movement

W. G. Anderson, President
M. S. Page, Executive Secretary

3. Interview with Bernice Reagon

Bernice Reagon, then Bernice Johnson, was a student at the all-black Albany State College and secretary of the local NAACP youth chapter when Charles Sherrod and Cordell Reagon first came to Albany. This is an excerpt from a 1986 interview with Bernice Reagon by the Eyes on the Prize *production team.*

Growing up in Albany, I learned that if you bring black people together, you bring them together with a song. To this day, I don't understand how people think they can bring anybody together without a song.

Now, the singing tradition in Albany was congregational. There were not soloists, there were song leaders.

When you ask somebody to lead a song, you're asking them to plant a seed. The minute you start the song, then the song is created by everybody there. It's almost like a musical explosion that takes place. But the singing in the movement was different from the singing in church. The singing is the kind of singing where you disappear.

The song-singing I heard in Albany I'd never heard before in my life, in spite of the fact that I was from that congregational singing culture. The only difference was that in Albany, Georgia, black people were doing some stuff around being black people. I know a lot of people talk about it being a movement and when they do a movement they're talking about buses and jobs and the ICC ruling, and the Trailways bus station. Those things were just incidents that gave us an excuse to be something of ourselves. It's almost like where we had been working before we had a chance to do that stuff was in a certain kind of space, and when we did those marches and went to jail, we expanded the space we could operate in, and that was echoed in the singing. It was a bigger, more powerful singing. . . .

After this first march, we're at Union Baptist Church, Charlie Jones [of SNCC] looks at me and said, "Bernice, sing a song." And I started "Over My Head I See Trouble in the Air." By the time I got to where "trouble" was supposed to be, I didn't see any trouble, so I put "freedom" in there. And I guess that was the first time I really understood using what I'd been given in terms of songs. I'd always been a singer but I had always, more or less, been singing what other people taught me to sing. That was the first time I had the awareness that these songs were mine and I could use them for what I needed them to. This sort of thing was important because I ended up being arrested in the second wave of arrests in Albany, Georgia. And I was in jail. And when we got to jail, Slater King was already in jail, and he said, "Bernice, is that you?" And I said, "Yeah." And he said, "Sing a song."

The voice I have now, I got the first time I sang in a movement meeting, after I got out of jail. Now I'm past that first meeting in Union Baptist, I've done "Lift Every Voice and Sing." I am a song leader, I lead every song in jail, but I did not lead the songs in jail in the voice I have now. The voice I have now I got that night and I'd never heard it before in my life. At that meeting, they did what they usually do. They said, "Bernice, would you lead us in a song?" And I did the same first song, "Over My Head I See Freedom in the Air," but I'd never heard that voice before. I had never been that me before. And once I became that me, I have never let that me go.

I like people to know when they deal with the movement that there are these specific things, but there is a transformation that took place inside of the people that needs to also be quantified in the picture. And the singing is just the echo of that. If you have a people who are transformed and they create the sound that lets you know they are new people, then certainly you've never heard it before. They have also never heard it before, because they've never been that before.

When I was in the mass meetings, I would be part of a group up at the front leading the songs. There would be Rutha Harris, Andrew Reed, Charlie Jones, Cordell Reagon, Charles Sherrod. We were all young people. The meetings always started with these freedom songs and the freedom songs were in-between all of the activities of the mass meetings. Most of the mass meeting was singing—there was more singing than there was talking. Most of the work that was done in terms of taking care of movement business had to do with nurturing the people who had come, and there would be two or three people who would talk but basically songs were the bed of everything. I'd had songs in college and high school and church, but in the movement all the words sounded differently. "This Little Light of Mine, I'm Going to Let It Shine," which I'd sung all my life, said something very different: "All in the street, I'm going to let it shine." I'd never even heard that before, 'cause, I mean, who would go into the street? That was not where you were supposed to be if you were an upstanding Christian person. "All in the jailhouse, I'm going to let it shine"— all of these new concepts of where, if you said it, this is where you could be.

What I can remember is being very alive and very clear, the clearest I've ever been in my life. I knew that every minute, I was doing what I was supposed to do. That was the way it was in jail, too, and on the marches. In "We Shall Overcome" there's a verse that says "God is on our side," and there was a theological discussion that said maybe we should say, "We are on God's side." God was lucky to have us in Albany doing what we were doing. I mean, what better case would he have? So it was really like God would be very, very happy to be on my side. There's a bit of arrogance about that, but that was the way it felt.

I think Albany settled the issue of jail and I think songs helped to do that because in the songs you could just name the people who were trying to use this against you—Asa Kelley, who was the mayor, Chief Pritchett, who was the police. This behavior is new behavior for black people in the United States of America. You would every once in a while have a crazy black person going up against some white person and they would hang him. But this time, with a song, there was nothing they could do to block what we were saying. Not only did you call their names and say what you wanted to say, but they could not stop your sound. Singing is different than talking because no matter what they do, they would have to kill me to stop me from singing, if they were arresting me. Sometimes they would plead and say, "Please stop singing." And you would just know that your word is being heard. There was a real sense of platformness and clearly empowerment, and it was like just saying, "Put me in jail, that's not an issue of power. My freedom has nothing to do with putting me in jail." And so there was this joy.

4. Letter from Albany Merchant Leonard Gilberg to Albany Police Chief Laurie Pritchett

July 23, 1962

One of the Albany Movement's tactics was to mount a boycott against many downtown white businesses in the hope that pressure on the pocketbook would achieve what appeals to whites' consciences had not produced. Leonard Gilberg's letter to Chief Pritchett was written during a period of mass protests that took place during July and August 1962.

Dear Chief Pritchett:

In order to inform you as to the situation business-wise for myself and other merchants with whom I have spoken, I am sure you will find the following to be true.

At least 90 to 95% of all the negro business I have enjoyed in past years has been lacking for the last 7 months due to an obvious boycott on the part of the negroes and threats and coercion toward other negroes not in sympathy with the movement to keep them from shopping downtown in Albany.

Now to top all this off, their constant harassment, sit-ins, demonstrations, marching, etc. are keeping all people both white and negro from Albany. Many customers have told me direct that they would not come to Albany from out of town due to fear of demonstrations in Albany and local people have said that they ask their wives and children to stay out of town for the same reason.

Our business is at present suffering an approximate 50% decrease due to lack of customer traffic in Albany and it is an intolerable situation. This fear of mob violence and demonstration has made our situation a dire one. Any aid you can give us in the matter will be greatly appreciated and our thanks to you for the wonderful manner in which you have handled these past events.

Very truly yours,
GILBERG's
Leonard Gilberg

5. "Birmingham: People in Motion"

When the Southern Christian Leadership Conference mounted its campaign of mass protests in Birmingham, Alabama, in April and May 1963, the core of the movement's support came from the Alabama Christian Movement for Human Rights, led by Reverend Fred Shuttlesworth, one of King's cofounders of the SCLC. Birmingham: People in Motion, *the booklet from which these excerpts were taken, was published in 1966 on the occasion of the ACMHR's tenth anniversary.*

In May 1956 Alabama politicians "stood on the beach of history and tried to hold back the tide." They outlawed the National Association for the Advancement of Colored People, in a desperate attempt to halt the movement for Negro equality. But their action had precisely the opposite effect. For almost immediately the Negroes of Birmingham came together to form a movement which during the last ten years has transformed life in Birmingham— which has shaken America.

"They could outlaw an organization, but they couldn't outlaw the movement of a people determined to be free," said the Rev. Fred L. Shuttlesworth, president of the new group. And at a mass meeting called by a committee of Negro ministers, the Alabama Christian Movement for Human Rights (ACMHR) was born. Many Negroes in "the Johannesburg of North America" were afraid to join. But many others echoed the sentiments of Mrs. Rosa Walker, one of the first members: "I was frightened, but I figured we needed help to get us more jobs and better education. And we had the man here to help us."

In its original statement of principles, the ACMHR stated:

> As free and independent citizens of the United States of America, we express publicly our determination to press forward persistently for freedom and democracy, and the removal from our society of any forms of second-class citizenship. . . . We Negroes shall never become enemies of the white people. But America was born in the struggle for Freedom from Tyranny and Oppression. We shall never bomb any homes or lynch any persons; but we must,

because of history and the future, march to complete
freedom with unbowed heads, praying hearts, and an
unyielding determination.

———

The new organization's first efforts were directed toward getting
the City of Birmingham to hire Negroes as policemen. When
petitions and delegations failed, a suit was filed against the
Personnel Board, demanding the right of Negroes to take examinations for all civil service jobs. But it was not to be until ten
years later, after months of picketing and marching outside city
hall and the county courthouse, that the first four Negro policemen
were hired.

In its first year, the movement also filed suit in federal court
on behalf of a Milwaukee couple arrested because they sat in the
"white" waiting room in the city's railway station.

Both these actions followed the pattern of court action established by the NAACP, and indeed, suits have always been one of
the ACMHR's most effective weapons. But in December 1956 the
movement entered a new phase, and took on the character it was
to retain—of a movement of people putting their bodies into a
challenge to the system.

It was in December, 1956 that the U.S. Supreme Court ruled
that bus segregation in Montgomery was illegal. This was a climax
to the historic yearlong Montgomery bus protest.

Immediately, the ACMHR announced that a group of its
members would test segregation laws in their city by attempting
to integrate Birmingham buses. The protest was scheduled for
December 26.

But Christmas night, the night before the protest, the home of
Rev. Shuttlesworth was bombed. The bed in which he was sleeping
was directly over the spot where the bomb went off. The bed was
blown to bits, but he escaped unhurt. Members of the ACMHR
say he was saved to lead the movement.

Shuttlesworth took a neighbor who was hurt in the explosion
to the hospital. Then he took a bus home—and he rode in front.
The bombing strengthened the determination of his followers in
the same way.

"On the 25th day of December, that's when they blew up Rev.

Shuttlesworth's house," says Mrs. Walker. "And when I went to the meeting the next morning Rev. Shuttlesworth was the first thing I saw. And I knowed as how their house was blowed up, and I couldn't figure out how he was there. And I said then, that I'm going into it. And I went into it on that day."

More than 250 others "went into it" with Mrs. Walker. Twenty-one of them were arrested that day, one the following day. They were convicted and fined, and they then filed suit in federal court, in January, 1957.

The question of desegregating the buses wasn't over until late 1959. At that time, federal court rulings held the police were wrong in arresting Negroes who rode the buses integrated in 1958 and the Milwaukee couple who sat in the railroad station in 1959. But the segregation signs were still up, and by now ACMHR people knew that court rulings only come to life when people put their bodies on the line in a challenge to the old ways.

———————

The victories were important and gave people the knowledge that they do have strength, but as yet life in Birmingham had not really changed. Ever since the movement began leaders had received threats of death over the telephone and through the mail. Phones rang all night and strange cars circled the blocks where leaders of the movement lived. Every night after the first bombing in December, 1956, volunteer guards sat all night watching the Shuttlesworth house and church.

Police joined in the harassment. They tapped the telephones and searched and arrested guards at the Shuttlesworth home. Every non-white who came through his street was stopped and questioned. One man was arrested for distributing literature in alleged violation of Alabama's anti-boycott law. Each week city detectives attended the ACMHR mass meetings. They stopped and searched members leaving the meetings and charged them with blocking traffic. One man, the Rev. Charles Billups, was arrested on a charge of interfering with the entrance of a detective at a meeting; it was said he "touched the officer's coat." Later he was tied to a tree and beaten by the Ku Klux Klan. Other ACMHR members were threatened with loss of their jobs, and some were actually fired.

During 1960 and 1961 the ACMHR filed a variety of suits—to desegregate the parks and schools, open airport eating facilities, and to stop the police from attending ACMHR meetings.

1961 ended with victories in the courts.

A federal court ruled that the ordinance forbidding whites and Negroes to play any games together—baseball, checkers, or dominoes—was unconstitutional. Shuttlesworth described the ordinance as "the backbone of Birmingham segregation" and noted that it was the first time a local federal judge had ruled against segregation without a higher court order. "Even here, the light appears," he said.

But a court ruling ordering the desegregation of public parks was turned to defeat for both Negro and white citizens of Birmingham when the city commissioners closed down the parks.

It was early in 1962 that the pressure which finally cracked the solid white wall of opposition of the city's power structure began to build up. . . .

In the spring, Birmingham Negro college students and the ACMHR put on an effective selective buying campaign against the downtown stores. Their demands were desegregation of public accommodations and hiring of Negro clerks. Newspapers ignored the boycott but business leaders admitted privately it hurt them badly. Negro leaders claimed it was eighty per cent effective. Connor retaliated by cutting off the city relief payments, most of which go to Negroes.

The break came when the Rev. Martin Luther King, Jr. announced plans to hold SCLC's 1962 convention in Birmingham . . . [In] order to avert demonstrations . . . Birmingham business leaders sent delegates to confer with SCLC. SCLC replied that whether there would be demonstrations in Birmingham was a matter for local civil rights leaders to decide. So Birmingham business leaders were forced to talk to Shuttlesworth for the first time. . . .

Business leaders had decided that some changes would have to be made if the city's economy was to avoid drastic damage. They found themselves pitted against the city's political leaders, who were unbending in their extreme segregationist position.

6. Wiretap Transcript of Phone Conversation Between Martin Luther King, Jr., and Coretta Scott King
April 15, 1963

During the Birmingham protest campaign, Martin Luther King, Jr., intentionally allowed himself to be arrested and jailed for leading a demonstration on Good Friday, April 12. King's aides, particularly Wyatt T. Walker, executive director of the SCLC, encouraged Coretta Scott King to phone President John F. Kennedy to seek federal reassurance concerning her husband's safety. When President Kennedy returned Mrs. King's call on Monday, April 15, he informed her that federal inquiries were being made and that King's jailers had told the FBI that they would allow him to phone his wife. When he did call, the Birmingham police recorded and transcribed the Kings' conversation, excerpts of which appear here.

MR. KING: I just read your lovely letter.

MRS. KING: You just got it?

MR. KING: Yes.

MRS. KING: I just got a call from the President and he told me you were going to call me in a few minutes.

MR. KING: Who was that? (At this point King talked with his two children, Marty and Yoki.)

MRS. KING: Are you being guarded?

MR. KING: Yes.

MRS. KING: Did they give you a time limit?

MR. KING: Not exactly, but [they] hear everything, you know. Who did you say called you?

MRS. KING: Kennedy, the President.

MR. KING: Did he call you direct?

MRS. KING: Yes, and he told me you were going to call in a few minutes. It was about thirty minutes ago. He called from Palm Beach. I tried to phone him yesterday.

MR. KING: Is that known?

MRS. KING: It's known here; I just got it.

MR. KING: Let Wyatt know.

MRS. KING: The Executive in Birmingham?

MR. KING: Yes, do that right now.

MRS. KING: Is your spirit all right?

MR. KING: Yes. I've been alone, you know.

MRS. KING: Yes, I know that. Are things pretty good?

MR. KING: Uh huh.

MRS. KING: Now, he told me the F.B.I. talked with you last night, is that right?

MR. KING: No. No.

MRS. KING: They sent them in there, they must have talked with some of the others. They sent them in last night. I talked with Bobby last night. He called twice and told me he would call me today, and it was the President, himself, and he assured me of his concern. He asked if we had any complaints and said if we did to be sure and let them know.

MR. KING: Be sure and get that to the Reverend. I think it will make a very good statement.

MRS. KING: He's very sympathetic and kept saying, "How are you, I understand you have a little baby." He said things might get better with the new administration. This is a problem.

MR. KING: Is it being carried well?

MRS. KING: Not too well here, still not too well. There was a good program today with Dick . . . Arnell. . . .

MR. KING: What about the *Constitution*—that's not important, it's what they say.

MRS. KING: They have been carrying articles. Yesterday they had something about the sixty. The [Atlanta Daily] *World* has had front page about every day recently, but it was not accurate. They said the boycott was not effective. There was something this morning about yesterday. It's been carried pretty good. They had a picture last night, of A.D. [King—Martin's brother]. I think with the *National* it's been pretty good; it's been pretty good today.

MR. KING: When you get this over it will help.

MRS. KING: Yes.

———————

MR. KING: . . . I'll probably come out in the next day or so. Be sure to get in touch with the Reverend. I think this gives it a new dimension.

MRS. KING: I just thought about it yesterday, and I told the Reverend and he tried to get to you, but there was no choice. . . .

7. "Letter from Birmingham City Jail"
Martin Luther King, Jr.

While King was in jail after his Good Friday arrest, an open letter from eight "liberal" white Birmingham clergymen who characterized the demonstrations as "unwise and untimely" appeared in the **Birmingham News**. *King's "Letter from Birmingham City Jail," dated April 16, 1963, though not widely disseminated until a month later, soon became a classic of protest literature.*

My Dear Fellow Clergymen,

While confined here in the Birmingham City Jail, I came across your recent statement calling our present activities "unwise and untimely." Seldom, if ever, do I pause to answer criticism of my work and ideas. . . . But since I feel that you are men of genuine good will and your criticisms are sincerely set forth, I would like to answer your statement in what I hope will be patient and reasonable terms.

I think I should give the reason for my being in Birmingham, since you have been influenced by the argument of "outsiders coming in." I have the honor of serving as president of the Southern Christian Leadership Conference, an organization operating in every Southern state with headquarters in Atlanta, Georgia. We have some 85 affiliate organizations all across the South. . . . Several months ago our local affiliate here in Birmingham invited us to be on call to engage in a nonviolent direct action program if such were deemed necessary. We readily consented.

_____

In any nonviolent campaign there are four basic steps: 1) collection of the facts to determine whether injustices are alive; 2) negotiation; 3) self-purification; and 4) direct action. We have gone through all of these steps in Birmingham. . . . Birmingham is probably the most thoroughly segregated city in the United States. Its ugly record of police brutality is known in every section of the country. Its unjust treatment of Negroes in the courts is a notorious reality. There have been more unsolved bombings of Negro homes and churches in Birmingham than in any city in this nation. These are the hard, brutal, and unbelievable facts. On the basis of these conditions Negro leaders sought to negotiate with the city fathers. But the political leaders consistently refused to engage in good faith negotiation.

Then came the opportunity last September to talk with some of the leaders of the economic community. In these negotiating sessions certain promises were made by the merchants—such as the promise to remove the humiliating racial signs from the stores. On the basis of these promises Reverend Shuttlesworth and the leaders of the Alabama Christian Movement for Human Rights agreed to call a moratorium on any type of demonstrations. As the weeks and months unfolded we realized that we were the victims of a broken promise. The signs remained. As in so many experiences of the past, we were confronted with blasted hopes, and the dark shadow of a deep disappointment settled upon us. So we had no alternative except that of preparing for direct action, whereby we would present our very bodies as a means of laying our case before the conscience of the local and national community. We were not unmindful of the difficulties involved. So we decided to go through a process of self-purification. We started having workshops on nonviolence and repeatedly asked ourselves the questions, "Are you able to accept the blows without retaliating?" "Are you able to endure the ordeals of jail?"

You may well ask, "Why direct action? Why sit-ins, marches, etc.? Isn't negotiation a better path?" You are exactly right in your call for negotiation. Indeed, this is the purpose of direct action. Nonviolent direct action seeks to create such a crisis and establish such creative tension that a community that has constantly refused to negotiate is forced to confront the issue.

My friends, I must say to you that we have not made a single gain in civil rights without determined legal and nonviolent pressure. History is the long and tragic story of the fact that privileged groups seldom give up their privileges voluntarily. Individuals may see the moral light and give up their unjust posture; but as Reinhold Niebuhr has reminded us, groups are more immoral than individuals.

We know through painful experience that freedom is never voluntarily given by the oppressor; it must be demanded by the oppressed. Frankly I have never yet engaged in a direct action movement that was "well timed," according to the timetable of those who have not suffered unduly from the disease of segregation. For years now I have heard the word "Wait!" It rings in the ear of every Negro with a piercing familiarity. This "wait" has almost always meant "never." It has been a tranquilizing Thalidomide, relieving the emotional stress for a moment, only to give birth to an ill-formed infant of frustration. We must come to see with the distinguished jurist of yesterday that "justice too long delayed is justice denied." We have waited for more than 340 years for our constitutional and God-given rights. The nations of Asia and Africa are moving with jetlike speed toward the goal of political independence, and we still creep at horse and buggy pace toward the gaining of a cup of coffee at a lunch counter.

I guess it is easy for those who have never felt the stinging darts of segregation to say wait. But when you have seen vicious mobs lynch your mothers and fathers at will and drown your sisters and brothers at whim; when you have seen hate-filled policemen curse, kick, brutalize, and even kill your black brothers and sisters with impunity; when you see the vast majority of your 20 million Negro brothers smothering in an airtight cage of poverty in the midst of an affluent society; when you suddenly find your tongue twisted and your speech stammering as you seek to explain to your six-year-old daughter why she can't go to the public amusement park that has just been advertised on television, and see the tears welling up in her little eyes when she is told that Funtown is closed to colored children, and see the depressing clouds of inferiority begin to form in her little mental sky, and see her begin to distort her little personality by unconsciously developing a bitterness toward white people; when you have to concoct an answer for a five-year-old son who is asking in agonizing pathos: "Daddy, why do white people treat colored people so mean?"; when you take a cross country drive and find it necessary to sleep night after night in the uncomfortable corners of your automobile because no motel will accept you; when you are humiliated day in and day out by nagging signs reading "white" men and "colored"; when your first name becomes "nigger" and your middle name becomes "boy" (however old you are) and your last name becomes "John," and when your wife and mother are never given the respected title of "Mrs."; when you are harried by day and haunted by night by the fact that you are a Negro, living constantly at tip-toe stance, never quite knowing what to expect next, and plagued with inner fears and outer resentments; when you are forever fighting a degenerating sense of "nobodiness"—then you will understand why we find it difficult to wait. There comes a time when the cup of endurance runs over, and men are no longer willing to be plunged into an abyss of injustice where they experience the bleakness of corroding despair. I hope, sirs, you can understand our legitimate and unavoidable impatience.

———

I must make two honest confessions to you, my Christian and Jewish brothers. First, I must confess that over the last few years I have been gravely disappointed with the white moderate. I have almost reached the regrettable conclusion that the Negroes' great stumbling block in the stride toward freedom is not the White Citizens' "Counciler" or the Ku Klux Klanner, but the white moderate who is more devoted to "order" than to justice; who prefers a negative peace which is the absence of tension to a positive peace which is the presence of justice; who constantly says "I agree with you in the goal you seek, but I can't agree with your methods of direct action"; who paternalistically feels that he can set the timetable for another man's freedom; who lives by the myth of time and who constantly advises the Negro to wait until a "more convenient season." Shallow understanding from people of good will is more frustrating than absolute misunderstanding from people of ill will. Lukewarm acceptance is much more bewildering than outright rejection.

———

You spoke of our activity in Birmingham as extreme. At first I was rather disappointed that fellow clergymen would see my nonviolent efforts as those of the extremist. I started thinking about the fact that I stand in the middle of two opposing forces in the Negro community. One is a force of complacency made up of Negroes who, as a result of long years of oppression, have been so completely drained of self-respect and a sense of "somebodi-ness" that they have adjusted to segregation, and of a few Negroes in the middle class who, because of a degree of academic and economic security, and because at points they profit by segregation, have unconsciously become insensitive to the problems of the masses. The other force is one of bitterness and hatred and comes perilously close to advocating violence. It is expressed in the various black nationalist groups that are springing up over the nation, the largest and best known being Elijah Muhammad's Muslim movement. This movement is nourished by the contem-porary frustration over the continued existence of racial discrim-ination. It is made up of people who have lost faith in America, who have absolutely repudiated Christianity, and who have con-cluded that the white man is an incurable "devil."

———

The Negro has many pent-up resentments and latent frustrations. He has to get them out. So let him march sometime; let him have his prayer pilgrimages to the city hall; understand why he must have sit-ins and freedom rides. If his repressed emotions do not come out in these nonviolent ways, they will come out in ominous expressions of violence. This is not a threat; it is a fact of history.

So I have not said to my people, "Get rid of your discontent." But I have tried to say that this normal and healthy discontent can be channeled through the creative outlet of nonviolent direct action.

In spite of my shattered dreams of the past, I came to Birmingham with the hope that the white religious leadership of this community would see the justice of our cause and, with deep moral concern, serve as the channel through which our just grievances could get to the power structure. I had hoped that each of you would understand. But again I have been disappointed.

I have heard numerous religious leaders of the South call upon their worshippers to comply with a desegregation decision because it is the law, but I have longed to hear white ministers say follow this decree because integration is morally right and the Negro is your brother. In the midst of blatant injustices inflicted upon the Negro, I have watched white churches stand on the sideline and merely mouth pious irrelevancies and sanctimonious trivialities. In the midst of a mighty struggle to rid our nation of racial and economic injustice, I have heard so many ministers say, "Those are social issues with which the Gospel has no real concern," and I have watched so many churches commit themselves to a completely other-worldly religion which made a strange distinction between body and soul, the sacred and the secular.

I hope this letter finds you strong in the faith. I also hope that circumstances will soon make it possible for me to meet each of you, not as an integrationist or a civil rights leader, but as a fellow clergyman and a Christian brother. Let us all hope that the dark clouds of racial prejudice will soon pass away and the deep fog of misunderstanding will be lifted from our fear-drenched communities and in some not too distant tomorrow the radiant stars of love and brotherhood will shine over our great nation with all of their scintillating beauty.

Yours for the cause of Peace and Brotherhood,

M. L. King, Jr.

8. The Birmingham Truce Agreement
May 10, 1963

This is the text of the written agreement reached after a week of intensive negotiations between the protest leaders and representatives of Birmingham's business leaders and merchants. The SCLC and ACMHR agreed to halt demonstrations in exchange for certain beginnings of racial change. The accord, energetically encouraged by the presence in Birmingham of U.S. Assistant Attorney General Burke Marshall, a close advisor to both Robert and John Kennedy, was, relative to existing conditions in Birmingham, a significant step forward. Nonetheless, it covered a very modest set of particulars, and several years, rather than several months, passed before the city of Birmingham moved forward in any meaningful fashion with regard to nondiscriminatory job opportunities—both public and private—for its black citizens.

The Birmingham Truce Agreement

1. Within 3 days after close of demonstrations, fitting rooms will be desegregated.
2. Within 30 days after the city government is established by court order, signs on wash rooms, rest rooms and drinking fountains will be removed.
3. Within 60 days after the city government is established by court order, a program of lunchroom counter desegregation will be commenced.
4. When the city government is established by court order, a program of upgrading Negro employment will be continued and there will be meetings with responsible local leadership to consider further steps.

Within 60 days from the court order determining Birmingham's city government, the employment program will include at least one sales person or cashier.

Within 15 days from the cessation of demonstrations, a Committee on Racial Problems and Employment composed of members of the Senior Citizens' Committee will be established, with a membership made public and the publicly announced purpose of establishing liaison with members of the Negro community to carry out a program of up-grading and improving employment opportunities with the Negro citizens of the Birmingham community.

9. President John F. Kennedy's Nationally Televised Speech
June 11, 1963

The greatest impact of the Birmingham demonstrations was national rather than local. Similar protests against racially discriminatory public accommodations spread across the South, and large sympathy demonstrations in support of the Birmingham campaign took place in cities all across America. Several weeks after the climax and settlement of the Birmingham protests, Alabama governor George C. Wallace unsuccessfully sought to block the desegregation of the University of Alabama by obstructing the registration of two black students a federal court had ordered admitted to the university. Only President Kennedy's deployment of federalized National Guard troops ensured the peaceful admission of the two. That evening the president went on nationwide television to comment on his actions and offer a ringing endorsement of the black civil rights activism that the Birmingham protests demonstrated. Within hours of Kennedy's important address, Mississippi NAACP leader Medgar Evers was shot from ambush and killed outside his home in Jackson.

This nation was founded by men of many nations and backgrounds. It was founded on the principle that all men are created equal; and that the rights of every man are diminished when the rights of one man are threatened.

It ought to be possible, therefore, for American students of any color to attend any public institution they select without having to be backed up by troops. It ought to be possible for American consumers of any color to receive equal service in places of public accommodation, such as hotels and restaurants, and theaters and retail stores, without being forced to resort to demonstrations in the street.

And it ought to be possible for American citizens of any color to register and to vote in a free election without interference or fear of reprisal.

It ought to be possible, in short, for every American to enjoy the privileges of being American without regard to his race or his color.

This is not a sectional issue. Difficulties over segregation and discrimination exist in every city, in every state of the Union, producing in many cities a rising tide of discontent that threatens the public safety.

Nor is this a partisan issue. In a time of domestic crisis, men of goodwill and generosity should be able to unite regardless of party or politics.

This is not even a legal or legislative issue alone. It is better to settle these matters in the courts than on the streets, and new laws are needed at every level. But law alone cannot make men see right.

We are confronted primarily with a moral issue. It is as old as the Scriptures and is as clear as the American Constitution. The heart of the question is whether all Americans are to be afforded equal rights and equal opportunities; whether we are going to treat our fellow Americans as we want to be treated.

If an American, because his skin is dark, cannot eat lunch in a restaurant open to the public; if he cannot send his children to the best public schools available; if he cannot vote for the public officials who represent him; if, in short, he cannot enjoy the full and free life which all of us want, then who among us would be content to have the color of his skin changed and stand in his place?

Who among us would then be content with the counsels of patience and delay? One hundred years of delay have passed since President Lincoln freed the slaves, yet their heirs, their grandsons, are not fully free. They are not yet freed from the bonds of injustice; they are not yet freed from social and economic oppression.

And this nation, for all its hopes and all its boasts, will not be fully free until all its citizens are free.

Now the time has come for this nation to fulfill its promise.

The events in Birmingham and elsewhere have so increased the cries for equality that no city or state or legislative body can prudently choose to ignore them.

The fires of frustration and discord are burning in every city, North and South. Where legal remedies are not at hand, redress is sought in the streets in demonstrations, parades and protests, which create tensions and threaten violence—and threaten lives.

We face, therefore, a moral crisis as a country and a people. It cannot be met by repressive police action. It cannot be left to increased demonstrations in the streets. It cannot be quieted by token moves or talk. It is a time to act in the Congress, in your state and local legislative body, and, above all, in all of our daily lives.

I am, therefore, asking the Congress to enact legislation giving all Americans the right to be served in facilities which are open to the public—hotels, restaurants and theaters, retail stores and similar establishments. This seems to me to be an elementary right.

I'm also asking Congress to authorize the Federal Government to participate more fully in lawsuits designed to end segregation in public education. We have succeeded in persuading many districts to desegregate voluntarily. Dozens have admitted Negroes without violence.

Other features will also be requested, including greater protection for the right to vote.

But legislation, I repeat, cannot solve this problem alone. It must be solved in the homes of every American in every community across our country.

In this respect, I want to pay tribute to those citizens, North and South, who've been working in their communities to make life better for all.

They are acting not out of a sense of legal duty but out of a sense of human decency. Like our soldiers and sailors in all parts of the world, they are meeting freedom's challenge on the firing line, and I salute them for their honor—their courage.

10. Original Text of Speech to Be Delivered at the Lincoln Memorial
John Lewis

The August 28, 1963, March on Washington, conceived as a protest against the federal government's relative disinterest in the economic plight of black Americans, was transformed by the time it took place into a rally of support for the civil rights legislation President Kennedy had sent to the Congress after his June 11 speech. SNCC Chairman John Lewis, however, in the advance text of his prepared remarks for the event, strongly dissented from any endorsement of the Kennedy administration's new stance. Reluctantly bowing to last-minute pressure from other civil rights leaders, Lewis, with the aid of other SNCC leaders, revised his speech to tone down several of the strongest statements. These are excerpts from the original version, before it was altered for delivery at the Lincoln Memorial.

We march today for jobs and freedom, but we have nothing to be proud of. For hundreds and thousands of our brothers are not here. They have no money for their transportation, for they are receiving starvation wages . . . or no wages, at all.

In good conscience, we cannot support the administration's civil rights bill, for it is too little, and too late. There's not one thing in the bill that will protect our people from police brutality.

This bill will not protect young children and old women from police dogs and fire hoses, [for] engaging in peaceful demonstrations. . . .

The voting section of this bill will not help thousands of black citizens who want to vote. It will not help the citizens of Mississippi, of Alabama, and Georgia, who are qualified to vote, but lack a 6th Grade education. "One man, one vote," is the African cry. It is ours, too. (It must be ours.)

We are now involved in . . . revolution. This nation is still a place of cheap political leaders who build their careers on immoral compromise and ally themselves with open forms of political, economic and social exploitation. What political leader here can stand up and say, "My party is the party of principles"? The party of Kennedy is also the party of Eastland. The party of Javits is also the party of Goldwater. Where is *our* party?

In some parts of the South we work in the fields from sun-up to sun-down for $12 a week. In Albany, Georgia, nine of our leaders have been indicted not by Dixiecrats but by the Federal Government for peaceful protest. But what did the Federal Government do when Albany's Deputy Sheriff beat Attorney C. B. King and left him half dead? What did the Federal Government do when local police officials kicked and assaulted the pregnant wife of Slater King, and she lost her baby?

It seems to me that the Albany indictment is part of a conspiracy on the part of the Federal Government and local politicians in the interest of expediency.

I want to know, which side is the Federal Government on?

The revolution is at hand, and we must free ourselves of the chains of political and economic slavery. The non-violent revolution is saying, "We will not wait for the courts to act, for we have been waiting for hundreds of years. We will not wait for the President, the Justice Department, nor Congress, but we will take matters into our own hands and create a source of power, outside any national structure that could and would assure us a victory." To those who have said, "Be Patient and Wait," we must say that, "Patience is a dirty and nasty word." We cannot be patient, we do not want to be free gradually, we want our freedom, and we want it now. We cannot depend on any political party, for both the Democrats and the Republicans have betrayed the basic principles of the Declaration of Independence.

We all recognize the fact that if any radical social, political and economic changes are to take place in our society, the people, the masses, must bring them about. In the struggle we must seek more than civil rights; we must work for the community of love, peace and true brotherhood. Our minds, souls, and hearts cannot rest until freedom and justice exist for *all the people*.

The revolution is a serious one. Mr. Kennedy is trying to take the revolution out of the street and put it in the courts. Listen, Mr. Kennedy, Listen, Mr. Congressman, listen, fellow citizens, the black masses are on the march for jobs and freedom, and we must say to the politicians that there won't be a "cooling-off" period.

––––––––––

We won't stop now. All of the forces of Eastland, Barnett, Wallace, and Thurmond won't stop this revolution. The time will come when we will not confine our marching to Washington. We will march through the South, through the Heart of Dixie, the way Sherman did. We shall pursue our own "scorched earth" policy and burn Jim Crow to the ground—nonviolently. We shall fragment the South into a thousand pieces and put them back together in the image of democracy. We will make the action of the past few months look petty. And I say to you, WAKE UP AMERICA!

MISSISSIPPI: IS THIS AMERICA? (1962–1964)

Introduction by Clayborne Carson

Many student activists saw Mississippi as the stronghold of segregation and thus the ultimate testing ground for their idealism and commitment. The Freedom Riders who spent much of the summer of 1961 in Mississippi jails were the first wave of activists who entered the Mississippi movement, but the most determined assault came from Student Nonviolent Coordinating Committee (SNCC) "field secretaries" who first arrived late in the summer to establish a beachhead in McComb. The director of SNCC's project in McComb was Robert Moses, a schoolteacher from Harlem who had attended graduate school at Harvard. Influenced by Ella Baker's belief in group leadership, Moses established a model for community organization that would be followed in other communities. Stressing the need to work with local black leaders, Moses played down his own leadership role and sought to build the confidence of black residents who would carry on the struggle after SNCC had left. Moses later guided the voting rights campaign of the statewide Council of Federated Organizations (COFO), but he continued to emphasize the need for Mississippi residents to lead the suffrage effort and to see his role as a catalyst for the development of indigenous leadership.

Moses encouraged the emergence of a confident, resilient group of black leaders in Mississippi, but white resistance remained strong, and few blacks were added to the voter rolls. Indeed, antiblack violence, such as the killing of Herbert Lee in 1961, received little attention outside the state, and civil rights workers' calls for federal protection were largely ignored during the early 1960s. In 1963, the continuing violence and intimidation, as well as the assassination in Jackson of National Association for the Advancement of Colored People (NAACP) field secretary Medgar Evers, led Moses to rethink his initial opposition to the use of white student volunteers from outside the state. Recognizing that northern public opinion was not much affected by violence against Mississippi blacks, he surmised that the presence of white students might provide a protective shield against the more blatant acts of racial intimidation.

Moses followed the suggestion of white lawyer and activist Allard Lowenstein and, in the fall of 1963, planned a mock election similar to a black protest vote which Lowenstein had observed in South Africa. Lowenstein recruited white students, mostly from Stanford and Yale, to assist the effort, which would demonstrate the desire of blacks to vote. The mock election was considered a success, because over 80,000 blacks participated and attacks against civil rights workers decreased. Local blacks gained confidence, and Moses immediately began considering the idea of bringing a larger number of whites to the state during the following summer. He and other SNCC workers felt that the large-scale involvement of whites from prominent northern colleges and families would restrain white violence or perhaps, if violence occurred, provide a confrontation between federal and state authorities. Many black organizers on the COFO staff resisted the plan to use large numbers of whites, however, believing that it would hamper their long-term effort to build self-confident local black leadership. Despite this opposition, COFO voted to support a major project that would bring as many as a thousand volunteers to the state during the summer of 1964.

The 1964 Summer Project succeeded in greatly increasing national awareness of the extent of racial oppression in Mississippi, but it also exposed serious internal tensions in the movement to achieve civil rights reforms. Even as volunteers were arriving in the state in June, they learned that three civil rights workers— two whites, Andrew Goodman and Michael Schwerner, and a black, James Chaney—were missing after being released from the Philadelphia, Mississippi, jail. They had gone to nearby Meridian to investigate a church bombing. The killings led to an investigation by the FBI, which had responded unenthusiastically to previous SNCC requests to investigate attacks on black Mississippians. Following a massive search involving military personnel, the bodies of the three men were found buried in an earthen dam. Months later, a group of whites that included police officials were implicated in the murders. They were eventually convicted of interfering with the civil rights of the victims.

The Summer Project, which continued despite the disappearance of the three workers, brought accomplishments and disappointments. Volunteers and COFO workers gained extensive experience in community organizing and in developing black-controlled institutions. Among the most successful aspects of the project were the "freedom schools," which used innovative teaching techniques to improve the academic and political skills of black children—and some adults—and to enhance their knowledge of Afro-American history. Both teachers and students alike were positively influenced by this unique educational experience, which inspired the subsequent free schools movement in the urban North.

Another important aspect of the Summer Project was the development of the Mississippi Freedom Democratic Party (MFDP), a political organization intended to challenge the legitimacy of the regular, all-white Mississippi delegation to the Democratic convention in Atlantic City, held in August 1964. The MFDP hoped to unseat the regulars by affirming its loyalty to the expressed principles of the national party and proclaiming its support of the reelection of President Lyndon B. Johnson. Despite MFDP's adherence to state regulations and its considerable support among northern delegates at the convention, the challenge did not succeed. The MFDP delegation voted to reject a compromise offered by Democratic leaders, who proposed that the challengers accept two at-large seats rather than the full recognition they sought.

The rejection of the compromise was a major turning point in the history of the southern black movement. It strengthened the belief of some activists that the Summer Project had been an unsuccessful experiment. Bitterness over the outcome of that convention challenge exacerbated many of the racial tensions that had festered during the summer's unprecedented interactions between black activists and white volunteers in Mississippi. Many black organizers in SNCC became increasingly dubious about the merits of interracialism as a strategy of black advancement and more determined to seek fundamental social change rather than merely civil rights legislation. The fall of 1964 was a period of reassessment for SNCC and other civil rights organizations, and the ideological ferment that occurred during the period provided hints of the ideological debates that dominated the late 1960s.

The struggle in Mississippi had brought black residents closer to the goal of voting rights, but as with other social movements, new objectives and concerns had emerged in the process of pursuing initial goals. After the summer, organizers confronted the vexing question of how to alter the basic living conditions of poor blacks. Were traditional political processes adequate or was it necessary to build new black-controlled institutions? Organizers also critically examined their tactics, political assumptions, and organizing techniques to ensure that they were consistent with their desire to build new bases of black power rather than remain forever dependent on the goodwill of white liberals. While white volunteers returned from the summer in Mississippi with greater militancy and distrust of elite-controlled institutions, many black organizers began to move in a separatist direction. A SNCC delegation's tour of Africa during the fall of 1964 brought the organization into contact with the black nationalist ideology of Malcolm X, who met with SNCC workers in Kenya and later in Selma, Alabama. Both the lessons of experience and the influences of Malcolm and African nationalist leaders shaped the development of new black-controlled institutions, such as the Lowndes County Freedom Organization (LCFO) in Alabama. The struggle to achieve the vote for black Mississippi provided a stimulus for subsequent movements seeking a radical transformation of American society.

1. "Mississippi: 1961–1962"

Robert Moses

During the 1950s, NAACP members in Mississippi had faced fierce opposition to their efforts to encourage black voter registration, and in 1955, Reverend George Lee had been ambushed and killed after protesting against black disenfranchisement. Another early pioneer was Amzie Moore, a World War II veteran who, after the war, organized blacks to resist a series of racist killings designed to ensure that returning black soldiers did not disrupt the "southern way of life." In 1960, Moore invited Robert Moses to bring students to the state in order to launch a voting rights campaign, and in 1961 Moses returned to McComb, population thirteen thousand.

. . . I first came South July, 1960, on a field trip for SNCC, went through Alabama, Mississippi and Louisiana gathering people to go to the October conference. That was the first time that I met Amzie Moore. At that time we sat down and planned the voter registration drive for Mississippi. I returned in the summer of 1961 to start that drive. We were to start in Cleveland, Mississippi in the delta. However, we couldn't; we didn't have any equipment; we didn't even have a place at that time to meet. So we went down to McComb at the invitation of C. C. Bryant, who was the local head of the NAACP. And we began setting up a voter registration drive in McComb, Mississippi.

What did we do? Well, for two weeks I did nothing but drive around the town talking to the business leaders, the ministers, the people in the town, asking them if they would support ten students who had come in to work on a voter registration drive. We got a commitment from them to support students for the month of August and to pay for their room and board and some of their transportation while they were there. . . . This means that we went around house-to-house, door-to-door in the hot sun everyday because the most important thing was to convince the local townspeople that . . . we were people who were responsible. What do you tell somebody when you go to their door? Well, first you tell them who you are, what you're trying to do, that you're working on voter registration. You have a form that you try to get them to fill out. . . .

Now we did this for about two weeks and finally began to get results. That is, people began to go down to Magnolia, Mississippi, which is the county seat of Pike County and attempt to register. In the meantime, quite naturally, people from Amite and Walthall County, which are the two adjacent counties to Pike County, came over asking us if we wouldn't accompany them in schools in their counties so they could go down and try to register also. And this point should be made quite clear, because many people have been critical of going into such tough counties so early in the game. . . . The problem is that you can't be in the position of turning down the tough areas because the people then, I think, would simply lose confidence in you; so, we accepted this.

We planned to make another registration attempt on the 19th of August. . . . This was the day then that Curtis Dawson and Preacher Knox and I were to go down and try to register. This was the day that Curtis Dawson drove to Steptoe's, picked me up and drove down to Liberty and we were to meet Knox at the courthouse lawn, and instead we were to walk through the town and on the way back were accosted by Billy Jack Caston and some other boys. I was severely beaten. I remember very sharply that I didn't want to go immediately back into McComb because my shirt was very bloody and I figured that if we went back in we would probably be fighting everybody. So, instead, we went back out to Steptoe's where we washed down before we came back into McComb.

Well, that very same day, they had had the first sit-in in McComb, so when we got back everybody was excited and a mass meeting was planned for that very night. And Hollis [Watkins] and Curtis [Hayes] had sat down in the Woolworth lunch counter in McComb and the town was in a big uproar. We had a mass meeting that night and made plans for two things: one, the kids made plans to continue their sit-in activity, and two, we made plans to go back down to Liberty to try to register some more. We felt it was extremely important that we try and go back to town immediately so the people in that county wouldn't feel that we had been frightened off by the beating and before they could get a chance there to rally their forces.

Accordingly, on Thursday, August 31, there was more activity in Liberty and McComb. In McComb, there were more sit-ins, in Liberty, another registration attempt coupled with an attempt by us to find the person who had done the beating and have his trial. Well, it turned out that we did find him, that they did have his trial, that they had a six-man Justice of the Peace jury, that in a twinkling of an eye the courthouse was packed. That is, the trial was scheduled that day and in two hours it began and in those two hours farmers came in from all parts of the county bearing their guns, sitting in the courthouse. We were advised not to sit in the courthouse except while we testified, otherwise we were in the back room. After we testified, the sheriff came back and told us that he didn't think it was safe for us to remain there while the jury gave its decision. Accordingly, he escorted us to the county line. We read in the papers the next day that Billy Jack Caston had been acquitted.

To top it all off, the next week John Hardy was arrested and put in jail in Walthall County. He had been working there for two weeks and they had been taking people down, and finally one day he had taken some people down to the registrar's office, had walked in, they had been refused the right to register, and he had asked the registrar why. The registrar recognized him, took the gun out of his drawer and smacked John on the side of his head with a pistol. John staggered out onto the street and was walking down the street when he was accosted by the sheriff who arrested him and charged him with disturbing the peace. . . .

. . . A couple of days before John Hardy was arrested, we had gone back into Amite County to Liberty. This time I was not beaten, but Travis Britt was. I think that was on the 5th of September, and I stood by and watched Travis get pummeled by an old man, tall, reedy and thin, very, very, very mean with a lot of hatred in him. . . . At that particular occasion, Travis and I had been sitting out front of the courthouse and then decided to move around back because the people began to gather out front.

Finally, everybody, about 15 people, gathered around back and began questioning Travis and myself. . . . They were asking him where he was from and how come a nigger from New York City could think that he could come down and teach people down here how to register to vote and have all those problems up there in New York City, problems of white girls going with nigger boys and all such like that. . . . Well, the Travis Britt incident followed by the John Hardy incident in Walthall County just about cleaned us out. The farmers in both those counties were no longer willing to go down; people in Pike County and McComb were in an uproar over the sit-in demonstrations and the fact that Brenda Travis, a sixteen-year-old girl, was in jail, and for the rest of the month of September we just had a tough time. Wasn't much we could do. The kids were in jail; people were in jail on the sit-in charges, had a $5,000 bail over their heads, and the problem was to raise that money and get them out of jail, and then sit down and see if we couldn't collect the pieces together.

Well, we got through September aided in great measure by some of the lawyers from the Justice Department who finally began to come in investigating the voting complaints. They stayed in for about a two-week period and while they were there they gave a lot of support and confidence to the people of the Negro community and allowed us to go back into Walthall and Amite Counties and to interview all the people who had been involved in the voter registration campaign and raise some hope that perhaps something would be done.

And then, finally, the boom lowered, on September 31: Herbert Lee was killed in Amite County. . . . The Sunday before Lee was killed, I was down at Steptoe's with John Doar from the Justice Department and he asked Steptoe was there any danger in that area, who was causing the trouble and who were the people in danger. Steptoe had told him that E. H. Hurst who lived across from him had been threatening people and that specifically he, Steptoe, Herbert Lee and George Reese were in danger of losing their lives. We went out, but didn't see Lee that afternoon. At night John Doar and the other lawyers from the Justice Department left. The following morning about 12 noon, Doc Anderson came by the Voter Registration office and said a man had been shot in Amite County. . . . I went down to take a look at the body and it was Herbert Lee; there was a bullet hole in the left side of his head just above the ear. . . .

Our first job was to try to track down those people . . . who had been at the shooting, who had seen the whole incident. . . . Essentially, the story was this: they were standing at the cotton gin early in the morning and they saw Herbert Lee drive up in his truck with a load of cotton, E. H. Hurst following behind him in an empty truck. Hurst got out of his truck and came to the cab on the driver's side of Lee's truck and began arguing with Lee. He began gesticulating towards Lee and pulled out a gun which he had under his shirt and began threatening Lee with it. One of the people that was close by said that Hurst was telling Lee, "I'm not fooling around this time, I really mean business," and that Lee told him, "Put the gun down. I won't talk to you unless you put the gun down." Hurst put the gun back under his coat and then Lee slid out on the other side, on the offside of the cab. As he got out, Hurst ran around the front of the cab, took his gun out again, pointed it at Lee and shot him. . . . Hurst was acquitted. He never spent a moment in jail. In fact, the sheriff had whisked him away very shortly after the crime was committed. I remember reading very bitterly in the papers the next morning, a little short article on the front page of the *McComb Enterprise Journal,* said that the Negro had been shot in self-defense as he was trying to attack E. H. Hurst. That was it. You might have thought he had been a bum. There was no mention that Lee was a farmer, that he had a family, that he had nine kids, beautiful kids, that he had been a farmer all his life in Amite County and that he had been a very substantial citizen. It was as if he had been drunk or something and had gotten into [a] fight and gotten shot. . . . Now we knew in our hearts and minds that Hurst was attacking Lee because of the voter registration drive, and I suppose that we all felt guilty and felt responsible, because it's one thing to get beat up and it's another thing to be responsible, or to participate in some way in a killing.

Shortly after Lee was killed, the kids were released from jail who had been in jail for a month on the sit-in cases, including Brenda.

Brenda was not allowed to go back in the school and in early October she and 115 students marched out and marched downtown. It's no doubt in my mind that part of the reason for the march, part of the reason for the willingness of so many students to do it, was the whole series of beatings culminating in the killing that had taken place in that area. Well, needless to say, the white community was completely on edge by this time. 115 students stopped in front of the city hall to begin praying one by one, Brenda first, then Curtis, then Hollis, then Bobby Talbort and then finally all of us herded up the steps and into the city courthouse, and Bob Zellner, who was the only white participant, was attacked on the steps as he went up and then the mob outside, waiting, milling around, threatening, and inside, the police brought the people down, the white people, the so-called good citizens of the town, to come down and take a look at this Moses guy, and they would come down and stand at the front of the jail and say, "Where's Moses?" . . .

We were finally taken up one by one into a kind of kangaroo court which they held upstairs which was crowded with citizens from the town: the sheriff, the local county attorney, the local judges. . . . Well, they let all the kids who were under 18 off, and took those who were over 18 down to the county jail and we stayed in jail for several days. . . .

We were let out a few days later on a bail bond, and swept back into the problems in McComb where the balance of the hundred students who had marched out were now being required to fill out a slip saying that they would not participate in any more demonstrations in order to get back in the school. Most of them were refusing to do so, and the community was again in an uproar. . . . We finally decided to set up make-shift classes for them. We opened up Nonviolent High in McComb. That was pretty funny. We had about fifty to seventy-five kids in a large room trying to break them down with the elements of algebra and geometry, a little English, and even a little French, a little history, I think Deon taught physics and chemistry, and [Charles] McDew took charge of history, and I did something with math. . . . And we carried on our classes for a week or two weeks, until finally we got word from Campbell College in Jackson that they would accept them all and that they would make provisions for them immediately.

Well, we spent most of the month of November and on into December in jail; we . . . then regrouped to decide what could be done and what projects we needed to carry out next, how we could pick up the pieces. We had, to put it mildly, got our feet wet. We now knew something of what it took to run a voter registration campaign in Mississippi; we knew some of the obstacles we would have to face; we had some general idea of what had to be done to get such a campaign started. First there were very few agencies available in the Negro community that could act as a vehicle for any sort of campaign. The Negro churches could not in general be counted on; the Negro business leaders could also not in general be counted on except for under-the-cover help; and, in general, anybody who had a specific economic tie-in with the white community could not be counted on when the pressure got hot. Therefore, our feeling was that the only way to run this campaign was to begin to build a group of young people who would not be responsible economically to any sector of the white community and who would be able to act as free agents. And we began to set about doing this. . . .

2. "To Praise Our Bridges"

Fannie Lou Hamer

In the state where Emmett Till had been lynched, enormous courage was required to attempt to register to vote. Successful organizers in SNCC, CORE, and other groups worked diligently and patiently to gain the confidence of black Mississippi residents and then to instill in those residents the necessary confidence to lead their own struggle for equal rights and political power. Mrs. Fannie Lou Hamer became one of the movement's most effective leaders. These are excerpts from her 1967 autobiography, which was taped and edited by Julius Lester and Maria Varela of SNCC.

I was born October sixth, nineteen and seventeen in Montgomery County, Mississippi. My parents moved to Sunflower County when

I was two years old, to a plantation about four and a half miles from here, Mr. E. W. Brandon's plantation.

. . . My parents were sharecroppers and they had a big family. Twenty children. Fourteen boys and six girls. I'm the twentieth child. All of us worked in the fields, of course, but we never did get anything out of sharecropping.

My life has been almost like my mother's was, because I married a man who sharecropped. We didn't have it easy and the only way we could ever make it through the winter was because Pap had a little juke joint and we made liquor. That was the only way we made it. I married in 1944 and stayed on the plantation until 1962 when I went down to the courthouse in Indianola to register to vote. That happened because I went to a mass meeting one night.

Until then I'd never heard of no mass meeting and I didn't know that a Negro could register and vote. Bob Moses, Reggie Robinson, Jim Bevel and James Forman were some of the SNCC workers who ran that meeting. When they asked for those to raise their hands who'd go down to the courthouse the next day, I raised mine. Had it up as high as I could get it. I guess if I'd had any sense I'd a-been a little scared, but what was the point of being scared? The only thing they could do to me was kill me and it seemed like they'd been trying to do that a little bit at a time ever since I could remember.

Well, there was eighteen of us who went down to the courthouse that day and all of us were arrested. Police said the bus was painted the wrong color—said it was too yellow. After I got bailed out I went back to the plantation where Pap and I had lived for eighteen years. My oldest girl met me and told me that Mr. Marlow, the plantation owner, was mad and raising sand. He had heard that I had tried to register. That night he called on us and said, "We're not going to have this in Mississippi and you will have to withdraw. I am looking for your answer, yea or nay?" I just looked. He said, "I will give you until tomorrow morning. And if you don't withdraw you will have to leave. If you do go withdraw, it's only how I feel, you might still have to leave." So I left that same night. Pap had to stay on till work on the plantation was through. Ten days later they fired into Mrs. Tucker's house where I was staying. They also shot two girls at Mr. Sissel's.

That was a rough winter. I hadn't a chance to do any canning before I got kicked off, so didn't have hardly anything. I always can more than my family can use 'cause there's always people who don't have enough. That winter was bad, though. Pap couldn't get a job nowhere 'cause everybody knew he was my husband. We made it on through, though, and since then I just been trying to work and get our people organized.

I reckon the most horrible experience I've had was in June of 1963. I was arrested along with several others in Winona, Mississippi. That's in Montgomery County, the county where I was born. I was carried to a cell and locked up with Euvester Simpson. I began to hear the sound of licks, and I could hear people screaming. . . .

After then, the State Highway patrolmen came and carried me out of the cell into another cell where there were two Negro prisoners. The patrolman gave the first Negro a long blackjack that was heavy. It was loaded with something and they had me lay down on the bunk with my face down, and I was beat. I was beat by the first Negro till he gave out. Then the patrolman ordered the other man to take the blackjack and he began to beat. . . .

. . . After I got out of jail, half dead, I found out that Medgar Evers had been shot down in his own yard.

———————

I've worked on voter registration here ever since I went to that first mass meeting. In 1964 we registered 63,000 black people from Mississippi into the Freedom Democratic Party. We formed our own party because the whites wouldn't even let us register. We decided to challenge the white Mississippi Democratic Party at the National Convention. We followed all the laws that the white people themselves made. We tried to attend the precinct meetings and they locked the doors on us or moved the meetings and that's against the laws they made for their ownselves. So we were the ones that held the real precinct meetings. At all these meetings across the state we elected our representatives to go to the National Democratic Convention in Atlantic City. But we learned the hard way that even though we had all the law and all the righteousness on our side—that white man is not going to give up his power to us.

We have to build our own power. We have to win every single political office we can, where we have a majority of black people.

———————

The question for black people is not, when is the white man going to give us our rights, or when is he going to give us good education for our children, or when is he going to give us jobs—if the white man gives you anything—just remember when he gets ready he will take it right back. We have to take for ourselves.

3. "Interim Report of the United States Commission on Civil Rights"
April 16, 1963

The kinds of harassment suffered by Mrs. Hamer and others received little national attention, and voting rights workers became increasingly angry about the failure of the federal government to protect them or the local blacks in the movement. The 1963 report of the U.S. Commission on Civil Rights, from which these excerpts are taken, was important in the process of publicizing the extent of racial repression in Mississippi.

Since October 1962, the open and flagrant violation of constitutional guarantees in Mississippi has precipitated serious conflict which, on several occasions, has reached the point of crisis. The United States Commission on Civil Rights has become increasingly alarmed at the defiance of the Constitution. Each week brings fresh evidence of the danger of a complete breakdown of law and order.

Citizens of the United States have been shot, set upon by vicious dogs, beaten and otherwise terrorized because they sought to vote. Since October, students have been fired upon, ministers have been assaulted and the home of the Vice Chairman of the State Advisory ittee of this Commission has been bombed. Another member and his wife were jailed on trumped up charges after their home had been defiled. Even children, at the brink of starvation, have been deprived of assistance by the callous and discriminatory acts of Mississippi officials administering Federal funds.

All this affronts the conscience of the Nation.

The Commission notes the action taken by the President of the United States in employing the force necessary to assure compliance with the court decrees in the University of Mississippi case. It is mindful of the unequivocal public statements of the President expressing his belief that discriminatory practices are morally wrong. The Commission, nevertheless, believes that the President should, consistent with his Constitutional and statutory authority, employ to the fullest the legal and moral powers of his office to the end that American citizenship will not continue to be degraded in Mississippi.

4. "Freedom Summer"
Sally Belfrage

The Summer Project of 1964 was a major test of interracialism in the southern struggle, for it led to an unprecedented degree of involvement by white activists in Mississippi's black communities. Sally Belfrage took part in the second of two training sessions for the six hundred student volunteers—"eighty-five percent white, one hundred percent middle class," as she put it—in Oxford, Ohio, and was then assigned to Greenwood, Mississippi. Her book Freedom Summer *was published in 1965.*

In describing the then Chairman of SNCC, with whom he was sharing a Mississippi jail cell, Bob Moses wrote in 1961 that "McDew . . . has taken on the deep hates and deep loves which America, and the world, reserve for those who dare to stand in a strong sun and cast a sharp shadow." This could as well describe many SNCC Negroes, whose deep hates and loves were often translated into simple whites and blacks. They were automatically suspicious of us, the white volunteers; throughout the summer they put us to the test, and few, if any, could pass. Implicit in all the songs, tears, speeches, work, laughter, was the knowledge secure in both them and us that ultimately we could return to a white refuge.

———

But we didn't *have* to come, did we? We could have stayed at home and gone to the beach, or earned the money we so badly needed for next semester at old Northern White. And here we are: We Came. Among all the millions who could have realized their responsibility to this revolution, we alone came. Few Northern Negroes even came. We came. Don't we earn some recognition, if not praise? *I want to be your friend, you black idiot,* was the contradiction evident everywhere.

SNCC is not populated with Toms who would wish to be white . . . who fill closets with bleaches and straighteners, who lead compromise existences between reality and illusion. They accept their color and are engaged in working out its destiny. To bend to us was to corrupt the purity of their goal.

———

It was the policy of the Summer Project to limit its activities this side of the Civil Rights Act, and not to engage in testing the law or desegregating public facilities. . . . There were people in Greenwood, however, particularly young admirers of Silas Mc-Ghee, who were quite unmoved by the idea of registering voters. The bill had been passed, and they wanted to see it work. Without COFO help or supervision, teenagers began to make forays over the tracks on their own. As the weeks passed, their frustration fed on itself, white outrage increased, and violence rose nearer to the surface daily.

Meanwhile, Silas and Jake [McGhee] kept going to the movies. On July 25 their house was shot into; on July 26 they went to the Leflore Theater. They had been joined near the end of the month by their elder half-brother Clarence Robinson, a six-foot-six paratrooper (again on furlough and still out on bail). Clarence had a thirty-six-inch reach and a 136 I.Q., and his Army hat was reinforced with a silver dollar sewn under the emblem: picked on in a bar once, he had swung the hat and downed two men. He walked down the street in his uniform like Wild Bill Hickok on the way to a duel, cool, tough, infinitely menacing.

He spoke at a mass meeting one night, using his voice as he used his body, with precision and power. "When I went in the Army in April of 1952, I raised my right hand and they told me that I was fighting for my country and my brothers, my sisters, my mother, and my fellow man. And after approximately four months of basic training to teach me how to fight, they sent me to Korea. Now when I come back here and try to go to the Leflore Theater, me and my two brothers, when I got ready to leave, there was a whole *mob* out there. . . ."

_____

". . . We walked to this car. I opened the rear door, let my two brothers in, and I stood outside for approximately thirty seconds looking around. Nobody threw a brick at me. They could have, they could have knocked my brains out. I'm the same as anybody else, I can be killed, very easy. But they didn't do it. Why? Because I showed that I didn't mind being hit. That if I could get the man that wants to hit me within my thirty-six-inch *reach* [he demonstrated], I'll prove to him that I'm a better man than he is. We left from the theater, because there were incidents. When you go to the theater you've got to expect incidents. Why? Because the white man is scared of you!"

The "incidents" had been reported to the national SNCC office as they occurred, and most of the mass meeting audience already knew what had happened. The brothers had seen the movie in peace that night—largely because those who objected to their presence inside were on the picket line outside. But when the movie finished there were nearly two hundred whites waiting for them in the street. The McGhees tried to call for a taxi but none would come. The manager ordered them to leave: the theater was closing. They couldn't risk walking. There was one alternative, to call the SNCC office. Two of our cars volunteered to go down to get them while the office phoned the FBI, relating the facts to local agent Schaum. Schaum, responding that the FBI would not give protection, was told that the purpose of the call was to request FBI witnesses on the scene. Schaum refused to commit himself. . . .

When the cars arrived at the Leflore from the office, the

McGhees, inside in the lobby, asked two policemen on duty to escort them through the mob. The policemen took them outside; then one of them had a look at the crowd and said, "You got yourself into this, you can get yourself out." The brothers were abandoned between point one and point two.

They made their way toward the car. As they reached it, the whites began to scream at them. They managed to get inside, but the mob, cheated, closed in on them. A bottle was thrown at the rear window with such force that it broke through and sprayed the brothers with glass. Jake was hit by particles in the eye. Instead of returning to the office, they drove to the hospital, where Jake was admitted to the emergency ward.

In the office calls came in on every phone, and the staff, like synchronized parts of a machine, answered them and phoned out again. One of the two cars returned, its occupants reporting that they had been followed by a car of whites and that those at the hospital were in danger. The office sent another car to the hospital. When it arrived, Judy Richardson called in to say that they had been shot at from a roadhouse on the way, a white teen-agers' hangout. . . . At the hospital they found a throng of whites milling around, of whom at least five were seen (by Clarence, who knew such things) to be armed with .22 rifles and .38 pistols. After Jake was treated and discharged, a group trying to drive away was threatened with bricks and sticks and blocked at the exit by a car full of white men. They returned to the hospital.

Something had to be done to avert a shooting war. The people in COFO were anxious for peace in which to conduct their work, but events were no longer in their control. The teen-agers were mesmerized by the brothers McGhee, and felt more and more uninterested in the tameness of the Freedom School, the Freedom Party: they wanted direct action. The Freedom School teachers, sensing this, invited Clarence Robinson to come to the Friendship Church to debate with Bob Zellner. The audience had defined the confrontation as "Nonviolence against Violence"; but Bob began by mentioning that he and Clarence would "just have a little discussion on the different approaches to social change." . . .

"It has been proven time and time again," Clarence said, "that when a man fights back, he is not attacked. Now, I've never been the one to start a fight. But if someone is pushing me, I have to defend myself. You got to learn to stay flexible, to fight when you have to, but *only* when you have to."

Bob's respect for Clarence was immediately apparent; he clearly didn't want to argue with him publicly. He began by quoting Gandhi: "If you can't be nonviolent, be violent rather than a coward." Then: "Because we're organized we have to be nonviolent. We don't have the strength, even if we wanted to, to carry guns and fight back. We're facing organizations with more resources, more money, and with unlimited access to weapons."

CLARENCE: "I'm not talking about carrying guns. If everybody did that, pretty soon you'd have a revolution on your hands. And I'm not saying we should go out there and *start* a lot of violence. I'm saying that you only resort to violence after you have done everything possible to avoid it." Speaking to the children, and pointing to Bob: "This man can't go to the Leflore Theater and integrate it for you, because he's white." . . .

BOB: "There's more guts per person in the McGhees than in any other family you'll ever meet. They're trying to desegregate the Leflore and they're doing a great job. But we feel that our concentration has to be on voter registration now. Integrating all the movies in the South won't achieve anything basic."

CLARENCE: "You got to act in areas that people understand, not just a nebulous political argument beyond them all. This house-to-house activity is fine, but people are afraid of what they can't grasp. They never *have* voted, they don't know what it's all about. But they know they can't go to that movie. . . ."

The children broke in then. A solemn, composed girl of about sixteen raised her hand and spoke. "You say," she addressed Bob, "that we have to wait until we get the vote. But you know, by the time that happens the younger people are going to be too old to enjoy the bowling alley and the swimming pool. And the Civil Rights Act was passed this month." A little girl added, "Yeah, and do you mean we jus' s'pose to let The Man beat on our head?"

BOB: "Look, I try to be a disciplined man. That means I try to do what I say I'm goin' to do. When I joined with SNCC I said I'd behave nonviolently. I didn't say how I'd think, how I'd feel.

But the reason I know I can do this, that I *can* behave nonviolently, is that I've done it. I was in McComb, Mississippi, in sixty-one. McComb is not a Freedom School or a playpen. I had eighteen men beatin' me, stompin' on me while the cops held my arms. They tried to pull my eyes out by the roots. And I was nonviolent, not only because I said I'd be, but because there were about five hundred people watching, and what am I goin' to do with five hundred people?"

CLARENCE: "If anyone has the guts to raise their right hand and say they'll be nonviolent, I respect that. I haven't got the guts to do that. If he's able to do this and maintain it, that's a fine thing."

Clarence said that actual weapons were not the issue: "They bring trouble with the law, violations of the Sullivan Act. The point is you *got* a weapon—you got two hands and two feet, and I don't mean using them to run on. Only four people can get on a man at one time. If you bring certain death to the first *two,* then you won't have much trouble with the others. I'm just talking about if you're attacked, and you can do some damage, the next time they'll be a little more *cautious.* . . .

"Then there's this argument they're always having in the movement, you know, about what you are supposed to do if you're nonviolent and you're in a house where the man has a gun, and 'letting him do the dirty work' if you're attacked, and should he have that gun at all if you're involved. Well, all I'm saying is that in a case like that, I'm not doing your dirty work for you; I'm defending *my* right to have whom *I* want in *my* house."

BOB: "I agree. I don't see where you get off tellin' somebody else to be nonviolent because you are." And he wanted to clear a few things up. "The way I am, I'd flatten anybody who came at me on the street. But when you're pledged to the discipline of a mass movement, you got to behave as you promised."

The children sat digesting it all for a while, then the same girl who had spoken before raised her hand and Bob recognized her. "How is it," she asked, "that SNCC has moved from a militant position to a rather subdued one?"

There was a little coughing. Bob said, "It depends on your

definition of the word 'militant.' This is a policy worked out by the most militant people in the South today. As far as we're concerned, we're doing one of the most militant things anybody could be doing: building a new political structure."

5. "Mississippi at Atlantic City"
Charles M. Sherrod

The culmination of Freedom Summer came in August when the Mississippi Freedom Democratic Party delegates attempted to be recognized as the official delegation to the Democratic National Convention in Atlantic City, New Jersey. These are excerpts from SNCC leader Charles Sherrod's account of events before and during the convention, which nominated Lyndon Johnson, who had become president after the November 22, 1963, assassination of John F. Kennedy.

It was a cool day in August beside the ocean. Atlantic City, New Jersey, was waiting for the Democratic National Convention to begin. In that Republican fortress history was about to be made. High on a billboard smiling out at the breakers was a picture of Barry Goldwater and an inscription "In your heart you know he's right." Later someone had written underneath, "Yes, extreme right." Goldwater had had his "moment," two weeks before on the other ocean. This was to be L.B.J.'s "moment," and we were to find out that this was also his convention.

No one could say that we were a renegade group. We had tried to work within the structure of the state Party. In fact, we were not only trying to be included in the state Party, but we also sought to insure that the state Party would remain loyal to the candidates of the National Democratic Party in November.

No one could say that we had not tried. We had no alternative but to form a State Party that would include everyone.

So sixty-eight [Freedom Democratic Party] delegates from Mississippi—black, white, maids, ministers, carpenters, farmers, painters, mechanics, schoolteachers, the young, the old—they were ordinary people but each had an extraordinary story to tell. And they could tell the story! The Saturday before the convention began, they presented their case to the Credentials Committee, and through television, to the nation and to the world. No human being confronted with the truth of our testimony could remain indifferent to it. Many tears fell. Our position was valid and our cause was just.

But the word had been given. The Freedom Party was to be seated without voting rights as honored guests of the Convention. The [MFD] Party caucused and rejected the proposed "compromise." The slow and now frantic machinery of the administration was grinding against itself. President Johnson had given Senator Humphrey the specific task of dealing with us. They were desperately seeking ways to seat the regular Mississippi delegation without any show of disunity. The administration needed time!

Sunday evening, there was a somewhat secret meeting held at the Deauville Hotel, for all Negro delegates. The MFDP was not invited but was there. In a small, crowded, dark room with a long table and a blackboard, some of the most prominent Negro politicians in the country gave the "word," one by one. Then an old man seated in a soft chair struggled slowly to his feet. It was the black dean of politics, Congressman Charles Dawson of Chicago.

Unsteady in his voice, he said exactly what the other "leaders" had said: (1) We must nominate and elect Lyndon B. Johnson for President in November; (2) we must register thousands of Negroes to vote; and (3) we must follow leadership—adding, "we must respect womanhood"—and sat down.

With that a little woman, dark and strong, Mrs. Annie Devine from Canton, Mississippi, standing near the front, asked to be heard. The Congressman did not deny her. She began to speak.

"We have been treated like beasts in Mississippi. They shot us down like animals." She began to rock back and forth and her voice quivered. "We risk our lives coming up here . . . politics must be corrupt if it don't care none about people down there . . . these politicians sit in positions and forget the people put them there." She went on, crying between each sentence, but right after her witness, the meeting was adjourned.

. . . Here we were in a life-death grip, wrestling with the best political strategists in the country. We needed only eleven votes for a minority report from the Credentials Committee. . . .

A compromise was suggested by [Congresswoman] Edith Green (D.-Ore.), a member of the Credentials Committee. It was acceptable to the Freedom Party and could have been the minority report: (1) Everyone would be subjected to a loyalty oath, both the Freedom Party and the Mississippi regular party; (2) Each delegate who took the oath would be seated and the votes would be divided proportionally. It was minimal; the Freedom Party would accept no less.

The administration countered with another compromise. It had five points. (1) The all-white Party would take the oath and be seated; (2) The Freedom Democratic Party would be welcomed as honored guests of the Convention; (3) Dr. Aaron Henry and Rev. Edwin King, Chairman and National Committeeman of the Freedom Democratic Party respectively, would be given delegate status in a special category of "delegates at large"; (4) The Democratic National Committee would obligate states by 1968 to select and certify delegates through a process without regard to race, creed, color or national origin; and (5) The Chairman of the National Democratic Committee would establish a special committee to aid the states in meeting standards set for the 1968 Convention. . . .

The "word" had come down for the last time. We had begun to lose support in the Credentials Committee. This came mainly as a result of a squeeze play by the administration.

It was Tuesday morning when the Freedom Democratic Party delegation was hustled to its meeting place, the Union Temple Baptist Church. You could cut through the tension; it was so apparent. People were touchy and on edge. It had been a long fight; being up day and night, running after delegations, following leads, speaking, answering politely, always aggressive, always moving. Now, one of the most important decisions of the convention had to be made.

. . . The hot day dragged on; there were speeches and speeches and talk and talk—Dr. Martin Luther King, Bayard Rustin, Senator Wayne Morse, Edith Green, Jack Pratt, James Farmer, James Forman, Ella Baker, Bob Moses. Some wanted to accept the compromise and others did not. A few remained neutral and all voiced total support whatever the ultimate decision. But time had made the decision. The day was fast spent when discussion was opened to the delegation.

The administration had succeeded in baiting us into extended discussion and this was the end. . . .

The [administration's] proposal was rejected by the Freedom Democratic Delegation; we had come through another crisis with our minds depressed and our hearts and hands unstained. Again we had not bowed to the "massa." We were asserting a moral declaration to this country that the political mind must be concerned with much more than the expedient; that there are real issues in this country's politics and "race" is one.

We could have accepted the compromise, called it a victory and gone back to Mississippi, carried on the shoulders of millions of Negroes across the country as their champions. But we love the ideals of our country; they mean more than a moment of victory. We are what we are—hungry, beaten, unvictorious, jobless, homeless, but thankful to have the strength to fight. This is honesty, and we refuse to compromise here. It would have been a lie to accept that particular compromise. It would have said to blacks across the nation and the world that we share the power, and that is a lie! The "liberals" would have felt great relief for a job well done. The Democrats would have laughed again at the segregationist Republicans and smiled that their own "Negroes" were satisfied. That is a lie! We are a country of racists with a racist heritage, a racist economy, a racist language, a racist religion, a racist philosophy of living, and we need a naked confrontation with ourselves.

6. Student Nonviolent Coordinating Committee Brief Report on Guinea

James Forman

In the fall of 1964, SNCC accepted an invitation from the government of Guinea—extended through entertainer and activist Harry Belafonte—to visit Africa. The SNCC delegation was composed of James Forman, John Lewis, Bob Moses, Dona Richards, Prathia Hall, Julian Bond, Ruby Doris Robinson, Bill Hansen, Donald Harris, Mathew Jones, and Fannie Lou Hamer. These excerpts are from a report to his colleagues at home by James Forman.

CONAKRY, GUINEA . . . SEPTEMBER 23, 1964

Today our group had a meeting with Diallo Alpha who is the director general of the Ministry of Information and Tourism. This ministry is one of the largest in the Guinean government. . . .

We asked Diallo if he had any suggestions for us as to what we could do with helping the cause of Guinea. He told us of a trip he took to the United States. He said that he had had a press conference in New York and on that basis as well as other bases he was invited in February to visit the President. The President asked him what the United States could do to aid Guinea. He told the President that the U.S. should give moral support to the Guinea cause. The President replied that he was the first foreign visitor who had only asked for moral support. The implication is that other visitors, foreign, had asked for some sort of technical assistance or money. Diallo said that he would never forget those words. He also said that Pierre Salinger asked him what he thought of the United States. He told Pierre that he had a bizarre opinion that he would rather not give but that if he insisted on an answer he (Diallo) would give it. Pierre asked him to be frank. Diallo said that the main concern he had was about the relative unconcern and lack of information that people in America had about affairs outside of their own country. He went on to say that we could do a lot to help Africa by explaining what we had seen.

We had not read something, we had seen it with our own eyes, and this makes a difference. When we got home people were not simply going to want to read a book about Africa, but would want to hear from us what occurred and what we saw. In our conference he stated that our country is noted for this tendency and that we should explain what we had seen. We told him we would do this and would send him information on a regular basis.

After this, Diallo went into a discussion of his pending trip to the United States. He stated that he wanted to observe the revolution in Negro affairs that was about to take place. He said that he really felt that the American government after the election was going to move forward to grant full rights to the Negroes. He asked us what we thought about the election. Moses, who speaks French, began an explanation of the fact that Negroes in the South really do not vote for the most part: they are denied this right. Diallo halted him and pulled out a paper he had written or was in the process of writing. In this paper he had based some conclusions on what he had read in the journals, Robert White's book, and some speeches of "pastor" Luther King, as he called him. All of us began to explain some realities of the American political system, the historical development of the denial of the right to vote, especially in Mississippi. After this, Mrs. Hamer began to explain her difficulties with registration and voting, translated by myself. It was not difficult to do. Although one, or at least myself, cannot put into French her exact words or the words of anyone else. There was a long discussion on the realities of the South and some explanations of what existed in the North in terms of realities for the Negro. We included a description of machine politics and their relations to the Negro.

This discussion helped to clear up some misconceptions Diallo had. Following this he asked about the "two tendencies in the Negro struggle": that of Pastor Luther King and of Malcolm X. We all smiled and told him there were more than these two tendencies. We diagramed a line from right to left stating what we thought were the positions of the various civil rights groups mentioning only the five major groups. Diallo immediately understood the significance of this diagram and began to discern why "Pastor King" was constantly used on television.

We related to him other relevant factors about the movement

in the United States, including what we thought were differences between our position and that of other civil rights groups. The interview ended after three hours with Diallo giving Mrs. Hamer a present: a musical instrument found only in Africa. . . .

CONAKRY . . . SEPTEMBER 26, 1964

Our group met with President Sékou Touré last night in the cas. This is one of the presidential homes existing in Guinea. . . .

I suggested we should concentrate on three prior arranged points: (1) what Touré felt [was] the significance of our trip to Africa; (2) to tell something about our efforts in the South; and (3) to discuss ways of establishing relationships with Guinea and other African countries—what he thought of this and how he thought it could be carried out.

We began discussing the second point first, which probably should have been the order in the first place. There was some description by me in French as to the nature of the movement; some historical development, and then some analysis of why we differed in part from some of the other civil rights groups in the United States. This point was considered most important because the day before we had talked to the Minister of Information who was not at all informed on the barest difference between the Movements in the United States and had thought in fact that Martin Luther King was the leader of all the Negroes in the United States. We described to Touré as we did to Diallo that there was a line from right to left which could be used to somewhat pinpoint the positions of the civil rights groups, especially the principal five. This we did. Afterwards there were some expressions by the members of the group. Harry told the President that there existed in the United States at one time a group of people who were militant, but the McCarthy period helped to end their potentialities. He especially referred to Dr. W. E. B. Du Bois, and to Paul Robeson. But he found that in SNCC there existed an answer to the type of militant leadership that was needed in the Negro liberation struggle in the United States.

The President began by saying, "Bon." We all laughed for it was something disarming. He thanked us for coming and stated that our struggle was not just ours and that there existed a great relationship between what we do in the United States: what happens in Africa and the converse is true. He began by saying that our struggle was not only social, economic and human, but that it is really a political problem created by history and history itself would decide its future. Or there must be an historical solution. If we agreed upon this, then there should be an analysis of the three principal points.

(1) No solution of a problem can come about unless there is a consciousness that the problem exists. A poor man without a consciousness of the problem cannot help himself. But a rich man, even if he has a social consciousness about human conditions, can do more to help solve problems than someone who is poor. We must set a goal and move toward that goal step by step. We must be educated and informed about the nature of the problem. There are two types of political consciousness. The first is absolute. It says that if you reject discrimination, you will never submit to it under any circumstances. One is firm and does not deviate from his position. The second position is relative. The struggle is relative to the situation. It is practical. It helps if you are going forward. He gave an example of a man who wanted to take a stick and hit someone over the head. That takes physical courage: but political courage involves the study of events step by step. One must be working on A but preparing for B and C, and see that these steps will lead to a larger objective.

(2) The second point which must be firmly understood is that of organization. We must not underestimate the role of organization. He took the example of the table in front of him on which there were peanuts and some boiled peeled potatoes. He said that he could lift the table himself, but that if all of the 20 or more of us who were around the table began to pull in different directions, probably none of us would be able to lift it. We must work to bring people in the Movement. Even if someone himself does not respond the way we think he should, he may have relatives who will become committed. (This point is probably important from an experiential point of view in that the Chief of State is from a very wealthy family in Guinea from which he has broken.)

Now, what is the structure of injustice in the United States? The rich exploit the poor. It is a question of economics. There are even black men who exploit other black men: they may well be more dangerous than some whites. Segregation is simply an effect. We will never get rid of that effect until we rid ourselves of the cause. Our organization must attack the cause of segregation. Take the example of a factory where there are 1,000 workers: 800 white, 200 black. They are all exploited. Rather than talk about "liberty for the black" we must pose the problem for all. It is true that in particular situations you will want to speak directly to the black people and point out their own frustration and exploitation. However, this problem should be posed as human so that support can be obtained. If an organization is efficient it must fight against all causes, not just questions of social differences, but economic. We must study the world situation of exploitation. We should aim at specific goals and not fix a date. If a date is fixed then opportunism sets in. What is a century to wait and work for if you feel it is right?

(3) A third very important factor for any movement is that those who are selected to represent you are carefully selected because the quality of their actions will affect society in one way or another. This point should not be underestimated.

Now the conditions in America are different than they are in Africa. Despite the period of colonialism Africa has remained true to its values. Colonialism tried to make a difference but it did not. African society could not develop unless it is supported by its values. African society can be vertical, i.e. go up, but the situation with the Negro in America is different. Here progress is horizontal. It is important to remember that from the very beginning, the Negro was cut off from all value systems. He was forced to live in a society where all the conceptions of values were foreign to him. One's advancement under these circumstances was blocked. Also, it has to be remembered that the United States is not unitary, and that each state is almost a little entity unto itself. This has tremendous implications in postulating tactics. We must develop a consciousness from a study of the whole society. From these two situations, of course, and from the structure in America—as elsewhere—there is something called the grand conscience for *lui-meme*—a person trying to create a place for himself. He sees the structure vertically as that of achieving his own ambitions. There are a few and this must be further developed: a political consciousness to change the whole system. It may well be that in this struggle you may have to fight more against the blacks than the others.

Now, let us consider the situation from the point of view of strategy. Don't pose the problem as one of emancipation of black people. We must emancipate the whole community so that aspirations can be shared by all. The situation is social, political, and economic. We must study to try to find the best solution. In the black community we might tell people they are exploited because they are black. It gives the movement a broad base. The whole community will know that your victory will be their victory.

From the point of view of tactics: The social structure is not one. Examine it state by state. From this study you select different means for each state. It would be wrong politics to impose a common attitude on the people. *The diversity of American society must be reflected in our organization.* We cannot forget the actions of the everyday struggle in the various sections. These daily confrontations will develop a consciousness. (This is important from my point of view with respect to the Civil Rights Law—especially the Public Accommodations Section.)

It is fundamental that we see the problem as the system. Do not try to stress the contradictions in the black community. On the national plane, however, we must try to project unity. If we try to solve our internal contradictions, we will lose. Look at the system.

At this point the President asked what time it was and said we could continue the discussion at a later time. . . .

7. "The Trip"
John Lewis and Donald Harris

After the rest of the SNCC delegation returned to the United States, John Lewis and Donald Harris continued on a month-long tour of Liberia, Ghana, Zambia, Kenya, Ethiopia, and Egypt. This is an excerpt from a report dated December 14, 1964, written by Lewis and Harris.

GHANA

. . . There were two factors that we had to deal with while in Ghana. The first was the fact that the Non-Allied Nations conference was taking place in Cairo at the time, drawing most of the important government, party, journalist, and exiled freedom fighters away to Egypt. Even so, those that were left in Accra were wholly receptive and helpful to us and as soon as people arrived back in Ghana [they] put us in touch with them. In this regard, it seems we were exceptionally lucky and fortunate. The second thing we had to cope with was that Malcolm X had just left Ghana some few days before we arrived and had made fantastic impressions. Because of this, very often people's first attitude or impression of us was one of skepticism and distrust. Among the first days we were in Accra someone said, "Look, you guys might be really doing something—I don't know, but if you are to the right of Malcolm, you might as well start packing right now 'cause no one'll listen to you." Among the first questions we were continually asked was, "What's your organization's relationship with Malcolm's?" We ultimately found that this situation was not peculiar to Ghana; the pattern repeated itself in every country. After a day of this we found that we must, immediately on meeting people, state our own position in regards to where we stood on certain issues—Cuba, Vietnam, the Congo, Red China and the U.N., and what SNCC's role, guidelines, and involvement in the Rights Struggle was. Malcolm's impact on Africa was just fantastic. In every country he was known and served as the main criteria for categorizing other Afro-Americans and their political views. Only because we were able to point out quite directly SNCC's involvement in the Struggle, that is, programs, successes, John's involvement in the March (and the cutting of his speech) and the fact that we were on the Continent attempting to bridge the gap between Africa and the States were we able to gain the kind of respect and create the kind of interest that was vital to the trip.

ZAMBIA

. . . Zambia was an important and significant stop on our trip. For the nationalists it is the closest free spot outside South Africa; it is the place where those fleeing from the terror and ruthless oppression of apartheid can first rest, walk the streets without fear, meet friends and receive aid from a people and a government who all too well know the evils and oppressions of white settlers and colonial rule. At the same time, it is also the point where dedicated and committed men left to return to South Africa; after being trained and drilled for many months sometimes thousands of miles away, this was the beginning of a long and dangerous journey. But most important, those Africans returning to South Africa were bringing new skills with which to keep the fight going . . . new knowledge of demolition, plastic bomb warfare or sabotage. This, that is Zambia, was their last refuge before entering a hell beyond description for any man who had the audacity to be born with a skin that was black. Because of these factors, the nationalists were anxious for news; eager for us to write and send aid or anything . . . just to know that the effort and lives that they are expending are also being heard and supported. In many ways the Pan-Africanist Congress is not much different from SNCC (. . . was?).

They are poor, angry, frustrated, and almost powerless human beings fighting against governments and systems thousands of miles away. Whatever we do to help them will be a significant step in helping our own struggle here.

KENYA

. . . The first person we saw on arrival at our hotel was Malcolm X, who had just come in from Tanzania with Kenyatta. This was a chance meeting, but in many ways a very important meeting.

We spent the rest of that day and evening as well as a good part of the following day talking with Malcolm about the nature of each of our trips. At that point [he] had been to eleven countries, talked with eleven heads of state, and had addressed the parliaments in the majority of these countries. Although he was very tired he planned to visit five more countries. He felt that the presence of SNCC in Africa was very important and that this was [a] significant and crucial aspect of the "human rights struggle" that the American civil rights groups had too long neglected. He pointed out (and our experience bears him correct) that the African leaders and people are strongly behind the Freedom Movement in this country; that they are willing to do all they can to support, encourage, and sustain the Movement; but they will not tolerate factionalism or support particular groups or organizations within the Movement as a whole. It was with this in mind that he formed his Organization of Afro-American Unity.

Discussion also centered around Malcolm's proposed plan to bring the case of the Afro-American before the General Assembly of the United Nations and hold the United States in violation of the Human Rights Charter. The question was at that time (and ultimately was evident) that support from the civil rights voices in this country was not forthcoming and the American black community was too [splintered] to attempt such a move without looking like complete asses and embarrassing our most valuable allies. We departed with Malcolm giving us some contacts and the hope that there would be greater communication between the O.A.U.A. (the U.S. version) and SNCC.

PROPOSALS:

1. That SNCC establish an international wing—specifically, an African Bureau or Secretariat.

During the course of the trip we established contact with nineteen different countries, sixteen of which are on the continent of Africa. It seems eminently important that these contacts be utilized to their best advantage, not only for SNCC, but for the Movement as a whole. Although the "Civil rights leaders" have not yet recognized the necessity of a strong link between the Freedom Movement here and the various Liberation Movements in Africa, we in SNCC have been teaching what is called "Negro and African history" completely disregarding the potential of the many African embassies and thousands of African students already in the country. The growing importance of the Afro-Asian countries, their particular political and economic ideologies as well as their increasing influence in world opinion must be communicated to the people that we work with. SNCC and the entire Movement has a need to increase its scope. We have left publicity, interpretation of situations, and the statements of position to chance as far as other countries are concerned. It seems needless to say that we, that is, Afro-Americans in this country, are not in such an advantageous position that we can leave these things to luck. With such a bureau, it seems clear that forces outside the country could be infinitely more effective in putting pressure on the U.S. Government, thus helping our struggle as well as their own.

2. That the function of the African Bureau or Secretariat be to maintain and increase SNCC's contacts with Africa specifically, but also with any other countries or groups of people in other countries who can be helpful to us and the Cause.

A great lack in the Rights Movement has been the complete failure to utilize the great number of African diplomats that are constantly in this country, in Washington and in New York. No move of the least significance has been attempted to involve the thousands of African students that study in the U.S. each year in any of the many projects we have. No attempt has been made to even make them fully aware of what is going on in the American South (although many Africans know more about what is happening than many Afro-Americans do.)

3. That the African Bureau or Secretariat should be closely tied to or linked with the present communications department of SNCC.

In view of the fact that much of the said bureau would be writing to and receiving communications from international contacts it would be advantageous to have both departments closely allied. The importance of an international mailing list that was sent out regularly from Atlanta that would include news releases, Student Voices, and any other SNCC publications is evident. Certainly keeping in touch with the African embassies by mail as well as by phone bears consideration. Also informing our contacts in this country what kind of support or relationship we have with these new countries could have many ramifications with the press and government of this country.

4. That at least two people be assigned to work full-time with the African Bureau or Secretariat and that one of these two persons be available to travel between Atlanta, Washington, and New York.

Certainly there is enough to do right now in confirming the contacts already established as well as making new ones that two people working full-time would have their hands full. The necessity for one of these persons to be available to travel to the various embassies in Washington as well as to the missions and the U.N. sessions in New York is essential. This kind of job, that is, talking with these brothers and attempting to involve them more in what is going on in the South, is one that requires personal confrontation. It cannot be done, seriously, that is, by phone or by mail or by having four and five different people communicating with someone and, in SNCC tradition, telling them four or five different things.

8. "To Mississippi Youth"
Malcolm X

On December 31, 1964, Malcolm X spoke to a group of teenagers visiting Harlem from McComb, Mississippi. This is a brief excerpt from that speech.

In my opinion, the greatest accomplishment that was made in the struggle of the black man in America in 1964 toward some kind of real progress was the successful linking together of our problem with the African problem, or making our problem a world problem. Because now, whenever anything happens to you in Mississippi, it's not just a case of somebody in Alabama getting indignant, or somebody in New York getting indignant. The same repercussions that you see all over the world when an imperialist or foreign power interferes in some section of Africa . . . nowadays, when something happens to black people in Mississippi, you'll see the same repercussions all over the world. I wanted to point this out to you because it is important for you to know that when you're in Mississippi, you're not alone. . . . We here in the Organization of Afro-American Unity are with the struggle in Mississippi one thousand per cent. We're with the efforts to register our people in Mississippi to vote one thousand per cent. But we do not go along with anybody telling us to help nonviolently. . . . You get freedom by letting your enemy know that you'll do anything to get your freedom; then you'll get it. It's the only way you'll get it.

9. "From Protest to Politics: The Future of the Civil Rights Movement"
Bayard Rustin

After the Mississippi Summer Project, veteran civil rights leader Bayard Rustin was one of many who became concerned about the radical direction of black activism. Rustin, an organizer of the 1963 March on Washington, had been considered a radical himself in his early years, but by 1964 he had become convinced that, in order for blacks to continue advancing, they must build alliances with liberal and labor forces in the Democratic party. This is an excerpt from an article he wrote for **Commentary** *(February 1965).*

. . . In Mississippi, thanks largely to the leadership of Bob Moses, a turn toward political action has been taken. More than voter registration is involved here. A conscious bid for *political power* is being made, and in the course of that effort a tactical shift is being effected: direct-action techniques are being subordinated to a strategy calling for the building of community institutions or power bases. Clearly, the implications of this shift reach far beyond Mississippi. What began as a protest movement is being challenged to translate itself into a political movement.

It is now concerned not merely with removing the barriers to full *opportunity* but with achieving the fact of *equality*. From sit-ins and freedom rides we have gone into rent strikes, boycotts, community organization, and political action. As a consequence of this natural evolution, the Negro today finds himself stymied by obstacles of far greater magnitude than the legal barriers he was attacking before: automation, urban decay, *de facto* school segregation. These are problems which, while conditioned by Jim Crow, do not vanish upon its demise. They are more deeply rooted in our socio-economic order; they are the result of the total society's failure to meet not only the Negro's needs, but human needs generally.

I believe that the Negro's struggle for equality in America is essentially revolutionary. While most Negroes—in their hearts—unquestionably seek only to enjoy the fruits of American society as it now exists, their quest cannot *objectively* be satisfied within the framework of existing political and economic relations. The young Negro who would demonstrate his way into the labor market may be motivated by a thoroughly bourgeois ambition and thoroughly "capitalist" considerations, but he will end up having to favor a great expansion of the public sector of the economy. At any rate, that is the position the movement will be forced to take as it looks at the number of jobs being generated by the private economy, and if it is to remain true to the masses of Negroes.

How are these radical objectives to be achieved? The answer is simple, deceptively so: *through political power.*

Neither . . . [the civil rights protest] movement nor the country's twenty million black people can win political power alone. We need allies. The future of the Negro struggle depends on whether the contradictions of this society can be resolved by a coalition of progressive forces which becomes the *effective* political majority in the United States.

———————

Here is where the cutting edge of the civil rights movement can be applied. We must see to it that the reorganization of the "consensus [Democratic] party" proceeds along the lines which will make it an effective vehicle for social reconstruction, a role it cannot play so long as it furnishes Southern racism with its national political power. (One of Barry Goldwater's few attractive ideas was that the Dixiecrats belong with him in the same party.) And nowhere has the civil rights movement's political cutting edge been more magnificently demonstrated than at Atlantic City, where the Mississippi Freedom Democratic Party not only secured recognition as a bona fide component of the national party, but in the process routed the representatives of the most rabid racists— the white Mississippi and Alabama delegations. While I still believe that the FDP made a tactical error in spurning the compromise, there is no question that they launched a political revolution whose logic is the displacement of Dixiecrat power. They launched that revolution within a major political institution and as part of a coalitional effort.

CHAPTER SIX

BRIDGE TO FREEDOM (1965)

Introduction by David J. Garrow

Following the 1964 passage of the landmark Civil Rights Act, Martin Luther King, Jr., and his colleagues in the Southern Christian Leadership Conference (SCLC) rightfully concluded that the next federal legislative goal of the black freedom struggle in the South should be congressional passage of a strong voting rights statute that would provide for direct federal action and intervention guaranteeing southern blacks widespread access to registration and the ballot. Despite the passage of previous laws—particularly the Civil Rights Acts of 1957 and 1960—aimed at protecting southern blacks' right to vote, in many heavily black southern counties few, if any, black citizens were registered to vote due to discriminatory practices employed by white voter registrars.

One Alabama county with a record of consistent opposition to black voting was Dallas, whose county seat was Selma, a small city of twenty-seven thousand people fifty miles west of Montgomery, Alabama's capital. Despite its strongly segregationist politics, Dallas County had several hundred registered black voters as of 1964, thanks very largely to the long-term efforts of the Dallas County Voters' League (DCVL), the local black civic organization, and its two long-time leaders, Amelia and Samuel Boynton (the latter died in 1963). Mrs. Boynton, a courageous and dedicated woman, also had been instrumental in convincing the Student Nonviolent Coordinating Committee (SNCC) to make Selma, like McComb and Albany before it, one of those southern locales where a small number of full-time SNCC workers was deployed.

The succession of SNCC workers that began in 1963 met a violently hostile reception from white officials, particularly short-tempered Dallas County Sheriff James G. Clark, Jr., and a some-times mixed welcome from Selma's black community. Clark's deputies and white volunteer "possemen" almost literally sur-rounded the first black community mass rally when it took place in May 1963. Likewise, an October 1963 Freedom Day voter registration effort, which brought hundreds of prospective black registrants to the downtown county courthouse on one of the few dates of the month when Alabama laws required voter registrars to open their offices, met with stiff resistance from Clark's lawmen.

By late 1964, in the aftermath of the disheartening experience at Atlantic City's Democratic National Convention, SNCC's com-mitment of people and resources to an active project in Selma seemed, to local black leaders like Mrs. Boynton and DCVL President Rev. F. D. Reese, to be weakening. Committed to keeping up some initiatives, Mrs. Boynton proposed to the SCLC's staff, who long had known of her invaluable work in Selma, that King and his organization make Selma their next national focal point. King, convinced that any campaign for a strong federal voting rights statute would need such a focus, quickly accepted Mrs. Boynton and the DCVL's invitation to come to Selma and take on trigger-tempered Sheriff Clark.

Throughout January and February 1965, the SCLC's staff, in conjunction with several SNCC workers who also had continued organizing efforts in Selma, mounted an ongoing series of dem-onstrations targeted at the Dallas County courthouse, which contained the offices of both the registrar and the combative Sheriff Clark. When initial police restraint made for low-key national news coverage of the Selma drive, King chose to be arrested and jailed to draw more attention to the protests. As demonstrations continued into mid-February, Sheriff Clark en-gaged in picturesque tactics that drew some news coverage to the campaign on several occasions, but SCLC decided to expand some of its efforts to the nearby small town of Marion, seat of Perry

County. There, on Wednesday evening, February 17, a small civil rights march was attacked by lawmen and one participant, Jimmy Lee Jackson, was shot by an Alabama state trooper. Several days later Jackson died, and Marion activists, in conjunction with the SCLC staff, decided that a fitting movement response to his death would be a mass pilgrimage from Selma to the Alabama state capitol in Montgomery.

The march was scheduled for Sunday, March 7. The SCLC leaders, King and Ralph Abernathy, were in Atlanta preaching at their respective churches, and the six-hundred-person column was led by the SCLC's Hosea Williams and SNCC chairman John Lewis. After crossing the Edmund Pettus Bridge over the Alabama River on the eastern edge of downtown Selma, the marchers' path was blocked by scores of Alabama state troopers and Clark's local lawmen. The troopers' commander instructed the marchers to turn around and walk back into Selma; when the column did not move, the gas-masked lawmen walked forward, pushing marchers to the ground and striking others with billy clubs as tear gas canisters were fired at the peaceful parade. Within seconds the scene was a bloody rout with mounted possemen chasing the marchers back across the bridge into Selma. More than fifty participants were treated at local hospitals.

Television footage of the eerie and gruesome attack produced immediate national outrage. King issued a public call for civil rights supporters across the nation to come to Selma to show their support and join a second attempted march; congressmen of both parties called upon President Lyndon B. Johnson to intervene in Alabama and to speedily put voting rights legislation before Congress. Johnson's Justice Department aides already had been hard at work preparing a comprehensive voting rights bill, but the "bloody Sunday" attack and the national reaction to it spurred the White House to press for a faster completion of the drafting process.

At the same time, Attorney General Nicholas deB. Katzenbach and other administration officials strongly lobbied King to postpone the second march attempt until a federal court hearing and decision on the protesters' plea for government protection against any further brutalities could take place. King found himself painfully torn between the federal requests, from men who had committed themselves to spur passage of the voting rights legislation—his top goal—and the desire of hundreds of movement supporters who had poured into Selma for an immediate second march. Faced with those competing pressures, King in the end led the second march out to the place where the first column had been attacked, and then, when faced with another wall of lawmen, King called the group to kneel and pray and then turned the procession around and marched back into Selma. None of the marchers or King's civil rights colleagues had been informed of his intention to turn around. His less-than-forthright behavior and his sometimes contradictory characterizations of his actions brought down on his head an angry deluge of private criticism, especially from SNCC workers. The "Tuesday turnaround," as the event came to be called, pushed the underlying strategic and organizational tensions between SCLC and SNCC to a higher level than had ever been reached before.

On Monday evening, March 15, as King and his colleagues waited in Selma for the expected federal court approval of a fully protected march to Montgomery, President Johnson addressed a joint session of Congress on national television to announce that his voting rights legislation was ready and that his administration was committed. He said that "we shall overcome . . . a crippling legacy of bigotry and injustice." Congressional leaders promised that the administration's bill would receive speedy consideration and endorsement from representatives who, with only a modest number of exceptions, were more than ready to support a legislative remedy for voting discrimination that Selma's televised brutalities had so effectively highlighted.

Following federal court approval and the deployment of substantial numbers of Federal Bureau of Investigation agents and federalized National Guardsmen, the third attempt at a march from Selma to Montgomery got under way on Sunday, March 21, under heavy government protection and even heavier international news coverage. Walking an average of some ten miles a day, sometimes in heavy rain, and camping at night in open fields under simple tents, the marchers arrived in Montgomery on Tuesday, March 25, and held a large rally on the steps of the

Alabama state capitol. Hours later, one participating white volunteer, Viola Liuzzo, a Michigan housewife, was shot and killed by Klansmen as she drove between Selma and Montgomery.

Little more than four months later, on August 6, 1965, the Voting Rights Act of 1965 was signed into law. In ensuing years, the black voter registration gains it made possible and the discriminatory election techniques it voided allowed black southerners in many small towns and rural counties to enjoy meaningful participation and representation in the American electoral process for the first time in their lives.

1. "Early Attempts at Betterment"
Amelia Platts Boynton

Amelia Boynton, wife of long-time Dallas County Voters League leader Samuel William "Bill" Boynton, was a local-level activist who played a crucial role in involving SNCC, and later the SCLC, in the struggle in Selma. She wrote about her experiences in **The Bridge Across Jordan** *(1979).*

For many years Negro leaders had tried to arouse the blacks and get them to realize that they were taxpayers and citizens who had the right to vote. For many years we urged black citizens to call on the local governments of Selma and Dallas County and ask for these rights. But it was like striking the pendulum offbeat. We got no results until 1965.

During the late 1920's a group of Selma and Dallas County black citizens formed the first city-county organization that unified them for one common cause—becoming registered voters. But the Dallas County Voters' League (DCVL) went to sleep for lack of enough interest. In 1936, just before election time, the DCVL members were called together by my husband Bill, and another attempt was made to serve the black community. C. J. Adams, a railroad clerk, was elected president again. He was truly the most dynamic person Selma had had, but most Negroes were afraid to follow him. They knew he was right, but the point was to please the "white folks," or they knew their lives would be in danger.

Mr. Adams was finally forced to leave Selma because of the economic pressure imposed by the whites, and afterward Bill became head of the League. He continued as president until his death in 1963. The harder the DCVL worked to get Negroes registered the harder the county, city and state worked to throw up barriers so high as to make registration impossible. In 1963 there were only 180 registered Negroes in the county, though clinics and schools had been held for several years. We found that other methods had to be used to break the complacency of the adults. If we succeeded, other parts of the South might do likewise. As Negroes gained political strength, they would certainly be able to gain more of their constitutional rights.

All the candidates running for local and state office were segregationists who preached their segregation when necessary to gain votes in the white community. It was usually unnecessary to mention it because it was the standard pattern, and seemingly no one was concerned with breaking it. That is, until 1954, when the Supreme Court ruled that schools should be desegregated with all deliberate speed. But Negroes were only fighting for the privilege to vote. We held regular meetings, and just before an election we would arrange to vote as a bloc for our candidates. Then our votes would count; if they did not listen to us we would not support them. Selecting the lesser of the evils to vote for was in most cases a toss-up.

2. "Selma, Alabama"
Bernard Lafayette

Bernard Lafayette and his wife, Colia Liddell Lafayette, were among the first young SNCC workers to go into Selma. This is an excerpt from an interview conducted by Guy and Candie Carawan for their book **Freedom Is a Constant Struggle** *(1968).*

Colia and I first went to Selma in February 1963. It was sort of our honeymoon; we'd been married about six weeks. The first

SNCC worker there came back and said that we might as well scratch Selma off the list because the people there just weren't ready for a movement. We didn't get any different impression when we were there. We had trouble finding a place to live; most people were afraid to put us up. But we worked on this assumption: no matter how bad a place is, some people got courage. Those people are gonna be warm and friendly to you.

It was Mrs. Amelia Boynton who befriended us. We used her office and began to work. The first thing we did was to just try to get people to loosen up, to talk about registration and to realize they needed to vote. We set up classes teaching people how to fill out the registration forms. We knew that the forms are irrelevant in terms of voting and have nothing to do with whether a person is qualified to vote or not. But it's a psychological thing to build people's confidence. They have to feel themselves that they can fill out the form before they feel they can go down and try to register.

We tried to get people around the city to come, but it was slow. So we went out in the rural. The people out there are close to the earth, they're very religious and warm and friendly. And mostly they're unafraid. They own most of their own property and their little stores. They work hard and they want to see a future for their children. So we got these people to go and try to register to vote first.

Then we used this as a leverage to try to embarrass many of the people in the city. City folks are sometimes critical and skeptical about country people. So we pointed out that these people were really getting ahead. When these city people began to go down it was really sort of a birth of a movement.

Between February and September we got about 2,000 people to go down and try to register and about 600 of them actually did get registered.

By this time we had the people teaching each other. When one person learned to fill out the form, he was qualified to help somebody else. We had recruited some local workers too. We didn't really have to be there anymore.

We went back to school that Fall. Worth Long and James Love were the SNCC workers who took over in Selma. The situation continued to develop and I would get little bits of news from there.

In the Fall of 1964 James Bevel and SCLC moved into Alabama and began to build on making Selma a national issue of Voter Registration.

I went back in 1965 to help with some of the planning and strategy. I saw some great changes. Many, many people had gone to jail—people you never would have expected to stand up. Some of the kids I had worked with—whose parents, grandparents and teachers had all argued with them, threatened them and disciplined them—would run up to me:

"Guess what happened! Man, my grandmother went to jail! Man, I can't believe it . . . my grandma's in jail!"

The principal of one high school who had told the kids he would lower their grades if they participated in the Movement, actually led a march of teachers asking for the right to vote. Many of the informers—Negroes who used to carry messages downtown to the white people—were still message-carriers, but they were now bringing messages to us. So I saw a whole city change. Large numbers of adults were participating, both from Selma and from surrounding areas.

3. "A Letter from a Selma, Alabama, Jail"

Martin Luther King, Jr.

A major part of King's and the SCLC's political strategy for the Selma protest campaign involved drawing national news media attention to the political plight of Selma's largely disenfranchised black citizens. On February 1, 1965, King himself was purposefully arrested and jailed as part of the SCLC's strategy for drawing national attention to the Selma situation. Even before he was incarcerated, the SCLC had prepared a fund-solicitation advertisement for publication in The New York Times *that was designed to remind readers of King's already famous 1963 "Letter from a Birmingham Jail." This letter is part of the advertisement, which appeared in* The New York Times *on February 5, the same day King emerged from jail.*

February 1, 1965.

Dear Friends:

When the King of Norway participated in awarding the Nobel Peace Prize to me he surely did not think that in less than sixty days I would be in jail. He, and almost all world opinion will be shocked because they are little aware of the unfinished business in the South.

By jailing hundreds of Negroes, the city of Selma, Alabama, has revealed the persisting ugliness of segregation to the nation and the world. When the Civil Rights Act of 1964 was passed many decent Americans were lulled into complacency because they thought the day of difficult struggle was over.

Why are we in jail? Have you ever been required to answer 100 questions on government, some abstruse even to a political scientist specialist, merely to vote? Have you ever stood in line with over a hundred others and after waiting an entire day seen less than ten given the qualifying test?

THIS IS SELMA, ALABAMA. THERE ARE MORE NEGROES IN JAIL WITH ME THAN THERE ARE ON THE VOTING ROLLS.

But apart from voting rights, merely to be a person in Selma is not easy. When reporters asked Sheriff Clark if a woman defendant was married, he replied, "She's a nigger woman and she hasn't got a Miss or a Mrs. in front of her name."

This is the U.S.A. in 1965. We are in jail simply because we cannot tolerate these conditions for ourselves or our nation.

We need the help of all decent Americans. Our organization, SCLC, is not only working in Selma, Ala., but in dozens of other Southern communities. Our self-help projects operate in South Carolina, Georgia, Louisiana, Mississippi and other states. Our people are eager to work, to sacrifice, to be jailed—but their income, normally meager, is cut off in these crises. Your help can make the difference. Your help can be a message of unity which the thickest jail walls cannot muffle. With warmest good wishes from all of us.

Sincerely,
MARTIN LUTHER KING, JR.

4. "Midnight Plane to Alabama: Journey of Conscience"
George B. Leonard

Thousands of Americans were shocked and outraged when they first saw the television news film depicting Alabama lawmen's violent attack on the marchers as they attempted to cross the Edmund Pettus Bridge on "bloody Sunday," March 7, 1965. Journalist George B. Leonard was one of the hundreds who rushed to Selma the next day. These are excerpts from an article he wrote for **The Nation.**

. . . The chief function of the current Negro movement has been to awaken a nation's conscience. . . .

Such an awakening is painful. It may take years to peel away the layers of self-deception that shut out reality. But there are moments during this process when the senses of an entire nation become suddenly sharper, when pain pours in and the resulting outrage turns to action. One of these moments came, not on Sunday, March 7, when a group of Negroes at Selma were gassed, clubbed and trampled by horses, but on the following day when films of the event appeared on national television.

The pictures were not particularly good. With the cameras rather far removed from the action and the skies partly overcast everything that happened took on the quality of an old newsreel. Yet this very quality, vague and half silhouetted, gave the scene the vehemence and immediacy of a dream. The TV screen showed a column of Negroes standing along a highway. A force of Alabama state troopers blocked their way. As the Negroes drew to a halt, a toneless voice drawled an order from a loudspeaker: In the interests of "public safety," the marchers were being told to turn back. A few moments passed, measured out in silence, as some of the troopers covered their faces with gas masks. There was a lurching movement on the left side of the screen; a heavy phalanx of troopers charged straight into the column, bowling the marchers over.

A shrill cry of terror, unlike any sound that had passed through a TV set, rose up as the troopers lumbered forward, stumbling sometimes on fallen bodies. The scene cut to charging horses, their hoofs flashing over the fallen. Another quick cut: a cloud of tear gas billowed over the highway. Periodically the top of a helmeted head emerged from the cloud, followed by a club on the upswing. The club and the head would disappear into the cloud of gas and another club would bob up and down.

Unhuman. No other word can describe the motions. The picture shifted quickly to a Negro church. The bleeding, broken and unconscious passed across the screen, some of them limping alone, others supported on either side, still others carried in arms or on stretchers. It was at this point that my wife, sobbing, turned and walked away, saying, "I can't look any more."

We were in our living room in San Francisco watching the 6 P.M. news. I was not aware that at the same moment people all up and down the West Coast were feeling what my wife and I felt, that at various times all over the country that day and up past 11 P.M. Pacific Time that night hundreds of these people would drop whatever they were doing, that some of them would leave home without changing clothes, borrow money, overdraw their checking accounts; board planes, buses, trains, cars; travel thousands of miles with no luggage; get speeding tickets, hitchhike, hire horse drawn wagons; that these people, mostly unknown to one another, would move for a single purpose: to place themselves alongside the Negroes they had watched on television.

Within the next several hours I was to meet many of these travelers and we were to pass the time telling one another how and why we had decided to come. My own decision was simple. I am a Southerner living away from the South. Many of my friends and relatives have remained there to carry on the grinding day-after-day struggle to rouse the drugged conscience of a stubborn and deluded people. They are the heroes. A trip to Alabama is a small thing.

I had, of course, any number of excellent reasons for *not* going to Selma, not the least of which was a powerful disinclination to be struck on the head and gassed. But as I raised that point and every other negative argument, a matter-of-fact voice answered: "You better get down there."

At midnight, the San Francisco airport was nearly deserted.

Three men stood at the Delta Air Lines counter, a Negro and a white man in business suits, and a tall, fair Episcopalian priest. I sensed something dramatic about the tall man. . . . I introduced myself and learned that the priest was going to Selma, that he had decided to go only that night, that he had no idea how he was going to get from Birmingham, where the flight ended, to Selma, ninety miles south. I told him I had wired to both Avis *and* Hertz for cars at Birmingham, somehow I would get him to Selma.

Flight 808 to Dixie rose into the cloudless California night. As in countless other flights across America, I pressed my head to the window and wondered at the wilderness below. This nation, the most automated, urbanized civilization in the world, consists mostly of open space. Yet this is appropriate, for America is still unfinished; it is still a huge, untidy experiment, a series of hopeful statements ending with question marks.

Dawn came in Dallas as we waited between planes. The night had brought other flights in from the West; each had its cargo of pilgrims. All of us trooped aboard a rakish, shining Convair 880 for Birmingham—a score of clergymen both Negro and white, a lawyer from Palo Alto, a psychiatrist from Los Angeles, a Bay Area matron who had had a bit too much to drink, a young couple from Berkeley.

Inside the plane, a plump Negro minister from Los Angeles named Bohler kept leaping to his feet to introduce himself and everyone within earshot to each new passenger, most of whom were bound for Selma. Twice he told us that the previous night he had been wanting to go "more than anything," and that the phone had rung at about 10:30 with news that he had been given a ticket—at which he had murmured, "Oh, He's answered my prayers so quickly!" One of Bohler's companions admitted that "when I told my wife, all she said was buy as much insurance as possible."

In Birmingham . . . the airport was in turmoil. People from all over the nation were streaming in. Many others, we learned, were landing in Atlanta, still more in Montgomery. I picked up my car and loaded my passengers and started out on a tricky, uneasy 90 miles through hostile territory.

———

In the back was an older couple who had sat in front of me on the plane from Dallas.

———

"We watched the news," Ruth Morris said, "and then we went in and sat down and were eating dinner. Our home is right on the ocean. It's a very pleasant place to live, rather gay in color. Our dining room is warm and gay and we were sitting down to a very good dinner. We felt sort of guilty about being there enjoying ourselves after what we had just seen on TV.

"We both said it at the same time, it just seemed to come out of the blue: Why are we sitting here? Then I said, 'I'll pack,' and Bull said, 'I'll call for reservations.' "

———

We entered Selma . . . and we stayed on dirt roads all the way to the Negro church district that was our destination. As we pulled to a stop, three slim young Negro women walked past our car. One of them leaned over to us and said with absolute simplicity: "Thank you for coming." . . .

The scene inside the church burst upon me. Every seat, every aisle was packed. They were shoulder to shoulder—the Princeton professor and the sharecropper's child, the Senator's wife and the elderly Negro mammy.

———

A doctor from New York was speaking: he was giving us, with scientific enthusiasm, our medical briefing. "Tear gas will *not* keep you from breathing. You may *feel* like you can't breathe for a while. Tear gas will not make you *permanently* blind. It may blind you *temporarily*. Do *not* rub your eyes." I looked around at the amused but somber smiles. The doctor's enthusiasm was carrying him away. "If you become unconscious, be sure somebody stays with you." A delighted, outraged laugh rose throughout the church. The doctor laughed, too. "I mean, if you see someone become unconscious, be sure to stay with him." He got the day's greatest ovation.

Outside, in hazy sunlight, the marchers formed. . . . They moved in voiceless exaltation. I exchanged smiles with Jim Forman who walked arm in arm with Dr. King in the front rank. And behind them were all those with whom I had traveled. . . .

America's conscience has been sleeping, but it is waking up. . . . A trip to Alabama is a small thing, but out of many such acts, let us hope, may come a new America. I smiled at my friends and stepped into the ranks.

5. SNCC–SCLC Relations
James Forman

SNCC executive secretary James Forman was one of those movement activists who was most greatly troubled by the differences in political strategy that distinguished the SCLC from SNCC and by King's handling of the extremely difficult situation the movement found itself faced with on Monday night, March 8, and Tuesday, March 9, when federal officials pleaded with King to postpone any second march attempt while hundreds of movement supporters, newly arrived in Selma, eagerly but ominously looked forward to a renewed effort to march to Montgomery. This excerpt is from a chapter in Forman's first book, Sammy Younge, Jr.: The First Black College Student to Die in the Black Liberation Movement *(1968).*

. . . SCLC decided to devote almost all of its organizational energy to a massive right-to-vote campaign, with headquarters in Selma. SNCC, already based in Selma, agreed to cooperate in this new venture. . . . But disagreement on such key issues as concepts of leadership, working methods, and organizing voters for independent political action versus Democratic Party politics, bred conflict between SNCC and SCLC staffs in Alabama.

As the vote campaign intensified, accompanied by innumerable arrests and beatings, the proposal emerged for a march on the Alabama Capitol to demand the vote, as well as new state elections. Basically SNCC was opposed to a Selma-Montgomery march because of the likelihood of police brutality, the drain on resources, and the frustrations experienced in working with SCLC. At a lengthy meeting of its executive committee on March 5 and 6, SNCC voted not to participate organizationally in the march scheduled for Sunday, March 7. However, it encouraged SNCC staffers to do so on a non-organizational basis if they so desired. SNCC was also to make available radios, telephone lines, and certain other facilities already committed by our Alabama staff.

Then we heard that Dr. King would not appear at the march he himself had called. Without his newsworthy presence, it seemed likely that the lives of many black people would be even more endangered. We therefore mobilized three carloads of staff workers from Mississippi, two-way radios, and other protective equipment. At our national office in Atlanta, a group of SNCC people—including Alabama project director Silas Norman and Stokely Carmichael, whose subsequent election as SNCC chairman was largely the result of his work in Alabama—chartered a plane rather than make the five-hour drive to Selma. Since we had heard of King's absence only after the marchers had begun to assemble, none of SNCC's people were able to arrive for the march itself. But it seemed important to have maximum support in the event that violence developed that evening. While our various forces headed for Selma, we tried repeatedly, but unsuccessfully, to contact Dr. King, to find out his reasons for not appearing and to discuss the situation.

Our fears proved all too well-founded: hundreds, including SNCC chairman John Lewis, were beaten, whipped, and tear-gassed by Jim Clark's deputies and Alabama state troopers at the bridge that Sunday.

A new attempt to march was scheduled for the following Tuesday; SCLC also filed a suit seeking to enjoin the Alabama Highway Patrol and Sheriff Jim Clark from interfering with the march. I arrived in Montgomery early Monday evening and found James Farmer, then director of CORE [Congress of Racial Equality], also at the airport. A. D. King, Martin's brother, told us that we were wanted at a meeting. Gathered there were Martin Luther King, Ralph Abernathy, Andrew Young, Hosea Williams, and Bernard Lee of SCLC, together with Fred Gray and Solomon Seay, Jr., Montgomery attorneys.

Farmer and I were informed that Judge Frank Johnson of the Federal Court of the Middle District had promised the SCLC lawyers that if Tuesday's march from Selma to Montgomery was canceled, he would hold a hearing Thursday on the injunction suit which SCLC had filed. Judge Johnson's other conditions were that there be no demonstrations in Montgomery and that the march not proceed in any way before or during the hearing. He expected an answer by 9:00 P.M., said Fred Gray.

The group assembled wanted to know what James Farmer and I had to say. It was clear that the consensus was to accept Judge Johnson's offer; Hosea Williams was the only SCLC leader pushing for the march. Farmer stated that, while he had come down to march and emotionally understood the position of Hosea, rationally he had to agree with waiting until Thursday. I stated that, first, I had not come to march and, second, I had not yet talked with our Alabama staff, so none of my remarks could be binding. With these reservations, I offered my analysis of the situation: that the Judge's offer was legal blackmail. There was no guarantee of getting the injunction and no deadline for the completion of hearings on it. "So many times in the past," I added, "we have seen movements killed by placing the question in the courts, waiting for weeks or months to get an injunction—or just a hearing on one."

Martin Luther King decided to accept the Judge's condition. The march would be postponed.

The entire group left immediately for Brown's Chapel in Selma. There, to my amazement, King pledged before a mass meeting that the march would begin the next morning at eight o'clock!

Not having had a chance to talk with the SNCC staff, I decided not to raise any questions about King's announcement publicly. When asked to speak, I talked about the need for organizing politically when the vote was won. Immediately afterward, I met with the SNCC staff who were disturbed to hear of the way people had been misled.

Later, SCLC held a meeting to reconsider the decision against marching; the SNCC staff attended. After three hours, Dr. King was convinced that he should reverse his position. He telephoned Attorney General Nicholas Katzenbach at 4:30 A.M. to tell him that the march would proceed. According to King, they talked over forty-five minutes and Katzenbach was angry. "I really had to preach to him," said King. I then decided to participate in the march, as King urged, hoping that events might continue to move him away from the U.S. government. Developments in the years which followed, and in particular Dr. King's stand on the Vietnam war, indicate that this did take place to a considerable degree.

As we had anticipated, Judge Johnson issued a court order a few hours later against the march or any type of demonstration. Katzenbach had not sat idly by. But we knew it was impossible to enjoin a whole town and we also felt that, at this point, people had to move. We therefore urged that anyone who had not actually been served papers under the court order should participate. . . .

Hundreds stood ready to march, including many Northern supporters. But once again we were fooled. After crossing the bridge, going a few yards beyond the spot where people had been beaten on the previous Sunday, and then kneeling in prayer, Dr. King turned the march around and led it back to Selma. This was done, according to my own information and the press coverage of the time, in compliance with a "compromise" agreement made between the Administration and Dr. King through the intermediacy of LeRoy Collins, director of the Federal Community Relations Service. King did not inform the marchers of that agreement. Needless to say, people were dismayed, baffled, and angry.

Back in Selma, Dr. King stated that all marches in Selma or Montgomery would be postponed pending the outcome of the injunction suit. This was on Tuesday, March 9. Relations between SNCC and SCLC were at a very low point. We began holding meetings of the SNCC staff, as well as meetings between SNCC and SCLC, to resolve our difficulties. . . .

6. Personal Letter from Muriel and Art Lewis to Her Mother

Selma, Alabama, March 19, 1965

In Selma, as in Montgomery, Albany, and Birmingham in previous years, the white population was not monolithically segregationist. In each city there lived a few—albeit not many—white natives or longtime residents who knew that segregation and racial discrimination were wrong and sought to find ways in which they could successfully help speed their elimination. In Selma the two best known white moderates or liberals were auto dealer Art Lewis and his wife, Muriel, who wrote this letter, circulated among several dozen of their friends and relatives across the country.

Dear Mother,

This letter is being written to all our friends, relatives and a few acquaintances to try and explain our personal position in "the Selma situation." There are some few of you who understand the situation completely and our role in it, but for the most part we think you believe that we are either disinterested, not involved, partial segregationists, rednecks, fools, courageous or possibly even moderate or liberal in our thinking. We feel that we must set the record straight, as no story in recent years has so completely stirred the nation, or had such complete coverage.

This is almost the end of the ninth week of racial demonstrations in this locale, and for most of that time we have been walking on eggshells, balancing on a very thin tightrope while trying to do what we believe is right and just. But we must act differently, and think differently because Selma is our home, we love it and its people and we want to continue to live here.

We have long been aware of the white racist group in Selma (and it is very large), and we have worked in a small way to change this through overthrowing the political machine that has ruled this city and county for many many years. There has been some success along these lines; our new young Mayor, Joe Smitherman; the head of the City Council, Carl Morgan; and three other councilmen were elected partly through our efforts and support. Art is one of the few nonpolitical figures who can still talk with the Mayor, but sadly these past weeks none of his advice has been accepted. Prior to these past few months, there was a good line of communication between the Mayor and the local negro leaders. For the first time there had been biracial talks, and we can only hope that in time these will resume. The history of Selma is too long to go into now; let me get down to the Lewises.

. . . Until the riot on the bridge on our terrible black Sunday we kept our views quiet. We could be called moderates but not liberals, for we believe in the rights of the negroes, their right to free speech and their right to demonstrate in *moderation*. We know that Selma has been used for the sole purpose of bringing national attention to the rights of the negroes, and we were well aware that there was a perfect setup here with "the villain" Jim Clark, and when Martin Luther King arrived there was the hero. Among the press, the negroes and some whites they are known as "the devil and deLawd."

Anyhow, the past few weeks we have become more vocal. I started by talking with my friends. There are a pitiful few who feel as we do, and when the tensions become almost unbearable we have only each other with whom to talk. One of the great problems in the city is the lack of strong, nonpolitical, white, moderate leaders. We have known that there was formed a nucleus of old-family (important) business and professional men who are moderates, but they have [been] and are still meeting in secret. We too need a leader and we know to be successful he must have certain qualifications. Art does not quite fit these, because of the fact that we have only lived here 23 years (and so are still outsiders), we are Jewish and there is a health problem to consider. I personally have taken to writing letters to editors to try and show that Selma has human beings here who do not condone violence. So far the only one printed (that I know of) was in our Selma paper and that in re. the rights of local citizens to work with the CRS [Community Relations Service] to help our city attain what is right and to ensure peace. This one letter has had surprising results. I have been contacted by a group of local people who are too liberal and too new in town to have any long lasting effect, and as expected there has been a little hate mail. . . .

. . . We realize that we can no longer be afraid to speak out, but that does not mean that we are no longer a bit fearful, and we do not—nor should you, condemn our moderate friends for their silence. We know that this area is full of potential violence, not only from the radical whites, but from the many militant negroes. We go anywhere and everywhere in Selma, except Sylvan St., [and] we go about the necessary day to day activities, but for weeks we have thought of nothing else, have talked of nothing else. The tension has been ever present, and it will be here for a long long time. The name Selma will soon drop from the headlines, but we are working for a long range program of understanding between the races and for lasting peace.

From our friends and relatives we have heard very little, and we have needed all the love and support possible. Some few of you have been concerned and kind and to you we have tried to make our ordeal seem much less than it has been. A very few of you have seen fit to question our motives and thoughts during this time. We hope that you will continue to acknowledge us, or we shall be truly lost, and you should not feel shame at writing SELMA on an envelope. There are decent people everywhere, and this town is no exception.

We are confused, more than ever tonight. We must live with ourselves, but we also want to live here. It would be so easy to be quiet, but it would not let us sleep any easier than we do now. All we ask from you is partial understanding, and compassion. We hope that you will never be faced with a crisis in your lives that even remotely resembles this, and we hope that you will understand the purpose of this letter. We ask that you do not show it to your friends or even talk about it; this information is for the people who mean something important to us.

With fondest regards,
Muriel and Art Lewis

7. "Our God Is Marching On!"
Martin Luther King, Jr.

Martin Luther King, Jr., spoke from the steps of the state capitol before a crowd of more than twenty-five thousand at the conclusion of the Selma-to-Montgomery march, on March 25, 1965.

My dear and abiding friends, Ralph Abernathy, and to all the distinguished Americans seated here on the rostrum, my friends and co-workers of the state of Alabama and to all of the freedom-loving people who have assembled here this afternoon, from all over our nation and from all over the world.

Last Sunday, more than eight thousand of us started on a mighty walk from Selma, Alabama. We have walked on meandering highways and rested our bodies on rocky byways. Some of our faces are burned from the outpourings of the sweltering sun. Some have literally slept in the mud. We have been drenched by the rains.

Our bodies are tired, and our feet are somewhat sore, but today as I stand before you and think back over that great march, I can say as Sister Pollard said, a seventy-year-old Negro woman who lived in this community during the bus boycott and one day she was asked while walking if she wanted a ride and when she answered, "No," the person said, "Well, aren't you tired?" And with her ungrammatical profundity, she said, "My feets is tired, but my soul is rested."

And in a real sense this afternoon, we can say that our feet are tired, but our souls are rested.

They told us we wouldn't get here. And there were those who said that we would get here only over their dead bodies, but all the world today knows that we are here and that we are standing before the forces of power in the state of Alabama saying, "We ain't goin' let nobody turn us around."

The Civil Rights Act of 1964 gave Negroes some part of their rightful dignity, but without the vote it was dignity without strength.

Once more the method of nonviolent resistance was unsheathed from its scabbard and once again an entire community was mobilized to confront the adversary. And again the brutality of a dying order shrieks across the land. Yet Selma, Alabama, became a shining moment in the conscience of man.

There never was a moment in American history more honorable and more inspiring than the pilgrimage of clergymen and laymen of every race and faith pouring into Selma to face danger at the side of its embattled Negroes.

Confrontation of good and evil compressed in the tiny community of Selma generated the massive power to turn the whole nation to a new course. A president born in the South had the sensitivity to feel the will of the country, and in an address that will live in history as one of the most passionate pleas for human rights ever made by a president of our nation, he pledged the might of the federal government to cast off the centuries-old blight. President Johnson rightly praised the courage of the Negro for awakening the conscience of the nation.

On our part we must pay our profound respects to the white Americans who cherish their democratic traditions over the ugly customs and privileges of generations and come forth boldly to join hands with us. From Montgomery to Birmingham, from Birmingham to Selma, from Selma back to Montgomery, a trail wound in a circle and often bloody, yet it has become a highway up from darkness. Alabama has tried to nurture and defend evil, but the evil is choking to death in the dusty roads and streets of this state.

So I stand before you this afternoon with the conviction that segregation is on its deathbed in Alabama and the only thing uncertain about it is how costly the segregationists and Wallace will make the funeral.

Our whole campaign in Alabama has been centered around the right to vote. In focusing the attention of the nation and the world today on the flagrant denial of the right to vote, we are exposing the very origin, the root cause, of racial segregation in the Southland.

The threat of the free exercise of the ballot by the Negro and the white masses alike resulted in the establishing of a segregated society. They segregated southern money from the poor whites; they segregated southern mores from the rich whites; they segregated southern churches from Christianity; they segregated southern minds from honest thinking; and they segregated the Negro from everything.

We have come a long way since that travesty of justice was perpetrated upon the American mind. Today I want to tell the city of Selma, today I want to say to the state of Alabama, today I want to say to the people of America and the nations of the world: We are not about to turn around. We are on the move now. Yes, we are on the move and no wave of racism can stop us.

We are on the move now. The burning of our churches will not deter us. We are on the move now. The bombing of our homes will not dissuade us. We are on the move now. The beating and killing of our clergymen and young people will not divert us. We are on the move now. The arrest and release of known murderers will not discourage us. We are on the move now.

Like an idea whose time has come, not even the marching of mighty armies can halt us. We are moving to the land of freedom.

Let us therefore continue our triumph and march to the realization of the American dream. Let us march on segregated housing, until every ghetto of social and economic depression dissolves and Negroes and whites live side by side in decent, safe and sanitary housing.

Let us march on segregated schools until every vestige of segregated and inferior education becomes a thing of the past and Negroes and whites study side by side in the socially healing context of the classroom.

Let us march on poverty . . . until no starved man walks the streets of our cities and towns in search of jobs that do not exist.

Let us march on ballot boxes, march on ballot boxes until race baiters disappear from the political arena. Let us march on ballot boxes until the Wallaces of our nation tremble away in silence.

Let us march on ballot boxes, until we send to our city councils, state legislatures, and the United States Congress men who will not fear to do justice, love mercy, and walk humbly with their God. Let us march on ballot boxes until all over Alabama God's children will be able to walk the earth in decency and honor.

For all of us today the battle is in our hands. The road ahead is not altogether a smooth one. There are no broad highways to lead us easily and inevitably to quick solutions. We must keep going.

My people, my people, listen! The battle is in our hands. The battle is in our hands in Mississippi and Alabama, and all over the United States.

So as we go away this afternoon, let us go away more than ever before committed to the struggle and committed to nonviolence. I must admit to you there are still some difficulties ahead. We are still in for a season of suffering in many of the black belt counties of Alabama, many areas of Mississippi, many areas of Louisiana.

I must admit to you there are still jail cells waiting for us, dark and difficult moments. We will go on with the faith that nonviolence and its power transformed dark yesterdays into bright tomorrows. We will be able to change all of these conditions.

Our aim must never be to defeat or humiliate the white man but to win his friendship and understanding. We must come to see that the end we seek is a society at peace with itself, a society that can live with its conscience. That will be a day not of the white man, not of the black man. That will be the day of man as man.

I know you are asking today, "How long will it take?" I come to say to you this afternoon however difficult the moment, however frustrating the hour, it will not be long, because truth pressed to earth will rise again.

How long? Not long, because no lie can live forever.

How long? Not long, because you still reap what you sow.

How long? Not long. Because the arm of the moral universe is long but it bends toward justice.

How long? Not long, 'cause mine eyes have seen the glory of the coming of the Lord, trampling out the vintage where the grapes of wrath are stored. He has loosed the fateful lightning of his terrible swift sword. His truth is marching on.

He has sounded for the trumpets that shall never call retreat. He is lifting up the hearts of man before His judgment seat. Oh, be swift, my soul, to answer Him. Be jubilant, my feet. Our God is marching on.

WE THE PEOPLE:
THE STRUGGLE CONTINUES

Vincent Harding

On March 25, 1965, as thousands of marchers poured into the concourse of Montgomery's Dexter Avenue, moving like a dark and light river toward the capitol at the far end of the thoroughfare, they carried among themselves a symbolic power too forceful to overlook. Many layers of history and meaning were caught up in this convergence of people, time, and place, this climax of another stage in the long, black-led journey toward a more perfect union.

After four days of marching through rain, mud, sunshine, and sudden chills, carrying their American flags, accompanied by federalized guard units and army personnel, still always aware of the presence of danger, but always singing their songs ("Oh, Wallace! Segregation's got to fall . . . you never can jail us all"), they had finally come to Montgomery.

This city represented many realities, each spiraling into the other. It had been the first capital of the Confederacy, stark symbol of the South's blood-red, Civil War resistance to the demands for black freedom. But now, marching toward the capitol were also many of the human sources of the city's transformation. Here, among the thousands of persons spreading all over the streets, were hundreds of women and men who represented the historic black determination to "swamp the foundations" of injustice, to possess the land, and to re-create the meaning of Montgomery. As they marched down Dexter Avenue, such persons were living signs of a continuing struggle to define and live out freedom, a struggle that had been going on, in its most recent manifestation, for a century.

A. Philip Randolph was there, perhaps the oldest of the long-time freedom-moving contingent, continuing a tradition he had carried on ever since World War I. Ralph Bunche, first black American Nobel Peace Prize winner, a direct link to the powerful days of Howard University in the 1930s, had joined the line on that day. So had Roy Wilkins, bearing witness to the persistent presence of the National Association for the Advancement of Colored People (NAACP) for more than half a century in the struggle to re-create the Union. Bayard Rustin, veteran of the national and international nonviolent movements for peace and justice, returned to the city where he had first helped Martin Luther King, Jr. In the line, too, was John Lewis, SNCC chairman, his head still bandaged from the Pettus Bridge beating, representing the new generation of black students who had given a powerful, decisive impetus to the movement. He marched along with Stokely Carmichael, the tall indefatigable young organizer from Harlem and Trinidad who already dreamed of what *black power* might be like. (Perhaps, in his own way, Malcolm—now beyond even El-Hajj Malik El-Shabazz—was also there, marching, testifying.) And, of course, courageous local leaders like Mrs. Amelia Boynton and Reverend Fred Reese of Selma reminded the world that it was their commitment, and the persistent determination of grass-roots leaders like them everywhere, which usually formed the base of every attempt to reshape the nation in the direction of democracy, justice, and freedom.

But who could have marched on Dexter Avenue that day bearing more dreams and memories than Rosa Parks and Martin and Coretta King and Ralph and Juanita Abernathy and the thousands of black Montgomerians who just ten years earlier had brought a new moment to the historic struggle? Following their lead, in less than a decade, an aroused southern black community, eventually joined by white allies from everywhere, had confounded all the conventional wisdom about who they were and what power they did or did not possess. In the process they had surprised and shaken their nation and encouraged millions of people around the world.

Disciplined by a profound sense of place, deep reservoirs of religious faith, a commitment to nonviolence, and an American optimism, this black-shaped force had lifted up the richest implications of the 1954 Supreme Court decision and joined its faith in God to a faith in democracy and, finally, in themselves. Thus armed, they had taken on in direct confrontation the harsh and often murderous system of legalized and quasi-legal segregation in the South and had broken its essential power. In the process they had made it impossible for the United States ever to return to its explicit, pre–World War II commitment to black submissiveness, white domination, and a schizophrenic democracy. Rising from the bottom, they had pressed the nation forward.

By 1965 they had smashed almost all of the humiliating "colored" and "white" signs, and though the unsigned realities still persisted, though the supporters of the old order swore never to give up, the audacious power of a religiously inspired human freedom movement was against them. Now churches, schools, courthouses, registration lists, restrooms, motels, U.S. military units, some political offices, parks, pools, beaches—every public facility and restroom—were all feeling the rising force of the flooding black movement.

In the course of their struggle, these black marchers had also been freeing white people all over the South and North, opening the locked doors for both the prisoners and the wardens. Indeed, an observer needed only to look at the parading, celebrating, marching lines as they made their way toward the capitol that day in order to see one of the most powerful and pervasive effects of the post-1954 black freedom struggle. Clearly, it had opened the way for the white religious communities of the nation to respond more fully to their God of truth, justice, and love. Priests and rabbis, Catholic sisters and Orthodox bishops, monks and laypeople of every persuasion were in the lines, joining their lives in the search for a just community, a more perfect union, assuming that the quest for such human community was an act of divine communion. Thus the singing, preaching, believing black movement had once more brought into the streets its long tradition of liberation spirituality, theology, and action, and thousands of white sisters and brothers were set free to begin anew, set free by the descendants of America's slaves.

It was the same for young white people. The Montgomery bus boycott had begun at a time when all the keepers of the societal wisdom were identifying white young folks (the only ones they saw) as "the silent generation." College students of the period were put down as a set of fearful, self-centered youth, cowed by the domestic anti-Communist crusades of the "cold war," refusing to take risks or to live with political ideologies. Into the midst of these analyses walked the black children and teenagers who took the words of *Brown* v. *Board of Education of Topeka* and transmuted them into costly deeds, testifying to the presence of far more than the wise men had seen. Then, while commissions and academic conferences were continuing to explain why college students were obsessed by panty-raids and telephone-booth-stuffing contests, a creative black youth storm blew into the face of official public segregation, becoming sit-ins and Freedom Rides and dangerous voter registration organizing and campaigning.

Black youth were on fire in the cause of justice, living on subsistence salaries (when the checks arrived), standing in solidarity with the people under threat, drawing much of it to themselves. Quickly, the power of their commitment, the audacity of their movement, and the justice of their cause began to draw thousands of white young people out of their hiding places into the light of the surging movement toward a new society. The white youth were never the same again, as many went on to challenge their universities, their government, and eventually their own souls. (Again, in spite of the conventional wisdom of our own time, it is likely that the last has not been heard from some of the men and women whose young lives were transformed in the crucible of the black-led freedom movement.) In Selma they were present, looking for the America that had not yet come into being in their lives. Indeed, white Americans of every age were responding to the power of the challenging black surge. They understood that it was also a movement for their liberation from a distortion of democracy. That was why Viola Liuzzo came from Detroit, to serve, to risk, and finally, to die.

Of course, the powerful dynamic of the movement had moved

not only white youth, religious peoples, and other citizens who were believers in justice, but it had insistently, amazingly, challenged the major institutions of our national government as well. So not only had the highest courts been forced to face the meaning of the Constitution and its Preamble, but now presidents, Congresses, and political parties were pressed to decide how they would stand, what they would say, what they would do in response to the black challenge to re-create America, to redefine "we the people." Now, all over the world, wherever women and men honored the hope of social justice, the southern black freedom movement was a source of inspiration, and its songs—especially "We Shall Overcome"—began to be heard everywhere.

At the same moment, as one might expect, the black community was re-creating, repossessing, and challenging itself, discovering the possibilities of a power that had long been denied, from within and without. One fascinating aspect of this self-renewal was evidenced in the fact that the black people of the North had gained new respect for the courage and creativity of their supposedly backward relatives in the churning precincts of the South. Indeed, faithful to a long tradition among many freedom-obsessed peoples, a stunning dialectic had been set in motion: A people determined to change the world around them had begun again, as well, to change the world within them, to take into themselves the words of their song, words as old as humankind: "The truth shall make us free." For now the marchers could hopefully envision the freedom of their children and their grandchildren, could see the new beauty about to be born as a result of their costly, risky struggles, and could repeat the words of the black woman of the bus boycott: "My feets is tired, but my soul is rested." Indeed, all through the South, a fascinating testimony was constantly repeated: Wherever the freedom movement heightened its activities in a black community, at the same time, the crime rate in that community plummeted to its lowest levels.

So the history and the hope the marchers brought into Montgomery that day were long and deep, at once centuries old and yet less than a decade into their newest motion. Of course, a decade is a short time in the development of human struggles for justice, especially when their highest goal has been defined as "redeeming the soul of America," especially when they intend "to [inject] new meaning into the veins of history and of civilization," especially when their major weapons are courage, hope, commitment, and intelligent, powerful love.

Martin Luther King, Jr., whose greatest gift may well have been his capacity to imbibe, transform, and return to the people their best hopes and dreams, understood how short a time a decade was. He knew this was especially the case for people whose unarmed struggle pits them against fierce opponents in persons and structures, sets them against systems of inertia and fear. So that Thursday afternoon, when he finally stood on the steps of the capitol in Montgomery, rounding off a century, closing out a decade, facing the exultant crowd, he clearly understood the great pride of the people in what they had already accomplished to "establish justice, insure domestic tranquility, provide for the common defense, and promote the general welfare," as well as to "secure the blessings of liberty" to themselves and their posterity. At the same moment, he realized that civil rights acts, voter registration laws, and the smashing of outward signs were only the end of the beginning of the long journey toward a new America.

Working from that consciousness and from his own deep sense of compassion and courage, the black leader urged the responsive crowd of some twenty-five thousand persons—as well as the onlooking nation and world—to keep moving on the long journey. He knew, of course, that "The road ahead is not altogether a smooth one." He said, "There are no broad highways to lead us easily and inevitably to quick solutions." But he pressed on, challenging the crowd, the nation: "We must keep going."

Within the context of such a statement, we can understand that what is usually called the "civil rights movement" was only one element—albeit a crucial, necessary element—of what many persons considered a larger, deeper, historically grounded movement: the struggle—often led by black people—to transform America, its values, institutions, and people, toward a more perfect union. (Thus the grass-roots-level leaders and participants rarely spoke of fighting for "civil rights." More often they saw themselves as true freedom fighters, and the songs which ran deep into the soul of the movement were not called "civil rights songs" but "freedom songs," and all through the nights the chant, "Everybody wants free-e-e-DOM!" went out.)

As a result, there could be a real sense of pride and joy when in the summer of 1965 Congress finally passed the Voting Rights Bill and it was signed into law. Everybody knew how fully this governmental action had been spurred by the confrontations on Pettus Bridge, by the march to Montgomery, by the deaths on the way. But there was also a sense of sobriety when in that same summer the fires of Watts broke loose. There had been intimations of such volatility in Birmingham in 1963 and in Harlem and other scattered cities in 1964, but Watts was the great explosion which some people (like Malcolm X) had been sensing for years. Indeed, anyone who looked at the conditions of the black urban communities, anyone who recognized the all-too-American commitment to violent solutions then being acted out in Vietnam, anyone who felt the increasing white resistance to deep probes into the structural problems of the nation—anyone with such insights knew that something like Watts was coming.

In a sense, the rounding off of the classic southern phase of the movement in Selma that spring and the summertime explosion in black Los Angeles (as well as in places like Chicago and Philadelphia) proved to mark a turning point. From there on, the growing attention, energies, and action of the black freedom movement were geared toward the North, toward the cities, toward the problems of political powerlessness, economic exploitation, social disruption (from within and without), and explosive, sometimes cathartic rage. All of this was set in the context of what most movement leaders considered a cruel, unjust, and wasteful war being waged by the United States against the Vietnamese people. Finally, the entire domestic setting was shaped and fundamentally influenced by the powerful black nationalist fervor which was emerging with sometimes volcanic force in the black communities everywhere, especially after the February 1965 assassination of Malcolm X.

By the middle of 1966, all of these transitional elements were drawn together in Mississippi in what was called the March Against Fear. Late in the spring of that year, James Meredith, the somewhat reluctant hero of the hard struggle to integrate the University of

Mississippi, had decided to set off on this solitary march down through the heart of his native state. After he fell victim to a shotgun blast at the beginning of his march, other movement leaders attempted to continue, but the strains among them concerning the future of the freedom struggle, concerning the role of white allies, concerning outspoken criticism of the federal government, were too great for all of them to go into Mississippi together. So the march developed as a fascinating encounter among the Student Nonviolent Coordinating Committee (SNCC), the Southern Christian Leadership Conference (SCLC), and the Congress of Racial Equality (CORE), against the background of white Mississippi's continuing, sometimes brutal resistance to the movement of history. The most powerful result of the march was likely the emergence of SNCC's call for *black power,* identified primarily with its radical, charismatic, and often provocative new chairperson, Stokely Carmichael, veteran of Alabama's hard organizing campaigns and many other battlegrounds in the South.

In that same explosive period of transition, SNCC and other movement forces were also attracted to another kind of charisma. This was identified with the young, California-based Black Panther Party and their dramatic projection of the necessity of "picking up the gun" in the defense of the black communities of the North against the familiar force of police arrogance and brutality. King, meanwhile—against much powerful advice—followed his compassion and had gone into Chicago to try to find some way to use his movement experience and contacts to challenge the harsh world of poverty, political powerlessness, and despair that he found in the northern urban black communities. Of course, these were often communities where women and men had no deeply projected sense of place, no history of sustained, disciplined, and often victorious struggles for change. Coming out of such a setting in the South, King thought he could use his southern movement resources and transform them in such a way as to organize a real challenge to the powerful, paternalistic political machine of Mayor Richard Daley, thereby suggesting a ray of hope to Afro-Americans locked in similar situations across the North. Great resistance to this new vision emerged in the white communities of the North, and many black northerners were ambivalent as well.

Meanwhile, the summer explosions in the black communities of

America continued. By 1967, when thousands of U.S. troops had to be called out to control the two major uprisings of that summer, in Newark, New Jersey, and Detroit, Michigan, many persons were talking of the possibility of seeing widespread racial warfare erupt in America. But for the black participants in the rebellions they never quite took on that character, for these men and women were striking out more against the enveloping hopelessness of their situation than against white persons as individuals. The deaths in the riots were overwhelmingly black, usually at the hands of police or other enforcers of law and order. From the perspective of many black persons, if a war existed, it was between the forces of unjust law and crippling order that were so often set against the northern, urban black need to break out into fresh air, into a new sense of what it means to be taken seriously as "we the people," as shapers of their own destiny and that of the nation.

In a parallel movement, King, SNCC, and CORE had decisively and often harshly identified the war in Vietnam (and the American president who was obsessed with winning it) as a major obstacle to any real national attempt to deal with the problems of structural racism, poverty, militarism, and political powerlessness. Indeed, the black freedom workers made it clear that they considered all of these aspects of the nation's way of life to be part of the bloody, entangling web in Vietnam, part of the obstruction to the necessary, continuing internal movement toward a more perfect union.

In a sense, King was a repository of much of the symbolic and actual energies that had now flowed from the southern black freedom movement into the larger, less definable task of "redeeming the soul of America." In the last year of his life, King was calling more and more for what he loosely identified as "a revolution of values" in the United States. But he was going further as well. For by that time it was clear to him, he said, that

> the black revolution is much more than a struggle for the rights of Negroes. It is forcing America to face all its interrelated flaws—racism, poverty, militarism and materialism. It is exposing the evils that are rooted deeply in the whole structure of our society. It reveals systemic rather than superficial flaws and suggests that radical reconstruction of society itself is the real issue to be faced.

By the time of his assassination, King was consumed with the compassionate, ambiguous search for the way to "radical reconstruction" of this country he loved so deeply. Constantly facing the threat of death and the reality of harsh criticism from many former allies, he groped for a way which would challenge the best energies and indignation of the black community—especially its young people—and move them into a higher level of nonviolence than had yet been discovered in the freedom struggle. He was no longer dependent on the goodwill of the federal government's leaders toward him and his cause. For by 1967–68 there was almost none. Instead, King sought to recruit the poor and their allies of every community—Appalachian whites, Native Americans, Hispanics, as well as northern and southern black people, rural and urban together. These were the persons who had gained very little in concrete benefits from the victories of the southern movement.

But in those years, the shadow of assassination seemed to fall everywhere. On April 4, 1968, its movement cut short King's attempt to organize a Poor People's Campaign. At its best this was meant to be an audacious, multiracial movement of America's poor people and their friends to challenge the unfriendly, Vietnam-obsessed federal government with massive civil disobedience in the search for economic justice, for a more perfect union, for a nonviolent revolution. King had seen the faces of the poor. Like the grass-roots SNCC organizers of an earlier time, like Malcolm X, he had felt more and more deeply the needs of the locked-out. Thus, he had gone beyond civil rights to try to take on the structural problems of racism, poverty, militarism, materialism, and paranoid anticommunism in American life. But he could not go beyond the edges of his own life, and, therefore, left much undone, much to be done.

At the same time, other persons who had been deeply involved in the freedom struggle were losing energy, focus, vision, and direction. Some, facing a time of assassinations, murderous police riots, and extensive government subversion, were losing courage and hope. Others had drifted into self-destructive ways of life, deeply wounded veterans of a long and costly struggle. SNCC was in organizational disarray. CORE was fighting a series of harsh internal battles. It was simply not clear how persons and organizations, rising out of the traditions of the black-led freedom struggle, might confront and respond to the need for "radical reconstruction" of the nation's life systems. In other words, it was hard to know how to keep going, how to keep eyes on the prize. It was especially difficult for many persons to find the internal resources necessary for venturing onto new, uncertain, and dangerous ground.

As part of the black search for the way ahead, the period surrounding King's assassination saw an electric outpouring of black energy, creativity, and activism. Conferences and conventions flourished in a spirit reminiscent of the early days of the post–Civil War Reconstruction, bringing together politics, religion, economics, and culture. Black caucuses erupted in almost every predominantly white organization, often accompanied by hard, confrontative stands over issues of power, control, financing, and direction. (Some of the most vigorous of these caucuses sprang up in the churches, both Protestant and Roman Catholic. They were the sources of much of the black theology movement which broke through the traditions of a white, Euro-American theology which had previously made many self-assured, but unfounded, claims to universalism.) Black Power conventions in Newark— while the odor of burning was still in the air—and then in Philadelphia were transmuted in 1970 into the first Congress of African Peoples in Atlanta, a testimony to the powerful revival of black nationalism and Africa-consciousness. Of course it was also a testimony to the transformation that was at work in Atlanta itself: A Congress of African People in Joe Louis Auditorium at Morris Brown College in Atlanta! Surely the times were changing.

During this period, many conferences were called by teachers, parents, students, and others which convened scholars, activists, political leaders, and many professionals to engage in vibrant, sometimes marvelously unscholarly discussions and debates on the need for black history and black studies in American life. White academic institutions in the North, feeling a postassassination pressure unlike any they had known before, were pushed to find black faculty, to recruit black students, to discover black-focused curriculum, and campuses rocked with confrontational actions.

Small, often creative, independent black institutions, especially those intent on the education of children, on the repossession of young minds, sprang up in hundreds of locations across the nation. Regularly they claimed the names, words, and traditions of Du Bois, Garvey, Robeson, Ida B. Wells, and other historical figures as they searched for a past on which to build their vision of the future. It was a time of powerful, sometimes abrasive cultural renaissance—matched in power and scope only by the highest days of the Universal Negro Improvement Association—as poets, playwrights, graphic artists, dancers, and musicians seemed to be flourishing everywhere in the early 1970s. If nothing more, their presence seemed to suggest that the coming "radical reconstruction" of America would have to include systems of culture and belief, systems of education and identity, especially as these were revisioned and re-created by black people.

Much of the thrust and energy of this period was caught up in the first National Black Political Convention held in March 1972, in Gary, Indiana, a new beachhead city for the rising force of another black electoral power. Symbolically enough, the convention was called by the gifted, charismatic black artist and nationalist, Amiri Baraka (LeRoi Jones); by one of the representatives of traditional black congressional power, U.S. Representative Charles Diggs of Detroit (who had courageously attended the Mississippi trial of Emmett Till's murderers in 1955); and by the newly elected mayor of Gary, Richard Hatcher, host of the exciting, historic gathering.

Most persons among those hundreds who attended from across the country had some sense of agreement with the preamble to the convention's declaration: "We stand on the edge of history. We cannot turn back." Although interpretations of that announcement were varied, it was easy to forget the differences in the midst of the high energy of the convention. Indeed, some persons thought they might be witnessing the beginning of a new age in the black freedom struggle, or at least a new stage, when toward the end of the convention they were treated to this sight: On the stage, Jesse Jackson, Coretta Scott King, Shirley Chisholm (the first black woman elected to the U.S. House of Representatives), Baraka, Diggs, Hatcher, and others stood with clasped hands raised high, suggesting the prospects of a new union of forces for the transformation of black and white America.

Unfortunately, the millennium was not at hand. Much traditional politics and many personal agendas stood in the way. So it was necessary to deal with King's 1965 warning again: "There are no broad highways to lead us easily and inevitably to quick solutions." So, many persons left Gary and continued to move into the ambiguous years of the 1970s, sometimes guided only by the conviction that "we must keep going." Perhaps that was all that was possible for anyone to know with any certainty while moving on the edge of history.

As black men and women pressed on beyond Gary, trying to find ways to respond to the internal and external challenges of past, present, and future, they chose a number of alternatives, many bearing familiar elements of earlier times in the freedom movement. Some went the way of traditional American political participation, believing that the rising black numbers would somehow make a difference in a system still dominated by unprincipled compromise, the overwhelming desire for reelection, and a blindness to the needs for "radical restructuring." Others moved toward independent black institutions, finding their way to traditional black settings, or creating new ones. Many persons became deeply involved in organizations and movements focused on African liberation, participating in the continuing drama of the search for independence and for unity in the homeland. Sometimes they also seemed to be signaling a belief that the possession of this land had proved impossible—or at least incompatible with their sense of black integrity. Meanwhile a relative few developed scenarios for armed rebellion in the United States and some of them tried at times to live that out, often with disastrous results.

For a time, a significant movement of black people continued into the Nation of Islam. Then, after the death of the Honorable Elijah Muhammad, the organization went through a series of radical changes, leading finally to the creation of a breakaway, revivalist movement headed by Minister Louis Farrakhan. These transformations and internal divisions made it difficult for many seekers, and some turned toward the path of more traditional Islam. (Indeed, a significant number of movement activists from the 1960s are now seriously engaged in religious communities.)

In the course of the 1970s, powerful debates were carried on in some circles of the black community over the relative merits of black nationalism and black Marxism as adequate ways to the future. Some of this proved enlightening and it opened up important issues concerning the "radical reconstruction" of the nation that King called for; however, other aspects of the debate were far more focused on personalities than on issues, always a dangerous trend. Indeed, by the end of the 1970s it was especially clear that black people needed to be wary of all cults of personality. For they watched in horror as the story unfolded concerning one such cult, led by James Jones, a renegade white Christian minister, and learned how hundreds of largely poor, religiously committed African-Americans had been driven to a terrible mass suicide in Guyana. But the death of Jonestown also carried the continuing, insistent message that men and women of every kind wanted and needed to be called to transformation, to work for the re-creation of themselves and their society, wanted to develop that work on some spiritually nourishing base in community with others. In other words, all over America, among many peoples, a deep hunger existed to participate actively in the search for a more perfect union.

As a result, much of the debate over affirmative action, self-help, government aid, entitlements, and other important recent issues somehow seemed to miss the depth and power of the call that was coming from many persons for a way to engage in the re-creation of their personal lives and the life of their nation. Perhaps the continuing hope for such an alternative was part of what drew so many Chicago citizens to the powerful campaign that made Harold Washington the first black mayor of the city in 1983. Perhaps it was this hope that made Jesse Jackson's presidential candidacy so compelling in the following year. Here was the great-grandson of slaves boldly entering the arena of presidential politics and offering to lead a nation badly in need of some direction. For Jackson and those who searched with him to find a way to challenge, and perhaps transform America, many of the issues I raised (in *The Other American Revolution*) at the beginning of the 1980s are still relevant. Referring to the 1970s as "a long, hard winter to endure," I asked:

If we are actually in the midst of so elemental a time of turning, if indeed we stand at the edge of history, then the central question for us all, but especially for those of us who are young, is, how shall we live responsibly in this momentous period of humankind's evolution? In the light of what we have seen and been and done over the last twenty years, what is our best response to this hour, to our forebears, to our children—to our own deepest hopes and human longings? Considering the lessons of the 1970s, how do we move forward?

Do we turn aside into divisionary and essentially private pursuits, refusing to face our need for solidarity and community, resisting the struggle-honed development of our own most humane and creative selves? Or do we move forward, emerging renewed and enlarged out of the spiritual pilgrimages of this decade, ready to advance in the company of our brothers and sisters into the uncharted arena of the new time?

At the edge of history, how shall we move? Do we continue to trail behind the most revolutionary insights that our struggle has already achieved? Do we turn away from the radical directions that Malcolm, Martin, and Fannie Lou had already approached in the 1960s? Or do we stand with them, move with them, move beyond them, move on for them and for ourselves and our children to remake this nation?

Absorbing the meaning of the 1970s, do we ignore the call of Gary? Or do we take its best insights and press on to create our own courageous summons to the newest stages of our struggle? How do we take all that we have learned and move it into the deeper internal spaces of our beings which this decade of winter has allowed us to explore? How, from so spacious and solid a center do we then move forward, beyond our best actions, beyond our best dreams, to participate fully in the creation of a fundamentally new reality, in ourselves, in our people, in this nation, and in this world?

These are no longer wild and visionary questions. The winter of our constrictions is finally passing. Are we ready for all the necessary birth pangs, all the searching floodlights, all the unexpected new pathways of spring?

Because the questions remain alive among us (when we allow ourselves to be alive with them), it may be helpful to close this section with the words of the poem "Creation-Spell" by Ed Bullins.

Into your palm I place the ashes
Into your palm are the ashes of your brothers
burnt in the Alabama night
Into your palm that holds your babies
into your palm that feeds your children
into your palm that holds the work tools
I place the ashes of your father
here are the ashes of your husbands
Take the ashes of your nation
and create the cement to build again
Create the spirits to move again
Take this soul dust and begin again.

Is it possible that beginning again, building again on the foundation of the long historic struggle for freedom—in every generation—is the only way to "possess this land," to possess ourselves, to create, and to re-create, a more just, compassionate, and perfect union for ourselves and our posterity? Is that possibly what it means to keep your eyes on the prize?

CHAPTER SEVEN

THE TIME HAS COME (1964–1966)

Introduction by Clayborne Carson

The increasingly militant black protests of the early 1960s fostered a new sense of racial pride and self-confidence among African-Americans. Many observers attributed the rise of this new racial consciousness to the influence of northern black nationalists, such as Elijah Muhammad, leader of the black religious group the Nation of Islam, and Malcolm X, the Nation of Islam's most effective spokesman. Although these influences were important, the new black consciousness also grew out of the experiences of activists in the southern struggle. Rather than northern black nationalism supplanting earlier civil rights militancy, the emergent ideas of the southern struggle merged with developing themes of the long-established northern black nationalist and separatist movements.

From the beginning of the modern southern freedom struggle, it had transformed the racial attitudes and identities of black participants. When Martin Luther King addressed Montgomery blacks in December 1955, he correctly predicted that the boycott movement would alter the treatment of blacks in future history books: "Somebody will have to say, 'There lived a race of people, of black people . . . people who had the moral courage to stand up for their rights.'" In 1960, Nashville student activist Diane Nash discovered that she and other sit-in protesters had become part of "a group of people suddenly proud to be called 'black.'" SNCC's use of the black panther symbol in Lowndes County, Alabama, also symbolized the increasingly militant spirit of the southern black struggle. By the mid-1960s, in short, a new racial consciousness—a positive identification with African-American history and an optimism about the destiny of the race—was evident among black veterans of the southern struggle.

Besides drawing on their own experiences, some black civil rights activists increasingly absorbed the ideas of Elijah Muhammad, Malcolm X, and other northern advocates of black nationalism. After passage of the Civil Rights Acts of 1964 and 1965, organizers in the Deep South recognized that they still confronted major problems similar to those of northern blacks. They appreciated Malcolm's effectiveness in overcoming the psychological and cultural legacies of black oppression. Malcolm had instilled a positive sense of racial identity among northern urban blacks. As the objectives and class composition of the black struggle broadened, SNCC organizers in the Deep South sought ways to deal with the deeply rooted feelings of racial inferiority that were the legacy of southern racism. Recognizing the need to build enduring locally controlled institutions, they sought to develop the leadership abilities of southern blacks. Determined to avoid making black residents dependent on outside organizers, they worked closely with local leaders, adopting the slogan, "Our job is to work ourselves out of a job." After the 1964 Mississippi Summer Project, organizers confronted the difficult issue of whether white volunteers could work effectively in black communities without undermining local leadership. Would the presence of whites reinforce feelings of racial dependence? They also questioned whether interracial activism and appeals for federal intervention would be effective in seeking economic and political rather than civil rights goals. One of the results of the disillusionment felt by many activists after the Democratic Convention in Atlantic City was the desire to create alternative, independent, black-led political institutions, such as the Lowndes County Freedom Organization. In the spring of 1966, a SNCC position paper suggested the future direction of black militancy by insisting that "white participation, as practiced in the past, is now obsolete." Effective organizing in black communities, the authors argued, required a climate in which blacks could advance themselves without the inhibiting presence of whites. The paper called for "a mystique" of black leadership: "If we are to proceed toward true liberation, we must cut ourselves off from white people. We must form our own institutions, credit unions, co-ops, political parties, write our own histories." Soon after the position paper was written, SNCC's new chair, Stokely Carmichael, popularized the Black Power slogan when he publicly challenged King's interracial strategy during a march through Mississippi that began after the attempted assassination of James Meredith.

The growing racial militancy among black activists had sources outside as well as inside the civil rights movement. Conclusions drawn from years of organizing in southern communities often coincided with the concepts associated with the northern black nationalist movements. Malcolm X, in particular, became an increasingly significant source of ideas for black militants after he left the Nation of Islam and openly challenged the apolitical and accommodationist views of the Nation's leader, Elijah Muhammad. Malcolm's chance meeting in Africa during the fall of 1964 with touring SNCC representatives John Lewis and Don Harris was only one of a series of interactions during 1964 and 1965 involving Malcolm and young black civil rights activists. Shortly before his assassination in February 1965, Malcolm addressed Selma demonstrators at the invitation of SNCC. After his death, Malcolm's ideas regarding the need for racial pride, pan-African unity, and black control of black community institutions became increasingly popular among blacks.

By the end of 1966, the interracial coalition that had supported earlier civil rights reforms disintegrated as a result of a "white backlash" against black demands and a divisive debate over the Black Power slogan. Although many journalists and political leaders attacked Malcolm, Carmichael, and other Black Power advocates, the ideas of such leaders quickly gained support in black communities. King, Roy Wilkins of the NAACP, and Whitney Young of the Urban League joined most white leaders in denouncing black separatist sentiments. But Carmichael, Floyd McKissick of CORE, Congressman Adam Clayton Powell, and many others competed to define the ideas behind the slogan. The 1967 Black Power Conference in Newark, New Jersey, initiated a series of gatherings that would establish a new ideological foundation for African-American politics in subsequent decades.

Many of the ideas associated with the Black Power slogan—the importance of positive racial identity, study of black history, and recognition of the need for black-controlled institutions—eventually became widely accepted. Black Power had many different definitions, however, and ideological disputes undermined racial unity even among black leaders who called for it. Agreement on the need for black power and pride did not prevent bitter and sometimes deadly conflicts between advocates of revolutionary nationalism and advocates of cultural nationalism, between black socialists (or African communalists) and black capitalists, and between militant protesters and dissenters and proponents of electoral politics. Countless new groups and leaders appeared during the last half of the 1960s, reflecting the growing diversity within black political life. The political debate also prompted and reflected a transformation of African-American culture as black artists and writers sought to clarify the meaning of "blackness." Perhaps the most significant cultural leaders of the period were poet and dramatist LeRoi Jones, who changed his name to Amiri Baraka, and cultural theorist Maulana Karenga, founder of the California-based US group and one of the organizers of the 1967 Newark Conference. Other important definers of the new "black aesthetic" included Sonia Sanchez, Addison Gayle, Jr., Larry Neal, and Haki Madhubuti (formerly Don L. Lee). In short, the debate over Black Power ignited an exciting, unpredictable, and tumultuous period of African-American intellectual and cultural development.

1. "Message to the Grass Roots"
Malcolm X

A prefatory note in Malcolm X Speaks, *edited by George Breitman, explains the context for this speech, delivered shortly before Malcolm X's break with Elijah Muhammad and the Nation of Islam: "In late 1963, the Detroit Council for Human Rights announced a Northern Negro Leadership Conference to be held in Detroit on November 9 and 10. When the council's chairman, Rev. C. L. Franklin, sought to exclude black nationalists and Freedom Now Party advocates from the conference, Rev. Albert B. Cleage, Jr., resigned from the council and, in collaboration with the Group On Advanced Leadership (GOAL), arranged for a Northern Negro Grass Roots Leadership Conference. This was held in Detroit at the same time as the more conservative gathering, which was addressed by Congressman Adam Clayton Powell among others. The two-day Grass Roots conference was climaxed by a large public rally at the King Solomon Baptist Church, with Rev. Cleage, journalist William Worthy, and Malcolm X as the chief speakers. The audience, almost all black and with non-Muslims in the great majority, interrupted Malcolm with applause and laughter so often that he asked it to desist because of the lateness of the hour. A few weeks after the conference, President Kennedy was assassinated and Elijah Muhammad silenced Malcolm X. This is, therefore, one of the last speeches Malcolm gave before leaving Muhammad's organization. . . . But it is not a typical Black Muslim speech. Even though Malcolm continued to preface certain statements with the phrase, 'The Honorable Elijah Muhammad says,' he was increasingly, in the period before the split, giving his own special stamp to the Black Muslims' ideas, including the idea of separation."*

We want to have just an off-the-cuff chat between you and me, us. We want to talk right down to earth in a language that everybody here can easily understand. We all agree tonight, all of the speakers have agreed, that America has a very serious problem. Not only does America have a very serious problem, but our people have a very serious problem. The only reason she has a problem is she doesn't want us here. And every time you look at yourself, be you black, brown, red or yellow, a so-called Negro, you represent a person who poses such a serious problem for America because you're not wanted. Once you face this as a fact, then you can start plotting a course that will make you appear intelligent, instead of unintelligent.

What you and I need to do is learn to forget our differences. When we come together, we don't come together as Baptists or Methodists. You don't catch hell because you're a Baptist, and you don't catch hell because you're a Methodist. You don't catch hell because you're a Methodist or Baptist, you don't catch hell because you're a Democrat or Republican, you don't catch hell because you're a Mason or an Elk, and you sure don't catch hell because you're an American; because if you were an American, you wouldn't catch hell. You catch hell because you're a black man. You catch hell, all of us catch hell, for the same reason.

So we're all black people, so-called Negroes, second-class citizens, ex-slaves. You're nothing but an ex-slave. You don't like to be told that. But what else are you? You are ex-slaves. You didn't come here on the "Mayflower." You came here on a slave ship. In chains, like a horse, or a cow, or a chicken. And you were brought here by the people who came here on the "Mayflower," you were brought here by the so-called Pilgrims, or Founding Fathers. They were the ones who brought you here.

We have a common enemy. We have this in common: We have a common oppressor, a common exploiter, and a common discriminator. But once we all realize that we have a common enemy, then we unite—on the basis of what we have in common. And what we have foremost in common is that enemy—the white man. He's an enemy to all of us. I know some of you all think that some of them aren't enemies. Time will tell.

In Bandung back in, I think, 1954, was the first unity meeting in centuries of black people. And once you study what happened at the Bandung conference, and the results of the Bandung conference, it actually serves as a model for the same procedure you and I can use to get our problems solved. At Bandung all the nations came together, the dark nations from Africa and Asia. Some of them were Buddhists, some of them were Muslims, some of them were Christians, some were Confucianists, some were atheists. Despite their religious differences, they came together.

Some were communists, some were socialists, some were capital-ists—despite their economic and political differences, they came together. All of them were black, brown, red or yellow.

The number-one thing that was not allowed to attend the Bandung conference was the white man. He couldn't come. Once they excluded the white man, they found that they could get together. Once they kept him out, everybody else fell right in and fell in line. This is the thing that you and I have to understand. And these people who came together didn't have nuclear weapons, they didn't have jet planes, they didn't have all of the heavy armaments that the white man has. But they had unity.

They were able to submerge their little petty differences and agree on one thing: That one African came from Kenya and was being colonized by the Englishman, and another African came from the Congo and was being colonized by the Belgian, and another African came from Guinea and was being colonized by the French, and another came from Angola and was being colonized by the Portuguese. When they came to the Bandung conference, they looked at the Portuguese, and at the Frenchman, and at the Englishman, and at the Dutchman, and learned or realized the one thing that all of them had in common—they were all from Europe, they were all Europeans, blond, blue-eyed and white skins. They began to recognize who their enemy was. The same man that was colonizing our people in Kenya was colonizing our people in the Congo. The same one in the Congo was colonizing our people in South Africa, and in Southern Rhodesia, and in Burma, and in India, and in Afghanistan, and in Pakistan. They realized all over the world where the dark man was being oppressed, he was being oppressed by the white man; where the dark man was being exploited, he was being exploited by the white man. So they got together on this basis—that they had a common enemy.

And when you and I here in Detroit and in Michigan and in America who have been awakened today look around us, we too realize here in America we all have a common enemy, whether he's in Georgia or Michigan, whether he's in California or New York. He's the same man—blue eyes and blond hair and pale skin—the same man. So what we have to do is what they did. They agreed to stop quarreling among themselves. Any little spat that they had, they'd settle it among themselves, go into a huddle—don't let the enemy know that you've got a disagreement.

Instead of airing our differences in public, we have to realize we're all the same family. And when you have a family squabble, you don't get out on the sidewalk. If you do, everybody calls you uncouth, unrefined, uncivilized, savage. If you don't make it at home, you settle it at home; you get in the closet, argue it out behind closed doors, and then when you come out on the street, you pose a common front, a united front. And this is what we need to do in the community, and in the city, and in the state. We need to stop airing our differences in front of the white man, put the white man out of our meetings, and then sit down and talk shop with each other. That's what we've got to do.

I would like to make a few comments concerning the difference between the black revolution and the Negro revolution. Are they both the same? And if they're not, what is the difference? What is the difference between a black revolution and a Negro revolution? First, what is a revolution? Sometimes I'm inclined to believe that many of our people are using this word "revolution" loosely, without taking careful consideration of what this word actually means, and what its historic characteristics are. When you study the historic nature of revolutions, the motive of a revolution, the objective of a revolution, the result of a revolution, and the methods used in a revolution, you may change words. You may devise another program, you may change your goal and you may change your mind.

Look at the American Revolution in 1776. That revolution was for what? For land. Why did they want land? Independence. How was it carried out? Bloodshed. Number one, it was based on land, the basis of independence. And the only way they could get it was bloodshed. The French Revolution—what was it based on? The landless against the landlord. What was it for? Land. How did they get it? Bloodshed. Was no love lost, was no compromise, was no negotiation. I'm telling you—you don't know what a revolution is. Because when you find out what it is, you'll get back in the alley, you'll get out of the way.

The Russian Revolution—what was it based on? Land; the landless against the landlord. How did they bring it about? Bloodshed. You haven't got a revolution that doesn't involve bloodshed. And you're afraid to bleed. I said, you're afraid to bleed.

As long as the white man sent you to Korea, you bled. He sent you to Germany, you bled. He sent you to the South Pacific to fight the Japanese, you bled. You bleed for white people, but when it comes to seeing your own churches being bombed and little black girls murdered, you haven't got any blood. You bleed when the white man says bleed; you bite when the white man says bite; and you bark when the white man says bark. I hate to say this about us, but it's true. How are you going to be nonviolent in Mississippi, as violent as you were in Korea? How can you justify being nonviolent in Mississippi and Alabama, when your churches are being bombed, and your little girls are being murdered, and at the same time you are going to get violent with Hitler, and Tōjō, and somebody else you don't even know?

If violence is wrong in America, violence is wrong abroad. If it is wrong to be violent defending black women and black children and black babies and black men, then it is wrong for America to draft us and make us violent abroad in defense of her. And if it is right for America to draft us, and teach us how to be violent in defense of her, then it is right for you and me to do whatever is necessary to defend our own people right here in this country.

The Chinese Revolution—they wanted land. They threw the British out, along with the Uncle Tom Chinese. Yes, they did. They set a good example. When I was in prison, I read an article— don't be shocked when I say that I was in prison. You're still in prison. That's what America means: prison. When I was in prison, I read an article in *Life* magazine showing a little Chinese girl, nine years old; her father was on his hands and knees and she was pulling the trigger because he was an Uncle Tom Chinaman. When they had the revolution over there, they took a whole generation of Uncle Toms and just wiped them out. And within ten years that little girl became a full-grown woman. No more Toms in China. And today it's one of the toughest, roughest, most feared countries on this earth—by the white man. Because there are no Uncle Toms over there.

Of all our studies, history is best qualified to reward our research. And when you see that you've got problems, all you have to do is examine the historic method used all over the world by others who have problems similar to yours. Once you see how they got theirs straight, then you know how you can get yours straight. There's been a revolution, a black revolution, going on in Africa. In Kenya, the Mau Mau were revolutionary; they were the ones who brought the word "Uhuru" to the fore. The Mau Mau, they were revolutionary, they believed in scorched earth, they knocked everything aside that got in their way, and their revolution also was based on land, a desire for land. In Algeria, the northern part of Africa, a revolution took place. The Algerians were revolutionists, they wanted land. France offered to let them be integrated into France. They told France, to hell with France, they wanted some land, not some France. And they engaged in a bloody battle.

So I cite these various revolutions, brothers and sisters, to show you that you don't have a peaceful revolution. You don't have a turn-the-other-cheek revolution. There's no such thing as a non-violent revolution. The only kind of revolution that is nonviolent is the Negro revolution. The only revolution in which the goal is loving your enemy is the Negro revolution. It's the only revolution in which the goal is a desegregated lunch counter, a desegregated theater, a desegregated park, and a desegregated public toilet; you can sit down next to white folks—on the toilet. That's no revolution. Revolution is based on land. Land is the basis of all independence. Land is the basis of freedom, justice, and equality.

The white man knows what a revolution is. He knows that the black revolution is world-wide in scope and in nature. The black revolution is sweeping Asia, is sweeping Africa, is rearing its head in Latin America. The Cuban Revolution—that's a revolution. They overturned the system. Revolution is in Asia, revolution is in Africa, and the white man is screaming because he sees revolution in Latin America. How do you think he'll react to you when you learn what a real revolution is? You don't know what a revolution is. If you did, you wouldn't use that word.

Revolution is bloody, revolution is hostile, revolution knows no compromise, revolution overturns and destroys everything that gets in its way. And you, sitting around here like a knot on the wall, saying, "I'm going to love these folks no matter how much they hate me." No, you need a revolution. Whoever heard of a revolution where they lock arms, as Rev. Cleage was pointing out beautifully, singing "We Shall Overcome"? You don't do that in a revolution. You don't do any singing, you're too busy swinging. It's based on land. A revolutionary wants land so he can set up his own nation, an independent nation. These Negroes aren't asking for any nation—they're trying to crawl back on the plantation.

When you want a nation, that's called nationalism. When the white man became involved in a revolution in this country against England, what was it for? He wanted this land so he could set up another white nation. That's white nationalism. The American Revolution was white nationalism. The French Revolution was white nationalism. The Russian Revolution too—yes, it was—white nationalism. You don't think so? Why do you think Khrushchev and Mao can't get their heads together? White nationalism. All the revolutions that are going on in Asia and Africa today are based on what?—black nationalism. A revolutionary is a black nationalist. He wants a nation. I was reading some beautiful words by Rev. Cleage, pointing out why he couldn't get together with someone else in the city because all of them were afraid of being identified with black nationalism. If you're afraid of black nationalism, you're afraid of revolution. And if you love revolution, you love black nationalism.

To understand this, you have to go back to what the young brother here referred to as the house Negro and the field Negro back during slavery. There were two kinds of slaves, the house Negro and the field Negro. The house Negroes—they lived in the house with master, they dressed pretty good, they ate good because they ate his food—what he left. They lived in the attic or the basement, but still they lived near the master; and they loved the master more than the master loved himself. They would give their life to save the master's house—quicker than the master would. If the master said, "We got a good house here," the house Negro would say, "Yeah, we got a good house here." Whenever the master said "we," he said "we." That's how you can tell a house Negro.

If the master's house caught on fire, the house Negro would fight harder to put the blaze out than the master would. If the master got sick, the house Negro would say, "What's the matter, boss, *we* sick?" *We* sick! He identified himself with his master, more than his master identified with himself. And if you came to the house Negro and said, "Let's run away, let's escape, let's separate," the house Negro would look at you and say, "Man, you crazy. What you mean, separate? Where is there a better house than this? Where can I wear better clothes than this? Where can I eat better food than this?" That was that house Negro. In those days he was called a "house nigger." And that's what we call them today, because we've still got some house niggers running around here.

This modern house Negro loves his master. He wants to live near him. He'll pay three times as much as the house is worth just to live near his master, and then brag about "I'm the only Negro out here." "I'm the only one on my job." "I'm the only one in this school." You're nothing but a house Negro. And if someone comes to you right now and says, "Let's separate," you say the same thing that the house Negro said on the plantation. "What you mean, separate? From America, this good white man? Where you going to get a better job than you get here?" I mean, this is what you say. "I ain't left nothing in Africa," that's what you say. Why, you left your mind in Africa.

On that same plantation, there was the field Negro. The field Negroes—those were the masses. There were always more Negroes in the field than there were Negroes in the house. The Negro in the field caught hell. He ate leftovers. In the house they ate high up on the hog. The Negro in the field didn't get anything but what was left of the insides of the hog. They call it "chitt'lings" nowadays. In those days they called them what they were—guts. That's what you were—gut-eaters. And some of you are still gut-eaters.

The field Negro was beaten from morning to night; he lived in a shack, in a hut; he wore old, castoff clothes. He hated his master. I say he hated his master. He was intelligent. That house Negro loved his master, but that field Negro—remember, they were in the majority, and they hated the master. When the house caught on fire, he didn't try to put it out; that field Negro prayed for a wind, for a breeze. When the master got sick, the field Negro prayed that he'd die. If someone came to the field Negro and said, "Let's separate, let's run," he didn't say, "Where we going?" He'd say, "Any place is better than here." You've got field Negroes in America today. I'm a field Negro. The masses are the field Negroes. When they see this man's house on fire, you don't hear the little Negroes talking about "*our* government is in trouble." They say, "*The* government is in trouble." Imagine a Negro: "*Our* government"! I even heard one say "*our* astronauts." They won't even let him near the plant—and "*our* astronauts"! "*Our* Navy"— that's a Negro that is out of his mind, a Negro that is out of his mind.

Just as the slavemaster of that day used Tom, the house Negro, to keep the field Negroes in check, the same old slavemaster today has Negroes who are nothing but modern Uncle Toms, twentieth-century Uncle Toms, to keep you and me in check, to keep us under control, keep us passive and peaceful and nonviolent. That's Tom making you nonviolent. It's like when you go to the dentist, and the man's going to take your tooth. You're going to fight him when he starts pulling. So he squirts some stuff in your jaw called novocaine, to make you think they're not doing anything to you. So you sit there and because you've got all of that novocaine in your jaw, you suffer—peacefully. Blood running down your jaw, and you don't know what's happening. Because someone has taught you to suffer—peacefully.

The white man does the same thing to you in the street, when he wants to put knots on your head and take advantage of you and not have to be afraid of your fighting back. To keep you from fighting back, he gets these old religious Uncle Toms to teach you and me, just like novocaine, to suffer peacefully. Don't stop suffering—just suffer peacefully. As Rev. Cleage pointed out, they say you should let your blood flow in the streets. This is a shame. You know he's a Christian preacher. If it's a shame to him, you know what it is to me.

There is nothing in our book, the Koran, that teaches us to suffer peacefully. Our religion teaches us to be intelligent. Be peaceful, be courteous, obey the law, respect everyone; but if someone puts his hand on you, send him to the cemetery. That's a good religion. In fact, that's that old-time religion. That's the one that Ma and Pa used to talk about: an eye for an eye, and a tooth for a tooth, and a head for a head, and a life for a life. That's a good religion. And nobody resents that kind of religion being taught but a wolf, who intends to make you his meal.

This is the way it is with the white man in America. He's a wolf—and you're sheep. Any time a shepherd, a pastor, teaches you and me not to run from the white man and, at the same time, teaches us not to fight the white man, he's a traitor to you and me. Don't lay down a life all by itself. No, preserve your life, it's the best thing you've got. And if you've got to give it up, let it be even-steven.

The slavemaster took Tom and dressed him well, fed him well and even gave him a little education—a *little* education; gave him a long coat and a top hat and made all the other slaves look up to him. Then he used Tom to control them. The same strategy that was used in those days is used today, by the same white man. He takes a Negro, a so-called Negro, and makes him prominent, builds him up, publicizes him, makes him a celebrity. And then he becomes a spokesman for Negroes—and a Negro leader.

I would like to mention just one other thing quickly, and that is the method that the white man uses, how the white man uses the "big guns," or Negro leaders, against the Negro revolution. They are not a part of the Negro revolution. They are used against the Negro revolution.

When Martin Luther King failed to desegregate Albany, Georgia, the civil-rights struggle in America reached its low point. King became bankrupt almost, as a leader. The Southern Christian Leadership Conference was in financial trouble; and it was in trouble, period, with the people when they failed to desegregate Albany, Georgia. Other Negro civil-rights leaders of so-called national stature became fallen idols. As they became fallen idols, began to lose their prestige and influence, local Negro leaders began to stir up the masses. In Cambridge, Maryland, Gloria Richardson; in Danville, Virginia, and other parts of the country, local leaders began to stir up our people at the grass-roots level. This was never done by these Negroes of national stature. They control you, but they have never incited you or excited you. They control you, they contain you, they have kept you on the plantation. As soon as King failed in Birmingham, Negroes took to the streets. King went out to California to a big rally and raised I don't know how many thousands of dollars. He came to Detroit and had a march and raised some more thousands of dollars. And recall, right after that Roy Wilkins attacked King. He accused King and

CORE [Congress of Racial Equality] of starting trouble everywhere and then making the NAACP [National Association for the Advancement of Colored People] get them out of jail and spend a lot of money; they accused King and CORE of raising all the money and not paying it back. This happened; I've got it in documented evidence in the newspaper. Roy started attacking King, and King started attacking Roy, and Farmer started attacking both of them. And as these Negroes of national stature began to attack each other, they began to lose their control of the Negro masses.

The Negroes were out there in the streets. They were talking about how they were going to march on Washington. Right at that time Birmingham had exploded, and the Negroes in Birmingham—remember, they also exploded. They began to stab the crackers in the back and bust them up 'side their head—yes, they did. That's when Kennedy sent in the troops, down in Birmingham. After that, Kennedy got on the television and said "this is a moral issue." That's when he said he was going to put out a civil-rights bill. And when he mentioned civil-rights bill and the Southern crackers started talking about how they were going to boycott or filibuster it, then the Negroes started talking—about what? That they were going to march on Washington, march on the Senate, march on the White House, march on the Congress, and tie it up, bring it to a halt, not let the government proceed. They even said they were going out to the airport and lay down on the runway and not let any airplanes land. I'm telling you what they said. That was revolution. That was revolution. That was the black revolution.

It was the grass roots out there in the street. It scared the white man to death, scared the white power structure in Washington, D.C., to death; I was there. When they found out that this black steamroller was going to come down on the capital, they called in Wilkins, they called in Randolph, they called in these national Negro leaders that you respect and told them, "Call it off." Kennedy said, "Look, you all are letting this thing go too far." And Old Tom said, "Boss, I can't stop it, because I didn't start it." I'm telling you what they said. They said, "I'm not even in it, much less at the head of it." They said, "These Negroes are doing things on their own. They're running ahead of us." And that old shrewd fox, he said, "If you all aren't in it, I'll put you in it. I'll put you at the head of it. I'll endorse it. I'll welcome it. I'll help it. I'll join it."

A matter of hours went by. They had a meeting at the Carlyle Hotel in New York City. The Carlyle Hotel is owned by the Kennedy family; that's the hotel Kennedy spent the night at, two nights ago; it belongs to his family. A philanthropic society headed by a white man named Stephen Currier called all the top civil-rights leaders together at the Carlyle Hotel. And he told them, "By you all fighting each other, you are destroying the civil-rights movement. And since you're fighting over money from white liberals, let us set up what is known as the Council for United Civil Rights Leadership. Let's form this council, and all the civil-rights organizations will belong to it, and we'll use it for fund-raising purposes." Let me show you how tricky the white man is. As soon as they got it formed, they elected Whitney Young as its chairman, and who do you think became the co-chairman? Stephen Currier, the white man, a millionaire. Powell was talking about it down at Cobo Hall today. This is what he was talking about. Powell knows it happened. Randolph knows it happened. Wilkins knows it happened. King knows it happened. Every one of that Big Six—they know it happened.

Once they formed it, with the white man over it, he promised them and gave them $800,000 to split up among the Big Six; and told them that after the march was over they'd give them $700,000 more. A million and a half dollars—split up between leaders that you have been following, going to jail for, crying crocodile tears for. And they're nothing but Frank James and Jesse James and the what-do-you-call-'em brothers.

As soon as they got the setup organized, the white man made available to them top public-relations experts; opened the news media across the country at their disposal, which then began to project these Big Six as the leaders of the march. Originally they weren't even in the march. You were talking this march talk on Hastings Street, you were talking march talk on Lenox Avenue, and on Fillmore Street, and on Central Avenue, and on 32nd Street and 63rd Street. That's where the march talk was being talked. But the white man put the Big Six at the head of it; made them the march. They became the march. They took it over. And the first move they made after they took it over, they invited Walter Reuther, a white man; they invited a priest, a rabbi, and an old white preacher, yes, an old white preacher. The same white element that put Kennedy into power—labor, the Catholics, the Jews, and liberal Protestants; the same clique that put Kennedy in power, joined the march on Washington.

It's just like when you've got some coffee that's too black, which means it's too strong. What do you do? You integrate it with cream, you make it weak. But if you pour too much cream in it, you won't even know you ever had coffee. It used to be hot, it becomes cool. It used to be strong, it becomes weak. It used to wake you up, now it puts you to sleep. This is what they did with the march on Washington. They joined it. They didn't integrate it, they infiltrated it. They joined it, became a part of it, took it over. And as they took it over, it lost its militancy. It ceased to be angry, it ceased to be hot, it ceased to be uncompromising. Why, it even ceased to be a march. It became a picnic, a circus. Nothing but a circus, with clowns and all. You had one right here in Detroit—I saw it on television—with clowns leading it, white clowns and black clowns. I know you don't like what I'm saying, but I'm going to tell you anyway. Because I can prove what I'm saying. If you think I'm telling you wrong, you bring me Martin Luther King and A. Philip Randolph and James Farmer and those other three, and see if they'll deny it over a microphone.

No, it was a sellout. It was a takeover. When James Baldwin came in from Paris, they wouldn't let him talk, because they couldn't make him go by the script. Burt Lancaster read the speech that Baldwin was supposed to make; they wouldn't let Baldwin get up there, because they know Baldwin is liable to say anything. They controlled it so tight, they told those Negroes what time to hit town, how to come, where to stop, what signs to carry, what song to sing, what speech they could make, and what speech they couldn't make; and then told them to get out of town by sundown. And every one of those Toms was out of town by sundown. Now I know you don't like my saying this. But I can back it up. It was a circus, a performance that beat anything Hollywood could ever do, the performance of the year. Reuther and those other three devils should get an Academy Award for the best actors because they acted like they really loved Negroes and fooled a whole lot of Negroes. And the six Negro leaders should get an award too, for the best supporting cast.

2. "Malcolm"
Sonia Sanchez

The poet, playwright, and teacher Sonia Sanchez first encountered Malcolm X in the early 1960s when she was working with the Congress of Racial Equality in New York. She wrote this tribute to him shortly after his assassination in February 1965.

Do not speak to me of martyrdom
of men who die to be remembered
on some parish day.
I don't believe in dying
though I too shall die
and violets like castanets
will echo me.

Yet this man
this dreamer,
thick-lipped with words
will never speak again
and in each winter
when the cold air cracks
with frost, I'll breathe
his breath and mourn
my gun-filled nights.

He was the sun that tagged
the western sky and
melted tiger-scholars
while they searched for stripes.
He said, "Fuck you white
man. we have been
curled too long. nothing
is sacred now. not your

white face nor any
land that separates
until some voices
squat with spasms."

Do not speak to me of living.
life is obscene with crowds
of white on black.
death is my pulse.
what might have been
is not for him/or me
but what could have been
floods the womb until I drown.

3. "Black Belt Election: New Day A'Coming"

Stokely Carmichael and Charles V. Hamilton

In the immediate aftermath of the Selma-to-Montgomery march, several SNCC workers—including future chairman Stokely Carmichael (now Kwame Turé), who had already earned his organizing spurs in the Mississippi Delta in 1963 and 1964, focused their efforts on Lowndes County, Alabama, the hard-core segregationist stronghold lying between Selma and Montgomery and through which the marchers had passed. This is an excerpt from Black Power: The Politics of Liberation in America *(1967), by Carmichael and political scientist Charles V. Hamilton.*

. . . In March, 1965, not one black person was even registered to vote; over the next twenty months, close to 3,900 black people had not only registered but also formed a political organization, held a nominating convention and slated seven of their members to run for county public office. . . . If ever the political scientists wanted to study the phenomenon of political development or political modernization in this country, here was the place: in the heart of the "black belt," that range of Southern areas characterized by the predominance of black people and rich black soil.

Most local black people readily admit that the catalyst for change was the appearance in the county in March and April, 1965, of a handful of workers from SNCC. They had gone there almost immediately after the murder of Mrs. Viola Liuzzo, on the final night of the Selma to Montgomery March. Mrs. Liuzzo, a white housewife from Detroit, had been driving marchers home when she was shot down by Klansmen on that same Highway 80 in Lowndes County. For the black people of Lowndes, her murder came as no great surprise: Lowndes had one of the nation's worst records for individual and institutional racism, a reputation for brutality that made white as well as black Alabama shiver. In this county, eighty-one percent black, the whites had ruled the entire area and subjugated black people to that rule unmercifully. Lowndes was a prime area for SNCC to apply certain assumptions learned over the years of work in rural, backwoods counties of the South.

SNCC had long understood that one of the major obstacles to helping black people organize structures which could effectively fight institutional racism was *fear*. The history of the county shows that black people could come together to do only three things: sing, pray, dance. Any time they came together to do anything else, they were threatened or intimidated. For decades, black people had been taught to believe that voting, politics, is "white folks' business." And the white folks had indeed monopolized that business, by methods which ran the gamut from economic intimidation to murder.

The situation in Lowndes was particularly notable inasmuch as civil rights battles had been waged on an extensive scale in two adjoining counties for years: in Dallas County (Selma) and in Montgomery County. The city of Montgomery had seen a powerful movement, led by Dr. Martin Luther King, Jr., beginning in 1955 with the bus boycott. But Lowndes County did not appear affected by this activity. This is even more striking when one considers that at least seventeen percent of the black people in Lowndes work in Montgomery and at least sixty percent of the black people do their major shopping there. Lowndes was a truly totalitarian society—the epitome of the tight, insulated police state. SNCC people felt that if they could help crack Lowndes, other areas—with less brutal reputations—would be easier to organize. This might be considered a kind of SNCC Domino Theory.

There were several black organizations in Lowndes County, all centered around the church. . . . Some of the most politically-oriented people who subsequently formed the Lowndes County Freedom Organization were those experienced in the internal politics of the church. The ability and power of these local leaders, however, rested inside the black community and was geared toward religious and social affairs only. Many people who were very political *inside* those organizations were unwilling to enter the *public* political arena. They were afraid.

The black people most respected by the whites in Lowndes County were the school teachers and the two high school principals. But, as in many southern communities, they were at the mercy of the white power structure. They held their positions at the sufferance of the whites; the power they had was delegated to them by the white community. And what the master giveth, the master can take away. The power of the black principals and teachers did not come from the black community, because that community was not organized around public political power. In this sense, they were typical "Negro Establishment" figures.

The question of leadership in the county was crucial. If there was to be a sustained political assault on racism, the black people would have to develop a viable leadership group. The white-established Negro leaders—the teachers, principals—were looked up to by the black community because they could get certain things done. They could intercede with the white man, and they had certain overt credentials of success: a big car, a nice house, good clothes. The black ministers constituted another source of leadership. They have traditionally been the leaders in the black community, but their power lay inside the black community, not with the white power structure. In some cases, they could ask white people to do certain things for black people, but they did not have the relative power possessed by the white-made leaders. The ministers, likewise, could invoke the authority of God; they were, after all, "called to preach the gospel," and, therefore, their word had almost a kind of divine authority in the black community.

———————

There was another set of leaders in the black community of Lowndes County. This was a group of middle-aged ladies, who knew the community well and were well known. They were to play a very important role in the political organization of the blacks. They had considerable influence in the black community—being staunch church members, for example—but they possessed no power at all with the white community.

Economically, Lowndes County is not noted for its equitable distribution of goods and income. The average income of blacks, most of them sharecroppers and tenant farmers, is about $985 per year. Eighty-six white families own ninety percent of the land. Inside the black community, there were in 1965 few people who had running water in their houses; only about twenty families had steam heat, and the rest got by with stove burners and wood fireplaces to keep warm. The economic insecurity of the latter is obvious, yet as we have seen, even the "Negro Establishment" faced disaster if they started meddling in "white folks business."

Against these odds, there had somehow been in Lowndes County a long history of black men who started to fight—but were always cut down. Mr. Emory Ross, who later became an active participant in the Lowndes County Freedom Organization, had a father who was a fighter. He was shot at several times; his house riddled with bullets; his home burned down at one time. But he continued to struggle, and he was able to impart his determination to his son.

There were a few more like him. Spurred by the demonstrations and Dr. King's presence in Selma in early 1965, some seventeen brave people rallied around Mr. John Hulett, a lifelong resident of the County, to form the Lowndes County Christian Movement for Human Rights in March of that year. SNCC workers began moving around the county shortly afterward, talking a strange language: "Political power is the first step to independence and freedom." "You can control this county politically." It was exceptionally difficult at first to get black people to go to the courthouse to register—the first step. The fight at that point was waged simply in terms of being able to establish within the black community a sense of the *right* to fight racial oppression and exploitation. This was a battle of no small proportion, because black people in this county—many of them—did not even feel that they had the *right* to fight. In addition, they felt that their fight would be meaningless. They remembered those who had been cut down.

From March to August, 1965, about fifty to sixty black citizens made their way to the courthouse to register and successfully passed the registration "test." Then, in August, the 1965 Voting Rights Act was passed and federal "examiners" or registrars came into the county. No longer did a black man face literacy tests or absurdly difficult questions about the Constitution or such tactics as rejection because one "t" was not properly crossed or an "i" inadequately dotted. The voting rolls swelled by the hundreds. . . .

The *act* of registering to vote does several things. It marks the beginning of political modernization by broadening the base of participation. It also does something the existentialists talk about: it gives one a sense of being. The black man who goes to register is saying to the white man, "No." He is saying: "You have said that I cannot vote. You have said that this is my place. This is where I should remain. You have contained me and I am saying 'No' to your containment. I am stepping out of the bounds. I am saying 'No' to you and thereby I am creating a better life for myself. I am resisting someone who has contained me." That is what the first act does. The black person begins to live. He begins to create his *own* existence when he says "No" to someone who contains him.

But obviously this is not enough. Once the black man has knocked back centuries of fear, once he is willing to resist, he then must decide how best to use that vote. To listen to those whites who conspired for so many years to deny him the ballot would be a return to that previous subordinated condition. He must move independently. The development of this awareness is a job as tedious and laborious as inspiring people to register in the first place. In fact, many people who would aspire to the role of an organizer drop off simply because they do not have the energy, the stamina, to knock on doors day after day. That is why one finds many such people sitting in coffee shops talking and theorizing instead of organizing.

The SNCC research staff discovered an unusual Alabama law which permits a group to organize a potential political party on a county-wide basis. . . . The black people of Lowndes County and SNCC then began the hard work of building a legitimate, independent political party with no help from anyone else. Virtually the entire country condemned this decision; it was "separatism";

it was traditionally doomed "third-party politics" and the only way to succeed was through one of the two established parties. Some even said that the black voters of Lowndes County should support the Democratic party out of gratitude for being given the vote. But the Democratic party did not give black people the right to vote; it simply stopped denying black people the right to vote.

In March, 1966, the Lowndes County Freedom Organization was born with the immediate goals of running candidates and becoming a recognized party. In building the LCFO, it was obviously wise to attempt first to recruit those black people who owned land and were therefore somewhat more secure economically than those without property. But there were few of them. Those without property, merely sharecropping on white-owned plantations, were subject to being kicked off the land for their political activity. This is exactly what had happened at the end of December, 1965; some twenty families were evicted and spent the rest of the winter living in tents, with temperatures often below freezing. Their fate, and it was shared by others later, intensified the fear, but it also served to instill a sense of the tremendous need to establish an independent base of group power within the community. That base could lend support, security. Thus, despite the ever-present threat of loss of home and job and even possibly life, the black people of Lowndes County continued to build. Mass meetings were held weekly, each time in a different part of the county. Unity and strength, already developing over the winter, grew.

In May, 1966, the time arrived to put up black candidates in the primary election. . . .

The black people of Lowndes County were ready and made themselves even readier. Workshops were held, with SNCC's assistance, on the duties of the sheriff, the coroner, the tax assessor, tax collector and members of the Board of Education—the offices up for election. Booklets, frequently in the form of picture books, were prepared by SNCC and distributed over the county. People began to see and understand that no college education or special training was needed to perform these functions. They called primarily for determination and common sense, and black people in Lowndes had long since shown that they possessed these qualities.

The campaign which followed was hardly a typical American political campaign. There were no debates (or offers to debate) between the candidates; black candidates certainly did not canvass white voters and no white candidates made open appeals for black votes.

[Despite tremendous LCFO efforts, on election day, Nov. 8, 1966, all of the black candidates lost to their white competitors by margins of roughly 600 votes—2,200 to 1,600. Nonetheless, the LCFO drew clear lessons from the experience.]

The new Lowndes County Freedom Party is also aware that somehow it must counteract the economic dependence which so seriously impedes organizing. It must begin thinking of ways to build a "patronage" system—some sort of mechanism for offering day-to-day, bread-and-butter help to black people immediately in need. A prime example occurred on election day at 1 P.M., when a black family's home was completely destroyed by fire; fourteen children, ranging in age from four to eighteen, and two adults were left homeless and penniless. Immediate assistance in the form of clothes, food, and dollars coming from the Party would have been politically invaluable. It is true that the Party does not have the local resources to help every family burned out of their homes or kicked off the land or in need of a job, but it must begin to move in that direction. Such "patronage" should always be identified as coming from the Party. If necessary (and it undoubtedly will be necessary), drives in selected northern communities could be launched to help until the Party can show more substantial victories. Only so many black people will rush to the banner of "freedom" and "blackness" without seeing some way to make ends meet, to care for their children.

One way or another, the fact is that the John Huletts of the South will participate in political decision-making in their time and in their land. November 8, 1966, made one thing clear: some day black people will control the government of Lowndes County. For Lowndes is not merely a section of land and a group of people, but an idea whose time has come.

4. Lowndes County Freedom Organization Pamphlet

These are excerpts from a pamphlet prepared by the LCFO for use in educating black potential voters in Lowndes County.

VOTING

What Is the Vote?

Voting is the way a citizen chooses people to represent him in his county, state and federal government. When a citizen votes, he speaks for himself about things that concern his own welfare.

Why Vote?

If you don't vote, you give up your right to decide for yourself how you want things to be done in your government. Your voice never gets heard in politics if you don't vote.

How Does Voting Work?

First, you have to be registered. This means you have to go to have your name put on a list along with others who want to vote in elections in your county or state. Then you must pay the poll tax.

Can You Vote?

Yes. Any person can be a qualified voter if he or she is at least 21 years old, has lived in the state at least one year, in the county six months and in the precinct three months.

POLITICS

What Is Politics?

Politics is the coming together of people to make decisions about their lives. For example, who is going to be sheriff, who will be elected to the school board, who will be the mayor of your city.

However, in the past, Negroes have not been permitted to practice politics. A few people, most of them white, have worked in politics to benefit themselves.

How Have We Been Kept Out of Politics?

1. Certain laws and practices have kept Negroes from voting.
2. Negroes have been kept out of political parties.
3. Negroes have been beaten when they tried to register to vote, and told time and time again that politics and voting were "white folks' business."
4. They have told us that we are not "qualified" to practice politics, that we are not "qualified" to run our own lives! Everyone knows if he will think about it that each and every grown man and woman is just as "qualified" as anyone else to decide what he wants his life to be like. There may be some information that some of us need in order to decide how to go about making our lives what we want them to be, but we can get that information and we can learn it just as well as anyone else can.
5. They have told us that Negroes "just can't stick together."

Why Come Together?

When you come together you can determine who from your own community can do the thing you want done. If you don't come together, the people who have been running the show will put their own candidates up and vote for programs that will benefit them only and you will have no say at all.

What Can You Do When You Come Together?

If you are a qualified elector (voter), that is, if you have registered to vote and paid the poll tax for 2 years, you can form your own political organization.

How Can People Work Together in a Political Organization?

First of all, we have to stick together. Then we should decide what are our common needs. We can decide this by asking ourselves, "Will this program or this candidate help us and people like ourselves?" Once you have a political organization you can go out and talk to your neighbors and friends and even to strangers, and find others who are willing to work with you.

Why Form a Political Organization?

When you form a political organization you can nominate for office candidates of your own choosing, and in the general election, you can vote to put your candidate into office.

How Do You Form a Political Organization in Lowndes County, Alabama?

1. Alabama law says you cannot be a member of a political organization if you are not a qualified elector ** that is, you must be registered to vote and must have paid your poll tax.

2. Alabama law says that any organization of qualified electors can nominate candidates. The date for such meetings is May 3, 1966. The candidates must be nominated at this meeting. The general public may attend this mass meeting, but only members of the political organization may participate in the meeting.

In Lowndes County, you can nominate candidates for the offices of county sheriff, county tax assessor, county tax collector, county school board members, and circuit solicitors. Any qualified elector can run for these offices.

3. If they are running for a county office, the names of the candidates you choose at the mass meeting on May 3, 1966 must be sent to the probate judge of your county *at least 60 days before the date of the general election* (November 8, 1966). This certificate must contain the name of each person nominated and the office for which he was nominated, and must be signed by the president and recording secretary of the mass meeting. If the mass meeting of the organization nominates candidates for state or district the names of the candidates must be sent to the secretary of state instead of the probate judge. House District 29 (Lowndes and Autauga counties) can elect 1 representative to the House. Senate District 20 (Lowndes, Butler, Crenshaw and Covington) can elect 1 Senator.

4. If a candidate nominated by the organization at a mass meeting receives 20% or more of the vote cast in the . . . November 8, 1966 election for that office, the organization is declared by Alabama law to be a political party for and within the county.

If a candidate nominated for a state or district office receives 20% or more of the vote cast for that office in the state or district, the organization is declared by Alabama law to be a party for and within that state or district.

Alabama law says that if you nominate and run your own candidates, you cannot vote in either the Democratic or Republican primaries.

What Are the Rights and Privileges of a Political Organization?
Alabama law states that any political organization having a candidate on the ballot may appoint a person to watch at each polling place. The poll-watcher shall be permitted to be present at the place where the ballots are cast from the time the polls are opened until the ballots are counted and certificates of the result of the election are signed by the inspectors. The watchers shall be permitted to see the ballots as they are called during the count.

NOW IS THE TIME!

If ever we in Lowndes County had a chance to come together to make political decisions about our own lives—now is the time!

If ever there was a time for Negroes to leave the white supremacy Democratic party of Alabama alone—now is the time!

If ever we had a chance to do something about the years of low pay, beatings, burnings of homes, denial of the right to vote, bad education and washed-out roads—now is the time!

Join the
Lowndes County Freedom Organization
Rt.1, Box 191
Hayneville, Alabama

5. "How the Black Panther Party Was Organized"

John Hulett

Following are excerpts from a speech by John Hulett, chairman of the Lowndes County Freedom Organization, given in Los Angeles on May 22, 1966, at a meeting sponsored by a group of anti–Vietnam War committees.

. . . Some time ago, we organized a political group of our own known as the Lowndes County Freedom Organization, whose emblem is the black panther.

We were criticized, we were called communists, we were called everything else, black nationalists and whatnot, because we did this. Any group which starts at a time like this to speak out for what is right—they are going to be ridiculed. The people of Lowndes County realized this. Today we are moving further. . . .

Too long Negroes have been begging, especially in the South, for things they should be working for. So the people in Lowndes County decided to organize themselves—to go out and work for the things we wanted in life—not only for the people in Lowndes County, but for every county in the state of Alabama, in the Southern states, and even in California.

You cannot become free in California while there are slaves in Lowndes County. And no person can be free while other people are still slaves, nobody.

In Lowndes County, there is a committee in the Democratic Party. This committee not only controls the courthouse, it controls the entire county. When they found out that the Negroes were going to run candidates in the primary of the Democratic Party on May 3, they assembled themselves together and began to talk about what they were going to do. Knowing this is one of the poorest counties in the nation, what they decided to do was change the registration fees in the county.

Two years ago, if a person wanted to run for sheriff, tax collector or tax assessor, all he had to do was pay $50 and then he qualified to be the candidate. This year, the entrance fee is about $900. If a person wants to run, he has to pay $500 to run for office. In the primary, when they get through cheating and stealing, then the candidate is eliminated. So we decided that we wouldn't get into such a primary because we were tired of being tricked by Southern whites. After forming our own political group today, we feel real strong. We feel that we are doing the right thing in Lowndes County.

We have listened to everybody who wanted to talk, we listened to them speak, but one thing we had to learn for ourselves. As a group of people, we must think for ourselves and act on our own accord. And this we have done.

Through the years, Negroes in the South have been going for the bones while whites have been going for the meat. The Negroes of Lowndes County today are tired of the bones—we are going to have some of the meat too.

At the present time, we have our own candidates which have been nominated by the Lowndes County Freedom Organization. And we fear that this might not be enough to avoid the tricks that are going to be used in Lowndes County against us. . . .

In Lowndes County, the sheriff is the custodian of the courthouse. This is a liberal sheriff, too, who is "integrated," who walks around and pats you on the shoulder, who does not carry a gun. But at the same time, in the county where there are only 800 white men, there are 550 of them who walk around with a gun on them. They are deputies. This is true; it might sound like a fairy tale to most people, but this is true.

After talking to the sheriff about having the use of the courthouse lawn for our mass nominating meeting, not the courthouse but just the lawn, he refused to give the Negroes permission. We reminded him that last year in August, that one of the biggest Klan rallies that has ever been held in the state of Alabama was held on this lawn of this courthouse. And he gave them permission. A few weeks ago an individual who was campaigning for governor—he got permission to use it. He used all types of loudspeakers and anything that he wanted.

But he would not permit Negroes to have the use of the courthouse. For one thing he realized that we would build a party—and if he could keep us from forming our own political group then we would always stand at the feet of the Southern whites and of the Democratic Party. So we told him that we were going to have this meeting, we were going to have it here, on the courthouse lawn. And we wouldn't let anybody scare us off. We told him, we won't expect you to protect us, and if you don't, Negroes will protect themselves.

Then we asked him a second time to be sure he understood what we were saying. We repeated it to him the second time. And then we said to him, sheriff, if you come out against the people, then we are going to arrest you.

And he said, I will not give you permission to have this meeting here. I can't protect you from the community.

Then we reminded him that according to the law of the state of Alabama, that this mass meeting which was set up to nominate our candidates must be held in or around a voters' polling place. And if we decide to hold it a half a mile away from the courthouse, some individual would come up and protest our mass meeting. And our election would be thrown out.

So we wrote the Justice Department and told them what was going to happen in Lowndes County.

All of a sudden the Justice Department started coming in fast into the county. They said to me, John, what is going to happen next Tuesday at the courthouse?

I said, We are going to have our mass meeting. And he wanted to know where. And I said on the lawn of the courthouse.

He said, I thought the sheriff had told you you couldn't come there. And I said, Yes, but we are going to be there.

Then he wanted to know, if shooting takes place, what are we going to do. And I said, that we are going to stay out here and everybody die together.

And then he began to get worried, and I said, Don't worry. You're going to have to be here to see it out and there's no place to hide, so whatever happens, you can be a part of it.

And then he began to really panic. And he said, There's nothing I can do.

And I said, I'm not asking you to do anything. All I want you to know is we are going to have a mass meeting. If the sheriff cannot protect us, then we are going to protect ourselves. And I said to him, through the years in the South, Negroes have never had any protection, and today we aren't looking to anybody to protect us. We are going to protect ourselves.

That was on Saturday. On Sunday, at about 2 o'clock, we were having a meeting, and we decided among ourselves that we were going to start collecting petitions for our candidates to be sure that they got on the ballot. The state laws require at least 25 signatures of qualified electors and so we decided to get at least 100 for fear somebody might come up and find fault. And we decided to still have our mass meeting and nominate our candidates.

About 2:30, here comes the Justice Department again, and he was really worried. And he said he wasn't satisfied. He said to me, John, I've done all I can do, and I don't know what else I can do, and now it looks like you'll have to call this meeting off at the courthouse.

And I said, we're going to have it.

He stayed around for a while and then got in his car and drove off, saying, I'll see you tomorrow, maybe. And we stayed at this meeting from 2:30 until about 11:30 that night. About 11:15, the Justice Department came walking up the aisle of the church and said to me, Listen. I've talked to the Attorney General of the state of Alabama, and he said that you can go ahead and have a mass meeting at the church and it will be legal.

Then we asked him, Do you have any papers that say that's true, that are signed by the Governor or the Attorney General? And he said no. And we said to him, Go back and get it legalized, and bring it back here to us and we will accept it.

And sure enough, on Monday at 3 o'clock, I went to the courthouse and there in the sheriff's office were the papers all legalized and fixed up, saying that we could go to the church to have our mass meeting.

To me, this showed strength. When people are together, they can do a lot of things, but when you are alone you cannot do anything. . . .

There are 600 Negroes in the county who did not trust in themselves and who joined the Democratic Party. We warned the entire state of Alabama that running on the Democratic ticket could not do them any good, because this party is controlled by people like Wallace; and whoever won would have to do what these people said to do. . . .

Now, to me, the Democratic Party primaries and the Democratic Party is something like an integrated gambler who carries a card around in his pocket and every now and then he has to let somebody win to keep the game going. To me, this is what the Democratic Party means to the people in Alabama. It's a gambling game. And somebody's got to win to keep the game going every now and then. . . .

I would like to say here, and this is one thing I'm proud of, the people in Lowndes County stood together, and the 600 people who voted in the Democratic primary have realized one thing, that they were tricked by the Democratic Party. And now they too are ready to join us with the Lowndes County Freedom Organization whose emblem is the black panther.

We have seven people who are running for office this year in our county; namely, the coroner, three members of the board of education—and if we win those three, we will control the board of education—tax collector, tax assessor, and the individual who carries a gun at his side, the sheriff.

Let me say this—that a lot of persons tonight asked me, Do you really think if you win that you will be able to take it all over, and live?

I say to the people here tonight—yes, we're going to do it. If we have to do like the present sheriff, if we have to deputize every man in Lowndes County 21 and over, to protect people, we're going to do it.

There was something in Alabama a few months ago they called fear. Negroes were afraid to move on their own, they waited until the man, the people whose place they lived on, told them they could get registered. They told many people, don't you move until I tell you to move and when I give an order, don't you go down and get registered. . . .

Then all the people were being evicted at the same time and even today in Lowndes County, there are at least 75 families that have been evicted, some now are living in tents while some are living in one-room houses—with 8 or 9 in a family. Others have split their families up and are living together with their relatives or their friends. But they are determined to stay in Lowndes County, until justice rolls down like water.

Evicting the families wasn't all—there were other people who live on their own places who owe large debts, so they decided to foreclose on these debts to run Negroes off the place. People made threats—but we're going to stay there, we aren't going anywhere.

I would like to let the people here tonight know why we chose this black panther as our emblem. Many people have been asking this question for a long time. Our political group is open to whoever wants to come in, who would like to work with us. But we aren't begging anyone to come in. It's open, you come, at your own free will and accord.

But this black panther is a vicious animal as you know. He never bothers anything, but when you start pushing him, he moves backwards, backwards, and backwards into his corner, and then he comes out to destroy everything that's before him.

Negroes in Lowndes County have been pushed back through the years. We have been deprived of our rights to speak, to move, and to do whatever we want to do at all times. And now we are going to start moving. On November 8 of this year, we plan to take over the courthouse in Hayneville. And whatever it takes to do it, we're going to do it.

We've decided to stop begging. We've decided to stop asking for integration. Once we control the courthouse, once we control the board of education, we can build our school system where our boys and girls can get an education in Lowndes County. There are 89 prominent families in this county who own 90 percent of the land. These people will be taxed. And we will collect these taxes. And if they don't pay them, we'll take their property and sell it to whoever wants to buy it. And we know there will be people who will buy land where at the present time they cannot buy it. This is what it's going to take.

We aren't asking any longer for protection—we won't need it—or for anyone to come from the outside to speak for us, because we're going to speak for ourselves now and from now on. And I think not only in Lowndes County, not only in the state of Alabama, not only in the South, but in the North—I hope they too will start thinking for themselves. And that they will move and join us in this fight for freedom. . . .

6. "From Black Consciousness to Black Power"

Cleveland Sellers with Robert Terrell

On June 5, 1966, James Meredith began to walk from Memphis, Tennessee, to Jackson, Mississippi, to serve as an example of individual courage so that other blacks in the state would overcome their fear and actively seek to exercise their right to vote. A shotgun blast abruptly ended Meredith's march, but only provoked in members of SNCC, the SCLC, and CORE a fierce determination to resume the trek from where Meredith had been ambushed. It was during this march that the slogan Black Power, symbolizing a radical new departure in the civil rights movement, was first proclaimed and embraced by young blacks grown weary of the slow pace of legislative and legalistic progress. Cleveland Sellers was program secretary of SNCC during the period of the Meredith march. This is an excerpt from Sellers's 1973 autobiography, The River of No Return.

. . . What is Black Consciousness? More than anything else, it is an attitude, a way of seeing the world. Those of us who possessed it were involved in a perpetual search for racial meanings . . . the construction of a new, black value system. A value system geared to the unique cultural and political experience of blacks in this country.

Black Consciousness signaled the end of the use of the word *Negro*. . . . Black Consciousness permitted us to relate our struggle to the one being waged by Third World revolutionaries in Africa, Asia and Latin America. It helped us understand the imperialistic aspects of domestic racism. It helped us understand that the problems of this nation's oppressed minorities will not be solved without revolution.

We were in Little Rock, Arkansas, talking with Project Director Ben Greenich and some of his staff when a lawyer came up and told us that James Meredith had been killed.

Even though I'd always believed that Meredith's intention to march across Mississippi in order to prove that blacks didn't have to fear white violence any longer was absurd, I was enraged.

We didn't find out until two hours later that Meredith had not actually been murdered. The pellets from the shotgun, which had been fired from about fifty feet, had only knocked him unconscious. . . .

When we arrived at the hospital the next afternoon, Dr. [Martin Luther] King and CORE's new national director, Floyd McKissick, were visiting Meredith. Stanley [Wise], Stokely [Carmichael] and I joined them. . . . Meredith had agreed that the march should be continued without him.

Later that afternoon, a group, which included Stokely, Stanley Wise, Dr. King, McKissick and me, drove out on the highway to the spot where Meredith had been ambushed, and we walked for about three hours. We wanted to advertise that the march would be continued.

Late that night, a planning meeting was held at the Centenary Methodist Church, whose pastor was an ex-SNCC member, the Reverend James Lawson. The meeting was attended by representatives from all those groups interested in participating in the march, including Roy Wilkins and Whitney Young, who had flown in earlier in the day.

Participants in the meeting were almost immediately divided by the position taken by Stokely. He argued that the march should deemphasize white participation, that it should be used to highlight the need for independent, black political units, and that the Deacons for Defense, a black group from Louisiana whose members carried guns, be permitted to join the march.

Roy Wilkins and Whitney Young were adamantly opposed to Stokely. They wanted to send out a nationwide call to whites; they insisted that the Deacons be excluded and they demanded that we issue a statement proclaiming our allegiance to nonviolence.

Despite considerable pressure, Dr. King refused to repudiate Stokely. Wilkins and Young were furious. Realizing that they could not change Stokely's mind, they packed their briefcases and announced that they didn't intend to have anything to do with the march. . . .

The march began in a small way. We had few people, maybe a hundred and fifty. That was okay. We were headed for SNCC territory and we were calling the shots.

The Deacons for Defense served as our bodyguards. Their job was to keep our people alive. . . .

We had our first major trouble with the police on June 17, in Greenwood. It began when a contingent of state troopers arbitrarily decided that we could not put up our sleeping tent on the grounds of a black high school. When Stokely attempted to put the tent up anyway, he was arrested. Within minutes, word of his arrest had spread all over town. The rally that night, which was held in a city park, attracted almost three thousand people—five times the usual number.

Stokely, who'd been released from jail just minutes before the rally began, was the last speaker. He was preceded by McKissick, Dr. King and Willie Ricks. Like the rest of us, they were angry about Stokely's unnecessary arrest. Their speeches were particularly militant. When Stokely moved forward to speak, the crowd greeted him with a huge roar. He acknowledged his reception with a raised arm and clenched fist.

Realizing that he was in his element, with his people, Stokely let it all hang out. "This is the twenty-seventh time I have been arrested—and I ain't going to jail no more!" The crowd exploded into cheers and clapping.

"The only way we gonna stop them white men from whuppin' us is to take over. We been saying freedom for six years and we ain't got nothin'. What we gonna start saying now is Black Power!"

The crowd was right with him. They picked up his thoughts immediately.

"BLACK POWER!" they roared in unison.

Willie Ricks, who is as good at orchestrating the emotions of a crowd as anyone I have ever seen, sprang into action. Jumping to the platform with Stokely, he yelled to the crowd, "What do you want?"

"BLACK POWER!"

"What do you want?"

"BLACK POWER!!"

"What do you want?"

"BLACK POWER!! BLACK POWER!!! BLACK POWER!!!!"

Everything that happened afterward was a response to that moment. More than anything, it assured that the Meredith March Against Fear would go down in history as one of the major turning points in the black liberation struggle.

———————

From SNCC's point of view, the march was a huge success. Despite the bitter controversy precipitated by Stokely's introduction of Black Power, we enjoyed several important accomplishments: thousands of voters were registered along the route; Stokely emerged as a national leader; the Mississippi movement acquired new inspiration, and major interest was generated in independent, black political organizations.

7. "What We Want"

Stokely Carmichael

Stokely Carmichael had been elected chairman of SNCC in May 1966. These are excerpts from his essay "What We Want" in the New York Review of Books *(September 22, 1966).*

One of the tragedies of the struggle against racism is that up to now there has been no national organization which could speak to the growing militancy of young black people in the urban ghetto. There has been only a civil rights movement, whose tone of voice was adapted to an audience of liberal whites. It served as a sort of buffer zone between them and angry young blacks. None of its so-called leaders could go into a rioting community and be listened to. In a sense, I blame ourselves—together with the mass media—for what has happened in Watts, Harlem, Chicago, Cleveland, Omaha. Each time the people in those cities saw Martin Luther King get slapped, they became angry; when they saw four little black girls bombed to death, they were angrier; and when nothing happened, they were steaming. We had nothing to offer that they could see, except to go out and be beaten again. We helped to build their frustration.

An organization which claims to be working for the needs of a community—as SNCC does—must work to provide that community with a position of strength from which to make its voice heard. This is the significance of black power beyond the slogan.

Black power can be clearly defined for those who do not attach the fears of white America to their questions about it. We should begin with the basic fact that black Americans have two problems: they are poor and they are black. All other problems arise from this two-sided reality: lack of education, the so-called apathy of black men. Any program to end racism must address itself to that double reality.

The concept of "black power" is not a recent or isolated phenomenon: It has grown out of the ferment of agitation and activity by different people and organizations in many black communities over the years. Our last year of work in Alabama added a new concrete possibility. In Lowndes County, for example, black power will mean that if a Negro is elected sheriff, he can end police brutality. If a black man is elected tax assessor, he can collect and channel funds for the building of better roads and schools serving black people—thus advancing the move from political power into the economic arena. In such areas as Lowndes, where black men have a majority, they will attempt to use it to exercise control. This is what they seek: control. Where Negroes lack a majority, black power means proper representation and sharing of control. It means the creation of power bases from which black people can work to change statewide or nationwide patterns of oppression through pressure from strength—instead of weakness. Politically, black power means what it has always meant to SNCC: the coming-together of black people to elect representatives and *to force those representatives to speak to their needs.* It does not mean merely putting black faces into office. A man or woman who is black and from the slums cannot be automatically expected to speak to the needs of black people. Most of the black politicians we see around the country today are not what SNCC means by black power. The power must be that of a community, and emanate from there.

Ultimately, the economic foundations of this country must be shaken if black people are to control their lives. The colonies of the United States—and this includes the black ghettoes within its borders, north and south—must be liberated. For a century, this nation has been like an octopus of exploitation, its tentacles stretching from Mississippi and Harlem to South America, the Middle East, southern Africa, and Vietnam; the form of exploitation varies from area to area but the essential result has been the same—a powerful few have been maintained and enriched at the expense of the poor and voiceless colored masses. This pattern must be broken. As its grip loosens here and there around the world, the hopes of black Americans become more realistic. For racism to die, a totally different America must be born.

White America will not face the problem of color, the reality of it. The well-intended say: "We're all human, everybody is really decent, we must forget color." But color cannot be "forgotten" until its weight is recognized and dealt with. White America will not acknowledge that the ways in which this country sees itself are contradicted by being black—and always have been. Whereas most of the people who settled this country came here for freedom or for economic opportunity, blacks were brought here to be slaves. When the Lowndes County Freedom Organization chose the black panther as its symbol, it was christened by the press "the Black Panther Party"—but the Alabama Democratic Party, whose symbol is a rooster, has never been called the White Cock Party. No one ever talked about "white power" because power in this country *is* white. All this adds up to more than merely identifying a group phenomenon by some catchy name or adjective. The furor over that black panther reveals the problems that white

America has with color and sex; the furor over "black power" reveals how deep racism runs and the great fear which is attached to it.

I have said that most liberal whites react to "black power" with the question, What about me?, rather than saying: Tell me what you want me to do and I'll see if I can do it. There are answers to the right question. One of the most disturbing things about almost all white supporters of the movement has been that they are afraid to go into their own communities—which is where the racism exists—and work to get rid of it. They want to run from Berkeley to tell us what to do in Mississippi; let them look instead at Berkeley. They admonish blacks to be nonviolent; let them preach nonviolence in the white community. They come to teach me Negro history; let them go to the suburbs and open up freedom schools for whites. Let them work to stop America's racist foreign policy; let them press this government to cease supporting the economy of South Africa.

There is a vital job to be done among poor whites. We hope to see, eventually, a coalition between poor blacks and poor whites. That is the only coalition which seems acceptable to us, and we see such a coalition as the major internal instrument of change in American society. SNCC has tried several times to organize poor whites; we are trying again now, with an initial training program in Tennessee. It is purely academic today to talk about bringing poor blacks and whites together, but the job of creating a poor-white power bloc must be attempted. The main responsibility for it falls upon whites.

But our vision is not merely of a society in which all black men have enough to buy the good things of life. When we urge that black money go into black pockets, we mean the communal pocket. We want to see money go back into the community and used to benefit it. We want to see the cooperative concept applied in business and banking. We want to see black ghetto residents demand that an exploiting store keeper sell them, at minimal cost, a building or a shop that they will own and improve cooperatively;

they can back their demand with a rent strike, or a boycott, and a community so unified behind them that no one else will move into the building or buy at the store. The society we seek to build among black people, then, is not a capitalist one. It is a society in which the spirit of community and humanistic love prevail. . . .

8. "Black Power: A Voice Within"
Ruth Turner Perot

Ruth Turner Perot was special assistant to the national director of CORE when she wrote the 1967 essay "Black Power: A Voice Within" from which this excerpt is taken.

. . . Black power to CORE means the organization of the black community into a tight and disciplined group, for six purposes:

1. Growth of political power.
2. Building economic power.
3. Improvement of self-image.
4. Development of Negro leadership.
5. Demanding federal law enforcement.
6. Mobilization of Negro consumer power.

Let me give some examples of how CORE programs the concept:

- In Baltimore, MFU, an independent union organized by CORE, raised wages of nearly 100 members, workers regular labor unions did not want to organize, from 35¢ to $1.50.
- Baltimore, CORE's 1966 Target City, also demonstrated black power in the November elections. As a result of intensive mobilizing and organizing by CORE and other groups, Negroes switched 35 to 1 to vote for Republican [Spiro] Agnew over "Home is your castle" [George P.] Mahoney. Mahoney was defeated. We were so effective, in fact, that the Ku Klux Klan has chosen Baltimore as [its] Target City.
- CORE ran eight Negro candidates for school board elections

in Democratic primaries in Louisiana. All won, first time since Reconstruction.

- Also—Louisiana (Opelousas)—Sweet potato cooperative. 375 farmers, 15 white, growing and marketing their sweet potato crops. This is economic black power.
- Watts, Operation Bootstraps, "Learn, Baby, Learn." 12 teenagers, graduates of [a] computer course, have set up their own business, offering up-to-date skills for pay.
- Freedom School in Baltimore and plans for Black Arts and Afro-American Institute. A place where black people learn of history and contributions to world culture and civilization. Power of self-knowledge. Also in Baltimore, a leadership training [program] for neighborhood people.
- As a result of CORE insistence, federal examiners sent to South Carolina and Mississippi counties. Result: registration climbed.

We believe that these building blocks will become a bulwark that will protect the next Adam Clayton Powell, multiplied many times over. There is no other choice. If power for the powerless is not achieved so that changes within its structure can be made, this nation will not survive.

CHAPTER EIGHT

TWO SOCIETIES (1965–1968)

Introduction by Darlene Clark Hine

The documents in this chapter explore the course of the civil rights movement in two northern urban centers—Chicago, Illinois, and Detroit, Michigan—in 1966 and 1967. The title also connotes the differences, tensions, and contradictions permeating the lives of white and black residents in these cities. What connects the disparate documents and individual testimonies of observers and participants in the struggles for full equality is the fact that the North was as plagued by racial segregation as was the South. In Chicago, political negotiations between civil rights leaders and the Daley machine over housing segregation characterize much of the struggle. In Detroit, a deadly race riot resulted in tremendous loss of life and the destruction of millions of dollars in property as African-Americans made known their frustration and dissatisfaction with a long history of police violence and employment discrimination.

In January 1966 the Southern Christian Leadership Conference drafted a proposal for the development of a nonviolent action movement in the greater Chicago area. In the proposal SCLC officials opined that Chicago with its housing segregation and limited educational opportunities was "the prototype of the northern urban race problem." Having defined the Chicago problem specifically as "simply a matter of economic exploitation" that was manifested in education, building trades unions, real estate, banks and mortgage companies, slum landlords, the welfare system, federal housing agencies, the courts, the police, the political system, the city administration, and the federal government, SCLC reiterated its philosophical approach to social change. The proposal indicated that SCLC would depart from its usual strategy of concentration on a single issue at a time and instead focus on all of these issues simultaneously. Actually, the fight for open housing would soon become a major priority, and mass marches the major tactic for bringing the issue to public attention.

Dr. Martin Luther King, Jr., and SCLC, working in cooperation with the Coordinating Council of Community Organizations, on July 10, 1966, led several thousand marchers to the City Hall from a large rally at Soldier Field. Upon arrival, King posted a list of twenty-four demands on Mayor Richard J. Daley's front door. The demands included a call for an end to racial discrimination as practiced by real estate boards, banking institutions, businesses, unions, and political institutions. One demand called for the governor to prepare a new $2 minimum wage law and another demand threatened a selective buying campaign against businesses that boycott black products. The posting of demands was largely a symbolic gesture.

Similarly, the ten-point agreement of the Subcommittee to the Conference on Fair Housing convened by the Chicago Conference on Religion and Race reflected more shadow than substance. According to the agreement—reached as a result of a series of "summit meetings" between leaders of the Chicago Freedom Movement and city leaders and signed by both Daley and King— the city pledged to urge the 1967 session of the state legislature to adopt fair housing legislation, while the Chicago Commission on Human Relations attempted "to require every real estate broker to post a summary of the city's policy on open housing and the requirement of the Fair Housing Ordinance in a prominent position in his place of business." Unarguably, the sentiment pointed in the right direction, but there was little political muscle to force compliance to open housing practices in the greater Chicago area.

Initially Congress of Racial Equality member Linda Bryant Hall was elated that Dr. Martin Luther King, Jr., had accepted the invitation from Chicago civil rights leaders to bring the movement to the "Windy City." Like thousands of other blacks, Hall chafed under the unwritten codes of residential segregation, represented most graphically by the violence visited upon any black person daring to move into surrounding white suburbs, especially Cicero. However, when King called off a planned demonstration into the feared Cicero after the ten-point agreement had been signed, Hall's elation turned to ambivalence. As revealed in her insightful interview, the civil rights movement strategies that had worked in the South produced limited results in a northern environment, where a diversified population of blacks had more complex relations with the political structure and adhered to varied strategies for social change. She questions the efficacy of King's model for addressing the multifaceted problems of the urban North, and shares her enthusiasm for the emerging ideology of Black Power. The Cicero march took place without King, and as Hall notes, it was different from the traditional King-led demonstrations.

The participation of community people determined to fight back and eschew the doctrine of nonviolence signaled a major difference between the Cicero march and SCLC-orchestrated demonstrations in the South. The events in Detroit further underscore the growth of divergent ideologies competing for support within black communities in northern urban areas. In 1967, few would have predicted the explosion that shattered illusions of peace and tranquility in Detroit.

The excerpt from the autobiography of Roger Wilkins, who served as head of the Community Relations Service of the U.S. Justice Department, is an eyewitness account of the course of the rebellion and the responses of ostensibly peacekeeping agencies, including the Michigan Guard, the Michigan State Police, and the Detroit Police Department.

Wilkins's status as a government official affords a unique angle of vision, permitting glimpses into the deeper motivations that informed the political vacillations of state and national leaders. Moreover, his telling asides also point out the differences between middle-class blacks who themselves queried "What do *they* want?" and those African-Americans whose demands for "jobs and dignity" fed the rebellion.

In the aftermath of the Detroit rebellion, President Lyndon B. Johnson appointed an eleven-member National Advisory Commission on Civil Disorders, headed by Illinois governor Otto Kerner. The commission released a report in February 1968 that delineated the factors contributing to the outbreak of racial violence throughout the country. The commission warned that America was "moving towards two societies, one black, one white— separate and unequal." In the report the commission took pains to lay responsibility for the urban explosions at the doorstep of a racist white society. In speaking of the ghetto, the report charged that "white institutions created it, white institutions maintain it, and white society condones it." Few of the report's recommendations were implemented.

1. "A Proposal by the Southern Christian Leadership Conference for the Development of a Nonviolent Action Movement for the Greater Chicago Area"

Known as the Chicago Plan and dated January 5, 1966, this was the SCLC's working document for its Chicago campaign, to be conducted in conjunction with the Chicago-based Coordinating Council of Community Organizations (CCCO).

Chicago is a city of more than a million Negroes. For almost a century now it has been the northern landing place for southern migrants journeying up from the Mississippi Delta. It was the Promised Land for thousands who sought to escape the cruelties of Alabama, Mississippi and Tennessee; yet, now, in the year 1966, the cycle has almost reversed. Factories moving South, employment and opportunities on the increase, and recent civil rights legislation are rapidly disintegrating the cruelties of segregation. The South is now a land of opportunity, while those who generations ago sang, "Going to Chicago, sorry but I can't take you," now sink into the depths of despair.

Educational opportunities in Chicago, while an improvement over Mississippi, were hardly adequate to prepare Negroes for metropolitan life. A labor force of some 300,000 have found little beyond low paying service occupations open to them, and those few who possessed skills and crafts found their ranks rapidly being depleted by automation and few opportunities for advancement and promotion. In 1960 Negroes, who represented twenty-three percent of the population, accounted for forty-three percent of the unemployed. This was not including the thousands of new migrants and young adult males who were entering the laboring market, but who had not yet made their way to an unemployment office, knowing full well in advance that only a few dirty jobs were available to them.

Those few Negroes who were fortunate enough to achieve professional and managerial status found themselves victimized in their search for adequate housing. Two distinct housing markets were maintained by Chicago real estate interests, carefully separate and controlled; and those who were able to make what should have been a living wage, found that they had to pay ten to twenty percent more on rental of homes, purchase of property, and insurance and interest rates than their white counterparts.

Langston Hughes asks, "What happens to a dream deferred?" But these dreams were not deferred, they were denied and repudiated by vicious though subtle patterns of exploitation. So the dreams do not "dry up like raisins in the sun." They decay like sun-ripened oranges that are devoured by worms and birds until they fall to the ground, creating a rotten mess. But centuries ago Victor Hugo proclaimed that, "When men are in darkness, there will be crime; but those who have placed them in darkness are as much responsible for the crime as those who commit it." And so the social consequences of our repudiated dreams, denied opportunities and frustrated aspirations are very much present.

Chicago is not alone in this plight, but it is clearly the prototype of the northern urban race problem.

PAST APPROACHES

During the past two years there has been a conscientious and creative attempt to dramatize the evils of this system of northern segregation by the Coordinating Council of Community Organizations. CCCO and its member groups have worked in a united action program and through independent organizational activities to call attention to the various sore spots in Chicago society. Negotiations have taken place with the school board, city officials, labor movement, real estate interests and many other points of power in the high command of Chicago metropolitan life. These efforts represent the foundation stones upon which any movement must build. The CCCO "Get Rid of [Schools Superintendent] Willis Campaign" is as significant as any campaign ever organized in this country. A similar campaign held in Fort Wayne, Indiana, Louisville, Kentucky, or Atlanta, Georgia, would have indeed met with unparalleled success in the area of school desegregation; but before the Goliath of Chicago their efforts made only limited impact.

The problems of Chicago, indeed the problems of the northern city, demand something new.

THE SCLC PHILOSOPHY OF SOCIAL CHANGE

In our work in the South two principles have emerged. One, the crystallization of issues, and two, the concentration of action.

In Birmingham we confronted the citadel of southern segregation. In 1963 not one aspect of Birmingham community life was desegregated. In approaching this complex segregated society, the issue was simplified deliberately to: Segregation. Early newspaper critiques challenged the simplification and offered a thousand rationalizations as to why such complex problems could not be dealt with so simply and suggested a hundred more "moderate, responsible" methods of dealing with our grievances. Yet it was the simplification of the issue to the point where every citizen of good will, black and white, north and south, could respond and identify that ultimately made Birmingham the watershed movement in the history of the civil rights struggle.

The second point was the concentration of action, and we chose lunch counters, a target which seemed to most social analysts the least significant but one to which most people could rally. It was a target wherein one might achieve some measure of change yet which sufficiently involved the lines of economic and social power to a point beyond itself—to the larger problem.

The concentration of action led to an immediate local victory at the level of the lunch counter, but pointed beyond the lunch counter to the total problem of southern segregation and produced a ten-title legislative victory on a national level in the Civil Rights Act of 1964.

THE PROBLEM IN CHICAGO

For the past months the SCLC staff has been working in Chicago trying to apply the SCLC philosophy to the problem of Chicago. Their work has been concerned with strengthening community organizations and recruiting new forces to join in a nonviolent movement, but they have also given a great deal of thought to the crystallization and definition of the problem in Chicago in terms which can be communicated to the man on the street, who is most affected. The Chicago problem is simply a matter of economic exploitation. Every condition exists simply because someone profits by its existence. This economic exploitation is crystallized in the SLUM.

A slum is any area which is exploited by the community at large or an area where free trade and exchange of culture and resources is not allowed to exist. In a slum, people do not receive comparable care and services for the amount of rent paid on a dwelling. They are forced to purchase property at inflated real estate value. They pay taxes, but their children do not receive an equitable share of those taxes in educational, recreational and civic services. They may leave the community and acquire professional training, skills or crafts, but seldom are they able to find employment opportunities commensurate with these skills. And in the rare occasions when they do, opportunities for advancement and promotion are restricted. This means that in proportion to the labor, money and intellect which the slum pours into the community at large, only a small portion is received in return benefits. [James] Bevel and our Chicago staff have come to see this as a system of internal colonialism, not unlike the exploitation of the Congo by Belgium.

This situation is true only for Negroes. A neighborhood of Polish citizens might live together in a given geographic area, but that geographic area enters into free exchange with the community at large; and at any time services in that area deteriorate, the citizens are free to move to other areas where standards of health, education and employment are maintained.

As we define and interpret the dynamics of the slum, we see the total pattern of economic exploitation under which Negroes suffer in Chicago and other northern cities.

1. Education: $266 per year is the average investment per Negro child; per white pupil it is $366 in the city of Chicago. Suburban communities spend anywhere from $450 to $900 per pupil annually. Hence, slum education is designed to perpetuate the inferior status of slum children and prepare them only for menial jobs in much the same way that the South African apartheid educational philosophy does for the African.

2. Building Trades Unions: Building trades unions bar Negroes from many employment opportunities which could easily be learned by persons with limited academic training.

3. Real Estate: Real Estate Boards restrict the supply of housing available to Negroes to the result that Negro families pay an average $20 per month more in rent and receive fewer services than persons in other neighborhoods.

4. Banks and Mortgage Companies: Banks and mortgage companies charge higher interest rates and in many instances even refuse to finance real estate in slum communities and transitional communities, making the area easy prey for loan sharks.

5. Slum Landlords: Slum landlords find a most lucrative return on a minimum investment due to inefficient enforcement of city building codes as well as inadequate building codes, over-crowding of living space, and a tax structure on slum property which means the more you let the building run down, the less you pay in taxes.

6. The Welfare System: The welfare system contributes to the breakdown of family life by making it more difficult to ob-

tain money if the father is in the household and subjects families to a dehumanized existence at the hand of an impersonal self-perpetuating bureaucracy.

7. Federal Housing Agencies: Federal housing agencies will not insure loans for purchasing real estate in Negro communities and make little or no money available for financing any low-cost housing or renovation of present housing.

8. The Courts: The courts are organized as a tool of the economic structure and political machine. Judges are political appointees and subject to political influence.

9. The Police: The police are little more than "enforcers" of the present system of exploitation and often demonstrate particular contempt for poor Negroes, so that they are deprived of any sense of human dignity and the status of citizenship in order that they may be controlled and "kept in line."

10. The Political System: The established political system deprives Negroes of political power and, through patronage and pressure, robs the community of its democratic voice in the name of a Democratic Machine.

11. The City Administration: The city administration refuses to render adequate services to the Negro community. Street cleaning, garbage collection and police protection are offered menially, if at all.

12. The Federal Government: The federal government has yet to initiate a creative attempt to deal with the problems of megalopolitan life and the results of the past three centuries of slavery and segregation on Negroes.

CONCENTRATION OF ACTION

There are two possible ways to concentrate on the problems of the slum: one would be to focus on a single issue, but another is to concentrate all of our forces and move in concert with a nonviolent army on each and every issue.

In the South concentration on one issue proved feasible because of a general pattern of state and local resistance. However, in Chicago we are faced with the probability of a ready accommodation to many of the issues in some token manner, merely to curtail the massing for forces and public opinion around those issues. Therefore, we must be prepared to concentrate all of our forces around any and all issues.

MOBILIZATION OF FORCES

Presently our movement constitutes the member organizations of CCCO and the staff resources of SCLC. Some time has been spent strengthening and orienting these present forces, but they must be supplemented immediately by additional power factors which will help us organize and raise issues before the entire Chicago community.

Foremost among these power factors is the church. The church constitutes a ready ally for a nonviolent movement, because basically we are raising questions of human rights for those who are numbered among the children of God but who have been denied these rights by the structures of our society. This has already begun through the work of Jesse Jackson, Rev. Clay Evans and three Baptist Ministers Conferences.

During the month of January an effort should be made to involve every minister in the city in at least an informational meeting concerning the plans for a nonviolent movement in Chicago. This can be accompanied through meetings with existing minsters conferences, convocations at seminaries in the area, and special efforts to reach the Roman Catholic community through the Catholic Interracial Council and the offices of the Archdiocese.

Students in the fifty-one colleges in the Chicago area are another potential force for the movement. We must also count the entire Negro high school population as an available force to be mobilized. This mobilization should be carried out by concentrating first on key area schools (areas to be defined) with the understanding that contacts are being made in other schools who may be organized for supporting action in a few days time.

There should be approximately 100,000 unemployed Negroes in the city of Chicago, a considerable percentage of these would be young men between the ages of sixteen and twenty-five. Many of these are in gangs or are drifting idly from corner to corner. This group must [be] mobilized into an action unit, prepared to demonstrate whenever the occasion seems tactically important. Their organization must be in their own behalf and must focus on meaningful employment and training opportunities through which they might achieve active participation in our society.

In two or three selected neighborhoods, household units must be organized into some type of union to end slums (or householders union, tenant union, or community union). These neighborhoods would be organized on a door-to-door basis to bargain collectively with landlords and the city in an effort to change the conditions which create slums. It would provide protection against eviction and exploitation and help resolve many immediate problems, but its main function would be to band together to demand that the conditions which create slums be ended. This would be a tremendous power in dealing with both political and economic factors which affect life in the slums.

Some explorations are under way in Longdale, East Garfield Park, Kenwood and Englewood.

Developmental Approach to Action

In our present understanding of the nature of slums and the nature of a movement, the task of developing an action program which involves the whole of Chicago and encompasses many issues should not be too difficult. From the bases of power, which are discussed in the previous section, we will have the forces which can be mobilized to dramatize issues as they occur.

During the first phase of the movement organization and education are the primary purposes. This will be done largely through mass meetings, neighborhood rallies and work shops and should continue through the month of February. Demonstrations must also be thought of as educational and organizational tools, and there may be some occasions which call for demonstrations. When this is the case, it must be clear that the purpose of the demonstration is to dramatize and so define this incident as one link in the chain of economic exploitation which occurs in slum life.

Phase 2: By the first of March, community response and live issues should have evolved to the point where some consensus has been reached around specific targets. At this point we should be able to develop the detailed day-by-day strategy which would seek to demonstrate the total chain which enslaves us. Demonstrations should be scheduled at points which should reveal the agents of exploitation and paint a portrait of the evils which beset us in such a manner that it is clear the world over what makes up a slum and what it is that destroys the people who are forced to live in a slum.

Phase 3: By the first of May we should be ready to launch the phases of massive action, but just as no one knew on January 2, 1965, that there would be a march from Selma to Montgomery by March of that year, so now we are in no position to know what form massive action might take in Chicago. However, as we begin to dramatize the situation, we will be led into forms of demonstration which will create the kind of coalition of conscience which is necessary to produce change in this country.

OBJECTIVES

Our objectives in this movement are federal, state and local. On the federal level we would hope to get the kind of comprehensive legislation which would meet the problems of slum life across this nation. At the state level, we should expect the kinds of tax reforms, updating of building codes, open occupancy legislation and enforcement of existing statutes for the protection of our citizens. On the local level we would hope to create the kind of awareness in people that would make it impossible for them to [be] enslaved or abused and create for them the kind of democratic structures which will enable them to continually deal with the problems of slum life. Among these would be active community organizations, a coordinated and powerful civil rights movement, religious institutions which are prepared to minister to persons in urban society as well as to the structures of that society. We would also hope that from this would emerge several pilot projects and institutions which might be of some permanent significance.

There are very few cultural, recreational and vocational facilities available to youth in this country to match the kinds of sports pavilions which exist in other countries of the world. One need only think of what it would have meant to Harlem and the whole world had New York's Lincoln Center been constructed between Central Park and 125th Street. A whole region would have been reclaimed. Perhaps the city of Chicago might be influenced to devote a similar portion of its resources to the cultural and recreational life of its underprivileged youth and centers like Lincoln Center in New York or Opportunities Industrialization Centers of Philadelphia might be outgrowths of our years of movement in Chicago.

2. Demands Placed on the Door of Chicago City Hall by Martin Luther King, Jr.
July 10, 1966

REAL ESTATE BOARDS AND BROKERS

1. Public statements that all listings will be available on a nondiscriminatory basis.

BANKS AND SAVINGS INSTITUTIONS

1. Public statements of a nondiscriminatory mortgage policy so that loans will be available to any qualified borrower without regard to the racial composition of the area.

THE MAYOR AND CITY COUNCIL

1. Publication of headcounts of whites, Negroes and Latin Americans for all city departments and for all firms from which city purchases are made.

2. Revocation of contracts with firms that do not have a full scale fair employment practice.

3. Creation of a citizens review board for grievances against police brutality and false arrests or stops and seizures.

4. Ordinance giving ready access to the names of owners and investors for all slum properties.

5. A saturation program of increased garbage collection, street cleaning, and building inspection services in the slum properties.

POLITICAL PARTIES

1. The requirement that precinct captains be residents of their precincts.

CHICAGO HOUSING AUTHORITY AND THE CHICAGO DWELLING ASSOCIATION

1. Program to rehabilitate present public housing including such items as locked lobbies, restrooms in recreation areas, increased police protection and child care centers on every third floor.

2. Program to increase vastly the supply of low-cost housing on a scattered basis for both low and middle income families.

BUSINESS

1. Basic headcounts, including white, Negro and Latin American, by job classification and income level, made public.

2. Racial steps to upgrade and to integrate all departments, all levels of employment.

UNIONS

1. Headcounts in unions for apprentices, journeymen and union staff and officials by job classification. A crash program to remedy any inequities discovered by the headcount.

2. Indenture of at least 400 Negro and Latin American apprentices in the craft unions.

GOVERNOR

1. Prepare legislative proposals for a $2.00 state minimum wage law and for credit reform, including the abolition of garnishment and wage assignment.

ILLINOIS PUBLIC AID COMMISSION AND THE COOK COUNTY DEPARTMENT OF PUBLIC AID

1. Encouragement of grievance procedures for the welfare recipients so that recipients know that they can be members of and represented by a welfare union or a community organization.
2. Institution of a declaration of income system to replace the degrading investigation and means test for welfare eligibility.

FEDERAL GOVERNMENT

1. Executive enforcement of Title I of the 1964 Civil Rights Act regarding the complaint against the Chicago Board of Education.
2. An executive order for Federal supervision of the nondiscriminatory granting of loans by banks and savings institutions that are members of the Federal Deposit Insurance Corporation or by the Federal Deposit Insurance Corporation.
3. Passage of the 1966 Civil Rights Act without any deletions or crippling amendments.
4. Direct funding of Chicago community organizations by the Office of Economic Opportunity.

PEOPLE

1. Financial support of the Freedom Movement.

2. Selective buying campaigns against businesses that boycott the products of Negro-owned companies.

3. Participation in the Freedom Movement target campaigns for this summer, including volunteer services and membership in one of the Freedom Movement Organizations.

3. "Agreement of the Subcommittee to the Conference on Fair Housing Convened by the Chicago Conference on Religion and Race"

This is the text of the agreement reached on August 26, 1966, between the Chicago Freedom Movement and the city of Chicago.

This subcommittee has been discussing a problem that exists in every metropolitan area in America. It has been earnestly seeking immediate, practical, and effective steps which can be taken to create a fair housing market in metropolitan Chicago.

In the City of Chicago itself, the policy of fair housing has been established by the clear statement of purpose in the Chicago Fair Housing Ordinance enacted in 1963. It provides:

1. It is hereby declared the policy of the City of Chicago to assure full and equal opportunity to all residents of the City to obtain fair and adequate housing for themselves and their families in the City of Chicago without discrimination against them because of their race, color, religion, national origin or ancestry.

2. It is further declared to be the policy of the City of Chicago that no owner, lessee, sublessee, assignee, managing agent, or other person, firm or corporation having the right to sell, rent or lease any housing accommodation, within the City of

Chicago, or any agent of any of these, should refuse to sell, rent, lease or otherwise deny or withhold from any person or group of persons such housing accommodations because of the race, color, religion, national origin or ancestry of such person or persons or discriminate against any person because of his race, color, religion, national origin or ancestry in the terms, conditions, or privileges of the sale, rental or lease of any housing accommodation or in the furnishing of facilities or services in connection therewith.

The subcommittee has addressed itself to methods of making the Chicago Ordinance work better, the action which can be taken by various governmental groups, the role of the Chicago Real Estate Board, and how to make further progress towards fair housing in the months ahead. It would be too much to expect complete agreement on either the steps to be taken or their timing. Nevertheless, the representatives at the meetings have undertaken specific and affirmative measures to attack the problem of discrimination in housing. Carrying out these commitments will require substantial investments of time and money by both private and public bodies and the wholehearted effort of many Chicagoans of good will, supported by the cooperation of thousands of others.

In the light of the commitments made and program here adopted and pledged to achieve open housing in the Chicago metropolitan community, the Chicago Freedom Movement pledges its resources to help carry out the program and agrees to a cessation of neighborhood demonstrations on the issue of open housing so long as the program is being carried out.

The subcommittee believes that the program can be a major step forward. It has confidence that this program, and the more extensive measures bound to flow from it, will achieve the objective of affording every resident "full and equal opportunity to obtain fair and adequate housing without discrimination because of race, color, religion, national origin or ancestry."

The participants in this conference have committed themselves to the following action:

1. The Chicago Commission on Human Relations is already acting to require every real estate broker to post a summary of

the City's policy on open housing and the requirements of the Fair Housing Ordinance in a prominent position in his place of business. To obtain full compliance with the Fair Housing Ordinance, the Commission will give special emphasis to multiple complaints and will follow up on pledges of non-discrimination resulting from prior conciliation proceedings. The Commission will increase its enforcement staff and has already requested budgetary increases to support a significantly higher level of effective enforcement activity. This will include year-around inquiry to determine the extent of compliance in all areas of the City, but without placing undue burdens on any broker's business. The Commission will initiate proceedings on its own motion where the facts warrant. It will act on all complaints promptly, ordinarily initiating an investigation within 48 hours, as is now the case. In order to facilitate proceedings on complaints, it has changed its rules to provide for the substitution of attorneys for Commissioners to preside in conciliation and enforcement hearings. Where a formal hearing justifies such action under the ordinance, the license of an offending broker will be suspended or revoked.

The City will continue its consistent support of fair housing legislation at the State level and will urge the adoption of such legislation at the 1967 session of the State Legislature.

2. In a significant departure from its traditional position, the Chicago Real Estate Board announced at the August 17 meeting that its Board of Directors had authorized a statement reading in part as follows:

As a leadership organization in Chicago, we state the fundamental principle that freedom of choice in housing is the right of every citizen. We believe all citizens should accept and honor that principle.

We have reflected carefully and have decided we will—as a Chicago organization—withdraw all opposition to the philosophy of open occupancy legislation at the state level—provided it is applicable to owners as well as to brokers—and we reserve the right to criticize detail as distinguished from philosophy—and we will request the state association of Real Estate Boards to do likewise but we cannot dictate to them.

While not willing to dismiss its appeal from the decision of the Circuit Court of Cook County upholding the validity of the City's Fair Housing Ordinance, the Board has committed itself effectively to remind its members of their duty to obey the ordinance and to circulate to them the interpretation of the ordinance to be furnished by the Chicago Commission on Human Relations. The individual representatives of the Board also committed themselves to join other realtors to participate in a continuing organization, should one be formed, to promote effective action implementing the principle of freedom of choice in housing.

3. The Chicago Housing Authority will take every action within its power to promote the objectives of fair housing. It recognizes that heavy concentrations of public housing should not again be built in the City of Chicago. Accordingly, the Chicago Housing Authority has begun activities to improve the character of public housing, including the scattering of housing for the elderly across the city, and initiation of a leasing program which places families in the best available housing without regard to the racial character of the neighborhood in which the leased facilities are provided. In the future, it will seek scattered sites for public housing and will limit the height of new public housing structures in high density areas to eight stories, with housing for families with children limited to the first two stories. Wherever possible, smaller units will be built.

In addition, in order to maximize the usefulness of present facilities and to promote the welfare of the families living in them, a concerted effort will be made to improve the opportunities for satisfactory community life in public housing projects. In order to achieve this improvement the participation of all elements in the surrounding communities will be actively enlisted and utilized.

4. The President of the Cook County Board of Commissioners has advised the chairman of the subcommittee by letter that the Cook County Department of Public Aid will make a renewed and persistent effort to search out the best housing for recipients available within the ceilings authorized by the legislature, regardless of location. Each employee of the Department will be reminded that no recipient is to be prohibited or discouraged from moving into any part of Cook County because of his race, color or national origin. The Department will not be satisfied if recipients live in

less satisfactory accommodations than would be available to them were they of a different race, color or national origin.

Department employees will be instructed to report any discriminatory refusal by real estate brokers to show rental listings to any recipient to the Chicago Commission on Human Relations or the State Department of Registration and Education through the Chief of the Bureau of Housing of the Public Aid Department. Department employees will also encourage recipients who encounter discrimination in dealing with brokers to report such experiences to the same agencies. The Chief of the Bureau of Housing will maintain close follow-up on all matters that have been thus reported.

5. The Urban Renewal Program has had some success in achieving stable residential integration in facilities built in renewal developments, with the cooperation of property owners, property managers, community organizations, and neighbors to that end. The Urban Renewal Program will devote itself to producing the same results in its relocation activities and will earnestly solicit the support of all elements of the community in the City, County and metropolitan area in these efforts.

In relocating families, the Department of Urban Renewal will search out the best housing available regardless of location. Each employee of the Department will be reminded that no family is to be prohibited or discouraged from moving into any part of the Chicago metropolitan area because of his race, color, or national origin. Department employees will be instructed to report any discriminatory refusal by a real estate broker to show listings, to the Chicago Commission on Human Relations or the State Department of Registration and Education through the Director of Relocation. They will also encourage families who encounter discrimination in dealing with a broker to report such experiences to the same agencies. The Director of Relocation will maintain a close follow-up on all matters that have been thus reported.

6. The Cook County Council of Insured Savings Associations, by letter, and the Chicago Mortgage Bankers Association, at the Committee meeting on August 17, 1966, have affirmed that their policy is to provide equal service and to lend mortgage money to all qualified families, without regard to race, for the purchase of housing anywhere in the metropolitan area.

7. Assistant Attorney General Roger Wilkins, head of the Community Relations Service of the United States Department of Justice, has advised the chairman of the subcommittee that the Service will inquire into the questions raised, under existing law, with respect to service by the Federal Deposit Insurance Corporation and the Federal Savings and Loan Insurance Corporation to financial institutions found guilty of practicing racial discrimination in the provision of financial service to the public. While the matter is a complex one, it will be diligently pursued.

8. The leaders of the organized religious communities in the metropolitan area have already expressed their commitment to the principle of open housing.

The Chicago Conference on Religion and Race, which is co-sponsored by the Catholic Archdiocese of Chicago, the Church Federation of Greater Chicago, the Chicago Board of Rabbis and the Union of American Hebrew Congregations, pledges its support to the program outlined and will enlist the full strength of its constituent bodies and their churches and synagogues in effecting equal access to housing in the metropolitan area for all people. They pledge to:

1. Educate their membership on the moral necessity of an open and just community.
2. Urge owners to sell or rent housing without racial restriction.
3. Support local real estate offices and lending institutions in their cooperation with this program.
4. Cooperate with and aid in the establishment of responsible community organizations and support them in the implementation of these programs.
5. Undertake to secure peaceful acceptance and welcome Negro families prior to and at the time of their entrance into any community.
6. Use their resources to help make housing available without racial discrimination.
7. Establish, within 30 days, one or more housing centers, with the assistance of the real estate and housing industry and financial institutions, to provide information and help in finding suitable housing for minority families and to urge them to take advantage of new housing opportunities.

9. The representatives of the Chicago Association of Commerce and Industry, the Commercial Club, the Cosmopolitan Chamber of Commerce, Chicago Mortgage Bankers Association, Metropolitan Housing and Planning Council, Chicago Federation of Labor and Industrial Union Council, and other secular groups represented in these discussions recognize that their organizations have a major stake in working out the problems of fair housing. Each such representative welcomes and pledges support to the program outlined in this report. Further, each undertakes to secure the support of his organization and its members, whether individuals, corporations, locals or groups, for the program and their participation in it, including education of their members on the importance to them of fair housing throughout the Chicago metropolitan area.

10. The Chicago Conference on Religion and Race will initiate forthwith the formation of a separate, continuing body, sponsored by major leadership organizations in the Chicago metropolitan area and built on a nucleus of the representatives of the organizations participating here. This body should accept responsibility for the execution and action programs necessary to achieve fair housing. It should be headed by a board consisting of recognized leaders from government, commerce, industry, finance, religion, real estate, labor, the civil rights movement, and the communications media. Its membership should reflect the diverse racial and ethnic composition of the entire Chicago metropolitan community.

The proposed board should have sufficient stature to formulate a strong and effective program and to provide adequate financing and staff to carry out that program. To the extent of available resources, it should carry forward programs such as, but not limited to, the convening of conferences on fair housing in suburban communities to the end that the policy of the City of Chicago on fair housing will be adopted in the whole Chicago metropolitan area. There must be a major effort in the pulpits, in the school systems, and in all other available forums to educate citizens of the metropolitan area in the fundamental principle that freedom of choice in housing is the right of every citizen and in their obligations to abide by the law and recognize the rights of others regardless of race, religion, or nationality. The group should assist in the drafting of fair housing laws and ordinances. It should make clear the stake that commerce, industry, banking, real estate, and labor, indeed all residing in the metropolitan area, have in the peaceful achievement of fair housing. The group should emphasize that the metropolitan housing market is a single market. The vigor and growth of that market is dependent upon an adequate supply of standard housing available without discrimination. The group should promote such practical measures as the development of fair housing centers after the model now being established by the Chicago Conference on Religion and Race. The group should in the immediate future set up specific goals for achievement of fair housing in the Chicago metropolitan area. Finally, the board should regularly review the performance of the program undertaken by governmental and non-governmental groups, take appropriate action thereon, and provide for public reports.

Although all of the metropolitan areas of the country are confronted with the problem of segregated housing, only in Chicago have the top leaders of the religious faiths, commerce, and industry, labor and government sat down together with leaders in the civil rights movement to seek practical solutions. With the start that has been made, the subcommittee is confident that the characteristic drive of Chicagoans to achieve their goals, manifest in the Chicago motto of "I Will," will enable the Chicago metropolitan area to lead the rest of the nation in the solution of the problems of fair housing.

> Respectfully submitted,
> THOMAS G. AYERS,
> Chairman

4. Interview with Linda Bryant Hall

Linda Bryant Hall, a Chicago native, was a member of the Congress of Racial Equality in 1966 when the Southern Christian Leadership Conference began to work with the Coordinating Council of Community Organizations. This is an excerpt from a 1989 interview with Hall by the Eyes on the Prize *production team.*

INTERVIEWER: How did you feel when Dr. King came to Chicago?

LINDA BRYANT HALL: Well, when I first heard that Dr. King was going to come to Chicago, I was elated. I said, Oh, my gosh, Chicago is going to get involved in all of this. You know, Dr. King has got a powerful following, a powerful message, and he's going to bring it to Chicago to help with the movement here. We sure need it. I was looking forward to his coming.

INT: Now, what were the differences between the southern communities and the northern community that he was coming to here in Chicago?

L.B.H.: Well, I didn't really understand how different the communities were until he came and the people he brought with him, I got a chance to meet them, and see what kinds of people they were. In the South I got the impression that that community was more monolithic. After he came here, it was quite obvious—at least to me—that this was a more diversified community and the tactics were going to have to be a little different here. What happened is that when he came in, I think what he tried to do was to try and take that kind of style he had operated with in the South and just plant it down here in Chicago, as if it worked there, it would work here, too. Not taking into consideration the differences that would be here.

. . . We had blacks who lived in Chicago public housing, we had blacks who lived in very poor slum areas, and we had blacks who lived on Chicago's gold coast—one of the richest communities in the world. But they all had a commonality: They all needed Dr. King here to help their voices be heard. All of us wanted Dr. King to come. I mean, to this day, I realize that I was a very lucky person to get to meet him, and know him.

INT: . . . So, what is the difference between what King is used to doing in the South and what he is faced with here in the North in terms of the diversity and the largeness of the black community here?

L.B.H.: . . . Each community had an organization already existing and each community had a plan and each community had their own kinds of goals set. We were working together in a group called Triple CO [CCCO], headed by Al Raby. At that time, we had just decided that we need an umbrella group. And, therefore, we came up with Triple CO, and all the community groups got together, and tried to pool our resources. When King came, though, what he wanted to do was just work with that one umbrella group. And then not understand that each group within that group had a program of its own—had leaders of its own, had its own kind of direction that it was going in; but we all had a common goal. But we needed somebody like King. We needed him to lend us his strength, to lend us his name. And we wanted him to come and join our movement—not come in and lead it, because we already had leaders. So, when he came in to try and discount what was already here, I think, he offended quite a few people.

INT: Give me a sense of problems you had with Dr. King basing his movement in the church, as he did in the South.

L.B.H.: . . . In Chicago—as I said—there are people who are very diversified. And some people in Chicago didn't even believe in churches, didn't believe in God; I mean, they were avowed atheists; and for someone to come in now and ask them to come into the church and follow his movement through that mechanism, it didn't wash so well with a lot of people. And then, too, the churches might have—in Chicago—represented something different from what they did in the South. In Chicago, the churches, many of the black churches—not all of them—many of them had very close connections to the political machine. The political machine supported many of the churches. I mean they did so much as buy the pews where the people set. They provided the church with a storefront. They provided the minister, in some cases, with a salary. So for him, now, to turn to the community people who had been fighting against this kind of setup and say, Come and follow me—you know, it just wouldn't go over.

INT: When you heard Stokely [Carmichael] issue that call for "Black Power," what did that mean to you as a member of CORE?

L.B.H.: When I heard Stokely stand up and say "Black Power," and he said it with so much force, and he wasn't ashamed to say it, and he said it with so much energy, that I knew that that was what I needed . . . that was the call I needed to adhere to. And so many others of us in CORE, at the same time, felt that way. He said it in a way that it said, I'm not ashamed of it. Yes, that's what I want. Put it right out here on the table, you know; this is what it is, this is what it's about: "Black Power"—let's pick that up, and deal with that. And they thought it was a challenge to those in the movement who were less militant . . . to either deal with that, or to step out and say, I'm not backing it, one way or the other. But it was an exciting time for us, because we felt, yeah, these people all over the country are feeling just like we're feeling right here; they want "Black Power."

INT: What role did organizations like CORE, which are more militant, play in getting King to be more militant?

L.B.H.: Groups like CORE made Dr. King, I think, more militant—kept him more to the left than he probably would have been if we had not been around. Whenever we decided we were going to do something very radical, such as our march into Cicero, that made Dr. King have to say, Well, maybe it's not such a bad idea—because Dr. King was not going to denounce us, as we were not going to denounce him. We had to show unity, even though we were at different points. So when we decided that we were going to do something very militant, like support "Black Power," Dr. King and his people, they had to look at "Black Power" and say, What is this? Is this something good here; is this something that we ought to be looking at? . . .

INT: When Dr. King called off the march [to Cicero on September 4, after the open housing agreement had been signed], how did you feel?

L.B.H.: When he called off the march, we were surprised; we were shocked. This is the march we looked forward to. The other marches were nice. But the one in Cicero had special meaning for us. The Cicero community has been a very hostile community to blacks for years—ever since I can remember. And I looked forward to the time that I could march down those streets in defiance of all those people there. When I was a little girl, we were told never go to Cicero—and, especially, don't go there by yourself. So when Dr. King said he wasn't going to march in that neighborhood, I said, My gosh, well, what's it all about? This is *the* neighborhood to march in. They've been known to have "toughs" in that neighborhood, and even some gangster connections there. But we were saying, you know, we're talking to all of those white bigots, and whether they're Mafia people, or whether they're just, ah, some white hecklers, we want them to know, yeah, we're going to come to Cicero; Cicero's got to yield, too, like the rest of the country.

So when we decided that we were going to go that morning when we gathered for the march, we had made this big statement, saying we were going to defy Dr. King and march to Cicero. Well, that took a lot more than just conversation to do. So we got in the park at the gathering point, where we had announced to the city in public press releases, we were going to march. There were practically more reporters than there were people; there were about six or seven of us who showed up to go on this march, and we just knew we were going to fall flat on our faces, and just, this is going to be the ultimate in embarrassment. We waited around, we were supposed to start I think about twelve o'clock; we waited around and waited around and waited around until, finally, we had to go. And it became obvious no more people were going to come. Just at that point, I think the community almost felt sorry for us—the community people: They started to show up. Well, these were the people who lived adjacent to Cicero, too. So they sort of knew the relationship of Cicero with Chicago; and especially with Cicero with blacks. And so they started to fall in line. We hadn't knocked on anybody's door. We hadn't leafleted that neighborhood; we had not done all of the kinds of community organization things that it takes to get this kind of march going; but, yet, and still these people just sort of started to come out of their houses. They had been sitting in cars watching, you know, the reporters and the newspeople around, the cameramen and all, and they were watching. But then the kids were playing basketball, they decided to come, go with us. I guess what happened is that everybody really was just tagging along to see who was there and what was going to happen.

As we got into Cicero, the hecklers got so bad that everybody decided, well, you know, I'm not going to let my people go over there and maybe I need to go with them. I think it was sort of a groundswell. The next thing I knew it was just at least a couple of thousand people going into Cicero. And once you got in there, you couldn't come back by yourself, so you had to stick with the march. So as we got into Cicero, we noticed that the National

Guard had been alerted, of course. [Chicago CORE president Bob] Lucas had promised the city that there was going to be no violence. Now, how he could promise somebody there was going to be no violence, I don't know. But that's the only way they were going to give us the permit to march. So we decided we would go on and tell them, yeah, nobody's going to riot, nothing's going to happen; and in fact, on our part, nothing did happen. When we got there, we noticed that all of the bayonets and the guns that were out were aimed at the marchers and not at the hecklers. The hecklers were throwing bottles and rocks and spitting and calling us all kinds of filthy names and doing some other things that I wouldn't even repeat. But what happened is that people became so excited and [there] was a closeness in that march. Even the Chicago police, I think, saw some of the things that were going on and felt that those things were unjust, and they decided, for the first time—Chicago police did not beat the marchers, did not throw the marchers around. Chicago police decided to protect us. Because, it was obvious who the National Guard were there to protect; they were there to protect Cicero and those people who were heckling us.

INT: How was the character of the Cicero march different from Dr. King's . . . marches in Chicago?

L.B.H.: Well, Dr. King's marches in Chicago were usually made up of movement people. This march was community people. These people had not attended any workshops on nonviolence; they had not listened to any lectures on love and loving your fellow man and all; they were just people who were angry about what was happening and wanted to do something. And when they all decided to go on this march, and people started to throw bricks and bottles at us, a couple of people caught the bricks and threw them back, threw rocks back; they even would jump in-between a lady sometimes. Women who were on the march were very protected. . . . These people were saying, you know, Yeah, we're going to come to Cicero and we're not going to go limp. We're going to march through Cicero, and we're going to march to the point that we said we were going to march to, and we're going to come back. And that in itself was a triumph, because people just didn't do that in Cicero.

5. "Profiles of Disorder . . . Detroit"

This is an excerpt from the Report of the National Advisory Commission on Civil Disorders. *President Lyndon Johnson had appointed the eleven-man commission—known popularly as the Kerner Commission for its chair, Illinois governor Otto Kerner—on July 27, 1967, before troops had been pulled out of Detroit. The commission issued its report in February 1968.*

On Saturday evening, July 22, the Detroit Police Department raided five "blind pigs." The blind pigs had their origin in prohibition days, and survived as private social clubs.

———

Police expected to find two dozen patrons in the [fifth] blind pig. That night, however, it was the scene of a party for several servicemen, two of whom were back from Vietnam. Instead of two dozen patrons, police found 82. Some voiced resentment at the police intrusion.

An hour went by before all 82 could be transported from the scene. The weather was humid and warm . . . and despite the late hour, many people were still on the street. In short order, a crowd of about 200 gathered.

———

On 12th Street, with its high incidence of vice and crime, the issue of police brutality was a recurrent theme. A month earlier the killing of a prostitute had been determined by police investigators to be the work of a pimp. According to rumors in the community the crime had been committed by a Vice Squad officer.

At about the same time, the killing of Danny Thomas, a 27-year-old Negro Army veteran, by a gang of white youths, had inflamed the community.

———

A few minutes after 5:00 A.M., just after the last of those arrested had been hauled away, an empty bottle smashed into the rear window of a police car. A litter basket was thrown through the window of a store. Rumors circulated of excess police force used by the police during the raid. A youth, whom police nicknamed "Mr. Greensleeves" because of the color of his shirt, was shouting: "We're going to have a riot!" and exhorting the crowd to vandalism.

At 5:20 A.M. Commissioner [Ray] Girardin was notified. He immediately called Mayor Jerome Cavanagh. Seventeen officers from other areas were ordered into the 10th Precinct. By 6:00 A.M. police strength had grown to 369 men. Of these, however, only 43 were committed to the immediate riot area. By that time the number of persons on 12th Street was growing into the thousands and widespread window-smashing and looting had begun.

———

By 7:50 A.M., when a 17-man police commando unit attempted to make the first sweep, an estimated 3,000 persons were on 12th Street. They offered no resistance. As the sweep moved down the street, they gave way to one side, and then flowed back behind it.

A shoe store manager said he waited vainly for police for two hours as the store was being looted. At 8:25 A.M. someone in the crowd yelled "The cops are coming!" The first flames of the riot billowed from the store. Firemen who responded were not harassed. The flames were extinguished.

By mid-morning, 1,122 men . . . had reported for duty. Of these, 540 were in or near the six-block riot area. One hundred and eight officers were attempting to establish a cordon. There was, however, no interference with looters.

———

Numerous eyewitnesses interviewed by Commission investigators tell of the carefree mood with which people ran in and out of stores, looting and laughing, and joking with the police officers. Stores with "Soul Brothers" signs appeared no more immune than others.

———

A police officer in the riot area told Commission investigators that neither he nor his fellow officers were instructed as to what they were supposed to be doing. Witnesses tell of officers standing behind saw-horses as an area was being looted—and still standing there much later, when the mob moved elsewhere. A squad from the commando unit, wearing helmets with face-covering visors and carrying bayonet-tipped carbines, blockaded a street several blocks from the scene of the riot. Their appearance drew residents into the street. Some began to harangue them and to question why they were in an area where there was no trouble. . . .

By that time a rumor was threading through the crowd that a man had been bayoneted by the police. Influenced by such stories, the crowd became belligerent. . . . Numerous officers reported injuries from rocks, bottles, and other objects thrown at them. Smoke billowed upward from four fires, the first since the one at the shoe store early in the morning. When firemen answered the alarms, they became the target for rocks and bottles.

At 2:00 P.M. Mayor Cavanagh met with community and political leaders at police headquarters. Until then there had been hope that, as the people blew off steam, the riot would dissipate. Now the opinion was nearly unanimous that additional forces would be needed.

A request was made for state police aid. By 3:00 P.M. 360 officers were assembling at the armory. At that moment looting was spreading from the 12th Street area to other main thoroughfares.

Some evidence that criminal elements were organizing spontaneously to take advantage of the riot began to manifest itself. . . .

A spirit of carefree nihilism was taking hold. To riot and to destroy appeared more and more to become ends in themselves. Late Sunday afternoon it appeared to one observer that the young people were "dancing amidst the flames."

In the midst of the chaos there were some unexpected individual responses.

Twenty-four-year-old E.G., a Negro born in Savannah, Georgia, had come to Detroit in 1965 to attend Wayne State University. Rebellion had been building in him for a long time. . . .

When a friend called to tell him about the riot on 12th Street, E.G. went there expecting "a true revolt," but was disappointed as soon as he saw the looting begin: "I wanted to see the people really rise up in revolt. When I saw the first person coming out of the store with things in his arms, I really got sick to my stomach and wanted to go home. Rebellion against the white suppressors is one thing, but one measly pair of shoes or some food completely ruins the whole concept."

At 4:20 P.M. Mayor Cavanagh requested that the National Guard be brought into Detroit. . . . The first troops were on the streets by 7:00 P.M.

At 7:45 P.M. the mayor issued a proclamation instituting a 9:00 P.M. to 5:00 A.M. curfew. At 9:07 P.M. the first sniper fire was reported. Following his aerial survey of the city, Governor [George] Romney, at or shortly before midnight, proclaimed that "a state of public emergency exists" in the cities of Detroit, Highland Park, and Hamtramck.

By 2:00 A.M. Monday, Detroit police had been augmented by 800 State Police officers and 1,200 National Guardsmen. An additional 8,000 Guardsmen were on the way. Nevertheless, Governor Romney and Mayor Cavanagh decided to ask for federal assistance.

Shortly before noon the President of the United States authorized the sending of a task force of paratroopers to Selfridge Air Force Base, near the city.

As the riot alternately waxed and waned, one area of the ghetto remained insulated. On the northeast side the residents of some 150 square blocks inhabited by 21,000 persons had, in 1966, banded together in the Positive Neighborhood Action Committee (PNAC). With professional help from the Institute for Urban Dynamics, they had organized block clubs and made plans for the improvement of the neighborhood. In order to meet the need for recreational facilities, which the city was not providing, they had raised $3,000 to purchase empty lots for playgrounds. Although opposed to urban renewal, they had agreed to co-sponsor with the Archdiocese of Detroit a housing project to be controlled jointly by the archdiocese and PNAC.

When the riot broke out, the residents, through the block clubs, were able to organize quickly. Youngsters, agreeing to stay in the neighborhood, participated in detouring traffic. While many persons reportedly sympathized with the idea of a rebellion against the "system," only two small fires were set—one in an empty building.

During the daylight hours Monday, nine more persons were killed by gunshots elsewhere in the city, and many others were seriously or critically injured. Twenty-three-year old Nathaniel Edmonds, a Negro, was sitting in his back yard when a young white man stopped his car, got out, and began an argument with him. A few minutes later, declaring he was "going to paint his picture on him with a shotgun," the white man allegedly shot-gunned Edmonds to death.

Mrs. Nannie Pack and Mrs. Mattie Thomas were sitting on the porch of Mrs. Pack's house when police began chasing looters from a nearby market. During the chase officers fired three shots from their shotguns. The discharge from one of these accidentally struck the two women. Both were still in the hospital weeks later.

At 11:20 P.M. the President signed a proclamation federalizing the Michigan National Guard and authorizing the use of the paratroopers.

Within hours after the arrival of the paratroopers the area occupied by them was the quietest in the city, bearing out General [John L.] Throckmorton's view that the key to quelling a disorder is to saturate an area with "calm, determined, and hardened professional soldiers." Loaded weapons, he believes, are unnecessary. Troopers had strict orders not to fire unless they could see the specific person at whom they were firing. Mass fire was forbidden.

During five days in the city, 2,700 Army troops expended only 201 rounds of ammunition, almost all during the first few hours, after which even stricter fire discipline was enforced. (In contrast, New Jersey National Guardsmen and State police expended 13,326 rounds of ammunition in three days in Newark.) . . .

General Throckmorton ordered the weapons of all military personnel unloaded, but either the order failed to reach many National Guardsmen, or else it was disobeyed.

———

With persons of every description arming themselves, and guns being fired accidentally or on the vaguest pretext all over the city, it became more and more impossible to tell who was shooting at whom. Some firemen began carrying guns. One accidentally shot and wounded a fellow fireman. Another injured himself.

———

On a number of occasions officers fired at fleeing looters, then made little attempt to determine whether their shots had hit anyone.

———

Prosecution is proceeding in the case of three youths in whose shotgun deaths law enforcement personnel were implicated following a report that snipers were firing from the Algiers Motel. In fact, there is little evidence that anyone fired from inside the building. Two witnesses say that they had seen a man, standing outside of the motel, fire two shots from a rifle. The interrogation of other persons revealed that law enforcement personnel then shot out one or more street lights. Police patrols responded to the shots. An attack was launched on the motel.

———

Although by late Tuesday looting and fire-bombing had virtually ceased, between 7:00 and 11:00 P.M. that night there were 444 reports of incidents. Most were reports of sniper fire.

———

In all, more than 7,200 persons were arrested. Almost 3,000 of these were picked up on the second day of the riot, and by midnight Monday 4,000 were incarcerated in makeshift jails.

Of the 43 persons who were killed during the riot, 33 were Negro and 10 were white. Seventeen were looters, of whom two were white. Fifteen citizens (of whom four were white), one white National Guardsman, one white fireman, and one Negro private guard died as a result of gunshot wounds. Most of these deaths appear to have been accidental, but criminal homicide is suspected in some.

Two persons, including one fireman, died as a result of fallen power lines. Two were burned to death. One was a drunken gunman; one an arson suspect. One white man was killed by a rioter. One police officer was felled by a shotgun blast when his gun, in the hands of another officer, accidentally discharged during a scuffle with a looter.

Action by police officers accounted for 20 and, very likely, 21 of the deaths. Action by the National Guard for seven, and, very likely, nine. Action by the Army for one. Two deaths were the result of action by store owners. Four persons died accidentally. Rioters were responsible for two, and perhaps three of the deaths; a private guard for one. A white man is suspected of murdering a Negro youth. The perpetrator of one of the killings in the Algiers Motel remains unknown.

Damage estimates, originally set as high as $500 million, were quickly scaled down. The city assessor's office placed the loss— excluding business stock, private furnishings, and the buildings of churches and charitable institutions—at approximately $22 million. Insurance payments, according to the State Insurance Bureau, will come to about $32 million, representing an estimated 65 to 75 percent of the total loss.

By Thursday, July 27, most riot activity had ended. The paratroopers were removed from the city on Saturday. On Tuesday, August 1, the curfew was lifted and the National Guard moved out.

6. "A Man's Life"
Roger Wilkins

Roger Wilkins was director of the U.S. Justice Department's Community Relations Service (CRS), serving under Attorney General Ramsey Clark, during the period this excerpt from his 1982 autobiography describes.

Something happened that night [shortly after the early-July Newark rioting] that Eve and I could not control. We started talking about Newark, about the deaths of the black people there and the wanton use of force against them. We talked about our sense of betrayal, our sense of outrage at America. The more we talked, the more intense Eve and I became about our judgment that the late fifties and the early sixties hadn't changed America after all. This generation of white Americans just couldn't take the humanity of poor black Americans seriously. Our words came tumbling out of us.

We were not attacking Ramsey [Clark] as he sat on our couch sipping a brandy. He agreed with much of what we were saying. He was just the catalyst for the expression of our despair. It took about two hours before it all ran out of us. Then we had a little more brandy and sat there quietly, suffering in the gloom of our vision of America. About eleven, Ramsey rose to go home. We watched him walk across the quiet street. The tall slender frame of the Attorney General of the United States was stooped. His head was down and his jacket thrown over his shoulder. He walked that way until he reached his old Oldsmobile convertible, got in and drove away.

Eve and I felt terrible. We had invited our friend over for a peaceful evening. Instead, he had received a load of our pain. We felt sorry for him. We felt sorry for our country. . . .

A few weeks later, on a Sunday night, Jim Madison, the head of the conciliation division of CRS, called me to say that his field man in Detroit had reported that trouble had erupted earlier that night when a cop had shot a black at an unlicensed drinking place, or "blind pig," in the middle of the black section of town.

"How bad is the trouble?" I asked. "How widespread?"

"We don't know that yet," he replied.

"Well, report it to the situation room at the Department," I said, "and let me know what else you hear."

I heard nothing more from him before I went to bed that night, but at about five the phone rang. It was Ramsey.

"We've had a pretty bad night in Detroit. Governor Romney has been on the phone with the President several times asking for federal troops. The President wants us at eight. We'd better meet in my office at six-thirty."

Warren Christopher, the brand-new Deputy Attorney General from California, was in Ramsey's office that morning, as were John Doar and George Culberson, my deputy. As in so many other crises, we sat there in that small corner office where Ramsey worked, just behind the grand one he used for ceremony, with insufficient information to make the judgments we knew had to be made. George and I reported the fragmentary information we had collected from the field. Widespread burning and looting and shooting, a few deaths. We didn't know how many or which side they were on.

Ramsey had similar information. In addition, he had the President's accounts of his conversations with Governor Romney. Though Romney wanted federal troops, he was unwilling to make the necessary declaration that the situation was beyond the state's control. What he hadn't said, of course, was that he was planning to run for President on the Republican ticket in 1968 and he didn't want such an admission on the record. The President, on the other hand, didn't want to use extreme measures unless emergency conditions really warranted them.

I stood up and rubbed the head of Lincoln that Ramsey kept on a window sill as I often did when we were squeezed into an awful corner. There's got to be some better way to run a country than this, I thought as I stared down at the gathering morning traffic at the corner of Tenth and Constitution.

When it was time to go over to the White House, Clark, Doar, Christopher and I went. Culberson went back to the office to try to collect more information on what was going on in Michigan. We were directed to the Cabinet Room and a couple of minutes after we settled in our chairs, the President came in with Robert McNamara, Secretary of Defense. The President went over the information he had and described his dealings with Romney. He wasn't very charitable about the Governor's behavior so far, which he characterized as a bit hysterical and substantially uninformed. During the middle of the meeting, Cyrus Vance, who had just resigned as Deputy Secretary of Defense because of a serious back problem, walked into the room.

Then Johnson went around the room and asked everyone for an opinion. I thought we shouldn't send any troops in until we could get some high-level civilians on the ground to see what was really going on. Others thought the President couldn't wait that long for fear of inviting the charge that he had fiddled while Detroit burned. After a little more discussion, the President announced that he was going to send a civilian team in to head the operation. Vance would lead the team, which was to include Christopher, Doar and me, from Justice, and Dan Henkin, a press spokesman, from Defense. He would send the 82nd up to Detroit, but they would be stationed outside the city, at the Michigan State Fair Grounds, until we civilians decided that they were needed.

Then Johnson delivered a fierce monologue about what he didn't want to happen. If the troops were ordered into Detroit, he didn't want them walking around with loaded guns unless their commanders thought there was a sufficient emergency for them to carry them. No bayonets. No bullets.

"I don't want my troops shooting some ni—" he glanced sharply at me and stopped. Then he started again, "—some pregnant woman."

Then he pulled a phone from its cradle by his chair under the cabinet table, handed it to Ramsey and had him call Governor Romney to inform him of the plan.

As we were being dismissed, the President touched my arm, looked at me for a long moment and then said, "Have a safe trip, Roger."

It was his way of saying that he was sorry that he had almost said "nigger" in front of me. I was amused, because I was sure it was one of the mainstays of his uninhibited vocabulary.

At the door of the Cabinet Room, John Doar and I paused to use the phone there to start the arrangements for our trip.

"Who are you taking with you?" John asked me.

"Nobody," I answered. "I already have a man there. If I get

there and find I need other people, I'll send for them. Who're you taking?"

John mentioned three names. I knew the first two, but I asked about the third.

"Who's Jesse Queen?"

"Don't you know Jesse Queen?" John said. "He's a Negro, *but* he's soft-spoken and he takes orders well."

I just looked at him and then turned to the phone to tell my office that I wouldn't be in that day.

Smoke was rising from Detroit when our plane flew over it. There were plenty of flames licking high as we came down the freeway on our way to police headquarters at 300 Beaubien.

"It's a great town if you're a fire buff," Christopher told Ramsey later on the phone.

We then met with Governor Romney, Mayor Jerome Cavanagh, the head of the Michigan National Guard, and the police super-intendent. They didn't know what to do. They had no moves planned. We were astonished to learn that the Guard Commander had thousands of troops in reserve, despite Romney's assertion that federal troops were needed. What was the level of violence, we wanted to know. Well, they didn't exactly know. The fire department was reporting a high incidence of sniper fire. So was the National Guard. It was dangerous out there. A blanket curfew had been imposed. Liquor stores were closed for the duration. They didn't know what else to do. I had never seen as impotent a group of men in my life. It was clear that the whole thing was in our hands.

When the troops got on the ground, Cy decided to bring them into town to patrol the east side of the city, freeing the Guard and the local and state police to handle the west side, where most of the action had occurred. What we needed most at that point was information more reliable than the hysterical reporting of the fire department about the level of violence in the city. I was the community-relations guy. I was the guy with a field man on the ground. I was it. My job was to go out and get the smell and the feel of the city, find the significant blacks, take their temperature and forge the links between our group and the black community.

The pattern of our days was set. We would get to our headquarters in the police department by seven-thirty, eat lunch at our desks and go back to the hotel at about five-thirty. We'd clean up and reassemble in the Vances' suite—Gay Vance was there with Cy—for cocktails. Since bars and liquor stores were closed, Mayor Cavanagh had provided Cy with a good supply of booze. Then we'd have dinner together in the hotel dining room. At about seven-thirty, we'd leave Gay Vance—a gracious, charming and attractive lady—and go back to work at headquarters. Everybody but the duty man—we took turns at that—would break at twelve-thirty or one to go back to the hotel to sleep. The man on duty had to stay at the office all night to handle any emergencies and to wake the rest of us if all hell broke loose.

The cocktail-dinner break became a ritual. It was the one oasis in a long and grubby day. We always did it together. We all looked forward to it.

When I made my rounds of the city at night, it was eerie. There was no traffic on the streets, and the city was very dark, because the National Guard and the police had shot out many of the street lights for cover. There were armed checkpoints all over the city. There is no experience quite like being stopped at gunpoint by armed and uniformed men in the middle of an American city. I would ride with my field man, who was also black, in his civilian car. As we approached checkpoints I would pull out my leather-encased Justice Department identification, hold it out the window and call out "Department of Justice." I was not going to risk being shot by a scared kid with a rifle in his hands.

I saw no evidence of the sniping that the fire department talked so much about. Occasionally, there were gunshots, but invariably, when we checked them out, we found they came from some trigger-happy Guardsman who had just shot out a street light. There was danger in the streets, though, and it came from the forces of law and order. I quickly learned that I was safest on the east side of town where the disciplined Army units were on patrol. The west side was downright frightening. The Michigan Guard was made up of white country kids who didn't know the city and were scared of blacks. If they hadn't been so dangerous with loaded rifles in their hands, they would have been ludicrous with those baby faces under their battle helmets. Moreover, Michigan State Police were pretty rough customers, and the Detroit Police had a long-standing reputation for brutality against blacks.

One night I was riding out on one of Detroit's main west side arteries, with two black staff members, when a convoy of seven state and local police cars went screaming by in the opposite direction. They screamed at us to get off the streets because there was sniping in the direction from which they had come. We headed for the sniping, but didn't see any. Finally, we decided to cruise down a side street to see what was happening when the convoy caught up with us, lights flashing and sirens screaming. They flagged us down at the corner of a large avenue, just as an old white Buick with a black man and woman in the front seat and two black children in the back turned into it.

"Come out of the car with your hands up," somebody shouted at us with a bullhorn.

The three of us came out of the car, credentials out, hands up shouting, "Department of Justice, Department of Justice."

We found ourselves surrounded by more than twenty armed white men aiming loaded rifles, shotguns and pistols at us.

"You're curfew breakers. What the hell are you doing on the streets?" a rough voice demanded.

"Department of Justice, Department of Justice," we kept yelling.

The blacks in the other car hadn't come out immediately, and I saw and heard cursing men go in after them and the ripping of clothing. The cops hadn't responded to our identifying shouts and shouted obscenities at us behind raised rifles.

Thirty-five years old and dead at the corner of Grand River and Joy Road, I thought. My father had died when he was thirty-five.

After the longest, stillest moment of my life, the cop who was in charge understood what we had been yelling. He motioned for his men to lower their firearms and stopped the others from snatching the people out of the Buick. It turned out that the man in the Buick had a special pass to be out at night because he did essential work at a G.M. plant, and his wife and two children had picked him up there to take him home. The officers apologized to us and told us they had to be careful, but advised us to get off the streets because they were so dangerous.

We got back in our cars, and the old Buick, which had a broken spring in the rear, went on off down Grand River, spewing exhaust fumes in its wake.

"Motherfuckers," I heard the man yell as his car limped on down the street. When I got back to headquarters, and made my report, including that incident, the three-star general who was in charge of the troops looked at me for a long time and then said, "Jesus, Roger, you're lucky to be alive."

Echoes of Los Angeles. The Detroit police killed a lot of black people during the Algiers Motel incident that night.

Detroit was full of black consciousness and intellectual ferment in the summer of 1967. A number of the major black thinkers lived there. One of them was the Reverend Albert Cleage, who started as a Congregational minister, but who by that time had renamed his church the Church of the Black Madonna. He was one of the black people I thought it important for Vance to meet if he were to have a full understanding of what was going on in the city. It was ironic that Cleage, one of the major apostles of black consciousness, was a very light-skinned man with light eyes.

Vance masked his surprise when Cleage met him at the church door. The two men were cordial to each other and got on easily. After they had talked for a while about the problems of blacks in Detroit, the minister offered to show Vance through his church.

"What denomination are you?" Cleage asked.

"Episcopalian," Vance replied.

"Oh, it's about the same," Cleage said.

Some black-consciousness thinkers felt that whites had done a terrible psychological thing to blacks by giving us a white god. During the riot, somebody had gone onto the grounds of a white monastery located in the heart of the black west-side area and had painted the face and hands of a statue of Jesus a deep, rich brown. Cleage chatted about such things with Vance as he headed him down the aisle toward the back of the church. When we got there, Cleage turned us around. Since I knew what we would see, I watched Vance's face. It blanched and his mouth dropped open.

Above the altar of this church, where a stained glass window might have been, was a huge oil painting of a Madonna against a background of deep blue. She was holding a baby. Both she and the baby had Africanoid features and were shiny black.

"Very impressive," Vance managed to say.

"Yes, I think so," Cleage said.

In addition to restoring order, we tried to put a group of prominent and powerful whites together with a representative group of black leaders so they could begin a process of improving the lives of the poor blacks in the city. Everybody told us that the key to such an effort was Walker Cisler, then head of the Detroit Edison Company. Cisler was said to be the mover who made things happen in Detroit.

One afternoon, after John Doar and I had spent the day at the federal prison in Milan, Michigan, interviewing people who had been arrested during the rioting, we learned that a meeting with Walker Cisler had been arranged. He had invited Mr. Vance to the Detroit Yacht Club for dinner.

"The Detroit Yacht Club?" I asked John, who had taken the call.

"Yes," John said. "I thought you ought to know that."

The Detroit Yacht Club was notorious among Detroit blacks. It didn't allow them to eat there.

"We're going to dinner there tonight. I thought you ought to know that," John repeated. "And I think Mr. Vance wants you to call him at the hotel."

So, I called Cy at the hotel. He asked how it had gone at the penitentiary, and I told him. He then said he'd see me back at the headquarters later in the evening. Everybody else in the group went to Cisler's dinner at the Detroit Yacht Club—as part of a mission that had black people, their lives and their aspirations, at the center of it all.

But many good things came out of Detroit. Cisler and some others helped form the New Detroit Committee, which still exists as part of the National Urban Coalition; it has done many constructive things in the city over the years. The auto companies opened up a number of jobs and instituted innovative training programs. Henry Ford became deeply involved over a long period of time in the affairs of the inner city. After a while, the embers cooled, the troops went back South, and we returned to Washington.

On one of our last nights in the city, John Doar and Warren Christopher decided that they wanted to join me on my nightly rounds to make sure that the city was now as calm as I had been reporting it to be. We got a driver and a car from the federal motor pool and set out. The driver, who was black, was clearly reluctant to be out on those eerie streets at night, but he had no choice. Christopher sat up in front next to him, and Doar sat behind him. I sat in the back behind the driver.

At the first checkpoint we reached, the Guardsman approached the car from the passenger side and he could see Christopher and Doar. He asked politely for their credentials and passed us through quickly. At the next checkpoint, the Guardsman approached from the driver's side, and he could see only two blacks. Perhaps because the car had federal motor pool markings on the door, perhaps because there were white men in the car, and perhaps because I was tired, I was sloppy. I didn't have my credentials in my hand as he came up to the car and I reached inside my suit pocket for them as he was standing there. Suddenly I felt cold steel on my neck.

"Don't move another muscle," the Guardsman said.

I froze with my hand in my pocket. Doar and Christopher quickly identified us, and the man removed the muzzle of the gun from my neck. Months later Christopher remarked at a meeting how different it was when the car had been approached on the black side from how it had been when approached from the white side. I was glad he remembered.

On one of our last nights in the city, when things had calmed down, I arranged to have dinner with my college roommate Dr. John Loomis and his wife, Suane. I met them at the home of one of her affluent relatives, who was also a doctor. The major north-south arteries on the west side were typical slum-commercial and had been hit very hard in the arson and the looting. Yet a number of the east-west streets between these major arteries contained some of the finest housing then available to black people. Suane's relatives lived on such a street only a few blocks each way from some of the major devastation areas. Before we went out to dinner, the relatives, John, Suane and I discussed the riot. It was going along quietly when the lady of the house, who had many diamonds on her fingers, turned to me and demanded:

"What is it that *they* want?"

I looked at her for a long time. This was the kind of middle-class Negro that I'd been running from all my life. Diamonds on her fingers, Cadillacs in her garage, and brown skin stretched across her strong boned face. What do *they* want?

"Jobs and dignity, I guess," I replied.

"Well, there's not much dignity in burning and looting," she replied haughtily. I closed my eyes. I had to go through this with white people all the time.

"No, I suppose not," I said without opening my eyes, "but I guess there's also not much dignity in sitting there quietly while the society chokes the life out of you and your children."

CHAPTER NINE

POWER!
(1966–1968)

Introduction by Gerald Gill

From 1966 through 1968, organizing campaigns on behalf of political and community empowerment in northeastern, midwestern, and western urban centers came to characterize the changing nature of African-American protest. These campaigns ranged from essentially reformist efforts by blacks to gain electoral office in locales where blacks were a near majority, if not majority, of the population to efforts deemed more radical to hold institutions to accountability or to exercise more complete forms of self-determination.

Owing to demographic changes in population from World War II through the mid-1960s, urban centers in the Northeast, the Midwest, and the far West came to be the home of more and more black residents. Yet, with the number of black residents approaching or exceeding 50 percent of the population in a growing number of cities, political power and decision making still remained in the hands of white elected officials. Increasingly, black voters came to complain about the nature of client-patron relations in urban centers. Although registered black voters gave their support to white political elites, they were not necessarily rewarded with improved city services, an improved stock of housing, better schools, and better community-police relations.

While the urban rebellions from 1964 through 1967 would

highlight both the frustrations and the unmet expectations of black city dwellers across the country, campaigns were under way in 1967 in two cities that would end with electoral victories for Richard Hatcher and Carl Stokes. In a 1967 campaign equally as historic as that being waged simultaneously in Cleveland, Ohio, city council member Richard C. Hatcher sought to become mayor of Gary, Indiana. Pledging to rid the midsized industrial city of "graft, corruption, inefficiency, poverty, racism and stagnation," Hatcher had to run against a Democratic incumbent, a hostile county machine, and a Republican challenger referred to in his campaign literature as "100 percent American." On November 7, 1967, by a less than two-thousand-vote margin, Richard Hatcher was elected mayor and, following his inauguration in January 1968, he would hold that office for twenty years.

November 7, 1967, would also witness the election of Carl Stokes as mayor of Cleveland. Stokes, a former assistant police prosecutor and three-term state representative, had finished second in the citywide race for mayor in 1965. In the aftermath of the Hough rebellion and increased racial tensions in the city in 1966–1967, Stokes announced his second campaign for the mayoral office. While already enjoying support in several of the city's black neighborhoods, Stokes sought to solidify his base by encouraging a summer-long registration campaign and by establishing contacts among voters on the predominantly white West Side. Stokes defeated the incumbent Ralph Locher in the primary and faced Republican candidate Seth Taft in the general election. Although he was the official Democratic Party nominee in a largely Democratic city, Stokes was no shoo-in. While debating Taft in a joint appearance on the West Side, Stokes, in the minds of several members of his campaign staff, committed a near fatal faux pas when he accused Taft of interjecting the issue of race into a campaign Taft characterized as heretofore devoid of racial fears. Nonetheless, Stokes persevered and, like Hatcher, won a very close election. His inauguration later in November made him the first black mayor of a major American city.

The registering and the mobilizing of black voters to help elect a black candidate to office would be only one strategy used on behalf of political empowerment in the late 1960s. The victories of Hatcher and Stokes, followed in succession by ongoing municipal successes in cities across the country since the late 1960s served to illustrate one facet of Bayard Rustin's hope that movement activities would progress "from protest to politics." But electoral successes, then and now, would not suffice as other forms of empowerment, forms viewed by many as more radical, came to the fore. While the Watts rebellion of 1965 revealed the dissatisfaction of many black residents of south central Los Angeles, the grievances and frustrations of blacks living in California were not readily known to most national black spokespersons.

In 1966, Huey P. Newton and Bobby Seale, two students at Merritt College in Oakland, California, formed the organization the Black Panther Party for Self-Defense. Borrowing the name and emblem of the Lowndes County, Alabama, independent party and heavily influenced by the writings of Frantz Fanon, Malcolm X, and Mao Tse-tung, the two Panther leaders espoused an ideology based on revolutionary nationalism and self-defense. In October 1966, Newton and Seale spelled out the party's aims: self-determination, full employment, decent housing, an end to exploitation, exemption from military service for black males, and an end to "police brutality and murder."

Early activities of the party were focused on the monitoring of the activities and behavior of the Oakland Police Department toward blacks. Viewed as local heroes by many Oakland blacks and as adversaries by the police, the Black Panthers were gaining local and statewide attention. While the male Panthers' uniform— black leather jacket, black trousers, and black beret—was appealing to many, the coverage given to Panther activities frightened many. In May 1967, to show their opposition to proposed state legislation prohibiting the carrying of loaded weapons, members of the Black Panther Party carried weapons into the California State Legislature. This one event, while given decidedly negative coverage in most of the electronic and print media, did provide national exposure to the Black Panther Party.

Further support for the organization came when Eldridge Cleaver, a newly paroled inmate, joined the party early in 1967. Cleaver soon became the party's chief publicist as the minister of information and resident intellectual (Seale was the chairman of the party and Newton was the minister of defense). The party established an official publication, the weekly newspaper *The Black*

Panther, and the party's activities were publicized through expanded distribution of the paper, through Cleaver's writings in white radical publications, and through his best-selling collection of essays, *Soul on Ice*. By early 1968, local chapters of the Black Panther Party were being established all across the country. By 1968, the party was starting to move beyond its image as a self-defense, revolutionary nationalistic organization. Rejecting the preachings of black nationalist and cultural nationalist spokespersons, party leaders called for the creation of coalitions with white revolutionaries in armed struggles for change. Yet, in addition to revolutionary bravado, party chapters initiated free breakfast programs for schoolchildren, free health clinics, black liberation schools, and ongoing attempts to bring about civilian control of police departments.

The efforts undertaken by individual chapters of the Black Panther Party in pursuit of community control of institutions were not alterably different in aim and in intent from those undertaken by parents, organizers, and community activists in several cities who were seeking to make public school systems more responsive to and more accountable to their local charges. While organizers and activists in New York City had called for school desegregation, even going so far as to stage a one-day school boycott in February 1964, by 1966 school desegregation in the nation's largest city had become a moot issue. Instead, residents of the Ocean Hill–Brownsville section of Brooklyn came to support the idea of more parental and community involvement in the operation of neighborhood schools. Enjoying initial support from the United Federation of Teachers, from the office of Mayor John Lindsay, and from the Ford Foundation, Ocean Hill–Brownsville was to be a test site in school decentralization. A newly created governing board—composed of parents, representatives from community organizations and institutions, and teachers—would oversee the operation of schools in the district. Rhody McCoy, a longtime teacher in the city's school system, was chosen as the district's superintendent.

As school year 1967–1968 began, McCoy wished to implement personnel and policy changes—the appointing of three principals of color, the hiring of school aides and monitors from the neighborhood, increased control of the curricula offerings, and increased accountability. Differences, ideological and procedural, led the teachers' representatives to withdraw from the local board and to participate in a suit against the hiring of new principals. Tensions worsened as McCoy sought the transfer of nineteen teachers and administrators whom he and the governing board deemed hostile to "community control." The teachers and administrators balked at reassignment without a hearing and their cases were upheld in special arbitration.

As the community board chose not to accept the return of the teachers, the teachers' union, the United Federation of Teachers, went out on strike during September 1968. Tensions became further inflamed as teachers from schools in Ocean Hill–Brownsville contended that they had received anti-Semitic leaflets. The leaflets were duplicated for wider dissemination and the teachers' strike and the whole debate over "community control" and "decentralization" became cast as a matter of black anti-Semitism. Faced with the continuing strike and with growing citywide polarization over the charge of anti-Semitism in Ocean Hill–Brownsville, the board of education intervened by suspending the local governing board, placing the district under trusteeship, removing those principals hired by the board, and reinstating the teachers whose transfers were sought.

The quest for community control and political empowerment would have mixed results in the years from 1966 to 1968, but would shape and help determine ongoing strategies in the 1970s and 1980s. The victories by Hatcher and Stokes in 1967 would set the stage for how blacks could gain electoral control of city hall in cities as varied as Atlanta, Detroit, and Los Angeles and more recently in New York and Seattle. And, while the Black Panther Party never envisioned its message of control and empowerment as supportive of electoral reforms, the campaigns in Oakland ironically would set the stage for Bobby Seale's campaign for mayor and Lionel Wilson's election as Oakland's first black mayor. Moreover, while the Ocean Hill–Brownsville experiment in school decentralization and community control was short-lived, its effects would be long-lasting on the parents, the students, and community residents who would become involved in other campaigns—electoral as well as local organizing—on behalf of the empowerment of Ocean Hill–Brownsville's, Brooklyn's, and the city of New York's people of color.

1. "Taking Over"
Carl B. Stokes

In this selection from his 1973 autobiography, Carl Stokes outlines one episode during his 1967 campaign for mayor. In a relatively controversial decision, Stokes met with Martin Luther King, Jr., in an effort to persuade King not to alienate white potential voters by staging marches in Cleveland during the course of the mayoral campaign.

. . . You learn to expect the unexpected in politics, you even try to plan for it. But how could I have ever dreamed that suddenly a threat to all my plans, my attempt to put black people in power in the eighth largest city in the country, would appear in the form of Dr. Martin Luther King, Jr., the most honored black leader in America?

I had put together a delicate, not to say precarious, structure. No one outside my campaign organization, and few on the inside, understood quite how it worked. The principles were elegantly simple. I had on paper what was out there, where the votes were, both for and against us. And I had in my head the things I knew had to be done to protect the votes for me and neutralize the votes against me. The delicacy of the structure lay in the proportion of my base vote; or, taken the other way, I had to keep the sixty-two percent white population from using its strength against me.

In 1967, Dr. King's great career was at a low point. He had just come out of Cicero, Illinois, with great disappointments, discovering just how profound are the white man's hatred and prejudice. He desperately needed a victory. The near-success we had in Cleveland in 1965 had swept the nation, and in 1967 all the national political writers were covering the Cleveland mayoral race. They wrote articles on our organization, the use of the business community, the registration drives. It began to look like we would win. Dr. King let us know he wanted to come.

We had been through it before. In the late spring the so-called Big Six, the major civil-rights figures, had announced they were coming to Cleveland that summer to register every black voter and energize the black community. Well, we already had the black community organized, mobilized and energized. If the Big Six came to Cleveland with their various rhetorics, they would create an energy that would in turn create an opposite and probably more than equal counter-energy. [Friend and campaign manager] Dr. [Kenneth] Clement and I had flown to New York and met with those men in a motel right at La Guardia Airport. We had explained to them that they could only bring problems for us. We were juggling a delicate situation that could, with the slightest wrong move, come down around our heads. We had asked them not to come. We had understood why they wanted to come. Cleveland was where the action was, at the focus of the eyes of the black world. Remember that at the same time Richard Hatcher was running for mayor of Gary, Indiana; but Gary was predominantly black. A victory in Gary was inevitable, therefore comparatively dull. The real action was in Cleveland. But fortunately we had managed to head off the move.

When Dr. King made his decision, Dr. Clement tried to talk to some of his aides, to convince them that we already had a winner, but that it could be lost if black pride started prodding white fears. Dr. Clement told them that we had for the first time the opportunity to seize real power by winning a city hall. Dr. King's coming would only release the haters and the persons looking for an issue to excite racist reaction to what we were doing.

He was not successful. Dr. King came to town. W. O. Walker arranged a meeting between Dr. King and me in his *Call & Post* office. I had met Dr. King at various national conferences since 1965, but we had never worked together. I felt a towering respect for the man, even awe. Facing down the bigots in Cleveland is one thing, but I knew I would never have had the nerve to walk across that Selma bridge or lead the people against Birmingham's Bull Connor. King's courage was of a different order from mine, suitable to different places, different actions.

In our meeting, I explained to Dr. King that I had carefully put this whole campaign together. I had worked to get actual white votes. I couldn't afford to do anything to aggravate the white voter. There was too much at stake. We had everything together, and if nothing foreign was introduced we knew how to handle the situation.

"Martin," I told him, "if you come in here with these marches and what not, you can just see what the reaction will be. You saw it in Cicero and other Northern towns. We have got to win a political victory here. This is our chance to take over a power that is just unprecedented among black people. But I'm very concerned that if you come here you're going to upset the balance we've created. You're going to create problems that we do not have now and may not be able to handle. I would rather that you not stay."

How on earth can any black American say that to Martin Luther King? I can tell you it was hard. But I knew I had my own way to make it hard for whites to live with their own prejudices. I knew that Dr. King and I wanted the same things. Finally, I knew my own situation, my own town, and I knew I had it in my hand. Once I got it, I knew I could do things that no civil-rights march ever did.

"Carl, I know just what you mean," he said. "We discussed this at SCLC headquarters before I came out here. But I am responding to the invitation of the United Pastors."

The United Pastors was a group of about a dozen ministers who were in an internal struggle with other ministers and were bidding to establish their own community leadership.

"I understand that, Dr. King, but they're thinking about promoting their group, while the question here is whether or not a black man takes over audacious power."

He listened to me, but I could see that he was going to stay. He needed to be on the scene of a victory.

"I will have to stay," he said, "but I promise you there will be nothing inflammatory. We'll try to do a job here and our people will get in touch with your people, and any time that you feel there is something harmful to your overall campaign, just let me know."

Dr. King did limit his visits and he did conduct his activities in a very restrained manner. He helped a great deal in not creating more problems than those posed by his mere presence. And those problems were real. Letters with the signature of the Democratic Party county chairman, Albert S. Porter, went out, saying that the election of Carl Stokes would mean turning over the city to Martin Luther King, a calamity that was meant to sound on the order of turning over a daughter or sister.

Ever since Dr. King's death, I have had to grapple with the problem of dealing with a small group of black leaders who grew out of the SCLC movement, because they knew of my not wanting Dr. King here. Asking Dr. King not to stay was one of the toughest decisions I ever had to make. It was a confrontation with a man whose recorded words I turn to for solace and inspiration at moments of depression. But it came down to the hard game of politics—whether we wanted a cause or a victory. I wanted to win. Our people needed me to win. I had been the architect for a unique assembly of interests, and I knew with one wrong move it would be just another house of cards.

2. Interview with Thompson J. "Mike" Gaines

Thompson J. "Mike" Gaines, a longtime member of the Congress of Racial Equality, volunteered in the 1965 and 1967 Stokes campaigns. This excerpt is from a 1988 interview with Gaines by the Eyes on the Prize *production team.*

I went to Washington in 1963 for the march, and I came back inspired by Dr. King's speeches and his philosophy on how to get things done. I was a very angry man at the inequities in our society. And from him, I really began to feel that violence was not the way to redress our grievances. So, naturally, when Carl Stokes announced that he would be a candidate for mayor, myself and hundreds of other people felt that this would be a good way to redress our grievances through the democratic process.

Most of your so-called political leaders went into hiding when this young black man decided to rock the political structure in Cleveland, Ohio. These were the black political leaders. It was very simple: They had been leading the white establishment to believe that they had the black vote under their control and under their command, and in turn, they were getting their rewards—

you know, patronage or what have you. But there was nothing coming down to the general black community. And when I say "coming down," the things that we wanted was better police protection, housing code enforcement, and things to maintain our community. We had a number of black councilmen at that time— off the top of my head, I know we had at least six or seven—but only one of them stood up for Carl Stokes. His name was James Bell, and he is now deceased.

So we did things quietly. We didn't call up the television station and say, "We are now trying to register black people today." We just went out and got the job done. And therefore we kind of caught the white community asleep. Because I don't think they realized we had the voting power we actually had. But in 1965, we also had a number of blacks that simply didn't come to the polls, because they simply didn't have the confidence that a black could win.

We would knock on doors and ask for signatures, and the first thing so many people would ask is, "Is he qualified?" Now mind you, here is a young black attorney that graduated from college, had his degree. At one time the president of our council was a high school dropout. And we've also had a mayor who was a high school dropout.

There was a certain segment of people who felt this can't be, the people just won't elect a black man. This is what was so hard in the role that I played, as well as hundreds of others, in knocking on doors to get people to sign petitions or come out and vote. It was just difficult to get people to believe in themselves, that we can do this if you just come out and vote. We brought out the fact that there must be something to the opportunity or the privilege of voting, and we would point out that people in the South were giving up their lives, sacrificing themselves for this right, being abused, driven off of their farmlands, off of sharecropper farmlands, because they were seeking to vote. Now we pointed out to the people that if these people are willing to make this big of a sacrifice to register to vote, and here in the North you have this opportunity, why can't you? And this worked in most cases. This was enough leverage to get the people to register to vote.

3. Interview with Geraldine Williams

Activist Geraldine Williams, an officer of the Nonpartisan Voters League, was instrumental in convincing Carl Stokes to run for mayor in 1965 and worked on both his campaigns. This is from a 1988 interview by the Eyes on the Prize *production team.*

INTERVIEWER: What people made up the Stokes campaign in '67? Where was the support coming from?

GERALDINE WILLIAMS: Well, in '67 it came from all over, since Carl had demonstrated that he could win. It came from labor. It came from white elected officials, black elected officials. And it also came from all over the country. We sent out letters and flyers and things to other politicians in other cities and so forth and so on. And we got a lot of money in for the '67 campaign from people all over the United States. Since this was really something different, something new, something momentous, I guess they wanted to get in on the action. We were all idealists. We appealed to all the people that had ideals that politics could really be better. So they sent us money.

INT: Could you talk about the voter education work you had to do after the primary?

G.W.: Well, you see, a lot of people had just registered. And they knew nothing whatsoever about voting. We had stressed so much that you must vote for Carl in the primary or you won't get a second chance. Now, if you don't put him on the ballot you can forget the whole deal. So they went out and voted for him. I think that was October the third. Okay. We said, "Now, we got to get them back to the polls again November seventh." So we had telephone banks going and we would call them and we would visit them. We'd have the block captains go see 'em, the block supervisors. And they'd tell us, "Already voted for him." We said, "Oh, my God. We got to do a voter education campaign." We said, "Yes, but you just put him on the ticket. You've got to go back again and vote to be sure that he's the mayor." And that was a job. Because we had all these new registered voters that had never voted before and we had a job on our hands.

INT: Will you tell us about the second debate [with Republican Seth Taft], at John Marshall High School on the west side? What did Stokes say?

G.W.: There were very few blacks over there to start out with, I think just a handful of us from the campaign. Blacks don't go on the west side too much. I mean, we never did feel too welcome. And Stokes introduced the matter of race into the campaign. I guess it took Seth quite by surprise, and he said, "Well, well, well, I guess if you don't vote for Carl Stokes, you're a racist." And our hearts just sank because that was his very best remark of the whole night. I'm sure that Carl introducing this into the campaign caught him by surprise, but he certainly rose to the occasion, you can believe that. And it scared us to death and then you could just sort of feel the hostility. And we were very glad to get back to the east side and get out of that high school.

INT.: What happened the next day?

G.W.: Oh, the next day when Carl showed up in the office, nobody spoke to him because they thought he'd really torn his custom-made britches. You know, I mean he shouldn't have done that! And he was trying to explain to us why he did and he always has a reason for everything that he does. Nobody bought it. So we sort of boycotted him that day, we wouldn't speak to him. But it was all right after that.

INT: Was it particularly significant that a black man won the mayoral race? Did that seem like an important step?

G.W.: Oh, yes, it was a first! I mean, it was quite important. We had done something that hadn't been done anyplace in the country before, and since folks laughed at us in '65 and we pulled it off in '67, I guess we felt pretty smug about it. Yeah, we were very happy about it. And we said, if it can be done here, it can be done other places. I've always felt that we started the trend, and I've always been very happy about that. 'Cause after then, black mayors jumped up all over.

4. "The Founding of the Black Panther Party" and "Patrolling"

Huey P. Newton

When Huey P. Newton and Bobby Seale founded the Black Panther Party in October 1966, they named their new organization after the emblem that the Lowndes County Freedom Organization in Alabama had come to be known by. These are excerpts from two chapters of Newton's **Revolutionary Suicide** *(1973).*

We had seen Watts rise up the previous year. We had seen how the police attacked the Watts community after causing the trouble in the first place. We had seen Martin Luther King come to Watts in an effort to calm the people, and we had seen his philosophy of nonviolence rejected. Black people had been taught nonviolence; it was deep in us. What good, however, was nonviolence when the police were determined to rule by force? . . . We had seen all this, and we recognized that the rising consciousness of Black people was almost at the point of explosion. . . .

Out of this need sprang the Black Panther Party. Bobby [Seale] and I finally had no choice but to form an organization that would involve the lower-class brothers.

All that summer we circulated in the Black communities of Richmond, Berkeley, Oakland, and San Francisco. Wherever brothers gathered, we talked with them about their right to arm. In general, they were interested but skeptical about the weapons idea. . . . The way we finally won the brothers over was by patrolling the police with arms.

Before we began the patrols, however, Bobby and I set down in writing a practical course of action. . . .

I started rapping off the essential points for the survival of Black and oppressed people in the United States. Bobby wrote them down, and then we separated those ideas into two sections, "What We Want" and "What We Believe. . . ."

. . . This is the program we wrote down:

OCTOBER 1966
BLACK PANTHER PARTY
PLATFORM AND PROGRAM
WHAT WE WANT
WHAT WE BELIEVE

1. *We want freedom. We want power to determine the destiny of our Black Community. . . .*

2. *We want full employment for our people. . . .*

3. *We want an end to the robbery by the capitalists of our Black Community. . . .*

4. *We want decent housing, fit for shelter of human beings. . . .*

5. *We want education for our people that exposes the true nature of this decadent American society. We want education that teaches us our true history and our role in present-day society. . . .*

6. *We want all Black men to be exempt from military service. . . .*

7. *We want an immediate end to POLICE BRUTALITY and MURDER of Black people. . . .*

8. *We want freedom for all Black men held in federal, state, county and city prisons and jails. . . .*

9. *We want all Black people when brought to trial to be tried in court by a jury of their peer group or people from their Black communities, as defined by the Constitution of the United States. . . .*

10. *We want land, bread, housing, education, clothing, justice, and peace. And as our major political objective, a United Nations-*

supervised plebiscite to be held throughout the Black colony in which only Black colonial subjects will be allowed to participate, for the purpose of determining the will of Black people as to their national destiny.

We started now to implement our ten-point program. Interested primarily in educating and revolutionizing the community, we needed to get their attention and give them something to identify with. This is why the seventh point—police action—was the first program we emphasized. . . . This is a major issue in every Black community. The police have never been our protectors. Instead, they act as the military arm of our oppressors and continually brutalize us. Many communities have tried and failed to get civilian review boards to supervise the behavior of the police. . . . We recognized that it was ridiculous to report the police to the police, but we hoped that by raising encounters to a higher level, by patrolling the police with arms, we would see a change in their behavior. Further, the community would notice this and become interested in the Party. Thus our armed patrols were also a means of recruiting.

At first, the patrols were a total success. Frightened and confused, the police did not know how to respond, because they had never encountered patrols like this before. They were familiar with the community-alert patrols in other cities, but never before had guns been an integral part of any patrol program. With weapons in our hands, we were no longer their subjects but their equals.

Out on patrol, we stopped whenever we saw the police questioning a brother or a sister. We would walk over with our weapons and observe them from a "safe" distance so that the police could not say we were interfering with the performance of their duty.

The Black Panthers were and are always required to keep their activities within legal bounds. . . . So, we studied the law about weapons and kept within our rights. . . .

. . . The police, invariably shocked to meet a cadre of disciplined and armed Black men coming to the support of the community, reacted in strange and unpredictable ways. In their fright, some of them became children, cursing and insulting us. We responded in kind, calling them swine and pigs, but never cursing—this would be cause for arrest—and we took care not to be arrested with our weapons.

In addition to our patrols and confrontations with the police, I did a lot of recruiting in pool halls and bars, sometimes working twelve to sixteen hours a day. I passed out leaflets with our ten-point program, explaining each point to all who would listen.

This recruiting had an interesting ramification in that I tried to transform many of the so-called criminal activities going on in the street into something political, although this had to be done gradually. Instead of trying to eliminate these activities—numbers, hot goods, drugs—I attempted to channel them into significant community actions. . . . Many of the brothers who were burglarizing and participating in similar pursuits began to contribute weapons and material to community defense. In order to survive they still had to sell their hot goods, but at the same time they would pass some of the cash on to us. That way, ripping off became more than just an individual thing.

Gradually the Black Panthers came to be accepted in the Bay Area community. We had provided a needed example of strength and dignity by showing people how to defend themselves. More important, we lived among them. They could see every day that with us the people came first.

5. "Seize the Time"
Bobby Seale

In this selection from his 1968 autobiography, Bobby Seale, chairman of the Black Panther Party, describes the party leadership's decision to stage the May 1967 protest at the California State Capitol as well as the reactions to that dramatic action.

One Monday morning Huey called me up and said, "Bobby, come over to the house right quick." I went over to the house. Huey showed me the papers. He said, "Look here, Mulford is up in the legislature now, trying to get a bill passed against us. We don't care about laws anyway, because the laws they make don't serve us at all. He's probably making a law to serve the power structure. He's trying to get some kind of law passed against us." He said, "I've been thinking. Remember when I told you we have to go in front of a city hall, in front of a jail, or do something like we did in Martinez, to get more publicity, so we can get a message over to the people?" This was Huey's chief concern, getting the message over to the people.

So Huey says, "You know what we're going to do?" "What?" "We're going to the Capitol." I said, "The *Capitol*?" He says, "Yeah, we're going to the Capitol." I say, "For what?" "Mulford's there, and they're trying to pass a law against our guns, and we're going to the Capitol steps. We're going to take the best Panthers we got and we're going to the Capitol steps with our guns and forces, loaded down to the gills. And we're going to read a message to the world, because all the press is going to be up there. The press is always up there. They'll listen to the message, and they'll probably blast it all across this country. I know, I know they'll blast it all the way across California. We've got to get a message over to the people."

Huey understood a revolutionary culture, and Huey understood how arms and guns become a part of the culture of a people in the revolutionary struggle. And he knew that the best way to do it was to go forth, and those hungry newspaper reporters, who are shocked, who are going to be shook up, are going to be blasting that news faster than they could be stopped. I said, "All right, brother, right on. I'm with you. We're going to the Capitol." So we called a meeting that night, before going up to the Capitol, to write the first executive mandate for the Black Panther Party. Huey was going to write Executive Mandate Number One.

This executive mandate was the first major message to *all* the American people, and *all* the black people, in particular, in this country, who are living in the confines of this decadent system. Eldridge and Huey and all of us sat down, and it didn't take us long. We weren't jiving. No time at all, not like some of the intellectuals and punks that have to take ten days before they can write an executive mandate to put things together. I don't think it was fifteen minutes before we whipped that executive mandate out, looked it over, and Eldridge corrected it, got things together. The executive mandate was the first message, the first major message made by the Black Panther Party, coming from the Minister of Defense, Huey P. Newton. Huey told me to organize the brothers, tell them to get their guns and be at the office tomorrow morning, at nine o'clock. "We're going to leave at ten o'clock. We're going to leave at ten o'clock sharp." . . .

On May 2, 1967, we went across the bridge to Sacramento with a caravan of cars. We wound up right in front of the Capitol building. There were thirty brothers and sisters. Six sisters and twenty-four brothers. Twenty of the brothers were armed.

Huey P. Newton was not with us. The brothers felt we could not risk Huey getting shot or anything, so we voted that he would stay behind in Oakland. We voted Huey down and wouldn't let him come.

When I first drove up, I didn't know where the steps were. The Capitol looked about a block or so away from me. I didn't know whether this was the right place or not, because we were specifically looking for the Assembly of the State of California. The reason I didn't know is because of an old thing they'd taught me in school about the Capitol in Washington, D.C. The dome, a round dome, you know, it was supposed to be the "omnipotent area," as brother Eldridge Cleaver puts it. It's the top, and it was supposed to be made up of two houses.

So I assumed it was the same as Washington, D.C. I didn't know if I was going to the right place or not. But I said, "Look, there's some cameramen up there." Huey said there's always cameramen around these places, so I thought, "This is probably it." The other brothers had parked their cars and had come back around to where we were. We got out of the car and got all our guns out. You know we always follow the laws. As soon as the brothers got out of the car, they were putting rounds into the chambers because Huey and I researched those laws in the past. We had to follow the law to the letter. There was a fish-and-game code law that you couldn't have a loaded shotgun or rifle in a car. That didn't refer to a pistol, but to a shotgun or a rifle.

The loaded rifle or shotgun meant an unexpended cartridge in the chamber. The law also read that unexpended cartridges in the magazine do not constitute a loaded gun. That is, bullets that haven't been fired do not constitute a loaded gun, even if they are in the magazine. But if there is an unexpended cartridge or bullet inside the chamber of a rifle or a shotgun, then it is considered loaded. The brothers got out of the car, and you could see brothers, just jacking rounds off into the chambers.

A lot of people were looking. A lot of white people were shocked, just looking at us. I know what they were saying: "Who in the hell are those niggers with these guns? Who in the hell are those niggers with these guns? What are they doing?"

One or two white people, they probably passed it off, "Oh this is just a gun club," and this is where Bob Dylan gets down on Mr. Jones, "You don't know what's going on." Because this was getting to be a colossal event and those people did not know what the hell was going on. Some of them did look at us like we were a gun club. But a lot of them only had questions on their faces of, "What the hell are those damn niggers doing with these goddam rifles?" They actually stopped and looked at us and stood up there around the Capitol, and stared up from the grass and looked at us. I didn't pay a damn bit of attention to them because we knew our constitutional rights and all that stuff about the rights of citizens to have guns. The Second Amendment to the Constitution of the United States, and no police or militia force can infringe upon that right; it states that specifically.

Anyway, all the brothers got up, and I said, "All right, brothers, let's roll." We started walking and moving. We didn't walk in military form. We just moved. We were scattered all across the sidewalk. We were not in any rank, but we held our guns straight up because Huey had taught us not to point a gun at anyone—not only was it unsafe, but there was a law against just the pointing of a gun.

So all the brothers had that stuff down. They all had their guns pointed straight up in the air or pointed straight down to the ground as they carried them. We were walking up the sidewalk. I remember a brother in the background saying, "Look at Reagan run." I thought that he was just referring to something symbolic, but I did find out later on, after all this shit was over, that

[Governor Ronald] Reagan *was* over there with a bunch of kids. We'd walked almost up this long twenty-foot-wide sidewalk leading up to the first steps of the Capitol, and one of the dudes said, "Look at Reagan run." Now this is very important, because we found out later that Reagan had had with him 200 Future Youth, Future Leaders they call them. He was speaking to them on the lawn of the Capitol. I was looking straight up at the front of the Capitol building and I saw a couple of cameramen running around up there.

I found out later that Reagan had righteously spotted us. One of the brothers saw Reagan turn around and start trotting away from the whole scene because here came all these hardfaced brothers. These brothers were off the block; righteous brothers off the block. From what they call the nitty gritty and the grass roots. You could look at their faces and see the turmoil they've lived through. Their ages ranged anywhere from sixteen, which was about the youngest we had there—that was Bobby Hutton— all the way down to myself, thirty-one. I guess I was about the oldest.

We righteously walked on up to the first stairs, and then we walked on up to the next stairs. Bobby Hutton was on my right side and Warren Tucker was on my left side. Bobby Hutton had a 12-gauge shotgun, a High Standard 12-gauge pump shotgun, that's what Bobby Hutton had. And Warren Tucker had a .357 Magnum. We walked all the way up, and they stayed right next to me.

We got to the stairs. Now personally I do not remember reading Executive Mandate Number One on the stairs, as I was ordered to do. I don't remember reading it there, but the brothers told me and everybody told me that I did in fact read it.

I'm on the stairs and I'm trying to make my mind up about going in. It wasn't any long process by which I had to make up my mind. Huey's emphasis on going into the Capitol was based on the fact that there might be a string of National Guards and policemen there, in case they found out we were coming. I heard the security guard over there talking to two brothers, when I glanced over there a second time, and I heard him say, "You aren't violating anything with your gun, so if you want to, you can go inside." And that made my mind up for me. But I also made up my mind in another context too. That I personally wanted to see the area where a citizen has a right to observe the legislature. I read in the paper that Mulford was an assemblyman from the Sixteenth Assembly District in Oakland, so it was the Assembly that I wanted to see. I waved to all the brothers. I said, "All right, brothers, come on, we're going in there. We're going inside."

The brothers were scattered all out in front of the Capitol. One of the cameramen walked up to me. "Are you going inside the Capitol?" he said. I said, "Yeah, we're going inside." And I snatched the door open, and me and Bobby Hutton and the rest of the brothers walked through that door. Warren Tucker was on my left and brother Bobby Hutton, with his 12-gauge shotgun, was on my right. We walked off into the lobby area. All around, to my right, to my left, everywhere, there were people, predominantly white people, who looked shocked. Man, they were shocked.

As we began to walk, I noticed one thing. They moved and stepped aside, and I saw some with their mouths hanging open, just looking, and they were saying with their eyes and their faces and expressions, "Who in the hell are these niggers with these guns?" And some of them were just saying, "Niggers with guns, niggers with guns," and I pointed those out as enemies because they were confused. I saw three or four faces that really caught what was going on. They must have been in the Assembly and heard Mulford talking about us because they frowned their faces up and looked at us like a bunch of pig racists, like I've seen racist pigs look at me and Huey, like they wanted to kill us.

I saw a long hall in front of me, a very long hall. I said, "We're looking for the Assembly." I saw a sign that said "Senate" and had an arrow that pointed to the right. But I was looking for the Assembly and I hadn't seen any sign. So I walked on. As we walked down the hall, cameramen were running from our left and from our right, around Bobby and around Tucker, jumping in front of us taking flicks and clicking flicks. Cameramen with movie cameras were shooting, but that didn't make any difference. I just tightened up and squeezed the mandate I had rolled up and kept walking. I stopped and said, "Where in the hell's the

Assembly? Anybody in here know where you go in and observe the Assembly making these laws?" Nobody said anything. Then somebody hollered out, "It's upstairs on the next floor."

We went up to the second floor and started walking again. By this time there were many cameramen in front of us, backing up and taking pictures of us walking down the hall. Movie cameramen, still cameramen, regular cameras. Bulbs were flashing all over the place. I got about midway down the hall when I saw a gate. I didn't relate to the gate at first, but I turned around and asked a reporter, "Could you please tell me where I go to observe the Assembly making the laws? I want to go there. I want to see Mulford supposedly making this law against black people." That's what I was thinking to myself—I want to *see this*. So he said, "Straight down, sir." I went ahead and saw this gate. As I was approaching the gate, when I was about five or six feet from it, this pig jumped out, this state pig, and said, "Where the hell are you going?" I said, "I'm going to observe the Assembly. What about it?"

"You can't come in here!"

"What the hell you mean, I can't come in here? You gonna deny me my constitutional right? Every citizen's got a right to observe the Assembly. What's wrong with you?" And while the conversation was going on, the reporters were vamping inside the gate. And so many reporters were trying to get in there, they bammed and knocked the pig all up against the wall. Trying to get pictures. The only thing that was in front of me was the pig, and just a little gate. Swing gate, like a swinging door, but it was only about three feet high. When the reporters vamped all over the pig, he just moved out of the way, and I just proceeded to move on.

As I proceeded to move, the reporters always had a way for me to travel. I noticed the way to go was to the right, so I moved to the right, and as I moved to the right, I could see a kind of heavyset short man, about five-foot six inches or five-foot seven. As I approached a big door that was three or four times as tall as I was, he was opening the door. He was opening the door in a manner of, "Yes, sir, you *sure can* come in. Come right on in, sir! You have the *gun*!" That's what he was saying. You have the gun. Come in. And he opened the door in a very humble manner.

Like a servant. Like a vassal. That's the way he opened that door. He was scared.

I walked inside, and as I did, I saw a lot of what we call "back seats." Back seats in a theater. Inside the Assembly, I looked to the left and I looked to the right. I walked to my left. There was an aisle over there. Cameramen and reporters jumped all in front of me. Something funny about the cameramen and reporters getting up in that aisle to my left. A lot of them came in another door. Because I know they weren't in front of me when I hit that door. They must have come in another door.

As I was walking to my left, I remember hearing this speaker, the Assembly speaker, saying, "Get those cameramen out of here, they're not supposed to be in here." As I got to the aisle, Eldridge Cleaver was there all of a sudden. Eldridge Cleaver was there, and Warren Tucker was halfway up the aisle, with a .357 Magnum on his side. I glanced up, and I saw some so-called black representatives in the legislature who we refer to as "Toms, sellouts, bootlickers."

They were looking at the man as if to say, "Why did they have to come here?" They hated us being there, those bootlickers. I looked at those bootlickers, those Uncle Toms, very intensely. I didn't care for them because they never represented us there. And this kind of humble-shoulderedness and looking back, "Well, here they are, they're here. What are they doing here?"

Someone was saying, "This is not where you're supposed to be. This is not where you're supposed to be." We were trying to decide whether to stay there on the floor of the Assembly or go upstairs. We were trying to discuss that in a very short span of time, in less than a minute. The next thing I know, a pig and Bobby Hutton passed behind my back. Bobby was cussing out the pig who had snatched his gun out of his hand. He had snuck up behind him and snatched his gun out of his hand. Bobby Hutton was cussing the pig back, "What the hell you got my gun for? Am I under arrest or something? If I'm not under arrest, you give me my gun back. You ain't said I was under arrest." He was remembering very well what Huey had taught. Always ask if you are under arrest. And if you're not under arrest, then you stand on your constitutional rights.

So I turned and ran up to the side of the pig and said, "Is this man under arrest? What the hell are you taking his gun for?" He said, "You're not supposed to be in here. This is not where you're supposed to be." I asked him, "Is he under arrest? If he ain't under arrest, what the hell you got his gun for?" Another pig walks up and hands this same pig a gun, which I recognized as the same gun which Mark Comfort had had, a 30-.06. I walked out of those big doors—this pig, me, and Bobby. Bobby was on one side and I was on the other side, Bobby cussing the pig out, calling him all kind of motherfuckers, and telling them to give him his gun back if he ain't under arrest.

Just as we got to the elevator, the pig grabbed hold of my right shoulder. I kept asking him if I were under arrest. He pushed me, and when he pushed I went into the elevator. I said, "All right, we're under arrest, brothers. We must be under arrest. Come on in, let's go." Because just before the pig grabbed me, he said I wasn't under arrest. So I think I accepted this kind of informal thing of him arresting us at this point. Then it flashed in my mind. The mandate . . . the message that Huey sent . . . I haven't read it. I gotta read the message, I gotta read the message. So nine or ten of the brothers just crowded in the elevator with guns, and some reporters got on that elevator too. We went down to the first floor and we went to the right, into a little room with a counter. The room was about ten feet long and six feet wide. All of a sudden I saw all these cameramen poking their cameras in the doors. I said, "Yeah . . . the mandate." The message that Huey told me to read. The message. Gotta get the message over. So I pulled the message out and opened it up, and I read the whole thing. In the background Bobby Hutton was cussing the pigs out and telling them to give him his gun back: "You give me my gun back. You ain't placing me under arrest. You give me my gun back. You ain't placing me under arrest." That might have been mentioned three or four times. He called the pigs all kind of motherfuckers, which even came over on TV, I heard later on.

At this point, after I finished reading the message, right at this point, a black pig walked in. A nigger pig, a "Negro" pig walked in. As he was passing in front of me I said, "Look man, are we under arrest or not?" And he says, "No, you're not under arrest." "Then dammit," I said, "give these black brothers back their guns." At this point he said, "They're going to get back their guns." I said, "Well, give them back to them!" And Bobby Hutton tore into them, "Bastard, load my gun back up. You unloaded my gun. I seen you unload. You unloaded my gun. Load it back up, just like you had it. Give me my gun back."

I glanced over at the counter there, and they were doing something to the guns, the 30-.06 and Bobby Hutton's pump shotgun. Next thing I knew they had the guns back in their hands. I was looking at all these cameramen. They asked me some questions. Somebody said to read it again. Said he didn't catch it. I read the mandate again, right inside that little room. When I finished reading it, I figured it was time to go. So I said, "Let's go." We cut out and came out the door. Then some cameraman walked up to me and asked me to read the message once more. So I read it again. First I was on the upper steps in front of the Capitol. I read it and then I got down to the lower steps and read the message still another time. I said, "All right, brothers, let's go."*

At that time I knew that what Huey P. Newton was saying about the colossal event had occurred. Because many, many cameramen

---

*Executive Mandate Number One
Statement by the Minister of Defense
Delivered May 2, 1967, at Sacramento,
California, State Capitol Building*

The Black Panther Party for Self-Defense calls upon the American people in general and the black people in particular to take careful note of the racist California Legislature which is now considering legislation aimed at keeping the black people disarmed and powerless at the very same time that racist police agencies throughout the country are intensifying the terror, brutality, murder, and repression of black people.

At the same time that the American government is waging a racist war of genocide in Vietnam, the concentration camps in which Japanese Americans were interned during World War II are being renovated and expanded. Since America has historically reserved the most barbaric treatment for non-white people, we are forced to conclude that these concentration camps are being prepared for black people who are determined to gain their freedom by any means necessary. The enslavement of black people from the very beginning of this country, the genocide practiced on the American Indians and the confining of the survivors on reservations, the savage lynching of thousands of black men were there. Many, many people had covered this event of black people walking into the Capitol, and registering their grievance with a particular statement. A message, Executive Mandate Number One, that Huey P. Newton had ordered me to take to the Capitol, to use the mass media as a means of conveying the message to the American people and to the black people in particular. We walked out and got to the car and brother Eldridge Cleaver came up behind me. And Eldridge said, "Brother, we did it. We did it, man. We put it over." I said, "That's right, brother, we sure did."

So I said, "All right, brothers and sisters, let's go. Let's get out of this town." I remember telling everybody, "The sisters and brothers cooked some chicken." The brothers were crowding up. Some of them were slightly behind us, and I said, "Let's go. We gonna go eat all this fried chicken that we got here, 'cause I'm hungry and it's hot in this town. It's hot, brother." So I went and got in my car, and I looked back for those people who'd parked behind me.

I opened the car door and asked the people if they were ready

------

and women, the dropping of atomic bombs on Hiroshima and Nagasaki, and now the cowardly massacre in Vietnam, all testify to the fact that toward people of color the racist power structure of America has but one policy: repression, genocide, terror, and the big stick.

Black people have begged, prayed, petitioned, demonstrated, and everything else to get the racist power structure of America to right the wrongs which have historically been perpetrated against black people. All of these efforts have been answered by more repression, deceit, and hypocrisy. As the aggression of the racist American government escalates in Vietnam, the police agencies of America escalate the repression of black people throughout the ghettoes of America. Vicious police dogs, cattle prods, and increased patrols have become familiar sights in black communities. City Hall turns a deaf ear to the pleas of black people for relief from this increasing terror.

The Black Panther Party for Self-Defense believes that the time has come for black people to arm themselves against this terror before it is too late. The pending Mulford Act brings the hour of doom one step nearer. A people who have suffered so much for so long at the hands of a racist society, must draw the line somewhere. We believe that the black communities of America must rise up as one man to halt the progression of a trend that leads inevitably to their total destruction.

to go. "Let's go," they said. "All right, brothers and sisters. Let's go," I hollered. As I pulled out, I asked, "Where's everybody else?" "They're around the corner," somebody said. "Some of them tried to park around the corner." So we drove around the corner. Further on, down a long, long block, I stopped and made sure that all of our people and all of our cars were in a line behind me. Warren Tucker, who was driving the second or third car, hollered to me, "Hey man, this car is hot." He was driving my '54 Chevy. "It needs some water in it, so we can cool it down." The engine was running hot because there was something wrong with the radiator.

"Later for that," I said. "We're going outside of town. We'll eat that chicken, and we'll get water later on." So I took off in the right-hand lane. Just before the corner, I noticed a sign: SAN FRANCISCO—TURN RIGHT. I stopped for the light and noticed a service station across the street. I debated in my mind. I decided that we'd go ahead and get the water. Instead of turning right, I waited until the green light came on and went straight across the street, and turned up into the service station. The rest of the brothers and sisters rolled into the station and just sat there. It was very, very hot. It was burning up. I decided to take off my leather jacket, but to take off my jacket I had to get out of the car.

As I was opening the door, I looked up and saw a pig at the corner walking south on the sidewalk from his car. He had his gun in his hand. I jumped out. I came on out of the car. I walked straight toward him. I stopped and he stopped. I said, "Now wait a minute." I said, "Now first thing you have to do is you have to put that gun away. Put it back in that holster. If you want to make an arrest you can make an arrest, but you better put that gun away." And the next thing I heard was brothers jacking rounds, jacking shells off into the chambers of their guns. When they saw the pig walking up with that gun, they started jacking rounds off. I said, "Put that gun away!" I looked him dead cold in his eyes. He was a scared pig, with his gun out. He took his gun, after hearing all the rounds, and me telling him to put his gun back, he slid his gun back into his holster, and kept his hands off of it. Right on!

Then I looked up and there was another pig who had walked

up near. He'd parked his motorcycle, and jumped on his little radio. I can't remember what the hell he said on his radio but he looked back at me. "We got a right," he said, "we got a right to have identification." I said, "Maybe you do have a right to identification, but you just make sure you keep your damn guns in your holsters!" The next thing I knew, other pigs were driving up. I heard something come over that radio that said, "Arrest them all. On anything. Arrest them all on anything." That's what it said. Then he asked me where I had been. I said we'd been to the Capitol. "Why? What about it?" You know what he asked me? He said, "What are you, a gun club?" I said, "No, we're the Black Panther Party. We're black people with guns. What about it?"

As I began to move away, I saw a lot of pigs coming up; plainclothesmen jumping out of cars, cars in the middle of the streets, everything. I still wasn't disturbed by them at all. I was just walking. Some plainclothesman came up. "You got any identification?" I said, "Yeah, I got identification." I saw a pig opening a door of one of the cars. I ran over to the car. I said, "Keep your hands off."

I turned around and two pigs were sneaking up behind Sherman Forte. Before I could say anything, they grabbed hold of both of his arms, and one of the pigs snatched his pistol out of his holster. And I said, "Is he under arrest?" "Yeah, he's under arrest." I said, "Take the arrest, Sherman."

The pig asked me again about identification. I went to my back pocket to pull out my wallet, and when I did that the pig, almost simultaneously, grabbed my right arm, and another pig grabbed my left arm and said, "You're arrested for carrying a concealed weapon." Then he snatched my gun out of my holster, holding my arms. They handcuffed me readily, and began to move me to the car.

They drove me to the Sacramento police station. As we came out of the elevator there, one pig grabbed the handcuffs and pushed them up real high—real high, so it hurt and pained. And he ran me right up against the wall and said, "Now you stand there with your face against the wall." That's what the pig said. And my face *hit that wall*. The wall was very cool. It was a soothing cool. I was glad to lay my face against this cool wall. Sherman Forte was to my left. I looked over at him. "What about it, brother?" "Ah man, it's nothing," he said. "It's all right." "Yeah," I said. "Going to be all right."

They took me to a cell. I asked myself, "Did I fuck up?" I didn't know. I was very tired. I got on the other side of the door, three or four feet away from it, lay down, and righteously fell off to sleep.

Somebody was unlocking the cell. There was Eldridge. "Oh, goddam it." That hurt me. That hurt me bad. I said, "Goddam, Eldridge is arrested!" I knew that was bad. Eldridge was on parole. I said, "Eldridge isn't going to get out of jail." I felt so bad. I said, "Man, they got you arrested. You might have to go back to prison." Eldridge said, "Fuck it. It was worth it, because we did it."

6. Interview with Dolores Torres

In December 1966 Dolores Torres, whose three children and a niece she was raising attended public school in Ocean Hill–Brownsville, was joined by other activists from around New York City in a sit-in at the Board of Education. When the Ocean Hill–Brownsville experimental district was formed, she was elected a parent representative to the local governing board. This is an excerpt from a 1988 interview with Torres by the Eyes on the Prize *production team.*

I can't talk about affluent white parents, or even affluent black or Puerto Rican parents. But poor people tend to say, "Well, these are the educated people. They're supposed to know what they're doing." And we just tend to sit back. But see, at the time, there were things going on. If I saw something going on and I knew it wasn't right, I would find out from other parents if they had seen similar things. And it just spread.

What happened was they told us the kids would have to go on double shifts. I had two going in the morning and two going in the afternoon. The school was overcrowded to an extreme. There wasn't much learning, wasn't much education going on. So we started going to PTA meetings, and meeting with other parents to decide what to do about this.

We were going down to 110 Livingston Street [the headquarters of the New York City Board of Education] to complain about the situation in the school. And they would just cut the mikes on us, you know. We would lodge complaints, and nothing was done about it. As I said, the [teachers'] union was dominating the schools. There was nothing done about it. We filed such and such about such and such a teacher, and we find that this has been going on for a little while, and there was nothing they would do. And we just got fed up with it. One night, we went down there for a meeting, and they started turning off the mikes like they usually did, and we just took over. We took over their seats. That particular night, it was a dramatic thing, but it was something that had to be done. Because we had no voice power. No voice power at all.

I don't think I was surprised. I knew that, eventually, it would happen. Because if you're not getting any kind of satisfaction, and you have kids in the school system and they aren't being taught, then eventually you're just going to rebel. And that's what we had to do. It wasn't something that was actually planned. We just kept saying, "Well, they're not representing us. Maybe we should represent ourselves."

7. "A JHS 271 Teacher Tells It Like He Sees It"

Charles S. Isaacs

Although the controversy at Ocean Hill–Brownsville was often depicted and later remembered as a conflict between a predominantly black and Latino governing board and the predominantly Jewish teachers' union, nearly three out of four teachers hired by the governing board during the teachers' strike of fall 1968 were white. In this account of his experiences as a Jewish nonunion teacher in Ocean Hill–Brownsville, Charles Isaacs describes the dedication of many of his black and white colleagues teaching at JHS 271, the increasing tensions between the union and nonunion teachers, and the mounting cries of anti-Semitism. His article appeared in the November 24, 1968, issue of the New York Times Magazine.

Landlord, landlord
My roof has sprung a leak.
Don't you 'member I told you about it
Way last week?

Landlord, landlord
These steps is broken down.
When you come up yourself
It's a wonder you don't fall down.

Ten bucks you say I owe you?
Ten bucks you say is due?
Well, that's Ten Bucks more'n I'll pay you
Till you fix this house up new.

What? You gonna get eviction orders?
You gonna cut off my heat?
You gonna take my furniture and
Throw it in the street?

Um-huh! You talking high and mighty.
Talk on—till you get through.
You ain't gonna be able to say a word
If I land my fist on you.

Police! Police!
Come and get this man!
He's trying to ruin the government
And overturn the land!

Copper's whistle!
Patrol bell!
Arrest.

Precinct station.
Iron cell.
Headlines in press:

Man Threatens Landlord
Tenant Held; No Bail
Judge Gives Negro 30 Days in County Jail

1. Who is the man in the poem?
2. Why is he angry? Should he be?
3. What does he do to the landlord? Was he justified in doing so?
4. What happens to him? Does he deserve the penalty?
5. Would it happen if he were white? Why? Why not?
6. Does this poem remind you of things that happen here in Ocean Hill–Brownsville? What?
7. Why do you think Mr. Mayer has used this poem in your class?

A social-studies lesson at J.H.S. 271

The above poem is "Ballad of the Landlord," by the late Afro-American poet Langston Hughes, and it has dual relevance to the Ocean Hill–Brownsville story. Replace the landlord with the educational establishment, the tenant with the black parent, and the leaky roof with a history of inferior education—then write a sequel to the poem. The sequel will be about an educational system crumbling from its own inner decay, a bureaucracy which is afraid to enter the ghetto without police protection, and a community which will settle for no less than the freedom to rebuild for itself. The tenant decides to raze the old structure and build a new one, with a new construction company of his own choice. That is where my colleagues and I come into the story.

When Jonathan Kozol, author of *Death at an Early Age,* taught a lesson similar to the one quoted to his Boston public-school students, he was fired; no JHS 271 teacher will be dismissed for teaching that lesson. Whether we label this change "innovation," "academic freedom," or "dangerous," it illustrates the new outlook to education which the Ocean Hill–Brownsville experiment in community involvement has brought about, the type of teacher it has attracted, and the threat which produced a massive effort to destroy it before it began. Despite the concessions granted the striking teachers' union over last weekend, the sense of innovation lingers in the air.

Actually, although innovation is a major purpose of decentralization, we have a basically traditional program at JHS 271; we have few formal changes that other schools could not copy if they were so inclined. There are many reasons for this, perhaps the most prominent of which is the pressure to get more children into decent high schools. Last year, only nine out of 491 graduates went on to the "better" schools. The parents of my eighth-grade students have this very much on their minds, and many of them want community-controlled schools just so their children will be able to enter the better high schools and colleges. In discussions with these parents, it is difficult to discuss the new math, or doing away with old-fashioned grammar lessons; they want their children to learn the 3 R's. In this respect, these black and Puerto Rican parents are no different from white parents; they don't want their children to be used as guinea pigs.

The experiment has had an educational effect on many of the parents and will, in time, bring about a change in the community's basic conservatism. At one meeting, a father stood up to ask a question. He said that when he "was a boy," he wouldn't talk back to a teacher because he would get "whupped" both at home and in school if he did; he wanted to know why we didn't encourage more "whupping." He was answered by a young black college student who explained that the awe and fear of authority figures felt by children in a bygone era is counter-productive today.

The reply received considerably more applause than the question, but, sitting on the speakers' panel, I was wondering how that parent would react if his child came home and told him what he learned in "Charlie's class" that day. I had told my students that they were allowed to address me by my first name, and I had done this precisely to break down the wall of fear that usually exists between student and teacher. (It is a monument to the past that so many children have found it impossible to take advantage of this familiarity.)

Other frustrations to real innovation have been police in the schools, the uncertainty of not knowing whether school will be open or closed tomorrow, and the general tension which these have created. But there have been two more basic obstacles.

The first of these has been the presence of reporters, a presence which transforms any situation into something different from what it would otherwise be. The daily mass media understand an orderly hallway, suits and ties, but no psychodrama, or *dashikis*. As one teacher explained: "Of course we have to make the children go up the 'Up' staircase, and down the 'Down' staircase; there might be a television camera at the end of the stairs." To experiment means to accept the risk of possible failure, and no one wants to take the risk of falling flat on his face in 60 million living rooms.

An even more fundamental obstacle is built into the very nature of the project. Our experiment will be evaluated in terms of the established conventional criteria: reading scores, discipline, standardized achievement tests, etc., some of which measure what they are intended to measure, for middle-class children. We have a problem when these criteria fail to measure the extent to which a child has been educated, when they simply test rote memorization, stifling of initiative and training in sitting through standardized examinations. Unleashed creativity, or a critical outlook, for example, would probably lower a child's score on these exams, rather than raise them.

If the conventional criteria measure the wrong things, their effect is harmful to our students, yet they will determine to a great extent whether or not we will ever be free to develop our own yardsticks. In effect, we must miseducate the children before we will be allowed to educate them.

If we succeed where others have failed, the explanation will not lie in minor reforms of a decadent educational system. If the children learn now, it will be because they want to more than ever before. It will be because they do feel the sense of community which is developing, and because their parents now participate actively in their education. They know that their teachers have faith in them, and, most important of all, they are learning to have faith in themselves. Appeals to manhood and to pride in blackness are far better motivational and disciplinary tools in JHS 271 than threats of suspension or detention.

In order to encourage these positive factors, the faculty is trying to become truly close to the students and their families. One *Saturday*, we arranged for free buses and took 600 children on a trip to Bear Mountain. No red tape, no waiting period, and, of course, no pay for the teachers; they were having too good a time themselves even to consider it.

A large group of teachers attend all open community meetings, and the teacher-community solidarity at these gatherings strengthens all of us; at one meeting, the only speaker to receive a standing ovation was Fran Aurello, a white teacher. We have been arranging informal get-togethers with the parents at school and in their homes, and every teacher is pledged to get acquainted with the parents of all his students. All this takes time, but the possibilities for the future, as well as our successes, in this short period of time are lost on none of us.

Our assistant principals have offered an interesting comparison between the "old" supervisory personnel and those who will replace them. In September, when I began teaching, we had five assistant principals, including one Negro, who were imposed on us by the central Board of Education, and two who were hired by the local governing board. Since I had not known at first that any of our staff was of the former group, my initial experiences with them shook my faith in the experiment more than a little. One spent an entire staff meeting instructing the teachers that our major function was to discipline, regiment, and routinize the children. Another admonished the staff to wear rubber-soled shoes, as she did, so we could "sneak up on the children in the halls." Still another barged into the middle of an orderly class to exclaim: "Close those windows! If a child falls out, *we'll* really be in a fix." If this was experimentation, I thought, how much worse could things have been before?

It was not long before I found out that these people were not part of the experiment, did not want to participate in the experiment, and were, in fact, sabotaging the experiment by forcing students and teachers simply to refuse to implement such repressive policies. Finally, unable to influence their staff in any way, they were kind enough to transfer voluntarily out of the district as a group.

That left us with John Mandracchia, an experienced administrator who transferred into the district last February, and Albert Vann, an acting (uncertified) assistant principal who doubles as president of the African-American Teachers Association. Mandracchia is that rare individual who managed to survive in the so-called merit system despite substantial merit. He is white, forty years old, and lives in the suburbs; yet he has no trouble in relating to black people or young people, including pupils, and seems to understand the problems of the cities. Few teachers wake up at 4:45 each morning, as he does, and stay late every afternoon. He once slept in school overnight because he did not have time for his daily four hours of driving.

Mandracchia is an exception to the rule that a life-time of being white, combined with a career within the New York City School System, will prevent anyone from becoming a competent supervisor in a black school. Still, when I asked him what he thought our major administrative innovation was, he said: "For the first time, black kids have the opportunity to identify with black leadership in their schools."

Al Vann is one of those black leaders. Ten years in the system have taught him to hate it, and his battle against it seems to have brought wrath down upon him. One newspaper reported that he arrived at school at 9 one morning and organized and led a parent-teacher march through the community beginning at 9:02. Anyone who could have organized that march in two minutes certainly should throw a scare into the system.

It is perhaps because of fear, mixed with a generous portion of racism, that the press, the UFT [United Federation of Teachers], and the Board of Education credit Vann with having instigated many unfriendly actions, some of which never even took place. These allegations have led him, and three other teachers, into the Board of Education's "due process" mechanism for transfer and dismissal. Vann is a forceful, popular figure who is capable of instilling awe, respect, terror, or pride in any of the children as the situation demands. He sees his future, that of his organization, the ATA [African-American Teachers Association], as well as that of his people, bound up in the struggle for community control.

While most of our teachers are part of this struggle, some are apprehensive about the ATA's role in it. Just [as] a narrow, "careerist" view of self-interest corrupted the UFT and forced it to oppose quality education in order to protect its membership, it is feared that the ATA might simply replace the unresponsive white bureaucracy with a similar black one, in order to further the career goals of its constituency. Here, Vann faces the dilemma which all black leaders must eventually come to grips with: Is he to advance himself within the existing system, or will he remain a part of that community, at whatever cost to his own career?

Les Campbell, another "black militant" facing accusations before the Board of Education, teaches Afro-American history. In a sense, both he and the course (four times a week for all students) are innovations. Both are objected to by the central system, and descriptions of both are usually distorted.

When I first met Campbell, I hardly knew what to expect: physically, vocally, and intellectually, he seemed far larger than the norm, and, supposedly, he had no use for whites. Two months of conversation and observation have discredited the latter speculation and confirmed the former. Campbell wants to see the institutions that dominate the lives of black people controlled by those people, not by white colonial masters, but he recognizes the role that can be played by white allies in the struggle.

His suspicion of the "white liberal" arises out of a history of double-cross and meaningless rhetoric, and seems to be shared by his true constituency, the black community. I expected more distrust than I actually found. I was almost disappointed.

When the UFT press releases proclaimed that "hate whitey" was being taught in Campbell's classes, I had to find out for myself. I walked into a class five minutes after it began, and took a seat in the back of the room. Campbell was showing a series of slides on the origins of African civilization. They portrayed the recent anthropological discoveries suggesting man's origin in the Olduvai Gorge in central Africa, depicted the builders of ancient Egyptian culture, including their Negroid features, and led the class into a discussion of the social institutions of some of the early, highly developed African civilizations.

The course will trace the African people from this point through the European invasion, forced emigration to the New World, slavery and slave revolt, to the present day, none of which is covered in conventional history texts or courses. According to Campbell, it is designed to answer the questions: "Who am I? Where have I been? Who and where am I today?" If the white man turns out to be the villain in this story, such is the testimony of history. If things are different today, if the children will have reason to expect anything different in the future, they must be educated by their own, and by the black faculty's everyday interaction with the white faculty. This is no insignificant part of our job.

The white teachers (70 per cent of the faculty) are an interesting, diverse group of individuals. In addition to being younger and better educated, we have less experience in working for the system, and more in working against it, than any other faculty in the city. Forty per cent of us are Jewish (some Orthodox), 30 per cent will need draft deferments in order to continue teaching, 25 per cent have never taught before; all are licensed by the central board, and nearly all are "committed" to social changes. Many sections of the country are represented, as are most major colleges and universities. Alan Kellock, a teacher of Afro-American history, is writing a doctoral dissertation for the University of Wisconsin in that field; Sandy Nystrom is a former white organizer for the Mississippi Freedom Democratic Party; Stu Russell is a returned Peace Corps volunteer; Steve Bloomfield is an organizer of the Brooklyn Heights Peace and Freedom Party.

My own background is simply this: grammar school in Brooklyn, bar mitzvah, suburban high school, Long Island University, marriage, law school at the University of Chicago. My father owns a parking lot; my mother is a working housewife. While they spend most of their time explaining me to their friends and neighbors, they actually enjoy suburban life. In another day, my twenty-third birthday would not have found me teaching in the ghetto. This generation, though, has grown up at a unique time in history. I am not alone in being a contradiction to my upbringing.

While many of us have done our best to disestablish the Establishment, no single ideology unites us, no plan of action is taken without heated debate. We do not even agree on a single analysis of the situation in which we are engaged. The school has set the stage for an interesting day-to-day drama involving the complex relationship between this group and the more united black faculty.

One observer of the opening of school noted a "checkerboard" seating pattern in the teachers' cafeteria, black teachers together at some tables, white teachers at others; this pattern, for instance, has since broken down somewhat into one of agreement on—and interest in—whatever issue is being fought out in any particular part of the room. We are integrated now, but not by pretending that black is the same as white; it is, rather, integration born out of respect for individual and group differences, and pride in, as well as recognition of, one's own heritage. We form a mixture, not a solution—a smorgasbord, not a melting pot.

The moment of truth, in this respect, came for many white teachers when we decided to organize the faculty and elect a steering committee. The black teachers demanded equal representation on the committee even though they were a numerical minority; there would be a black caucus to whom the black representatives would be responsible, and a white caucus to elect the white representatives. Some (not all) white teachers objected to this plan, maintaining that it would institutionalize race differences, and instead proposed at-large elections, based on traditional "color-blind" integration.

A long debate ensued, with Campbell calling the "at-large" plan "a step backward in the fight for black self-determination," while himself being charged with "segregationism" and "separatism." When someone suggested a vote on which plan to accept, his proposal had broad support.

At this point, Steve Mayer, a white teacher, pointed out that, in a vote on the question, the white majority would be deciding whether or not the blacks were to have self-determination. Most of us recognized this as the colonial situation we were all determined to avoid, and the vote no longer was necessary. The two caucuses met separately, elected their representatives, and the steering committee was formed. The two-caucus system has lessened racial tensions on the committee rather than having exacerbated them, and its work has been made more effective by removing the fiction on which it would otherwise have rested.

Despite whatever tension has existed among the faculty—and I think this tension has been constructive—we have been united on a few major issues and goals: we are for community control of schools; we want to educate the children; and we want the power structure (UFT, Board of Education, politicians, Selective Service) to leave our experiment alone so that we can make it work.

It was in this context that the transferred UFT teachers were put back into the school, along with a force of about 3,000 armed police bodyguards. It was absurd to think that an agreement between the UFT and the Board of Education, with community representation excluded, could have made either the community or the faculty accept those teachers back with open arms. It was more absurd to think the intimidating presence of the police would help. There had to be harassment on both sides, and there was. The harassment was petty, though, and, to the best of my knowledge, it never escalated to threats on people's lives, no matter what the newspaper stories supposedly leaked from a still-unreleased report by impartial observers may have said.

Examples sound absurd when repeated. One of the UFT teachers for instance, walked into the middle of a math class I was teaching, marched to the center of the room, and began picking papers up off the floor. I asked: "What are you doing here? You're disrupting my class." In reply, he told me that he was not disrupting the class, but I was. Then, with the students (thirteen to fifteen years old) looking at him—their eyes filled, some with amazement, some with hatred, some with confusion—I walked toward the door, opened it for him, and told him to leave. He went to the door, but rather than leave, he started rummaging in the wastebasket, for no apparent reason. Finally, he straightened up, turned to the class, belched loudly and walked out. Barely containing myself, I slammed the door shut.

Presumably he had wanted to disrupt the class and provoke either me or a student into taking a swing at him. If so, he succeeded in his first objective, and almost succeeded in the second.

After he had left the room, the students, miles from algebra by this time, released the accumulated tension by applauding and, after quieting down, they asked questions: "Why can't the kids take care of them?" "Why did they have to come back? Everything was going so good!" These questions may not display a high degree of political sophistication, but they certainly raise doubts as to whether teachers like the one who disrupted my class can ever be effective in one of our classrooms.

Sometimes, the UFT teachers did not even have to take overt action to arouse our ire. The air of arrogance with which they carried themselves was described by one nonunion teacher this way: "It's as though they're saying, 'We're back. We won. You lost. Ha! Ha! Ha!'" When the mathematics staff gathered for a departmental meeting, we found three UFT people smugly waiting in the room, their arms folded. We caucused for a few minutes, then walked out to meet some place else, leaving them alone with two of our "old" assistant principals. At the time, this seemed the only way to prevent a real incident from occurring, so high were feelings running during those days. If this was harassment, I plead guilty.

All of the abuse was verbal. We told them what we thought of them, and they reciprocated. Perhaps the UFT leadership has forgotten the distinction explained in the old "sticks and stones" rhyme. The entire issue of harassment was best summed up by the Rev. C. Herbert Oliver, the chairman of the governing board, when he said, "I wish people wouldn't interpret an exclamation of 'Drop Dead!' as a threat on their lives."

All discussions of harassment evolve into allegations of anti-Semitism. The UFT's skillful use of this issue exploited legitimate fears of the liberal Jewish community and turned potential supporters against us. I have spent up to eighteen hours a day in the Ocean Hill–Brownsville community, and I have never experienced any racial or religious slur against me there, nor has anyone with whom I have spoken, nor have I seen any "hate" literature besides that which is distributed by the UFT.

On the contrary, the community and the governing board have demonstrated again and again that these fears are unfounded. On the day before Rosh Hashanah, the governing board distributed to all the children in our schools a leaflet explaining the holiday, what it means to the Jewish people, and why all the city schools are closed on that day. As far as I know, no other school district has taken the trouble to do this.

The issue of black anti-Semitism is a major element in the black-Jewish confrontation which threatens to devastate New York City. Yet, here in Ocean Hill–Brownsville, in the eye of the storm, the problem seems not to exist. I read in the UFT literature and in the Jewish press about "black racism," but I have never experienced it in Ocean Hill, and, to my knowledge, neither has anyone else on the faculty. While the storm rages around Ocean Hill–Brownsville, it is not about Ocean Hill–Brownsville. But one fact of life does stand out: this issue of anti-Semitism, true or false, preys on the fears of the one ethnic group that, united behind it, could destroy us; if this happens, I expect a real problem of black anti-Semitism, and the cycle of self-fulfilling prophecy will be complete.

Unfortunately, there seems to be no effective way to discredit the UFT charges. Rumors abound in the Jewish community of armed hordes of "black Nazis." Recently, I spoke in Forest Hills to a group of Jewish parents who were understandably concerned about this issue. The meeting was organized by a veteran of concentration camps who hoped that I could relate my personal experiences to the parents, and lead a discussion of facts, rather than of wild accusations. He meant well, but the mission was pretty hopeless. These parents simply could not—or would not—believe that the charges of anti-Semitism had no basis in fact. Sometimes, they went to great lengths of logical distortion in order to continue believing what they had been told. One woman said: "You only tell us what you've seen. Shouldn't you tell us about what you haven't seen?"

This is not, however, to say that I have not been threatened. Each time my name or picture appears on television or in the newspapers, I receive a flurry of anonymous letters and, sometimes, telephone calls, all trying to put into question my job, my health, my sanity, or my continued existence. I have been called everything from "scab" to "Commie bastard" to "nigger-lover lout." One letter said: "I hope you can live with yourself. Have you been intimidated yet?" Another put a "black curse" on me; another placed the hopes of the Jewish people in not producing any more like myself. All this is sad and childish, but it does not indicate that there is an organized campaign in the white, Jewish community against me.

Black people hate the "Uncle Tom" more than any white man, and this is probably how the white racists feel about me. Depending on their particular problems, they feel that I am a traitor to my race, my religion, my neighborhood, my family, or any combination of these. It was interesting that, during our confrontations with large contingents of police and UFT pickets, the black parents spent most of their energy haranguing and lecturing the Negro cops, while the white UFT pickets harassed the white "scabs" far more than the black ones.

A year ago, I never thought that I would be crossing picket lines today. I have always supported unions, and I led a nine-day student strike at Long Island University's Brooklyn Center while I was student-body president there. Since I did not believe in the teachers' strike, I had decided not to let the pickets disturb me. Nevertheless, they did. The few pickets on the line that first day spouted more hate in two minutes than I had heard in my lifetime, and it shook me up. I knew that this could not continue long without, at the very least, making my teaching less effective.

The next day, as I approached the picket line, the UFT teachers began their catcalls. I walked to the middle of the line, turned my back, folded my arms, and simply stood there while they poured out their verbal venom. I heard a surprising number of references to my personal past, and I wanted to turn and ask where they get all this information, but I didn't. After five or ten minutes (it seemed much longer), their catharsis ended, the chanting and raving stopped—and I walked on.

It could be that my little nonviolent confrontation with the pickets made them realize how foolish they really were; they have not bothered me since. But I still don't enjoy crossing picket lines, and, after a couple of weeks, I found another route to the school.

The police, while they were at school in large numbers, were less easy to avoid. They stationed themselves on streets and roofs, in the school, in toilets, and in our meetings. During the first weeks of school, our attendance was lower than we expected, and a team of teachers canvassed the parents to find out what was keeping the children home. The answer they most frequently received was: "I don't want to send my kids into an armed camp," and no one could blame the parents for being apprehensive. The children had to squeeze through police barricades in order to reach the front door, and parents were not permitted to accompany them; more than one parent was beaten for insisting that she be allowed to bring her child into school. Even teachers were asked for identification; since none of us had any, we sometimes had to circle the block to find an entrance where there was less resistance.

The police were drawn from all over the city, from Yankee Stadium to Staten Island, they were working overtime, and they did not seem happy to be there. There was also a great deal of confusion at critical moments. At one demonstration, while we were retreating from one line of police advancing in front of us, we turned and found out we were also supposed to be retreating from those behind us. The result was blood and chaos. One quiet morning, I myself was arrested because of a similar mixup. One officer said to move on; another said to stay; whatever I did, I had to end up in jail.

I spent that entire day in the stationhouse, the paddy wagon, and the courthouse, and this afforded me an opportunity to find out how the police themselves felt about what they were doing. One cop I spoke to was, more than anything else, angry. It was his fourteenth consecutive day of work, he was miles from his precinct, and he knew there were too many police on the scene. He didn't understand why he had to keep parents out of their schools and take abuse from those who hated him for being there. Nevertheless, he would be back the next day and the day after that; he wanted that pension.

And this is where we came in. The cop, the teacher, the landlord—all want to collect the rent while the roof leaks, the house decays, and the tenant boils.

> Landlord, landlord
> My roof has sprung a leak.
> Don't you 'member I told you about it
> Way last week?

8. Interview with Karriema Jordan

In 1968 Karriema Jordan was in the eighth grade at JHS 271 and a member of the African-American Students Association. This is an excerpt from a 1989 interview with Jordan by the Eyes on the Prize *production team.*

I was born Theresa Jordan, that's true. But slave names were out. You know, Jordan was the slave master's name, and Theresa was some—I don't know. So everybody adopted African names. I adopted mine from a book that I read in a summer program. The book was on African civilizations, and one of the women in that book was Nabowiah. So I thought Nabowiah was a great name. She was a woman prophet. My name was Nabowiah Weusi. Weusi meant black. So I adopted that name. Everybody called me Nabi. But I met an African brother who said to me that I was not an African prophet, a woman prophet, and that was sacrilege, you know. So he decided to name me Karriema, which is a person in the Koran who did good deeds for the prophet Mohammed. I didn't oppose it. One name to me was just as good as the other, as long as it was African. So I kept the name Karriema.

During the fall of 1968, I was totally amazed to get up in the morning, walk, meet my friend Sia. Coming from the Howard Avenue side, we had to go through barricades to get to the school. We'd look out on the rooftops, across the street from the school: the cops were there with their riot helmets and their nightsticks and helicopters, and the playground was converted into a precinct, and walking up to the school you have just mass confusion. You have the community people out there. You have the UFT. You have the black teachers on the inside. You were just amazed. You couldn't believe this was happening, you know, and you just went to school.

[With so many new black teachers at JHS 271], you learned a lot more. You identified more. You learned that teachers were human beings, not some abstract something. They stayed after school. At three o'clock, they didn't run downstairs and punch out. You know, they gave you more time. I mean, you felt more accepted. You weren't an outsider in your own school. They were part of your environment. I mean, they were black. You can identify with them and they can identify with you. It's as simple as that. There's no big mystery, you know.

9. "Anti-Semitism?—A Statement by the Teachers of Ocean Hill–Brownsville to the People of New York"

This advertisement appeared in **The New York Times,** *November 11, 1968.*

This statement, prepared by the teachers of the Ocean Hill–Brownsville demonstration school district now teaching there, is designed to clarify some issues with respect to racism and particularly anti-Semitism. At first, we thought that only the several hundred Jewish teachers in the district should sign it, but then we realized that, in view of the persistent charges of racial polarization, all of us, Jewish and non-Jewish, white and black, should join to set the record straight about the scurrilous charges that have been leveled against our board.

It is time to scotch the rumors and hysteria about anti-Semitism, racism, and revolution being the underlying causes of the problems of Ocean Hill–Brownsville. Statistically, 70 per cent of the 541 teachers teaching the 8,500 youngsters in Ocean Hill–Brownsville are white, 50 per cent of this percentage are Jewish, and all are certified by the Board of Education. What we want to do is to teach the children entrusted to us without having to live and work behind a wall of fear and mistrust that Mr. [Albert] Shanker [president of the United Federation of Teachers] has helped to build around us.

THE UFT WALL OF FEAR

In an effort to tag the Ocean Hill–Brownsville governing board with anti-Semitism, the UFT is engaged in a massive publicity campaign and is distributing UFT reprints of anti-Semitic literature. The most talked-about is the one that refers to "Middle Eastern murderers."

This is actually a composite reprint of two separate leaflets. One, signed by the purported chairman of fictitious "JHS 271 Parents Community Council," is anti-UFT and urges the exclusion of whites from teaching black or Puerto Rican children.

The other section, with its anti-Semitic references, is reproduced from a different, anonymous leaflet surreptitiously inserted in some teachers' mailboxes during the May walkout (strike) that followed the involuntary transfer of the nineteen teachers.

Blending these two leaflets together in this fashion is intended to imply that the demand for community control of education in a black community means: (1) firing all white teachers, (2) virulent anti-Semitism, (3) support for these doctrines by our board.

WHAT THE NEW YORK CIVIL LIBERTIES UNION SAYS

On the basis of its own study of this piece of propaganda, the New York Civil Liberties Union has concluded: "The UFT is trying to pin responsibility for the anti-white and anti-Semitic sentiments in these leaflets on the Ocean Hill–Brownsville decentralization program. This is a smear tactic reminiscent of the days of Senator Joseph McCarthy."

Mr. Shanker is using propaganda of this type to win the support of white teachers and parents in this battle against our governing board.

We, the undersigned teachers, are living proof that such charges are false on all accounts.

WHAT HAS THIS TO DO WITH OUR GOVERNING BOARD?

We state unequivocally that by their words and actions they have shown that they will not tolerate any form of anti-Semitism. Furthermore, we resent the continued allegations that are being made against the governing board when we know that they are untrue.

Here are the words of the Ocean Hill–Brownsville governing board on this matter:

> The Ocean Hill–Brownsville governing board, as well as the entire Ocean Hill–Brownsville demonstration school district, has never tolerated nor will it ever tolerate anti-Semitism in any form. Anti-Semitism has no place in our hearts or minds and indeed never in our schools.
>
> While certain anti-Semitic literature may have been distributed outside our school buildings, there is absolutely no connection between these acts and the thoughts and intents of the Ocean Hill–Brownsville governing board. We disclaim any responsibility for this literature and have in every way sought to find its source and take appropriate action to stop it.

The acts of the board, however, are more important than their words. When the governing board recruited 350 new teachers last summer, more than 50 per cent of them were Jewish. Are these anti-Semitic actions?

WHAT IS OUR BOARD REALLY DOING?

The truth about our board is that it is trying to provide, against powerful opposition, the basis for a real breakthrough in the urgent problem of providing good education not only for the black and Puerto Rican children of our city but for all the children.

We feel that education is one of the best ways to curb anti-Semitism and racism. But there is an even better way to end both anti-Semitism and anti-Negro prejudices. Black people will be turned away from anti-Semitism and white will be turned away from anti-Negro feelings only through the establishment of trust and confidence between both groups in day-to-day relationships.

We, the teachers of Ocean Hill–Brownsville, are working together with parents and administrators to teach the children of this community. We approach the children with an expectation of success, which we communicate to them and to which they are responding. In this way we are establishing relationships of mutual trust and respect, which we believe are the best ways to end prejudice now and in the future.

WHY DOES MR. SHANKER PERSIST IN THESE FALSE CHARGES?

By this time, it is evident that the city-wide strike has neither trade-union, moral, nor educational justification. Mr. Shanker's continuance of the strike now finds him in opposition to: the Board of Regents, the state commission of education, the Board of Education, the superintendent of schools, the United Parents Association, and the leaders of most major educational institutions in and around the city of New York. Not to mention more than 1 million children.

Why is this so? Because it is now clear that the strike no longer has anything to do with the return of the disputed teachers. Whatever might have been the situation earlier, the governing board on its own—recognizing its responsibility to the other children of New York, as well as to those of our district—made it clear on October 23 that the disputed teachers will be fully accepted and given actual classroom assignments:

> We recognize that each of the seventy-nine teachers returning by order of the Board of Education will be assigned actual classroom assignments with actual students, which was the fact in seven of our eight schools since the last strike of the UFT and actually achieved at JHS 271 before this last strike. Each principal will respect the aforesaid assignments.

WHOM DOES MR. SHANKER TRUST?

Mr. Shanker's final argument is that the governing board cannot be believed because of previous experiences. Let us be clear: all the previous "experiences" arose out of agreements Mr. Shanker made with the Central Board of Education, which they both tried (with incredible insensitivity) to cram down the throat of the Ocean Hill–Brownsville governing board. Now the governing board itself has accepted the return of the teachers and has agreed to "cooperate to achieve a peaceful atmosphere."

Moreover, the state Board of Regents has pledged every resource at its command to the satisfactory return of the disputed teachers, and has promised it will establish guidelines on the protection of the rights of teachers.

Mr. Shanker has now stated that the only thing he would accept is the elimination (at least for the foreseeable future) of the governing board's administrator, Rhody McCoy, and all the principals of our schools. This Mr. Shanker cannot have, and the education of 1 million children ought not to be sacrificed to his determination to wreck the first bright hope of bringing quality education to the black and Puerto Rican children in New York.

An Invitation to See for Yourselves

We, the teachers of Ocean Hill–Brownsville, invite you to visit our schools. We would like to have ministers and rabbis, educators and laymen of every color and creed come and see what we are doing. We are proud of what has been going on in our classrooms, and the children and parents are proud, too.

We would like to share with you our dream of what real community education can provide for the future of all our children.

CHAPTER TEN

THE PROMISED LAND
(1967–1968)

Introduction by David J. Garrow

In early 1967 Martin Luther King, Jr., was considerably more pessimistic about the future—about the future of the black freedom struggle, about the future of American society, and about his own individual future—than he had been two years earlier after the triumphant Selma-to-Montgomery march and the enactment of the landmark Voting Rights Act of 1965.

In part King's troubled prognosis was the product of the enervating and at times depressing experiences he had had during the Chicago Freedom Movement of 1966, when the Southern Christian Leadership Conference's large-scale commitment to helping advance the desegregation of one of America's largest and toughest northern cities had resulted only in a paper agreement with city authorities that many movement participants and onlookers found inadequate and disappointing.

In part, too, King's worried expectations stemmed from the aftermath of the massive urban disorders that had struck the Watts section of Los Angeles in August 1965 and other northern ghettos, such as Cleveland's Hough neighborhood, in the summer of 1966. The 1966 state and congressional elections had witnessed a conservative, Republican resurgence against liberal Democrats associated with the "Great Society" domestic programs of President Lyndon B. Johnson, and many commentators suggested that

"Black Power" and the urban disorders had been a major factor in producing that political turnaround. The election of outspoken segregationist Lester Maddox as governor of King's home state of Georgia especially upset him, but King's downcast state of mind was also in part the product of the physically and mentally exhausting public schedule that he endured day after day, week after week, with hardly any time off from the stresses and tensions of his public role in the entire decade reaching all the way back to the Montgomery boycott of 1955–1956.

But, more than anything else at the outset of 1967, Martin Luther King, Jr., was troubled and preoccupied by America's involvement in the war in Vietnam. King had spoken out against U.S. involvement, and especially about the massive military scale of American operations, as early as March 1965, but when his sharp criticisms during August and September 1965 had drawn harsh attacks from close allies of the Johnson administration he had largely terminated his public comments. In private, however, the war continued to weigh heavily on King's conscience, not only because of how it swallowed up government funds that otherwise could make "Great Society" domestic programs truly meaningful, and not only because of the disproportionate frontline combat burdens that seemed to be borne by black fighting men, but also and most powerfully because of how the war and America's aggressive sponsorship of it contradicted the ethic of nonviolence, an ethic to which King's deep and life-central commitment had been further intensified, in his mind, by the moral burden and obligation stemming from his 1964 receipt of the Nobel Peace Prize. In early 1967 King vowed that he would remain silent no longer, that his obligation to speak the truth about the error of America's ways far outweighed the political damage he would suffer from attacking a war that very, very few prominent Americans so far had questioned. But in early April, when King's newly energized stance on the war first drew significant press attention, the extent and intensity of the hostile attacks—including criticism from the NAACP—nonetheless surprised and upset King. However, unlike in 1965, King persevered and continued to speak against the war throughout the balance of 1967 and into the early months of 1968.

King's worries and concerns about where America was headed at home also intensified during the spring and summer of 1967, and were most painfully and traumatically strengthened by the massive riots and ensuing urban warfare that swept the ghettos of Newark and Detroit in July. King's commitment to nonviolence led him to deplore the disorders without hesitance, but he coupled his remarks with equally strong criticisms about the absence of government interest in meaningfully tackling the deteriorating urban conditions that gave rise to the anger and despair in which the riots themselves were rooted.

The scope and intensity of those disorders, combined with the energetic calls for control and repression that then issued from many political officeholders, convinced King anew that an uncompromisingly explicit effort for economic opportunity and social justice in American society had to be mounted immediately. With at first no detailed outline of what he hoped to generate, King issued a major call for a mass protest in the nation's capital, what he termed a "Poor People's Campaign" that would highlight the extent to which Americans of all races and ethnicities, rural as well as urban, were suffering stunted lives as a result of poor schooling, inadequate food and health care, bad housing, and an absence of jobs—and all at a time when the nation was spending millions of dollars to kill people, military and civilian, in Vietnam.

King and his aides in the SCLC spent the winter of 1967–1968 attempting to put together and agree on a moderately detailed strategic game plan for this spring campaign targeted at the federal government—both president and Congress—in Washington. By early February, however, SCLC's efforts to recruit thousands of participants for the campaign, both from poor rural counties in the Mississippi Delta and from inner city ghettos in New York, Newark, and Philadelphia, were only slowly taking shape, and some on King's staff—principally James Bevel and Jesse Jackson—were suggesting that the larger game plan be rethought.

King, however, was totally committed to plunging ahead with the campaign and with an intensive recruitment of participants, even if SCLC's preparatory work so far had left much to be desired. When a request came from a longtime friend, Memphis pastor James Lawson, that King lend his presence and voice to a newly begun strike for recognition and decent wages by the city's nearly all-black sanitation work force, King readily consented to add Memphis to his already overcrowded schedule. Tremendously impressed on that first visit by the energy and spirit of the nascent Memphis movement, King agreed to return and lead a major protest march even though SCLC's own staff, fully occupied with Poor People's Campaign recruiting, would not be able to join in organizing it. When that march ended in violent turmoil—and one death—as a result of intense animus that young Memphis black militants harbored toward the adult leadership that had invited King and sponsored the protest, King was both publicly embarrassed and privately traumatized. While critics both black and white suggested that the Memphis disruption indicated how any Poor People's Campaign descent upon Washington could not avoid similar riot and ruin, King himself worried that nonviolence's day might temporarily be at an end and concluded that his only alternative would be to return to Memphis and lead a successful, fully peaceful march, even if so doing would distract his—and all of SCLC's—attention from the Poor People's Campaign planning. On April 3, 1968, King returned to Memphis for the final time.

King's SCLC associates tried to cope with the wrenching emotional trauma of King's assassination by continuing the Poor People's Campaign, but the ensuing early summer encampment in Washington encountered most of the problems, and few if any of the successes, that King and his colleagues had anticipated. Both President Johnson and the Congress offered no meaningful responses to the campaign's policy demands, and most of America seemed either indifferent to or unsupportive of the campaign's efforts. News media coverage often focused primarily if not exclusively on the internal troubles of the campaign's encampment, Resurrection City, and when the federal government finally closed down the short-lived "city on the Mall," even many participants acknowledged that the campaign had been a disappointing failure, notwithstanding the justice of its goals.

The years 1967 and 1968 were among the movement's most trying times. King was dead, many of America's cities had once-vibrant neighborhoods that were now in ruins, and thousands of people, black and white and most especially Asian, continued to die each week in Vietnam. But King's message of peace with justice, of nonviolence and economic change, would outlive both the man and the shambles of the Poor People's Campaign.

1. "A Time to Break Silence"
Martin Luther King, Jr.

King's most famous—and to his critics the most notorious—of his major antiwar speeches condemning America's involvement in Vietnam was delivered on April 4, 1967, in New York's Riverside Church. King brought together in this speech the full panoply of his reasons for finding America's involvement wrong and immoral, and its tough language and intense tone captures the emotional intensity that underlay King's early dissent from American policy. These are excerpts from the speech.

I come to this magnificent house of worship tonight because my conscience leaves me no other choice. I join with you in this meeting because I am in deepest agreement with the aims and work of the organization which has brought us together: Clergy and Laymen Concerned about Vietnam. The recent statement of your executive committee are the sentiments of my own heart and I found myself in full accord when I read its opening lines: "A time comes when silence is betrayal." That time has come for us in relation to Vietnam.

The truth of these words is beyond doubt but the mission to which they call us is a most difficult one. Even when pressed by the demands of inner truth, men do not easily assume the task of opposing their government's policy, especially in time of war. Nor does the human spirit move without great difficulty against all the apathy of conformist thought within one's own bosom and in the surrounding world. Moreover when the issues at hand seem as perplexed as they often do in the case of this dreadful conflict we are always on the verge of being mesmerized by uncertainty; but we must move on.

Some of us who have already begun to break the silence of the night have found that the calling to speak is often a vocation of agony, but we must speak. We must speak with all the humility that is appropriate to our limited vision, but we must speak. And we must rejoice as well, for surely this is the first time in our nation's history that a significant number of its religious leaders have chosen to move beyond the prophesying of smooth patriotism to the high grounds of a firm dissent based upon the mandates of conscience and the reading of history. Perhaps a new spirit is rising among us. If it is, let us trace its movement well and pray that our own inner being may be sensitive to its guidance, for we are deeply in need of a new way beyond the darkness that seems so close around us.

Over the past two years, as I have moved to break the betrayal of my own silences and to speak from the burnings of my own heart, as I have called for radical departures from the destruction of Vietnam, many persons have questioned me about the wisdom of my path. At the heart of their concerns this query has often loomed large and loud: Why are you speaking about war, Dr. King? Why are you joining the voices of dissent? Peace and civil rights don't mix, they say. Aren't you hurting the cause of your people? they ask. And when I hear them, though I often understand the source of their concern, I am nevertheless greatly saddened, for such questions mean that the inquirers have not really known me, my commitment or my calling. Indeed, their questions suggest that they do not know the world in which they live.

I come to this platform tonight to make a passionate plea to my beloved nation. This speech is not addressed to Hanoi or to the National Liberation Front. It is not addressed to China or to Russia.

Since I am a preacher by trade, I suppose it is not surprising that I have several reasons for bringing Vietnam into the field of my moral vision. There is at the outset a very obvious and almost facile connection between the war in Vietnam and the struggle I, and others, have been waging in America. A few years ago there was a shining moment in that struggle. It seemed as if there was a real promise of hope for the poor—both black and white—through the Poverty Program. There were experiments, hopes, new beginnings. Then came the build-up in Vietnam and I watched the program broken and eviscerated as if it were some idle political plaything of a society gone mad on war, and I knew that America would never invest the necessary funds or energies in rehabilitation of its poor so long as adventures like Vietnam continued to draw men and skills and money like some demoniacal destructive suction tube. So I was increasingly compelled to see the war as an enemy of the poor and to attack it as such.

Perhaps the more tragic recognition of reality took place when it became clear to me that the war was doing far more than devastating the hopes of the poor at home. It was sending their sons and their brothers and their husbands to fight and to die in extraordinarily high proportions relative to the rest of the population. We were taking the black young men who had been crippled by our society and sending them 8,000 miles away to guarantee liberties in Southeast Asia which they had not found in Southwest Georgia and East Harlem. So we have been repeatedly faced with the cruel irony of watching Negro and white boys on TV screens as they kill and die together for a nation that has been unable to seat them together in the same schools. . . .

My third reason moves to an even deeper level of awareness, for it grows out of my experience in the ghettos of the North over the last three years—especially the last three summers. As I have walked among the desperate, rejected and angry young men I have told them that Molotov cocktails and rifles would not solve their problems. I have tried to offer them my deepest compassion while maintaining my convictions that social change comes most meaningfully through non-violent action. But they asked—and rightly so—what about Vietnam? They asked if our own nation wasn't using massive doses of violence to solve its problems, to bring about the changes it wanted. Their questions hit home, and I knew that I could never again raise my voice against the violence of the oppressed in the ghettos without having first spoken clearly to the greatest purveyor of violence in the world today—my own government. . . .

For those who ask the question, "Aren't you a Civil Rights leader?" and thereby mean to exclude me from the movement for peace, I have this further answer. In 1957 when a group of us formed the Southern Christian Leadership Conference, we chose as our motto: "To save the soul of America." We were convinced that we could not limit our vision to certain rights for black people, but instead affirmed the conviction that America would never be free or saved from itself unless the descendants of its slaves were loosed completely from the shackles they still wear.

_____

And as I ponder the madness of Vietnam and search within myself for ways to understand and respond in compassion my mind goes constantly to the people of that peninsula. I speak now not of the soldiers of each side, not of the junta in Saigon, but simply of the people who have been living under the curse of war for almost three continuous decades now. I think of them too because it is clear to me that there will be no meaningful solution there until some attempt is made to know them and hear their broken cries.

_____

They watch as we poison their water, as we kill a million acres of their crops. They must weep as the bulldozers roar through their areas preparing to destroy the precious trees. They wander into the hospitals, with at least 20 casualties from American firepower for one Vietcong-inflicted injury. They wander into the towns and see thousands of the children, homeless, without clothes, running in packs on the streets like animals. They see the children degraded by our soldiers as they beg for food. They see the children selling their sisters to our soldiers, soliciting for their mothers. . . .

Perhaps the more difficult but no less necessary task is to speak for those who have been designated as our enemies. What of the National Liberation Front—that strangely anonymous group we call VC or Communists? What must they think of us in America when they realize that we permitted the repression and cruelty of Diem which helped to bring them into being as a resistance group in the South? What do they think of our condoning the violence which led to their own taking up of arms? How can they believe in our integrity when now we speak of "aggression from the North" as if there were nothing more essential to the war? How can they trust us when now we charge them with violence after the murderous reign of Diem, and charge them with violence while we pour every new weapon of death into their land? Surely we must understand their feelings even if we do not condone their actions. Surely we must see that the men we supported pressed them to their violence. Surely we must see that our own computerized plans of destruction simply dwarf their greatest acts.

How do they judge us when our officials know that their membership is less than 25 per cent Communist and yet insist on giving them the blanket name? What must they be thinking when they know that we are aware of their control of major sections of Vietnam and yet we appear ready to allow national elections in which this highly organized political parallel government will have no part? They ask how we can speak of free elections when the Saigon press is censored and controlled by the military junta. And they are surely right to wonder what kind of new government we plan to help form without them—the only party in real touch with the peasants. They question our political goals and they deny the reality of a peace settlement from which they will be excluded. Their questions are frighteningly relevant. Is our nation planning to build on political myth again and then shore it up with the power of new violence?

Here is the true meaning of value and compassion and non-violence when it helps us to see the enemy's point of view, to hear his questions, to know his assessment of ourselves. For from his view we may indeed see the basic weaknesses of our own condition, and if we are mature, we may learn and grow and profit from the wisdom of the brothers who are called the opposition.

So, too, with Hanoi. In the North, where our bombs now pummel the land, and our mines endanger the waterways, we are met by a deep but understandable mistrust. To speak for them is to explain this lack of confidence in western words, and especially their distrust of American intentions now. In Hanoi are the men who led the nation to independence against the Japanese and the French, the men who sought membership in the French common-wealth and were betrayed by the weakness of Paris and the willful-ness of the colonial armies. It was they who led a second struggle against French domination at tremendous costs, and then were persuaded to give up the land they controlled between the 13th and

17th parallel as a temporary measure at Geneva. After 1954 they watched us conspire with Diem to prevent elections which would have surely brought Ho Chi Minh to power over a united Vietnam, and they realized they had been betrayed again. . . .

At this point I should make it clear that while I have tried in these last few minutes to give a voice to the voiceless on Vietnam and to understand the arguments of those who are called enemy, I am as deeply concerned about our own troops there as anything else. For it occurs to me that what we are submitting them to in Vietnam is not simply the brutalizing process that goes on in any war where armies face each other and seek to destroy. We are adding cynicism to the process of death, for they must know after a short period there that none of the things we claim to be fighting for are really involved. Before long they must know that their government has sent them into a struggle among Vietnamese, and the more sophisticated surely realize that we are on the side of the wealthy and the secure while we create a hell for the poor.

If we continue there will be no doubt in my mind and in the mind of the world that we have no honorable intentions in Vietnam. It will become clear that our minimal expectation is to occupy it as an American colony and men will not refrain from thinking that our maximum hope is to goad China into a war so that we may bomb her nuclear installations. If we do not stop our war against the people in Vietnam immediately, the world will be left with no other alternative than to see this as some horribly clumsy and deadly game we have decided to play.

In order to atone for our sins and errors in Vietnam, we should take the initiative in bringing a halt to this tragic war. I would like to suggest five concrete things that our Government should do immediately to begin the long and difficult process of extricating ourselves from this nightmarish conflict:

1. End all bombing in North and South Vietnam.
2. Declare a unilateral cease-fire in the hope that such action will create the atmosphere for negotiation.

3. Take immediate steps to prevent other battlegrounds in Southeast Asia by curtailing our military build-up in Thailand and our interference in Laos.
4. Realistically accept the fact that the National Liberation Front has substantial support in South Vietnam and must thereby play a role in any meaningful negotiations and in any future Vietnam government.
5. Set a date that we will remove all foreign troops from Vietnam in accordance with the 1954 Geneva Agreement.

Part of our ongoing commitment might well express itself in an offer to grant asylum to any Vietnamese who fears for his life under a new regime which included the Liberation Front. Then we must make what reparations we can for the damage we have done. We must provide the medical aid that is badly needed, making it available in this country if necessary.

Meanwhile we in the churches and synagogues have a continuing task while we urge our Government to disengage itself from a disgraceful commitment. We must continue to raise our voices if our nation persists in its perverse ways in Vietnam. We must be prepared to match actions with words by seeking out every creative means of protest possible.

2. "Conversation with Martin Luther King"

On the evening of March 25, 1968, Dr. Martin Luther King, Jr., appeared at the sixty-eighth annual convention of the Rabbinical Assembly. He responded to questions submitted in advance to Rabbi Everett Gendler, who chaired the meeting. These are excerpts from the transcript of what was said that evening, beginning with the words of Professor Abraham Joshua Heschel.

DR. HESCHEL: Where does moral religious leadership in America come from today? The politicians are astute, the establishment is proud, and the market place is busy. Placid, happy, merry, the people pursue their work, enjoy their leisure, and life is fair.

People buy, sell, celebrate and rejoice. They fail to realize that in the midst of our affluent cities there are districts of despair, areas of distress.

Where does God dwell in America today? Is He at home with those who are complacent, indifferent to other people's agony, devoid of mercy? Is He not rather with the poor and the contrite in the slums?

Dark is the world for me, for all its cities and stars. If not for the few signs of God's radiance, who could stand such agony, such darkness?

Where in America today do we hear a voice like the voice of the prophets of Israel? Martin Luther King is a sign that God has not forsaken the United States of America. God has sent him to us. His presence is the hope of America. His mission is sacred, his leadership of supreme importance to every one of us.

The situation of the poor in America is our plight, our sickness. To be deaf to their cry is to condemn ourselves.

Martin Luther King is a voice, a vision and a way. I call upon every Jew to harken to his voice, to share his vision, to follow in his way. The whole future of America will depend upon the impact and influence of Dr. King.

May everyone present give of his strength to this great spiritual leader, Martin Luther King.

DR. KING: I need not pause to say how very delighted I am to be here this evening and to have this opportunity of sharing with you in this significant meeting, but I do want to express my deep personal appreciation to each of you for extending the invitation. It is always a very rich and rewarding experience when I can take a brief break from the day-to-day demands of our struggle for freedom and human dignity and discuss the issues involved in that struggle with concerned friends of good will all over our nation. And so I deem this a real and a great opportunity. . . .

I am not going to make a speech. We must get right to your questions. I simply want to say that we do confront a crisis in our nation, a crisis born of many problems. We see on every hand the restlessness of the comfortable and the discontent of the affluent, and somehow it seems that this mammoth ship of state is not moving toward new and more secure shores but toward old, destructive rocks.

It seems to me that all people of good will must now take a stand for that which is just, that which is righteous. Indeed, in the words of the prophet Amos, "Let justice roll down like the waters and righteousness like a mighty stream."

Our priorities are mixed up, our national purposes are confused, our policies are confused, and there must somehow be a reordering of priorities, policies and purposes. I hope, as we discuss these issues tonight, that together we will be able to find some guidelines and some sense of direction.

RABBI EVERETT GENDLER: We begin now with some of the batches of questions. And since the question of confusion came up, and the problem of politics, perhaps we can begin with two or three questions which are rather immediate and relate to some very recent developments. One question is, "At this point, who is your candidate for President?" One question is, "If as it now seems Johnson and Nixon are nominated, do you have any suggestions as an alternative for those seeking a voice in the profound moral issues of the day?" And a third question in this general area of immediacy, "Would you please comment on Congressman [Adam Clayton] Powell's charge that you are a moderate, that you cater to Whitey, and also his criticism that you do not accept violence?" Some criticism! . . .

DR. KING: . . . On the first question, I was about to say that I don't endorse candidates. That has been a policy in the Southern Christian Leadership Conference. We are a non-partisan organization. However, I do think the issues in this election are so crucial that it will be impossible for us to absolutely follow the past policy. I do think the voters of our nation need an alternative in the 1968 election, but I think we are in bad shape finding that alternative with simply Johnson on the one hand and Nixon on the other hand. I don't see the alternative there. Consequently, I must look elsewhere. I think in the candidacy of both Senator Kennedy and Senator McCarthy we see an alternative. It is not definite, as you know, that President Johnson will be renominated. Of course, we haven't had a situation since 1884 when an incumbent President was not renominated, if he wanted the nomination. But these are different days and it may well be that something will happen to make it possible for an alternative to develop within the Democratic party itself.

I think very highly of both Senator McCarthy and Senator Kennedy. I think they are both very competent men. I think they are relevant on the issues that are close to our hearts, and I think they are both dedicated men. So I would settle with either man being nominated by the Democratic party.

On the question of Congressman Powell and his recent accusation, I must say that I would not want to engage in a public or private debate with Mr. Powell on his views concerning Martin Luther King. Frankly, I hope I am so involved in trying to do a job that has to be done that I will not come to the point of dignifying some of the statements that the Congressman has made.

I would like to say, however, on the question of being a moderate, that I always have to understand what one means. I think moderation on the one hand can be a vice; I think on the other hand it can be a virtue. If by moderation we mean moving on through this tense period of transition with wise restraint, calm reasonableness, yet militant action, then moderation is a great virtue which all leaders should seek to achieve. But if moderation means slowing up in the move for justice and capitulating to the whims and caprices of the guardians of the deadening status quo, then moderation is a tragic vice which all men of good will must condemn.

I don't see anything in the work that we are trying to do in the Southern Christian Leadership Conference which is suggestive of slowing up, which is suggestive of not taking a strong stand and a strong resistance to the evils of racial injustice. We have always stood up against injustices. We have done it militantly. Now, so often the word "militant" is misunderstood because most people think of militancy in military terms. But to be militant merely means to be demanding and to be persistent, and in this sense I think the non-violent movement has demonstrated great militancy. It is possible to be militantly non-violent.

On the question of appealing to "Whitey," I don't quite know what the Congressman means. But here again I think this is our problem which must be worked out by all people of good will, black and white. I feel that at every point we must make it very clear that this isn't just a Negro problem, that white Americans have a responsibility, indeed a great responsibility, to work passionately and unrelentingly for the solution of the problem of racism, and if that means constantly reminding white society of its obligation, that must be done. If I have been accused of that, then I will have to continue to be accused.

Finally, I have not advocated violence. The Congressman is quite right. I haven't advocated violence, because I do not see it as the answer to the problem. I do not see it as the answer from a moral point of view and I do not see it as the answer from a practical point of view. I am still convinced that violence as the problematic strategy in our struggle to achieve justice and freedom in the United States would be absolutely impractical and it would lead to a dead-end street. We would end up creating many more social problems than we solve, and unborn generations would be the recipients of a long and desolate night of bitterness. Therefore, I think non-violence, militantly conceived and executed, well-organized, is the most potent weapon available to the black man in his struggle for freedom and human dignity.

RABBI GENDLER: Having raised several points that some of the questions referred to, we may proceed by a further exploration of some of these elements, Dr. King, and perhaps we could begin with several questions that relate to your evaluation of the internal mood of the black community.

Let me share some of the formulations of these questions with you. "How representative is the extremist element of the Negro community?" "How do we know who really represents the Negro community?" "If we are on a committee and there is a Negro militant and a Negro moderate, how shall a concerned white conduct himself?"

"What is your view of the thinking in some Negro circles which prefers segregation and separatism, improving the Negro's lot within this condition? How do you see Black Power in this respect?"

"Black militants want complete separation. You speak of integration. How do you reconcile the two?"

"How can you work with those Negroes who are in complete opposition to your view, and I believe correct view, of integration?"

DR. KING: Let me start off with the question, "How representative are the extremist elements in the black community?" I assume when we say extremist elements we mean those who advocate violence, who advocate separation as a goal. The fact is that these persons represent a very small segment of the Negro community at the present time. I don't know how the situation will be next year or the year after next, but at the present time the vast majority of Negroes in the United States feel that nonviolence is the most effective method to deal with the problems that we face.

Polls have recently revealed this, as recently as two or three months ago. *Fortune* magazine conducted a pretty intensive poll, others have conducted such polls, and they reveal that about 92 percent of the Negroes of America feel that there must be some nonviolent solution to the problem of racial injustice. The *Fortune* poll also revealed that the vast majority of the Negroes still feel that the ultimate solution to the problem will come through a meaningfully integrated society.

Now let me move into the question of integration and separation by dealing with the question of Black Power. I've said so often that I regret that the slogan Black Power came into being, because it has been so confusing. It gives the wrong connotation. It often connotes the quest for black domination rather than black equality. And it is just like telling a joke. If you tell a joke and nobody laughs at the joke and you have to spend the rest of the time trying to explain to people why they should laugh, it isn't a good joke. And that is what I have always said about the slogan Black Power. You have to spend too much time explaining what you are talking about. But it is a slogan that we have to deal with now.

I debated with Stokely Carmichael all the way down the highways of Mississippi, and I said, "Well, let's not use this slogan. Let's get the power. A lot of ethnic groups have power, and I didn't hear them marching around talking about Irish Power or Jewish Power; they just went out and got the power; let's go out and get the power." But somehow we managed to get just the slogan.

I think everybody ought to understand that there are positives in the concept of Black Power and the slogan, and there are negatives.

Let me briefly outline the positives. First, Black Power in the positive sense is a psychological call to manhood. This is desperately needed in the black community, because for all too many years black people have been ashamed of themselves. All too many black people have been ashamed of their heritage, and all too many have had a deep sense of inferiority, and something needed to take place to cause the black man not to be ashamed of himself, not to be ashamed of his color, not to be ashamed of his heritage. . . .

The word black itself in our society connotes something that is degrading. It was absolutely necessary to come to a moment with a sense of dignity. It is very positive and very necessary. So if we see Black Power as a psychological call to manhood and black dignity, I think that's a positive attitude that I want my children to have. I don't want them to be ashamed of the fact that they are black and not white.

Secondly, Black Power is pooling black political resources in order to achieve our legitimate goals. I think that this is very positive, and it is absolutely necessary for the black people of America to achieve political power by pooling political resources. In Cleveland this summer we did engage in a Black Power move. There's no doubt about that. I think most people of good will feel it was a positive move. The same is true of Gary, Indiana. The fact is that Mr. [Richard] Hatcher could not have been elected [mayor] in Gary if black people had not voted in a bloc and then joined with a coalition of liberal whites. In Cleveland, black people voted in a bloc for Carl Stokes [for mayor], joining with a few liberal whites. This was a pooling of resources in order to achieve political power.

Thirdly, Black Power in its positive sense is a pooling of black economic resources in order to achieve legitimate power. And I think there is much that can be done in this area. We can pool our resources, we can cooperate, in order to bring to bear on those who treat us unjustly. We have a program known as Operation Breadbasket in SCLC, and it is certainly one of the best programs we have. It is a very effective program and it's a simple program. It is just a program which demands a certain number of jobs from the private sector—that is, from businesses and industry. It demands a non-discriminatory policy in housing. If they don't yield, we don't argue with them, we don't curse them, we don't burn the store down. We simply go back to our people and we say that this particular company is not responding morally to the question of jobs, to the question of being just and humane toward the black people of the community, and we say that as a result of this we must withdraw our economic support.

That's Black Power in a real sense. We have achieved some very significant gains and victories as a result of this program, because the black man collectively now has enough buying power to make the difference between profit and loss in any major industry or concern of our country. Withdrawing economic support from those who will not be just and fair in their dealings is a very potent weapon.

Political power and economic power are needed, and I think these are the positives of Black Power.

I would see the negatives in two terms. First, in terms of black separatism. As I said, most Negroes do not believe in black separatism as the ultimate goal, but there are some who do and they talk in terms of totally separating themselves from white America. They talk in terms of separate states, and they really mean separatism as a goal. In this sense I must say that I see it as a negative because it is very unrealistic.

The fact is that we are tied together in an inescapable network of mutuality. Whether we like it or not and whether the racist understands it or not, our music, our cultural patterns, our poets, our material prosperity and even our food, are an amalgam of black and white, and there can be no separate black path to power and fulfillment that does not ultimately intersect white routes. There can be no separate white path to power and fulfillment, short of social disaster, that does not recognize the necessity of sharing that power with black aspirations for freedom and justice.

This leads me to say another thing, and that is that it isn't enough to talk about integration without coming to see that integration is more than something to be dealt with in esthetic or romantic terms. I think in the past all too often we did it that way. We talked of integration in romantic and esthetic terms and it ended up as merely adding color to a still predominantly white power structure.

What is necessary now is to see integration in political terms where there is sharing of power. When we see integration in political terms, then we recognize that there are times when we must see segregation as a temporary way-station to a truly integrated society. There are many Negroes who feel this; they do not see segregation as the ultimate goal. They do not see separation as the ultimate goal. They see it as a temporary way-station to put them into a bargaining position to get to that ultimate goal, which is a truly integrated society where there is shared power.

I must honestly say that there are points at which I share this view. There are points at which I see the necessity for temporary segregation in order to get to the integrated society. I can point to some cases. I've seen this in the South, in schools being integrated and I've seen it with Teachers' Associations being integrated. Often when they merge, the Negro is integrated without power. The two or three positions of power which he did have in the separate situation passed away altogether, so that he lost his bargaining position, he lost his power, and he lost his posture where he could be relatively militant and really grapple with the problems.

And this is why I think it is absolutely necessary to see integration in political terms, to see that there are some situations where separation may serve as a temporary way-station to the ultimate goal which we seek, which I think is the only answer in the final analysis to the problem of a truly integrated society.

I think this is the mood which we find in the black community, generally, and this means that we must work on two levels. In every city we have a dual society. This dualism runs in the economic market. In every city, we have two economies. In every city, we have two housing markets. In every city, we have two school systems. This duality has brought about a great deal of injustice, and I don't need to go into all that because we are all familiar with it.

In every city, to deal with this unjust dualism, we must constantly work toward the goal of a truly integrated society while at the same time we enrich the ghetto. We must seek to enrich the ghetto immediately in the sense of improving the housing conditions, improving the schools in the ghetto, improving the economic conditions. At the same time, we must be working to open the housing market so there will be one housing market only. We must work on two levels. We should gradually move to disperse the ghetto, and immediately move to improve conditions within the ghetto, which in the final analysis will make it possible to disperse it at a greater rate a few years from now.

RABBI GENDLER: Perhaps we could share now a few questions relating to some of the domestic issues of poverty. A couple of them ask about the Kerner Report. "If the Kerner Report recommendations are implemented, will it make a difference?" "What is your opinion of the report of the Kerner Commission?"

Another raises the question of people of good intentions wanting to deal with slum problems and hardly knowing what to do, feeling that most of the simple tutoring and palliative efforts in the community may not amount to much, given the entire context of the system. It speaks of the power structure, the establishment finding funds for supersonic transports, moon projects, technological developments which are mere luxuries, for Vietnam, but not for those pressing needs which affect millions here at home. "Can you suggest why the establishment seems to work this way? Is it an accident or does it have deeper causes? What seem to you the minimal changes needed in the system in order to achieve some greater measure of social justice and equality?"

And perhaps related to this is the question of some of the realistic goals of the poor peoples' campaign to be held in Washington beginning April 22nd.

DR. KING: Thank you. I want to start this answer by reiterating something that I said earlier, and that is that we do face a great crisis in our nation. Even though the President said today that we have never had it so good, we must honestly say that for many people in our country they've never had it so bad. Poverty is a glaring, notorious reality for some forty million Americans. I guess it wouldn't be so bad for them if it were shared misery, but it is poverty amid plenty. It is poverty in the midst of an affluent society, and I think this is what makes for great frustration and great despair in the black community and the poor community of our nation generally.

In the past in the civil rights movement we have been dealing with segregation and all of its humiliation, we've been dealing with the political problem of the denial of the right to vote. I think it is absolutely necessary now to deal massively and militantly with the economic problem. If this isn't dealt with, we will continue to move as the Kerner Commission said, toward two societies, one white and one black, separate and unequal. So the grave problem facing us is the problem of economic deprivation, with the syndrome of bad housing and poor education and improper health facilities all surrounding this basic problem.

This is why in SCLC we came up with the idea of going to Washington, the seat of government, to dramatize the gulf between promise and fulfillment, to call attention to the gap between the dream and the realities, to make the invisible visible. All too often in the rush of everyday life there is a tendency to forget the poor, to overlook the poor, to allow the poor to become invisible, and this is why we are calling our campaign a poor peoples' campaign. We are going to Washington to engage in non-violent direct action in order to call attention to this great problem of poverty and to demand that the government do something, more than a token, something in a large manner to grapple with the economic problem.

We know, from my experiences in the past, that the nation does not move on questions involving genuine equality for the black man unless something is done to bring pressure to bear on Congress, and to appeal to the conscience and the self-interest of the nation.

I remember very well that we had written documents by the Civil Rights Commission at least three years before we went to Birmingham, recommending very strongly all of the things that we dramatized in our direct action in Birmingham. But the fact is that the government did not move, Congress did not move, until we developed a powerful, vibrant movement in Birmingham, Alabama.

Two years before we went into Selma, the Civil Rights Commission recommended that something be done in a very strong manner to eradicate the discrimination Negroes faced in the voting area in the South. And yet nothing was done about it until we went to Selma, mounted a movement and really engaged in action geared toward moving the nation away from the course that it was following.

I submit this evening that we have had numerous documents, numerous studies, numerous recommendations made on the economic question, and yet nothing has been done. The things that we are going to be demanding in Washington have been recommended by the President's Commission on Technology, Automation and Economic Progress. These same things were recommended at our White House Conference on Civil Rights. The Urban Coalition came into being after the Detroit riot, and recommended these things.

The Kerner Commission came out just a few days ago recommending some of the same things that we will be demanding. I think it is basically a very sound, realistic report on the conditions, with some very sound recommendations, and yet nothing has been done. Indeed, the President himself has not made any move toward implementing any of the recommendations of that Commission. I am convinced that nothing will be done until enough people of good will get together to respond to the kind of movement that we will have in Washington, and bring these issues out in the open enough so that the Congressmen, who are in no mood at the present time to do anything about this problem, will be forced to do something about it.

I have seen them change in the past. I remember when we first went up and talked about a civil rights bill in 1963, right after it had been recommended by President Kennedy on the heels of the Birmingham movement. [Senator] Dirksen was saying that it was unconstitutional, particularly Title I dealing with integrated public accommodations. He was showing us that it was unconstitutional. Yet we got enough people moving—we got rabbis moving, we got priests moving, we got Protestant clergymen moving, and they were going around Washington and they were staying on top of it, they were lobbying, they were saying to Mr. Dirksen and others that this must be done.

Finally, the Congress changed altogether. One day when Senator Russell saw that the civil rights bill would be passed and that the Southern wing could not defeat it, he said, "We could have blocked this thing if these preachers hadn't stayed around Washington so much."

Now the time has come for preachers and everybody else to get to Washington and get this very recalcitrant Congress to see that it must do something and that it must do it soon, because I submit that if something isn't done, similar to what is recommended by the Kerner Commission, we are going to have organized social disruption, our cities are going to continue to go up in flames, more and more black people will get frustrated, and the extreme voices calling for violence will get a greater hearing in the black community.

So far they have not influenced many, but I contend that if something isn't done very soon to deal with this basic economic problem to provide jobs and income for all America, then the extremist voices will be heard more and those who are preaching non-violence will often have their words falling on deaf ears. This is why we feel that this is such an important campaign.

We need a movement now to transmute the rage of the ghetto into a positive constructive force. And here again we feel that this movement is so necessary because the anger is there, the despair is growing every day, the bitterness is very deep, and the leader has the responsibility of trying to find an answer. I have been searching for that answer a long time, over the last eighteen months.

I can't see the answer in riots. On the other hand, I can't see the answer in tender supplications for justice. I see the answer in an alternative to both of these, and that is militant non-violence that is massive enough, that is attention-getting enough to dramatize the problems, that will be as attention-getting as a riot, that will not destroy life or property in the process. And this is what we hope to do in Washington through our movement.

We feel that there must be some structural changes now, there must be a radical re-ordering of priorities, there must be a de-escalation and a final stopping of the war in Vietnam and an escalation of the war against poverty and racism here at home. And I feel that this is only going to be done when enough people get together and express their determination through that togetherness and make it clear that we are not going to allow any military-industrial complex to control this country.

One of the great tragedies of the war in Vietnam is that it has strengthened the military-industrial complex, and it must be made clear now that there are some programs that we can cut back on—the space program and certainly the war in Vietnam—and get on with this program of a war on poverty. Right now we don't even have a skirmish against poverty, and we really need an all out, mobilized war that will make it possible for all of God's children to have the basic necessities of life.

RABBI GENDLER: . . . One [last question] is, "What can we best do as rabbis to further the rights and equal status of our colored brethren?" Another is, "What specific role do you think we as rabbis can play in this current civil rights struggle? What role do you see for our congregants? How can all of us who are concerned participate with you in seeking this goal of social justice?"

DR. KING: Thank you very much for raising that because I do think that is a good note to end on, and I would hope that somehow we can get some real support, not only for the over-all struggle, but for the immediate campaign ahead in the city of Washington.

Let me say that we have failed to say something to America enough. I'm very happy that the Kerner Commission had the courage to say it. However difficult it is to hear, however shocking it is to hear, we've got to face the fact that America is a racist country. We have got to face the fact that racism still occupies the throne of our nation. I don't think we will ultimately solve the problem of racial injustice until this is recognized, and until this is worked on.

Racism is the myth of an inferior race, of an inferior people, and I think religious institutions, more than any other institutions in society, must really deal with racism. Certainly we all have a responsibility—the federal government, the local governments, our educational institutions. But the religious community, being the chief moral guardian of the over-all community, should really take the primary responsibility in dealing with this problem of racism, which is largely attitudinal.

So I see one specific job in the educational realm: destroying the myths and the half-truths that have constantly been disseminated about Negroes all over the country and which lead to many of these racist attitudes, getting rid once and for all of the notion of white supremacy.

I think also I might say, concerning the Washington campaign, that there is a need to interpret what we are about or will be about in Washington because the press has gone out of its way in many instances to misinterpret what we will be doing in Washington.

There is a need to interpret to all of those who worship in our congregations what poor people face in this nation, and to interpret the critical nature of the problem. We are dealing with the problem of poverty. We must be sure that the people of our country will see this as a matter of justice.

The next thing that I would like to mention is something very practical and yet we have to mention it if we are going to have movements. We are going to bring in the beginning about 3,000 people to Washington from fifteen various communities. They are going to be poor people, mainly unemployed people, some who are too old to work, some who are too young to work, some who are too physically disabled to work, some who are able to work but who can't get jobs. They are going to be coming to Washington to bring their problems, to bring their burdens to the seat of government, and to demand that the government do something about it.

Being poor, they certainly don't have any money. I was in Marks, Mississippi, the other day and I found myself weeping before I knew it. I met boys and girls by the hundreds who didn't have any shoes to wear, who didn't have any food to eat in terms of three square meals a day, and I met their parents, many of whom don't even have jobs. But not only do they not have jobs, they are not even getting an income. Some of them aren't on any kind of welfare, and I literally cried when I heard men and women saying that they were unable to get any food to feed their children.

We decided that we are going to try to bring this whole community to Washington, from Marks, Mississippi. They don't have anything anyway. They don't have anything to lose. And we decided that we are going to try to bring them right up to Washington where we are going to have our Freedom School. There we are going to have all of the things that we have outlined and that we don't have time to go into now, but in order to bring them to Washington it is going to take money.

They'll have to be fed after they get to Washington, and we would hope that those who are so inclined, those who have a compassion for the least of these God's children, will aid us financially. Some will be walking and we'll be using church busses to get them from point to point. Some will be coming up on mule train. We're going to have a mule train coming from Mississippi, connecting with Alabama, Georgia, going right on up, and in order to carry that out you can see that financial aid will be greatly needed.

But not only that. We need bodies to bring about the pressure that I have mentioned to get Congress and the nation moving in the right direction. The stronger the number, the greater this movement will be.

We will need some people working in supportive roles, lobbying in Washington, talking with the Congressmen, talking with the various departments of government, and we will need some to march with us as we demonstrate in the city of Washington. Some have already done this, like Rabbi Gendler and others. When we first met him it was in Albany, Georgia, and there along with other rabbis and Protestant clergymen and Catholic clergymen we developed a movement. And there have been others—as I said earlier, Rabbi Heschel in Selma and other movements.

The more of this kind of participation that we can get, the more helpful it will be, for after we get the 3,000 people in Washington, we want the non-poor to come in in a supportive role. Then on June fifteenth we want to have a massive march on Washington. You see, the 3,000 are going to stay in Washington at least sixty days, or however long we feel it is necessary, but we want to provide an opportunity once more for thousands, hundreds of thousands of people to come to Washington, reminiscent of [the] March [in] 1963 when thousands of people said we are here because we endorse the demands of the poor people who have been here all of these weeks trying to get Congress to move. We would hope that as many people in your congregations as you can find will come to Washington on June fifteenth.

You can see that it is a tremendous logistics problem and it means real organization, which we are getting into. We would hope that all of our friends will go out of their way to make that a big day, indeed the largest march that has ever taken place in the city of Washington.

These are some of the things that can be done. I'm sure I've missed some, but these are the ones that are on my mind right now and I believe that this kind of support would bring new hope to those who are now in very despairing conditions. I still believe that with this kind of coalition of conscience we will be able to get something moving again in America, something that is so desperately needed.

RABBI GENDLER: I think that all of us, Dr. King, recall the words of Professor Heschel at the beginning of this evening. He spoke of the word, the vision, and the way that you provide. We certainly have heard words of eloquence, words which at the same time were very much to the point, and through these I think we have the opportunity now to share more fully in your vision.

As for the way, it is eminently clear that the paths you tread are peaceful ones leading to greater peace. You may be sure that not only have we heard your words and not only do we share your vision, but many of us will take advantage of the privilege of accompanying you in further steps on the path that all of us must tread.

Thank you, Dr. King.

3. "I See the Promised Land"
Martin Luther King, Jr.

One of King's most famous orations, perhaps second only to his August 28, 1963, "I Have a Dream" speech at the March on Washington, is his April 3, 1968, "mountaintop" speech delivered at the Mason Temple in Memphis the night before his death.

Thank you very kindly, my friends. As I listened to Ralph Abernathy in his eloquent and generous introduction and then thought about myself, I wondered who he was talking about. It's always good to have your closest friend and associate say something good about you. And Ralph is the best friend that I have in the world.

I'm delighted to see each of you here tonight in spite of a storm warning. You reveal that you are determined to go on anyhow. Something is happening in Memphis, something is happening in our world.

As you know, if I were standing at the beginning of time, with the possibility of general and panoramic view of the whole human history up to now, and the Almighty said to me, "Martin Luther

King, which age would you like to live in?"—I would take my mental flight by Egypt through, or rather across the Red Sea, through the wilderness on toward the promised land. And in spite of its magnificence, I wouldn't stop there. I would move on by Greece, and take my mind to Mount Olympus. And I would see Plato, Aristotle, Socrates, Euripides and Aristophanes assembled around the Parthenon as they discussed the great and eternal issues of reality.

But I wouldn't stop there. I would go on, even to the great heyday of the Roman Empire. And I would see developments around there, through various emperors and leaders. But I wouldn't stop there. I would even come up to the day of the Renaissance, and get a quick picture of all that the Renaissance did for the cultural and esthetic life of man. But I wouldn't stop there. I would even go by the way that the man for whom I'm named had his habitat. And I would watch Martin Luther as he tacked his ninety-five theses on the door at the church in Wittenberg.

But I wouldn't stop there. I would come on up even to 1863, and watch a vacillating president by the name of Abraham Lincoln finally come to the conclusion that he had to sign the Emancipation Proclamation. But I wouldn't stop there. I would even come up to the early thirties, and see a man grappling with the problems of the bankruptcy of his nation. And come with an eloquent cry that we have nothing to fear but fear itself.

But I wouldn't stop there. Strangely enough, I would turn to the Almighty, and say, "If you allow me to live just a few years in the second half of the twentieth century, I will be happy." Now that's a strange statement. But I know, somehow, that only when it is dark enough, can you see the stars. And I see God working in this period of the twentieth century in a way that men, in some strange way, are responding—something is happening in our world. The masses of people are rising up. And wherever they are assembled today, whether they are in Johannesburg, South Africa; Nairobi, Kenya; Accra, Ghana; New York City; Atlanta, Georgia; Jackson, Mississippi; or Memphis, Tennessee—the cry is always the same—"We want to be free."

And another reason that I'm happy to live in this period is that we have been forced to a point where we're going to have to grapple with the problems that men have been trying to grapple with through history, but the demands didn't force them to do it. Survival demands that we grapple with them. Men, for years now, have been talking about war and peace. But now, no longer can they just talk about it. It is no longer a choice between violence and nonviolence in this world; it's nonviolence or nonexistence.

That is where we are today. And also in the human rights revolution, if something isn't done, and in a hurry, to bring the colored peoples of the world out of their long years of poverty, their long years of hurt and neglect, the whole world is doomed. Now, I'm just happy that God has allowed me to live in this period, to see what is unfolding. And I'm happy that he's allowed me to be in Memphis.

I can remember, I can remember when Negroes were just going around as Ralph has said, so often, scratching where they didn't itch, and laughing when they were not tickled. But that day is all over. We mean business now, and we are determined to gain our rightful place in God's world.

And that's all this whole thing is about. We aren't engaged in any negative protest and in any negative arguments with anybody. We are saying that we are determined to be men. We are determined to be people. We are saying that we are God's children. And that we don't have to live like we are forced to live.

Now, what does all of this mean in this great period of history? It means that we've got to stay together. We've got to stay together and maintain unity. You know, whenever Pharaoh wanted to prolong the period of slavery in Egypt, he had a favorite, favorite formula for doing it. What was that? He kept the slaves fighting among themselves. But whenever the slaves get together, something happens in Pharaoh's court, and he cannot hold the slaves in slavery. When the slaves get together, that's the beginning of getting out of slavery. Now let us maintain unity.

Secondly, let us keep the issues where they are. The issue is injustice. The issue is the refusal of Memphis to be fair and honest in its dealings with its public servants, who happen to be sanitation workers. Now, we've got to keep attention on that. That's always the problem with a little violence. You know what happened the other day, and the press dealt only with the window-breaking. I read the articles. They very seldom got around to mentioning the fact that one thousand, three hundred sanitation workers were on strike, and that Memphis is not being fair to them, and that Mayor Loeb is in dire need of a doctor. They didn't get around to that.

Now we're going to march again, and we've got to march again, in order to put the issue where it is supposed to be. And force everybody to see that there are thirteen hundred of God's children here suffering, sometimes going hungry, going through dark and dreary nights wondering how this thing is going to come out. That's the issue. And we've got to say to the nation: we know it's coming out. For when people get caught up with that which is right and they are willing to sacrifice for it, there is no stopping point short of victory.

We aren't going to let any mace stop us. We are masters in our nonviolent movement in disarming police forces; they don't know what to do. I've seen them so often. I remember in Birmingham, Alabama, when we were in that majestic struggle there we would move out of the 16th Street Baptist Church day after day; by the hundreds we would move out. And Bull Connor would tell them to send the dogs forth and they did come; but we just went before the dogs singing, "Ain't gonna let nobody turn me round." Bull Connor next would say, "Turn the fire hoses on." And as I said to you the other night, Bull Connor didn't know history. He knew a kind of physics that somehow didn't relate to the transphysics that we knew about. And that was the fact that there was a certain kind of fire that no water could put out. And we went before the fire hoses; we had known water. If we were Baptist or some other denomination, we had been immersed. If we were Methodist, and some others, we had been sprinkled, but we knew water.

That couldn't stop us. And we just went on before the dogs and we would look at them; and we'd go on before the water hoses and we would look at it, and we'd just go on singing "Over my head I see freedom in the air." And then we would be thrown in the paddy wagons, and sometimes we were stacked in there like sardines in a can. And they would throw us in, and old Bull would say, "Take them off," and they did; and we would just go in the paddy wagon singing, "We Shall Overcome." And every now and then we'd get in the jail, and we'd see the jailers looking through the windows being moved by our prayers, and being moved by our words and our songs. And there was a power there which Bull Connor couldn't adjust to; and so we ended up transforming Bull into a steer, and we won our struggle in Birmingham.

Now we've got to go on to Memphis just like that. I call upon you to be with us Monday. Now about injunctions: We have an injunction and we're going into court tomorrow morning to fight this illegal, unconstitutional injunction. All we say to America is, "Be true to what you said on paper." If I lived in China or even Russia, or any totalitarian country, maybe I could understand the denial of certain basic First Amendment privileges, because they hadn't committed themselves to that over there. But somewhere I read of the freedom of assembly. Somewhere I read of the freedom of speech. Somewhere I read of the freedom of the press. Somewhere I read that the greatness of America is the right to protest for right. And so just as I say, we aren't going to let any injunction turn us around. We are going on.

We need all of you. And you know what's beautiful to me, is to see all of these ministers of the Gospel. It's a marvelous picture. Who is it that is supposed to articulate the longings and aspirations of the people more than the preacher? Somehow the preacher must be an Amos, and say, "Let justice roll down like waters and righteousness like a mighty stream." Somehow, the preacher must say with Jesus, "The spirit of the Lord is upon me, because he hath anointed me to deal with the problems of the poor."

And I want to commend the preachers, under the leadership of these noble men: James Lawson, one who has been in this struggle for many years; he's been to jail for struggling; but he's still going on, fighting for the rights of his people. Rev. Ralph Jackson, Billy Kyles; I could just go right on down the list, but time will not permit. But I want to thank them all. And I want you to thank them, because so often, preachers aren't concerned about anything but themselves. And I'm always happy to see a relevant ministry.

It's alright to talk about "long white robes over yonder," in all of its symbolism. But ultimately people want some suits and dresses and shoes to wear down here. It's alright to talk about "streets flowing with milk and honey," but God has commanded us to be concerned about the slums down here, and his children who can't eat three square meals a day. It's alright to talk about the new Jerusalem, but one day, God's preacher must talk about the New York, the new Atlanta, the new Philadelphia, the new Los Angeles, the new Memphis, Tennessee. This is what we have to do.

Now the other thing we'll have to do is this: Always anchor our external direct action with the power of economic withdrawal. Now, we are poor people, individually, we are poor when you compare us with white society in America. We are poor. Never stop and forget that collectively, that means all of us together, collectively we are richer than all the nations in the world, with the exception of nine. Did you ever think about that? After you leave the United States, Soviet Russia, Great Britain, West Germany, France, and I could name the others, the Negro collectively is richer than most nations of the world. We have an annual income of more than thirty billion dollars a year, which is more than all of the exports of the United States, and more than the national budget of Canada. Did you know that? That's power right there, if we know how to pool it.

We don't have to argue with anybody. We don't have to curse and go around acting bad with our words. We don't need any bricks and bottles, we don't need any Molotov cocktails, we just need to go around to these stores, and to these massive industries in our country, and say, "God sent us by here, to say to you that you're not treating his children right. And we've come by here to ask you to make the first item on your agenda—fair treatment, where God's children are concerned. Now, if you are not prepared to do that, we do have an agenda that we must follow. And our agenda calls for withdrawing economic support from you."

And so, as a result of this, we are asking you tonight, to go out and tell your neighbors not to buy Coca-Cola in Memphis. Go by and tell them not to buy Sealtest milk. Tell them not to buy— what is the other bread?—Wonder Bread. And what is the other bread company, Jesse? Tell them not to buy Hart's bread. As Jesse Jackson has said, up to now, only the garbage men have been feeling pain; now we must kind of redistribute the pain. We are choosing these companies because they haven't been fair in their hiring policies; and we are choosing them because they can begin the process of saying, they are going to support the needs and the rights of these men who are on strike. And then they can move on downtown and tell Mayor Loeb to do what is right.

But not only that, we've got to strengthen black institutions. I call upon you to take your money out of the banks downtown and deposit your money in Tri-State Bank—we want a "bank-in" movement in Memphis. So go by the savings and loan association. I'm not asking you something that we don't do ourselves at SCLC. Judge [Benjamin] Hooks and others will tell you that we have an account here in the savings and loan association from the Southern Christian Leadership Conference. We're just telling you to follow what we're doing. Put your money there. You have six or seven black insurance companies in Memphis. Take out your insurance there. We want to have an "insurance-in."

Now these are some practical things we can do. We begin the process of building a greater economic base. And at the same time, we are putting pressure where it really hurts. I ask you to follow through here.

Now, let me say as I move to my conclusion that we've got to give ourselves to this struggle until the end. Nothing would be more tragic than to stop at this point, in Memphis. We've got to see it through. And when we have our march, you need to be there. Be concerned about your brother. You may not be on strike. But either we go up together, or we go down together.

Let us develop a kind of dangerous unselfishness. One day a man came to Jesus; and he wanted to raise some questions about some vital matters in life. At points, he wanted to trick Jesus, and show him that he knew a little more than Jesus knew, and through this, throw him off base. Now that question could have easily ended up in a philosophical and theological debate. But Jesus immediately pulled that question from mid-air, and placed it on a dangerous curve between Jerusalem and Jericho. And he talked about a certain man, who fell among thieves. You remember that a Levite and a priest passed by on the other side. They didn't stop to help him. And finally a man of another race came by. He got down from his beast, decided not to be compassionate by proxy. But with him, administered first aid, and helped the man in need. Jesus ended up saying, this was the good man, this was the great man, because he had the capacity to project the "I" into the "thou," and to be concerned about his brother. Now you know, we use our imagination a great deal to try to determine why the priest and the Levite didn't stop. At times we say they were busy going to church meetings—an ecclesiastical gathering—and they had to get on down to Jerusalem so they wouldn't be late for their meeting. At other times we would speculate that there was a religious law that "One who was engaged in religious ceremonials was not to touch a human body twenty-four hours before the ceremony." And every now and then we begin to wonder whether maybe they were not going down to Jerusalem, or down to Jericho, rather to organize a "Jericho Road Improvement Association." That's a possibility. Maybe they felt that it was better to deal with the problem from the causal root, rather than to get bogged down with an individual effort.

But, I'm going to tell you what my imagination tells me. It's possible that these men were afraid. You see, the Jericho road is a dangerous road. I remember when Mrs. King and I were first in Jerusalem. We rented a car and drove from Jerusalem down to Jericho. And as soon as we got on that road, I said to my wife, "I can see why Jesus used this as a setting for his parable." It's a winding, meandering road. It's really conducive for ambushing. You start out in Jerusalem, which is about 1200 miles, or rather 1200 feet above sea level. And by the time you get down to Jericho, fifteen or twenty minutes later, you're about 2200 feet below sea level. That's a dangerous road. In the days of Jesus it came to be known as the "Bloody Pass." And you know, it's possible that the priest and the Levite looked over that man on the ground and wondered if the robbers were still around. Or it's possible that they felt that the man on the ground was merely faking. And he was acting like he had been robbed and hurt, in order to seize them over there, lure them there for quick and easy seizure. And so the first question that the Levite asked was, "If I stop to help this man, what will happen to me?" But then the Good Samaritan came by. And he reversed the question: "If I do not stop to help this man, what will happen to him?"

That's the question before you tonight. Not, "If I stop to help the sanitation workers, what will happen to all of the hours that I usually spend in my office every day and every week as a pastor?" The question is not, "If I stop to help this man in need, what will happen to me?" "If I do not stop to help the sanitation workers, what will happen to them?" That's the question.

Let us rise up tonight with greater readiness. Let us stand with a greater determination. And let us move on in these powerful days, these days of challenge to make America what it ought to be. We have an opportunity to make America a better nation. And I want to thank God, once more, for allowing me to be here with you.

You know, several years ago, I was in New York City autographing the first book that I had written. And while sitting there autographing books, a demented black woman came up. The only question I heard from her was, "Are you Martin Luther King?"

And I was looking down writing, and I said yes. And the next minute I felt something beating on my chest. Before I knew it I had been stabbed by this demented woman. I was rushed to Harlem Hospital. It was a dark Saturday afternoon. And that blade had gone through, and the X-rays revealed that the tip of the blade was on the edge of my aorta, the main artery. And once that's punctured, you drown in your own blood—that's the end of you.

It came out in the *New York Times* the next morning, that if I had sneezed, I would have died. Well, about four days later, they allowed me, after the operation, after my chest had been opened, and the blade had been taken out, to move around in the wheel chair in the hospital. They allowed me to read some of the mail that came in, and from all over the states, and the world, kind letters came in. I read a few, but one of them I will never forget. I had received one from the President and the Vice-President. I've forgotten what those telegrams said. I'd received a visit and a letter from the Governor of New York, but I've forgotten what the letter said. But there was another letter that came from a little girl, a young girl who was a student at the White Plains High School. And I looked at that letter, and I'll never forget it. It said simply, "Dear Dr. King: I am a ninth-grade student at the White Plains High School." She said, "While it should not matter, I would like to mention that I am a white girl. I read in the paper of your misfortune, and of your suffering. And I read that if you had sneezed, you would have died. And I'm simply writing you to say that I'm so happy that you didn't sneeze."

And I want to say tonight, I want to say that I am happy that I didn't sneeze. Because if I had sneezed, I wouldn't have been around here in 1960, when students all over the South started sitting-in at lunch counters. And I knew that as they were sitting in, they were really standing up for the best in the American dream. And taking the whole nation back to those great walls of democracy which were dug deep by the Founding Fathers in the Declaration of Independence and the Constitution. If I had sneezed, I wouldn't have been around in 1962, when Negroes in Albany, Georgia, decided to straighten their backs up. And whenever men and women straighten their backs up, they are going somewhere, because a man can't ride your back unless it is bent. If I had sneezed, I wouldn't have been here in 1963, when the black people of Birmingham, Alabama, aroused the conscience of this nation, and brought into being the Civil Rights Bill. If I had sneezed, I wouldn't have had a chance later that year, in August, to try to tell America about a dream that I had had. If I had sneezed, I wouldn't have been down in Selma, Alabama, to see the great movement there. If I had sneezed, I wouldn't have been in Memphis to see a community rally around those brothers and sisters who are suffering. I'm so happy that I didn't sneeze.

And they were telling me, now it doesn't matter now. It really doesn't matter what happens now. I left Atlanta this morning, and as we got started on the plane, there were six of us, the pilot said over the public address system, "We are sorry for the delay, but we have Dr. Martin Luther King on the plane. And to be sure that all of the bags were checked, and to be sure that nothing would be wrong with the plane, we had to check out everything carefully. And we've had the plane protected and guarded all night."

And then I got into Memphis. And some began to say the threats, or talk about the threats that were out. What would happen to me from some of our sick white brothers?

Well, I don't know what will happen now. We've got some difficult days ahead. But it doesn't matter with me now. Because I've been to the mountaintop. And I don't mind. Like anybody, I would like to live a long life. Longevity has its place. But I'm not concerned about that now. I just want to do God's will. And He's allowed me to go up to the mountain. And I've looked over. And

I've seen the promised land. I may not get there with you. But I want you to know tonight, that we, as a people will get to the promised land. And I'm happy, tonight. I'm not worried about anything. I'm not fearing any man. Mine eyes have seen the glory of the coming of the Lord.

4. "My Last Letter to Martin"
Ralph David Abernathy

This is the text of a sermon delivered by Ralph Abernathy on Sunday, April 7, 1968, at the West Hunter Street Baptist Church, Atlanta. Abernathy was King's closest aide and companion, reaching all the way back to the onset of the Montgomery bus boycott in December 1955. Although Abernathy was not always a major strategist or decision maker within SCLC, his emotional closeness to King, and King's choice of him as his designated successor, automatically made Abernathy president of SCLC following King's assassination.

Martin,

I miss you and it has been just a few days. I thought I would write you a short letter. It is probably more for my good than it is for yours. I hope it will not be too long before you read it. In Heaven I know you have so much to do, so many people to see. And I know many of them have already been looking and waiting for you. It wouldn't surprise me Martin, if God didn't have a special affair just to introduce his special activist black son to so many others like you that have gone on ahead. I know you wouldn't believe that could happen but then you did not understand how wonderful you are.

But look up these black friends and talk to the ones you and I have talked about; and the ones that you and I led; and the ones who so gallantly followed your leadership. Say thanks to those prophets we quoted all over America and everywhere else that they asked for us. Give a special word from me to Peter, the man who was once sand, but Jesus made him a rock. Give my warmest felicitations to my favorite apostle, John, who loved my Master so much until he stood with his mother at the foot of the Cross. Pass my greetings on to Isaiah, who had the prophetic vision to see the coming of a Saviour whose name would be Wonderful, a Mighty Counselor, an Everlasting Father, and a Prince of Peace. Stop by and chat with Hosea. And find Mahatma K. Gandhi, the man who inspired us so much in our struggle to free black people through the philosophy and techniques of nonviolence. And in the midst of your conversations, Martin, mention me. Look up Bartholomew. For some strange reason I always liked him.

But, above all, I want you to see Jesus. Go to the throne and tell how thankful we are. Yes, go see Jesus, and tell Him about us down here, all of us, and all of our families, and how we have sustained ourselves in the many battles all through our lives. Tell Him how much we love Him. Tell Him how His name is music in our ears. Tell Him how at His name our knees will forever bow and our tongues will always confess. Tell Him that we follow not only His words but we follow His life, for His footprints lead to Bethany, for that's where He stayed; but they lead to Gethsemane, for it was there He prayed. They lead to Calvary where salvation was complete. There we were saved by His grace.

Then, Martin, go from the throne and find the Rev. George Lee, that stalwart hero who could barely read and write, who was shot down on the streets of Belzoni, Miss., simply because he wanted to vote. Check with Medgar Evers, who was shot down by mean and cruel white men, who thought they could turn us around by taking the life of this young man. Check with William Moore, another casualty in Alabama. And then Jimmy Lee Jackson, who died on the battlefield of Alabama. Oh, I wish you would look up Mrs. Viola Liuzzo, a white woman who was killed, you remember, on Highway 80; and then check with Jonathan Daniels, a young theological Catholic student who died in Haynesville, Ala., down in Lowndes County, standing up for the rights of black people. James Reeb should be seen also, Martin. For James Reeb, a Unitarian minister, was beaten to death when he came to march for us in Selma. And don't forget Michael Schwerner and Andrew Goodman and James Chaney. You remember those three freedom fighters that they killed in Mississippi and buried their bodies beneath an earthen dam. Express our thanks to them. And then, Martin, don't forget the four little innocent girls who died in a Sunday School class in the 16th Street Baptist Church in Birmingham. They've been waiting to hear from us. Give them a good and complete report. And tell them that you left your people on your way. And we're determined that we ain't gonna let nobody turn us around.

And then, Martin, find Frederick Douglass, that great and marvelous human personality who lived in even more difficult times than we live today. Check with Nat Turner, and Marcus Garvey, for they, too, are heroes in our crusade. And oh, I wish that you would pause long enough at the mansion that is occupied by Abraham Lincoln, the man who freed us from physical bondage here in this country. Then, Martin, we owe a great debt of gratitude to John Fitzgerald Kennedy who less than five years ago, young as you were, brilliant as you were, filled with new ideas as you were, was shot down and killed as you were in cold blood by a mean, vicious and angry society. And don't forget Malcolm X. Look for Malcolm X, Martin. Remember our God is a loving God and he understands things we don't think that he understands. Malcolm may not have believed what we believe and he may not have preached but he was a child of God and he was concerned about the welfare of his people. And then, Martin, please do not forget about all of those who died across Alabama, Mississippi, Louisiana, Chicago, and New York, and all other places where men have died for the liberty and justice of other men. Martin, it may seem like a big order, but if you find one of them, he will know where the rest are. And he will take you to them. I know that they have founded the grand international company of freedom fighters, and can't wait to introduce you to take over the final hours.

A man on Hunter Street said, "I envy the way that he died. He will be with so many who have died like he did."

I know that you have a lot to talk about and you will have a wonderful time, but, remember, your brother, Ralph, will be coming along one day. One thing, we won't have any critics up there, Martin. I don't think they will make it, that they will be there. Every day will be Sunday. None but the righteous will see God.

The day after I last saw you in Memphis, I remembered you from the first time I saw you. It was in Montgomery, Ala. This was a very jovial memory. In fact, I first saw you in church. You were still a student at Crozier Theological Seminary. You were preaching at the Ebenezer Baptist Church. Even then you moved me. You remember that you were preaching that Sunday on the subject of "The Christian and the Faith." Afterwards when everybody was shaking hands with you, I shook your hand, also. And I remembered your handshake. It was warm and strong. It was soft and tender. I liked you even then.

Strangely enough, Martin, the second time I saw you was at Spelman's Sisters Chapel. You were well-dressed and you were giving your attention to a very pretty lady. You escorted her there in the prime of your life. I need not remind you that it wasn't Coretta, for this was long before she came into your life. You were young, then. You were a student and you were just playing the field. How different now, dear friend. You had come there to see others. Now others are coming to see you. I know you can hardly believe it as you look down on us and see those long silent lines of people waiting in the cool evening, the early mornings, the springtime noon, and even in the weary midnight hours, passing under the budding green trees past your silent bier. Well, Martin, if you ever had any moments of doubt about whether people loved you, now in the time of death, you no longer have to doubt. You kept the faith with them, and you brought us through the dark and difficult days and nights of our movement. Now they keep it with you throughout the night, around the clock. Today so much is happening in Sisters Chapel, the second place where I saw you. And even more will happen in the Ebenezer Baptist Church and the Morehouse Quadrangle and all across the world in the days and the years to come.

It was after that third time, Martin, that I met you when we really became fast friends. You will remember this meeting. It was in my home, the parsonage of the First Baptist Church in Montgomery. We were never separated until the other day, as you know. I was right behind you there as I have always been. I don't know why they got you and left me. I can't help but talk about it. I ran to you as quickly as I could and I said, "It's me, Ralph." You rolled your eyes around in your head, and, even with your jaw shot out and your vocal cords gone, you still tried to talk to me. Those were some of the last thoughts. You who had been our spokesman couldn't speak any more. But don't worry, Martin, for they're playing your words all around the world and this will continue for a few days. But you may be assured that we won't ever let your words die. Like the words of our Master, Jesus Christ, they will live in our minds and our hearts and in the souls of black men and white men, brown men and yellow men as long as time shall last.

Let me go back to our third meeting. It was so different in that third meeting. You had arrived to become the new pastor of the Dexter Avenue Baptist Church in Montgomery. I left the parsonage and came over to greet you. You remember you had picked up that great preacher, Vernon Johns, by accident, and brought him back to preach at the First Baptist Church. He had preceded you at Dexter and everyone was happy to see you two together. The great old preacher, Vernon Johns, with his quick wit and pervading wisdom, served as a softening force to our personal thoughts and feelings. We became real friends and true companions that afternoon. Thank God we have remained so through the years. That was the beginning. Our families spent many nights and days together. We were at one house and then the other house, discussing the great issues and ideals, simply because there were no restaurants or motels or hotels that we could go in on a non-discriminatory basis. Those were fighting times for thought and for planning. We got to know each other very well and we got to know the souls of each other in those moments. As I write, I realize that God made us good friends so that he could later make us a working team. As a man in the Movement says, God knows what he is doing. That stays on my mind these days. But I wish so very much that it were the other way. Looking back, things seem clearer now than ever before. Dates come to me. How people looked is clearer, and the meaning of some events that have come to me with greater emphasis.

It was early in the morning on December 2nd when I received a telephone call from E. D. Nixon, a Pullman porter, who told me how Mrs. (Rosa) Parks had been jailed, fingerprinted and mugged like a common criminal. He said to me that something ought to be done because this woman only wanted to sit down on the bus. And she refused to give her seat to a white man. But, before doing anything, I checked with you, Martin. Upon your suggestion, I went into action, began organizing the ministers, calling meetings. And from that day until now, our lives have been in action together. I remember how we talked together about who should be the leader of the new movement. You had not been in Montgomery very long. You were just out of the seminary and some people wanted me because they knew me. And I was president of many organizations in Montgomery. And I could have forced myself to be the leader. But I never, as you know, Martin, wanted to be the leader. I only wanted to stand with you, as Caleb stood with Moses.

From the grand action of the Montgomery movement, our lives were filled with the action of doing God's will in village, hamlet and city. We used to talk theology and then we learned to do theology. It was great. It has been great, Martin. Remember Gee's Bend down in Wilcox County, Ala.? Remember that day we stopped at a little filling station and bought jars of pickled pig's feet and some skins in Mississippi because they would not serve us at a restaurant. Remember, Martin, they wouldn't let us eat downtown? But our staff in that little crowded black man's country store had a fellowship, a *kononia*, together. We had a purpose and we had a universal sense of love that they did not have downtown. Some of my experiences with you will never be forgotten. You will recall how we went to Greensboro, N.C., when the sit-ins broke out, and how we sat in, in order that black men might stand up all over the world. You remember the Freedom Rides and how we were incarcerated and how we were forced to spend the night in the First Baptist Church in Montgomery with thousands of our followers while angry mobs stood on the outside. You remember the Albany movement and how Police Chief [Laurie] Pritchett and his forces tried to turn us around, and a divided Negro community became disgusted and despondent? You said to me, "Ralph, we must go on, anyhow." You remember Bull Connor brought out his vicious dogs, his fire engines and his water hoses and tried to stop us in Birmingham. But it was you, Martin, who said to me, "Ralph, don't worry about the water, because we've started a fire in Birmingham that water can't put out."

You will recall Savannah, Ga., and how we went there to the aid and rescue of Hosea Williams. Hosea is still with me and he has promised to be to me, Martin, what I tried to be to you. You remember the March of Washington, when more than 250,000 Americans and people from all over the world came to hear you talk about "I Have a Dream"? You remember Danville, Va., and how they put us in jail? You remember St. Augustine, Fla., and Hoss Manuei when he said that he did not have any evil vices whatever? He did not drink liquor, he did not chase after women, he did not smoke. His only hobby was beating and killing niggers. But we knew how to deal with Hoss and we changed him from a Hoss into a mule. You remember how we worked on Bull Connor and changed him from a bull into a steer? You remember how we marched across Edmund Pettus Bridge in Selma and the state troopers lined across upon the orders of Gov. George Wallace and said that we could not pass. But we kept on marching. And when we got there, it opened up, like the Red Sea opened up for Moses and his army. You remember how Mayor [Richard] Daley tried to stop us in Chicago. But we would not let him turn us around.

My dear friend, Martin, now that you have gone, there are some special thoughts that come to me during this Lenten season. There are so many parallels. You were our leader and we were your disciples. Those who killed you did not know that you loved them and that you worked for them as well. For, so often, you said to us: "Love your enemies. Bless them that curse you and pray for them that despitefully use you." They did not know, Martin, that you were a good man, that you hated nobody. But you loved everybody. They did not know that you loved them with a love that would not let you go. They thought they could kill our movement by killing you, Martin.

But Martin, I want you to know that black people loved you. Some people say that they were just burning and looting in the cities of the nation at the time. But you and I know that just folk, poor people, have had a hard time during these difficult days in which we have lived on this earth. And, in spite of the burning, I think they are saying: "He died for us." It may seem that they are denying our nonviolence for they are acting out their frustrations. And even a man of good, as you were, was killed in such an evil world as we live in today. And they are merely seeking to express their frustrations. They do not see a way out.

But I want you to know, Martin, that we're going to point to them a way. That was the frustration of Jerusalem during this same season nearly 2,000 years ago. But we know, Martin, because we love people, that, after the venting of frustration, there will be the need for reconciliation. There you will be invisible but real. Black and white will need you to take them from their shame and reconcile them unto you and unto our Master, Jesus Christ. Your words of love are there and we will be there to follow your leadership. There has been a crucifixion in our nation, but here in this spring season as we see the blossoms and smell the fresh air we know that the Resurrection will shortly appear.

When the Master left the disciples, they felt gloom at first. Then they gathered themselves together in a fellowship. They must. . . . Many grew up overnight. They were covered with their ancient words and with despair. We promise you, Martin, just as the disciples tarried in that upper room, that we're going to wait until the power comes from on high. We're going to wait until the Holy Ghost speaks and when the Holy Ghost comes and when the Holy Ghost speaks, we're going to speak as Peter spoke. And others will be converted and added to the movement and God's kingdom will come. We promise you, Martin, that we will tighten our fellowship and cover our word. Don't worry, my friend. We will pull our load. We will do our best. With the help of our friends and above all with the help of God. The Poor People's March will be our first attempt to properly do your will for the poor people of this nation. Just a few lines from your friend and your fellow freedom fighter.

Sincerely,
Ralph

5. "On the Case in Resurrection City"
Charlayne A. Hunter

Charlayne A. Hunter (now Charlayne Hunter-Gault) was one of the two black students who integrated the University of Georgia in 1961. In 1968, as a participant-observer, she covered the Poor People's Campaign for Trans-Action *magazine on a grant from the Russell Sage Foundation. These are excerpts from her article.*

Resurrection City—where the poor had hoped to become visible and effective—is dead. And despite the contention of many people, both black and white, that it should never have been born, R.C. was, as its City Fathers had been quick to point out, a moment in history that may yet have a telling effect on the future of this country. For although Resurrection City was never really a city, per se, it functioned as a city, with all the elements of conflict that arise when public issues and private troubles come together.

The public issues were clear and could be articulated—at least in a general way—by most of the people who lived there. Handbills had helped residents formulate their statement of purpose. "What will the Poor People's Campaign do in Washington?" read one handbill. "We will build powerful nonviolent demonstrations on the issues of jobs, income, welfare, health, housing, human rights. These massive demonstrations will be aimed at government centers of power and they will be expanded if necessary. We must make the government face up to poverty and racism." If such a statement was not specific enough, residents—who in all probability found it difficult to always know just what the leaders had in mind (as did the leaders themselves)—would simply fend off the question with a statement like, "We know what the demands are." If pressed further, they would glare accusingly at the questioner, as if to further confirm his ignorance. (This technique of bluffing one's way into the offensive was initiated by the leader of the Poor People's Campaign, the Rev. Ralph Abernathy. The press was relentless in its efforts to get Mr. Abernathy to give out more specifics about his demands, but this was impossible for a long while simply because none had been formulated.)

The private troubles of those who came to live in R.C. were less clear, at least in the beginning. And as these troubles emerged— sometimes in the form of fights, rapes, thefts, and harassment— they became far more prominent than the cause or the individuals who came to fight for it. The outside world concerned itself with the disorganization and lack of leadership in the camp. And while this was certainly a valid concern, critics seemed to be missing one essential point—that the life styles of the poor vary, from individual to individual and from region to region. Long before coming to Resurrection City, leaders and followers had been conditioned by their backgrounds and the life styles they had established. That is why, for example, the first City Manager of R.C., Jesse Jackson—a 26-year-old Chicagoan and an official of the Southern Christian Leadership Conference (S.C.L.C.)—had more success with the Northern urban hustler than did Hosea Williams, the second City Manager, who came out of the South and had much more success with diffident rural blacks.

Most of the conflicts at the camp were caused by the ghetto youths whose lives in the asphalt jungles of the North led them to view Resurrection City as a camp-outing and an alfresco frolic. Surrounded by trees, grass, and open air, the Northern youths were among alien things, which (before the rain and mud) were hostile to them. The innocence of their Southern counterparts—for whom the trees, grass, open air, and mud are a way of life—was a challenge to the Northerners. With such easy, church-oriented prey, the hip cat from the North immediately went into his thing—taking advantage of the uninitiated. Southerners had the history of the movement behind them. They had produced the sit-ins, the Freedom Rides, the Bus Boycotts—the 1960s Direct Action Task Force. And yet much of the Southern mystique got beaten by the hard, hostile life style of the urban ghetto-dweller.

No one is quite sure how many people moved into Resurrection City, although there was an attempt to register people as they came in. The registration count was 6312, but the community was nothing if not mobile and there was no way to count the outflow.

The people came to the District from all sections of the country. They came in bus caravans and on trains. Some came from the South in the Mule Train (which was put into a regular train in Atlanta because the horses were giving out), some came from the nearby North in cars or on foot. They came representing the church. They came representing the community. They came representing street gangs—those that would fight and those that wouldn't. And many came representing themselves. Most came as followers. But, of necessity, a few emerged as leaders. Many came to participate in the campaign for as long as S.C.L.C. wanted them there, and then they planned to go home. Others came thinking of the North as a land of opportunity. And *they* came to stay forever.

Today, the site where Resurrection City stood is cleared. After the sun baked the mud dry, patches of growing grass were placed there, and although the land is not quite so green as it was before, it is just as it was when the architects began designing Resurrection City on paper back in April. Perhaps if they had it to do over, they would change a few things, because, by now, they would have learned about the differences in poverty—that poor people do not automatically respond positively to one another.

The design, on paper, had been impressive. Three architects (none of them Negroes), with the help of students of the Howard University School of Architecture (all of them Negroes), produced plans that called for modest A-frame structures, which could be built small enough for two and large enough for six or eight and which would house 3000 people for two to four months. The prefabricated units—25 percent of them A-frames and 75 percent of them dormitories—were to be assembled in Virginia by local white volunteers, then brought to Washington in trucks that would be unloaded next to the building sites, starting west and building eastward.

By the time the first stake for an A-frame was driven in by Mr. Abernathy [May 13], around a thousand people had already come into Washington and had been housed in coliseums and churches.

New Yorkers Go It Alone

During the first week, morale and energy and activity levels were high. But one of the first indications that the paper plans might not succeed came when the New York delegation insisted upon setting up shop in the most easternward section of the site. New Yorkers, independent, fast-paced, and accustomed to protests (like rent strikes) that require organization, were going to do things their own way. Though this meant that they had to carry their own wood all the way from the front of the site to the back, they set up their structures with record-breaking speed. Where it sometimes took three men working together an hour to put up an A-frame, in the New York contingent three men produced an A-frame in 15 minutes. There was, among *everyone,* a feeling of distrust for larger communities: Provincialism had reared its head.

After a week and a half of more or less organized endeavor, there followed a long stretch of bad weather. It rained every day, and rivers of thick, brown mud stood in doorways and flowed along the walkways from one end of the camp to the other. But although the mud and rain sapped some of the energy of some of the assemblers, it seemed to inspire creativity in others—the majority, in fact, since they were eager to get their houses built so that they could move in. More people came to R.C. than left. And although many had been evacuated to churches and schools—often long distances away—the Mexican-Americans and the Indians were the only contingents that chose to stay on high ground.

When the rains did not let up, the last vestiges of formal organization at R.C. slid unceremoniously into the mud. But those who had left returned, and others joined them, and all waded through. Wood that had been lost turned up as porches for the A-frame houses—luxuries not called for in the paper plans. "It was interesting to see this mass-produced, prefab stuff developing into color and rambunctiousness," one of the planners said.

By the time most of the A-frames had been filled, what existed on the site of the planned city was a camp rather than a community, with some areas so compounded with picket fences or solid fences that no outsider could get in. Walking or wading through the camp, one saw not only simple, unadorned A-frames, but split-levels and duplexes. Some were unpainted; others were painted simply (usually with yellows and burgundy); and still others were both mildly and wildly, reverently and irreverently, decorated with slogans. One house bore on its side a verse from the Bible: "And they said one to another, behold, this dreamer cometh. Come now therefore, and let us slay him, and cast him into some pit, and we will say, some evil beast hath devoured him; and we shall see what will become of his dreams. Genesis 37. Martin Luther King, Jr., 1929–1968." Others had such slogans as "Black Power on Time," "Soul Power," "United People Power, Toledo, Ohio," "Soul City, U.S.A.," and "The Dirty Dozen," on a building I figured was a dormitory. And, of course, the inevitable "Flower Power." "I Have a Dream" stickers appeared in most places, as well as pictures of Martin Luther King—usually enshrined beside the canvas-and-wood cots inside the houses.

SOME MOVERS AND DOERS

While the camp was virtually leaderless from a formal, organizational standpoint (Mr. Abernathy was always off traveling with a large entourage of S.C.L.C. officials), it did not lack individual movers and doers. One day, a discussion of the mud revealed such a person. Standing attentively at a press conference on a sunny day, with an umbrella over her head, Mrs. Lila Mae Brooks of Sunflower County, Miss., said, to no one in particular, "We used to mud and us who have commodes are used to no sewers." A tall, thin, spirited woman, Mrs. Brooks talks with little or no prompting. Observing that I was interested, she went on: "We used to being sick, too. And we used to death. All my children [she has eight] born sickly. But in Sunflower County, sick folks sent from the hospital and told to come back in two months. They set up 27 rent houses—rent for $25—and they put you out when you don't pay. People got the health department over 'bout the sewers, but Mayor said they couldn't put in sewers until 1972." She is 47, and for years has worked in private homes, cotton fields, and churches. In 1964 she was fired from a job for helping Negroes register to vote. For a while, she was on the S.C.L.C. staff, teaching citizenship. When she had a sunstroke, and later a heart attack, she had to go on welfare. (She is also divorced.) For three years, she got $40-a-month child support, and finally $73. She left her children with her mother, who is 80, and sister to come to the campaign.

"People in Sunflower asked my friends was I sick 'cause they hadn't seen me. Then they saw me on TV in Washington and said I'd better head back before the first or they'd cut off my welfare check. You go out the state overnight and they cut off your welfare check. But that's OK. I had to come. When S.C.L.C. chose me from Eastland's County, he met his match. I've seen so much. I've seen 'em selling food stamps and they tell you if you don't buy, they cut off your welfare check. And that stuff they sell there don't count—milk, tobacco, and washing powder. Well, how you gonna keep clean? All the welfare people know is what *they* need. I ain't raising no more white babies for them. Ain't goin' that road no more. I drug my own children through the cotton fields, now they talkin' 'bout not lettin' us go to Congress. Well, I'll stand on Eastland's toes. People from 12 months to 12 months without work. People with no money. Where the hell the money at? I say to myself, I'll go to Washington and find out. Talking about using it to build clinics. Then they make people pay so much at the clinics they get turned away. What the people gettin' ain't enough to say grace over. I done wrote to Washington so much they don't have to ask my name."

I asked Mrs. Brooks how long she planned to stay here. "I don't know honey," she said as she put her sunglasses on. "They might have to 'posit my body in Washington."

There were other women organizing welfare groups and working in the lunch halls, and still others, like Miss Muriel Johnson, a social worker on loan to S.C.L.C. from other organizations. This was her first movement and she was in charge of holding "sensitivity" sessions. When I asked her what a sensitivity session was, she said, "Well, you just can't take a bunch of people out and march them down Independence Avenue. All they know is that they're hungry and want something done about it. We got 150 to 200 people out a day into nonviolent demonstrations. We got to teach them to protect themselves and prepare for whatever. We have to explain situations to people. And we have to talk with them, not down to them. If they get something out of this training, they'll go home and do something."

LEON AND J.T.

Joining Mrs. Brooks and Miss Johnson were many other young men and women, among them college students who, like the students of the old movement (the early 1960's), believed that it was better for black boys and girls to give themselves immediately and fully to a worthwhile cause than to finish college. Many of them wore their hair natural and some wore buttons that said, "Doing it black." Young men like Leon and J.T., both S.C.L.C. organizers in the South, held no place in the movement hierarchy, but were, as the residents were fond of saying of anybody plugged in to what was going on, "on the case."

Leon and J.T. led demonstrations and boosted morale by taking part in the day-to-day problems and activities of Resurrection City. The difference between them and many of the other S.C.L.C. officials was that when R.C. residents were tired and smelly from marching eight miles to a demonstration and back, so were Leon and J.T. When residents went to bed wearing all their clothes and wrapped in blankets saturated with dampness, so did Leon and J.T. And if Leon and J.T. could still sing freedom songs the next day, then so could they. There were not, however, enough Leons and J.T.s. Many weeks had been spent building the Abernathy compound—a large frame structure surrounded by A-frames for his aides. But despite a ceremonial gesture of walking in with a suitcase and announcing that he was moving in, Mr. Abernathy never lived in R.C. Nor did his lieutenants. . . .

HOSEA'S GIFT OF RAP

The one S.C.L.C. higher-up always on the case was Hosea Williams, who early in the campaign became the City Manager. One of Hosea's major assets was the gift of rap.

One Sunday morning he was stopped by three well-dressed white men, one of whom said he was running for Congress from Florida and had come to R.C. because he felt he and his people ought to know about it. Soon after the conversation began, the man asked Hosea about his background, and if he was a Communist. Hosea was not offended by the question, but moved into it slowly. He denied being a Communist.

"What is Resurrection City all about?" Hosea asked rhetorically. "This is what you have to know. We are asking for jobs. Not welfare. Check the cat on the welfare rolls and you'll find his mother and daddy were on welfare.

"What we've got to have is a redefinition of work. As Lillian Smith indicated in her book, I think *Killers of the Dream*, what we have is a conflicting ideology in our value system. The reason I loved Dr. King was that he made $600,000 in one year and died a pauper. We have got to let scientists go to work and create jobs. I know it can be done. I was working as a research chemist for 14 years trying to rid this country of insects. I was born in Attapulgus, Ga. My father was a field hand and my mother worked in the white folks' house. I raised myself while she raised the white folks' children. And we got to get some help for the old. And we got to do something about this educational system. That's what produced the hippies. White colleges. I got more respect for the hippies than I have for the hypocrites.

"R.C. is just a place we have to sleep and get some food to fight a war—a nonviolent war. We are here for an economic bill of rights. Congress's job is to solve the problems. We are political analysts and psychiatrists and Congress is the patient."

———

Demonstrations were the one constant in R.C. Each demonstration I attended was different from another, not so much because the body of demonstrators changed as because of their usual tendency to "do what the spirit say do."

Although R.C. residents had been there before—to present demands for changes in the welfare system—my first demonstration was at the Department of Health, Education, and Welfare. The 200 demonstrators marched into the auditorium of the building and sent word that they wanted to see "Brother Cohen"—Wilbur J. Cohen, Secretary of Health, Education, and Welfare. An otherwise impressive delegation—including Assistant Secretary Ralph K. Huitt and Harold Howe II of H.E.W.'s Office of Education—was sent in, but was given short shrift. Led by Hosea, the demonstrators began to chant "We want Cohen," and Hosea turned from the second-string officials and told the crowd: "You might as well get comfortable," and before he had finished a young boy in gray trousers and a green shirt had taken off his tennis shoes, rolled up his soiled brown jacket into a headrest, and stretched out on the floor. As he closed his eyes, the crowd, led by Hosea, began singing "Woke Up This Morning With My Mind Set on Freedom." In between songs the crowd would chant "We want Cohen." An elderly lady from New Orleans, who after the march obviously had little strength left to stand and yell and chant, simply shook her head in time with whatever she happened to be hearing at the moment.

The more pressure the officials put upon Hosea to relent, the stronger the support from the crowd. Given the demonstrators' vote of confidence, he began to rap. "I never lived in a democracy until I moved to Resurrection City. But it looks like the stuff is all right."

"Sock soul, brother!" the people yelled.

"Out here," he continued, "they got the gray matter to discover a cure for cancer, but can't."

"Sock soul, brother!"

Then, to the tune of the song "Ain't Gonna Let Nobody Turn Me 'Round," Hosea led the group in singing, "Ain't Gonna Let the Lack of Health Facilities Turn Me 'Round." And at the end of the song—something like three hours after the demonstrators had demanded to see Cohen—the word spread through the auditorium: "Cohen's on the case."

Demonstrators who had spread throughout the building buttonholing anybody and everybody who looked important, demanding that they "go downstairs and get Cohen," filed back into the auditorium. And as Cohen appeared, an exultant cheer rose from the demonstrators—not for Cohen but for the point that they had won.

Before Cohen spoke, Huitt came to the microphone. He looked relieved. "I'd just like to say, before introducing the Secretary, that I haven't heard preaching and singing like that since I was a boy. Maybe that's what wrong with me." The crowd liked that and showed it. "Get on the case, brother," someone called. And as clenched black fists went into the air—a gesture that had come to stand for "Silence!" and succeeded in getting it—Cohen spoke:

"Welcome to your auditorium," he said, managing a smile. He proceeded to outline his response to the demonstrators' demands, which included changing the state-by-state system of welfare to a federally controlled one. When he had finished, he introduced a very polished, gray-haired, white matron sitting next to him as "our director of civil rights." A voice of a Negro woman in rags called out to her: "Get to work, baby."

———

SOLIDARITY DAY

The last demonstration I attended was on Solidarity Day. In that great mass of 50,000 or more people, I looked for the faces that I had come to know over the last few weeks. I saw only a few, and concluded that the veteran residents of R.C. just happened to be in places that I was not. Later, as the program dragged on and I became weary from the heat, I walked back into the city, expecting to find it empty. Instead I saw the people I had been looking for outside. J.T. and Leon and many others.

Harry Jackson, a cabinet-maker from Baltimore, sat in his usual place—inside the fenced-in compound of the Baltimore delegation. He was keeping watch over the two dormitories—women to the left, men to the right—and a frying pan of baked beans cooking on a small, portable grill. Since he was not out demonstrating, I asked him why he had come to R.C. in the first place. "We came because of the lack of association between the black man and the white man. If the system don't integrate itself, it will segregate itself all over again. Our group was integrated. We had one white fellow from the University of Massachusetts. But he hasn't been back."

This man, I thought, was probably typical of the majority of R.C. residents. They wanted things to get better, and felt that they would if people got together. The system didn't have to come down; it just needed overhauling. Still, the system had created the provincialism and distrust of larger communities that prompted Harry Jackson to remark as I was leaving, "I believe we should keep the people together who came together."

As I walked through Resurrection City, in the distance I could hear the sound of voices coming from the Lincoln Memorial—voices too distant to be understood. After a while, I ran across Leon and J.T. Leon said he was on the way to his A-frame.

"Why aren't you at the demonstration?" I asked. And barely able to keep his eyes open, he replied weakly, "My demonstration was all night last night. Up at the Agriculture Department. And I'll be there again, all night tonight. That's why I've just got to get some sleep."

A few days later, Jackson and Leon and J.T. and every other resident of Resurrection City were either arrested (for civil disobedience) or tear-gassed (for convenience) by policemen from the District of Columbia. The structures came down in less than half the time it took to put them up. Resurrection City was dead. Up on the hill, spokesmen for S.C.L.C. said they had achieved some of the goals of the campaign and were making progress toward achieving more. But the people were all—or mostly all— gone.

So, in the end, what did Resurrection City do? It certainly made the poor visible. But did it make them effective? Mr. Abernathy would have them believe that it did. And the people who believed him were, by and large, the ones who had come out of the same area that he had come from. An observer once said that Mr. Abernathy lived for the few hours when he could escape back to his church in Atlanta for Sunday services. This was home. Those who came out of that background were the ones who would have stayed in Washington until their leader said the job was done, working diligently all the while. But they, too, would be glad to get home.

The confrontations of rural Negroes, not only with officials and the police but with urban blacks as well, may have engendered in them a bit of cynicism—perhaps even a bit of militancy. But one suspects that the talk, for years to come, will be of how they went to Washington and, for all practical purposes, "stood on Eastland's toes."

For the urban-rural types, who were in a transitional position to begin with, the frustrations inherent in the system became only more apparent. Already leaning toward urban-type militancy, their inclinations were reinforced by the treatment that even the nonviolent received when those in control grew weary of them and their cause.

The urban people did not learn anything that they hadn't already known. Except, perhaps, about the differences that exist between them and their Southern brothers. They expected nothing, they gave little, and they got the same in return.

Resurrection City was not really supposed to succeed as a city. It was supposed to succeed in dramatizing the plight of the poor in this country. Instead, its greatest success was in dramatizing what the system has done to the black community in this country. And in doing so, it affirmed the view taken by black militants today—that before black people can make any meaningful progress in the United States of America, they have to, as the militants say, "get themselves together."

CHAPTER ELEVEN

AIN'T GONNA SHUFFLE NO MORE (1964–1972)

Introduction by Gerald Gill

The successes of freedom movement struggles in the early to mid 1960s would coincide with and later shape other emergent forms of consciousness, protest, and strategy. Whether witnessed in changing nomenclature (from *Negro* to *Black*), a growing interest in black history and culture, or increased calls for racial unity and solidarity, the years from 1964 to 1972 would be characterized by a growing sense of individual and collective affirmation of identity, of protest and ongoing struggle. These campaigns posed mounting challenges to the larger American community as well as the more staid institutions within the African-American community.

In 1960, Cassius Marcellus Clay won the Olympic gold medal in the light heavyweight division. Shortly after returning to his hometown of Louisville, Kentucky, Clay was refused service at a local restaurant. Stung by the rebuke, Clay, according to his autobiography, threw the medal into the Ohio River. Nonetheless, he chose to embark upon a professional boxing career. Advancing through the ranks of the heavyweight division, Clay quickly became a ranking contender. While his boxing skills were clearly evident, Clay also gained increasing attention for his amiable braggadocio and his pithy doggerel. In press and media interviews in 1963 and 1964, Clay referred to himself as "The Greatest" and would mock his opponents and brazenly predict in which round he would win. In early 1964 Clay defeated the then heavyweight champion, Sonny Liston, and became the new heavyweight champion.

Shortly after his victory, Clay announced that he was a member of the Nation of Islam and had changed his name to Muhammad Ali, a name given to him by the organization's head, the Honorable Elijah Muhammad. Ali's membership in the Nation of Islam and his friendship with Malcolm X made him even more unpopular among many persons who resented first his flamboyant personality and now his affiliation with a religious group they feared or detested.

With the escalation of the American war effort in Vietnam in 1966, Ali came under additional scrutiny. Initially, he had been deferred from the draft on the basis of having failed the Selective Service qualifying exam. In 1966, following the Selective Service System's lowering of the exam scores necessary for induction and following Ali's straightforward declaration "I got nothing against those Viet Congs," numerous letters, often vicious, were sent to Ali's draft board in Louisville, demanding his reclassification and induction. Upon his being reclassified later that year, Ali sought exemption from the draft on religious grounds. Citing the Koran and the teachings of the Honorable Elijah Muhammad, he contended that Muslims "don't take part in Christian wars or wars of any unbelievers." Ali's claim was turned down and he was ordered to report for induction in Houston, Texas, on April 28, 1967. Expressing his refusal to be inducted, he stated, "I am not going ten thousand miles from here to help murder and kill and burn another poor people simply to help continue the domination of white America." Convicted of draft evasion, Ali was sentenced to a five-year jail term and was stripped of his heavyweight title. Much of the national media, reflecting the sentiments and biases of a large segment of the American populace, viciously denounced Ali's decision to resist induction. However, throughout his almost four-year ordeal to have his conviction overturned, Muhammad Ali was revered by many blacks for his resolve in adhering to his beliefs and principles. Indeed, Ali's decision to resist induction was both educational and inspirational to countless critics of the war, and Ali became a personal hero to millions of Americans of all ages and races.

Among those most affected by Ali's courage were black college and university students. If Muhammad Ali's convictions allowed him to take a stand, then black students at historically black and predominantly white institutions could similarly take stands on behalf of their convictions. While students and former students from many of the historically black institutions had been involved in sit-in protests, Freedom Rides, demonstrations, and voter registration campaigns, most historically black institutions had been largely untouched by on-campus demands for institutional change before 1966. The murder of Sammy Younge, a SNCC organizer and a former student at Tuskegee Institute who was killed for attempting to use a "whites only" bathroom at a service station near the Tuskegee campus in January 1966, marked the stirrings of on-campus protests at historically black institutions. Although overshadowed in terms of national media attention by student protests at Berkeley, the University of Wisconsin, Columbia, and Harvard, black college campuses—campuses as varied as Texas Southern University, Voorhees College in South Carolina, and Central State University in Ohio, for example—were the sites of full-scale protest from 1966 to 1970 around increased student rights, curricular changes, and the overall aim, mission, and future direction of historically black institutions.

At Howard University in Washington, D.C., described by historian Walter Dyson as "the capstone of Negro education," burgeoning discontent began to manifest itself during academic year 1965–1966 over the lack of due process for students and the mandatory ROTC for freshman male students. That discontent became more focused, more demonstrative, and more confrontational over the course of the next two years as Howard, like most historically black institutions, witnessed the growing racial and political consciousness of its student body. Serving as a psychological as well as a political spur was Robin Gregory's winning of the "Miss Homecoming" title in the fall of 1966. Gregory's sporting an Afro and running a campaign that stressed both racial pride and an interest in black history represented a marked departure from previous winners.

Gregory's victory helped to crystallize a new mood of both protest and consciousness that emerged in the spring of 1967 when Howard students, chanting "America is the black man's battlefield," prevented General Lewis Hershey, the director of the Selective Service System, from speaking on campus. When university officials arbitrarily sought to discipline those they thought were behind the "Hershey incident," student leaders organized a one-day boycott of classes calling for the dropping of charges against those students called in for disciplinary hearings, the abolition of the mandatory comprehensive exams for seniors, the abolition of compulsory ROTC, the rescinding of the university policy statement on student protest, and no reprisals against faculty members involved in on-campus "political activity."

The administration's attempted purge of student leaders and quelling of on-campus protest led to more determined efforts on behalf of change among growing numbers of returning and incoming students. Frustrated by university officials' slowness to enact their desired changes, student leaders from several campus organizations sent an open letter to the university president demanding immediate changes in the university's top leadership, in courses taught, and in the mission and orientation of Howard. When administration officials failed to respond to the demands and later sought to punish student protesters, students took over and occupied the administration building. Negotiations ensued for several days before students won several of their demands, and promises from trustees to consider others.

Empowerment, whether expressed through Muhammad Ali's individual act or the collective protests of Howard University students, was the hallmark of much late 1960s protest by African-Americans. That quest continued but would extend beyond individual or local pockets of community struggle. Throughout the late 1960s and early 1970s, whether expressed in poetry, essays, or music, one heard refrains calling for a sense of national unity among African-Americans. Yet this call for unity was political as much as cultural. From the 1967 Black Power Conference in Newark onward, numerous meetings and congresses were held across the country that sought to attract spokespersons, from the more moderate to the more militant, to discuss the need for unity and solidarity. Following up on the impetus of these several meetings and with the 1972 presidential election approaching, there were mounting calls for a national black political convention. In March 1972, nearly 3,000 delegates from across the country gathered in Gary, Indiana, to attempt to draft a national black political agenda. For three days, the assembled delegates, whose ranks included elected officials, civil rights activists, trade unionists, community organizers, and members of Pan-Africanist organizations, debated among themselves. Finally the delegates ratified a document that called for increased political and economic empowerment, increased black involvement and participation in international concerns, and increased control of institutions within African-American communities.

From Muhammad Ali's struggle for the right to observe and to practice his religious beliefs, to the protests of Howard University students on behalf of wide-ranging curricular and institutional changes, to the efforts of the Gary delegates to draft and to ratify an agenda for increased empowerment, activists and organizers served notice that a new era had arrived. Characterized by a growing sense of racial pride and racial solidarity, African-Americans increasingly sought to challenge the status quo in both the larger American community and the African-American community. No longer wedded to the past, they sought to find more innovative, more creative, and more empowering methods to meet their needs, wants, and aspirations.

1. " '. . . I'm the Greatest,' a poem by Cassius Clay"

Part of Muhammad Ali's appeal as a rising heavyweight contender and later champion lay in the poems he would often recite before forthcoming bouts. In these poems, he would call attention to his talents and mockingly chide his opponents. In this 1963 poem (which appeared in Life *magazine), Ali, then known as Cassius Clay, tells of his importance to boxing, predicts that he will win the heavyweight championship, and marvels at his talent and prowess.*

This is a story about a man
With iron fists and a beautiful tan.

He talks a lot and he boasts indeed
Of a powerful punch and blinding speed.
The fight game was dying
And Promoters were crying
For someone to come along
With a new and different song.
Patterson was dull, quiet and sad,
And Sonny Liston was just as bad.
Then along came a kid named Cassius Clay,
Who said, "Liston, I'll take your title away."
This colorful fighter is something to see,
And heavyweight champ he's certain to be.
You get the impression while watching him fight
That he plays cat and mouse, then turns out the light.
What a frustrating feeling I'm sure it must be,
To be hit by blows you can't even see.
Where was he first? Where was he last?
How can you conquer a man so fast?
I'm sure his opponents have tried their best,
But one by one on the canvas they rest.
Everyone knew when Cassius wasn't around,
For quietness descended on the town.
If Clay says a mosquito can pull a plow,
Don't ask him how—
Hitch him up!

2. "The Greatest"
Muhammad Ali with Richard Durham

After having held the heavyweight championship for two years, Muhammad Ali came under increasing national scrutiny and criticism for his draft deferment and his comments against the Vietnam War. In these excerpts from his 1975 autobiography, Ali describes his efforts in 1966–1967 to be exempted from the armed forces and, when unsuccessful, his decision to refuse induction.

Of all the poems I wrote, all the words I spoke, all the slogans I shouted—"I'm the greatest!" . . . "I'm the prettiest!" . . . "I can't be beat!" . . . "He must fall in five!"—of all the controversies that aroused people against me or for me, none would have the effect on my life or change the climate around me like the "poem" I read on a TV hookup one warm February afternoon in Miami, 1966.

I was in training and looking forward to my third defense of the World Heavyweight Title. This time against six-foot-six Ernie "The Octopus" Terrell, so named because he wrapped his long arms like tentacles around his opponents, smothering their blows and hugging them half to death.

I had come out into the front yard of the little gray cement cottage that my White Southern Christian Millionaire Sponsors had rented in my name in the black section of Miami. A TV reporter had been set up to ask my reaction to the fact that the Louisville Draft Board had just promoted me from 1-Y, deferred status, to 1-A, making me eligible for immediate induction into the U.S. Army.

I gave it: "I ain't got no quarrel with the Viet Cong." Later, when they kept asking the same question, I rhymed it for them:

> Keep asking me, no matter how long
> On the war in Viet Nam, I sing this song
> I ain't got no quarrel with the Viet Cong . . .

I said more than that, of course, much more, and all evening, but those were the only words it seemed the world wanted to hear from me. They broke out in headlines across America and overseas—in London, Paris, Berlin, Zurich, Madrid, Hong Kong, Rome, Amsterdam—and for years afterwards their echo would rumble in the air around me. In fact, the rumbling began even before I got to sleep that night.

After the reporters left I took a ride over to a Miami Beach steakhouse, and when I came back my brother was in the doorway. He was beckoning me in a way I understood to mean he wanted no reporters to follow.

"The phones won't stop," he whispered as I brushed past him. "They gone crazy."

We had three phones and all three were ringing. I was reaching for the nearest one.

"Wait a minute." He tried to restrain me. "Let me answer. They all insane."

But I was already hearing a hard, mean voice on the other end of the line: "This you, Cassius?"

"No, sir," I said, feeling he should at least acknowledge my name. "This is Muhammad Ali."

"Muhammad, Cassius—whatever you call yourself, I heard you on TV!" he shouted. "You cowardly, turncoat black rat! If I had a bomb I would blow you to hell! I've got a message for you and your kind. . . ." I hung up, since I had already gotten the message, and picked up the kitchen phone. A woman's voice was hysterical: "Cassius Clay? Is that you? You better'n my son? You black bastard, you! I pray to God they draft you tomorrow. Draft you and shoot you on the spot! Listen to me. . . ."

I let her go to pick up the phone in the bedroom. This time it was a voice I knew. A deputy sheriff named Murphy who had escorted me around Miami Beach many times. He had a soft drawl, like a fatherly bigot: "Now, Cassius, you just done gone too far now. Somebody's telling you wrong. Them Jews and Dagos you got around you. Now, some of my boys want to come down and talk to you, for your own good."

I hung up and took the phone handed to me by my sparring partner, Cody Jones. There was only heavy breathing. Then: "You gonna die, nigger, before the night's out! You gonna die for that!" and more heavy breathing.

Those who had always wanted me to disappear from the scene reacted quickest. The first calls came mostly from the white side of Miami. But as the news spread across the time zones, other voices were saying, "That was mighty fine." . . . "I'm glad you said that." . . . "It's time someone spoke out."

And in the days that followed, calls came in from Kansas City, Omaha, St. Louis, Las Vegas, New York, Philadelphia. Housewives and professionals and plain everyday people—who I never heard from except when I pulverized somebody in the ring—thanked me for what I said. Students called from campuses, urging me to come and speak. It was a strange new feeling, and now, without planning or even wanting it, I was an important part of a movement I hardly knew existed.

For days I was talking to people from a whole new world. People who were not even interested in sports, especially prize-fighting. One in particular I will never forget: a remarkable man, seventy years older than me but with a fresh outlook which seemed fairer than that of any white man I had ever met in America.

My brother Rahaman had handed me the phone, saying, "Operator says a Mr. Bertrand Russell is calling Mr. Muhammad Ali." I took it and heard the crisp accent of an Englishman: "Is this Muhammad Ali?" When I said it was, he asked if I had been quoted correctly.

I acknowledged that I had been, but wondered out loud, "Why does everyone want to know what I think about Viet Nam? I'm no politician, no leader. I'm just an athlete."

"Well," he said, "this is a war more barbaric than others, and because a mystique is built up around a champion fighter, I suppose the world has more than incidental curiosity about what the World Champion thinks. Usually he goes with the tide. You surprised them."

I liked the sound of his voice, and told him I might be coming to England soon to fight the European champ, Henry Cooper, again.

"If I fight Cooper, who'd you bet on?"

He laughed. "Henry's capable, you know, but I would pick you."

I gave him back a stock answer I used on such occasions: "You're not as dumb as you look." And I invited him to ringside when I got to London.

He couldn't come to the fight, but for years we exchanged cards and notes. I had no idea who he was (the name Bertrand Russell had never come up in Central High in Louisville) until two years later when I was thumbing through a *World Book Encyclopedia* in the *Muhammad Speaks* newspaper office in Chicago and saw his name and picture. He was described as one of the greatest mathematicians and philosophers of the twentieth century. That very minute I sat down and typed out a letter of apology for my offhand remark, "You're not as dumb as you look," and he wrote back that he had enjoyed the joke.

A short time after I fought Cooper, when I had another fight prospect in London, I made plans for Belinda and me to visit him, but I had to explain to him that the outcome of my fight against being drafted to Viet Nam might hold me up. The letter he wrote back was sent to me in Houston:

> I have read your letter with the greatest admiration and personal respect.
>
> In the coming months there is no doubt that the men who rule Washington will try to damage you in every way open to them, but I am sure you know that you spoke for your people and for the oppressed everywhere in the courageous defiance of American power. They will try to break you because you are a symbol of a force they are unable to destroy, namely, the aroused consciousness of a whole people determined no longer to be butchered and debased with fear and oppression. You have my whole-hearted support. Call me when you get to England.
>
> Yours sincerely,
> Bertrand Russell

By the time I got his letter I had been convicted and my passport lifted, just as his had been in World War I. Four years later, when my passport was returned, the friend I had made with my remark in my front yard had died. I thought of him whenever I visited England and for years I kept a picture of his warm face and wide eyes. "Not as dumb as he looks."

———

I thought the letter was dead and buried, somewhere on a Houston street seven years ago. But I came across it when I was moving out of Cherry Hill, New Jersey, out of the old Spanish-style villa I had bought with the money I made from the first fight after my exile. I was going through stuff I had accumulated from my last three homes—my childhood home in Louisville, then Chicago and Philadelphia—to see what I wanted to keep, and what to throw away.

I found a faded red, white and blue jacket with KENTUCKY GOLDEN GLOVES CHAMPION on the back in pretty gold letters. I had walked all over Louisville wearing that jacket. I was fourteen years old, and it was the first big prize I had won. I threw the jacket into a box and opened the old chest of drawers where Belinda stored my papers. I pulled out a blue box, and a stack of letters spilled onto the floor.

Kneeling down to pick them up, I noticed the gold-and-green-trimmed letter from President Kwame Nkrumah of Ghana, the blue stationery from Premier Ahmed Ben Bella of Algeria, congratulations from President Charles de Gaulle of France, an invitation to Egypt from President Gamal Abdel Nasser, greetings from President François Duvalier of Haiti, King Faisal Abdel Aziz of Saudi Arabia, President Zulfikar Ali Bhutto of Pakistan, Prime Minister Jack Lynch of Ireland, and the long, plain white envelope I thought I'd thrown away. At first I was almost afraid to pick it up. I knew what it was and the memories it would bring back. I got a chilly feeling, and somehow it seemed as though the mailman had just delivered it, and the part of my life it represented was starting all over again.

I asked Belinda why she had put it there. "It belongs there," she insisted. "This is where I keep all the letters from heads of state."

Although I had gotten congratulations from all over the world after winning the Heavyweight Crown, at that time I was only the second American Heavyweight Champion who was never invited to the White House. Jack Johnson was the other. My only contact with an American President was this letter. It came on April Fool's Day, 1967, ten days after my title defense against Zora Folley. It read:

ORDER FOR TRANSFERRED MAN
TO REPORT FOR INDUCTION

FROM: The President of the United States
TO: Mr. Cassius Marcellus Clay, Jr.
AKA Muhammad Ali
5962 Ardmore Street
Houston, Texas 77021

Greetings:

Having heretofore been ordered to report for induction by Local Board No. 47, State of Kentucky, Louisville,

Kentucky, which is your Local Board of Origin, and having been transferred upon your own request to Local Board No. 61, State of Texas, Houston, Texas, which is your Local Board of Transfer for delivery to an induction station, you will therefore report to the last named Local Board at 3rd Floor, 701 San Jacinto St., Houston, Texas 77022 on April 28, 1967, at 8:30 A.M.

I had filed for draft exemption as a conscientious objector, telling the government that as a minister in the Nation of Islam ". . . to bear arms or kill is against my religion. And I conscientiously object to any combat military service that involves the participation in any war in which the lives of human beings are being taken." The claim was rejected in Louisville, and [attorney Hayden] Covington took the case to the Kentucky Appeal Board. He based my appeal on religious grounds, and the fact that blacks were not represented on the Selective Service Boards that judged me. In a special hearing, Circuit Court Judge Lawrence Grauman determined that my beliefs were sincere, and recommended that my claim be upheld.

A few days later South Carolina Democratic Representative L. Mendel Rivers told the Veterans of Foreign Wars, "If the theologian of Black Muslim power, Cassius Clay, is deferred by the board in Louisville, you watch what happens in Washington. . . . We are going to do something if that board takes your boy and leaves him [Clay] home to double-talk."

Covington convinced me to move to Houston. His sister, he said, was married to Selective Service Director General Lewis B. Hershey, and we hoped I could get a better deal in Texas. But if the deal I got in Houston was better because my lawyer's sister was married to the draft boss, I hate to think what might have happened elsewhere.

It was two weeks before the Houston Board turned down my appeal. Covington called me in Chicago. "It looks like trouble, Champ," he told me. "General Hershey has just predicted that you won't be deferred. This isn't like any case I've had before. Joe Namath can get off to play football and George Hamilton gets out because he's going with the President's daughter, but you're different. They want to make an example out of you."

When the cab swings up to an old courthouse, there's not a soul around.

"If this is where they're drafting people," the driver says, "nobody's showing up today." He rocks with laughter. "The war's on and nobody's showing up."

Covington almost screams, "Then it must be the other building. Hurry up!"

The driver steps on the gas, still laughing. "Nobody's showing up for the war. Ain't that a bitch?"

He pulls up to a large stone building, the U.S. Customs House, 701 Jacinto Street, where everybody has shown up for the war. People waiting for my arrival have jammed the sidewalk. When they see our cab drive up, they wave picket signs and scream, "Muhammad Ali, don't go!" . . . "Muhammad Ali!"

The steps of buildings all along the street are filled with people and the windows crowded with peering faces.

Some students from Texas Southern University are marching with banners that read STAY HOME, MUHAMMAD ALI! Across the street in a blue denim jacket and jeans stands [SNCC chairman] H. Rap Brown, holding up a clenched fist and surrounded by a group of young blacks shouting, "Hep! Hep! Don't take that step! Hep! Hep! Don't take that step!"

An elderly woman cuts through the crowd, grabs my hand and whispers, "Stand up, brother! We're with you! Stand up! Fight for us! Don't let us down!"

A band of long-haired hippies begin shouting, "We didn't go! You don't go! We didn't go! You don't go!"

Someone grabs my arm, and my lawyer says quietly, "It's the FBI. Go along." A group of policemen push the crowd back from the doors as I return Rap Brown's salute. I climb the step and the people begin to clap and cheer. Newspapermen and photographers are wedging their way through and crying out, "Muhammad, give us the answer!" . . . "Are you going in?" . . . "What's your last word?" . . . "What will your stand be?"

I remember one boy sitting in a corner with tears in his eyes. He's being forced to leave his wife and four children. He doesn't want to go, but he's afraid not to go. All he wants from me is my autograph.

A short, red-haired white boy comes over. "It's something to see you in person. I've read so much about you in the papers."

"Like what?" I ask.

"Well, about your religion. You hate white people, don't you?"

I shake my head. "Do I act like I hate anybody?"

"No." He says nothing more.

An officer walks into the room and there is an uneasy shuffle as everyone tries to pull himself together. My name is third.

Someone whispers, "This is it! This is it!"

"Go left, turn down the hall and go to Room I B," the officer says. "You'll be inducted into the United States Armed Forces! You'll be given further instructions when you get there."

The induction room had been used as a judge's chambers in earlier days and the floor was still covered with its original gold carpeting. A blond green-eyed officer, a little younger than myself, stands behind an oakwood rostrum with American flags on both sides. I'd see his name in the next day's newspapers: Lt. S. Steven Dunkley.

All eyes except Dunkley's are focused on me.

Without looking up from his papers, he orders, "The first four will line up in front and the next four will line up behind them."

We take our places, and I'm third from the left in the second row. I know that I'll be called next to the last to take the step.

A senior officer goes over to the lieutenant and whispers something in his ear. He looks up automatically, and when his eyes meet mine, I feel a knot rise in my throat.

The officers and orderlies had been chatting and joking when I entered, but now everything is quiet. A number of people I can't account for have stepped into the room, some wearing civilian clothes. The young officer at the podium clears his throat.

"Attention!"

We all straighten up somewhat, but the four in front are standing particularly erect. My palms are beginning to sweat.

Dunkley glances quickly around the room before reading his prepared statement. He's probably read it hundreds of times before, but now there is special emphasis in his voice. He tries to make sure that each word is clear: "You are about to be inducted into the Armed Forces of the United States, in the Army, the Navy, the Air Force or the Marine Corps, as indicated by the service announced following your name when called. You will take one step forward as your name and service are called and such step will constitute your induction into the Armed Forces indicated."

He pauses, and even though everyone else is watching me, it seems like he and I are the only ones in the room.

I'm sweating. I look around. It seems like everyone in the entire Induction Center has crept into the room. For months I've drilled myself for this moment, but I still feel nervous. I hope no one notices my shoulders tremble. . . .

The lieutenant has finished with the man on my left and everybody seems to brace himself. The room is still and the lieutenant looks at me intently. He knows that his general, his mayor and everybody in the Houston Induction Center is waiting for this moment. He draws himself up straight and tall.

Something is happening to me. It's as if my blood is changing. I feel fear draining from my body and a rush of anger taking its place.

I hear the politician again: "Who are you to judge?" But who is this white man, no older than me, appointed by another white man, all the way down from the white man in the White House? Who is he to tell me to go to Asia, Africa or anywhere else in the world to fight people who never threw a rock at me or America? Who is this descendant of the slave masters to order a descendant of slaves to fight other people in their own country?

Now I am anxious for him to call me. "Hurry up!" I say to myself. I'm looking straight into his eyes. There's a ripple of movement as some of the people in the room edge closer in anticipation.

"Cassius Clay—Army!"

The room is silent. I stand straight, unmoving. Out of the

corner of my eye I see one of the white boys nodding his head at me, and thin smiles flickering across the faces of some of the blacks. It's as if they are secretly happy to see someone stand up against the power that is ordering them away from their homes and families.

The lieutenant stares at me a long while, then lowers his eyes. One of the recruits snickers and he looks up abruptly, his face beet-red, and orders all the other draftees out of the room. They shuffle out quickly, leaving me standing alone.

He calls out again: "Cassius Clay! Will you please step forward and be inducted into the Armed Forces of the United States?"

All is still. He looks around helplessly. Finally, a senior officer with a notebook full of papers walks to the podium and confers with him a few seconds before coming over to me. He appears to be in his late forties. His hair is streaked with gray and he has a very dignified manner.

"Er, Mr. Clay . . ." he begins. Then, catching himself, "Or Mr. Ali, as you prefer to be called."

"Yes, sir?"

"Would you please follow me to my office? I would like to speak privately with you for a few minutes, if you don't mind."

It's more of an order than a request, but his voice is soft and he speaks politely. I follow him to a pale green room with pictures of Army generals on the walls. He motions me to a chair, but I prefer to stand. He pulls some papers from his notebook, and suddenly drops his politeness, getting straight to the point.

"Perhaps you don't realize the gravity of the act you've just committed. Or maybe you do. But it is my duty to point out to you that if this should be your final decision, you will face criminal charges and your penalty could be five years in prison and ten thousand dollars fine. It's the same for you as it would be for any other offender in a similar case. I don't know what influenced you to act this way, but I am authorized to give you an opportunity to reconsider your position. Selective Service regulations require us to give you a second chance."

"Thank you, sir, but I don't need it."

"It is required"—he never stops talking or looking at his notes—"that you go back into the induction room, stand before the podium and receive the call again."

"Sir, why should I go back out there and waste everybody's time—"

"It's the procedure," he cuts in. "I can't tell you what to do or not to do, but we must follow procedure."

I follow him back into the room, and notice that new faces have appeared. More military personnel, a stenographer and a number of men in civilian clothes, who, I learn later, are FBI agents.

A private hands me a note. "This is from your lawyer."

It's a copy of a letter from U.S. Attorney Morton Sussman.

> I am authorized to advise you that we are willing to enter into an agreement. If you will submit your client for induction, we will be willing to keep him here in the Houston area until all of your civil remedies are exhausted. Otherwise, he will be under criminal indictment. . . .

I crumple it up and stuff it in my pocket. One of the men in civilian clothes who has been watching me now turns and walks out the door. The green-eyed officer is still standing behind the rostrum, ready to read the induction statement. This time I'm closer to him. He's less than an arm's-reach away. I can see drops of sweat on his forehead.

"Mr. Cassius Clay," he begins again, "you will please step forward and be inducted into the United States Army."

Again I don't move.

"Cassius Clay—Army," he repeats. He stands in silence, as though he expects me to make a last-minute change. Finally, with hands shaking, he gives me a form to fill out. "Would you please sign this statement and give your reasons for refusing induction?" His voice is trembling.

I sign quickly and walk out into the hallway. The captain who originally ordered me to the room comes over. "Mr. Clay," he says with a tone of respect that surprises me, "I'll escort you downstairs."

When we reach the bottom of the steps, the television cameramen who had been held up by the guards focus their lights on us, while a platoon of military police scuffle to keep them behind a rope that blocks the end of the corridor.

"Muhammad," a reporter yells, "did you take the step? Are you in the Army?"

"Can we just have a minute, Champ?" another shouts. "What did you do? Can you just tell us yes or no?"

I keep walking with the captain, who leads me to a room where my lawyers are waiting. "You are free to go now," he tells us. "You will be contacted later by the United States Attorney's office."

I step outside and a huge crowd of people rush toward me, pushing and shoving each other and snapping away at me with their cameras. Writers from two French newspapers and one from London throw me a barrage of questions, but I feel too full to say anything. Covington gives them copies of a statement I wrote for them before I left Chicago. In it I cite my ministry and my personal convictions as reasons for refusing to take the step, adding that "I strongly object to the fact that so many newspapers have given the American public and the world the impression that I have only two alternatives in taking this stand—either I go to jail or go into the Army. There is another alternative, and that is justice."

By the time I get to the bottom of the front steps, the news breaks. Everyone is shouting and cheering. Some girls from Texas Southern run over to me, crying, "We're glad you didn't go!" A black boy standing next to H. Rap Brown shouts out, "You don't go, so I won't go!"

I feel a sense of relief and freedom. For the first time in weeks I start to relax. I remember the words of the reporter at the hotel: "How will you act?" Now it's over, and I've come through it. I feel better than when I beat the eight-to-ten odds and won the World Heavyweight Title from Liston.

[Attorney Chauncey] Eskridge pushes me to a cab waiting at the corner.

"You headin' for jail. You headin' straight for jail." I turn and an old white woman is standing behind me, waving a miniature American flag. "You goin' straight to jail. You ain't no champ no more. You ain't never gonna be champ no more. You get down on your knees and beg forgiveness from God!" she shouts in a raspy tone.

I start to answer her, but Covington pulls me inside the cab.

She comes over to my window. "My son's in Viet Nam, and you

no better'n he is. He's there fightin' and you here safe. I hope you rot in jail. I hope they throw away the key."

The judge who later hears my case reflects the same sentiment. I receive a maximum sentence of five years in prison and ten thousand dollars fine. The prosecuting attorney argues, "Judge, we cannot let this man get loose, because if he gets by, all black people will want to be Muslims and get out for the same reasons."

Four years later in June of 1970, the Supreme Court unanimously reverses that decision, 8-0, but now this is the biggest victory of my life. I've won something that's worth whatever price I have to pay. It gives me a good feeling to look at the crowd as we pull off. Seeing people smiling makes me feel that I've spoken for them as well as myself. Deep down, they didn't want the World Heavyweight Champion to give in, and in the days ahead their strength and spirit will keep me going. Even when it looks like I'll go to jail and never fight again.

"They can take away the television cameras, the bright lights, the money, and ban you from the ring," an old man tells me when I get back to Chicago, "but they can't destroy your victory. You have taken a stand for the world and now you are the people's champion."

Bertrand Russell writes to assure me: "The air will change. I sense it."

The World Boxing Authority doesn't take nearly as long as the Government to pass judgment on me. As soon as I get back to my hotel room, I hear a radio announcement that the WBA has stripped me of my title again and that they will hold an elimination tournament to determine my successor. The WBA took action against me back in 1965. And on April 28, 1967, the New York Boxing Commission is the first to take my license. This time it will take me more than seven years to get it back.

3. "Muhammad Ali—The Measure of a Man"

Muhammad Ali's decision to refuse induction into the armed forces would be both jeered and hailed. This is an editorial from **Freedomways,** *a New York–based magazine that described itself as "a quarterly review of the Negro freedom movement."*

In recent months, with increasing frequency, it has been necessary to use the Editorial pages of FREEDOMWAYS to call attention to attacks upon particular individuals by the Government as well as other agencies of power. This has been necessary because these instances symbolize and mirror the larger pattern of what is happening in America today.

Consequently, our last Editorial (Winter '67) dealt with the unseating of Congressman Adam Clayton Powell. More recently, the withdrawal of the world heavyweight boxing title from its rightful holder, Mr. Muhammad Ali, by the World Boxing Association and various state Athletic Commissions is the latest case in point.

This arrogant, presumptuous act by the moguls of the boxing business was effected in a matter of hours after Muhammad Ali refused induction into the Army at Houston, Texas. Mr. Ali is also threatened with indictment by the Federal Government because of his anti-draft stand. This attack upon Mr. Ali occurs at a time when voices are heard in the U.S. Congress demanding that dissent be crushed and the First Amendment ignored. The huge anti–Vietnam War demonstrations in New York and San Francisco this spring have obviously placed the question of stopping the war in Vietnam on the agenda of our time and can no longer be ignored.

Mr. Ali's case raises questions of great import for the entire country, and most especially for the 22,000,000 Americans of African descent. This is quite aside from any consideration of the blatant immorality of the particular war against the Vietnamese people which Muhammad Ali is protesting together with millions of other Americans. It is also aside from considering his constitutionally guaranteed right to practice his religious beliefs as a matter of conscience.

While we are not claiming any special privilege for Negro Americans, what we are challenging is the moral right of this nation, *based upon its record*, to insist that any black man must put on the military uniform, at any time, and go thousands of miles away from these shores to risk his life for a society which has historically been his oppressor.

Muhammad Ali, as Cassius Clay, fought for "his country" and won at the 1960 Olympics in Rome, only to return to his home town, Louisville, Kentucky, and be refused service at a lunch counter because he is a black man. Where was the Federal Government then, to uphold his human rights? And where is the Federal Government today as civil rights workers in Louisville face screaming mobs, throwing rocks and bottles at them as they peacefully march to end housing discrimination? We are reminded that the State of Kentucky established its fame and wealth in the American Republic by breeding race horses and Negroes (both for sale, of course).

Stripping Muhammad Ali of the heavyweight title, which he earned the hard way, happens to be considered good business by the money-grabbing jackals who control the boxing syndicates. By stealing the heavyweight crown from the champion, they hope they can stimulate competition and a new era of prosperity at the box office. Such are the ethics of "our glorious free enterprise system."

"*I won't wear the uniform*," declared the world heavyweight champion. Of all the rhetoric used to express opposition to the Vietnam War, these words may prove to be the most eloquent as a statement of personal commitment. They are words which should echo among the youth in every ghetto across this land. In taking his stand as a matter of conscience, the world heavyweight champion may be giving up a small fortune, but he has undoubtedly gained the respect and admiration of a very large part of humanity. That, after all, is the measure of a Man.

The Editors

4. Interview with Paula Giddings

In her effort to become the homecoming queen at Howard University in the fall of 1966, Robin Gregory broke tradition in both her personal grooming and in her campaign substance. Her victory, as described by fellow Howard student Paula Giddings, would signal a new era at one of the nation's oldest black educational institutions. This is an excerpt from a 1988 interview with Giddings by the Eyes on the Prize *production team.*

The traditional homecoming campaign was quite a ritual. Each sorority or fraternity, for example, had their candidates, and other organizations had candidates as well. During the days of the campaign, each candidate would appear on campus at certain times of the afternoon. All the candidates, of course, had to get new wardrobes with the latest fashions. They usually came rolling in in a latest model convertible. And everything was color-coordinated. And I remember working on the campaign, you always had to think of what color was the car, then the dress had to match the car, and the flowers had to match the dress that matched the car. So it was all very elaborate, and then there would be a demonstration talking about the candidate.

Of course, Robin Gregory had no car and always looked sharp, but she was certainly not wearing those elaborate dresses. She had an Afro, which of course was the statement that she made physically. And she was always flanked by two very handsome men, very serious, very well dressed in the way that the Fruit of Islam was dressed, with the bow ties. They always had their arms folded and would look straight ahead while Robin talked. And Robin talked about the movement. Robin talked about black politics. Robin was not the traditional homecoming queen candidate. She would also go around to the dorms in the evenings, which was something very, very different.

I was very excited about Robin's campaign. I'd always felt that there was something wrong with that other kind of traditional ritual that was going on. But at the same time I had divided loyalties, because I was a member of Delta Sigma Theta sorority and we had our own candidate, who was a very good friend of mine and who I worked on the campaign with. So many of us had these feelings back and forth. But all of us, with divided loyalties or not, felt very excited about Robin's campaign and about what it symbolized, not just in terms of politics but in terms of what women should be doing as well, the role of women. It was very, very important to us.

I remember being confronted with the kind of situation where when you passed by men, especially as an underclassman, as a freshman, sophomore, they would actually give you a grade. I mean, they would talk among themselves and say, "Well, that's an A," or "That's a B." There was a lack of respect in lots of instances. And there was a terrible degrading sense about all of that. And what Robin did was not only in terms of race but also talking about the role of women and what they should be doing and talking about and being taken very, very seriously, not just because of any physical attributes but because of her mind. And this I think was as important as the racial aspect of her campaign.

I remember very much the evening when the homecoming queen was crowned. I was in Cramton Auditorium, which was filled to the hilt. For the last time all the candidates were announced and went up on the stage in the auditorium. And the way the whole evening was set was very, very dramatic. What would happen after that is that the lights went down and all the candidates went behind the curtain, back of the stage. The ballot was actually secret balloting, so no one in the auditorium knew who was going to win. And the idea was that there was a throne, a high-backed throne, with its back to the audience, behind the curtain, and there was a revolving stage, so whoever would win would sit on that throne and then slowly revolve toward the audience.

The lights went down. The candidates went back. Then you heard the curtains open. And you heard the crank of the revolving stage begin. And as the stage revolved and turned around toward the audience, the lights began to come up at the same time. Well, before you saw Robin, you saw the way the lights cast a silhouette on the curtains, and you saw the silhouette of her Afro before you saw her. Well, the auditorium exploded. It was a wonderful moment. People started jumping up and screaming and some were raising their fists, then spontaneously a chant began. The chant was "Umgawa, Black Power, Umgawa, Black Power," and a chain was created. People started to march to the rhythm of "Umgawa, Black Power," and there was a line that went all the way around the auditorium, and more and more people joined the line. I did too as it went around the auditorium. And finally out the door and into the streets of Washington, D.C., past the campus and still chanting, "Umgawa, Black Power," and that was really the launching of that movement at Howard.

5. An Open Letter Sent to Howard President James M. Nabrit

While the protests of the preceding year had developed a growing racial and political consciousness among many Howard students, few on-campus changes had been realized. In February 1968, a group of undergraduate student leaders sent an open letter to university president James M. Nabrit describing their frustrations with his administration and demanding institutional and curricular changes. The demands contained in this letter would be among the core demands when students occupied the administration building in March.

Dear President Nabrit:

Howard University has always considered itself a source of leadership for the black community and for the black liberation movement in America. In earlier stages of that movement, the leaders whom Howard produced encouraged the masses to work hard, dress neatly and study diligently in order to prove to themselves and to the rest of society that they were as good as white men. It is a tragic testimony to the depth of our collective inferiority complex that we so long based the philosophy of our struggle on the importance of being accepted by others.

It is axiomatic where social movements are concerned that today's militants become tomorrow's moderates and conservatives. To give an extreme example, Abraham Lincoln, a radical in his time, is revealed as a reactionary white supremacist in the context of 1968. In the case of the black liberation movement in America, the Roy Wilkinses, the Whitney Youngs—and the James Nabrits are yesterday's militants and today's moderates and conservatives.

Black youth of today have learned that to be "just like a white man" is to acquire a synthetic identity and to hate one's true self. Black youth of today are conscious that they have been robbed of awareness of themselves by the white man's pervasive brainwash. Thus, the black leader of today must address himself to a new breed of youth and the black university of today must produce a new breed of leaders—leaders who take pride in their true identity and who will instill similar pride in others.

Unfortunately, Howard University has not yet committed itself to producing such leaders. It is desperately trying to remain an imitation white school turning out imitation white people.

It is time for the Howard University administration to recognize that the days of the movement based on bleaching, straightening, brainwashing and otherwise molding the black student into a strange and pathetic hybrid acceptable to whites are gone forever, despite the old guard's fond memories of them.

We therefore demand that Howard University begin to move towards becoming a black university by effecting the following changes:

1. We demand the immediate resignation of the following Howard administrators on the grounds of their incompetence and obvious unwillingness to work towards a black Howard University.
   a. President James Nabrit
   b. Vice President Stanton Wormley
   c. Liberal Arts Dean Frank Snowden
2. We demand the institution of the following curriculum changes by next semester.
   a. We demand that Howard should be the center of Afro-American thought. We demand that the economic, government, literature and social science departments begin to place more emphasis on how these disciplines may be used to effect the liberation of blackpeople in this country.
   b. We demand the institution of non-prerequisite courses in Negro History.
   c. We demand the immediate abolishment of Freshman Assembly. Black students are not culturally deprived. We

demand the immediate reinstatement of all Howard instructors who have been unjustifiably dismissed for their political activism including:

Dr. Nathan Hare   Dr. David Hammond
Dr. Andress Taylor   Dr. Harold Shipper
Samuel Carcione   Dr. Alan Lefcowitz
Keith Lowe   Dr. Ivan Eames

Measures must be instituted to insure that all instructors be given a fair hearing if considered for dismissal.

4. We demand the institution of a Black Awareness Research Institute at Howard University.

5. Students are trained to be leaders only by learning to accept responsibility. We demand therefore that student autonomy that is student control in matters that concern only students. Therefore we demand:

   a. The student judiciary and codification or rules presently submitted to the Faculty Senate Steering Committee should be immediately instituted.

   b. That students must be authorized to control the budgeting and expenditure of the student activity fee.

6. Howard must be made relevant to the black community. The University campus must be made more available to all black people and programs must be instituted to aid the black community in the struggle against oppression.

7. We demand that Howard personnel begin to treat students like black people should treat blackpeople, with respect and courtesy.

We allow you until February 29, exactly three weeks after the Orangeburg Massacre, to respond to our demands.

Sincerely,
Anthony Gittens, Political Director of Howard Univ. Ujamaa
Ewart Brown, President of the University Student Assembly
Adrienne Manns, Editor of the Hilltop
Barbara Penn, President of the LASC Student Council
And all other Concerned Black Students

6. Interview with Tony Gittens

Howard University student Tony Gittens, of the class of 1969, was features editor for the student newspaper, **The Hilltop,** *political director of the umbrella organization of student activist groups, Ujamaa, and one of the signatories of the open letter to President Nabrit. This is an excerpt from a 1988 interview with Gittens by the* **Eyes on the Prize** *production team.*

INTERVIEWER: When you got on [the Howard] campus, what disturbed you so much about what you found there?

TONY GITTENS: When I got to Howard, back in 1965, what disturbed me so much was the way . . . the Howard administration tended to treat students like children. As though we couldn't take care [of] ourselves and their job was to make us more cultured black people, that they felt that we were these Negroes from the field and that we were to be treated like kids. And I found that absolutely insulting. I found the whole idea of this, the largest, most prestigious black institution in the country, wanting to view itself as the black Harvard as opposed to setting out its own identity. . . .

INT: Why did you and other students begin to get into this Vietnam protest? What was your personal feeling in connection with that?

T.G.: Well, we were totally against the war. We were against the draft, we felt that the Vietnam War was totally unjust and that especially black people should have no role in the war. And Howard at that time had compulsory ROTC. That was another aspect of it that most men there found just absolutely appalling. We felt that Howard should not be a factory for black officers to go into the war. And that we were not going to just participate in it. And as a matter of fact we were going to say no to it. And so there were protests against that and to let the world know that black people were not going to participate in the war. Or at least were going to be strongly opposed to it.

INT: Will you talk a little bit about the black consciousness stuff that was going on outside the campus? How did that infect the campus? And was there an attempt by the administration to stop that from coming on campus?

T.G.: The whole Howard movement was impacted by what was going on outside of Howard. There was a lot of activity in the South. There were black colleges in the South where students were taking very militant, very firm stands against discrimination. And here there were the students of Howard, who were considered to be very middle class and sort of away from a lot of that. So there were some students at Howard who believed that that should not be the case and that in fact that Howard if it was to be a leader amongst black universities should take the firmest of stands. And we pushed to make Howard do that. And the resistance to that took the form of, for example, there were people who would come to Howard. There were organizers who wanted to have demonstrations here in Washington and they would come to Howard to try and get Howard students to participate. And there was always resistance on the part of the administration to such people coming on campus. There were speakers who we wanted to bring to Howard, toward the earlier days, not so much during the later days. And there was always resistance to these speakers being brought to Howard. So the university as a whole felt that it should not be in a controversial position. It stated in documents that they felt that a good deal of money was coming from the federal government to support Howard and Howard students therefore should not be antagonistic toward the government. We, on the other hand, felt that where Howard got its money was its own business and we were adults and able to make our own decisions and take our own stands on things.

INT: You talked at one point about how [the administration] was trying to keep the university separate from the community. Can you say something about that?

T.G.: Howard University is located in a community that parts of it are developed, but there's a whole strip along Georgia Avenue that's not very developed. And there's always been this conflict between what at that point were called block boys or gangs of kids who lived in the area, and Howard students whom they viewed as being middle class and snobbish. And our feeling was that the university had to relate to its immediate environment if it was going to live up to its mandate. We couldn't be creating officers for ROTC to go fight wars thousands of miles away and then have a community right at your door where there's all kinds of problems, economic problems and social problems and health problems, and not really do anything for them.

So we wanted the university to just, what we call, relate to the community. To have events that would be attractive enough for people in the area to come in, to have concerts and things. We wanted them to relate to all kinds of activities that were going on in the communities. There were social groups and church organizations that were doing things. We went out and we tried to participate in them and bring speakers in from those communities. We talked about all kinds of things that never really took place. But day-care centers . . . for young mothers. And med school doctors who would go out and spend some time working with people there. So that was what we were looking for. That was our utopia. For what the university should do for people who live right there.

INT: Talk about the [March 1968] takeover. . . .

T.G.: We had decided that we were going to have a sit-in in the administration building. . . . The university was going to have hearings again to try some students who had been more active on campus. So we had a rally in front of Douglas Hall. And we said that we were just tired of this, tired of the way we were being treated. And that we were going to have a sit-in in the administration building. And I remember different people gave speeches. And I gave the last speech. That was part of the plan. And we had these bags of food that we were carrying in. And I said, we're going to go in, and we're going to sit down. And we're not going to get up until they refuse to have these hearings. And I remember just walking off, walking away from the steps and going down. And I was out front and there were some people by my side. And then I remember turning around and just seeing all of these students. [LAUGHS] And it was just so movingly incredible. I mean, we had never been able to get this response before. . . . And I just realized that all these people were also tired. . . .

And we went into the first floor of the administration building.

And everybody sat down, just sat down. When we went in there, when we planned this the night before, we figured that we'd just sit on the first floor and that would be it. And we would just stay there. And then more students [came], people began to hear about it. And then the whole first floor was full. Then the whole second floor was filled. Then they went up the third floor. And the whole building was just filled with these students who had come out of the dormitories, come out of their classes to just participate in this. And it was incredible. It was just amazing. I mean, after all that time, all that work, that someone was actually listening. And so we just stayed there. It was then about noon and we stayed there and the newspapers began to hear about it and reporters began to show up. And the university, the people who worked there, just left. They just left the building to us.

And so then we said, Well, we have to organize this. So we had meetings. There was this group that we called the Central Committee. And we met and we started having chairmen of certain committees. There was a Sanitation Committee, there was a Communications Committee. And there was a Food Committee, and a Security Committee. There were all these committees that we made.

And there were just some incidents there that astounded me. Like the switchboards had to be manned. And so we just made an announcement. From somewhere someone came up with a PA system. . . . And all these women got up and went and took over the whole university switchboard. I remember looking into this room and they were just very professionally and efficiently running the switchboard. I said, How . . . ? And they said, You know, these students work, doing this kind of stuff part-time. And everyone was saying . . . that sorry, the university is closed today. The students have taken it over. And that went on for days. And they developed a schedule for taking care of that.

Then there was food that all these people from off campus, this community, who the university, up until then, had very little relationship with . . . began to bring food. Ladies would bring these bags of food. And churches would take up collections and bring us all this money. And then these cultural groups would come in and say, We want to do something. Can we perform? And there'd be plays and all kinds of things would go on. And people from around Washington would come and give all these supportive speeches and say, Whatever you want, let us know.

And then, people who could not get into the building, there are all these students outside of the building who were just there, just willing to participate. And signs were made. HOWARD UNIVERSITY, THE BLACK UNIVERSITY. Then teachers would come up. And they said, What can we do? And we had classes that were going on. Because some students were afraid they were getting behind. And these faculty members [were] saying, Don't worry about it. We'll take care of it. And people would come in and have seminars. . . .

We met every morning, and we met periodically to take care of the issues. It was just . . . an incredible experience to just show . . . the administration, these people who thought that we were kids, [they] were just so off-key, just so wrong about the whole thing.

INT: When you say they were off-key, what did it show the university?

T.G.: Well, I think that the demonstration showed the university, the administration there, that they were not dealing with helpless children. That they were dealing with people who were quite capable of taking care of themselves in a very serious, organized fashion. It also showed them that there were not just these few militant minority students who had these grievances with them. That in fact there were thousands of students who were disgruntled and were willing take a stand to put their education on the line. To let them know that they were just off base with understanding who it is they were and what they wanted out of their education, out of Howard University.

INT: Talk about the fear you had that the police might be called on campus. And what was the context of that fear? Had they been called on at other universities?

T.G.: There was some concern that the police would be called in. However, we felt that we had so much community support, that there was so much recognition on the part of the media who were covering this event . . . in the nightly news . . . that the university was not going to use any force to remove us.

INT: Why did you end the takeover? What did you accomplish?

T.G.: A couple of things happened that made us want to end the takeover. One was that we had gotten a lot of what we said that we came in there for. We told them what we wanted and the negotiations were very successful in our regard. We had made a very strong point about it. You couldn't see a lot of reason to stay there outside of just being belligerent. And we thought that that would be immature, to do that. So we decided that as we chose to go in, that we would be adult and mature and responsible enough to choose to go out. And we talked about it at length and came down one morning and just made the announcement that we felt that it was time to go. . . . There was no press there. We put all the press out. And we had an open mike and anybody could come up and say whatever they felt about it. There was some people who felt that we shouldn't go and then the vast majority said that we should. We took a voice vote.

And so we walked out. And we just left the place. We cleaned it. Put everything as much back in order as much as we could, as we recalled it, and we just walked out that day. And students went back to the dorm and we went back to doing what it is we did before we went in. . . .

I think that experience changed the life of every single Howard student that was on campus that day. Everyone felt proud. And as we walked out I felt very good. And the students tended to feel very, very good about themselves. . . . They just felt their whole self-image of what they were as Howard students just changed. They felt part of the whole world of black progress. So it was quite a wonderful feeling to have ended by choice and in such a positive way.

7. "The Nature and Needs of the Black University"
Gerald McWorter

One of the key demands of student protesters at Howard and on other historically black campuses was for such institutions to remake themselves into "black universities." In this 1968 essay, sociologist Gerald McWorter (now Abdul Alkalimat), then at Fisk University, put forth one model of "the Black University."

Revolutionary change for the liberation of a people from oppressive social structures is not the special function of one course of action, but, more likely, the result of several. And while education is generally hoped to be a liberating force on men's minds and bodies, ofttimes it has been used as a debilitating tool in the interests of an oppressive society. Accordingly, Kwame Nkrumah compares the colonial student educated for "the art of forming not a concrete environmental view of social political problems, but an abstract 'liberal' outlook," with the revolutionary student "animated by a lively national consciousness, (who) sought knowledge as an instrument of national emancipation and integrity." So it is becoming rather clear that educational institutions are vital to a liberation movement, a fact of modern times in anti-colonial movements in the Third World.

In the United States there is no question about the persistence of segregation, racism, and more subtle forms of neo-racism. As the pernicious oppression of racism is an organic part of the institutions, symbols, and values of Western industrial society, so it is firmly entrenched in the U.S.A. ("as American as apple pie"). An Afro-American liberation movement must subvert and/or supplant such a well-entrenched social system if it is to be a real source of radical change and not a false one.

My primary task in this discussion is an ideological consideration of the role of a university in the liberation of the Afro-American community. It must be clear that this role has to deal with today's world, as well as with what ought to be. And certainly, it must include the management of whatever social change is required to move effectively from the "is" to the "ought." The university is alive for people in the world (including all of the socio-economic and political hang-ups involved), and so must meet the challenge of responding creatively to whatever needs exist now for those people. But, at the same time, it must project itself as a prophetic institution calling into question all that which is inconsistent with its highest ideals, and organizing its activities to bring about the realization of its ideals. The focus of this discussion is on what *ought* to be, the prophetic social role of the *Black University*, for therein lies the fountainhead of revolutionary liberation.

We must be reminded of this same theme as stated by Dr.

W. E. B. Du Bois over 50 years ago in the 1910 Niagara Movement resolutions:

> And when we call for education, we mean real education . . . Education is the development of power and ideal. We want our children trained as intelligent human beings should be, and we will fight for all time against any proposal to educate black boys and girls simply as servants and underlings, or simply for the use of other people. They have a right to know, to think, to aspire. We do not believe in violence . . . but we do believe in . . . that willingness to sacrifice money, reputation, and life itself on the altar of right.

The Booker T. Washington–Du Bois dialectical opposition is relevant here, as it is the important example of the "is" versus the "ought" concerning educational ideology for Afro-Americans. Training people to fit in where they can (think of MDTA, Job Corps, etc.) might be acceptable for short term solutions, though not as Washington thought it to be. But the educational ideology of Du Bois is our prophecy, a rationale to build a Black University— the crucible of definitive social change.

In order that the idea of the new university and the notions of how we are to achieve it as a goal will be more clearly understood, it is important to discuss briefly the current social situation. The current situation is one charged with a great deal of expectancy on the part of many Afro-Americans, an expectancy frequently expressed by the emotional connotations of a term or phrase but usually not delineated in structural or programmatic terms. But this programmatic deficiency is not so much a shortcoming, for the exciting search for innovation and relevance is the first sign of progress. A major question, then, is what conditions give rise to this expectancy, this charged atmosphere crystallized around the term Black University?

A major trend in today's world is that, as oppressed people know that the world offers more than they have, and as they are able to get a little more of it, they also expect to get very much more. This has been called "the revolution of rising expectations." A figurative example: An Afro-American family gets a television set and enters as a spectator the world of affluent Euro-American society. It is not complicated to see that this would lead to the family wanting more than it has, much more. Just imagine how cruel it must be for poor oppressed Black people to watch the give-away quiz programs on which white people win appliances, furniture, and cars in 20 minutes or so. Then think of a scene of ghetto destruction during which people brave armed police to steal appliances, furniture, and cars in 20 minutes or so. Oppressed people see what is going on, and want "in" in the best way they can get "in" (yes, by any means necessary to do it right now!!).

Along with this developing desire to get more out of society there also is the increasing saliency of a nationalistic alternative to the system. The general components are militancy, self-determination, and a desire to identify with similar oppressed people throughout the world (who are *not* by accident mostly colored people). This alternative is grounded in communalism and finds its legitimacy from within Afro-America and not outside of it. Nationalism, in this context, means total concern for the community of common experience, so Afro-American Nationalism is grounded in the Black Experience. Communalism, meaning self-help cooperative efforts, is the ethic supporting the new alternative.

These two major trends cannot be viewed outside of the total context of world events, especially those events of particular relevance to the Afro-American community. The military-industrial machine of the Western powers is equally offensive and outraging in Vietnam and South Africa, in Santo Domingo and Ghana. But it seems apparent that peoples can only unite across the world in aspiring for the same universals—peace, freedom, and justice— while focusing their working activities on the social ills as manifested at home. If we are to reap a harvest of world brotherhood, then each man must first tend to his own garden. But for each garden to have its true meaning, the gardener must know his historical role and his relationship with all others working for the same harvest.

The two trends are general social sources of the cry for a Black University. While everyone is more or less for such a thing as a university, for some the quality of Blackness imbues the concept with polemical emotional intensity and conceptual ambiguity (or, in extreme cases, of racism). This must be cleared up if the dialogue is to continue. In reference to a university, Blackness must mean at least three things.

First, Blackness refers to the Afro-American community as the basic focus for the University. This in no way compromises or limits its universalistic orientation or its attempts to contribute to human progress: rather, it frees it to be relevant in the face of an unmet need reflecting the woeful limit of human progress.

A second, and more controversial point, considers the limits placed on participation in the University. Blackness does not categorically exclude all white people from the University; it redefines the standards for their participation and the possibility for their involvement. In much the same way that independent African countries have attempted to redefine the possible role of the European, so in the Black University the role of the white man must be redefined and carefully placed for the maximum good of all. Some white people will be necessary for the immediate future if for no other reason than the black community's own shortage of resources. But unconditional participation will have to be ended. The participation must be based on a commitment to the goals and aspirations of the Afro-American community, and the white participant must possess the sacrificial humility necessary for one historically and socially identified with the beast of Afro-American history and the system of oppression.

Last, Blackness is an affirmation of an identity independent of the historical human evils of modern nation states, and is closely tied to the emerging international identity of man in his struggle for a better life. Consider this revelation by Brother Malcolm X when on his pilgrimage to Mecca:

> "That morning was when I first began to reappraise the 'white man.' It was when I first began to perceive that 'white man' as commonly used, means complexion only secondarily; primarily it described attitudes and actions. In America, 'white man' meant specific attitudes and actions toward the black man, and toward all other non-white men. But in the Muslim world, I had seen men with white complexions were more genuinely brotherly than anyone else had ever been."

The relations between people must be allowed to grow and progress without the limiting problem of the national state. Who are we? Afro-Americans, men of the world. Why are we here? We were sent here to love. Where are we going? Toward the community of love, and if stopped we will continue "by any means necessary," because we must continue.

So much for prologue. What is the Black University idea all about? What are its goals? And what might it look like? The university focusing on the particular needs of the Afro-American community will be a center of learning. But, recognizing the alternatives noted above by Nkrumah, it must be based on an educational ideology grounded in an uncompromising goal of psychological independence from the oppressor (and his oppressive system), and as much structural independence as is necessary not only to survive in the world, but to prosper. So, education must be defined to specify these purposes as most important.

The American (U.S.A.) ethic of individualism is inclusive of both basic needs of men and the essence of a social style. All men are, to some extent, self-centered. But to build a social group process on self-centeredness is to hope for a just order through "antagonistic cooperation." The thrust of the Black University must be to overcome this subtle social warlike-state with the ethic of communalism. This means that instead of hoping for social progress through the individual merits of its students or faculty *qua* individuals, progress is to be viewed as a social process through which the community is uplifted with the aid of its contributing people. This then means that while students and faculty play a very vital role, they are co-workers alongside the equally important others, *e.g.*, the community organizer, the artist, the union organizer.

Moreover, the goal of the university must be one of service to the community. The students, faculty, and administration of the Black University must consider themselves as servants to the broader Afro-American community. Being a member of the University must be considered an honor, but more important this honor must be one involving responsibility to the total community and not simply focusing on the "I-made-it-because-I'm-smarter-than" kind of thinking. Being servants, status is not based on the academic credentials university people create for themselves;

rather it is on the extent to which the total community is able to reap benefits from the service provided.

The service of the Black University must not be one transmitted through mass communication or ritualistic ceremony but through a concrete programmatic movement toward liberation. The time when the Afro-American community must be arms-length from its institutions of higher education is over. The pimps, prostitutes, preachers, and Ph.D.'s must find a common bond to change themselves and weave an organic unity as the basis for liberation and a better life for all.

These goals must redefine two dangerously-pervasive patterns found among Afro-American faculty and students today. One of the patterns is for education to be simply a process of acclimation and adjustment to the white world. One goes to a white school to rub shoulders with *them,* "because, son, you got to make a livin' out in their world." Another pattern is the play-culture of friendship cliques and fraternity life. Whether it is mimicry of whites (think of Fort Lauderdale in the spring), or defection based on hopelessness, we must find the recipe for a revolutionary discipline consistent with our desire for immediate radical change. A free man is also (and must be) a responsible man, and so must Afro-American students and faculty be responsible to themselves by being responsible to the Black community.

The values of the Black University must support the liberation movement of Afro-Americans, oppressed people around the world, and all that prevents man from leading the good life. We must find a synthesis of efficient reason and purposive compassion. The value placed on scientific methods must be joined by an equally important value placed on empathy, *i.e.,* scientific detachment must be limited to method and technique, complemented with involvement and commitment. The students and faculty must be evangelical in their social roles and give new meaning to being a missionary for freedom. And finally, the Black University must impart to all who are associated with it the strength to be alone. The struggle against ignorance, just as with the struggle of power, is one within which the forces of good are often small in number and sparsely placed. An Afro-American of the Black University must have inner strength, positive historical identity, and a vision of the good, for only in having these traits will he be able to stand up in a world dominated by evil and be secure even in being alone.

Among its many functions, the university is most concerned with knowledge, both the accumulated information and insights of human history and the vision and process of new discovery. And it is knowledge about Afro-Americans that is most lacking, or biased and wrong, in all these respects. The Black University is based on the fundamental assumption that the Afro-American community is, in E. Franklin Frazier's words, "a little social world," a human universe heretofore misused or ignored by higher education. Consider these autobiographical comments by Dr. Du Bois:

> When I went South to Fisk, I became a member of a closed racial group with rites and loyalties, with a history and a corporate future, with an art and philosophy.
> Into this world I leapt with provincial enthusiasm. A new loyalty and allegiance replaced my Americanism: henceforth I was a Negro.

The Black University must respond creatively to just these realities which were true for Du Bois in 1880, and equally true for this author in the 1960's.

The knowledge of Afro-Americans, just as with Africa, is yet to be fully reclaimed. With the full scope of University activities (research, teaching, etc.), revision is needed to secure for colored peoples of the world their proper place in human history. This revision of educational materials is a process as much political as it is scholarly. With scholarly work a text of U.S.A. history can be written, but only with political influence will it be made available by getting it published, placed in a library, or adopted as recommended reading. However, in the present it would be foolish to think of throwing everything aside. Revision of *what is* must be a thorough job of systematic and rigorous scholarship backed by the concerted political efforts of Afro-American students, faculty, and the entire community.

But more important (and more difficult), there is a need to find new styles of scholarship, new forms of knowledge, new ways of knowing. These new developments must be consistent with what is to be known, and have utility for the liberation movement. There must be research on all aspects of the Black experience, research necessarily not limited to traditional scholarly disciplines, but open to the demands of the subject. For example, the "Blues" component of Afro-American culture demands a historian, musicologist, literary historian, sociologist, etc. The soul of a people must be reflected in the results of the research as well as the life style of the Black University. We must be in search of the "funky" sociologist, the "soulful" political scientist, and the University president who can "get down."

These are some of the necessary ingredients of a Black University. And while we can, at best, look to the future for its full realization, it is quite possible now to suggest a structural outline that reflects these fundamental assumptions about its social and intellectual role. The [author] . . . suggests three related colleges [the College of Liberal Arts, College of Afro-American Studies, and College of Community Life] concerned with distinct areas, though bound together in the idea of the University. Each would be organized around research, teaching, and practice. For every part of the University community there would be an advisory board of community representatives from all walks of life, with the task of providing policy suggestions and guidelines. This would insure the community of ties to the specific parts of the University.

As one enters the University he will be faced with a variety of degree programs and alternative courses of study. It is quite clear that the standard four-year college degree meets only a partial need for the Afro-American community. But even the student entering the College of Liberal Arts would have to work at least a year in one or more of the other two colleges in order to meet the requirements for graduation. The general principle might well be that, to meet the needs of today, the new programs will have to take less time; but those set up to meet the needs of tomorrow will have to take more time.

As a national institution engaged in activities found nowhere else, the component colleges of the Black University would be of great service to a wide variety of groups. Service professionals working with Afro-Americans face a challenge supported by sparse research and little experience. The College of Afro-American Studies, being a center of innovation and discovery concerning these problems, will conduct special courses and training programs so that students can supplement their training and experience with a concentrated program. There is a desperate need for social workers, teachers, lawyers, doctors, psychiatrists, etc. And the same kind of function is planned for the entire University.

There also must be connected with such a University a set of centers of International Study. They will be small centers specializing in specific areas in order that, together, they might constitute an international program without superficially missing the peculiar character of each part of the world. In addition, no such University could hope to function without an international conference center available to the University community, and accommodating other activities consistent with the aims and purpose of the University community and liberation movement. Afro-Americans are moving onto the international scene and so must have at their disposal a center where such meetings can be held.

As stated at the beginning of this discussion, there is no panacea for the Afro-American liberation movement, just as there can and will be no monolithic organizational structure. But there can be operational unity around such concepts as the Black University. The first step in moving toward this operational unity, moving toward the Black University, is to begin a creative and honest dialogue among Afro-Americans. But more than that, we need small bands of people in positions to act, to make steps, to be daring enough to risk failure (or worse, irrelevance). It will only be when these ideas can be referred to in concrete terms that definitive statements can be made, and the concrete reality of the Black University must begin today.

One last thought. The Afro-American community does not possess unlimited resources with which to carry on experiment after experiment. Each of us who can contribute to the Black University must ask himself what he is doing for it, what he is doing for this kind of operational unity. I am calling for all of the brothers and sisters in "other" colleges and university settings to come on home. And to those at home, let us get this thing together!!

8. "It's Nation Time"
Amiri Baraka

In this clarion call for racial solidarity, poet, playwright, and activist Amiri Baraka (formerly LeRoi Jones) expressed the growing sentiments of many black activists in the late 1960s and early 1970s. The recurrent cry "it's nation time" would be the beckoning call for a proposed national conference of black activists in 1972.

Time to get
together
time to be one strong fast black energy space
           one pulsating positive magnetism, rising
time to get up and
be
come
be
come, time to
        be come
        time to
        get up be come
        black genius rise in spirit muscle
        sun man get up rise heart of universes to be
future of the world
the black man is the future of the world
be come
rise up
future of the black genius spirit reality
        move
        from crushed roach back
        from dead snake head
        from wig funeral in slowmotion
        from dancing teeth and coward tip
        from jibberjabber patme boss patme smmich
when the brothers strike niggers come out
come out niggers
when the brothers take over the school
help niggers
come out niggers

all niggers negroes must change up
come together in unity unify
for nation time
it's nation time . . .
                  Boom
                  Booom
                  BOOOM
                  Boom
                  Dadadadadadadadadadad
                  Boom
                  Boom
                  Boom
                  Boom
                  Dadadadad adadadad
                              Hey aheee (soft)
                              Hey ahheee (loud)
                  Boom
                  Boom
                  Boom
sing a get up time to nationfy
singaa miracle fire light
sing a airplane invisibility for the jesus niggers come from
  the grave
for the jesus niggers dead in the cave, rose up, passt jewjuice
on shadow world
raise up christ nigger
Christ was black
krishna was black shango was black
           black jesus nigger come out and strike
              come out and strike boom boom
                Heyahheeee come out
             strike close ford
               close prudential burn the policies
             tear glasses off dead statue puppets even
                those
                  they imitate life
                    Shango buddah black
                hermes rasis black
                moses krishna
                        black
when the brothers wanna stop animals
come out niggers come out

come out niggers niggers niggers come out
help us stop the devil
help us build a new world

niggers come out, brothers are we
  with you and your sons your daughters are ours
  and we are the same, all the blackness from one black allah
    when the world is clear you'll be with us
      come out niggers come out
      come out niggers come out
It's nation time eye ime
      It's nation ti eye ime
           chant with bells and drum
           it's nation time

It's nation time, get up santa claus   (repeat)
  it's nation time, build it
    get up muffet dragger
      get up rastus for real to be rasta farari
      ras jua
        get up got here bow

          It's Nation
          Time!

9. "We Must Pave the Way: An Independent Black Political Thrust"
Richard Hatcher

Mayor Richard Hatcher delivered this keynote address at the National Black Political Convention in Gary, Indiana, on March 11, 1972. A co-convenor of the convention, Hatcher had been elected mayor of Gary in 1967, the same year Carl Stokes was elected in Cleveland.

As we look out over this vast and expectant assemblage, we can imagine how Moses and the people of Israel thrilled when they witnessed the parting of the Red Sea.

We picture the jubilation of Joshua and his soldiers at that last trumpet blast.

We experience the exultation of Noah when he gazed at Mount Ararat as the clouds parted and the sun shone down.

We know the spirit of triumph and determination that infused Dr. Du Bois and his fellow warriors at the first gathering of the Niagara movement.

Some of the white bourgeois news media have criticized us for welcoming all brothers and sisters. It is our convention. We shall determine who attends it. All black people are welcome. Thousands strong, we warmly embrace Angela Davis and Bobby Seale.

This convention can make history. Whether it does, will depend on what we do here today.

We must emerge from this convention with an independent national black political agenda: A dynamic program for black liberation, that in the process, will liberate all America from its current decadence.

Equally important, we must not leave this convention until we have built the mechanism to implement our program. Program must mesh with action. For this we must create a living organization.

And as we deliberate, as we plan, as we work—the banner waving over our head must proclaim "unity." Without that unity, all is lost.

Yes, we support marches and demonstrations . . . Yes, we support sit-ins . . . Yes, we support trade union activity . . . Yes, we support legal defense . . . Yes, we support radical action . . . Yes, we support all avenues to liberation. We know full well that political action is not the whole answer. But political action is an essential part of our ultimate liberation. And it is the political questions we shall pursue at this historic convention.

Our precious time together is limited. We must not waste it in fruitless dispute, ego trips, self-aggrandizement, or rhetoric uninformed by thought. Every word, every moment, we shall invest with the utmost meaning.

Poised at the exhilarating beginning of this historic convention, we must first probe our bitter political past. We dare not delude ourselves about the black role in the political life of this country. A people bent on freedom can ill afford to harbor illusions.

From reconstruction to the mid-1930's, we nestled in the white bosom of the Republican Party—a warm home for some, perhaps;

but a rocky bed for the sons and daughters of Africa. In the mid-30's, we took up residence in the hip pocket of the Democratic Party where we lodge uneasily to this day.

Our mythic heroes of Republican and Democratic stripe—Lincoln, Franklin Delano Roosevelt, John F. Kennedy—none of them moved in our behalf without tremendous pressure. Neither major party can claim our undying loyalty because of any blessings they heaped upon us.

So starved were we for recognition that when Teddy Roosevelt appointed a black man as collector of the Port of Charleston, the editor of the "Coloured American Magazine," overcome by this dubious honor, called it our greatest political triumph in 20 years. And he was probably right . . . appropriately, the new collector was named Crum. That's spelled C-R-U-M.

Desperate for voters after the Civil War, Republicans hastened to recruit us. And vote Republican we did—at least twice saving the presidency for our new masters. Early reconstruction Republican party platforms promised us real freedom, but the issue soon cooled, and so did the Republicans.

The Hayes-Tilden compromise of 1877 more than any other event, marked the end of our hopes for reconstruction, and set the stage for the terror to follow. Hayes, a Republican, beat Tilden for the presidency by just one electoral vote, causing a political uproar. In exchange for letting Hayes ascend peacefully to the presidency, the Republicans betrayed us and agreed to pull federal troops out of the south, leaving us to the mercy of our former masters.

It matters little that Teddy Roosevelt invited Booker T. Washington to the White House for dinner. He also permitted blacks to be barred from the Bull Moose Party convention.

Under another of our great Republican leaders, William Howard Taft, federal employees were segregated—a practice which his Democratic successor, Woodrow Wilson, not to be outdone, expanded and improved.

But we still hadn't learned all our lessons at Republican school. In 1924, W. E. B. Du Bois told us straight out. "Any black man," he said, "any black man who votes for the present Republican party out of gratitude or with any hope that it will do a single thing for the Negro is a born fool." Born fools all, we trooped to the polls and voted Coolidge in.

Hoover's message to us came through loud and clear; no blacks were allowed on his southern campaign committees. The Ku Klux Klan backed Hoover. So did we. Three weeks after his election, Hoover announced he would end black and tan political power in the south.

1936—the year of the big switch—Franklin Roosevelt and the depression moved us into the Democratic Party and there most of us have remained ever since. But life was no sweeter for us with the Democrats.

Only the threat of a black march on Washington pressured F.D.R. into ending employment discrimination in defense factories. And even with war raging, he refused to desegregate the armed forces.

Malcolm X said it—dixiecrats are nothing but Democrats in disguise. The Democrats never left the dixiecrats. It was the other way around.

And even our liberal friend, John Kennedy, stalled two years before ending discrimination in federally financed housing by a simple "stroke of the pen."

What of Johnson? He bragged about the black thirteen and a half percent of his federal work force—but he didn't tell us they were in the lowest paying jobs.

Democrats or Republicans . . . how much difference has it really made to black people?

In 1969, black median income was still only 60 per cent of white income; black unemployment was still twice that of white unemployment; and a black man with four years of high school still earned less money than a white man with an eighth grade education.

In our infinite patience, we have tried year after year, election after election, to work with the two major political parties. We believed the pledges, believed the platforms, believed the promises, each time hoping they would come true. Hoping we would not again be sold out . . . hoping . . . hoping . . . always hoping.

We are through believing. We are through hoping. We are through trusting in the two major white American political parties.

Hereafter, we shall rely on the power of our own black unity.

We shall no longer bargain away our support for petty jobs or symbolic offices.

If we are to support any political party, the price will now run high—very high.

First. We emphatically reject the role of advisor to the party's governing circles.

Advisors are impotent. We are strong.

Advisors do not vote on vital questions. We must have a vote in every decision which affects the party, black people and this country.

The two Richards, Nixon and Daley, as well as Mao Tse Tung, know that power is of the essence. We know that too. Anything short of our complete sharing of power is a sham and is unacceptable.

Second. Our sharing of power must take place on every political level, from precinct to ward, to county, to state, to Capitol Hill, to presidential cabinet.

Third. We are not concerned with minute tid-bits of political power. We must be accorded the largest share of political power resulting from the following tests:

Our proportionate contribution to the party's vote, or to the defeats that would occur were we to withhold that vote, or the importance of the black question on the American scene. Whichever of these tests yields the greatest amount of political representation, that is what we must have.

Fourth. We shall name our own candidates for public office and our own party and governmental committee members. No political party to which we attach ourselves may any longer pick and choose the Toms and Sallys among us.

Fifth. The political party with which we identify ourselves must work from the bottom up, not the top down.

Before critical national decisions are made, they must be discussed in every nook and cranny of this country, from the tar paper shacks in the Mississippi Delta, to the pine hovels in the Appalachian Hills, from the rank and fetid basement apartments of 47th Street to the barrios of Spanish Harlem.

The 1968 national party conventions made a mockery of the Democratic process. They were drunken carnivals run for the exclusive few. They debauched electoral politics, and shattered the idealistic hopes of youth.

In considering when a political party may lay claim to our support and fidelity, we come now to the sixth and final point. It is by far the most crucial.

Who does the party represent? For whose benefit does it exist? What arouses its indignation? For whom does it have compassion? Who are its allies, and who its enemies?

In short, what does the political party stand for? What is its ideology?

Preoccupation with power, while neglecting ideology, is the prelude to opportunism and betrayal.

This political convention will come to nought, it will be a disservice to the people, if the problems of power are permitted to overshadow the pressing issues of the day and our thoughtful solutions to them.

It is always a delicate balance we must maintain between the two—issues and program on one hand, power on the other. To neglect either is a disaster.

And so let us consider issues and program.

We demand that any party which asks our support acknowledge the inhumanity every black man, woman and child faces in a hundred different ways, each and every day of his existence, up and down the width and breadth of this vast country.

And we further demand that the party pledge, in bold script and deafening tones, the immediate liberation of black people from their long night of relentless indignities.

Poverty in the midst of opulence is madness. We demand employment, amply compensated, for every able man and woman, or else a governmental income which honorably sustains them.

Advanced education is not meant only for the children of the elite. We demand free college with adequate stipends, for every student who will but make the grade.

We would not house animals where many wretched people dwell. We demand, for every family, a place to live which does not affront the eyes nor offend the nostrils.

No sin is greater than the early maiming of a child's intellect and spirit. We demand a healthy system of public education in which our children can grow and flower.

The state of medical care in the country is a national disgrace. We demand the finest medical and hospital care for every human being, and the absence of the ability to pay should not influence the quality of care.

We demand the eradication of heroin from the ghetto, now eating away the vitals of black youth. White society would never tolerate it in such epidemic proportions in suburbia.

No political party which represents the interests of America's giant corporations, rather than the urgent needs of the people, may enlist black political power in its support.

These huge corporations, which dominate every facet of American existence, now proudly hasten to assure us that they are involved.

Oh, they are involved, alright!

They are involved in exploiting the men and women who work for them, exhausting them with speed ups, cruelly tossing them into the trash heap of retirement, and discriminating against blacks, Latin Americans and women as they hire and promote.

Yes, the corporations surely are involved!

They're involved ever so eagerly in gouging the consumer, exacting enormous profits from him, threatening his health and endangering his life with products both inferior and unsafe.

Behold, as well, the massive corporate involvement as they darken the skies, and poison the waters beyond redemption.

Witness their incredible underpayment of the local property tax, unconscionably shifting it to the little man, already buckling under a mountain of other burdens.

Yes, the corporations are mightily involved. Like dinosaurs, they gobble up the legislatures, both state and national. What does it matter that they destroy or mutilate legislation salutary to the people?

And if a mammoth corporation like I.T.T. wants justice, it is there on sale at the department of justice for a mere four-hundred thousand dollars. With equal ease, a bankrupt Lockheed can borrow two-hundred and fifty million dollars with government guarantee. Listen, black business man, try that out on your local small business administration.

Add it all up, and we most certainly agree with the corporations. They really are involved!

Hereafter, every political party must make up its mind. It cannot represent both the corporations and the people. As the party chooses, so shall we then choose the party.

Finally, we shall shun, like the plague, any political party which does not demand, in unmistakable terms, the immediate return to these shores, of every single American boy from those distant southeast Asian lands.

This horrible war, the ugliest page in our foreign history, could never have taken place without the overwhelming complicity of both political parties.

And it could not continue for another day without that same complicity.

That complicity has slaughtered and maimed over 360,000 American youth and millions of Indochinese, who, I need not remind you, are people of color; and people of color everywhere, no matter where they live, are our brothers and sisters.

And to what end this loathsome carnage? To prop up a cruel and corrupt tyranny in South Vietnam and to keep the mass of poor and aspiring peasants in their place. We black people know that syndrome all too well.

Our participation in that atrocious war is not an unfortunate mistake on the part of the American ruling class. Rather, it is part and parcel of an economic policy to make the world safe for American corporate penetration and to fill the coffers of the corporate treasuries.

That policy is designed to hold the Third World in a state of abject peonage and subjection.

Accordingly, we have shored up one quasi-fascist regime after another. Greece in 1947 and the Greek junta today; Chiang Kai-shek driven out of China by his own people in humiliating defeat, now the tyrant of Taiwan with billions of our assistance; Perón of Argentina in 1946; Syngman Rhee in South Korea in 1950; Batista in Cuba in 1952; and fresh from the Riviera, the playboy Diem in Vietnam in 1954. In each and every instance we fortified the forces of fascist repression in these unhappy lands.

We were also adept, through the CIA, at overthrowing governmentals friendly to their people; Dr. Mohammed Mossadegh of Iran in 1953, because he dared to nationalize his country's oil; Arbenz of Guatemala in 1954 because he wanted to give land to his people thereby endangering the swollen profits of United Fruit Company which extorted eight million stems of bananas a year from that country; and Premier Patrice Lumumba of the Congo, butchered because he refused to orbit within the American sphere.

The Kennedy and Johnson administrations supported seven military coups which overthrew constitutional governments in Latin America: El Salvador, Argentina, Peru, Guatemala, Ecuador, the Dominican Republic and Honduras.

Finally, we shall never forgive the massive support that a racist American government, and rapacious American corporations, have extended to the white barbarians who reign in the Union of South Africa, Angola, Rhodesia, and Mozambique.

You may be sure that the 436 million dollars our government just gave Portugal, in violation of the United Nations' embargo, will be fully used against our brothers in the guerrilla movement in Mozambique and Angola.

No self-respecting Afro-American can, without a sense of profound betrayal, offer one iota of further support to any political party which does not condemn American foreign policy with abhorrence, and pledge to end our savage repression of the struggling peoples of the third world.

This convention signals the end of hip pocket politics. We ain't in nobody's hip pocket no more!

We are through with any political party, and many of us, with any political system which is not irrevocably committed to our first principles, pursued in tenacious action: The liberation of black people at home and the end of exploitation abroad.

We say to the two American political parties: this is their last clear chance: they have had too many already.

These are not idle threats. Only senile fools would think them so.

The choice is theirs.

To ignore our demands is to will the consequences.

Those of us already disenchanted with the political system could conceivably turn to fearsome tactics, shattering the quiet routine of daily life.

Those of us still committed to a political solution may then cross the Rubicon and form a third party political movement.

I, for one, am willing to give the two major political parties one more chance in the year 1972. But if they fail us, a not unlikely prospect, we must then seriously probe the possibility of a third party movement in this country.

We have broken out of the two-party mold before. Except this time the rupture may well be permanent.

Free soil party . . . Virginia readjusters . . . Greenbackers and populists . . . blacks tried them all.

In our search for political impact we have held political conventions before. This is not the first time blacks have assembled to chart their political future.

1855, 1871, 1872 . . . these were years in which national black political conventions met in New York, Columbia, South Carolina and New Orleans.

We have even formed all-black parties. The great Frederick Douglass, despairing of justice from the Republican party, chaired the New York State Suffrage Association—a statewide black political party—which emerged in 1855. Pennsylvania blacks also disgusted with the regular Republicans, broke away in 1883 and formed the Colored Independent Party.

The Mississippi Freedom Democratic Party electrified the nation with its appearance at the 1964 Democratic National Convention.

Although the machinations of Johnson and Humphrey prevented the Freedom Democrats from unseating the regular Mississippi delegation, their demands sounded the death knell for future lily-white convention delegations.

The all Black Lowndes County Freedom Organization in Alabama, born in the travail of the 1960's southern freedom movement, raised the consciousness of poor black people by involving them politically.

Yes, we've looked beyond Republican and Democrat in our search for a political home . . . and many of our greatest leaders sick of the trickery of the established political parties, W. E. B. Du Bois, Paul Robeson, Benjamin Davis, Charlotta Bass, Charles Howard, Bill Patterson, and our own valiant sister, Angela, all, all looked outside the established parties to achieve their aspirations for their people.

And when, if they leave us no choice—and if we form a third

political movement, we shall take with us Chicanos, Puerto Ricans, Indians, Orientals, a wonderful kaleidoscope of colors.

And that is not all.

We shall also take with us the best of white America. We shall take with us many a white youth nauseated by the corrupt values rotting the innards of this society; many a white intellectual, revolted by the mendacity of the ruling ideology; many of the white poor, who have nothing to lose but the poverty which binds them; many a white ex-G.I. who dares to say "never again"; yes, and many of the white working class, too; we don't for a moment accept the movie character "Joe," or his television counterpart, "Bunker," as the prototype of the white man with the blue collar.

The sixties were an exciting decade: loaded with ferment, freedom rides, sit-ins, marches. It was all here—from the strains of "We Shall Overcome," sung warmly with arms linked—to the penetrating cries of black power, with fists raised.

We buried some wonderful brothers and sisters who strode, like giants, across the decade, sweeping away injustice before them.

And for each murdered martyr, a half-million black soldiers took his place.

The '70's will be the decade of an independent black political thrust.

Its destiny will depend on us.

How shall we respond?

Will we walk in unity or disperse in a thousand different directions?

Will we stand for principle or settle for a mess of pottage?

Will we act like free black men or timid shivering chattels?

Will we do what must be done?

These are the questions confronting this convention. And we— only we—can answer them.

History will be our judge.

10. "National Black Political Agenda. The Gary Declaration: Black Politics at the Crossroads"

After vigorous debate and deliberations, the delegates at the Gary convention ratified a comprehensive agenda. With provisions addressed to "black people" and to those black men and women holding or seeking to run for political office, the agenda put forth numerous initiatives, strategies, and tactics on behalf of increased political and economic empowerment, increased control over community institutions, and increased clout for African-Americans in national policy-making decisions and international developments. This excerpt from that fifty-five-page document, released to the public on May 19, 1972, the anniversary of Malcolm X's birth, includes the original call to the conference.

INTRODUCTION

The Black Agenda is addressed primarily to Black people in America. It rises naturally out of the bloody decades and centuries of our people's struggle on these shores. It flows from the most recent surgings of our own cultural and political consciousness. It is our attempt to define some of the essential changes which must take place in this land as we and our children move to self-determination and true independence.

The Black Agenda assumes that no truly basic change for our benefit takes place in Black or white America unless we Black people organize to initiate that change. It assumes that we must have some essential agreement on overall goals, even though we may differ on many specific strategies.

Therefore, this is an initial statement of goals and directions for our own generation, some first definitions of crucial issues around which Black people must organize and move in 1972 and beyond. Anyone who claims to be serious about the survival and liberation of Black people must be serious about the implementation of the Black Agenda.

What Time Is It?

We come to Gary in an hour of great crisis and tremendous promise for Black America. While the white nation hovers on the brink of chaos, while its politicians offer no hope of real change, we stand on the edge of history and are faced with an amazing and frightening choice: We may choose in 1972 to slip back into the decadent white politics of American life, or we may press forward, moving relentlessly from Gary to the creation of our own Black life. The choice is large, but the time is very short.

Let there be no mistake. We come to Gary in a time of unrelieved crisis for our people. From every rural community in Alabama to the high-rise compounds of Chicago, we bring to this Convention the agonies of the masses of our people. From the sprawling Black cities of Watts and Nairobi in the West to the decay of Harlem and Roxbury in the East, the testimony we bear is the same. We are the witnesses to social disaster.

Our cities are crime-haunted dying grounds. Huge sectors of our youth—and countless others—face permanent unemployment. Those of us who work find our paychecks able to purchase less and less. Neither the courts nor the prisons contribute to anything resembling justice or reformation. The schools are unable—or unwilling—to educate our children for the real world of our struggles. Meanwhile, the officially approved epidemic of drugs threatens to wipe out the minds and strength of our best young warriors.

Economic, cultural, and spiritual depression stalk Black America, and the price for survival often appears to be more than we are able to pay. On every side, in every area of our lives, the American institutions in which we have placed our trust are unable to cope with the crises they have created by their single-minded dedication to profits for some and white supremacy above all.

Beyond These Shores

And beyond these shores there is more of the same. For while we are pressed down under all the dying weight of a bloated, inwardly decaying white civilization, many of our brothers in Africa and the rest of the Third World have fallen prey to the same powers of exploitation and deceit. Wherever America faces the unorganized, politically powerless forces of the non-white world, its goal is domination by any means necessary—as if to hide from itself the crumbling of its own systems of life and work.

But Americans cannot hide. They can run to China and the moon and to the edges of consciousness, but they cannot hide. The crises we face as Black people are the crises of the entire society. They go deep, to the very bones and marrow, to the essential nature of America's economic, political, and cultural systems. They are the natural end-product of a society built on the twin foundations of white racism and white capitalism.

So, let it be clear to us now: The desperation of our people, the agonies of our cities, the desolation of our countryside, the pollution of the air and the water—these things will not be significantly affected by new faces in the old places in Washington, D.C. This is the truth we must face here in Gary if we are to join our people everywhere in the movement forward toward liberation.

WHITE REALITIES, BLACK CHOICE

A Black political convention, indeed all truly Black politics must begin from this truth: *The American system does not work for the masses of our people, and it cannot be made to work without radical fundamental change.* (Indeed, this system does not really work in favor of the humanity of anyone in America.)

In light of such realities, we come to Gary and are confronted with a choice. Will we believe the truth that history presses into our face—or will we, too, try to hide? Will the small favors some of us have received blind us to the larger sufferings of our people, or open our eyes to the testimony of our history in America?

For more than a century we have followed the path of political dependence on white men and their systems. From the Liberty Party in the decades before the Civil War to the Republican Party of Abraham Lincoln, we trusted in white men and white politics as our deliverers. Sixty years ago, W. E. B. Du Bois said he would give the Democrats their "last chance" to prove their sincere commitment to equality for Black people—and he was given white riots and official segregation in peace and in war.

Nevertheless, some twenty years later we became Democrats in the name of Franklin Roosevelt, then supported his successor Harry Truman, and even tried a "non-partisan" Republican General of the Army named Eisenhower. We were wooed like many others by the superficial liberalism of John F. Kennedy and the make-believe populism of Lyndon Johnson. Let there be no more of that.

BOTH PARTIES HAVE BETRAYED US

Here at Gary, let us never forget that while the times and the names and the parties have continually changed, one truth has faced us insistently, never changing: Both parties have betrayed us whenever their interests conflicted with ours (which was most of the time), and whenever our forces were unorganized and dependent, quiescent and compliant. Nor should this be surprising, for by now we must know that the American political system, like all other white institutions in America, was designed to operate for the benefit of the white race: It was never meant to do anything else.

That is the truth that we must face at Gary. If white "liberalism" could have solved our problems, then Lincoln and Roosevelt and Kennedy would have done so. But they did not solve ours nor the rest of the nation's. If America's problems could have been solved by forceful, politically skilled and aggressive individuals, then Lyndon Johnson would have retained the presidency. If the true "American Way" of unbridled monopoly capitalism, combined with a ruthless military imperialism could do it, then Nixon would not be running around the world, or making speeches comparing his nation's decadence to that of Greece and Rome.

If we have never faced it before, let us face it at Gary: The profound crisis of Black people and the disaster of America are not simply caused by men nor will they be solved by men alone. These crises are the crises of basically flawed economics and politics, and of cultural degradation. None of the Democratic candidates and none of the Republican candidates—regardless of their vague promises to us or to their white constituencies—can solve our problems or the problems of this country without radically changing the systems by which it operates.

THE POLITICS OF SOCIAL TRANSFORMATION

So, we come to Gary confronted with a choice. But it is not the old convention question of which candidate shall we support, the pointless question of who is to preside over a decaying and unsalvageable system. No, if we come to Gary out of the realities of the Black communities of this land, then the only real choice for us is whether or not we will live by the truth we know, whether we will move to organize independently, move to struggle for fundamental transformation, for the creation of new directions, towards a concern for the life and the meaning of Man. Social transformation or social destruction, those are our only real choices.

If we have come to Gary on behalf of our people in America, in the rest of this hemisphere, and in the Homeland—if we have come for our own best ambitions—then a new Black Politics must come to birth. If we are serious, the Black Politics of Gary must accept major responsibility for creating both the atmosphere and the program for fundamental, far-ranging change in America. Such responsibility is ours because it is our people who are most deeply hurt and ravaged by the present systems of society. That responsibility for leading the change is ours because we live in a society where few other men really believe in the responsibility of a truly humane society for anyone anywhere.

WE ARE THE VANGUARD

The challenge is thrown to us here in Gary. It is the challenge to consolidate and organize our own Black role as the vanguard in the struggle for a new society. To accept that challenge is to move independent Black politics. There can be no equivocation on that issue. History leaves us no other choice. White politics has not and cannot bring the changes we need.

We come to Gary and are faced with a challenge. The challenge is to transform ourselves from favor-seeking vassals and loud-talking, "militant" pawns, and to take up the role that the organized masses of our people have attempted to play ever since we came to these shores: That of harbingers of true justice and humanity, leaders in the struggle for liberation.

A major part of the challenge we must accept is that of redefining the functions and operations of all levels of American government, for the existing governing structures—from Washington to the smallest county—are obsolescent. That is part of the reason why nothing works and why corruption rages throughout public life. For white politics seeks not to serve but to dominate and manipulate.

We will have joined the true movement of history if at Gary we grasp the opportunity to press Man forward as the first consid-eration of politics. Here at Gary we are faithful to the best hopes of our fathers and our people if we move for nothing less than a politics which places community before individualism, love before sexual exploitation, a living environment before profits, peace before war, justice before unjust "order," and morality before expediency.

This is the society we need, but we delude ourselves here at Gary if we think that change can be achieved without organizing the power, the determined national Black power, which is neces-sary to insist upon such change, to create such change, to seize change.

Towards a Black Agenda

So when we turn to a Black Agenda for the seventies, we move in the truth of history, in the reality of the moment. We move recognizing that no one else is going to represent our interests but ourselves. *The society we seek cannot come unless Black people organize to advance its coming.* We lift up a Black Agenda recognizing that white America moves towards the abyss created by its own racist arrogance, misplaced priorities, rampant materialism, and ethical bankruptcy. Therefore, we are certain that the Agenda we now press for in Gary is not only for the future of Black humanity, but is probably the only way the rest of America can save itself from the harvest of its criminal past.

So, Brothers and Sisters of our developing Black nation, we now stand at Gary as people whose time has come. From every corner of Black America, from all liberation movements of the Third World, from the graves of our fathers and the coming world of our children, we are faced with a challenge and a call: Though the moment is perilous we must not despair. We must seize the time, for the time is ours.

We begin here and now in Gary. We begin with an independent Black political movement, an independent Black Political Agenda, an independent Black spirit. Nothing less will do. We must build for our people. We must build for our world. We stand on the edge of history. We cannot turn back.

To those who say that such an Agenda is "visionary," "utopian," and "impossible," we say that the keepers of conventional white politics have always viewed our situation and our real needs as beyond the realm of their wildest imaginations. At every critical moment of our struggle in America we have had to press relentlessly against the limits of the "realistic" to create new realities for the life of our people.

This is our challenge at Gary and beyond, for a new Black politics demands new vision, new hope and new definitions of the possible. Our time has come. These things are necessary. All things are possible.

CHAPTER TWELVE

A NATION OF LAW?
(1968–1971)

Introduction by Gerald Gill

The years from 1968 to 1971 were marked by growing polarization among American citizens. The demands for racial equality and voting rights that had characterized earlier freedom movement campaigns and the ongoing calls for racial solidarity and community empowerment of the late 1960s had made a growing number of white Americans, both inside and outside of government, fearful about the forms and prospects of future developments in race relations. Thus, a racial backlash began to develop, partially manifested in the Goldwater presidential campaign in 1964 and nurtured more fully in the Wallace and Nixon campaigns of 1968. Exploiting code words such as "law and order," Richard Nixon sought to gain support from those who wished to see more radical forms of dissent and dissatisfaction, whether in the forms of urban rebellions or in the appearance of more militant groups, quelled. Yet, in spite of a "changing mood," activists persevered and often took on new causes. Impressed by the writings of Malcolm X and Eldridge Cleaver and by a growing number of books, essays, and poems written by black men in state and federal prisons, some activists took on the cause of prisoners' rights. Arguing that many of those imprisoned were "political prisoners," individuals unjustly sentenced by a capitalistic political and legal system inherently biased against African-Americans, many activists across the country rallied in defense of those incarcerated.

While the legislative and executive branches of the federal government came to be belated supporters of civil rights legislation, other federal agencies, particularly the Federal Bureau of Investigation, were noted more for their inaction and overt hostility toward groups and individuals involved in freedom movement activities and in more radical initiatives on behalf of community empowerment. While the FBI had monitored the activities of an untold number of black leaders and spokespersons in the 1930s, 1940s, and early 1950s, once freedom movement activities intensified after 1960, the FBI increased its surveillance operations to include the monitoring of countless spokespersons and local organizers and nearly every organization from the more moderate to the more militant. In the spring of 1968, following the urging of Lyndon Johnson, the FBI expanded the scope of its counterintelligence program (known as COINTELPRO) to include alleged "Black Nationalist-Hate Groups." According to memos sent to FBI field offices across the country, local agents were to disrupt the development of any sort of coalition among "militant black nationalist groups," to prevent the emergence of a "messiah" who could "unify and electrify the militant black nationalist movement," and to prevent those organizations from winning any additional support and legitimacy from their followers, from the "responsible Negro community," and from whites.

Many of the FBI's efforts under the expanded COINTELPRO operation were directed against the Black Panther Party, particularly following the party's organizing successes in several urban centers in 1967–1968. In late 1968, Hoover called upon local agents "to exploit all avenues of creating . . . dissension within the ranks of the BPP" and called upon field offices to develop and send to bureau headquarters "imaginative and hard-hitting counterintelligence measures aimed at crippling the BPP." The Chicago branch of the party, headed by the charismatic and effective organizer Fred Hampton, was a prime target of the FBI. Local agents, fearing a possible alliance between the Black Panther Party and the Blackstone Rangers (a local gang), sought through manipulative letters to inflame antagonisms between the two groups. Local agents also sought to infiltrate the party's ranks through the use of informants and agent provocateurs. Again following the dictates of Hoover, agents in Chicago tried to destroy the Panthers' free breakfast program, to disrupt their liberation school, and to interrupt the distribution and selling of the party's newspaper. In addition, members of the Chicago police force who were in close contact with the local FBI office raided the Panthers' headquarters on several occasions.

In November of 1969 informant William O'Neal was asked to provide, and later delivered to his FBI contacts, a sketch of Hampton's apartment. Over the next two weeks, members of the Chicago police force and the state attorney general's office, provided with the apartment's floor plans, met to plan a raid of Hampton's apartment on the pretext of looking for "illegal weapons." In the early morning hours of December 4, 1969, fourteen Chicago police officers staged a raid on the apartment, killing Hampton and Mark Clark, of the Peoria branch of the Black Panthers, and wounding four other party members.

Initially, law enforcement officials contended that the police had fired in self-defense. However, independent investigations by representatives from the local news media pointed to numerous discrepancies in the "official" accounts. Still, an internal investigation by Chicago Police, the Cook County Coroner's office inquest, and grand jury investigations, all marked by perjury, cover-up, and obstruction of justice, issued no indictments for murder against any of the officers involved. Only after a long and trying appeal in federal court were the deaths and injuries of the Black Panther Party members partially resolved as a financial settlement of $1.85 million was awarded to the survivors of the attack and to the families of Hampton and Clark.

The murders of Hampton and Clark whetted further the arguments of radical and moderate activists alike against the tactics of police forces in what many viewed as the "Amerikan" police state. Their critiques also carried over to the American criminal justice system, a system, they argued, that falsely imprisoned and brutally dehumanized black male defendants. Spurred by the eloquent letters written by George Jackson, incarcerated at California's Soledad State Prison, activists and prisoners alike began to press for changes in the procedures and operations of the American criminal justice and penal systems.

In Attica State Prison in upstate New York, groups of inmates sought changes in their work conditions, their treatment, and in basic respect for their privacy and personhood. Their protests, summarized in a July 1971 manifesto to the commissioner of the state corrections system and to the governor, were acknowledged by talk of some future changes. On September 9, 1971, following a day of confrontation between several of the corrections officers and inmates, inmates from one wing of the prison seized control of that area. By late morning inmates had taken control of most of the facility and had taken approximately forty prison guards as hostages. The issuance of a first set of demands, which included the sending in of outside observers to help in the negotiations between correction system officials and the inmates, led to the beginning of an increasingly tense standoff at the prison.

While the observers, after consulting with the inmates, hammered out a list of twenty-eight points the commissioner said he would accept, Governor Nelson Rockefeller refused to grant blanket amnesty to the inmates, especially after one of the guards who had been held hostage and released died of wounds he suffered during the initial takeover. Rockefeller then ordered New York state troopers to storm the prison, and in the ensuing action thirty-nine inmates and nine of the hostages were killed by the gunfire of the troopers.

The federal and local crackdown on the Black Panther Party and the brutal putting down of the Attica Prison takeover combined to have a chilling impact on more radical forms of dissent. Yet these actions also led to the growing criticism of law enforcement agencies, criticisms voiced by moderate as well as more radical spokespersons. Increasingly, their criticisms pointed to the lack of respect for the constitutional rights that many law enforcement and political officials held for those holding views deemed radical or unpopular. While these crackdowns ostensibly were done to preserve "law and order," they contributed to the growing loss of trust and confidence that many were expressing in the honesty and efficacy of government at all levels.

1. "Fred Speaks"

By late 1968 and early 1969, twenty-one-year-old Fred Hampton, the charismatic leader of the Chicago chapter of the Black Panther Party, was developing a local and national reputation as an artful proponent of the party's program. In these excerpts from several of Hampton's speeches, he expounds upon the Party's call for armed revolutionary struggle, its setting up of free breakfast programs, and his overarching commitment the the "struggle for the people."

A lot of people get the word revolution mixed up and they think revolution's a bad word. Revolution is nothing but like having a sore on your body and then you put something on that sore to cure that infection. I'm telling you that we're living in a sick society. We're involved in a society that produces ADC victims. We're involved in a society that produces criminals, thieves and robbers and rapers. Whenever you are in a society like that, that is a sick society.

. . . We're gonna organize and dedicate ourselves to revolutionary political power and teach ourselves the specific needs of resisting the power structure, arm ourselves, and we're gonna fight reactionary pigs with international proletarian revolution. That's what it has to be. The people have to have the power—it belongs to the people.

. . . Unless people show us through their social practice that they relate to the struggle in Babylon, that means that they're not internationalists, that means that they're not revolutionaries. And when you're marchin' on this cruel war in Washington, all you radicals . . . we need to have some moratoriums on Babylon. We need to have some moratoriums on the Black community in Babylon and all oppressed communities in Babylon.

. . . We have to understand very clearly that there's a man in our community called a capitalist. Sometimes he's Black and sometimes he's white. But that man has to be driven out of our community because anybody who comes into the community to make profit off of people by exploiting them can be defined as a capitalist.

Any program that's brought into our community should be analyzed by the people of that community. It should be analyzed to see that it meets the relevant needs of that community.

. . . That's what the Breakfast for Children Program is. A lot of people think it's charity. But what does it do? It takes people from a stage to a stage to another stage. Any program that's revolutionary is an advancing program. Revolution is change.

. . . We say that the Breakfast for Children Program is a socialistic program. It teaches the people basically that—by practice. We thought up and let them practice that theory and inspect that theory. What's more important?

. . . And a woman said, "I don't know if I like communism, and I don't know if I like socialism. But I know that the Breakfast for Children Program feeds my kids. And if you put your hands on that Breakfast for Children Program . . ."

. . . You know, a lot of people have hang-ups with the Party because the Party talks about a class struggle. . . . We say primarily that the priority of this struggle is class. That Marx and Lenin and Che Guevara and Mao Tse-tung and anybody else that has ever said or knew or practiced anything about revolution always said that a revolution is a class struggle. It was one class—the oppressed, and that other class—the oppressor. And it's got to be a universal fact. Those that don't admit to that are those that don't want to get involved in a revolution, because they know as long as they're dealing with a race thing, they'll never be involved in a revolution.

. . . We never negated the fact that there was racism in America, but we said that the by-product, what comes off of capitalism, that happens to be racism . . . that capitalism comes first and next is racism. That when they brought slaves over here, it was to make money. So first the idea came that we want to make money, then the slaves came in order to make that money. That means, through historical fact, that racism had to come from capitalism. It had to be capitalism first and racism was a by-product of that.

. . . We may be in the minority, but this minority is gonna keep on shouting loud and clear: We're not gonna fight fire with fire, we're gonna fight fire with water. We're not gonna fight racism with racism, we're gonna fight racism with solidarity. We're not gonna fight capitalism with Black capitalism . . . we're gonna fight capitalism with socialism.

. . . We know that Black people are most oppressed. And if we didn't know that, then why in the hell would we be running around talking about the Black liberation struggle has to be the vanguard for all liberation struggles?

———————

Any theory you got, practice it. And when you practice it, you make some mistakes. When you make a mistake, you correct that theory, and then it will be corrected theory that will be able to be applied and used in any situation. That's what we've got to be able to do.

. . . A lot of us read and read and read, but we don't get any practice. We have a lot of knowledge in our heads, but we've never practiced it; and made any mistakes and corrected those mistakes so that we will be able to do something properly. So we come up with, like we say, more degrees than a thermometer but we are not able to walk across the street and chew gum at the same time. Because we have all that knowledge but it's never been exercised, it's never been practiced. We never tested it with what's really happening. We call it testing it with objective reality. You might have any kind of thought in your mind, but you've got to test it with what's out there. You see what I mean?

. . . The only way that anybody can tell you the taste of a pear is if he himself has tasted it. That's the only way. That's objective reality. That's what the Black Panther Party deals with. We're not into metaphysics, we're not idealists, we're dialectical materialists. And we deal with what reality is, whether we like it or not. A lot of people can't relate to that because everything they do is gauged by the way they like things to be. We say that's incorrect. You look and see how things are, and then you deal with that.

. . . We some Marxist-Leninist cussin' niggers. And we gonna continue to cuss, goddammit. 'Cause that's what we relate to. That's what's happening in Babylon. That's objective reality.

. . . You're dealing in subjectivity, because you're not testing it with objective reality. And what's wrong is that you don't go test it. Because if you test it, you'll get objective. Because as soon as you walk out there, a whole lot of objective reality will vamp down upon your ass.

―――――――

The community had a problem out there in California. There was an intersection where a lot of people were getting killed. . . . Let me tell you what Huey P. Newton did. Huey Newton went and got Bobby Seale, the Chairman of the Black Panther Party on a national level. Bobby Seale got his 9mm, that's a pistol. Huey P. Newton got his shotgun and got some stop signs and got a hammer. Went down to the intersection, gave his shotgun to Bobby, and Bobby had his 9mm. He said, "You hold this shotgun; anybody mess with us, blow their brains out." He put those stop signs up. There were no more accidents, no more problem.

. . . And I say anybody that comes into our community and sets up any type of situation that does not meet the needs of the masses, then I, Chairman Fred of the Black Panther Party, say that I'll take that nigger by his turtleneck and beat him to death with a Black Panther Newspaper! And you could kill him with the paper, because that paper has an ideology and if you don't read it you oughta read it.

. . . You don't want to get that Africanized, because as soon as you have to dress like somebody from Angola or Mozambique, then after you put on whatever you put on, and it can be anything from rags to something from Saks Fifth Avenue, you got to put on some bandoliers and some AR-15's and some 38's; you've got to put on some Smith and Wessons and some Colt 45's, because that's what they're wearin' in Angola and that's what they're wearin' in Mozambique.

. . . Anybody ever hear about Gloves on the South Side of Chicago? He's not white. Did you think [Gang Intelligence Unit Chief] Buckney's white? Buckney, who's taking all of your little brothers and all of your little sisters, and all of your little nephews, and he's gonna continue to take 'em. And if you don't do anything, he's gonna take your sons and your daughters. . . . We don't hear nobody running around talking about "I'm Benedict Arnold, III." Because Benedict Arnold's children don't want to talk about that they are his children. You hear people talking about they might be Patrick Henry's children, people that stood up and said, "Give me liberty or give me death." Or Paul Revere's cousin. Paul Revere said, "Get your guns, the British are coming." The British were the police.

. . . We say that we need some guns. There's nothing wrong with the guns in our community, there's just been a misdirection of guns in our community. For some reason or another, the pigs have all the guns, so all we have to do is equally distribute them. So if you see one that has a gun and you don't have one, then when you leave you should have one. That way we'll be able to deal with things right. I remember looking at TV and found that not only did the pigs not brutalize the people in western days, they had to hire bounty hunters to go arrest them because they had guns. Now they brutalize without even arresting them. They shoot somebody with no intention of arresting them. We need some guns. We need some guns. We need some guns. We need some force.

You can jail a revolutionary, but you can't jail the revolution. You can lock up a freedom fighter like Huey P. Newton, but you can't lock up freedom fighting. . . . Because if you do, you come up with answers that don't answer, explanations that don't explain, conclusions that don't conclude.

If you think about me and you think about me, niggers, and you ain't gonna do no revolutionary act, then forget about me. I don't want myself on your mind if you're not going to work for the people.

Like I always said, if you're asked to make a commitment at the age of 20, and you say I don't want to make no commitment only because of the simple reason that I'm too young to die, I want to live a little bit longer. What you did is . . . you're dead already.

You have to understand that people have to pay the price for peace. You dare to struggle, you dare to win. If you dare not struggle, then goddammit you don't deserve to win. Let me say to you peace if you're willing to fight for it.

Let me say in the spirit of liberation—I been gone for a little while, at least my body's been gone for a little while. But I'm back now, and I believe I'm back to stay.

I believe I'm going to do my job. I believe I was born not to die in a car wreck. I don't believe I'm going to die in a car wreck. I don't believe I going to die slipping on a piece of ice. I don't believe I going to die because I have a bad heart. I don't believe I'm going to die because I have lung cancer.

I believe I'm going to be able to die doing the things I was born for. I believe I'm going to die high off the people. I believe I'm going to die a revolutionary in the international revolutionary proletarian struggle. I hope each one of you will be able to die [in] the international revolutionary proletarian struggle, or you'll be able to live in it. And I think that struggle's going to come.

Why don't you live for the people.

Why don't you struggle for the people.

Why don't you die for the people.

2. Interview with Akua Njere (Deborah Johnson)

In this interview, Akua Njere (formerly Deborah Johnson) recalls her involvement with the Chicago chapter of the Black Panther Party. She is a survivor of the December 4, 1969, raid. At the time of her fiancé Fred Hampton's death, she was carrying his baby and subsequently gave birth to Fred Hampton, Jr. Njere's recollections as a female rank-and-file member of the party are especially useful, as she highlights local work assignments and to some degree gender relations within the Black Panther Party. The interview from which these excerpts are taken was published as a special supplement to the June 1990 issue of Burning Spear, *a publication of the African People's Socialist Party, Oakland, California.*

[QUESTION: What was your introduction to the Black Panther Party?]

AKUA NJERE: After high school I went to a city college, Wilson Junior College. At one point my brother brought a flyer home that said "Black Panthers Are Here." It had a panther on an 8½ × 11 white sheet of paper. The panther appeared to be walking across the page. I said, "Wow, I need to check this out and see what this is about."

In the meantime there was some organizing at my school. The Panthers were taking over some classes at that school because they felt that the education that we were given was not exposing the true nature of this decadent American society. It was not an education that allowed Africans to survive in this country. It did not educate us as to our true role in history. They had taken over these classes and there was interest there.

At some point I saw Fred Hampton on TV. It was a Ronnie Barrett talk show. Fred Hampton and some other Panthers were on the television show and Fred Hampton had taken it over. He decided what questions he would answer, how the interview would go, everything.

I sat there watching this brother. I sat on the edge of my seat because he went straight through the Party's 10 point program and platform, saying what our needs are and what our demands were. The thing that really impressed me about him was his sincerity, his dedication to his beliefs. In that interview I believed what the brother was saying, his honesty.

I knew that this was not a person who had read a lot of books, who had been involved in just developing a lot of theory. He was a brother who was involved in social practice. He stood on what his beliefs were and he would live, fight and die for those beliefs. . . .

It was like Fred Hampton was sitting in my living room talking to me. I talked to some other people and they got the same feeling. It was that kind of charisma that came across. You didn't have to be face to face.

Fred Hampton and a number of Panthers came over to speak at the college that I was attending. I tried to get some people to go with me, but they wouldn't. I was late getting there and the room was packed. So I got up to the front, right in Fred's face and he was talking. I was sitting there on the edge of my seat.

He did a long discussion about how people are being brutalized in the community, how African people are starving, our children are going to school hungry and are expected to learn, and we needed medical attention, and the government was murdering us at every turn.

Everything he said was true and he wasn't just talking, he was documenting, he was bringing us to the realization that everything he said was true. I just couldn't absorb it all. It was just so much. . . .

We went up to the cafeteria to meet. At that time there were only about three lunchroom tables of African people at the school.

At that time I was into doing a lot of poetry and short stories and stuff. My poetry was basically about the oppression the white government was putting on African people.

I had my little book and I went up to Fred and introduced myself. When I asked him what he thought about poetry, he said he really didn't like it. So I hid my book behind my back and said, "Me either Brother." That was the end of my writings.

We talked and he said, "Sister, you need to come to the Black Panther office. We're trying to feed children," and so on and so forth. I was really excited about it. I started going to the office and the rest is history—I have a 20-year-old son.

Q: Who were the people that the Black Panthers organized?

A.N.: Let me say this about the beauty of the work that Fred Hampton did. He was able to speak to every element of the oppressed community.

We had a number of struggles with people who felt that the workers as they existed in this country would be those who would bring about the revolution and what was labeled as the lumpen proletariat were considered the scum of the Earth. The lumpen proletariat were the people in the streets who survived by their wits, the chronically unemployed, the hustlers, the pimps, the alleged lowest element of the community.

In the Black Panther Party, we read everything, and Fred Hampton did too. We were attempting to provide socialism in the community, to lead to communism. But we didn't take the doctrines of Marx and Engels just across the board.

Fred Hampton knew that he could organize anybody. He talked to the brothers and sisters on the street. He talked to those in the classroom. He talked to those in the factories. He talked to those who were in business. He went to the churches. He organized and attempted to work with every element of our communities.

Fred Hampton was the originator of the concept of the Rainbow Coalition. He was the first person to come up with that concept in 1969. That was an effort to educate and politicize other poor and oppressed people throughout this world. He worked with and attempted to politicize the Young Patriots organization, which was a group of Appalachian whites in the near north area of Chicago, politicizing them and organizing them to recognize the leadership of the Black Revolution, the vanguard party, the Black Panther Party, and to work in their communities against this huge monster we had to deal with which is racism.

It was not their role to come in our community and dictate how our struggle should be waged. It was their obligation, their responsibility, to deal with racism with their brothers and sisters. So he politicized this group and had them working to organize breakfast programs and other programs and educational programs in their communities.

He also worked with the Young Lords organization, which at one point was a Puerto Rican gang. He was politicizing this group and having them recognize who the enemy really was. He had them recognizing that we are separated by design, that there are common issues that we can come together and organize on because we have a common oppressor.

Q: . . . How would you sum up your own work, how people responded to the Black Panthers?

A.N.: Initially, a number of people in the community bought what was fed to them every day by the print and electronic media. People were fearful of us because they were told that we were a gang. In some cases they were told that all we wanted to do was kill a pig every week and that we had no program.

The Black Panther Party began to go out in the community from day one. We talked to residents of the community to see what issues they were concerned about that affected their survival. We did not ask them to fill out questionnaires.

We started survival programs. We started breakfast programs. We started feeding the children in the community without asking how many children you got and how many different daddies of children you got or if you're getting an aid check. Those things were not important to us and we did not say we had to wait for federal funds. As a matter of fact we could not accept any federal funds at all because we felt that an enemy that was trying to destroy us would not give federal funds to a group that had no vested interest in that enemy's survival. . . .

We went out to the community and we found out that there was a disease called sickle cell anemia that very few people had heard of and that primarily affected Africans. That's why we hadn't heard of it: nobody cared about things that affected us, that were killing us and that we were dying from.

The Black Panther Party organized around these issues. The Black Panther Party was the first organization to do sickle cell testing. Following that a number of organizations started getting funds for testing and research.

We believe that the community learned. You can't just give them a bunch of free stuff. We had to educate and politicize the community. We knew that people didn't have an understanding of socialism or communism and that they might say they're against that, but people basically thought that children had a right to be fed and learn on a full stomach. . . .

We got doctors. We politicized the doctors and we let them know that public health is a priority over hospital wealth. We said it shouldn't be a question of how much insurance a person had or whether or not they had insurance or the money to pay. If people are sick and dying, then people have a right to treatment.

At our medical center the community came in. We had people who volunteered to be community liaison person. They would man our phones. We would train them how to fill out question- naires and how to do screening, and what questions to ask about sickle cell anemia.

So the community was concluding that all this stuff they're reading about these Panthers is opposite to our practice in the community. The people began to question the role the media played in the community. They began to question even more so a government that they knew was oppressing them.

They began to question the occupying force, the police force that was in their community constantly beating them and began to say, "We don't have to take this. Our life does not have to be like this. We have the right and we have the power to determine our own destiny. Our survival is not dictated by what they decide, what the government decides they will allow us to have. We have the power to create a revolution in this country."

The support continued to grow and people participated in the programs. Those who could not adopt the Party's philosophy wholesale could support the free prison bussing program. We had a free bussing program which allowed people in the community who had brothers and sisters and fathers and husbands in prisons and in jails to go visit their relatives in these prisons that were in downstate Illinois. People didn't have transportation for that.

We worked with them not as an agency coming in to solve the social ills of the community, but as their brother or sister next door who they grew up with, their brother and sister next door who they see out there getting beat in the head by the police just like the police just beat their son to death. So there was a kindred spirit there. There was a collective spirit. People began to see some light at the end of the tunnel.

Q: If you could, would you describe a typical day in terms of activities and work that you did as a member of the Party?

A.N.: First of all, everybody would have to get up at about 5:00 in the morning, and get ready to go to the breakfast program. We go mop the site and get the breakfast ready, get set up, have people stationed at their posts, make sure everybody is clean. Everybody was set for the program. We had literature there.

Children would sometimes start coming in at 6:30 in the morning. We'd feed the children. Then after the breakfast program we'd clean up the site and leave there and go sell our newspapers. From selling our newspapers we would read or we would have meetings in the community with different groups. We'd have lunch. We'd go back about 1:00 or 2:00 in the afternoon selling our papers again.

People had various areas of responsibility. . . . I worked on the breakfast program and also fundraising. . . .

We had to sell 200 papers a week minimum. We would come back and we would have political education classes three days a week. After the class we'd go to the bars and the lounges, selling the papers and just talking to people. We were visible in the community. People had no question about who we were. We weren't sitting in this office downtown. We were on West Madison which was in the heart of the African community, organizing the community and working with people.

People would bring folks together in their homes to learn about the programs of the Party and we would go through struggle with the people over some of the articles that were in the paper, over the 10 point program and platform.

Sometimes people would have problems with one of the points of our 10 point program, for example that we wanted freedom for all black men held in federal, state prisons and jails. They said, "Oh god, I don't want all them people out of jail, all these murderers and thieves and so on and so forth."

But Fred Hampton said and what the Black Panther Party would say is, "You got murderers and thieves sitting in the White House that are running this government. Release these small-time alleged criminals and let's lock up some of these big-time criminals who are murdering hundreds and thousands and millions of people all over the world."

We broke it down to them like that and showed them point for point how this government had destroyed us all over the world and they would say, "Well, I guess you got a point there." You bring people to the realization of where it's at right there at home.

Q: What were the difficulties and problems, the contradictions, as an African woman, as a revolutionary, during this period, trying to raise a son, a child alone? What can you now say in terms of the movement being able to learn from the difficulties that you had?

A.N.: Some of us did not have the support of our families when we joined the Party, because some people in our families did not understand what we were doing. But we went on and did what we had to do anyway. Eventually the families came around.

I was in the first group of women to become pregnant and have babies within the context of the Black Panther Party. There was nothing set up after the birth of Fred Hampton, Jr., [on December 29, 1969] that spoke to the issue of childcare, of how we would continue to function in the structure of the Party and continue to provide for our children. Before, when you were in the Party, you were by yourself, you could really sleep anywhere and you could work all night. But when you have the responsibility of children, you can't do that.

Somebody has to take that responsibility and I didn't feel that it was my role as a mother, a parent, to abdicate that responsibility to someone else. Not that I should be at home in a 24-hour housewife, mother role. There was no structure set up to work within the Party, to continue to work in the breakfast program, to continue to sell the newspaper. It was the demand to do it all or nothing. You would have to explain why you had to go take your child to the doctor, go through some struggle with that.

Because of the youth of the membership of the Party, because of the newness of the organization and again because it was the first group, we had no precedent to look to on how to deal with that issue. So it was due to our lack of knowledge and lack of having the practice of dealing with this issue that no viable solutions were set up. A lot of things that didn't happen or did happen spoke to the people's inability to deal with being a parent in the context of the revolutionary struggle.

A number of people left the Party. A number of new people came in and it was just really difficult for me to survive with a child without abdicating the responsibility of his growth and development to my mother, and I didn't think it was her full responsibility to take care of him while I continued.

I did, honestly, abdicate that responsibility to my mother for a period and would continue to try to work for the breakfast program, sell 200 newspapers and so on, but I didn't spend the time that needed to be spent with my son. Luckily I recognized what I was doing within a few months time.

There was some concern about my getting out of the Party because it wouldn't look good publicly. There was some concern by leadership that if I left the Party, it would appear as though the government had been successful in destroying the Party. But in all honesty, the government had been successful. The leadership that we had experienced and had followed under Fred Hampton was not there.

They had destroyed our movement, not just in Illinois, in Chicago with the murder of Fred Hampton. Just like this [snapping her fingers], starting from mid-'69, the government constantly had raids on our offices, and constantly incarcerated brothers and sisters. They were constantly in our offices piling up our breakfast donations and our medical supplies and setting them on fire in the office. They were raiding our offices all over the country.

There was a series of arrests. The arrests encompassed groups of folks, five, six, seven, eight, nine, ten people.

It was just like this, the government went through and destroyed the Black Panther Party.

So at that time when I had my son, the leadership was not there, nor was an apparatus set up for the childcare when a number of us had had babies at the same time in November, December, January. There were many babies born in the structure of the Black Panther Party but there was nothing set up to deal with that issue.

3. "Search and Destroy: A Report by the Commission of Inquiry into the Black Panthers and the Police"
Roy Wilkins and Ramsey Clark, Chairmen

Following the deaths of Fred Hampton and Mark Clark, several independent investigations into the murders were conducted. In 1973, the Commission of Inquiry into the Black Panthers and the Police, co-chaired by NAACP executive secretary Roy Wilkins and former attorney general Ramsey Clark, issued its report, **Search and Destroy,** *from which these excerpts are taken.*

PREFACE

Those of us who want to love our country are not anxious to ask whether our police are capable of murder. So we do not ask. We do not dare concede the possibility.

But we live here, and we are aware, however dimly, that hundreds of us are killed every year by police. We assume the victims are mad killers and that the officers fired in self-defense or to save lives.

Then came Orangeburg, the Algiers Motel incident, the Kent State killings, and reasonable persons were put on notice. Official conduct bears investigation. In a free society the police must be accountable to the people. Often, instead of seeking facts, we tend, largely in ignorance, to polarize, with ardent emotional commitment to the state and order on the one side and, equally passionately, to the oppressed and justice on the other.

Does the truth matter? If not, we are in an eternal contest of raw power. If it makes a difference, if it changes minds and hearts, can we find it?

This report pursues the truth of an episode that occurred early on December 4, 1969, at 2337 West Monroe Street in Chicago, Illinois. It was a time of darkness, cold, rage, fear, and violence. Facts are not easily found in such company.

The early dawn stillness had been broken at about 4:45 a.m. by heavy gunfire, eighty rounds or more, which lasted over a period of ten minutes. When it stopped, two young men, Fred Hampton and Mark Clark, were dead. Four other occupants of the premises, the Illinois Black Panther Party headquarters, were seriously wounded. Two police officers were injured, one by glass, the other by a bullet in the leg.

Of the total of perhaps one hundred shots fired that fatal night, probably one bullet was discharged by a Panther. It is possible that no Panther fired a shot, or that two or even three shots were fired by them. But it is highly unlikely that any Panther fired more than a single shot. The physical evidence does indicate that one shot was fired by them; and bullets fired inside a house make their mark.

Fred Hampton may or may not have been drugged or asleep throughout the episode; one can never be sure. Still, the probability is that he was unconscious at the time of his death. Nor can we be positive whether he was shot in the head by a policeman standing in full view of his prostrate body or by blind police gunfire from another room. But we must not weight the probabilities with our wishes. If Hampton never awakened, if he was murdered, it is better to know it. It tells us something we need to know. . . .

There is no chance that needed reforms will be made until the people have the opportunity and the will to understand the facts about official violence. Many will simply refuse to believe officials are capable of unlawful violence. Others will believe such violence and support it. But surely most Americans will not knowingly accept police lawlessness. If official violence is to be renounced, the truth must finally overcome our natural reluctance to incriminate government. It is our hope that this report will serve that end.

Of all violence, official violence is the most destructive. It not only takes life, but it does so in the name of the people and as the agent of the society. It says, therefore, this is our way, this is what we believe, we stand for nothing better. Official violence practices violence and teaches those who resist it that there is no alternative, that those who seek change must use violence. Violence, the ultimate human degradation, destroys our faith in ourselves and our purposes. When society permits its official use, we are back in the jungle.

There is a common thread that runs through the violence of B-52 raids in Indochina, police shooting students at Jackson State College in Mississippi, and the slaughter of prisoners and guards at Attica State Penitentiary in New York. We do not value others' lives as we do our own. The Vietnamese, the black students, the convicts and their guards are expendable. Until we understand that George Jackson and Mark Clark and Fred Hampton, as well as the victims of Kent State and nameless and faceless victims of Jackson State and on all sides in the Indochina war, are human beings equal in every way to our children and ourselves, we will see no wrong in using violence to control or destroy them.

Fred Hampton and Mark Clark were valuable young men. They could have enriched our lives. If they spoke of violence, suffered it, or used it, we should not be surprised. It was not foreign to their environment, nor did their government eschew it. And talented or not, violent or nonviolent, they were human beings whose lives and legal rights must be cherished by a just society. . . .

CONCLUSIONS

The Commission is of the opinion that it would have been improper to make actual findings of guilt; such conclusions should be made only after a trial during which the accused may exercise all of his rights. Rather, where the evidence suggests that a crime has been committed, the Commission has analogized its function to that of a grand jury, and has made findings of probable cause. It may be suggested that it was improper for the Commission even to have made findings of probable cause, since it does not have the power to compel testimony or to conduct a trial at which the accused may be exonerated. However, the circumstances surrounding the incident under investigation are so extraordinary that special measures seem called for. The existence of this Commission is itself a reflection of a widespread feeling that in this instance the legal system failed. . . .

The Plan for and Purposes of the Raid

The federal grand jury's *Report* concluded that the raid was "ill-conceived." The Commission considers that characterization of the raid to be a vast understatement, and has found that there is probable cause to believe that the predawn raid, carried out by officers with heavy armament but without tear gas, sound equipment, or lighting equipment, involved criminal acts on the part of the planners of the raid.

The infiltrator who reportedly informed the police and/or the FBI that illegal weapons were likely to be found in the Panthers' apartment was also reported to have informed them that the apartment was likely to be unoccupied at 8 p.m. on the evening preceding the raid. If the object of the raid had been, as stated, to search the premises for illegal weapons, that purpose could best have been accomplished without violence when the apartment was empty. Assuming that the search had disclosed illegal weapons, appropriate arrests could have been made thereafter.

Alternatively, the police could have surrounded the apartment and, communicating with the residents either by telephone or by loudspeaker, told them that the apartment was surrounded and ordered them to come out. The residents might have surrendered if given a chance. And the firepower available to the police department was surely more than ample to have permitted such an approach with no more danger to the police than was presented by the course of action actually followed.

Instead, however, the police chose to serve the warrant at 4:45

a.m., heavily armed and dressed in plainclothes. It is probable that the method chosen to execute the search warrant not only failed to avert violence, but instead actually maximized the likelihood of violence and clearly endangered the lives of the Panthers in the apartment. Moreover, it is probable that the purpose of the raid was to conduct a surprise attack on the Panthers, and that serving the search warrant was merely a guise.

The Commission finds that there is persuasive evidence that viable alternative methods of executing the search warrant did exist, methods which could have been utilized if the police officers and state's attorney had attempted to serve process in a manner respectful of the law.

The Opening Moments of the Raid—The First Shot

An analysis of the testimony by the police and by the Panther survivors about the events of the raid cannot be conclusive. The stories told by the police and the survivors are so fundamentally inconsistent that it is impossible to determine from the testimony what actually happened. However, the various narratives together with the physical evidence which has been available to the Commission have made several conclusions probable.

The question of the first shot was raised initially by the police, who claimed they were met by gunfire as they attempted to enter the apartment. The federal grand jury seemed to accept that theory, but never adequately addressed itself to the question. The result was to leave officially unanswered a question that was widely believed to be central and to justify the police use of gunfire, and at that time to imply that the police version of the first shot was correct.

The Commission finds that too little consideration was given by the federal grand jury, or by any other investigative body, to the ballistics report prepared by Mr. MacDonell. Although MacDonell relied on nonphysical evidence to reach his conclusion that Clark had not fired the first shot, and although that conclusion is therefore not definitive, it was a conclusion that, had a policeman rather than a Panther been the victim, would have been examined quite thoroughly by any investigative body. Instead, the federal grand jury characterized MacDonell's analysis as an "imaginative theory," a characterization which tends to discredit the analysis as sheer speculation. "Imaginative theories," however, when tested, often provide the crucial links between pieces of circumstantial evidence. MacDonell's theory was, instead, summarily dismissed.

Based on the evidence available to it, the Commission considers it probable that the first shot was fired neither by Mark Clark or Brenda Harris nor by Sergeant Groth or Officer Davis, but rather in the entrance hallway, apparently accidentally, by Officer Jones. Reference to such a shot is found both in the federal grand jury's *Report* and in the report prepared for the Commission by Mr. MacDonell, although little weight is given to it by either the federal grand jury or Mr. MacDonell.

More important, far too much weight has been given to the issue of who fired the first shot. First, there is considerable discrepancy as to the manner in which the police announced their presence at the apartment. While the Commission is of the opinion that the federal grand jury failed adequately to consider the controversy over who fired the first shot, the Commission also thinks that the significance of that issue has been highly exaggerated. Assuming, as is far from clear from the conflicting versions of the event, that the raiding officers did announce their presence and identify themselves as police, it is necessary to consider that it was 4:45 in the morning, the residents were asleep, and the police were in plainclothes. Under those circumstances, it is not unreasonable to suppose that anybody hearing an intruder entering his apartment is likely to reach for any available weapon— including a gun, if one is available—and use it. More importantly, the pattern of the shooting after the initial exchange of shots makes the question of the first shot seem relatively insignificant.

The Pattern of the Shooting

Approximately six shots were apparently fired as the police entered the living room through the front door—two by Sergeant Groth, three by Officer Davis, and one by Mark Clark. The FBI's ballistics analysis shows that during the remainder of the raid between seventy-seven and ninety-four shots were fired by the police—and none by the apartment's occupants. Accordingly, with the exception of one shot, the police testimony of gunfire directed at them from the occupants must be rejected.

The police testimony describes several orders for cease-fires, each of which was broken by shots fired by the occupants or by their shouts to "shoot it out." The evidence that no shots were fired by the occupants discredits the police testimony that they were returning fire; equally important, it discredits the police testimony that the occupants were advocating a shoot-out, for it is highly implausible that several calls to shoot it out could have been made without a shot being fired.

It was suggested to the police by the federal grand jury that police mistook the gunfire of other officers for firing by the Panthers. The fact that the police undoubtedly felt themselves endangered by the Panthers might have explained their propensity to shoot rather than to investigate. However, the police emphatically rejected the grand jury's suggestion. Moreover, that suggestion would not account for the police testimony that occupants of the apartment advocated a shoot-out. Since no shots were fired by the occupants, it is unlikely that the police testimony in that regard was true. If, however, the testimony of the officers that cries to "shoot it out" were heard is true, it seems far more likely that those cries were made by other police officers. If such was the case, those officers might well have intended the actual result— the killing and wounding of certain of the occupants.

Officer Gorman testified before the federal grand jury that as he fired his machine gun into the front bedroom, he saw one of the occupants aiming a gray shotgun at him, and the statement purportedly made by Blair Anderson shortly after the raid indicates that both he and Satchel had weapons. The Commission has been unable to establish the truth or falsity of that testimony. However, it seems likely that the occupants would have been able to fire at least one shot, if that had been their intent, while Gorman was firing into the closet. The front bedroom was a small room— approximately fourteen feet deep and seven feet wide. In it were two beds and a chest; the closet further reduced the actual space in the room. Three people were in the room; each of them was wounded several times. And while they were being wounded, not one shot was fired by any of them. Moreover, even if the occupants were armed, the Commission cannot condone the indiscriminate firing of a full round of thirty machine gun bullets into a room or the planning of a raid that would permit such an occurrence. There were other methods readily available to effect the arrests.

The Commission finds that attribution of culpability in the killing of Mark Clark and the wounding of Brenda Harris may be less clearly definable in the context of the already-begun raid. Clark apparently did fire at the police—regardless of whether his shot was the initial shot. Although Brenda Harris claims never to have touched a gun during the raid, the police testified that she did have one, and in the statement that she purportedly made to Andrew shortly after the raid she admitted that she had had, and had been attempting to fire, a shotgun. Moreover, the police knew *somebody* had fired at them, and a mistake by them as to who it had been may be understandable. The Commission is convinced, however, that both the killing of Clark and the wounding of Harris would have been avoided by proper planning, and that while no culpability is necessarily assignable to the officers who did the shooting, there is probable cause to believe that the planning of the raid was so inadequate as to constitute criminal conduct.

The Shooting of Fred Hampton

The death of Fred Hampton appears to the Commission to have been isolated from the killing of Mark Clark and the wounding of Brenda Harris on the one hand, and from the wounding of Ronald Satchel, Verlina Brewer, and Blair Anderson on the other. The Commission has concluded that there is probable cause to believe that Fred Hampton was murdered—that he was shot by an officer or officers who could see his prostrate body lying on the bed. Unfortunately, the inadequate investigation by the police and the other officials and their inadequate examination of the available evidence make it impossible to know which officer or officers actually fired the fatal bullets.

The Commission has been unable to determine whether the purpose, or a purpose, of the raid was specifically to kill Hampton. There is some evidence that Hampton was shot after the other occupants of the rear bedroom were removed. If that was not the sequence of events, it seems likely that he was the sole target of the police shooting from the doorway of the bedroom. Neither of those consequences, however, would establish that Hampton's death was an object of the raid.

On the other hand, the fact that Hampton appears from virtually all of the testimony never to have moved during the raid, the fact that after the police entered the apartment all the testimony placed him in bed, and the possibility that his failure to move was caused by his having been drugged are relevant to the question of the purpose of the raid.

Whether Hampton Was Drugged

The Commission has been unable to determine whether Hampton was drugged at the time of his murder, but considers it more probable than not that he was. The blood tests performed in connection with the second autopsy reportedly showed that Hampton had been drugged with a massive dose of secobarbital. The blood test reportedly conducted by the Cook County coroner failed to show the presence of any barbiturate, but there is a substantial doubt whether that test was ever conducted. The federal grand jury accepted as conclusive the findings of an FBI blood analysis which did not show the presence of any drugs. But the experts consulted by the Commission unanimously expressed the opinion that the FBI test, because of the embalming procedure used on Hampton's body, the instability of secobarbital in solution, and the long time during which the blood was stored without having been frozen, should not have been accepted as conclusive. In addition, certain of the experts concluded affirmatively that the blood did show the presence of a barbiturate, and that the FBI results were not just inadequate but wrong. In short, although the Commission has concluded that it is probable that Hampton was drugged, a final resolution of the issue is beyond the Commission's competence.

If Hampton was drugged, it would explain why, despite specific attempts to wake him, he was not awakened. Moreover, a finding that he was drugged might suggest that his death was an objective of the raid—that the police went to the apartment knowing that Hampton would be there and that he would be incapable of defending himself.

It seems unlikely that it will ever be known whether Hampton was drugged and whether his death was the major focus of the raid. The only investigative bodies who might have made that determination either failed to do so or have had their credibility so impeached that any conclusions reached by them must be disregarded. The Commission nonetheless considers it important to raise the issue because the facts compel that it be raised. The failure to raise it would be to hide from an unanswerable question solely because the most likely answers are not easy to accept.

State and Local Investigations

The performances following the raid of the various local law enforcement bodies which investigated the incident were singularly inadequate—in some cases by the admission of those official bodies. More important, however, is that some of those investigations—again by the admission of the investigators—were designed not to determine the facts but solely to establish the innocence of the police. It has been noted earlier that large segments of the black community had grown to distrust the police, as well as internal or other official investigations of police misconduct. The investigations of this raid confirm the validity of that mistrust.

The survivors of the raid have been widely condemned for their refusal to participate in certain of the official investigations. There is, however, not one hint that the participation by the survivors would have diminished the partiality and bias of any of those investigations, while there is much to suggest that their participation would have increased the acceptability of those investigations to the public. For example, despite the lack of evidence against the survivors and the substantial evidence against the police, it was the survivors and not the police who were initially indicted. And no investigation would have made available to the survivors the resources that were available to the state, or would otherwise have put the survivors and the police on equal footings. In short, the Commission has concluded that the refusal of the survivors to participate in the official investigations of the raid was understandable and justified. Until the black community at large has reason to think that blacks are being treated fairly by the police, and that police criminality will be dealt with justly by the law enforcement agencies, there is little chance of diminishing violence between police and blacks. If "the law" is designed to protect "the other side," then "the law" will inevitably be ignored.

The Commission considers that the performance by Special State's Attorney Barnabas Sears requires special comment. Mr. Sears, an established and respected lawyer, was appointed by Chief

Judge Power of the Cook County Criminal Court to investigate matters relating to the raid. When the Sears investigation failed to establish the innocence of the police—and instead resulted in the indictment of State's Attorney Hanrahan and thirteen other officials on charges of conspiring to obstruct justice—Sears became himself the subject of harsh treatment by Judge Power and by other members of Chicago and Illinois officialdom. The conclusion seems inescapable that Judge Power, too, was not impartial—that he intended Mr. Sears's investigation to exonerate the police regardless of the facts. Although the trial that followed from Mr. Sears's investigation resulted in the dismissal of charges against the indicted officials, the Commission questions whether that result would have followed if the resources of the state had been made more readily available to Mr. Sears rather than having been weighted against him.

The question of "Who polices the police?" is itself difficult. When it appears that law enforcement officials are working in unison, not for justice but solely to protect some of their own, the questions become that much more difficult. Who will judge the police? Who will judge the judges? And how can society expect the oppressed, or those who believe they are oppressed, to act when society's official avenues of recourse are closed to them?

Federal Law
The Commission finds that the raid of December 4, 1969, was not executed in compliance with the Fourth Amendment guarantees against unreasonable search and seizures; that there is probable cause to believe that the Civil Rights Statutes, Title 18, Sections 241 and 242, of the United States Code, were violated in the raid by the imposition of summary punishment on the Panthers with the intent to deny them their constitutionally protected rights to due process; and that the federal grand jury, in failing to return indictments against certain Chicago and Cook County police and other officials for their raid-related conduct, failed in its duty to proceed against violations of civil liberties.

Summary
The federal grand jury report found instances of official misfeasance, malfeasance, and nonfeasance related to investigations of

the raid. It also established what the Commission deems to be a prima facie case of illegal denial of the constitutional rights of the residents of the apartment. Nonetheless, the federal grand jury and the first state grand jury failed to return any indictments against the officials, and, instead, the first state grand jury indicted the survivors. The attitude of both grand juries appears to have been that the Panthers were dangerous, and, consequently, that any excesses by the police against them could be excused. The Commission deplores that approach.

One of the primary purposes of the criminal law is deterrence. If no attempt is made to prosecute the police in instances of apparent misconduct, such as appear to be present in this case, then it seems likely that police misconduct will continue in the future. It is perhaps too much to expect, at least until police service is thoroughly professionalized, that an officer in the course of a raid against people who he honestly believes intend to harm him would refrain from taking violent action to protect himself. To state that one understands, and perhaps is forced to accept, such a position does not, however, change the Commission's conclusion. It merely focuses attention on the culpable parties.

In other words, it would be perfectly proper to indict those officials who participated in the planning of the raid without indicting all of the participants, and if more evidence were obtained with respect to the roles of various of the officers, it might be proper to indict those police with respect to whom probable cause was found without indicting all of them. Clearly, however, it is unacceptable to conclude that because some of the police may not be guilty of any crime, none of them is. To follow such a course of action may well have the effect of increasing the number of instances of unjustified and unjustifiable police violence. The Commission is concerned, as all people must be, with the protection of police lives; it is also concerned, however, with the preservation of the lives of all persons, including those who may be suspected of having committed crimes. Summary execution is not tolerable; arbitrary punishment cannot be condoned. The best method for minimizing senseless killings and injuries seems to lie in establishing a situation where all people can expect justice; the Chicago incident seems calculated to foster a different result.

4. "The FBI's Efforts to Disrupt and Neutralize the Black Panther Party"

In the three-volume report issued in 1976 by the U.S. Senate's Select Committee to Study Governmental Operations (more commonly known as the Church Committee Report), readers were provided with a comprehensive examination of how government agencies monitored the activities of countless activists during the late 1960s and early 1970s. Based on a summation and presentation of FBI memos and reports, these excerpts detail how Chicago agents, making use of the strategy "divide and conquer," sought to engender tensions between the local chapter of the Black Panther Party and a gang known as the Blackstone Rangers, as well as how the FBI provided information that was used in the raid on Fred Hampton's apartment.

INTRODUCTION . . .

The Black Panther Party (BPP) was not among the original "Black Nationalist" targets. In September 1968, however, FBI Director J. Edgar Hoover described the Panthers as:

> the greatest threat to the internal security of the country.
> Schooled in the Marxist-Leninist ideology and the teaching of Chinese Communist leader Mao Tse-tung, its members have perpetrated numerous assaults on police officers and have engaged in violent confrontations with police throughout the country. Leaders and representatives of the Black Panther Party travel extensively all over the United States preaching their gospel of hate and violence not only to ghetto residents, but to students in colleges, universities and high schools as well.[3]

---

3. New York Times, 9/8/68.

By July 1969, the Black Panthers had become the primary focus of the program, and were ultimately the target of 233 of the total 295 authorized "Black Nationalist" COINTELPRO actions.[4]

Although the claimed purpose of the Bureau's COINTELPRO tactics was to prevent violence, some of the FBI's tactics against the BPP were clearly intended to foster violence, and many others could reasonably have been expected to cause violence.

This report focuses solely on the FBI's counterintelligence program to disrupt and "neutralize" the Black Panther Party. It does not examine the reasonableness of the basis for the FBI's investigation of the BPP or seek to justify either the politics, the rhetoric, or the actions of the BPP. This report does demonstrate, however, that the chief investigative branch of the Federal Government, which was charged by law with investigating crimes and preventing criminal conduct, itself engaged in lawless tactics and responded to deep-seated social problems by fomenting violence and unrest.

A. THE EFFORT TO PROMOTE VIOLENCE BETWEEN THE BLACK PANTHER PARTY AND OTHER WELL-ARMED, POTENTIALLY VIOLENT ORGANIZATIONS

The Select Committee's staff investigation has disclosed a number of instances in which the FBI sought to turn violence-prone organizations against the Panthers in an effort to aggravate "gang warfare." Because of the milieu of violence in which members of the Panthers often moved we have been unable to establish a direct link between any of the FBI's specific efforts to promote violence and particular acts of violence that occurred. We have been able to establish beyond doubt, however, that high officials of the FBI desired to promote violent confrontations between BPP members and members of other groups, and that those officials condoned tactics calculated to achieve that end. It is

---

4. This figure is based on the Select Committee's staff study of Justice Department COINTELPRO "Black Nationalist" summaries prepared by the FBI during the Petersen Committee inquiry into COINTELPRO.

deplorable that officials of the United States Government should engage in the activities described below, however dangerous a threat they might have considered the Panthers; equally disturbing is the pride which those officials took in claiming credit for the bloodshed that occurred.

---

2. The Effort to Promote Violence Between the Blackstone Rangers and the Black Panther Party

In late 1968 and early 1969, the FBI endeavored to pit the Blackstone Rangers, a heavily armed, violence-prone organization, against the Black Panthers.[46] In December 1968, the FBI learned that the recognized leader of the Blackstone Rangers, Jeff Fort, was resisting Black Panther overtures to enlist "the support of the Blackstone Rangers."[47] In order to increase the friction between these groups, the Bureau's Chicago office proposed sending an anonymous letter to Fort, informing him that two prominent leaders of the Chicago BPP had been making disparaging remarks about his "lack of commitment to black people generally." The field office observed:

---

46. There is no question that the Blackstone Rangers were well-armed and violent. The Chicago police had linked the Rangers and rival gangs in Chicago to approximately 290 killings from 1965–69. Report of Captain Edward Buckney, Chicago Police Dept., Gang Intelligence Unit, 2/23/70, p. 2. One Chicago police officer, familiar with the Rangers, told a Committee staff member that their governing body, the Main 21, was responsible for several ritualistic murders of black youths in areas the gang controlled. (Staff summary of interview with Renault Robinson, 9/25/75.)

47. Memorandum from Chicago Field Office to FBI Headquarters, 12/16/68. Fort also had a well-earned reputation for violence. Between September 1964 and January 1971, he was charged with more than 14 felonies, including murder (twice), aggravated battery (seven times), robbery (twice), and contempt of Congress. (Select Committee staff review of FBI criminal records.) A December 1968 FBI memorandum noted that a search of Fort's apartment had turned up a .22 caliber, four-shot derringer pistol. (Memorandum from Chicago Field Office to FBI Headquarters, 12/12/68, p. 2.)

Fort is reportedly aware that such remarks have been circulated, but is not aware of the identities of the individual responsible. He has stated that he would "take care of" individuals responsible for the verbal attacks directed against him.

Chicago, consequently, recommends that Fort be made aware that [name deleted] and [name deleted] together with other BPP members locally, are responsible for the circulation of these remarks concerning him. It is felt that if Fort were to be aware that the BPP was responsible, it would lend impetus to his refusal to accept any BPP overtures to the Rangers and *additionally might result in Fort having active steps taken to exact some form of retribution toward the leadership of the BPP*. [Emphasis added in Report.][48]

On about December 18, 1968, Jeff Fort and other Blackstone Rangers were involved in a serious confrontation with members of the Black Panther Party.

During that day twelve members of the BPP and five known members of the Blackstone Rangers were arrested on Chicago's South Side.[49] A report indicates that the Panthers and Rangers were arrested following the shooting of one of the Panthers by a Ranger.[49a]

That evening, according to an FBI informant, around 10:30 p.m., approximately thirty Panthers went to the Blackstone Rangers' headquarters at 6400 South Kimbark in Chicago. Upon their arrival Jeff Fort invited Fred Hampton, Bobby Rush and the other BPP members to come upstairs and meet with him and the Ranger leadership.[49b] The Bureau goes on to describe what transpired at this meeting:

> . . . everyone went upstairs into a room which appeared
> to be a gymnasium, where Fort told Hampton and Rush

---

48. Memorandum from Chicago Field Office to FBI Headquarters, 12/16/68, p. 2.

49. Letter Head Memorandum, 12/20/68.

49a. From confidential FBI interview with inmate at the House of Correction, 26th and California St. in Chicago, 11/12/69.

49b. Letterhead Memorandum, 12/20/68.

that he had heard about the Panthers being in Ranger territory during the day, attempting to show their "power" and he wanted the Panthers to recognize the Rangers' "power." Source stated that Fort then gave orders, via walkie-talkie, whereupon two men marched through the door carrying pump shotguns. Another order and two men appeared carrying sawed off carbines then eight more, each carrying a .45 caliber machine gun, clip type, operated from the shoulder or hip, then others came with over and under type weapons. Source stated that after this procession Fort had all Rangers present, approximately 100, display their side arms and about one half had .45 caliber revolvers. Source advised that all the above weapons appeared to be new.

Source advised they left the gym, went downstairs to another room where Rush and Hampton of the Panthers and Fort and two members of the Main 21 sat by a table and discussed the possibility of joining the two groups. Source related that Fort took off his jacket and was wearing a .45 caliber revolver shoulder holster with gun and had a small caliber weapon in his belt.

Source advised that nothing was decided at the meeting about the two groups actually joining forces, however, a decision was made to meet again on Christmas Day. Source stated Fort did relate that the Rangers were behind the Panthers but were not to be considered members. Fort wanted the Panthers to join the Rangers and Hampton wanted the opposite, stating that if the Rangers joined the Panthers, then together they would be able to absorb all the other Chicago gangs. Source advised Hampton did state that they couldn't let the man keep the two groups apart. Source advised that Fort also gave Hampton and Rush one of the above .45 caliber machine guns to "try out."

Source advised that based upon conversations during this meeting, Fort did not appear over anxious to join forces with the Panthers, however, neither did it appear that he wanted to terminate meeting for this purpose.[49c]

49c. *Ibid.*, pp. 3–4.

On December 26, 1968 Fort and Hampton met again to discuss the possibility of the Panthers and Rangers working together. This meeting was at a South Side Chicago bar and broke up after several Panthers and Rangers got into an argument.[49d] On December 27, Hampton received a phone call at BPP Headquarters from Fort telling him that the BPP had until December 28, 1968 to join the Blackstone Rangers. Hampton told Fort he had until the same time for the Rangers to join the BPP and they hung up.[49e]

In the wake of this incident, the Chicago office renewed its proposal to send a letter to Fort, informing FBI headquarters:

> As events have subsequently developed . . . the Rangers and the BPP have not only not been able to form any alliance, but enmity and distrust have arisen, to the point where each has been ordered to stay out of the other's territory. The BPP has since decided to conduct no activity or attempt to do recruiting in Ranger territory.[50]

The proposed letter read:

> Brother Jeff:
>
> I've spent some time with some Panther friends on the west side lately and I know what's been going on. The brothers that run the Panthers blame you for blocking their thing and *there's supposed to be a hit out for you.* I'm not a Panther, or a Ranger, just black. From what I see these Panthers are out for themselves not black people. I think you ought to know what they're up to, I know what I'd do if I was you. You might hear from me again.
>
> (sgd.) A black brother you don't know.
> [Emphasis added in Report.][51]

49d. FBI Special Agent Informant Report, 12/30/68.
49e. *Ibid.*
50. Memorandum from Chicago Field Office to FBI Headquarters, 1/10/69.
51. Memorandum from Chicago Field Office to FBI Headquarters, 1/13/69, p. 1.

The FBI's Chicago office explained the purpose of the letter as follows:

> It is believed the above may intensify the degree of animosity between the two groups and occasion Fort to take retaliatory action which could disrupt the BPP or lead to reprisals against its leadership.
>
> Consideration has been given to a similar letter to the BPP alleging a Ranger plot against the BPP leadership; however, it is not felt this would be productive principally because the BPP at present is not believed as violence prone as the Rangers to whom violent type activity— shooting and the like—is second nature.[52]

On the evening of January 13, 1969, Fred Hampton and Bobby Rush appeared on a Chicago radio talk show called "Hot Line." During the course of the program Hampton stated that the BPP was in the "process of educating the Blackstone Rangers."[52a] Shortly after that statement Jeff Fort was on the phone to the radio program and stated that Hampton had his facts confused and that the Rangers were educating the BPP.[52b]

On January 16, Hampton, in a public meeting, stated that Jeff Fort had threatened to blow his head off if he came within Ranger territory.[52c]

On January 30, 1969, [FBI] Director [J. Edgar] Hoover authorized sending the anonymous letter.[53] While the Committee staff could find no evidence linking this letter to subsequent clashes

---

52. *Ibid.*

52a. Memorandum from Special Agent to SAC, Chicago, 1/15/69.

52b. *Ibid.*

52c. Memorandum from Special Agent to SAC, Chicago, 1/28/69, reporting on informant report.

53. Memorandum from FBI Headquarters to Chicago Field Office, 1/30/69.

between the Panthers and the Rangers, the Bureau's intent was clear.[54]

B. THE EFFORT TO DISRUPT THE BLACK PANTHER PARTY BY PROMOTING INTERNAL DISSENSION

1. General Efforts to Disrupt the Black Panther Party Membership

In addition to setting rival groups against the Panthers, the FBI employed the full swing of COINTELPRO techniques to create rifts and factions within the Party itself, which it was believed would "neutralize" the Party's effectiveness.[55]

Anonymous letters were commonly used to sow mistrust. For example, in March 1969 the Chicago FBI Field Office learned that a local BPP member feared that a faction of the Party, allegedly led by Fred Hampton and Bobby Rush, was "out to get" him.[56] Headquarters approved sending an anonymous letter to Hampton which was drafted to exploit dissension within the BPP as well as to play on mistrust between the Blackstone Rangers and the Chicago BPP leadership:

Brother Hampton:

Just a word of warning. A Stone friend tells me [name deleted] wants the Panthers and is looking for somebody to get you out of the way. Brother Jeff is supposed to be

---

54. There are indications that a shooting incident between the Rangers and the Panthers on April 2, 1969, in a Chicago suburb may have been triggered by the FBI. According to Bobby Rush, coordinator of the Chicago BPP at the time, a group of armed BPP members had confronted the Rangers because Panther William O'Neal—who has since surfaced as an FBI informant—had told them that a Panther had been shot by Blackstone Rangers and had insisted that they retaliate. This account, however, has not been confirmed. (Staff summary of interview with Bobby Rush, 11/26/75.)

55. The various COINTELPRO techniques are described in detail in the Staff Report on COINTELPRO.

56. Memorandum from Chicago Field Office to FBI Headquarters, 3/24/69.

interested. I'm just a black man looking for blacks working together, not more of this gang banging.[57]

Bureau documents indicate that during this time an informant within the BPP was also involved in maintaining the division between the Panthers and the Blackstone Rangers.[57a]

In December 1968, the Chicago FBI Field Office learned that a leader of a Chicago youth gang, the Mau Mau's, planned to complain to the national BPP headquarters about the local BPP leadership and questioned its loyalty.[58] FBI headquarters approved an anonymous letter to the Mau Mau leader, stating:

Brother [deleted]:

I'm from the south side and have some Panther friends that know you and tell me what's been going. I know those two [name deleted] and [name deleted] that run the Panthers for a long time and those mothers been with every black outfit going where it looked like they was something in it for them. The only black people they care about is themselves. *I heard too they're sweethearts* and that [name deleted] has worked for the man that's why he's not in Viet Nam. Maybe that's why they're just playing like real Panthers. I hear a lot of the brothers are with you and want those mothers out but don't know how. The Panthers need real black men for leaders not freaks. Don't give up brothers. [Emphasis added in Report.][59]

A black friend.

---

57. Memorandum from FBI Headquarters to Chicago Field Office, 4/8/69.

57a. Memorandum from Chicago Field Office to FBI Headquarters, 1/28/69.

58. Memorandum from Chicago Field Office to FBI Headquarters, 12/30/68.

59. Memorandum from FBI Headquarters to Chicago Field Office, 1/30/69.

Information from Bureau files in Chicago on the Panthers was given to Chicago police upon request, and Chicago Police Department files were open to the Bureau.[165] A Special Agent who handled liaison between the FBI's Racial Matters Squad (responsible for monitoring BPP activity in Chicago) and the Panther Squad of the Gang Intelligence Unit (GIU) of the Chicago Police Department from 1967 through July 1969, testified that he visited GIU between three and five times a week to exchange information.[166] The Bureau and Chicago Police both maintained paid informants in the BPP, shared informant information, and the FBI provided information which was used by Chicago police in planning raids against the Chicago BPP.[167]

According to an FBI memorandum, this sharing of informant information was crucial to police during their raid on the apartment occupied by several Black Panther members which resulted in the death of the local Chairman, Fred Hampton, and another Panther:

> [Prior to the raid], a detailed inventory of the weapons and also a detailed floor plan of the apartment were furnished to local authorities. In addition, the identities of BPP members utilizing the apartment at the above address were furnished. This information was not available from any other source and subsequently proved to be of tremendous value in that it subsequently saved injury and possible death to police officers participating in a raid . . . on the morning of 12/4/69. The raid was based on the information furnished by the informant . . . [Emphasis added in Report.][168]

---

165. Special Agent deposition, 2/26/75, p. 90.

166. Special Agent deposition, 2/26/75, p. 84. The Agent also testified that other FBI agents in the Racial Matters Squad were also involved in the "free flow of information between the Racial Matters Squad and GIU," and that at one time or another, every agent had exchanged information with GIU.

167. Memorandum from Chicago Field Office to FBI Headquarters, 12/3/69, p. 2; memorandum from Special Agent to Chicago Field Office, 12/12/69.

168. Memorandum from Chicago Field Office to FBI Headquarters, 12/8/69.

5. "Angela Davis: An Autobiography"

Among the activists who supported the prisoners' rights movement of the late 1960s and early 1970s was Angela Davis. In this excerpt from her 1974 autobiography, Davis, an outspoken member of the American Communist party and a staunch crusader for racial and social justice, recounts the early days of her involvement in the prisoners' rights movement and her support of the efforts of the three inmates known as the Soledad Brothers, especially George Jackson.

Around the middle of February [1970] I picked up the Los Angeles *Times* and noticed on the front page a large photograph of three very striking Black men. Their faces were serene and strong, but their waists were draped in chains. Chains bound their arms to their sides and chains shackled their legs. "They are still trying to impress upon us that we have not yet escaped from bondage," I thought. Angry and frustrated, I began to read the story. It was about Soledad Prison.

Soledad Prison was a household word in the Black community. During my last two years in Los Angeles, I must have heard it a million times. There was San Quentin, there was Folsom—and there was Soledad. . . .

The L.A. *Times* article reported the indictment of George Jackson, John Clutchette and Fleeta Drumgo for the murder of a guard at Soledad Prison. An entire month had elapsed since the killing took place. Why had it taken so long to return the indictments? I wondered why the author had not commented on this time lag. The article reeked of deception and evasiveness. It seemed that the *Times* was trying to turn public opinion against the accused men even before the trial got started. If one accepted the article on its face, one would have come away with the assumption that the three men were guilty.

During the next three days, I kept thinking of the faces of those brothers. Three beautiful virile faces pulled out of the horrible anonymity of prison life.

A few weeks later, the Che-Lumumba Club was contacted about a meeting on the Soledad situation. It was being arranged by the

Los Angeles "Committee to Defend the Bill of Rights," which wanted to discuss the mounting of a mass campaign to free the three from Soledad.

I was drowning in work, but I simply couldn't stop thinking about those three haunting faces in the newspaper. I had to attend the meeting; even if I only became involved in a minimal way, at least I would be doing something.

The night of the meeting, Tamu, Patrice Neal—another club member—and I went down to the rundown old Victoria Hall. (It had been famous once for its swinging Saturday night dances. Now, in this hall, people were no longer having fun. They were talking about a very serious thing, about liberation.)

About a hundred people answered the call. Though they were predominantly Black, a sizeable number of white people had turned up as well. There were young people, older people and people who were obviously attending their first political meeting. There were those who had come because they had sons, husbands and brothers in Soledad Prison.

Seated behind the long tables stretched across the front of the hall were Fay Stender, lawyer for George Jackson, George's mother and sisters—Georgia, Penny and Frances Jackson—Inez Williams, Fleeta's mother, and Doris Maxwell, the mother of John Clutchette.

Speaking of Soledad, Fay Stender explained that from the warden down to the guards, the prison hierarchy had a long history of promoting racial enmity in the prison population. As long as the Black, Chicano and white prisoners were at each other's necks, the prison administration knew they would not have to worry about serious challenges to their authority.

As in an old Southern town, segregation in Soledad Prison was almost total. All activities were arranged so that racial mingling would not occur—or so that when it did occur, the prisoners would be in a posture of battle. With the collaboration of some of the white prisoners, Soledad had developed its own counterpart to the Ku Klux Klan—a group called the "Aryan Brotherhood." Tension in the prison was so thick that even the most innocuous meeting between the races was bound to set off an explosion.

Before January 13, 1970, exercise periods, like everything else, were segregated. On that day, with no explanation, the guards sent Black, Chicano and white prisoners to exercise together in the newly constructed yard. Not a single guard was assigned to accompany them. The explosion was inevitable. A fight erupted between a Black prisoner and a white prisoner, and within a few minutes, there was havoc.

O. G. Miller had the reputation of being a hardline racist, and was known to be an expert marksman. He was stationed in the gun tower that day. He carefully aimed his carbine and fired several times. Three men fell: W. L. Nolen, Cleveland Edwards, Alvin Miller. They were all Black. A few days later the Monterey County Grand Jury was convened to hear the case of O. G. Miller. As could have been predicted, he was absolved of all responsibility for the deaths of the three brothers. The Grand Jury ruled that he had done nothing more serious than commit "justifiable homicide."

There was a brutal familiarity about this story. As I listened to Fay Stender's narration, the specter of Leonard Deadwilder invaded my thoughts. As he was rushing his pregnant wife to the hospital in Los Angeles, a white handkerchief attached to the antenna to indicate an emergency, the cops stopped him for speeding and without even seeking an explanation, they shot him to death. It was called justifiable homicide by the courts. I remembered Gregory Clark, the eighteen-year-old Black child who was stopped by the police because "he didn't look like he fit the Mustang he was driving." Though Gregory Clark was himself unarmed, the cop said he moved in self-defense. As the brother lay defenseless, face down on a hot ghetto sidewalk, his hands cuffed behind him, he was shot in the back of the head. Later the courts ruled that the cop had committed "justifiable homicide."

"Justifiable Homicide"—these innocuously official words conjured up the untold numbers of unavenged murders of my people.

Fay Stender's story recaptured my attention. She was talking about the Soledad prisoners' proud attempts to challenge this judicial endorsement of a clearly racist assassination. Spontaneously and with the intense desperation of men in chains, the Black prisoners had shouted unexecutable threats meant for the assassin O. G. Miller, and banged angrily at the bars of their cells. Soledad Prison pulsated with resistance. A guard inadvertently stumbled into the brothers' fierce but chaotic rebellion and was engulfed by their collective desire for revenge. No one knew who pushed the guard over the railing.

This was the beginning of the story of George Jackson, John Clutchette and Fleeta Drumgo. There was no evidence that they had killed the guard. But there was evidence that George, John and Fleeta were "militants"; they had been talking with their fellow captives about the theory and practice of liberation. The prison bureaucracy was going to hold them symbolically responsible for the spontaneous rebellion enacted by the prisoners. They were charged with the murder of the guard. The prison hierarchy wanted to throw them into San Quentin's death chamber and triumphantly parade their gassed bodies before thousands of California prisoners, as examples of what the prison and the State did to those who refused to observe the silence of acceptance.

Fay Stender's legal analysis left us to suffer in the privacy of our individual emotions. But when Georgia Jackson began to speak, her voice brought a new dimension to our meeting, her words expressed her unashamed maternal pain. Georgia Jackson, Black, woman, mother; her infinite strength undergirded her plaintive words about her son.

When she began to talk about George, a throbbing silence came over the hall. "They took George away from us when he was only eighteen. That was ten years ago." In a voice trembling with emotion, she went on to describe the incident which had robbed him of the little freedom he possessed as a young boy struggling to become a man. He was in a car when its owner—a casual acquaintance of his—had taken seventy dollars from a service station. Mrs. Jackson insisted that he had been totally oblivious of his friend's designs. Nevertheless, thanks to an inept, insensitive public defender, thanks to a system which had long ago stacked the cards against young Black defendants like George, he was pronounced guilty of robbery. The matter of his sentencing was routinely handed over to the Youth Authority.

With angry astonishment I listened to Mrs. Jackson describe the sentence her son had received: One year to life in prison. One to life. And George had already done ten times the minimum. I was paralyzed by the thought of the absolute irreversibility of his last decade. And I was afraid to let my imagination trace out the formidable reality of those ten years in prison. A determination began to swell in me to do everything within the limits of the possible to save George from the gas chamber.

Fleeta Drumgo was his mother's only son. She spoke about her pain quietly but intensely, and appealed to us to rescue her son from his enemies. The mother of John Clutchette told us how she had received a note bearing the single word "Help." This was the first sign that the three brothers were being set up by the prison bureaucracy. Alone she could do nothing to help John, Fleeta or George. Only we, the people, could hope to stop the legal lynching which was planned for them.

By the time these women had finished, the prosecution appeared to have the logic and coherence of a conspiracy against the brothers—against them, their politics, their principles, their commitment. There was only one question: What were we prepared to do to prevent the consummation of the conspiracy? We addressed ourselves to the details of building a mass movement to fight for our brothers' freedom. The chairperson asked for volunteers to participate in the various subcommittees which needed to be set up—fund-raising, publicity, research, etc.

Although I already felt totally committed to George, John and Fleeta, I knew that I had too many responsibilities to assume a major role in the defense committee. The fight for my job raged on and was sending me up and down the California coast, exposing and challenging Ronald Reagan, and seeking support for our side. I was active in the Che-Lumumba Club, working in the area of political education. And, of course, I had to prepare for the two sets of lectures I was giving at UCLA. I was already killing myself trying to fulfill all these responsibilities. How could I possibly find time to be active on a day-to-day basis in the Soledad Brothers Defense Committee?

Even though these were my thoughts as the subcommittees were being constituted, my arm shot up when they asked for volunteers for the subcommittee on campus involvement. Something more elemental than timetables and prior commitments had seized me and made me agree to coordinate the committee's efforts in the local colleges and universities.

The decision had been made. How to find time was a secondary question. I thought about my initial reluctance to take on a substantial role. How presumptuous it had been to weight the outcome of the fight for my job against the outcome of the fight for the lives of these men. At UCLA I was fighting for my right as a Black woman, as a Communist, as a revolutionary, to hold on to my job. In Soledad Prison, George Jackson, John Clutchette, Fleeta Drumgo were fighting for their rights as Black men, as revolutionaries, to hold on to their *lives*. Same struggle. Same enemies.

The majority of the students and professors—except on the very reactionary campuses—agreed at least in principle with my academic freedom to teach, regardless of the fact that I was a Communist. I could utilize the widespread interest in the struggle around my job and the natural curiosity of people who wanted to see "a real, live, self-avowed Communist" to get onto the campuses and to call for support of the Soledad Brothers.

At the end of the meeting at Victoria Hall, the members of the campus subcommittee got together and decided to hold the first meeting the following week. I volunteered Kendra and Franklin's place on 50th Street. In the meantime we would try to recruit sympathetic students and professors from schools in the area to attend the meeting. We would try to devise proposals for the organizing efforts we were going to carry out in the Los Angeles academic community.

I left the meeting with a new sense of direction. I thought about George, John and Fleeta. We had to find some way to let them know that they were no longer alone. That soon there would be thousands of combative voices shouting "Free the Soledad Brothers" and thousands willing to fight for them.

———

Within a few short weeks, the campaign to free the Soledad Brothers was being talked about all over the Black community, the college campuses and Left political circles throughout the city. Our "Free the Soledad Brothers" buttons were being worn by many people. A brother in the BSU at UCLA had donated some silk-screen posters of the brothers, and a printing operation had produced masses of them at no cost to the committee. Wherever movement activities were going on—meetings, rallies, conferences—and at concerts and other events in the Black community, there were always committee activists, armed with literature, posters and buttons, inviting people to attend our weekly meetings at the 50th Street house. . . .

Our work was gaining momentum, and its impact on the community was growing stronger. The committee's numbers were increasing each week, reflecting the growth in strength of the broader defense campaign. I stepped up my own personal involvement. No requests for speaking engagements were turned down— but I made it clear that any speech I gave would be on the Soledad Brothers case, and whatever honorarium I received would be donated to the Soledad Brothers Defense Fund. Loyola College in L.A. Pasadena City College. University of San Francisco. University of the Pacific. Monterey Junior College. University of California at Santa Cruz. Palisades High School. There were also the churches and the social groups, including sororities and fraternities that were being stimulated by the growing political involvement of the sisters and brothers around them.

I had become so totally immersed in traveling and speaking engagements that when a pretrial hearing took place in Monterey County on May 8, I could not join the delegation from our committee. I had never seen the Soledad Brothers and had been looking forward to attending the hearing, if only to catch a glimpse of them. A few days earlier, I had received a message from George, saying that they were all eager to see us.

The Bay Area Soledad Committee had done an excellent job of mobilizing people to attend the hearing. The line outside Judge Campbell's courtroom stretched down the other end of the corridor. While it was good to see so many people already involved in the campaign, I was distressed by the fact that so few Black people were there. (Later, I discovered that the problem was the composition of the committee—it was active and had attracted numbers of enthusiastic members, but the Black people on the committee could be counted on one hand.)

When Georgia [Jackson] saw all the people, she told me that it didn't make sense for us to stand in this long line; the courtroom couldn't even seat all those already waiting. I had never felt so crushed. After all the shifting of schedules to make time for the hearing; after all the feverish running around to make sure we arrived on time; after all this, I wasn't going to get in. Full of rage, I saw myself standing outside the doors while the hearing took place, waiting breathlessly for some news of the proceedings.

Georgia tried to cheer me up by saying that there was still a chance that something could be arranged. [Cheryl] Dearmon and I took the hint, and when the bailiffs opened the doors for the families, we both slipped inconspicuously into the chambers.

Inside the crowded courtroom, the silence palpitated with the frustration of people powerfully stimulated by the tangible presence of the enemy. The redfaced bailiffs stationed along the walls stared at us with the hostility they had learned for their role. We waited. I hoped that something would soon happen to break this incredible tension before it exploded of its own accord.

Despite, or because of, this intense waiting, the sudden appearance of a fat, hard-looking uniformed white man startled us all. As he waddled through the door behind the bench, he epitomized the fascist atmosphere of this hearing. We knew already that Judge Campbell would try to tighten the knots of the conspiracy. He would try to lock the Brothers more securely into a fate leading unwaveringly to the death chamber. The presence of this Soledad guard was supposed to instill awe and fear in us. We were supposed to feel impotent before the apparatus he represented. We were supposed to already smell the odor of cyanide.

But we did not feel afraid, we did not feel impotent. And we vigorously applauded the heroes of our struggle as they strode proudly, courageously, powerfully into the courtroom. The chains draping their bodies did not threaten us; they were there to be broken, destroyed, smashed. The sight of those shackles designed to alarm us, to make the prisoners appear "dangerous," "mad," only made us itch to tear the metal from their wrists, their ankles. I knew that my own anger was shared by all. The bile rose in my throat. But more powerful than the taste of outrage was the dominating presence of the Brothers, for the Brothers were beautiful. Chained and shackled, they were standing tall and they were beautiful.

George looked even more vibrant than I had imagined. I had thought that the scars of the last decade would be immediately apparent. But there was not a trace of resignation, not the least stamp of the bondage in which he spent all the years of his adult life. He walked tall, with more confidence than I had ever seen before. His shoulders were broad and muscular, his tremendous arms sculptures of ancient strength, and his face revealed the depth of his understanding of our collective condition and his own refusal to be overwhelmed by this oppression. I could hardly believe the refreshing beauty of his smile. . . .

It was so wrong that they should be the ones to wear these clanging chains. Whatever the time it took, whatever the energy, these chains would be broken.

My communications with George became more regular. We too grew closer. As we agreed and disagreed with each other on political questions, a personal intimacy also began to develop between us. In his letters, which dealt for the most part with subjects such as the need to popularize communist ideas among the Black masses, the need to develop the prison movement, the role of women in the movement, etc., George also talked about himself, his past life, his own personal desires and aspirations, his fantasies about women, his feelings about me. "I've been thinking about women a lot lately," he once wrote. "Is there anything sentimental or otherwise wrong with that? That couldn't be. It's never bothered me too much before, the sex thing. I would do my exercise and the hundreds of katas, stay busy with something . . ."

I came to know George not only through the letters we exchanged, but also through the people who were close to him—through Jon and the rest of the Jackson family, through John Thorne, who, as his lawyer, saw him regularly. The closer I felt to George, the more I found myself revealing to those who knew George a side of me I usually kept hidden except from the most intimate of friends. In the letters I managed to get to him I responded not only to the political questions he posed; I also told him that my feelings for him had grown deeper than political commitment to struggle for his freedom; I felt a personal commitment as well.

George knew about the tons of hate mail which poured into my office at UCLA demanding that I be expelled from the university. He knew about the many threats which had been made on my life and was concerned for my safety. George was aware that whenever I appeared in a public situation, sisters and brothers from the Che-Lumumba Club did security duty. Yet, he didn't think this was enough. From his own experience—behind walls— he was convinced one could never be too vigilant. Besides, the sisters and brothers from Che-Lumumba were necessarily abstract for him. He had never seen them and knew them only through my letters. He knew and trusted Jonathan much more than anyone else on this side of the walls. He wrote me that he wanted Jon to stay with me as much as possible. Jon also received a message from his brother asking him to make sure that I was secure from the racists and reactionaries who might try to make me a martyr.

When George's book *Soledad Brother* was being prepared for publication, he asked me to read over the manuscript and make suggestions for improvements. The evening I received it, I thought I would skim through a few of the letters, saving the bulk of the book for another time. But once I got started, it was impossible to put the manuscript down until I had seen every word—from the first letter to the last. I was astounded. The formidable magnetism of the letters came not only from their content, not only from the way they traced George's personal and political evolution over the last five years—but even more from the way they articulated so clearly, so vividly, the condition of our people inside prison walls and outside. And in several passages George stated so precisely, so naturally, the reasons our liberation could only be achieved through socialism.

6. Letter from George Jackson

With the publication of his Soledad Brother *in 1970, inmate George Jackson came to be viewed as a thoughtful and authoritative voice against the American criminal justice and penal systems. In this letter to his lawyer, Fay Stender, Jackson points to the historic role of prisons, his sentencing and that of countless other black men for "political-economic" causes, and the brutal attempts to dehumanize those incarcerated. On August 21, 1971, Jackson was shot to death in San Quentin prison, where he had been transferred; prison officials claimed he was attempting to escape.*

Dear Fay,

On the occasion of your and Senator Dymally's tour and investigation into the affairs here at Soledad, I detected in the questions posed by your team a desire to isolate some rationale that would explain why racism exists at the prison with "particular prominence." Of course the subject was really too large to be dealt with in one tour and in the short time they allowed you, but it was a brave scene. My small but mighty mouthpiece, and the black establishment senator and his team, invading the state's maximum security row in the worst of its concentration camps. I think you are the first woman to be allowed to inspect these facilities. Thanks from all. The question was too large, however. It's tied into the question of why all these California prisons vary in character and flavor in general. It's tied into the larger question of why racism exists in this whole society with "particular prominence," tied into history. Out of it comes another question: Why do California joints produce more Bunchy Carters and Eldridge Cleavers than those over the rest of the country?

I understand your attempt to isolate the set of localized circumstances that give to this particular prison's problems of race is based on a desire to aid us right now, in the present crisis. There are some changes that could be made right now that would alleviate some of the pressures inside this and other prisons. But to get at the causes, you know, one would be forced to deal with questions at the very center of Amerikan political and economic life, at the core of the Amerikan historical experience. This prison didn't come to exist where it does just by happenstance. Those who inhabit it and feed off its existence are historical products. The great majority of Soledad pigs are southern migrants who do not want to work in the fields and farms of the area, who couldn't sell cars or insurance, and who couldn't tolerate the discipline of the army. And of course prisons attract sadists. After one concedes that racism is stamped unalterably into the present nature of Amerikan sociopolitical and economic life in general (the definition of fascism is: a police state wherein the political ascendancy is tied into and protects the interests of the upper class—characterized by militarism, *racism,* and imperialism), and concedes further that criminals and crime arise from material, economic, sociopolitical causes, we can then burn *all* of the criminology and penology libraries and direct our attention where it will do some good.

The logical place to begin any investigation into the problems of California prisons is with our "pigs are beautiful" Governor Reagan, a radical reformer turned reactionary. For a real understanding of the failure of prison policies, it is senseless to continue to study the criminal. All of those who can afford to be honest know that the real victim, that poor, uneducated, disorganized man who finds himself a convicted criminal, is simply the end result of a long chain of corruption and mismanagement that starts with people like Reagan and his political appointees in Sacramento. After one investigates Reagan's character (what makes a turncoat) the next logical step in the inquiry would be a look into the biggest political prize of the state—the directorship of the Department of Correction.

All other lines of inquiry would be like walking backward. You'll never see where you're going. You must begin with directors, assistant directors, adult authority boards, roving boards, supervisors, wardens, captains, and guards. You have to examine these people from director down to guard before you can logically examine their product. Add to this some concrete and steel, barbed wire, rifles, pistols, clubs, the tear gas that killed Brother Billingslea in San Quentin in February 1970 while he was locked in his cell, and the pick handles of Folsom, San Quentin, and Soledad.

To determine how men will behave once they enter the prison it is of first importance to know that prison. Men are brutalized by their environment—not the reverse.

I gave you a good example of this when I saw you last. Where I am presently being held, they never allow us to leave our cell without first handcuffing us and belting or chaining the cuffs to our waists. This is preceded always by a very thorough skin search. A force of a dozen or more pigs can be expected to invade the row at any time searching and destroying personal effects. The attitude of the staff toward the convicts is both defensive and hostile. Until the convict gives in completely it will continue to be so. By giving in, I mean prostrating oneself at their feet. Only then does their attitude alter itself to one of paternalistic condescension. Most convicts don't dig this kind of relationship (though there are some who do love it) with a group of individuals demonstrably inferior to the rest of society in regard to education, culture, and sensitivity. Our cells are so far from the regular dining area that our food is always cold before we get it. Some days there is only one meal that can be called cooked. We *never* get anything but cold-cut sandwiches for lunch. There is no variety to the menu. The same things week after week. One is confined to his cell 23½ hours a day. Overt racism exists unchecked. It is not a case of the pigs trying to stop the many racist attacks; they actively encourage them.

They are fighting upstairs right now. It's 11:10 a.m., June 11. No black is supposed to be on the tier upstairs with anyone but other blacks but—mistakes take place—and one or two blacks end up on the tier with nine or ten white convicts frustrated by the living conditions or openly working with the pigs. The whole ceiling is trembling. In hand-to-hand combat we always win; we lose sometimes if the pigs give them knives or zip guns. Lunch will be delayed today, the tear gas or whatever it is drifts down to sting my nose and eyes. Someone is hurt bad. I hear the meat wagon from the hospital being brought up. Pigs probably gave them some weapons. But I must be fair. Sometimes (not more often than necessary) they'll set up one of the Mexican or white convicts. He'll be one who has not been sufficiently racist in his attitudes. After the brothers (enraged by previous attacks) kick on this white convict whom the officials have set up, he'll fall right into line with the rest.

I was saying that the great majority of the people who live in this area of the state and seek their employment from this institution have overt racism as a *traditional* aspect of their characters. The only stops that regulate how far they will carry this thing come from the fear of losing employment here as a result of the outside pressures to control the violence. That is O Wing, Max (Maximum Security) Row, Soledad—in part anyway.

Take an individual who has been in the general prison population for a time. Picture him as an average convict with the average twelve-year-old mentality, the nation's norm. He wants out, he wants a woman and a beer. Let's say this average convict is white and has just been caught attempting to escape. They may put him on Max Row. This is the worst thing that will ever happen to him. In the general population facility there are no chains and cuffs. TVs, radios, record players, civilian sweaters, keys to his own cell for daytime use, serve to keep his mind off his real problems. There is also a recreation yard with all sorts of balls and instruments to strike or thrust at. There is a gym. There are movies and a library well stocked with light fiction. And of course there is work, where for two or three cents an hour convicts here at Soledad make paper products, furniture and clothing. Some people actually like this work since it does provide some money for the small things and helps them to get through their day— *without thinking* about their real problems.

Take an innocent con out of this general population setting (because a pig "thought" he may have seen him attempting a lock). Bring him to any part of O Wing (the worst part of the adjustment center of which Max Row is a part). He will be cuffed, chained, belted, pressured by the police who think that every convict should be an informer. He will be pressured by white cons to join their racist brand of politics (they *all* go under the nickname "Hitler's Helpers"). If he is predisposed to help black he will be pushed away—by black. Three weeks is enough. The strongest hold out no more than a couple of weeks. There has been *one* white man only to go through this O Wing experience without losing his balance, without allowing himself to succumb to the madness of ribald, protrusive racism.

It destroys the logical processes of the mind, a man's thoughts become completely disorganized. The noise, madness streaming from every throat, frustrated sounds from the bars, metallic sounds from the walls, the steel trays, the iron beds bolted to the wall, the hollow sounds from a cast-iron sink or toilet.

The smells, the human waste thrown at us, unwashed bodies, the rotten food. When a white con leaves here he's ruined for life. No black leaves Max Row walking. Either he leaves on the meat wagon or he leaves crawling licking at the pig's feet.

Ironic, because one cannot get a parole to the outside prison directly from O Wing, Max Row. It's positively not done. The parole board won't even consider the Max Row case. So a man licks at the feet of the pig not for a release to the outside world but for the privilege of going upstairs to O Wing adjustment center. There the licking process must continue if a parole is the object. You can count on one hand the number of people who have been paroled to the streets from O Wing proper in all the years that the prison has existed. No one goes from O Wing, Max Row straight to the general prison population. A man *must* go from Max Row to the regular adjustment center facility upstairs. Then from there to the general prison population. Only then can he entertain thoughts of eventual release to the outside world.

One can understand the depression felt by an inmate on Max Row. He's fallen as far as he can into the social trap, relief is so distant that it is very easy for him to lose his holds. In two weeks that little average man who may have ended up on Max Row for *suspicion* of *attempted* escape is so brutalized, so completely without holds, that he will never heal again. It's worse than Vietnam.

He's dodging lead. He may be forced to fight a duel to the death with knives. If he doesn't sound and act more zealous than everyone else he will be challenged for not being loyal to his race and its politics, fascism. Some of these cons support the pigs' racism without shame, the others support it inadvertently by their own racism. The former are white, the latter black. But in here as on the street black racism is a forced *reaction*. A survival adaptation.

The picture I have painted of Soledad's general population facility may have made it sound not too bad at all. That mistaken impression would result from the absence in my description of one more very important feature of the main line—terrorism. A frightening, petrifying diffusion of violence and intimidation is emitted from the offices of the warden and captain. How else could a small group of armed men be expected to hold and rule another much larger group except through *fear*?

We have a gym (inducement to throw away our energies with a ball instead of revolution). But if you walk into this gym with a cigarette burning, you're probably in trouble. There is a pig waiting to trap you. There's a sign "No Smoking." If you miss the sign, trouble. If you drop the cigarette to comply, trouble. The floor is regarded as something of a fire hazard (I'm not certain what the pretext is). There are no receptacles. The pig will pounce. You'll be told in no uncertain terms to scrape the cigarette from the floor with your hands. It builds from there. You have a gym but only certain things may be done and in specified ways. Since the rules change with the pigs' mood, it is really safer for a man to stay in his cell. . . .

Fay, have you ever considered what type of man is capable of handling absolute power? I mean how many would not abuse it? Is there any way of isolating or classifying generally who can be trusted with a gun and *absolute* discretion as to who he will kill? I've already mentioned that most of them are KKK types. The rest, all the rest, in general, are so stupid that they shouldn't be allowed to run their own bath. A *responsible* state government would have found a means of weeding out most of the savage types that are drawn to gunslinger jobs long ago. How did all these pigs get through?! Men who can barely read, write, or reason. How did they get through?! You may as well give a baboon a gun and set him loose on us!! It's the same in here as on the streets out there. *Who* has loosed this thing on an already suffering people? The Reagans, Nixons, the men who have, who own. Investigate them!! There are no qualifications asked, no experience necessary. Any fool who falls in here and can sign his name might shoot me tomorrow from a position thirty feet above my head with an automatic military rifle!! He could be dead drunk. It could really be an accident (a million to one it won't be, however), but he'll be protected still. He won't even miss a day's wages.

The textbooks on criminology like to advance the idea that prisoners are mentally defective. There is only the merest suggestion that the system itself is at fault. Penologists regard prisons as asylums. Most policy is formulated in a bureau that operates under the heading Department of Corrections. But what can we say about these asylums since *none* of the inmates are ever cured. Since in every instance they are sent out of the prison more damaged physically and mentally than when they entered. Because that is the reality. Do you continue to investigate the inmate? Where does administrative responsibility begin? Perhaps the administration of the prison cannot be held accountable for every individual act of their charges, but when things fly apart along racial lines, when the breakdown can be traced so clearly to circumstances even beyond the control of the guards and administration, investigation of anything outside the tenets of the fascist system itself is futile.

Nothing has improved, nothing has changed in the weeks since your team was here. We're on the same course, the blacks are fast losing the last of their restraints. Growing numbers of blacks are openly passed over when paroles are considered. They have become aware that their only hope lies in resistance. They have learned that resistance is actually possible. The holds are beginning to slip away. Very few men imprisoned for economic crimes or even crimes of passion against the oppressor feel that they are really guilty. Most of today's black convicts have come to understand that they are the most abused victims of an unrighteous order. Up until now, the prospect of parole has kept us from confronting our captors with any real determination. But now with the living conditions deteriorating, and with the sure knowledge that we are slated for destruction, we have been transformed into an implacable army of liberation. The shift to the revolutionary anti-establishment position that Huey Newton, Eldridge Cleaver, and Bobby Seale projected as a solution to the problems of Amerika's black colonies has taken firm hold of these brothers' minds. They are now showing great interest in the thoughts of Mao Tse-tung, Nkrumah, Lenin, Marx, and the achievements of men like Che Guevara, Giap, and Uncle Ho.

Some people are going to get killed out of this situation that is growing. That is not a warning (or wishful thinking). I see it as an "unavoidable consequence" of placing and leaving control of our lives in the hands of men like Reagan.

These prisons have always borne a certain resemblance to Dachau and Buchenwald, places for the bad niggers, Mexicans, and poor whites. But the last ten years have brought an increase in the percentage of blacks for crimes that can *clearly* be traced to political-economic causes. There are still some blacks here who consider themselves criminals—but not many. Believe me, my friend, with the time and incentive that these brothers have to read, study, and think, you will find no class or category more aware, more embittered, desperate, or dedicated to the ultimate remedy—revolution. The most dedicated, the best of our kind— you'll find them in the Folsoms, San Quentins, and Soledads. They live like there was no tomorrow. And for most of them there isn't. Somewhere along the line they sensed this. Life on the installment plan, three years of prison, three months on parole; then back to start all over again, sometimes in the same cell. Parole officers have sent brothers back to the joint for selling newspapers (the Black Panther paper). Their official reason is "Failure to Maintain Gainful Employment," etc.

We're something like 40 to 42 percent of the prison population. Perhaps more, since I'm relying on material published by the media. The leadership of the black prison population now definitely identifies with Huey, Bobby, Angela, Eldridge, and antifascism. The savage repression of blacks, which can be estimated by reading the obituary columns of the nation's dailies, Fred Hampton, etc., has not failed to register on the black inmates. The holds are being fast broken. Men who read Lenin, Fanon, and Che don't riot, "they mass," "they rage," they dig graves.

When John Clutchette was first accused of this murder he was proud, conscious, aware of his own worth but uncommitted to any specific remedial action. Review the process that they are sending this beautiful brother through now. It comes at the end of a long train of similar incidents in his prison life. Add to this all of the things he has witnessed happening to others of our group here. Comrade Fleeta spent eleven months here in O Wing for possessing photography taken from a newsweekly. It is such things that explain why California prisons produce more than their share of Bunchy Carters and Eldridge Cleavers.

Fay, there are only two types of blacks ever released from these places, the Carters and the broken men.

The broken men are so damaged that they will never again be suitable members of any sort of social unit. Everything that was still good when they entered the joint, anything inside of them that may have escaped the ruinous effects of black colonial existence, anything that may have been redeemable when they first entered the joint—is gone when they leave.

This camp brings out the very best in brothers or destroys them entirely. But none are unaffected. None who leave here are normal. If I leave here alive, I'll leave nothing behind. They'll never count me among the broken men, but I can't say that I am normal either. I've been hungry too long. I've gotten angry too often.

I've been lied to and insulted too many times. They've pushed me over the line from which there can be no retreat. I *know* that they will not be satisfied until they've pushed me out of this existence altogether. I've been the victim of so many racist attacks that I could never relax again. My reflexes will never be normal again. I'm like a dog that has gone through the K-9 process.

This is not the first attempt the institution (camp) has made to murder me. It is the most determined attempt, but not the first.

I look into myself at the close of every one of these pretrial days for any changes that may have taken place. I can still smile now, after ten years of blocking knife thrusts and pick handles of faceless sadistic pigs, of anticipating and reacting for ten years, seven of them in solitary. I can still smile sometimes, but by the time this thing is over I may not be a nice person. And I just lit my seventy-seventh cigarette of this twenty-one-hour day. I'm going to lay down for two or three hours, perhaps I'll sleep . . .

Seize the Time.

7. Attica Prisoners' Demands

Once the inmates of Attica prison took over the facility on Thursday, September 9, 1971, a committee of inmates drew up five demands as preconditions to end the takeover. These five demands would be broadened into "fifteen practical proposals" that would form the basis for the attempted negotiations among the prisoners, the committee of outside observers, state prison officials, and representatives from the governor's office.

THE FIVE DEMANDS

To the people of America

The incident that has erupted here at Attica is not a result of the dastardly bushwacking of the two prisoners Sept. 8, 1971 but of the unmitigated oppression wrought by the racist administration network of the prison, throughout the year.

WE are MEN! We are not beasts and do not intend to be beaten or driven as such. The entire prison populace has set forth to change forever the ruthless brutalization and disregard for the lives of the prisoners here and throughout the United States. What has happened here is but the sound before the fury of those who are oppressed.

' We will not compromise on any terms except those that are agreeable to us. We call upon all the conscientious citizens of America to assist us in putting an end to this situation that threatens the lives of not only us, but each and everyone of us as well.

We have set forth demands that will bring closer to reality the demise of these prisons, institutions that serve no useful purpose to the People of America but to those who would enslave and exploit the People of America.

Our Demands Are Such:

1. We want complete amnesty, meaning freedom from any physical, mental and legal reprisals.
2. We want now, speedy and safe transportation out of confinement, to a non-imperialistic country.
3. We demand that the FEDERAL GOVERNMENT intervene, so that we will be under direct FEDERAL JURISDICTION.
4. We demand the reconstruction of ATTICA PRISON to be done by inmates and/or inmate supervision.
5. We urgently demand immediate negotiation thru Wm. M. Kunstler, Attorney-at-Law, 588 Ninth Ave., NYC, Assemblyman Arthur O. Eve, of Buffalo, the Solidarity Committee, Minister Farrakhan of MUHAMMAD SPEAKS, Palante, The Young Lord's Party Paper, the Black Panther Party, Clarence Jones of the Amsterdam News, Tom Wicker of NY Times, Richard Roth of the Courier Express, the Fortune Society, David Anderson of the Urban League of Rochester, Blond-Eva Bond of NICAP, and Jim Ingram of Democrat Chronicle of Detroit, Mich. We guarantee the safe passage of all people to and from this institution. We invite *all the people* to come here and witness this degradation, so that they can better know how to bring this degradation to an end.

The Inmates of Attica Prison

THE FIFTEEN PRACTICAL PROPOSALS

Practical Proposals

1. Apply the New York State minimum wage law to all state institutions. STOP SLAVE LABOR.
2. Allow all New York State prisoners to be politically active, without intimidation or reprisals.
3. Give us true religious freedom.
4. End all censorship of newspapers, magazines, letters and other publications coming from the publisher.
5. Allow all inmates, at their own expense, to communicate with anyone they please.
6. When an inmate reaches conditional release date, give him a full release without parole.
7. Cease administrative resentencing of inmates returned for parole violations.
8. Institute realistic rehabilitation programs for all inmates according to their offense and personal needs.
9. Educate all correctional officers to the needs of the inmates, i.e., understanding rather than punishment.
10. Give us a healthy diet, stop feeding us so much pork, and give us some fresh fruit daily.
11. Modernize the inmate education system.
12. Give us a doctor that will examine and treat all inmates that request treatment.
13. Have an institutional delegation comprised of one inmate from each company authorized to speak to the institution administration concerning grievances (QUARTERLY).
14. Give us less cell time and more recreation with better recreational equipment and facilities.
15. Remove inside walls, making one open yard, and no more segregation or punishment.

8. "Negotiations and Failure"

Herman Badillo and Milton Haynes

At the request of Governor Nelson Rockefeller, U.S. Congressman Herman Badillo of the Bronx arrived at Attica on Friday, September 10, to serve on the observers' committee. These are excerpts from his account of his and other committee members' roles in attempting to serve as mediators in the four-day standoff before the New York state police were sent in to end the takeover. From A Bill of No Rights: Attica and the American Prison System, *by Herman Badillo and Milton Haynes.*

FRIDAY

. . . As a lawyer with some negotiating experience in the past, I felt the fact that the demands were listed on two separate sheets was an indication that the prisoners themselves wanted to negotiate. The demands were thus presented as two distinct lists, the first contradictory and propagandistic, the second a forthright statement of "practical proposals." It seemed to me there was a good basis for substantive discussions with the inmates.

An examination of the first list revealed its contradictory points: if the inmates were indeed demanding speedy and safe transportation to a "non-imperialist" country, why would they also demand a federal takeover of the prison, or the reconstruction of Attica? The practical proposals, on the other hand, were clear and consistent. . . .

It seemed evident from the way the demands were presented as two distinct documents, that the prisoners understood that some things could be negotiated, and some could not.

After [Commissioner of Correctional Services Russell] Oswald's presentation, Assemblyman Arthur Eve, who had already been at the prison for two days and involved in the negotiations up to that point, brought us up to date on his own activities. Eve indicated that we were going to have a major problem with the question of amnesty.

We adjourned our first caucus in the steward's room [an office being used by the observers] and decided to meet briefly with the prisoners in the yard. Even though all the Observers had not yet arrived, we felt it important to announce our arrival in the meantime. Without discussing it, we agreed on a black man as our spokesman—first it was Arthur Eve, and at another point it was Clarence Jones.

It was daylight when we first entered D-yard. The trip into rebel-held territory involved crossing a frontier like that between two foreign countries. From the administration building we walked through a tunnel, through A-block, towards the prisoners' section. At the gate to A-yard, we were handed over to prisoner escorts. The inmates had set up their own security system: we were searched at the gate, accompanied across A-yard, which was totally deserted, and into D-yard. Inside the crowded yard, inmate guards had linked arms to form a cordon around other prisoners who might interfere with our passage to the speaking platform, the bench where rebel leaders sat in the far corner of D-yard. Those of us who were known to the prisoners were greeted with cries of recognition. The fact of our arrival seemed to cheer the inmates substantially. We had given them hope of perhaps winning something out of the situation. The prisoners asked that we get the additional observers they had requested. . . .

Back in the steward's room, the committee decided to go over the entire set of proposals together. [William] Kunstler and several others had by now arrived. There seemed to be a great deal of confusion concerning the demands, so we sat down to determine our procedure for gathering the prisoners' proposals.

It was after 9 p.m. before we passed again from the perimeters of the prison controlled by state authorities, through the dark no-man's land that was A-yard, and into the littered confines of D-yard. There, amid the glare of television lights, the Committee of Observers, numbering almost thirty men—radicals and reactionaries; black men, white men, Puerto Rican men; state legislators, lawyers, ministers, reporters, and poverty fighters; all disparate in age and temperament and training—began negotiations with the 1,200 convicted, rebellious men.

The prisoners made it very clear from the outset that they would not agree to a negotiating committee of prisoners—all negotiations had to be conducted in the yard with every one of the inmates present. That seemed to indicate that this was no organized rebellion with leaders in strict control. The men insisted upon open discussions and wanted all the proceedings to be held in plain view with a microphone at the table so all could hear what was being said. . . .

This refusal to allow a committee to negotiate made the prospects of settling the rebellion more difficult. It is not easy to negotiate with a group of 1,200 people in an open yard at night. Moreover, our own committee was made up of as many as thirty people, some of whom were running in and out, while others spoke with small groups of inmates. Still other Observers were present for only part of the weekend. . . .

We all introduced ourselves to the inmates and, with Eve chairing what turned into a remarkable town meeting, we went down the list of demands, asking for comments and for a vote on each of the separate points. The vote demanding amnesty was practically unanimous.

There has been a great deal of discussion on the second point—speedy and safe transportation out of confinement to a non-imperialistic country. Indeed, reading and listening to news reports that weekend, one would have thought that the demand for transportation out of this country was an unalterable position of the inmates. But when the demand came up for a vote, it received support from fewer than twenty of the 1,200 prisoners. It was not a substantial question in the negotiations.

The demand for federal government intervention and for reconstruction of Attica prison also received little support.

However, when we turned to the second list, the "Practical Proposals," we began to get a real response. These were the issues the men in the yard cared about. The most sustained applause and the most enthusiastic vote was triggered by the demand, "Give us a doctor that will examine and treat all inmates who request treatment." . . .

After we had gone through the demands presented by the inmates, noting which ones had more support than others, we asked the men if there were any additional issues. After a discussion they agreed on the need for a Puerto Rican doctor for Spanish-speaking inmates, and the need for a narcotics program; they wanted a grand jury to investigate whether indeed guards were making a profit off the prison shop by selling products manufactured by the prisoners and keeping the money; they wanted black and Puerto Rican corrections officers; they wanted a Spanish library; and they wanted the removal of Superintendent Mancusi.

It was well past midnight by the time this meeting had taken its course. Inmates would stand up, some of them repeatedly, and tell us how bad conditions were, while we tried to write down what they wanted. It was a totally spontaneous, unrehearsed, and, I might say, unorganized operation. I took down the additional demands in my own handwriting. Various other members of the Observers' group had scraps of paper with notes about the added demands. By comparing our various handwritten notes we were able to come up with the demands to be worked out the next day with Oswald. It is important to remember the spontaneous, informal aspect of this process, for it shows once again that the rebellion was not really organized; the prisoners had not worked out all their demands in advance.

SATURDAY

. . . Saturday morning . . . a committee of about ten began work on drafting a revised version of the inmates' demands. We worked through the morning and into the afternoon. During the afternoon we called Commissioner Oswald in. By this time the commissioner was under enormous pressures. Corrections officials from other state institutions—even from other states—continued to call and demand that he put an immediate end to the Attica rebellion which, they claimed, was endangering the security of their own institutions. Furthermore, as more state officials and some of [Governor Nelson] Rockefeller's advisers arrived, the lines of authority became increasingly confused. . . .

While Oswald was negotiating points with the Observers' Committee, rumors were flying hot and heavy among troopers and corrections people. As early as that Saturday afternoon, reports were circulating of the emasculation of one hostage. A prisoner had reportedly fought his way from D-yard into A-block, which was controlled by state police. Previously Dunbar and Oswald had relied on information from those like Dr. Warren Hanson, who reported that the story of hostages being forced into a bathroom which was then set on fire was "nonsense." Now the corrections people would say: "We have sources of information behind the walls that you don't have."

It was in such an atmosphere that we negotiated with Oswald that afternoon. The commissioner did not attempt to deny that the prisoners were right on many points. He freely conceded that prisoners were denied religious freedom. He admitted that the Black Muslim religion was a legitimate faith, but that it was not so recognized in the prison, and that those who wanted to practice it were not allowed to do so. We pointed out to the commissioner that this happens to be a violation of the United States Constitution. . . .

Over the course of the afternoon we came to agreement on twenty-eight points. We then had them typed up. They constituted a remarkable document—to have been worked out in such an atmosphere, among such men, and in such great haste. Within twenty-four hours of our arrival at the prison we had, through the negotiations with the prisoners in the yard and with Oswald, agreed on all these very important points. . . .

While we were negotiating with the commissioner, something had happened which was to affect the whole course of later events: William Quinn, the injured guard, had died in Rochester Hospital at 4:30 p.m. A charge of homicide that could be leveled at any or all of the 1,200 men in the revolt was now added to the other amnesty problems. We were not informed of Quinn's death until a seven o'clock radio broadcast reported that Quinn had died of injuries suffered when inmates had thrown him from a second-story window at the beginning of the riot. (Every window in Attica, including those in the warden's office and in the steward's room where we negotiated, has heavy steel bars over it.) The prisoners themselves did not learn of Quinn's death until later in the evening.

The amnesty question was incalculably important for the inmates. Some of them had been involved in the riots in New York City prisons ten months earlier, and were thus acutely aware of the consequences of rebellion. In those riots, it had been agreed [that if] they gave up their hostages there would be no reprisals—yet television films and many newspaper photographs showed guards and police beating prisoners right after the rebellion collapsed. At least one leader at Attica, Herbert X. Blyden, had seventy-two counts of criminal indictments against him stemming from those riots. Consequently, the Attica inmates were not about to risk giving up the hostages only to find themselves at the mercy of furious corrections officers once everybody else had gone away. They wanted an Ombudsman there on a permanent basis, and they wanted unbreakable assurances against reprisals.

Saturday evening we received word that Bobby Seale, chairman of the Black Panther Party, had arrived outside the prison. . . . We reviewed for Seale what had taken place in the negotiations thus far, and showed him the twenty-eight points. We said it had been our intention, before he joined us, to re-enter the yard, report our progress to the prisoners, and recommend that they agree with the twenty-eight points.

Seale read the points at once, then made the valid reply that he was in no position to make a recommendation on such short notice; that the most he could do was accompany us into the yard. He would stay a short while, he informed us, explaining to the inmates that he had just arrived, that he was there only to let them know he had arrived, that he would be in touch with Huey P. Newton on the twenty-eight points, and that he would return the next morning. We all agreed that we would leave the yard with Seale after his brief appearance before the inmates.

Much to my surprise, the inmates' reception of Seale was guarded. Seale himself was unusually subdued—one could assume that having spent several years in prison, he felt depressed at re-entering the gates. There was applause for the Black Panther chairman when he entered the yard, but little satisfaction with what he had to say. He spoke for only a few minutes. He said simply that the Observers Committee would leave right away, that he would consult with Huey Newton before returning in the morning. One of the inmates—Roger Champen—stood up and complained that it was unfair of us to leave after only a few minutes—that the inmates had been waiting under great tension all day. At that point, Clarence Jones and Arthur Eve agreed to stay, and Jones began to read the twenty-eight points to the prisoners.

I left with Seale, as did all other elected officials except Eve. I did not see how we could possibly come to an agreement under the circumstances of that Saturday night. Even if we had come back to the yard with agreements on everything they asked for, the prisoners would have insisted on hearing what Seale would have to say Sunday morning. I felt, therefore, that it was the worst possible time to reveal the agreements we had reached with Oswald and with the Wyoming County district attorney. The inmates were bound to turn them down, or to say: wait and see what Seale recommends. I understood the prisoners' anger at our leaving but I felt that nothing worthwhile could be accomplished under the circumstances.

Oswald met Seale going out and thanked him on behalf of the state for coming. Kunstler escorted Seale to his car, then returned to the yard just as Clarence Jones finished reading the twenty-eight points. The inmates shouted down the twenty-eight points; then there was silence. It was surely one of the tensest moments in D-yard.

Then Brother Richard [X. Clark] rose to his feet. "You are now looking at a bunch of dead men," he said. "What amnesty means to us is what insurance means to your families." Another inmate summoned Kunstler to the microphone: "And what do you think, counselor?" William Kunstler is a man who arouses great emotion in people. His admirers hail his courage and his considerable abilities, while his detractors are outraged by the very mention of his name. He had been very effective earlier that Saturday during the drafting of the twenty-eight points. He arrived back in the prison yard at a moment when the Observers, out of control of the situation, felt quite anxious.

Kunstler addressed the inmates: "I'm speaking to you as a lawyer and that may destroy my credibility as a lawyer, but as a lawyer I can tell you that these twenty-eight points are the best we can do for you—at this time." Kunstler then sat down.

With the inmates shouting encouragement, Brother Richard then held aloft the sheet of paper listing the twenty-eight points and ripped it in half.

When the Observers' Committee members returned from the

yard, we talked the situation over for a while, then we adjourned until Seale's return.

It is important to note that, in their talks with newsmen outside the prison, members of the Observers' Committee had made many efforts to underscore the importance of eschewing the use of force and sticking with the negotiations. Kunstler had told Fred Ferretti of the *New York Times* and other journalists that "there is a good chance this could end," provided all parties, ". . . bargain in good faith." Kunstler also said—and this was in the *New York Times* that must have been on Nelson Rockefeller's breakfast table at Pocantico Hills that Sunday: "I hope the authorities don't precipitate tragedy, because there might be a two- or three-day negotiating span." . . .

SUNDAY

. . . Sunday, September 12, 1971, was an extraordinary day at Attica prison. Never had I seen such unbridled hatred as the men outside the prison demonstrated towards the Observers' Committee and the rebellious inmates. An armed force gathered during the day in the dispiriting drizzle that later changed to heavy rain. Evidence of impending violence lay everywhere—except in D-yard where, I am convinced, the prisoners had no idea of the state's decision to quit negotiating and apply armed force.

Tom Wicker has written: "The emphasis on guns and clubs during the crisis was incredible; it had to be seen to be believed . . . these guns, moreover, were in the hands of men who left no doubt they wanted to use them. Correction Commissioner Oswald's long delay of the assault and his effort to negotiate were met with anger and impatience by the prison staff; the Observers who were trying to prevent bloodshed saw hostility at every turn. A guard bringing them a box of food said as he put it down, 'If I'd known it was for you I wouldn't have brought it.' " . . .

It was into this kind of climate that Bobby Seale returned at 8:30 on Sunday morning. Oswald met him and asked what he was going to say inside. Seale said he could not recommend acceptance of the twenty-eight points. Oswald said that unless he promised to speak on behalf of the twenty-eight points, he would not allow Seale to return to D-yard. Seale walked out. . . .

After Seale left, we found ourselves with no place to go. The previous night I had feared just such an eventuality: Seale might not show up, or he might refuse to go back in, and we, having presented the results of our negotiations to the prisoners, would have no room to maneuver. It was necessary to come up with some alternative strategy since obviously we could not go back merely to tell the inmates that Seale was not returning.

Given the fact that they had rejected the twenty-eight points, our only recourse was to ask Rockefeller to come to Attica to meet with the Committee of Observers. It was not suggested by us, as later claimed by state officials, that Rockefeller come meet with the prisoners.

. . . If Rockefeller came, if he promised to enforce protection of prisoners' rights, and, *had* he shown the willingness for some form of executive amnesty, then the crisis might yet be resolved without force.

As the day degenerated into a series of preparations for an armed attack on the prison, a further reason emerged for calling in Rockefeller: It seemed to us that only Rockefeller's presence could avert a senseless massacre of both hostages and inmates.

Oswald had apparently given up on us the night before when we returned from the yard with the inmates' rejection of the twenty-eight points. There had been scarcely twenty-four hours of serious negotiations. But we had come a long way. The state had agreed to certain of the inmates' demands. Oswald had expected, unrealistically I think, that the issue would be solved as soon as his "generosity" became evident to the prisoners. The Observers lost credibility with Oswald when we failed to get the prisoners' agreement immediately. From Saturday evening on, his attitude was: There's nothing to discuss, we've agreed on these points and they've turned us down; from now on it's just a question of time until we go in.

After Seale left Attica, there was some question whether any of the Observers' Committee would be allowed back in the yard. Oswald said no legislators—meaning Eve, Dunne, Garcia, and me—would be allowed in. The strain was beginning to tell on members of the Observers' Committee as well. Eve had to demand that some committee members stop going to talk with the commissioner independently. Ours was a very diverse group representing many points of view, and containing many personalities. . . . It should be noted, after all the emphasis given our disputes and arguments, that in the most desperate and crucial hour—Sunday afternoon—we stood together unanimously.

The state had decided to use armed force to storm the prison that day. Commissioner Oswald has since admitted to members of Representative Pepper's Select House Committee on Crime that an attack on Sunday afternoon was "delayed at the last minute because of the Observers' pleas." By noon, we could see from our window that preparations for an attack were being made all around the prison.

About noon, a delegation of six observers—Eve, Kenyatta, Tom Soto, Jose Paris, G. I. Ortiz, and Reverend Florence—went down to the gate of D-Yard to keep the inmates posted on our efforts to get Rockefeller to come to meet with us. The prisoners had asked that Rockefeller come meet with them. The purpose of the subcommittee's visit was to inform Brother Richard that the Observers felt Rockefeller would not do that, but that we had asked him to come and participate in the Observers' Committee conversations and hoped he would comply with our request.

The area in the vicinity of D-gate was a sort of no-man's land. Observers who entered through the main prison gate crossed A-yard towards a series of gates that led through the overground tunnel into D-yard. It was at the entrance to A-yard, at the border between rebel and state territory, that the committee of six spoke with the inmates. The Observers selected Tom Soto as spokesman to explain the committee's actions to Brother Richard. While Soto talked at the gate, Deputy Commissioner Walter Dunbar stood right behind the Observers with several heavily-armed state troopers. They asked Dunbar to withdraw the trooper with the submachine gun. Reverend Florence said, "Hey, why don't you move behind us without those guns?" Another of the Observers suggested they form a line in front of the gate to block a clear shot of Brother Richard.

Soto explained our position to Brother Richard and, in the course of his discussion, handed the inmate leader a piece of paper drafted by the committee. Dunbar yelled, "Hey! You can't take that in with you." Accordingly, Brother Richard read the document, considered it, and handed it back, taking great care not to further aggravate relations between Observers' Committee members and Dunbar and the corrections officials. He then requested that a black newsman, a Puerto Rican newsman, Tom Wicker, and television reporters be allowed in to interview the hostages—the hostages wanted to talk with the press.

At the very moment members of this subcommittee were at the gate conferring with Brother Richard, Commissioner Oswald came in to tell the rest of us that he was drafting an ultimatum to the prisoners, and that under no circumstances would any members of the Observers' Committee be allowed back into the yard. . . .

—At 1:27, Tom Wicker, who had Rockefeller's telephone number at Pocantico Hills, put through a call and got the governor on the line. Wicker, then I, then Jones, and finally Dunne spoke to the governor. We all urged him to come to Attica to meet with us. We told him we did not want to discuss any prescribed agenda. He told us he could never agree on amnesty. I said we would not discuss the question of amnesty, that if he would only come and talk with us, we would gain additional time—it seemed clear from the movement around us that police officials were thinking of an attack. . . .

An attack that Sunday afternoon, I told Rockefeller, would likely result in a massacre, which might in turn lead to widespread violence. People all over the country were watching their television sets. I told him to consider the impact of that news bulletin in Harlem, Bedford-Stuyvesant, the South Bronx, Buffalo, Rochester, Detroit, Cleveland. I told him: "You need the time as much as we do, so the best way, while you set this machinery in motion, is—you come and meet with us. At least you will have been able to get an opinion from the scene, while if you rush in now, Mayor Lindsay is probably going to tell you he'll need National Guardsmen in New York."

Rockefeller had apparently not thought out that aspect of an attack. He said he would speak to his aide at Attica, Robert Douglass. I then turned the phone over to Clarence Jones and to Senator John Dunne, both of whom appealed urgently for him to come there and meet with us. Rockefeller said he would keep in touch. The call ended at 1:51 p.m. . . .

—At 2:09, the subcommittee returned from the gate. Clarence Jones, after his conversation with the Governor had gone downstairs and, conferring briefly with Brother Richard, had implied strongly that Rockefeller would visit the prison. When they returned, Wicker vigorously contested Jones' impression. I agreed that the governor was noncommittal in his remarks, though at least he had not turned us down outright.

—At 2:11, Oswald came back into the steward's room and read to us the following statement which was addressed to the inmates:

> As Commissioner of Correctional Services, I have personally met with you several times in areas under your control for the purposes of insuring the immediate safety of employee hostages and the safety of all others concerned during the current, difficult situation.
>
> As you all know, food, clothing, bedding and water, and medical care have been available to you. You have been able to meet with outside observers of your choice and representatives of the news media. A federal court order was obtained promptly to guarantee that there would be no administrative reprisals. Your representatives have been able to ascertain that no mistreatment of inmates has occurred.
>
> I urgently request you to release the hostages unharmed now, *and to accept the recommendations of the committee of outside observers, which recommendations were approved by me,* and join with me in restoring order to this institution.
>
> Only after these steps are taken am I willing to meet with a five-member committee chosen by you to discuss any grievances you may have and to create a mechanism by which you can be assured that the recommendations I have agreed to are implemented.
>
> All possible efforts have been made to deal fairly with your problems and grievances to resolve the present situation. All good faith is embodied in the proposed agreement I signed which is in your hands.
>
> It is in the interest of all concerned that you now respond affirmatively to this request.

Many committee members were angry and astonished that Oswald implied that the twenty-eight points were "the recommendations of the committee," and further, that he implied the Observers were party to his ultimatum. Eve exploded: "Man, you've just signed my death warrant!" Eve and other Observers said Oswald's statement would destroy any confidence the inmates had in us, and would endanger any members of the committee who met in the yard with inmates.

Oswald said that was immaterial since the Observers were not going to be permitted to re-enter the yard anyway. This intensified the already vigorous exchange between Oswald and other committee members. Several members of the group pleaded passionately with Oswald to let them return. After confessing with some anguish, "I've bent and I've bent and I can't compromise further. I'm walking through the tunnel of hell," he yielded. He agreed, "against the advice of every adviser in the state," to permit one last visit to the yard by the journalists (to interview the hostages) and several of the Committee of Observers.

At this time we learned from Oswald that Rockefeller's office had released a statement saying he would not come—in Oswald's words—"to meet with the inmates." Shortly afterward, we were given a mimeographed copy of Rockefeller's bristling statement.

> From the beginning of the tragic situation involving riots and hostages at the Attica Correctional Facility which imperil the lives of many persons, including thirty-nine innocent citizens and dedicated law-enforcement officers, I have been in constant, direct contact with Commissioner Oswald and my representatives at the scene. Every effort has been made by the state to resolve the situation and to establish order, hopefully by peaceable means.
>
> I have carefully considered the request conveyed to me by the Committee of Citizen Observers at Attica, as well as the demands of the inmates that I meet with them in the prison yard. I am deeply grateful to the members of the Committee for their long and courageous efforts to effect a peaceful settlement.
>
> The key issue at stake, however, is still the demand for total amnesty for any criminal act which may have occurred. I do not have the constitutional authority to grant such a demand, and I would not, even if I had the authority because to do so would undermine the very essence of our

free society—the fair and impartial application of the law. In view of the fact that the key issue is total amnesty—in spite of the best efforts of the Committee and in spite of Commissioner Oswald's major commitments to the inmates—I do not feel that my physical presence on the site can contribute to a peaceful settlement.

Rockefeller went on to reiterate his support for Oswald and to urge the prisoners to accept the twenty-eight points.

The Observers then agreed unanimously to send an appeal to Rockefeller, asking that he come to the prison to meet with us. Since pressure seemed to be running towards sending in the troopers, we then issued an appeal to the public, urging them to send Rockefeller telegrams asking him to meet us. . . .

Rockefeller had mentioned on the phone the pressure he was under to storm the prison. We hoped to have some impact by rounding up public support for another course. We drafted the statement under some pressure ourselves, but it was not a hasty or ill-considered document. Originally, Senator Dunne objected to the wording of the statement, and Tom Soto objected to the statement altogether since he did not see any point in trying to get Rockefeller to come. However, in order to avoid misunderstanding, we went around the room taking a vote on the final draft, and everyone voted to send the appeal out to the press immediately. . . .

I was designated to contact the press, and proceeded to do so, calling several agencies and attempting to tape a statement for CBS over the phone. However, when authorities discovered I was on radio with the appeal, they cut off our phone in the steward's room.

A delegation of Observers and news reporters re-entered the prison—for what was to be their last visit inside D-yard—at 2:55 p.m. The Observers' Committee hoped that showing the hostages on television, alive and unhurt, would dispel rumors of slain hostages and convince authorities that there was no need for haste. At about the same time, Oswald was outside the prison, reading the text of the ultimatum he was sending in to the more than one hundred members of the press. Unknown to Eve, Kunstler, Wicker, and other members of the Observers' Committee entering the prison yard, the inmates had already received the text of Oswald's statement and thought the Observers were trying to double-cross them. According to several reliable accounts, Brother Richard said, "I notice you can't look me in the eye, brothers." He then pulled from his pocket the ultimatum, implying that the Observers agreed with Oswald's position. "You lied to us. Some of the brothers want to kill you. You may not get out of here alive today." With understandable urgency, Eve, Kunstler, and Jose Paris of the Young Lords said they had not known about the note. It was under such circumstances that the Observers held their last consultation with the inmates. . . .

During this visit several of the hostages went before television film cameras to voice appeals to Rockefeller. Sergeant Edward Cunningham was one of those whose desperate plea to the governor was filmed: "I am speaking for all thirty-eight of us. We have been treated fairly by these men. I sleep on a mattress and they sleep on the ground. I think they should take all of those men off the roofs, along with their guns. There is more hardware here than there was at Mylai. I have eight children and two grandchildren. I want to live. I think Rocky should come here. If he doesn't, I'm dead. I also think immediate clemency should be given to all inmates involved in this affair." Asked if he was coerced, threatened, or otherwise forced to make his statements to the television cameras, Cunningham replied: "I, as do all these men, do this on my own free will." Cunningham was one of those who was to die in a hail of bullets the following morning. His plea, and that of several other hostages, came to nought. As the interview was being filmed, Oswald walked into the steward's room to tell us that there was great confusion, great distrust, and a very dangerous situation in D-yard because of the note he had sent in.

Our phone was cut off just after the subcommittee members returned from the yard at 6:18 p.m. This complete hardening of attitudes by the commissioner was a clear enough indication to us that our attempts had failed.

Correction officials were now treating congressmen of the United States, state representatives, and other committee members like prisoners. Our phone was dead. We were told to choose between leaving the prison or being locked in the steward's room, with a guard posted at our door.

We called Oswald in once again—this was early Sunday evening—and he blew up at us: "I've given everything and I've got nothing in return!" We all pleaded for more time. I asked him for one more day—for at least twenty-four hours. He refused. I then asked him to give us until nine o'clock Monday morning. He refused that, later saying he might give us until 7 a.m., but he wouldn't guarantee it. At one point, as Kunstler argued heatedly for more time, Oswald looked at him and said: "I can give you no assurances that there will not be action. There will be no more negotiations in D-block."

Tom Wicker, and reporters Dick Edwards of the *Amsterdam News* and Rudy Garcia of the *Daily News* went out into the pouring rain to brief other reporters outside the gates on their latest and last meeting with the inmates. Wicker reported that there was "absolute solidarity" among the inmates of all races. This brought a violent tirade of abuse from guards, police, and relatives present. Edwards reported that the bystanders shouted at Wicker: "Nigger-lover! You must live with niggers. Sonofabitch. What kind of white man are you? Standing on a platform with a nigger and help a nigger talking against your own. Why don't you talk about the unity of the guards? The police? You dirty double-crossing bastard. We ought to string you up." Kunstler and some of the other members of the committee left late that night to go to Batavia for some sleep. I stayed, fearing an attack during the night—Young Lord representatives and Black Panther men were staying overnight in the prison. They needed a public official to at least insure their safety in that nasty atmosphere.

Almost no one was able to sleep that night, though once in a while one of us would stretch out for a few minutes on one of the desks, or doze fitfully in the chairs around the steward's room.

So ended that tragic Sunday at Attica. Rockefeller had unaccountably snubbed the very mediators he had asked to go to the prison and left the problem in the hands of his own aides and advisors at the scene. In spite of our warnings to him that retaking the prison by force might very well result in a massacre, he had denied us a hearing.

As the Observers left the yard that afternoon for the last time, Brother Richard Clark had hugged and kissed each man goodbye, and said to them, "Tell my wife and children that I am ready to

die. I cannot live any longer as a caged beast. I know they are
going to kill us. Tell them we are doing this so, in the event my
children or grandchildren should slip along the way, they will not
have to live like dogs. Tell them it is better to die like a man than
to live like a dog."

MONDAY: THE STORMING OF THE PRISON

It was a drizzly, chilly morning at Attica with clouds hovering less
than two hundred feet above the prison walls. Those of us in the
steward's room awoke to the sounds of hundreds of blue-helmeted
state troopers gathering in the grassy area between the main gate
and A-block. We could hear them below, answering the roll,
fussing with their gas masks and their guns.

Commissioner Oswald came in at about 7:30 to tell us he was
about to give the inmates one hour's ultimatum. Oswald said they
planned to move in sometime around nine, and that if we did not
leave now, we would be held prisoner until it was over. We said
we would not leave, so two armed guards were posted at our
door, waving their guns at us. We were told there would be a gas
attack. We therefore asked for gas masks. The commissioner's
people said they could not find any extra gas masks, and we would
have to do the best we could.

At that point, I must say, we were all very concerned that we
might be shot by our guards. Their attitude was indescribably
hostile. We felt that if they could justify shooting us down in any
way, they would.

Seventeen of us were confined inside the little room, watching
the troopers make their preparations. There were to be no civilian
eyewitnesses to the assault. Senator Dunne had strongly urged
Oswald to let him observe the takeover, but his request was
peremptorily refused. As Oswald handed his final ultimatum to
the prisoners, control of events passed completely out of civilian
hands into the hands of the para-military leaders of the state
troopers and the National Guard.

At 8:50 a.m., Oswald's press aide, Gerald Houlihan, appeared
outside the prison gates to pass out copies of Oswald's latest
statement:

At 7:46 a.m. I delivered the attached memorandum to Brother Richard Clarke. In delivering it, I said: "Mr. Clarke, I earnestly implore you to give the contents of this memorandum your most careful consideration. I want to continue negotiations with you." Mr. Clarke said that a matter of this kind would have to be referred to the Peoples' Central Committee and that he would take it back to them. I reminded him that I would expect the answer within the hour.

Russell G. Oswald—Commissioner,
New York State Department of
Correctional Services

Too little is known about what was happening in D-yard at this moment. A voice vote was taken after Oswald's last ultimatum had been read over the microphone. The response was negative. Hostages report that some inmates shouted that the rebels should "kill the hostages and fight to the death." (Almost the same quotation came from the prisoners at Long Island City jail in New York the previous October, fifteen minutes before they surrendered against an overwhelming show of force.) The hostages were blindfolded, and some of them were bound hand-and-foot. Eight of the hostages according to their own statements, were taken to a trench dug by the inmates during the uprising. These hostages were being transferred as Oswald's last ultimatum expired at one minute after nine o'clock. By this time, two army CH-34 helicopters, which had been outside the grounds all weekend, had started to warm up their engines.

Oswald stayed in his office, entirely out of touch with what was happening in the yard. His only contact with events was through Deputy Commissioner Walter Dunbar, who had gone for one final meeting with the inmates.

Dunbar phoned from A-block to relay the prisoners' response to Oswald's ultimatum. His message was, "Negative. Negative! And now they've got the hostages at Times Square." That message was in turn relayed to Governor Rockefeller interrupting a discussion he was having with several state officials about an upcoming transportation bond issue. One of those at the meeting was Rockefeller's press secretary, Ronald Maiorana, who later told reporters that the decision to storm the prison 400 miles away was made "by people on the scene" in conference with the governor. "One of the things influencing the action decision was a report from Oswald that some prisoners were in an area known as Times Square and they were holding knives to the throats of some of the hostages."

At 8:56 the engines of the army helicopters stopped suddenly. An Attica fireman cursed: "They're shutting them down. I'll be a sonofabitch. It's a sin. Some lives are going to be sacrificed," he told a *Daily News* reporter, "but you've got to take a stand." The press contingent was being handled by a muscular guard with a nightstick who called reporters "Prisoner-oriented, ghoulish bastards," and complained about biased reporting of the event. He positioned state troopers shoulder-to-shoulder around the reporters to keep them tightly ensconced within a tight enclave.

A small, state police helicopter with a loudspeaker aboard started its engines at exactly nine o'clock. During these long and agonizing minutes—the attack did not begin until 9:43—the seventeen of us in the steward's room huddled together, crouched down, for fear a volley of bullets might cut us down. We were told that a truck with extra gas masks had lost the way and not arrived. In order to have some protection against the gas, we asked for water in which to soak our handkerchiefs. The guards balked at first, but they finally did bring some water.

William Kunstler arrived outside the heavily-guarded gates at 9:26, clutching a Buffalo newspaper with the headline: "Mood of Hostility Grips Attica as Talks Break Off." Kunstler was barred from entering the prison, and was left to stand watching in anguish as the smaller state police helicopter flew around the prison in ever tightening circles. Tom Wicker had made it inside just a few minutes earlier, barely before the deadline expired.

All that reporters outside the prison could do was to monitor walkie-talkie and radio transmissions off the blaring radios of state police cars. At 9:30, they heard the helicopter pilots chatting: "There's a 200-foot ceiling. The low stuff is coming in from the west. It'll be about 100 feet."

Then at 9:42, the voice of Captain Henry Williams took command of the assault. "All forces in position." One minute later, Williams ordered all electric power in the prison cut off. The clock in the steward's room came to a stop at 9:43:28. The power cut-off destroyed chances for a clear videotape recording of the takeover. State authorities say that when the videotape machine went on battery power—during the most important part of the takeover—the quality of the tape was so poor as to be worthless.

We watched as helicopters made their first low passes over D-yard. At 9:45, just as the helicopters were making their first sortie, Captain Williams directed over his radio: "Zero in on targets. Do not take action until the drop." Another voice cut in quickly: "The drop has been made. Jackpot One has made the drop." Williams shouted: "Move in! Move in! The drop has been made."

Clouds of tear gas rose from D-yard, quickly followed by the sound of canisters popping, and the snap of rifle fire. From the steward's room it was difficult to distinguish between the sound of gunfire and the tear-gas canisters going off. Within moments of the attack, a great wave of gas rolled across the yard and into our room, choking and blinding us. (CS or pepper gas stings the eyes and skin and gives one the sensation of suffocation.)

Tom Wicker has reported accurately, and I think most sensitively, on those minutes.

> ATTICA, N.Y. Sept. 13—At 9:43:28 this morning the power went off in the small littered steward's room on the second floor of the Attica Correctional Facility's administration building.
>
> The hands of an electric clock on the wall pointed to that second for almost two hours, while state policemen and other officers put a bloody end to a massive uprising by about 1,500 inmates—mostly black and Puerto Rican.
>
> To the 17 men in the room, the hands marked the moment of truth—the second when the end came for four days of emotional and exhausting effort to avoid the bloodshed that every one of them feared from the beginning. For 28 of the prisoners with whom they had vainly "negotiated" and for nine of the hostages the prisoners had been holding, death had been signaled. . . .
>
> Gazing out the window of the steward's room at the helmeted troopers and the drifts of gas floating across the prison grounds, two of the 17-member group, Representative Herman Badillo of New York City and this corre-

spondent, assured each other that they had done all they could—and each saw in the other's eye that the assurance was needed.

"There's always time to die," Mr. Badillo said. "I don't know what the rush was."

Behind him, at another window, a young lawyer and penologist named Julian Tepper said in a flat, tired voice, "I can see eight bodies on the ground dead."

Months later, the question still haunts me. There was no doubt in my mind that people were going to be massacred. I could not and I cannot see what was so urgent about bringing on a bloodbath. The prisoners were not going anywhere. They were out in a muddy yard in the rain, surrounded by high walls, and a tremendous armed force. They could have been starved out. The water could have been cut off, as was in fact, done at one point. They could have been saturated with tear gas—indeed, that was part of the attack that morning. There were any number of alternatives open to the state. But from the way state troopers lined up outside our window, we felt forced to crouch for fear they would shoot up into our room and say it was just part of the whole business. With such intensity loose down below, who could know where it would stop. We had no confidence that they were not going to kill us. Certainly, we had no confidence that they were not going to kill as many of the inmates as they could.

No one—except perhaps state police or Rockefeller's people at the scene—knows who gave the order to fire, or *if* there was an order to fire. We do know that troopers and deputies had been told that the prisoners had no conventional weapons or ammunition; possibly they would have knives, captured tear gas guns, and perhaps fire bombs. One witness to trooper briefings reported that forces were told to "watch out for your buddy," to be certain "the other guy" got it first. "If you encounter resistance, resist it." They were also told that all of the hostages were white. All the attack force was white—that left black men as the enemy. Rather than call in readily available black National Guardsmen from Buffalo, just twenty-five miles away, state authorities rounded up white troopers from places two hundred and more miles distant. Authorities know that white troopers would kill black and Puerto

Rican prisoners—but they could not count on black National Guardsmen to do the same.

After a period of gunfire and tear-gas canisters exploding, we could hear a broadcast from the state police helicopter: "Place your hands on your heads and surrender to the officer nearest you. You will not be hurt." The message was repeated again and again. According to all accounts that we can piece together, there was no resistance from the inmates after the gas was dropped. One hostage, Elmer Huehn, said that at the time of the assault his inmate guard whispered, "I don't have the heart to kill you," and shoved him to the ground, covering Huehn's body with his own.[1]

We were held in the steward's room until late morning, during which time the twenty-nine hostages who were rescued came streaming out of the prison gasping and coughing beside state troopers and corrections officers. Even with protecting gas masks, troopers were having trouble with the incapacitating gas.

From time to time during the attack, Deputy Commissioner Walter Dunbar would burst into the steward's room with reports on the state's maneuvers. With great gusto he explained to us that he was himself a military man and that, as a military man, he admired the state's operation, which was being carried out "with a minimum of casualties." His reports took the form of battle bulletins—"D-block has been recaptured," "There's hand-to-hand fighting in the cells," "We should be out in an hour," and so forth.

Shortly after noon, Dunbar came by the steward's room again, this time accompanied by several Republican legislators. He said

---

1. Even on the day following the assault, when it was widely believed that the prisoners had slashed the throats of eight hostages, there abounded a whole set of curiously touching stories about inmate ministrations to the hostages officials said were held at knifepoint. An inmate assigned to guard a twenty-three-year-old civilian employee named Ronald Kozlowski asked Kozlowski, as the helicopters circled, how he felt. Kozlowski said he felt sick, and the inmate gave him a Tums to settle his stomach. The inmate was dead a moment later, a bullet hole in his chest. Another hostage, reportedly held on the parapet, told Dr. Warren Hanson that the inmate had cut his bonds and told him to get down when the firing started.

that those of us who were elected officials—me, Garcia, Dunne and Eve, as well as those with him, Senator McGowan and Assemblyman Wemple—could have a tour of the freshly-secured prison yard. This sudden acknowledgement of our elective status came as something of a surprise because, for the last few hours, we had been prisoners just like the others; in Commissioner Oswald's own words: "prisoners of the state."

Dunbar then took us on a tour of D-yard. I recall vividly that I could hardly breathe because the air was still heavy with gas—and this was several hours after the attack. Dunbar pointed to a pool of blood and said this was where the hostages had been brought to be placed in execution positions. The reason people had to be killed and wounded, he told us, was that, when the tear gas was dropped, prisoners began cutting the throats of the hostages.[2] Not only had he, Dunbar, and others witnessed this, but authorities had videotape and gunsight films of the acts themselves. This was the reason for going in shooting—to prevent more hostages from being killed. He described how sharpshooters lined up on the roofs of surrounding blocks and skillfully picked off the prisoner-executioners without killing the hostages. He said that all the hostages had been killed by prisoners cutting their throats.

He showed us a big inmate, stretched prone on a table in the

---

2. A reader who did not follow the accounts of that day in newspapers or on radio and television should be aware that the version of the hostages' deaths related by officials at the prison for a full twenty-four hours was false. Gerald Houlihan—Oswald's press aide—and Deputy Commissioner Walter Dunbar told legislators and newsmen that the hostages' throats had been slashed, that one hostage had been emasculated, and that two of the hostages had been killed at least one day prior to the assault on the prison. All these details were false and were so proven by a state medical examiner the next day.

The state has since frequently claimed that the impression the hostages had died from slashed throats came from the press. Indeed, Oswald has become increasingly careless in his attempt to shift responsibility for the throat-slashing reports: On October 18, he told the Northeast Regional Conference of the Ladies of Charity that the false rumors were started because "news media were talking with anyone coming out of the gate." (Are Houlihan and Dunbar to be taken as "anyone coming out of the gate"?)

yard, forced to balance a football between his chin and chest. This man, Dunbar said, had been castrating a guard named Michael Smith, and stuffing the guard's sexual organs into his mouth— "Mau Mau style." Smith, it turned out later, had not been harmed in the action. At this point, of course, we had no way of knowing whether Dunbar's account was accurate or not. It was unthinkable that he was concocting all this for a sizeable group of public officials. Dunbar's account made it seem plausible that the troopers had of necessity gone in shooting—but was even this tale of inmate atrocity reason enough to justify the deaths of thirty-six men that morning, of the four others who died later, and the serious wounding of 110 prisoners?

It seemed to me even then that the state, with Dunbar's lurid account of the slayings, was attempting to establish the urgent necessity for going in shooting. It is important to remember that Dunbar's version was accepted by the press and the public for twenty-four hours. How much of an outcry against the massacre would there have been had the truth been known that day?

Arthur Eve also took that tour. His recollection of Dunbar's graphic account is very similar to mine: "When we were taken on the tour, we were taken on the second level, overlooking the yard. Deputy Commissioner Walter Dunbar—the number two man in the New York Correctional System under Russell Oswald—said, 'This is where we saw the inmates bring the hostages, put them in a position of execution'—and he said—'you know, we still didn't want to go in. We were still hoping they would give up the hostages. But what we saw,' Dunbar said, 'was one of the inmates took a knife and stuck the hostage in the stomach, and the hostage was dead and fell to the ground. The men got itchy and you could understand that it was difficult to restrain them. We replied— "Give us the hostages! Please!" And the inmates shouted—"This is our answer," and he slit the throat of another of the hostages. But the thing that really got us upset was when we saw an inmate take young Officer Smith, take a knife, castrate him, take the organs of his body and stuff them in his mouth—well, we just had to go in.'"

This castration story, and the enthusiasm with which it was repeated both in Attica, and far beyond, tells us perhaps more than we want to know about the psychology of the authorities and people at the scene. Even after doctors repeatedly declared there had been no mutilation of anyone's sexual organs, hostage or inmate, dead or alive—townspeople, guards, and troopers simply refused to believe it. Dr. Edlund, whose autopsies proved the hostages had died of gunshot wounds and of no other cause, finally got irritated when asked once too often about the sexual mutilation story. He snapped: "You don't have to be a medical expert to be able to determine if someone's genital organs have been mutilated."

Continuing his tour, Dunbar guided us to a spot where four black inmates, fully clothed, lay utterly still on the ground. About twenty other inmates, hands behind their heads, naked, were lying on the ground a short distance away. The residue of CS gas still on the grass severely irritated the prisoners' skin, giving it the sensation of being on fire, but the naked inmates were lying without twitching a muscle for fear of a beating. Eve asked if the four clothed inmates were dead. Dunbar said no, they were not—they were men who had been witnessed in the act of murdering hostages. It was at about this point of the tour that Arthur Eve swears he saw Elliot James Barkley alive.

Dunbar also showed us the hole in which, he declared, the body of one hostage had been buried—a hostage killed by inmates two days earlier, on Saturday. Someone asked if Dunbar and other corrections officials had known about this killing, and he answered, "Oh, yes, we had our sources." I'm not sure the question was raised at the moment, but several of us did wonder—if the authorities knew on Saturday that a hostage had been "killed," why did they continue to permit members of the Observers' team to visit the yard?

Apparently Dunbar, and the others who misled us that day, did not expect any of this to come to light. Authorities resisted the findings of the Monroe County medical examiner, John F. Edlund, with every resource available to them—even to the extent of bringing in two famous pathologists to check Dr. Edlund's findings. These pathologists agreed with Dr. Edlund in every particular.

Authorities must have calculated that they could get away with this monstrous lie. When the wrong medical examiner got hold of the bodies, did his job, and released his findings, the authorities were stunned. The story that prisoners had murdered the hostages would have served as a perfect explanation for shooting up the prison yard on Monday morning.

I mentioned that during the tour—hours after the morning assault—we could hardly breathe because of the gas residue. It was perfectly obvious that when this gas hit, it took effect immediately, rendering both prisoners and hostages absolutely helpless. Dunbar himself described the effects of pepper gas at close range: it produces such a strong sense of suffocation that virtually everyone clutches his throat and gasps for breath. Several state troopers, *wearing gas masks,* collapsed under the effects of the gas that morning. The prisoners were choking on the gas, and their hostages were choking on it also. Without guns, without gas masks, the prisoners were helpless. They were not about to kill the hostages—they could not have done so, even if they had wanted to.

Clearly the troopers could have entered the gassed prison yard with nightsticks and other non-lethal weapons and released the hostages without killing anybody. State authorities will not admit this. Once their story about the slashing of hostages' throats had collapsed, they tried to suggest that the inmates brought on the shooting by resisting the troopers' attack—as if the inmates were so superhuman that, without gas masks and unarmed, they had engaged these heavily-armed, masked state troopers in hand-to-hand fighting.

I see the picture of men struggling violently for breath, utterly helpless, and I see a trooper with a gas mask over his face, advancing through the clouds of tear gas. Wantonly, the trooper pulls the trigger. Why? The question persists in my mind, and keeps returning—in conversations, and in moments alone.

Why was there a need to kill anybody at Attica?

Our society must deal with the fact of the massacre and with its implications. Responsibility for the slayings does not rest with one man alone. *Every state official* who went along with the decision to send in troops, and *every trooper* who confronted the gassed inmates in the yard on Monday morning, had a choice before him. The governor of New York chose the security of state power over the lives of hostages, and inmates. Corrections officials from Oswald on down chose the brute assertion of their power over the very principles and ideals they had for so long professed. State troopers and guards chose revenge for mythical racial crimes over the prisoners' attempts to surrender peacefully.

A man has to be very callous to look at another man who is unarmed, under the influence of gas, and trying to surrender— and to shoot him cold. One does not need to take an extreme political position. The facts of Attica are extreme enough on their own: law enforcement officials deliberately chose to shoot to kill. Attica brought the tradition of Kent State and Mylai one step further.

Whether or not there were ever orders to shoot in any of these cases, the question remains: Why should a National Guardsman, a soldier, or a state trooper *follow* orders to shoot someone who is helpless? Why should he pull the trigger? How do men make that kind of judgment? What kind of fear and anger and hatred are we dealing with in the breasts of these men who wear uniforms and are our shields against lawlessness?

9. "The Brothers of Attica"
Richard X. Clark

Attica inmate Richard X. Clark served as a spokesman and leader during the rebellion. A veteran of the U.S. Navy and a member of the Nation of Islam, he was serving a four-year sentence for armed robbery—a crime, he states elsewhere in the book from which this excerpt is taken (The Brothers of Attica, 1973), he did not commit. Here he describes events after the prison was retaken.

As soon as we hit the door of D-block, two state troopers grabbed us. "You black bastards," they were screaming. They threw us inside the door and grabbed us behind the head, forcing us to our knees. They made us strip and then they started kicking us. "You black motherfuckers," they shouted, "get up!"

There were a whole bunch of correction officers beating us. They threw us down and made us keep our knees and elbows on the ground. I heard ribs crack and people being kicked. I heard troopers say, "Take the nigger into A-block."

They pointed at one of the brothers. "Oh, this is one of the intermediaries who cut their throats. Well, we'll cut his balls." And that was the first time I heard anything about throats being cut.

They forced us into A-block. They made us crawl in the mud and dirt. They kept the heels of their boots on our necks and hit us in the heads with the rifle butts. "Don't look up, nigger," they said. They didn't seem to realize that if we kept our heads in the mud, they couldn't recognize us. I remember the hardest thing for me was keeping my glasses on.

On the other side they were making sure inmates weren't someone they wanted to beat—someone who, they thought, played a role in the riot. They'd say, "There's that black son of a bitch. He had a lot to say."

They came to me and kicked me to the side. I tried to keep my glasses on. When they fell to the ground, someone stepped on them. Then they noticed my Timex watch. "Nigger, what are you doing with a watch?" they said. "Where'd you steal this from?" Then they stepped on that.

Someone else snatched my religious medal and threw it on the ground. There was some writing in Arabic on it. The guy said, "What are you, a Jew?"

Then someone said, "Hold that, man. That's that bastard Clark. He's one of the leaders." Someone else came up and stepped on my toes, and they ordered me to spread my cheeks. Then they threw cigarettes and bottles at me and tried to make me lose my balance.

The lieutenant came up and hit me in the kidneys to show he was a man. "Take him to the box," he said. "Don't kill him. Save him for the electric chair."

They grabbed me off the wall and marched me through the basketball court. There were six or seven of them holding me. They made me walk on glass, in water, up the stairs to A-block. There was a gauntlet of men, each with a stick. They beat me and tried to make me fall. "Here's the leader," they said.

The men were standing on both sides of a flight of stairs. But they were so disorganized that when they chased me up to the top, there were four more dudes there—Rice, Flynn and two others—big white honkies with big clubs. When I reached them, they told me to go downstairs again.

So here I am running up and down stairs. I get to the top, and

Rice and Flynn throw me down again. Then they ran me down the gallery and into a cell and locked me in, and so there I was in HBZ.

There was a bed and a rolled-up mattress. I stood up to the bars and watched and listened. All I heard was whimpering, and all I saw was a glimpse of naked buttocks, followed by a huge white Neanderthal. Then I heard the brothers coming in one by one. I heard one of them fall as they led them up the gallery. They broke a Spanish-speaking brother's arm in three places. Then they pulled him across the floor and you could hear his skin burning as it squeaked against the linoleum. There was one brother who had cerebral palsy. His arm was deformed. They kept hitting his arm.

Then it was night, and it was quiet. The guards were whispering just loud enough so you could hear them. One guard said he was going to kill a nigger. Another said, "I hear they only killed nine hundred." Someone else said, "Oh, I heard it was 925."

All through the night the guards kept coming through the gallery. Deputy Warden Pfeil stuck a gun into someone's cell and said, "What are you doing, nigger, sleeping? You're going to die in the morning." All through the night they were coming in with flashlights and guns drawn. They had pitchforks, knives and axes, some of them. "We sure got a lot of niggers in there," they said.

There was even a squad of police from Auburn. They were looking for a brother named Smitty who had been in the rebellion there. I don't know how they got there so fast, but they spent all night and the next day looking for him. They kept saying, "Smitty, where are you?" They said they were going to beat him because they didn't get a chance to beat him before.

This went on until Tuesday afternoon when the doctor came through. It was Sternberg, and he was taking names and numbers and asking what was the matter with you. When you told him, he said, "You should be dead."

Tuesday afternoon they fed us our first meal—cheese sandwiches and coffee. For the next two weeks they fed us just twice a day, two cheese sandwiches in the afternoon and cold cereal and coffee in the morning. We were kept in our cells twenty-four hours a day. I lost count of what day it was, but soon we started whispering to find out who was in there.

The next week they gave us pencils and paper and told us we could write home. Then the outside people started coming in, so they started giving us hot meals. The Goldman Committee, which was formed after the riot to protect inmates' civil rights, were the first ones inside.

They had taken our clothes and given us white overalls and white slippers, telling us we had to wear special uniforms. When we came out of our cells to talk to our lawyers or family, we had to walk with our arms folded in front of us. That was the only time we were allowed out of our cells. Any time you came out, it was one at a time. Two officers stood at the door. Before they let you out, they'd make you fold your arms.

After a month, we received our first shave. Two weeks later, we received our first haircut. Then on Wednesdays, every six weeks, they gave us another haircut. Every week they gave us a shave. The barber was an old white dude, and they would take us out one at a time to him. They had him so scared with stories they had fed him about us, he was afraid to nick us, so he used a safety razor.

On Thursdays we were taken outside for a shower. There were ninety-three men and just two showers. The showers started at nine a.m. and stopped at three. So we had about two minutes each under there.

They also had an outside facility called a strip cell. It was the size of two cells with four walls, with bars across the top instead of a roof. It was their idea of recreation. It was like a cement cage. And who wants to go out there in the cold with just those overalls. So we all just stayed in our cells, twenty-four hours a day.

No one knew how we were chosen. If you had come into contact with the authorities before, they picked you. Some guys had been at the negotiating table. Some brothers who had played only a minor role were there. And others, who had played significant roles in the revolt, were able to escape HBZ and go back with the prison population.

People think the riot at Attica was over on September 13. But ninety-two men are still in segregated cells at Attica or moved to other prisons throughout the state. The State of New York killed nine of its own men and to whitewash the crime tried to pin the murders on us. The ninety-three of us—myself included—are all facing possible charges of having killed a correction officer, which is a capital crime. If found guilty, we face the electric chair.

———————

Before September 9, 1971, I had had no serious prison infractions, and on February 8, 1972, I would have served two-thirds of my time—thirty-two months—and hence become eligible for conditional release. On November 16 I gave an interview to ten newsmen, while I was still in HBZ, attacking the prison authorities for their attack on the yard and their treatment of the men in HBZ.

The following day I was called before a time-allowance board meeting of prison officials, and on November 19 I was told I had lost a month of good prison time because of my record of serious infractions before the riot.

Herman Schwartz, my lawyer, wrote to Commissioner Russell Oswald to protest. On December 3, 1971, I received a letter from Oswald's office giving me back my lost month.

On December 13 I testified in Federal District Court about the retaliation exacted against me and the ninety-two others in HBZ. On December 22, the Department of Corrections reversed itself and took away the month of good time again.

On February 7 I appeared in Federal District Court of the Western District to protest losing the month. Judge John Henderson, ruling in my favor, told the Department of Corrections that it could not take away and give back a man's freedom so he had no idea when and if he was ever to get out of prison.

On February 8 I was conditionally released from Attica.

But I have been indicted on a charge of 34 (thirty-four) counts of first-degree kidnapping, which if convicted of just one—least of all, all thirty-four of them—I stand to do life in prison for each conviction.

CHAPTER THIRTEEN

THE KEYS TO THE KINGDOM (1974–1980)

Introduction by Gerald Gill

While the Supreme Court's decision in *Brown* v. *Board of Education* and Congress' later enactment of the 1964 Civil Rights Act and the 1965 Voting Rights Act were landmark victories in African-Americans' quest for freedom and equality, such judicial and legislative decrees alone would not ensure that African-Americans would be able to enjoy "equal protection of the laws" in terms of educational and economic opportunities. From the mid-1960s to the present, activists on the local level have engaged in continuous campaigns on behalf of the realization of equal opportunities in public school education and in access to institutions of higher education. As more black candidates won elective office, they sought to increase employment as well as economic opportunities for their black constituents. Facing increasing challenges from those who feared that the ongoing thrust for racial justice and for a more equitable economic order was going too far, movement activists, organizers, and elected officials persevered in their pursuit of justice and in their efforts to forestall the erosion of hard-won gains.

Although most Americans may have thought that the Supreme Court's decision in *Brown* would be applicable to southern and border state school districts which mandated de jure segregation, black parents and their supporters in northern, midwestern, and western cities and towns quickly realized that the High Court's decision could have legal bearing on the nature of de facto public school segregation in their hometowns. In Boston, for example, a small number of black parents had complained throughout the 1950s about the dilapidated and overcrowded conditions of public schools located in the city's predominantly black Roxbury and South End neighborhoods.

Emboldened by a federal district court judge's decision in 1961 that found the local board of education in New Rochelle, New York, guilty of maintaining an overwhelmingly Negro school through racial gerrymandering, black parents and NAACP representatives complained in increasing numbers to individual school principals, the superintendent of schools, and members of the Massachusetts Commission Against Discrimination about overcrowded classrooms, poor physical facilities, inadequate and outdated materials, more limited curricula offerings in the secondary schools, and the relatively large number of "substitute, inexperienced or 'unsuccessful' teachers" assigned to their neighborhoods. Such conditions, they argued, were directly attributable to de facto segregation of the Boston public schools.

In late spring of 1963, members of the Education Committee of the Boston NAACP publicly aired their grievances before the city's School Committee. The School Committee, then chaired by Louise Day Hicks, would not and did not accept the parents' and the NAACP's contention of segregated schools in Boston, precipitating a decade-long dispute between black parents and the NAACP on the one hand and the School Committee on the other.

From mid-1963 to 1965, black leaders in Boston helped to stage one-day boycotts and marches and established "Freedom Schools" to highlight their demands that the School Committee end "racial imbalance" in the school system. With the School Committee adamant in its refusal to accept de facto segregation, supporters of school desegregation were able to have the state legislature enact a Racial Imbalance Act in 1965 which required the state board of education to investigate and to monitor those school systems throughout the state that maintained local schools in which more than 50 percent of the pupils were black.

While the Boston School Committee and the state board would be in near continuous disagreement and lengthy litigation about

Boston's pupil assignment policies and the need for school deseg-regation, groups of black parents sought to avail themselves of the city's open enrollment policies. Beginning in 1965 Operation Exodus was established; under its aegis approximately 400 black students were bused to predominantly white schools throughout the city. In 1966, the Metropolitan Council for Educational Opportunity (METCO) was established; its program provided for 220 black pupils from Boston to be bused to select middle- and upper-middle-income suburban communities.

Finally, in 1972, a group of black parents at the insistence of the NAACP filed a suit in federal district court against the Boston School Committee in which they contended that the members of the School Committee had denied black children equal protection of the laws by maintaining a racially segregated school system. In 1974, federal district judge W. Arthur Garrity, upholding the parents' arguments, ordered the School Committee to develop a school desegregation plan that would require the citywide busing of students.

While busing plans had been and would be undertaken in cities such as Charlotte, North Carolina; Louisville, Kentucky; and Tampa, Florida, the reactions to busing in Boston among residents in several of the city's white working-class neighborhoods were more hardened, more hostile, and in the end more violent than in other locales. Fueled by race and class resentments, many white parents in predominantly Irish-American South Boston refused to send their children to the newly desegregated schools and sought by protest and defiance to have Judge Garrity's order overturned. Their protests, although strenuous and prolonged, did not succeed. Ultimately, a surface calm in race relations came to the city's public classrooms.

In addition to ongoing concerns about desegregation and equal educational opportunity, questions about academic opportunities and access to higher education came to be issues of concern from the late 1960s onward. How to increase economic opportunities so as to ensure equal opportunity in the workplace had been a concern for black labor and movement activists since the proposed March on Washington in 1941. Although the Truman, Eisen-hower, and Kennedy administrations took minimal action at best to address racial discrimination in employment by government contractors, it was not until 1965, when Lyndon Johnson issued Executive Order 11246, that the federal government required, through a clearly stated series of procedures, government contractors to take "affirmative action" in designing and implementing employment procedures to ensure that job opportunities were made available on a nondiscriminatory basis.

With Congress' later amending of Title VII of the 1964 Civil Rights Act to forbid discrimination on the state and local level and with city governments' establishing their own affirmative action plans, there were marked changes (especially in cities with black mayors) in the number of black municipal employees. In Atlanta, for example, newly elected mayor Maynard Jackson sought to increase the number of black municipal employees at all levels of city government. Upon Jackson's election in 1973, black workers comprised just over 40 percent of the city's work force; in 1978, they comprised 55.6 percent of the city workers. By 1978, approximately one-third of the employees at managerial grade were black and the percentage of black employees at the professional level had more than doubled from 1970 to over 40 percent. In just over a decade, the percentage of black police officers had risen from less than 10 percent to 33 percent.

However, the most controversial aspect of Jackson's efforts, at least in the minds of many white business leaders in the city, was his attempt to institute affirmative action policies in the city's purchasing and contracting procedures. Prior to his election, less than 5 percent of the city's business was conducted with minority-owned firms. To correct that discrepancy, Jackson moved to appoint a city contract compliance officer who would examine each bid submitted to ascertain if hiring goals for black workers and black subcontractors were being fulfilled. Although several companies balked at the new provisions, particularly as they applied to the construction of the city's international airport, many companies grudgingly or otherwise accepted the plan and soon nearly one-third of the city's business was going directly or indirectly to black-owned firms.

Just as the hiring policies in Atlanta and the establishment of efforts to devote more monies to black-owned businesses were race-conscious strategies designed to bring about a more equitable distribution of jobs, colleges and universities, particularly graduate and professional schools, began to devise race-sensitive or special minority admissions programs. Such programs, particularly those established in many professional schools in the late 1960s and early 1970s, were often specifically designed to recruit and to admit students from racial groups historically underrepresented in the health and legal professions. One such admissions program was that set up by the University of California at Davis' medical school, whereby up to sixteen seats out of a hundred in the first-year class were to be reserved for African-American, Native American, and Chicano students. In 1973 and again in 1974, Allan Bakke, an engineer in his late thirties, was rejected from more than ten medical schools, one of which was the school at Davis. With the assistance of an admissions officer at Davis who was sympathetic to his case, Bakke decided to file suit against the admissions program at Davis, contending that the plan violated his civil rights under the Fourteenth Amendment and the 1964 Civil Rights Act. As the suit made its way from federal district court to appeals and ultimately to the U.S. Supreme Court, the case brought wide and pronounced attention to the efficacy and the utility of affirmative action in general and special minority admissions programs in particular.

In June 1978, a divided Supreme Court issued its decision. In a 4–1–4 vote, the Court overturned the special minority admissions program at Davis and ordered Allan Bakke to be admitted to the medical school. In a second 4–1–4 decision, the Court stated that race as a means for diversifying a student body could be *a* factor used by admissions officers in the admissions process.

Policy concerns pertaining to racial redress and equity have become increasingly more difficult to adjudicate and to resolve in the years since 1974. Issues such as de facto school segregation in northern urban school districts and affirmative action programs in employment, education, and economic opportunities were and are more complex than the issues that characterized many of the freedom movement campaigns of the 1950s and 1960s. Thus, with more divided responses among Americans (even among some former allies), efforts to implement such programs and policies meet more determined resistance and less of a commitment or sympathetic hearing from the executive and judicial branches of the federal government. Yet, in spite of such opposition and challenge, activists have continued to go forward in the quest for equality, justice, and equity.

1. Statement to the Boston School Committee
June 11, 1963

Representatives from the Boston NAACP and concerned black parents, after continuing protests to school principals, the superintendent of schools, and representatives from the Massachusetts Commission Against Discrimination, appeared before the Boston School Committee in June 1963 to air their dissatisfaction with the "lack of educational opportunity" for black students in the city's schools. These are excerpts from the prepared statement delivered by Ruth Batson, chair of the Education Committee of the city's branch of the NAACP and a longtime parent-critic of the conditions in many of the city's predominantly black schools.

Madame Chairman, Members of the Boston School Committee:

The National Association for the Advancement of Colored People is an organization dedicated to the elimination of discrimination and prejudice from all phases of American life. Our goal is First Class Citizenship, and we will settle for nothing less. All immigrants to the American shores have suffered from discrimination, but in most cases, as soon as they lost their identifying accents, they were able to blend into the American culture and enjoy the fruits of our democratic system. The Negro, brought here in chains, bears visible identification of his race and we have spent our lives tearing down wall after wall of resistance raised in our path, because of our color.

One of the most frustrating and devastating obstacles confronting us, is the lack of educational opportunity. Education constitutes our strongest hope for pulling ourselves out of the inferior status to which society has assigned us. For, a boy of eight or nine years, who is receiving an inferior education today, will feel the effects at age thirty-five, forty-five and until he dies, as he struggles, as a father, to rear and educate his children. His lack of educational opportunity will make it impossible for him to motivate his children properly and thus, this burden is inherited by each succeeding generation. Since, you, our School Committee, are the caretakers of our educational school system, a job which each of you sought voluntarily, we are here tonight to express our dissatisfaction, to air our complaints and to make certain demands in connection with our schools.

I know that the word demand is a word that is disliked by many public officials, but I am afraid that it is too late for pleading, begging, requesting or even reasoning. The NAACP's concern with the plight of Negro pupils in the Boston schools is of long duration. Please allow me a few minutes to review. Several years ago, because of many complaints of a varying nature from parents, I received permission from the then superintendent, Dr. Haley, to visit and interview certain principals. I interviewed six principals of predominantly Negro schools. Three of these principals refused to acknowledge the existence of any problems. They tossed off the complaints parents had made and, in general, inferred that the NAACP was making a "mountain out of a molehill." One principal acknowledged that it could be true that his graduates, 99% Negro, might have difficulty in high school when competing with students from all over Boston, because he stated "Negroes do not make their kids learn." He said further that we should [be] like Jewish parents, who see that their children learn. Another principal told me that she just didn't think that Negroes could learn at the same rate as white children. She had just left a school in Roslindale which was an all white school, and felt that she could come to this conclusion. Another principal, very pleasant and affable, said that he saw no differences in children, and that he was sure that his attitude was reflected in his staff. Time has proven that this rather nonchalant attitude did not produce the results desired by the complaining parents.

We are here because the clamor from the community is too anxious to be ignored, the dissatisfaction and complaints too genuine and deep seated to be passed over lightly, and the injustices present in our school system hurt our pride, rob us of our dignity and produce results which are injurious not only to our future, but to that of our city, our commonwealth and our nation.

Paul Parks, a member of the Education Committee of the NAACP, has produced certain facts that call for serious attention. Mr. Parks' research brings out that there are 13 schools in Boston with predominantly Negro population. The youngest of these buildings was built in 1937. The rest were built in 1932, 1912, 1910, 1909, 1922, 1906, 1900, 1870 and 1868. According to the Sargent Report of May 1962, at least four of these buildings have been recommended to be abandoned because of health and safety reasons. Eight have been recommended to be renovated in order to meet present educational requirements.

We then make this charge . . . There is segregation in fact in our Boston Public School System. To be sure, the May 17, 1954 Supreme Court decision dealt with deliberate segregation, but there can be no misinterpretation of the language used in that decision which stated that the "separation of children solely on the basis of race generates a feeling of inferiority that may affect their hearts and minds in a way unlikely ever to be undone." The steady migration of Negroes to Boston has intensified this problem. The 1960 census showed a total Negro population of 112,000. 63,000 of that total live in Boston and 57,000 live in the Roxbury-Dorchester section of Boston. Our school population as of last Spring was 93,000 and of that approximately 14,000 are Negroes.

The NAACP's position on Northern School segregation is clear . . . we must work to reduce and eliminate school segregation wherever it exists. In the discussion of segregation in fact in our public schools, we do not accept residential segregation as an excuse for countenancing this situation. We feel that it is the responsibility of school officials to take an affirmative and positive stand on the side of the best possible education for all children. This "best possible education" is not possible where segregation exists. Inadequate educational standards, unequal facilities and discriminatory educational practices exist wherever there is school segregation.

Therefore, we state that it is imperative that the Boston School Committee take immediate steps to eliminate and reduce segregation from our school system. We recognize that some of the methods advised pose problems when related to younger children, therefore, we recommend that the immediate concentration be centered on our Jr. High Schools. There should be a review of the Open Enrollment plan which would allow transfers without the present limitations. This plan should be accompanied by rezoning designed deliberately to integrate our schools. Site selections and additions to existing school buildings must be planned to achieve integration. Segregation in fact is a problem existing in all urban communities today. This problem must be acknowledged and faced up to by all citizens and public officials.

The unjust conditions created by segregation should also come under our scrutiny tonight. There are many conditions that must be corrected as we move forward to give to Negro students what rightfully belongs to them.

We are indebted to the many known and unknown dedicated principals and teachers who have seen their duty clearly and have performed in the true spirit of their profession. We acknowledge and honor their presence in our system. However, too many others approach the Negro schools with their minds poisoned by stereotyped, preconceived notions of Negro people. They believe that Negroes are lazy, stupid and inferior. This attitude does not go unnoticed by the youngest Negro child . . . for at an early age our youngsters become skilled in their ability to recognize prejudice. This recognition is always accompanied by resentment, hostility and a feeling of humiliation. This is an unhealthy situation which cannot create an atmosphere in which the teacher is at his or her best, or where the child can perform at his highest level. We realize that teachers in these schools do teach under difficult conditions and these conditions should be remedied in order to encourage teachers not only to remain in these districts, but to improve the quality of their teaching. Training programs should be expanded to establish a liaison between the school administration and colleges from which we get our teachers so that they can start their teaching careers able to distinguish myth from reality. Such a program should create an understanding of the child in congested Negro school districts which would be [an] invaluable aid to well-meaning teachers who want to do a good job wherever they are assigned.

We also urge that permanent teachers be assigned to grades 1–3 and that the size of these classes be reduced to 25. I know that it is not necessary to stress the importance of a good beginning. Our teachers should have at their disposal sufficient supplies . . . books and other materials.

We should use books and other visual aids that include illustrations of people of all races. To use material depicting only white people is unrealistic in today's world. Please do not minimize the importance of this statement. It is important that the Negro child see recognition of himself as a person of worth and it is important that the white child see people of other races in a positive setting. This material is available and is being used in other school systems.

The statement often made by school officials to refute charges of discrimination—that we have a uniform curriculum—concerns thoughtful people. We know that needs vary from district to district. We know that many of our predominantly Negro schools are located in the older, underprivileged sections of Boston. We acknowledge that many of our children come from deprived homes. Many of our parents, handicapped by lack of training or formal education, are consumed with the day to day struggle of just trying to make ends meet. For many reasons that go hand in hand with deprivation, inadequate and dilapidated overcrowded housing, discrimination, bitterness and frustration, our schools must consider the plight of the pupil in these congested Negro areas. As a good teacher gears her program to the individual child, the school administration must gear its curriculum to the needs of the individual districts. We must have concentrated developmental reading programs in these schools in grades 1–8. In each school the programs for the gifted and the slow learners should be expanded and taught by qualified, specially trained teachers. The needs of the average child in this setting must not be overlooked. The curriculum must be enriched to enable this child to compete in a society where the removal of the barriers of segregation will force them to compete with those who have not been handicapped as they have been.

Because ghetto living produces children with problems, we

cannot emphasize too strongly the importance of the school adjustment counselors and the need for more such programs.

The vocational program should be expanded to include grade 7 and Negro children should be counselled by people who believe that America is the land of opportunity for all. To steer Negro students into certain trades or into certain training programs because the counselor believes other programs out of their reach is unfair, and this happens often in our schools. We are disturbed by the small number of our youngsters who take advantage of the cooperative programs. This we feel is the result of poor guidance programs, and the fact that many are discouraged from attending schools outside of their assigned school districts. This discouraging of students in the Industrial Arts courses prohibits them from gaining an entry into union and apprenticeship programs. We should see that all students, Negro and white, have the opportunity during specially observed weeks and in assemblies, to hear and see people of all races who have achieved in many fields. The value of this type of learning experience cannot be over emphasized and should be planned. This is something that can be accomplished without affecting our school budget and the dividends are great.

We feel that there should be no discrimination in the hiring or assigning of teachers. We take note of the fact that there is no Negro school principal in our system and ask you to examine the reasons for this.

We recommend that you accept in toto the section of the Sargent Report that refers to Roxbury and North Dorchester. This portion of the survey, we feel, will achieve maximum integration in this section of Boston.

We also urge that you review the system of intelligence testing in our schools. The Boston school system mainly uses a group test to determine the intelligence and capability of a child to learn. When we realize that many of the Negro children coming to Boston are from rural communities, we feel that a group test is unfair and does not give a true picture of ability. As a result of this kind of testing, many Negro children are declared slow learners and unteachable.

We are aware of the problems confronting this school administration. We, like any citizens, are vitally concerned with good sound educational policies. Our demands tonight have centered around de facto segregation and its evil effects because we know that this issue has not been faced by Boston school officials. This issue must be dealt with, if we are to move along with the plans and blueprints that proclaim a New Boston.

In the selection of a new superintendent, we see an opportunity to tackle a problem that is facing every major Northern city today. We regret that you chose to reject the proposal of the committee to aid in your selection, but we are encouraged by Dr. Hunt's role as consultant. In all frankness, we must say that we have seen no one with the present school administration who has demonstrated knowledge or ability to help in this problem. We feel strongly that the school committee should not limit itself to any section of this nation in its quest for the right person to fill this position. We do not believe that this man has to be a super man as indicated by a writer recently. We do believe, however, that he must be a person experienced in dealing with the problems of an urban community, who is sensitive to the needs of minority groups, who sees the community as an ally, and who is morally committed to the doctrine of the Fatherhood of God and the Brotherhood of Man.

We demand the right to discuss this selection in detail with Dr. Hunt and we demand that every applicant be examined thoroughly in regard to his background in the area of human relations. It might seem that we have placed the entire responsibility for the solving of these problems on your shoulders. Let me say that the community is also concerned and stands ready to work along with you. The school administration and the community must join forces [to] erase the faulty image they have of each other and work together if we are to be successful. You might question the ability of the community to rise to the occasion, and I answer that just as we rise to the occasion to pay our taxes (for which we get small return) . . . we will rise to the occasion to see that our children are no longer shortchanged in the education they receive.

Ruth Batson, Chairman Education Committee
NAACP, Boston Branch

Elizabeth Price, Barbara Elam, Erna Ballantyne,
Melvin King, Paul Parks

2. "Death at an Early Age"

Jonathan Kozol

In this searing account from his prize-winning book Death at an Early Age, *Jonathan Kozol writes of his academic year 1964–1965 experience as a fourth-grade teacher in an unnamed elementary school in a predominantly black neighborhood in Boston. Before the year was up, he was fired after teaching to his class Langston Hughes's poem "Ballad of a Landlord," which was not an "approved publication."*

The room in which I taught my Fourth Grade was not a room at all, but the corner of an auditorium. The first time I approached that corner, I noticed only a huge torn stage curtain, a couple of broken windows, a badly listing blackboard and about thirty-five bewildered-looking children, most of whom were Negro. White was overcome in black among them, but white and black together were overcome in chaos. They had desks and a teacher, but they did not really have a class. What they had was about one quarter of the auditorium. Three or four blackboards, two of them broken, made them seem a little bit set apart. Over at the other end of the auditorium there was another Fourth Grade class. Not much was happening at the other side at that minute so that for the moment the noise did not seem so bad. But it became a real nightmare of conflicting noises a little later on. Generally it was not until ten o'clock that the bad crossfire started. By ten-thirty it would have attained such a crescendo that the children in the back rows of my section often couldn't hear my questions and I could not hear their answers. There were no carpetings or sound-absorbers of any kind. The room, being large, and echoing, and wooden, added resonance to every sound. Sometimes the other teacher and I would stagger the lessons in which our classes would have to speak aloud, but this was a makeshift method and it also meant that our classes had to be induced to maintain an unnatural and otherwise unnecessary rule of silence during the rest of the time. We couldn't always do it anyway, and usually the only way out was to try to outshout each other so that both of us often left school hoarse or wheezing. While her class was reciting in unison you could not hear very much in mine. When she was talking alone I could be heard above her but the trouble then was that little bits of her talk got overheard by my class. Suddenly in the middle of our geography you could hear her saying:

"AFTER YOU COMPARE, YOU HAVE GOT TO BRING DOWN."

Or "PLEASE GIVE THAT PENCIL BACK TO HENRIETTA!"

Neither my class nor I could help but be distracted for a moment of sudden curiosity about exactly what was going on. Hours were lost in this way. Yet that was not the worst. More troublesome still was the fact that we did not ever *feel* apart. We were tucked in the corner and anybody who wanted could peek in or walk in or walk past. I never minded an intruder or observer, but to notice and to stare at any casual passer-by grew to be an irresistible temptation for the class. On repeated occasions I had to say to the children: "The class is still going. Let them have their discussion. Let them walk by if they have to. You should still be paying attention over here."

Soon after I came into that auditorium, I discovered that it was not only our two Fourth Grades that were going to have their classes here. We were to share the space also with the glee club, with play rehearsals, special reading, special arithmetic, and also at certain times a Third or Fourth Grade phonics class. I began to make head-counts of numbers of pupils and I started jotting them down:

Seventy children from the two regular Fourth Grades before the invasion.

Then ninety one day with the glee club and remedial arithmetic.

One hundred and seven with the play rehearsal.

One day the sewing class came in with their sewing machines and then that seemed to become a regular practice in the hall. Once I counted one hundred and twenty people. All in the one room. All talking, singing, yelling, laughing, reciting—and all at the same time. Before the Christmas break it became apocalyptic. Not more than one half of the classroom lessons I had planned took place throughout that time.

"Mr. Kozol—I can't hear you."

"Mr. Kozol—what's going on out there?"

"Mr. Kozol—couldn't we sing with them?"

One day something happened to dramatize to me, even more powerfully than anything yet, just what a desperate situation we were really in. What happened was that a window whose frame had rotted was blown right out of its sashes by a strong gust of wind and began to fall into the auditorium, just above my children's heads. I had noticed that window several times before and I had seen that its frame was rotting, but there were so many other things equally rotted or broken in the school building that it didn't occur to me to say anything about it. The feeling I had was that the Principal and custodians and Reading Teacher and other people had been in that building for a long time before me and they must have seen the condition of the windows. If anything could be done, if there were any way to get it corrected, I assumed they would have done it by this time. Thus, by not complaining and by not pointing it out to anyone, in a sense I went along with the rest of them and accepted it as something inevitable. One of the most grim things about teaching in such a school and such a system is that you do not like to be an incessant barb and irritation to everybody else, so you come under a rather strong compulsion to keep quiet. But after you have been quiet for a while there is an equally strong temptation to begin to accept the conditions of your work or of the children's plight as natural. This, in a sense, is what had happened to me during that period and that, I suppose, is why I didn't say anything about the rotting window. Now one day it caved in.

First there was a cracking sound, then a burst of icy air. The next thing I knew, a child was saying: "Mr. Kozol—look at the window!" I turned and looked and saw that it was starting to fall in. It was maybe four or five feet tall and it came straight inward out of its sashes toward the heads of the children. I was standing, by coincidence, only about four or five feet off and was able to catch it with my hand. But the wind was so strong that it nearly blew right out of my hands. A couple of seconds of good luck— for it was a matter of chance that I was standing there—kept glass from the desks of six or seven children and very possibly preserved the original shape of half a dozen of their heads. The ones who had been under the glass were terrified but the thing that I noticed with most wonder was that they tried very hard to hide their fear in order to help me get over my own sense of embarrassment and guilt. I soon realized I was not going to be able to hold the thing up by myself and I was obliged to ask one of the stronger boys in the class to come over and give me a hand. Meanwhile, as the children beneath us shivered with the icy wind and as the two of us now shivered also since it was a day when the mercury was hovering all morning close to freezing, I asked one of the children in the front row to run down and fetch the janitor.

When he asked me what he should tell him, I said: "Tell him the house is falling in." The children laughed. It was the first time I had ever come out and said anything like that when the children could hear me. I am sure my reluctance to speak out like that more often must seem odd to many readers, for at this perspective it seems odd to me as well. Certainly there were plenty of things wrong within that school building and there was enough we could have joked about. The truth, however, is that I did not often talk like that, nor did many of the other teachers, and there was a practical reason for this. Unless you were ready to buck the system utterly, it would become far too difficult to teach in an atmosphere of that kind of honesty. It generally seemed a great deal easier to pretend as well as you could that everything was normal and okay. Some teachers carried out this posture with so much eagerness, in fact, that their defense of the school ended up as something like a hymn of praise and adoration. "You children should thank God and feel blessed with good luck for all you've got. There are so many little children in the world who have been given so much less." The books are junk, the paint peels, the cellar stinks, the teachers call you nigger, and the windows fall in on your heads. "Thank God that you don't live in Russia or Africa! Thank God for all the blessings that you've got!" Once, finally, the day after the window blew in, I said to a friend of mine in the evening after school: "I guess that the building I teach in is not in very good condition." But to state a condition of dilapidation and ugliness and physical danger in words as mild and indirect as those is almost worse than not saying anything at all. I had a hard time with that problem—the problem of being honest and of confronting openly the extent to which I was compromised by going along with things that were abhorrent and by accepting as moderately reasonable or unavoidably troublesome things which, if they were inflicted on children of my own, I would have condemned savagely.

A friend of mine to whom I have confided some of these things has not been able to keep from criticizing me for what he thinks of as a kind of quiet collusion. When I said to him, for example, that the Reading Teacher was trying to do the right thing and that she was a very forceful teacher, he replied to me that from what I had described to him she might have been a very forceful teacher but she was not a good teacher but a very dangerous one and that whether she was *trying* to do the right thing or not did not impress him since what she *did* do was the wrong thing. Other people I know have said the same thing to me about this and I am certain, looking back, that it is only the sheer accident of the unexpected events which took place in my school during the last weeks of the spring that prompted me suddenly to speak out and to take some forthright action. I am also convinced that it is that, and that alone, that has spared me the highly specialized and generally richly deserved contempt which is otherwise reserved by Negro people for their well-intending but inconsistent liberal friends.

After the window blew in on us that time, the janitor finally came up and hammered it shut with nails so that it would not fall in again but also so that it could not open. It was a month before anything was done about the large gap left by a missing pane. Children shivered a few feet away from it. The Principal walked by frequently and saw us. So did supervisors from the School Department. So of course did the various lady experts who traveled all day from room to room within our school. No one can say that dozens of people did not know that children were sitting within the range of freezing air. At last one day the janitor came up with a piece of cardboard or pasteboard and covered over about a quarter of that lower window so that there was no more wind coming in but just that much less sunshine too. I remember wondering what a piece of glass could cost in Boston and I had the idea of going out and buying some and trying to put it in myself. That rectangle of cardboard over our nailed-shut window was not removed for a quarter of the year. When it was removed, it was only because a television station was going to come and visit in the building and the School Department wanted to make the room look more attractive. But it was winter when the window broke, and the repairs did not take place until the middle of the spring.

In case a reader imagines that my school may have been unusual and that some of the other schools in Roxbury must have been in better shape, I think it's worthwhile to point out that the exact opposite seems to have been the case. The conditions in my school were said by many people to be considerably better than those in several of the other ghetto schools. One of the worst, according to those who made comparisons, was the Endicott, also situated in the Negro neighborhood and, like my own school, heavily imbalanced. At Endicott, I learned, it had become so overcrowded that there were actually some classes in which the number of pupils exceeded the number of desks and in which the extra pupils had to sit in chairs behind the teacher. A child absent one day commonly came back the next day and found someone else sitting at his desk. These facts had been brought out in the newspapers, pretty well documented, and they were not denied by the School Department. Despite this, however, as in most cases like this, nothing had been done. When the parents of the Endicott children pressed the School Department to do something about it, a series of events transpired which told a large part of the story of segregation in a very few words.

The School Department offered, in order to resolve the problem, to buy a deserted forty-year-old Hebrew school and then allot about seven thousand dollars to furnish it with desks and chairs. Aside from the indignity of getting everybody else's castoffs (the Negroes already lived in former Jewish tenements and bought in former Jewish stores), there also was the telling fact that to buy and staff this old Hebrew school with about a dozen teachers was going to cost quite a lot of money and that to send the children down the street a couple of miles to a white school which had space would have saved quite a lot. The Hebrew school was going to cost over $180,000. To staff it, supply it with books and so forth would cost about $100,000 more. To send the children into available seats in nearby white classrooms (no new teachers needed) would have cost $40,000 to $60,000 for the year. The School Department, it seemed, was willing to spend something in the area of an extra $240,000 in order to put the Negro children into another segregated school. It was hard for me to believe, even after all I had seen and heard, that it could really be worth a quarter of a million dollars to anyone to keep the Negro children separate. As it happened, the School Committee dragged its heels so long and debated the issue in so many directions that most of the school year passed before anything of a final nature was decided. Meanwhile the real children in the real Endicott classrooms had lost another real year from their real lives.

3. *Tallulah Morgan* et al. v. *James W. Hennigan* et al.

After a decade-long battle with the Boston School Committee over its failure to provide equal educational opportunities for their children, a group of black parents filed a class action suit in federal court. These are excerpts from U.S. District Court Judge W. Arthur Garrity's June 1974 decision in the case, which found in favor of the parent plaintiffs and ordered the Boston School Committee to implement new school assignment plans making use of the busing of students.

. . . The court concludes that the defendants took many actions in their official capacities with the purpose and intent to segregate the Boston public schools and that such actions caused current conditions of segregation in the Boston public schools. The findings of fact stated in the preceding divisions of this opinion have described practices which have been ruled unconstitutional in many other cases. . . . In five of the categories of defendants' activities, described in divisions I–V, *ante,* the court concludes on the basis of evidence within each category that the defendants were acting with segregative intent. Only in division VI, *ante,* on Examination and Vocational Schools and Programs, has the court relied upon the burden-shifting principle discussed in the *Keyes* case at 413 U.S. 208–210. However, this principle is applicable generally and would be available to buttress the conclusions in divisions I–V if need be. The segregative consequences of many of the defendants' actions were scarcely contested, but were argued by the defendants to have been unforeseeable or beyond the defendants' power to prevent. The court has generally rejected these defenses for reasons stated either within numbered divisions of the opinion or in the part entitled Residential Segregation and Neighborhood Schools.

On the issue whether substantial portions of the system have been intentionally segregated by the defendants, the court concludes that they have. Plaintiffs have proved that the defendants intentionally segregated schools at all levels, e.g., secondary English, intermediate Lewenberg and elementary Hennigan; built new schools for a decade with sizes and locations designed to promote segregation; maintained patterns of overcrowding and underutilization which promoted segregation at 26 schools; and expanded the capacity of approximately 40 schools by means of portables and additions when students could have been assigned to other schools with the effect of reducing racial imbalance. How many students were intentionally separated on a racial basis cannot be stated with any degree of precision; but the annual totals were certainly in the thousands, including graduates of nine K–8 elementary schools and four middle schools by means of feeder patterns manipulated by the defendants, students attending most high schools and several junior highs by the same means, students making imbalancing transfers under the open enrollment policy and exceptions to the controlled transfer policy, students transported to perpetuate segregation, and students at schools identifiably black by means of assignment and transfer policies regarding faculty and staff. As explained in the *Keyes* case, at 201–202, segregative practices like these have obvious reciprocal effects. For example, by using feeder patterns to channel black students to English, defendants not only concentrated black students there but also made high schools which the black students might otherwise have attended more predominantly white. Similarly every segregative transfer under open enrollment or an exception to the controlled transfer policy, whether by a white or black student, increased segregation in the sending school as well as in the receiving school.

. . . Finally, defendants did not "adduce proof sufficient to support a finding that segregative intent was not among the factors that motivated their actions," *Id.*, at 210; nor produce "evidence supporting a finding that a lesser degree of segregated schooling" in any part of the system would not have resulted even if they had not acted as they did, *Id.*, at 211; nor demonstrate that any area of the city "is a separate, identifiable and unrelated section of the school district that should be treated as isolated from the rest of the district," *Id.*, at 213. In many instances defendants' evidence consisted of "allegedly logical, racially neutral explanations for their actions," *Id.*, at 210, which proved to be rationalizations. In view of the plaintiffs' proof of the defendants' pervasive practices which were intentionally segregative and their direct and reciprocal effects, the court concludes that the defendants' actions had a segregative impact far beyond the schools which were the immediate subjects of their actions. Indeed plaintiffs' evidence showed, independently of reciprocal effects, that some of defendants' practices had a segregative impact on entire levels of the school system. The court concludes that the defendants have knowingly carried out a systematic program of segregation affecting all of the city's students, teachers and school facilities and have intentionally brought about and maintained a dual school system. Therefore the entire school system of Boston is unconstitutionally segregated. Accordingly, this court will contemporaneously with this opinion file a partial judgment permanently enjoining the city defendants from discriminating upon the basis of race in the operation of the Boston public schools and ordering that they begin forthwith the formulation and implementation of plans to secure for the plaintiffs their constitutional rights.

4. Commencement Address at Howard University
Lyndon B. Johnson

This is an excerpt from the June 4, 1965, address in which President Lyndon B. Johnson announced the beginning of a new thrust in federal social policy on behalf of realizing equal opportunity in all areas of American life, setting the stage for what he would pronounce several months later in Executive Order 11246 regarding affirmative action.

I am delighted at the chance to speak at this important and this historic institution. Howard has long been an outstanding center for the education of Negro Americans. Its students are of every race and color and they come from many countries of the world. It is truly a working example of democratic excellence.

Our earth is the home of revolution. In every corner of every continent men charged with hope contend with ancient ways in the pursuit of justice. They reach for the newest of weapons to realize the oldest of dreams, that each may walk in freedom and pride, stretching his talents, enjoying the fruits of the earth.

Our enemies may occasionally seize the day of change, but it is the banner of our revolution they take. And our own future is linked to this process of swift and turbulent change in many lands in the world. But nothing in any country touches us more profoundly, and nothing is more freighted with meaning for our own destiny than the revolution of the Negro American.

In far too many ways American Negroes have been another nation: deprived of freedom, crippled by hatred, the doors of opportunity closed to hope.

In our time change has come to this Nation, too. The American Negro, acting with impressive restraint, has peacefully protested and marched, entered the courtrooms and the seats of government, demanding a justice that has long been denied. The voice of the Negro was the call to action. But it is a tribute to America that, once aroused, the courts and the Congress, the President and most of the people, have been the allies of progress.

Thus we have seen the high court of the country declare that discrimination based on race was repugnant to the Constitution, and therefore void. We have seen in 1957, and 1960, and again in 1964, the first civil rights legislation in this Nation in almost an entire century.

As majority leader of the United States Senate, I helped to guide two of these bills through the Senate. And, as your President, I was proud to sign the third. And now very soon we will have the fourth—a new law guaranteeing every American the right to vote.

No act of my entire administration will give me greater satisfaction than the day when my signature makes this bill, too, the law of this land.

The voting rights bill will be the latest, and among the most important, in a long series of victories. But this victory—as Winston Churchill said of another triumph for freedom—"is not the end. It is not even the beginning of the end. But it is, perhaps, the end of the beginning."

That beginning is freedom; and the barriers to that freedom are tumbling down. Freedom is the right to share, share fully and equally, in American society—to vote, to hold a job, to enter a public place, to go to school. It is the right to be treated in every part of our national life as a person equal in dignity and promise to all others.

But freedom is not enough. You do not wipe away the scars of centuries by saying: Now you are free to go where you want, and do as you desire, and choose the leaders you please.

You do not take a person who, for years, has been hobbled by chains and liberate him, bring him up to the starting line of a race and then say, "You are free to compete with all the others," and still justly believe that you have been completely fair.

Thus it is not enough just to open the gates of opportunity. All our citizens must have the ability to walk through those gates.

This is the next and the more profound stage of the battle for civil rights. We seek not just freedom but opportunity. We seek not just legal equity but human ability, not just equality as a right and a theory but equality as a fact and equality as a result.

For the task is to give 20 million Negroes the same chance as every other American to learn and grow, to work and share in society, to develop their abilities—physical, mental, and spiritual, and to pursue their individual happiness.

To this end equal opportunity is essential, but not enough, not enough. Men and women of all races are born with the same range of abilities. But ability is not just the product of birth. Ability is stretched or stunted by the family that you live with, and the neighborhood you live in—by the school you go to and the poverty or the richness of your surroundings. It is the product of a hundred unseen forces playing upon the little infant, the child, and finally the man.

This graduating class at Howard University is witness to the indomitable determination of the Negro American to win his way in American life.

5. Inaugural Address

Mayor Maynard Jackson

After a hard-fought mayoral campaign, one fraught with appeals by his opponent to the fears of many of the city's white residents, Mayor Maynard Jackson used his January 7, 1974, inaugural address to call for biracial cooperation among black and white Atlantans. While expressing his hope that Atlanta would serve as a trend-setter for what American cities could aspire to be in terms of continued economic growth and opportunity, Jackson also promised that his administration would develop policies and engage in efforts to ensure that all Atlantans, regardless of race or socioeconomic status, would share in the city's bounty.

Tonight we come together for a very special purpose. This Inauguration is more than just the swearing in of our newly elected officials. It is the positive reaffirmation that all Atlantans can work together for the good of our City. This affirmation is symbolized by the very nature of the Inaugural Program. Conceived, planned and executed by our citizens, this Inaugural Program brings together two important cultural traditions in the life of our City through the universal language of music. At the same time, this Inaugural joins our cultural and political lives in a new and vital union.

In another and perhaps more important sense, tonight's Inaugural symbolizes the full citizen participation which will be the style and the reality of this new administration. Tonight we are witnessing a "People's Inauguration." Over the next four years we shall work to create a People's administration, one that will afford even the poorest and most destitute person an alternative to agony. No longer will we necessitate Langston Hughes' plaintive cry of the masses,

> I swear to the Lord
> I still can't see
> Why Democracy means
> Everybody but me.

Your presence here is also a *strong* indication of your renewed faith in the electoral process. It is a *strong* indication of your hope for our future as a united City. Your presence is a *strong* indication of your belief in the promise of positive social and political change.

Such faith and hope indeed have become part of what is known as the "Atlanta Style." We use the Hartsfield slogan, "A City too busy to hate," but equally as important, we must ask during the difficult days ahead, are we a City too busy to love? That is no mere rhetorical question. For if we are to make this evening a meaningful beginning, we must make a conscious decision to start to change the way we live. We must do more than *say* we are concerned and that we care. We must begin to translate that concern into action, because we know that injustice and inequality are not vague and shadowy concepts that have no tangible dimensions. Behind every unjust act and behind all unequal treatment there are conscious decisions made by conscious men and women who choose not to care.

So, we must be a City of *love* and our definition of love must be a definition of *action*. Love must be strong economic growth and prosperity for *all*. Love must be giving the young a voice in City Government and restoring their faith in the electoral process. Love must be concern for the welfare of our senior citizens and a renewed commitment to make their years productive and rewarding for all of us. Love must be a balanced diet for all of our children. Love must be decent, safe and sanitary housing for all Atlantans. Love must be working to rid a community of the rats that attack babies while they sleep. Love must be a good education available to all who wish to learn. Love must be an open door to opportunity instead of a closed door of despair. Love must be good jobs, equal treatment and fair wages for all working people. Love must be safe streets and homes where our families can be secure from the threat of violence. Love must be a decision to care for the sick, the infirm and the handicapped. Love must be a city filled with people working together to improve the quality of all our lives. Love must be the absence of racism and sexism. Love must be a chance for everybody to be *somebody*.

To insure a clear reflection of this essential ethic, this administration must place priority upon serving the needs of the masses as well as the classes. The pending reorganization of our City

Government will be designed to open wide the doors of City Hall to all Atlantans and make our City Government more responsive to "people needs" and "people problems."

Foremost among our problems, other than the need for increased interracial communication, is *crime*. Regardless of where we live in Atlanta—Buckhead or Beaverslide, Peachtree Hills or Perry Homes, Cabbage Town or Collier Heights, Carver Homes or Cascade Heights—regardless of what one does for a living, regardless of the insularity one's money may afford, everybody is crime's victim. And we all must make certain that this dread disease does not cause our great city's demise.

An accurate diagnosis of our malady shows that, although some become criminals out of greed, all too often there are those who turn to crime because of the marginal existence of their daily lives. Twenty-five centuries ago, Aristotle, in his monumental work, *Politics,* told us that "poverty is the parent of crime." Martin Luther King, Jr., Ralph Ellison (*Invisible Man*), Franklin Delano Roosevelt, Michael Harrington (*The Other America*), Jule Sugarman and other 20th Century leaders of Social Planning, Criminology and Political Activism have documented the substantial causative relationship between poverty, its fellow determinants, and crime.

Atlanta must *see* that relationship. We must open our eyes if we are to begin to deal with the systematic eradication of poverty and the diminution of crime. We must render visible the invisible. We must *see* the other Atlanta, the one across the tracks, the "inner city" one, the Atlanta in the valleys and the shadows just beyond the first expressway exits one passes when leaving downtown.

If the "haves" do not help the "have nots," we will see the truth in the words of Alexander Stephens Jackson when he said, "The blight will fall on master and man equally, different only in phase." There can be no glittering International City as long as grim poverty and dangerous despair tarnish our glow. We must learn and remember that Atlanta's strength lies not in the power of its government, but in the power of the governed, and they demand the removal of the social cataracts from our governmental eyes.

This new direction means that we will not avoid the presence of crime in our City—and we will certainly not protect it. It means that we will face the tremendous human and financial costs which crime of every kind takes as a toll on our City. Therefore, we will work to create a law enforcement agency which is capable of moving efficiently without fear or favor to seek out the organizers and perpetrators of crime—whether they be on Broad Street or in board rooms. We will develop a police force which understands the kind of City we are seeking to build and is prepared to join this great adventure with us. We will respect it and require its respect of us.

We will be death on the drug trade. As far as a city is empowered, we will seek out the sources, the suppliers, the dealers, as well as the pushers and the addicts. Those who are criminals will be apprehended, convicted and penalized.

But we know, too, that crime is not solved ultimately by police, courts or prisons, that it can only be prevented by the creation of a new, vigorous moral spirit in the community. We can turn our children away from crime only as we turn our attention to them. Only as our own values become less materialistic can we convince them that nothing is important enough to steal. Only as we develop and *demonstrate* a new morality in every level of government, business and private life can we expect the young people of our city to break away from criminal temptations. Only as we help them to find new purposeful roles in society will they be prepared to give up the crutch and the false glamour of drugs.

So, in our great city, we will seek not only to punish crime with even-handed justice, but to prevent it with honest compassion and intelligent planning. We will do our utmost to create a new climate in which the need for crime, the romance of crime, the adventure of crime will be replaced with a sense of purpose and dedication to the building of a new kind of humane city.

Nowhere is that magnificent human potential more obvious than in Atlanta. Nowhere do men and women see more possibility for real change. For we stand, not so much as a gateway to the South, but as gateway to a new time, a new era, a new beginning for the cities of our land. It is a great moment for us. Many eyes are watching us; many cities are examining us.

Instead of falling prey to all the illnesses of urban life in America, Atlanta has the opportunity to lead the way to a new kind of life. It is awesome to consider, but true: we stand at a decisive point in history. Everyone knows that the Old South is dead forever. But in spite of much propaganda to the contrary, we have not yet seen the birth of a really New South. Now we stand with a choice: we can live as if this were simply the worst of times, as if there were no path for Atlanta save the terrible mistakes of the Urban North. Or we can strike out in still uncharted directions. We can become mired in the ruts of other cities, or we can develop an entirely new mural of urban life. If we dare to work, *we* can become the guides. *We* can create the new models. We can serve our city, our state, our section and our nation if we are prepared to create a new kind of city based on a new political vision shared in and worked toward by all Atlantans.

This is the task to which I have already set myself, the task I want to share with you. With your help, your prayers, your strength, your wisdom, your compassion, you, the Council and I *together* can show the world that here is a City too strong not to fight, too loving not to care, too great to turn away.

6. "Can Atlanta Succeed Where America Has Failed? An Exclusive *Atlanta* Magazine Interview with Mayor Maynard Jackson as He Completes His First 500 Days in Office."

Midway through his first administration, many of Mayor Maynard Jackson's initiatives for change had been resisted or thwarted by powerful segments within the Atlanta business community. In this interview, Jackson outlines some of the successes of his administration, some of his plans for future economic revitalization of the city, and the nature of his relationship with his critics in the business community.

Q: You said in an interview just after you were elected vice mayor in 1969 that you might have to do some things as spokesman for the black community that would upset part of the white community. What did you mean, and is that still the case now that you are mayor?

A: I don't recall the context in which I made the statement. I think that since becoming Mayor I have made my decisions based on what is good for the city as a whole, and not for one group as opposed to the other. But I would imagine, for example, in the area of equal employment, contract compliance and so forth, there might appear to be so-called "black decisions" that might not have the full consent of the white community.

An example of that is contract compliance. It is amazing to know that there is some minor—very minor—consternation among a few people in the white community about blacks' getting city contracts: getting them through the regular procedures, but getting contracts. There was some talk that last year we [City Hall] were trying to give all the contract work to blacks. In 1973, out of 83 construction contracts, four went to minority general contractors. That equals about 4.8 per cent. In 1974, out of 52 construction contracts, 13 went to minority general contractors. That's 25 per cent. Since an ordinance was passed last October, subcontractors must now comply with the EEOC regulations. And there has been a definite increase in the number of minority general contractors and subcontractors.

In dollar value, I suspect that out of the $73 million in contracts the City let last year, approximately 1 per cent went to minority contractors. Now if anxiety attaches when the black community gets 1 per cent of all contracts the City let last year, just imagine what happens when we double it to 2 per cent this year.

Let me give you the bottom line on this thing: What we have done is to set up basic systems that will guarantee fair competition to all people.

———

Q: Mr. Mayor, you have been in office approximately 500 days. What do you perceive that the public least understands about the way you function?
A: I think that in many sections of the white community, there is great anxiety about whether my decisions are purely racial. I think that was predictable. I think that is a natural consequence of the changes that we have seen by my election, by the election of a 50 per cent black Council, of a Board of Education that has five of

nine members being black. And by a city that is now predominantly black—about 55 per cent.

There is a peculiar anxiety which probably nobody was prepared to deal with, black or white: That's the anxiety which must attach to a white community which for the first time is a minority community. Black people have not [over the years] rolled over and taken all the negatives that go along with being a black minority, but there is some background, some history, of dealing with the fact of being a minority. In this case, a subjugated minority; an oppressed minority.

Whites on the other hand, although not an *oppressed* minority, are numerically the minority. They are not accustomed to dealing with that psychological fact, that phenomenon. Nor is the black community accustomed to dealing with a white minority.

Add those anxieties on top of the fact that you've got a brand new city charter. Most people don't have any appreciation of the impact of a new city charter on government: The first in a century. A badly needed change in our form of government. A radical change. From a weak mayor and Board of Aldermen with mixed legislative-executive powers in the executive branch—to a strict separation of powers: strong mayor and City Council.

We *are* the greatest city in the country, but we're not superhuman. [We have had] a complete reorganization from 26 to nine departments, a new administration. The mayor is black, half the Council is black, the mayor is new to his position, and of the Council members, eight are brand new. Package all this together in the year 1974 in America, with the economic situation the worst since the Depression. If we think that we're not going to miss a step, that we're not going to question ourselves, then we must be absolutely out of our minds.

Atlanta is, with all its questioning, with all its anxieties, still the best city in this country. And if you don't believe it, ask the folks in all other cities in the country, because they're the ones who convinced me. We still are very human, and we've got to learn to weep. We'll have to accommodate this tremendous change—more than any time in our history—with being patient with ourselves, and accommodate the new styles.

Another part of the new style is that even if there were not black people in this city, there would still be a radical change in how the white community deals with governmental issues. Because no longer is there a monolithic white community—if there ever was. Because now when you talk about the Northside, you talk about Northeast and Virginia-Highland, Morningside, Hope Park and many other communities. Those people, were there not a single black person around, would have fought the Power Structure tooth and nail over I-485. And would have won.

q: It has been agreed widely that the so-called Power Structure no longer has that degree of influence which it used to have even 10 years ago over decision-making. What role do they have? How do you get their input in the total decision-making process?

a: I seek their input pretty much as I do the input of what I call the third partner at the table. Historically, it's been City Hall and the business community. And those two groups made the decisions and others were brought to the table thereafter to ratify decisions that were previously made.

q: Wasn't the press involved in that too? Were they not elements of that triangulation of power?

a: In my opinion, no. In my opinion, the press was ancillary to the decision-making. The press was also used as a mechanism for garnering consensus.

q: The press became a spokesman rather than a third party?

a: Yes, I think so.

My approach is that it would be wrong to seek to exclude the business community. Atlanta would not function well that way, and I made this clear when I ran for office. I have sought in a consistent manner since becoming mayor, to pursue that end—i.e., to make sure that the business community and City Hall sat down together. I have probably pursued that more vigorously than any mayor has ever had to or has ever wanted to. Among the four modern mayors of Atlanta, Hartsfield and Allen didn't have to pursue it as much as Massell or Jackson had to. Massell, I think, in many ways chose not to because he was very heavily opposed by the white business community and only got 16 per cent of the white vote when he became mayor.

I, of course, have never played golf with those guys, have never been invited to their homes, didn't grow up with them, didn't go to school with them—so it was all uphill for me economically and racially. But I had the notion—to which I still cling, by the way, although with less fervor than I did originally—that it wouldn't matter as long as I showed my good faith, pursued honest coalitions with them, and as long as I made them understand that I wanted very much for the traditional coalition to continue with one amendment—and that was to bring the grass-roots community to the table as well.

Now grass roots to me means white and black. It means the middle-income, transportation-oriented groups, planning organizations, citywide league of neighborhoods—that whole movement—as well as blacks, middle income and low income. That's what I call the grass-roots, the masses of people.

I had to convince the business community of this: The fact that I'm bringing a third party to the table should not be taken by you as a threat. It does not mean that you and I are not going to talk. It does not mean that you and I won't consult regularly. It *does* mean that there is a third party here now. Then on the other hand I had to convince the grass-roots community that my frequent contacts with the business community did not mean that I was neglecting the grass-roots community. It's almost like you're in a balancing act constantly.

I feel that some of the people of the old guard, so to speak, are so inflexible that they find themselves now incapable of making the adjustment, even those who are able to say "Let's make the adjustment. It's for the good of Atlanta."

Q: What can be done to encourage white residents and businesses to remain in the city?

A: We have a new breed of "urban pioneer" moving back into the city and re-enrolling their children in the public schools. What they say is "We don't believe all that hogwash we hear about tremendous fears of being mugged every time you walk down a city street, because we work downtown. We know that there is a serious crime problem. We also know that the crime problem in the suburbs is accelerating at a far faster rate, and we also know the name of the game if you're going to fight crime is to have people living in the city. So it's more convenient. The energy crisis, if you want to call it a crisis, helps us to see the benefits of living close in. The housing is more than adequate. We have far better services. All the benefits are there, so we're going to live in the city. I think that's a vastly significant occurrence.

. . . I think also there will ease in the course of time some anxieties that some whites have.

Q: Mr. Mayor, it would be a fault of ours if we could not ask for some constructive suggestions that you might make to ease those anxieties.

A: The first thing is to make fair decisions. I honestly believe that some people have the crazy idea that blacks in Atlanta are going to "get back at" the white community for three and a half centuries of oppression. I have never entertained the idea, and I don't know of any single responsible black figure or person who is in any public position who has.

We can make an awful lot of decisions about where people will live, and more and more I think Atlanta's becoming the kind of city that will give women a fairer chance. I have appointed the very first women department heads, for example, in city government. The Civil Service Board is predominantly female because of my appointments. So is the License Review Board. My appointments have been 50-50 white and black across the board. I have nine commissioners. Five are white, four are black. I have appointed about 38 per cent female. That may have improved with some recent appointments. But that will improve.

Q: Will you deal with a sensitive perception? It does not come from us. There is a perception that if any position is voiced in opposition to yours, your response is that it leads to polarization, that it is a racial opposition.

A: Well, that perception is the result of some very careful and highly biased work by The Atlanta Constitution. Only once since I have been mayor have I ever accused anybody of being racist. Only once. That came at a press conference during the [Public Safety Commissioner Reginald] Eaves confirmation. I had just had a meeting in my office with a white member of City Council who had said that he was going to vote for the Eaves confirmation when I first announced it. I had told him "I appreciate the support, but I think you're going to encounter some real opposition in the white community if you do it." And he said, "Oh, I think you're just imagining that." [A few days later] he came in and said "some members of my church"—and he said they were white— "approached me and said 'Don't you dare vote for Eaves.' Some of them said 'Don't you dare vote for that nigger.' "

I went from that meeting with him into the press conference where somebody asked me not just about the [City] Council, but about the whole response, public and private: Do you think there's any racism involved? Well the obvious answer is yes. At no other time have I said that.

Q: At the end of an interview, we always give a subject an opportunity to say anything he wishes, within the constraint of his time, that we have not touched on—anything you wish to emphasize. The floor is yours.

A: This period of time is probably Atlanta's acid test. We're either going to live up to our advance billings, or we're going to flunk miserably. It all depends on whether black people and white people can get along with each other, and not become consumed in anxieties that are truly without basis in fact.

I have a prediction to make: Atlanta's going to *make* it. But I think it's going to be rough sledding for a while until people can get over anxieties that are at an extraordinarily high pitch.

Now I think that the economy of Atlanta will reflect the national economy. When times are rough in the nation, times are going to be rough here. And that's all that's really happening. But I think Atlanta's going to prosper.

I think that we're going to have to develop new forms of communication—broader, more comprehensive groups that communicate.

We have before us a challenge to have success in an area of concern—the racial area—where the nation as a whole has flunked. So the issue is, can Atlanta succeed where America has failed?

7. Amicus Curiae Brief in *Regents of the University of California* v. *Allan Bakke*

Bakke would be one of the most closely followed cases ever to come before the Supreme Court. After agreeing to hear the case, the Supreme Court received more than fifty amici curiae ("friend of the court") briefs filed on behalf of 117 organizations and institutions that sought to influence the Court's hearing and deciding of the case. These are excerpts from the brief filed by lawyers from the Howard University Law School on behalf of the historically black National Medical Association and National Bar Association as well as the National Association for Equal Opportunity in Higher Education, the research and advocacy group representing the nation's more than one hundred historically black and predominantly black colleges and universities.

Questions Presented

Is it constitutionally permissible for a state medical school to utilize as criteria for selection, among qualified applicants to study medicine, factors such as the applicant's race, sex, work experience, prior military experience and other background for the purpose of increasing the access of minority students to medical education, improving the quality of the medical education of all its students, and producing graduates best calculated to improve and extend medical care to the State's inhabitants? . . .

Argument . . .

II. THE USE OF RACIAL CLASSIFICATION TO PROMOTE INTEGRATION OR TO OVERCOME THE EFFECTS OF PAST DISCRIMINATION IS NEITHER "SUSPECT" NOR PRESUMPTIVELY UNCONSTITUTIONAL.

In the late sixties, the medical school at Davis, like many other medical and professional schools in this nation, realized that in order for their institutions to reflect a more heterogeneous enrollment, their traditional admissions criteria had to be changed.

. . . These schools found themselves in a segregated state even though many did not intentionally practice overt discrimination. Davis Medical School was among those schools which acted to alleviate a low minority enrollment. In fact, the University of California at Los Angeles did not graduate its first black medical student until 1970, or 51 years after being founded. Furthermore, the University of California at Los Angeles did not graduate its first black dentist until 1974, or 55 years after the founding of the Dental School. . . . Davis established a special admissions program to ameliorate its almost segregated medical school enrollment.

In the past ten years, both graduate and undergraduate schools have initiated so-called affirmative action programs in an effort to facilitate the increase of minorities in graduate and undergraduate institutions of higher learning. However, the need for affirmative action programs has become compelling in other work and professional areas of the society where minorities were nonexistent or in areas where their presence was so low as to border on the extinct.

Amici seeks reversal of the California State Supreme Court decision in *Bakke* because it is constitutionally erroneous. First, the California Supreme Court erroneously concluded that racial classification to promote integration is presumptively unconstitutional and "suspect." This conclusion is not the law as Amici understand it. In fact, as Judge Tobriner observed in his dissenting opinion below:

> The governing authorities . . . lend no support to the conclusion that the use of racial classifications to ameliorate segregated conditions is presumptively unconstitutional. . . . By failing to distinguish between *invidious racial classifications* and remedial or "benign" racial classifications, the [State court] majority utilize the wrong constitutional standard in evaluating the validity of the Davis special admissions program. [*Bakke* v. *Regents of University of California*, 553, P.2d 1152, 1173 (1976). (Tobriner, dissenting).]

The *Bakke* case removes scabs from old wounds brought on by invidious discrimination. For the arguments raised by *Bakke* ignore what the court must not ignore: that the history of this country is replete with judicial negation of the legal existence of black people. Hence, as *Bakke* argues that race, as an element of affirmative action programs, is unconstitutional—Amici, arguing the reverse, does not hesitate to remind the court of the dark past, and the accouterments of slavery which remain today. . . .

. . . Impact on the Professions of Law and Medicine for Black Americans: A Compelling State Interest

As illustrative of the broader issue involving affirmative action programs and their constitutional efficacy, this Court last term had before it the issue of affirmative action involving law school admission of black students. . . . Today, the Court is faced with another important professional aspect of the American society: the admission of minority applicants to medical schools as a result of affirmative efforts. As the following discussion points out, "The black legal community of this nation is small, far too small to address itself to the myriad and more complicated legal task which it is frequently called upon to undertake." . . . Likewise, the black medical community is small and is not capable of serving numerous blacks in need of medical care and treatment. The ominous threat of the extinction of other professions in which there are few or no blacks hangs in the balance if the opinion of this Court should side with those arguing that affirmative action programs are not constitutionally protected. . . .

In 1976, the total number of white lawyers in the United States was estimated to be 400,000 while the total number of black lawyers was approximately 7,500 or 1.8 percent of the profession. A 1976 Association of American Law Schools' survey of minority group students in legal education indicates a total of 5,503 Black Americans enrolled in approved law schools 1976–77 as compared with 5,127 in 1975–76 and 2,128 in 1969–70. The "largest absolute increase in first year enrollment was that for blacks [i.e., 2,045 (1975–76) to 2,128 (1976–77)]; however, the increase of 83 in the first year for black law students represented the smallest percentage increase of the six groups [i.e., Black American, Chicano, Puerto Rican, other Hispanic-American, Asian or Pacific Islander, Native American or Alaskan Native]." . . .

The available pool of black lawyers has increased in absolute numbers *but the percentage of blacks in the profession among all lawyers is not notably higher now than it was more than forty years ago.* According to the estimates in 1930, black lawyers comprised less than .007 percent of the entire profession. Although figures vary, it appears that compared with 159,735 white lawyers, there were between 1,175 and 1,230 black members of the bar. . . . In the words of Dr. Charles Houston, a prominent black jurist of the period, despite the fact that arguments could be made that "there [were] enough white lawyers to care for the ordinary legal business of the country," there was a "Need For Negro Lawyers." "Ordinary legal business" did not constitute the total work of attorneys in the United States then any more than it does now. "[W]here . . . pressure is greatest and racial antagonism most acute . . . the services of the Negro lawyer as a social engineer [were] needed." . . .

The need for Negro lawyers expressed by Dr. Charles Houston in 1935 has not changed in forty years even with recent affirmative action efforts. The society has continued to produce an abundance of white lawyers while the number of black lawyers, to say nothing of Americans of Spanish descent and American Indians, has remained static or inconsequential. . . . As Professor Griffin points out it is disquieting to know that blacks constitute 11.4 percent of the republic, yet comprise 1.8 percent of the republic's legal profession; and disquieting to know that Americans of Spanish descent make up 4.4 percent of the population and comprise 0.9 percent of the legal profession; and disquieting to know that the American Indian comprises 800,000, yet may count fewer than 325 Indian attorneys among its population. A recent report by the Vice President for Academic Administration at Temple University indicates that there is one black attorney for every 5,000 blacks as compared with one white attorney for every 750 whites. . . .

The number of black lawyers and law students has always been disproportionate to the needs of the black community and the nation. This problem has been addressed in major studies by black legal scholars since 1927. An examination of studies demonstrates clearly how gradually blacks have moved into the legal profession. . . .

A later "Black Lawyer's Study" prepared by Professor Jerome Shuman indicated that even by 1971, black lawyers comprised less than one percent of the entire profession due to both "inability to afford a legal education" and the "exclusionary practices of many of the law schools." . . . Hence, there has been some progress in the past six years, but not nearly enough effort to "jump and shout"!

It is clear from Shuman's study that by 1971, or 36 years after Houston's study, the number of black lawyers had increased by only 3,000 black attorneys. Today, there are approximately 7,500 black lawyers, as opposed to nearly 400,000 white attorneys. In 1935 there were 158,735 white attorneys. In short, there has been no significant increase in the black lawyer population, and the concerns voiced by Houston in 1935 remain constant in 1977. Indeed, Professor Tollett has concluded that "[U]ntil . . . oppressed minority groups approach proportional representation in law school and the bar, *preferential or special recruitment programs imperatively should continue apace.*" . . .

The impact of *Bakke* operates to summarily undermine the need and desire for equal opportunity in the field of medicine, also. Historically, the medical profession has been grossly underrepresented in terms of black participation and membership, thus demanding the necessity for greater black enrollment in medical schools. . . . A recent, yet unpublished statistical study prepared by Dr. Elizabeth Abramowitz of the Institute for the Study of Educational Policy is most illustrative of this theory. . . .

Dr. Abramowitz's study reveals a well-known fact that the need exists for "more doctors as health providers sensitive to the needs of black patients and as medical researchers studying health problems related to social class and race." Notwithstanding medical research, federal involvement with medical schools has centered around providing financial assistance for the training of those persons promising to work in underserved rural and urban communities. In spite of this attempt, however, the number of black doctors in the United States falls short of being described as negligible.

In 1974, for example, black doctors comprised 2 percent of all practicing doctors in the U.S., while at the same time, black citizens comprised 11% of all citizens. Keeping these figures in mind, if the only means of health service accessible to blacks emanated from the 6,600 black doctors, there would be only one black doctor for every 3,400 black persons. In comparing this situation with the then existing 330,000 white doctors, there would have been one white doctor for every 557 white persons. The result: the black doctor continues to be a limited resource in the medical delivery system for black and white patients, similarly.

The American Medical Association, hoping to alleviate this "supply" problem, endorsed the remedy of "increasing the number of black medical students to a figure roughly proportional to the black population." The goal set in the late 1960s, by the AMA, was to have 10 percent black enrollment in medical schools by the mid-1970s. In 1969, however, blacks totalled 2.8 percent of the 37,669 medical students, and by 1974, blacks totalled only 6 percent of the 53,554 medical students. Granted, that in this time span black enrollment in all medical schools increased 223 percent (from 1,038 in 1969 to 3,355 in 1974), however, black enrollment in all medical schools has not reached, and is not even near reaching, a comparable degree of similitude with the black population.

In 1969 only two historically black medical schools existed in the U.S., Howard University and Meharry Medical College, and these schools enrolled slightly less than one-half (46 percent) of all black medical students. However, by 1973, black enrollment in historically black medical schools accounted for 21 percent of all black medical students. In other words, between 1969 and 1972, the most significant increase in black enrollment in medical schools occurred on the campuses of historically and predominantly black medical schools.

This racial isolation in the fields of law and medicine is indicative of the racial isolation and non-access of blacks to other professional and highly technical fields.

It must follow, where a state decides within the exercise of its police power that there is a compelling state interest to correct this glaring tragedy on the promise of equality, that such a state policy is permitted under the Fourteenth Amendment.

8. *Regents of the University of California* v. *Allan Bakke* (The Supreme Court Judgment)
June 28, 1978

The two decisions rendered by the Supreme Court in the Bakke *case were complex efforts to reach majority opinions. In both decisions, Associate Justice Lewis Powell had to reach majority conclusions from among the four justices who wished to overrule the admissions plan at Davis and from the four justices who wished to uphold the admissions plan. In the opinion, while the admissions plan was ruled unconstitutional and Bakke was ordered admitted to the school, the Supreme Court also ruled that race could be a factor considered in decisions made by admissions committees in choosing students for undergraduate, graduate, and professional schools.*

Mr. Justice Powell announced the judgment of the Court.

This case presents a challenge to the special admissions program of the petitioner, the Medical School of the University of California at Davis. . . .

For the reasons stated in the following opinion, I believe that so much of the judgment of the California court holds petitioner's special admissions program unlawful and directs that respondent be admitted to the Medical School must be affirmed. . . .

I also conclude . . . the portion of the court's judgment enjoining petitioner from according any consideration to race in its admissions process must be reversed. . . .

Affirmed in part and reversed in part.

The Medical School of the University of California at Davis opened in 1968 with an entering class of 50 students. In 1971, the size of the entering class was increased to 100 students, a level at which it remains. . . . Over the next two years, the faculty devised a special admissions program.

The special admissions program operated with a separate committee, a majority of whom were members of minority groups. On the 1973 application form, candidates were asked to indicate whether they wished to be considered as "economically and/or educationally disadvantaged" applicants; on the 1974 form the question was whether they wished to be considered as members of a "minority group," which the Medical School apparently viewed as "Blacks," "Chicanos," "Asians," and "American Indians." . . . No formal definition of "disadvantaged" was ever produced, but the chairman of the special committee screened each application to see whether it reflected economic or educational deprivation. Having passed this initial hurdle, the applications then were rated by the special committee. . . . About one-fifth of the total number of special applicants were invited for interviews in 1973 and 1974. . . . The special committee then presented its top choices to the general admissions committee. The latter did not rate or compare the special candidates against the general applicants, but could reject recommended special candidates for failure to meet course requirements or other specific deficiencies. The special committee continued to recommend special applicants until a number prescribed by faculty vote were admitted. . . . [I]n 1973 and 1974 . . . the prescribed number of special admissions [was] 16.

From . . . 1971 through 1974, the special program resulted in the admission of 21 black students, 30 Mexican-Americans, and 12 Asians, for a total of 63 minority students. Over the same period, the regular admissions program produced one black, six Mexican-Americans, and 37 Asians, for a total of 44 minority students. Although disadvantaged whites applied to the special program in large numbers, none received an offer of admission through that process. Indeed, in 1974, at least, the special committee explicitly considered only "disadvantaged" special applicants who were members of one of the designated minority groups.

Allan Bakke is a white male who applied to the Davis Medical School in both 1973 and 1974. . . . His 1973 interview[er] . . . considered Bakke "a very desirable applicant to [the] medical school." Despite a strong benchmark score of 468 out of 500, Bakke was rejected. [In 1974, his] faculty interviewer . . . found Bakke "rather limited in his approach" to the problems of the medical profession and found disturbing Bakke's "very definite opinions which were based more on his personal viewpoints than upon a study of the total problem." . . . Again, Bakke's application was rejected. . . . In both years, applicants were admitted under the special program with grade point averages, MCAT scores, and benchmark scores significantly lower than Bakke's.

Petitioner prefers to view [the special admissions program] as establishing a "goal" of minority representation in the Medical School. Respondent, echoing the courts below, labels it a racial quota.

This semantic distinction is beside the point: The special admissions program is undeniably a classification based on race and ethnic background. To the extent that there existed a pool of at least minimally qualified minority applicants to fill the 16 special admissions seats, white applicants could compete for only 84 seats in the entering class, rather than the 100 open to minority applicants. Whether this limitation is described as a quota or a goal, it is a line drawn on the basis of race and ethnic status.

Although many of the Framers of the Fourteenth Amendment conceived of its primary function as bridging the vast distance between members of the Negro race and white "majority," the Amendment itself was framed in universal terms, without reference to color, ethnic origin, or condition of prior servitude. . . .

Over the past 30 years this Court has embarked upon the crucial mission of interpreting the Equal Protection Clause with the view of assuring to all persons "the protection of equal laws" in a Nation confronting a legacy of slavery and racial discrimination. . . .

Petitioner urges us to adopt for the first time a more restrictive view of the Equal Protection Clause and hold that discrimination against members of the white "majority" cannot be suspect if its purpose can be characterized as "benign." The clock of our liberties, however, cannot be turned back to 1868. It is far too late to argue that the guarantee of equal protection to *all* persons permits the recognition of special wards entitled to a degree of protection greater than that accorded others.

———————

There are serious problems of justice connected with the idea of preference itself. First, it may not always be clear that a so-called preference is in fact benign. Courts may be asked to validate burdens imposed upon individual members of a particular group in order to advance the group's general interest. Nothing in the Constitution supports the notion that individuals may be asked to suffer otherwise impermissible burdens in order to enhance the societal standing of their ethnic groups. Second, preferential programs may only reinforce common stereotypes holding that certain groups are unable to achieve success without special protection based on a factor having no relationship to individual worth. Third, there is a measure of inequity in forcing innocent persons in respondent's position to bear the burdens of redressing grievances not of their making.

———————

If it is the individual who is entitled to judicial protection against classifications based upon his racial or ethnic background because such distinctions impinge upon personal rights, rather than the individual only because of his membership in a particular group, then constitutional standards may be applied consistently. Political judgments regarding the necessity for the particular classification may be weighed in the constitutional balance . . . but the standard of justification will remain constant. This is as it should be, since those political judgments are the product of rough compromise struck by contending groups within the democratic process. When they touch upon an individual's race or ethnic background, he is entitled to a judicial determination that the burden he is asked to bear on that basis is precisely tailored to serve a compelling governmental [interest].

———————

In this case . . . there has been no determination by the legislature or a responsible administrative agency that the University engaged in a discriminatory practice requiring remedial efforts. Moreover, the operation of petitioner's special admissions program . . . prefers the designated minority groups at the expense of other individuals who are totally foreclosed from competition for the 16 special admissions seats in every Medical School class. Because of that foreclosure, some individuals are excluded from enjoyment of a state-provided benefit—admission to the Medical School—they otherwise would receive. When a classification denies an individual opportunities or benefits enjoyed by others solely because of his race or ethnic background, it must be regarded as suspect.

. . . The special admissions program purports to serve the purposes of: (i) "reducing the historic deficit of traditionally disfavored minorities in medical schools and in the medical profession"; (ii) countering the effects of societal discrimination; (iii) increasing the number of physicians who will practice in communities currently underserved; and (iv) obtaining the educational benefits that flow from an ethnically diverse student body. It is necessary to decide which, if any, of these purposes is substantial enough to support the use of a suspect classification.

. . . If petitioner's purpose is to assure within its student body some specified percentage of a particular group merely because of its race or ethnic origin, such a preferential purpose must be rejected not as insubstantial but as facially invalid. Preferring members of any one group for no reason other than race or ethnic origin is discrimination for its own sake. This the Constitution forbids.

. . . The State certainly has a legitimate and substantial interest in ameliorating, or eliminating where feasible, the disabling effects of identified discrimination. . . . That goal was far more focused than the remedying of the effects of "societal discrimination," an amorphous concept of injury that may be ageless in its reach into the past.

We have never approved a classification that aids persons perceived as members of relatively victimized groups at the expense of other innocent individuals in the absence of judicial, legislative, or administrative findings of constitutional or statutory violations. After such findings have been made, the governmental interest in preferring members of the injured groups at the expense of others is substantial, since the legal rights of the victims must be vindicated. In such a case, the extent of the injury and the consequent remedy will have been judicially, legislatively, or administratively defined. Also, the remedial action usually remains subject to continuing oversight to assure that it will work the least harm possible to other innocent persons competing for the benefit. Without such findings of constitutional or statutory violations, it cannot be said that the government has any greater interest in helping one individual than in refraining from harming another. Thus, the government has no compelling justification for inflicting such harm.

———

Hence, the purpose of helping certain groups . . . perceived as victims of "societal discrimination" does not justify a classification that imposes disadvantages upon persons like respondent, who bear no responsibility for whatever harm the beneficiaries of the special admissions program are thought to have suffered. To hold otherwise would be to convert a remedy heretofore reserved for violations of legal rights into a privilege that all institutions throughout the Nation could grant at their pleasure to whatever groups are perceived as victims of societal discrimination. That is a step we have never approved.

. . . Petitioner identifies . . . improving the delivery of health care services to communities currently underserved. It may be assumed that in some situations a State's interest in facilitating the health care of its citizens is sufficiently compelling to support the use of a suspect classification. But there is virtually no evidence in the record indicating that petitioner's special admissions program is either needed or geared to promote that goal. . . .

. . . The fourth goal asserted by petitioner is the attainment of a diverse student body. . . . Academic freedom, though not a specifically enumerated constitutional right, long has been viewed as a special concern of the First Amendment. The freedom of a university to make its own judgments as to education includes the selection of its student body.

———

Thus, in arguing that its universities must be accorded the right to select those students who will contribute the most to the "robust exchange of ideas," petitioner invokes a countervailing constitutional interest, that of the First Amendment. In this light, petitioner must be viewed as seeking to achieve a goal that is of paramount importance in the fulfillment of its mission.

. . . Physicians serve a heterogeneous population. An otherwise qualified medical student with a particular background—whether it be ethnic, geographic, culturally advantaged or disadvantaged—may bring to a professional school of medicine experiences, outlooks, and ideas that enrich the training of its student body and better equip its graduates to render with understanding their vital service to humanity.

Ethnic diversity, however, is only one element in a range of factors a university properly may consider in attaining the goal of a heterogeneous student body. Although a university must have wide discretion in making the sensitive judgments as to who should be admitted, constitutional limitations protecting individual rights may not be disregarded. . . .

. . . [P]etitioner's argument that this is the only effective means of serving the interest of diversity is seriously flawed. . . . Petitioner's special admissions program, focused *solely* on ethnic diversity, would hinder rather than further attainment of genuine diversity.

The experience of other university admissions programs, which take race into account in achieving the educational diversity valued by the First Amendment, demonstrates that the assignment of a fixed number of places to a minority group is not a necessary means toward that end. An illuminating example is found in the Harvard College program:

> In recent years Harvard College has expanded the concept of diversity to include students from disadvantaged economic, racial and ethnic groups. . . .
> . . . When the Committee on Admissions reviews the large middle group of applicants who are "admissible" and deemed capable of doing good work in their courses, the race of an applicant may tip the balance in his favor just as geographic origin or a life spent on a farm may tip the balance in other candidates' cases.

In such an admissions program, race or ethnic background may be deemed a "plus" in a particular applicant's file, yet it does not insulate the individual from comparison with all other candidates for the available seats. The file of a particular black applicant may be examined for his potential contribution to diversity without the factor of race being decisive when compared, for example, with that of an applicant identified as an Italian-American if the latter is thought to exhibit qualities more likely to promote beneficial educational pluralism. Such qualities could include exceptional personal talents, unique work or service experience, leadership potential, maturity, demonstrated compassion, a history of overcoming disadvantage, ability to communicate with the poor, or other qualifications deemed important. In short, an admissions program operated in this way is flexible enough to consider all pertinent elements of diversity in light of the particular qualifications of each applicant, and to place them on the same footing for consideration, although not necessarily according them the same weight. Indeed, the weight attributed to a particular quality may vary from year to year depending upon the "mix" both of the student body and the applicants for the incoming class.

This kind of program treats each applicant as an individual in the admissions process. The applicant who loses out on the last available seat to another candidate receiving a "plus" on the basis of ethnic background will not have been foreclosed from all consideration for that seat simply because he was not the right color or had the wrong surname. . . .

It has been suggested that an admissions program which considers race only as one factor is simply a subtle and more sophisticated—but no less effective—means of according racial preference than the Davis program. A facial intent to discriminate, however, is evident in petitioner's preference program and not denied in this case. No such facial infirmity exists in an admissions program where race or ethnic background is simply one element— to be weighed fairly against other elements—in the selection process. . . . And a Court would not assume that a university, professing to employ a facially nondiscriminatory admissions policy, would operate it as a cover for the functional equivalent of a quota system. In short, good faith would be presumed in the absence of a showing to the contrary in the manner permitted by our cases. . . .

. . . [W]hen a State's distribution of benefits or imposition of burdens hinges on ancestry or the color of a person's skin, that individual is entitled to a demonstration that the challenged classification is necessary to promote a substantial state interest. Petitioner has failed to carry this burden. For this reason, that portion of the California court's judgment holding petitioner's special admissions program invalid under the Fourteenth Amendment must be affirmed.

In enjoining petitioner from ever considering the race of any applicant, however, the courts below failed to recognize that the State has a substantial interest that legitimately may be served by a properly devised admissions program involving the competitive consideration of race and ethnic origin. For this reason, so much of the California court's judgment as enjoins petitioner from any consideration of the race of any applicant must be reversed.

With respect to respondent's entitlement to an injunction directing his admission to the Medical School, petitioner has conceded that it could not carry its burden of proving that, but for the existence of its unlawful special admissions program, respondent still would not have been admitted. Hence, respondent is entitled to the injunction, and that portion of the judgment must be affirmed.

9. *Regents of the University of California* v. *Allan Bakke* (Justice Marshall's Dissent)
June 28, 1978

*In a bitter dissenting opinion to the Supreme Court's decision to overturn the admissions plan at Davis, Associate Justice Thurgood Marshall (who had argued the **Brown** cases before this same Court a quarter century earlier) sought to remind his fellow justices of the historic legal and societal mistreatment of African-Americans and cited the need for the continuance of affirmative action programs as remedies for the effects of past and present discrimination.*

MR. JUSTICE MARSHALL.

I agree with the judgment of the Court only insofar as it permits a university to consider the race of an applicant in making admissions decisions. I do not agree that petitioner's admission's program violates the Constitution. For it must be remembered that, during most of the past 200 years, the Constitution as interpreted by this Court did not prohibit the most ingenious and pervasive forms of discrimination against the Negro. Now, when a State acts to remedy the effects of that legacy of discrimination, I cannot believe that this same Constitution stands as a barrier.

I

A

Three hundred and fifty years ago, the Negro was dragged to this country in chains to be sold into slavery. Uprooted from his homeland and thrust into bondage for forced labor, the slave was deprived of all legal rights. It was unlawful to teach him to read; he could be sold away from his family and friends at the whim of his master; and killing or maiming him was not a crime. The system of slavery brutalized and dehumanized both master and slave.[1]

The denial of human rights was etched into the American colonies' first attempts at establishing self-government. When the colonists determined to seek their independence from England, they drafted a unique document cataloguing their grievances against the King and proclaiming as "self-evident" that "all men are created equal" and are endowed "with certain unalienable Rights," including those to "Life, Liberty and the pursuit of Happiness." . . .

---

1. The history recounted here is perhaps too well known to require documentation. But I must acknowledge the authorities on which I rely in retelling it. J. H. Franklin, From Slavery to Freedom, (4th ed. 1974) (hereinafter Franklin); R. Kluger, Simple Justice (1975) (hereinafter Kluger); C. V. Woodward, The Strange Career of Jim Crow (3rd ed. 1974) (hereinafter Woodward).

The implicit protection of slavery embodied in the Declaration of Independence was made explicit in the Constitution, which treated a slave as being equivalent to three-fifths of a person for purposes of appointing representatives and taxes among the States. Art. I. §2. The Constitution also contained a clause ensuring that the "migration or importation" of slaves into the existing States would be legal until at least 1808. Art. I. §9, and a fugitive slave clause requiring that when a slave escaped to another State, he must be returned on the claim of the master. Art. IV. §2. In their declaration of the principles that were to provide the cornerstone of the new Nation, therefore, the Framers made it plain that "we the people," for whose protection the Constitution was designed, did not include those whose skins were the wrong color. . . .

The individual States likewise established the machinery to protect the system of slavery through the promulgation of the Slave Codes, which were designed primarily to defend the property interest of the owner in his slave. The position of the Negro slave as mere property was confirmed by this Court in *Dred Scott* v. *Sandford,* 19 How. 393 (1857), holding that the Missouri Compromise—which prohibited slavery in the portion of the Louisiana Purchase Territory north of Missouri—was unconstitutional because it deprived slave owners of their property without due process. The Court declared that under the Constitution a slave was property, and "[t]he right to traffic in it, like an ordinary article of merchandise and property, was guarantied to the citizens of the United States. . . ." *Id.,* at 451. The Court further concluded that Negroes were not intended to be included as citizens under the Constitution but were "regarded as beings of an inferior order . . . altogether unfit to associate with the white race, either in social or political relations; and so far inferior, that they had no rights which the white man was bound to respect. . . ." *Id.,* at 407.

B

The status of the Negro as property was officially erased by his emancipation at the end of the Civil War. But the long awaited emancipation, while freeing the Negro from slavery, did not bring him citizenship or equality in any meaningful way. Slavery was replaced by a system of "laws which imposed upon the colored race onerous disabilities and burdens, and curtailed their rights in the pursuit of life, liberty, and property to such an extent that their freedom was of little value." *Slaughter-House Cases,* 16 Wall. 36. 70 (1873). Despite the passage of the Thirteenth, Fourteenth, and Fifteenth Amendments, the Negro was systematically denied the rights those amendments were supposed to secure. The combined actions and inactions of the State and Federal Government maintained Negroes in a position of legal inferiority for another century after the Civil War.

The Southern States took the first steps to re-enslave the Negroes. Immediately following the end of the Civil War, many of the provisional legislatures passed Black Codes, similar to Slave Codes, which, among other things, limited the rights of Negroes to own or rent property and permitted imprisonment for breach of employment contracts. Over the next several decades the South managed to disenfranchise the Negroes in spite of the Fifteenth Amendment by various techniques, including poll taxes, deliberately complicated balloting process, property and literacy qualifications, and finally the white primary.

Congress responded to the legal disabilities being imposed in the Southern States by passing the Reconstruction Acts and the Civil Rights Acts. Congress also responded to the needs of the Negroes at the end of the Civil War by establishing the Bureau of Refugees, Freedmen, and Abandoned Lands, better known as the Freedmen's Bureau, to supply food, hospitals, land and education to the newly freed slaves. Thus for a time it seemed as if the Negro might be protected from the continued denial of his civil rights and might be relieved of the disabilities that prevented him from taking his place as a free and equal citizen.

That time, however, was short-lived. Reconstruction came to a close, and, with the assistance of this Court, the Negro was rapidly stripped of his new civil rights. . . .

The Court began by interpreting the Civil War Amendments in a manner that sharply curtailed their substantive protections. . . . [I]n the notorious *Civil Rights Cases,* 109 U.S. 3 (1883), the Court strangled Congress' efforts to use its power to promote racial equality. In those cases the Court invalidated sections of the Civil Rights Act of 1875 that made it a crime to deny equal access to "inns, public conveyances . . . theatres, and other places of public amusement." According to the Court, the Fourteenth Amendment gave Congress the power to prescribe only discriminatory action by the State. The Court ruled that the Negroes who were excluded from public places suffered only an invasion of their social rights at the hands of private individuals, and Congress had no power to remedy that. *Id.,* at 24–25. "When a man has emerged from slavery, and by the aid of beneficient legislation has shaken off the inseparable concomitants of that state," the Court concluded, "there must be some stage in the progress of his elevation when he takes the rank of a mere citizen, and ceases to be the special favorite of the laws. . . ." *Id.,* at 25. As Justice Harlan noted in dissent, however, the Civil War Amendments and Civil Rights Acts did not make the Negroes the "special favorite" of the laws but instead "sought to accomplish in reference to that race . . . what had already been done in every State of the Union for the White race—to secure and protect rights belonging to them as freemen and citizens; nothing more." *Id.,* at 61.

The Court's ultimate blow to the Civil War Amendments and to the equality of Negroes came in *Plessy* v. *Ferguson,* 163 U.S. 537 (1896). In upholding a Louisiana law that required railway companies to provide "equal but separate" accommodations for whites and Negroes, the Court held that the Fourteenth Amendment was not intended "to abolish distinctions based upon color, or to enforce social, as distinguished from political equality, or a commingling of the two races upon terms unsatisfactory to either." *Id.,* at 544. Ignoring totally the realities of the positions of the two races, the Court remarked:

> We consider the underlying fallacy of the plaintiff's argument to consist in the assumption that the enforced separation of the two races stamps the colored race with a badge of inferiority. If this be so, it is not by reason of anything found in the act but solely because the colored race chooses to put that construction upon it." *Id.,* at 551.

Mr. Justice Harlan's dissenting opinion recognized the bankruptcy of the Court's reasoning. He noted that the "real meaning" of the legislation was "that colored citizens are so inferior and degraded that they cannot be allowed to sit in public coaches occupied by white citizens." *Id.,* at 560. He expressed his fear that if like laws were enacted in other States, "the effect would be in the highest degree mischievous." *Id.,* at 503. Although slavery would have disappeared, the States would retain the power "to interfere with the full enjoyment of the blessings of freedom; to regulate civil rights, common to all citizens, upon the basis of race; and to place in a condition of legal inferiority a large body of American citizens. . . ." *Id.,* at 563.

The fears of Mr. Justice Harlan were soon to be realized. In the wake of *Plessy,* many States expanded their Jim Crow laws, which had up until that time been limited primarily to passenger trains and schools. The segregation of the races was extended to residential areas, parks, hospitals, theaters, waiting rooms and bathrooms. There were even statutes and ordinances which authorized separate phone booths for Negroes and whites, which required that textbooks used by children of one race be kept separate from those used by the other, and which required that Negro and white prostitutes be kept in separate districts. . . .

Nor were the laws restricting the rights of Negroes limited solely to the Southern States. In many of the Northern States, the Negro was denied the right to vote, prevented from serving on juries and excluded from theaters, restaurants, hotels, and inns. Under President Wilson, the Federal Government began to require segregation in Government buildings; desks of Negro employees were curtained off; separate bathrooms and separate tables in the cafeteria were provided; and even the galleries of the Congress were segregated. When his segregationist policies were attacked, President Wilson responded that segregation was "not humiliating but a benefit" and that he was "rendering [the Negroes] more safe in their possession of office and less likely to be discriminated against." . . .

The enforced segregation of the races continued into the middle of the 20th century. In both World Wars, Negroes were for the most part confined to separate military units; it was not until 1948 that an end to segregation in the military was ordered by President Truman. And the history of the exclusion of Negro children from white public schools is too well known and recent to require repeating here. That Negroes were deliberately excluded from public graduate and professional schools—and thereby denied the opportunity to become doctors, lawyers, engineers, and the like— is also well established. It is of course true that some of the Jim Crow laws (which the decisions of this Court had helped to foster) were struck down by this Court in a series of decisions leading up to *Brown* v. *Board of Education of Topeka,* 347 U.S. 483 (1954). . . . Those decisions, however, did not automatically end segregation, nor did they move Negroes from a position of legal inferiority to one of equality. The legacy of years of slavery and of years of second-class citizenship in the wake of emancipation could not be so easily eliminated.

II

The position of the Negro today in America is the tragic but inevitable consequence of centuries of unequal treatment. Measured by any benchmark of comfort or achievement, meaningful equality remains a distant dream for the Negro.

A Negro child today has a life expectancy which is shorter by more than five years than that of a white child.[2] The Negro child's mother is over three times more likely to die of complications in childbirth,[3] and the infant mortality rate for Negroes is nearly twice that for whites.[4] The median income of the Negro family is only 60% that of the median of a white family,[5] and the percentage of Negroes who live in families with incomes below the poverty line is nearly four times greater than that of whites.[6]

When the Negro child reaches working age, he finds that America offers him significantly less than it offers his white counterpart. For Negro adults, the unemployment rate is twice

---

2. U.S. Dept. of Commerce, Bureau of the Census, Statistical Abstract of the United States 65 (1977) (table 94).

3. *Id.,* at 70 (table 102).

4. *Ibid.*

5. U.S. Dept. of Commerce, Bureau of the Census, Current Population Reports, Series P-60. No. 107, at 7 (1977) (table 1).

6. *Id.,* at 20 (table 14).

that of whites,[7] and the unemployment rate for Negro teenagers is nearly three times that of white teenagers.[8] A Negro male who completes four years of college can expect a median annual income of merely $110 more than a white male who has only a high school diploma.[9] Although Negroes represent 11.5% of the population,[10] they are only 1.2% of the lawyers and judges, 2% of the physicians, 2.3% of the dentists, 1.1% of the engineers and 2.6% of the college and university professors.[11]

The relationship between those figures and the history of unequal treatment afforded to the Negro cannot be denied. At every point from birth to death the impact of the past is reflected in the still disfavored position of the Negro.

In the light of the sorry history of discrimination and its devastating impact on the lives of Negroes, bringing the Negro into the mainstream of American life should be a state interest of the highest order. To fail to do so is to ensure that America will forever remain a divided society.

III

I do not believe that the Fourteenth Amendment requires us to accept that fate. Neither its history nor our past cases lend any support to the conclusion that a University may not remedy the cumulative effects of society's discrimination by giving consideration to race in an effort to increase the number and percentage of Negro doctors.

A

This Court long ago remarked that

---

7. U.S. Dept. of Labor, Bureau of Labor Statistics, Employment and Earnings, January 1978, at 170 (table 44).

8. *Ibid.*

9. U.S. Dept. of Commerce, Bureau of the Census, Current Population Reports, Series P-60, No. 105, at 198 (1977) (table 47).

10. U.S. Dept. of Commerce, Bureau of the Census, Statistical Abstract of the United States 25 (table 24).

11. *Id.*, at 407–408 (table 662) (based on 1970 census).

"in any fair and just construction of any section or phrase of these [Civil War] amendments, it is necessary to look to the purpose which we have said was the pervading spirit of them all, the evil which they were designed to remedy. . . ." *Slaughter-House Cases,* 16 Wall., at 72.

It is plain that the Fourteenth Amendment was not intended to prohibit measures designed to remedy the effects of the Nation's past treatment of Negroes. The Congress that passed the Fourteenth Amendment is the same Congress that passed the 1866 Freedmen's Bureau Act, an act that provided many of its benefits only to Negroes. . . .

Since the Congress that considered and rejected the objections to the 1866 Freedmen's Bureau Act concerning special relief to Negroes also proposed the Fourteenth Amendment, it is inconceivable that the Fourteenth Amendment was intended to prohibit all race-conscious relief measures. It "would be a distortion of the policy manifested in that amendment, which was adopted to prevent state legislation designed to perpetuate discrimination on the basis of race or color," *Railway Mail Association* v. *Corsi,* 326 U.S. 88.94 (1945), to hold that it barred state action to remedy the effects of that discrimination. Such a result would pervert the intent of the framers by substituting abstract equality for the genuine equality the amendment was intended to achieve.

B

As has been demonstrated in our joint opinion, this Court's past cases establish the constitutionality of race-conscious remedial measures. Beginning with the school desegregation cases, we recognized that even absent a judicial or legislative finding of constitutional violation, a school board constitutionally could consider the race of students in making school assignment decisions. See *Swann* v. *Charlotte-Mecklenburg Board of Education,* 402 U.S. 1, 16 (1971); *McDaniel* v. *Barresi,* 402 U.S. 39.41 (1971). We noted, moreover, that a

"flat prohibition against assignment of students for the purpose of creating a racial balance must inevitably conflict with the duty of school authorities to disestablish dual school systems. As we have held in *Swann*, the Constitution does not compel any particular degree of racial balance or mixing, but when past and continuing constitutional violations are found, some ratios are likely to be useful as starting points in shaping a remedy. An absolute prohibition against use of such a device—even as a starting point—contravenes the implicit command of *Green* v. *County School Board*, 391 U.S. 430 (1968), that all reasonable methods be available to formulate an effective remedy." *Board of Education* v. *Swann*, 402 U.S. 43, 46 (1971).

As we have observed, "[a]ny other approach would freeze the status quo that is the very target of all desegregation processes." *McDaniel* v. *Barresi, supra*, at 41.

Only last Term, in *United Jewish Organizations* v. *Carey*, 430 U.S. 144 (1977), we upheld a New York reapportionment plan that was deliberately drawn on the basis of race to enhance the electoral power of Negroes and Puerto Ricans; the plan had the effect of diluting the electoral strength of the Hasidic Jewish Community. We were willing in *UJO* to sanction the remedial use of a racial classification even though it disadvantaged otherwise "innocent" individuals. In another case last Term, *Califano* v. *Webster*, 430 U.S. 313 (1977), the Court upheld a provision in the Social Security laws that discriminated against men because its purpose was " 'the permissible one of redressing our society's long standing disparate treatment of women.' " *Id,* at 317, quoting *Califano* v. *Goldfarb*, 340 U.S. 199, 209 n. 8 (1977) (plurality opinion). We thus recognized the permissibility of remedying past societal discrimination through the use of otherwise disfavored classifications.

Nothing in those cases suggests that a university cannot similarly act to remedy past discrimination.[12] It is true that in both *UJO*

---

12. Indeed, the action of the University finds support in the regulations promulgated under Title VI by the Department of Health, Education, and Welfare and approved by the President, which authorize a federally funded institution to take affirmative steps to overcome past discrimination against groups even where the institution was not guilty of prior discrimination. 45 CFR 80.3 (b) (6) (ii) (1977).

and *Webster* the use of the disfavored classification was predicated on legislative or administrative action, but in neither case had those bodies made findings that there had been constitutional violations or that the specific individuals to be benefited had actually been the victims of discrimination. Rather, the classification in each of those cases was based on a determination that the group was in need of the remedy because of some type of past discrimination. There is thus ample support for the conclusion that a university can employ race-conscious measures to remedy past societal discrimination, without the need for a finding that those benefited were actually victims of that discrimination.

IV

While I applaud the judgment of the Court that a university may consider race in its admissions process, it is more than a little ironic that, after several hundred years of class-based discrimination against Negroes, the Court is unwilling to hold that a class-based remedy for that discrimination is permissible. In declining to so hold, today's judgment ignores the fact that for several hundred years Negroes have been discriminated against, not as individuals, but rather solely because of the color of their skins. It is unnecessary in 20th century America to have individual Negroes demonstrate that they have been victims of racial discrimination; the racism of our society has been so pervasive that none, regardless of wealth or position, has managed to escape its impact. The experience of Negroes in America has been different in kind, not just in degree, from that of other ethnic groups. It is not merely the history of slavery alone but also that a whole people were marked as inferior by the law. And that mark has endured. The dream of America as the great melting pot has not been realized for the Negro; because of his skin color he never even made it into the pot.

These differences in the experience of the Negro make it difficult for me to accept that Negroes cannot be afforded greater protection under the Fourteenth Amendment where it is necessary to remedy the effects of past discrimination. In the *Civil Rights Cases, supra,* the Court wrote that the Negro emerging from slavery must cease "to be the special favorite of the laws." 109 U.S., at 25; see p. 5. *supra.* We cannot in light of the history of the last century yield to that view. Had the Court in that case and others been willing to "do for human liberty and the fundamental rights of American citizenship, what it did . . . for the protection of slavery and the rights of the masters of fugitive slaves," *id.,* at 53 (Harlan, J., dissenting), we would not need now to permit the recognition of any "special wards."

Most importantly, had the Court been willing in 1896, in *Plessy* v. *Ferguson,* to hold that the Equal Protection Clause forbids differences in treatment based on race, we would not be faced with this dilemma in 1978. We must remember, however, that the principle that the "Constitution is colorblind" appeared only in the opinion of the lone dissenter. 163 U.S., at 559. The majority of the Court rejected the principle of color blindness, and for the next 60 years, from *Plessy* to *Brown* v. *Board of Education,* ours was a Nation where, *by law,* an individual could be given "special" treatment based on the color of his skin.

It is because of a legacy of unequal treatment that we now must permit the institutions of this society to give consideration to race in making decisions about who will hold the positions of influence, affluence and prestige in America. For far too long, the doors to those positions have been shut to Negroes. If we are ever to become a fully integrated society, one in which the color of a person's skin will not determine the opportunities available to him or her, we must be willing to take steps to open those doors. I do not believe that anyone can truly look into America's past and still find that a remedy for the effects of that past is impermissible.

It has been said that this case involves only the individual, Bakke, and this university. I doubt, however, that there is a computer capable of determining the number of persons and institutions that may be affected by the decision in this case. For example, we are told by the Attorney General of the United States that at least 27 federal agencies have adopted regulations requiring recipients of federal funds to take *"affirmative action* to overcome the effects of conditions which resulted in limiting participation . . . by persons of a particular race, color, or national origin." Supplemental Brief for the United States as *Amicus Curiae* 16 (emphasis added). I cannot even guess the number of state and local governments that have set up affirmative action programs, which may be affected by today's decision.

I fear that we have come full circle. After the Civil War our government started several "affirmative action" programs. This Court in the *Civil Rights Cases* and *Plessy* v. *Ferguson* destroyed the movement toward complete equality. For almost a century no action was taken, and this nonaction was with the tacit approval of the courts. Then we had *Brown* v. *Board of Education* and the Civil Rights Acts of Congress, followed by numerous affirmative action programs. *Now*, we have this Court again stepping in, this time to stop affirmative action programs of the type used by the University of California.

10. "Whites Say I Must Be on Easy Street"
Nell Irvin Painter

From the decision rendered in the **Bakke** *case up until the present, the continuance of affirmative action programs in education, employment, and economic opportunities remains one of the most hotly debated policy issues in the United States. In this 1981* **New York Times** *"Hers" column, historian Nell Irvin Painter responds to those critics of affirmative action—many white and some black—who view such programs as a form of "preferential treatment" for otherwise "unqualified" and "underqualified" individuals.*

I've always thought affirmative action made a lot of sense, because discrimination against black people and women was prolonged and thorough. But I've been hearing talk in the last several years that lets me know that not everyone shares my views. The first time I noticed it was shortly after I had moved to Philadelphia, where I used to live. One evening I attended a lecture—I no longer remember the topic—but I recall that I arrived early and was doing what I did often that fall. I worked at polishing my dissertation. In those days I regularly carried chapters and a nicely sharpened pencil around with me. I sat with pencil and typescript, scratching out awkward phrases and trying out new ones.

Next to me sat a white man of about 35, whose absorption in my work increased steadily. He watched me intently—kindly—for several moments. "Is that your dissertation?" I said yes, it was. "Good luck in getting it accepted," he said. I said that it had already been accepted, thank you.

Still friendly, he wished me luck in finding a job. I appreciated his concern, but I already had a job. Where? At Penn, for I was then a beginning assistant professor at the University of Pennsylvania. "Aren't you lucky," said the man, a little less generously, "you got a job at a good university." I agreed. Jobs in history were, still are, hard to find.

While cognizant of the job squeeze, I never questioned the justice of my position. I should have a job, and a good one. I had worked hard as a graduate student and had written a decent dissertation. I knew foreign languages, had traveled widely and had taught and published. I thought I had been hired because I was a promising young historian. Unlike the man beside me, I didn't think my teaching at a first-rate university required an extraordinary explanation.

"I have a doctorate in history," he resumed, "but I couldn't get an academic job." With regret he added that he worked in school administration. I said I was sorry he hadn't been able to find the job he wanted. He said: "It must be great to be black and female, because of affirmative action. You count twice." I couldn't think of an appropriate response to that line of reasoning, for this was the first time I'd met it face to face. I wished the lecture would start. I was embarrassed. Did this man really mean to imply that I had my job at his expense? The edge of competition in his voice made me squirm.

He said that he had received his doctorate from Temple, and yet he had no teaching job, and where was my degree from? "Harvard," I said. It was his time not to reply. I waited a moment for his answer, then returned to my chapter.

Now I live in North Carolina, but I still hear contradictory talk about affirmative action. Last spring I was having lunch with some black Carolina undergraduates. One young woman surprised me by deploring affirmative action. I wondered why. "White students and professors think we only got into the University of North Carolina because we're black," she complained, "and they don't believe we're truly qualified." She said that she knew that *she* was qualified and fully deserved to be at Carolina. She fulfilled all the regular admissions requirements. It was the stigma of affirmative action that bothered her; without it other students wouldn't assume she was unqualified.

Another student said that the stigma of affirmative action extended to black faculty as well. She had heard white students doubting the abilities of black professors. Indeed, she herself tended to wait for black professors to disprove her assumption that they did not know their fields. She was convinced that without affirmative action, students would assume black faculty to be as good as white.

That's what I've been hearing from whites and blacks. White people tell me I must be on easy street because I'm black and female. (I do not believe I've ever heard that from a black person, although some blacks believe that black women have an easier time in the white world than black men. I don't think so.) White people tell me, "You're a twofer." On the other side of the color line, every black student knows that he or she is fully qualified— I once thought that way myself. It is just the other black people who need affirmative action to get in. No one, not blacks, not whites, benefits from affirmative action, or so it would seem.

Well, I have, but not in the early 1960's, when I was an undergraduate in a large state university. Back then, there was no affirmative action. We applied for admission to the university like everyone else; we were accepted or rejected like everyone else. Graduate and undergraduate students together, we numbered about 200 in a student body of nearly 30,000. No preferential treatment there.

Yet we all knew what the rest of the university thought of us, professors especially. They thought we were stupid because we were black. Further, white women were considered frivolous students; they were only supposed to be in school to get husbands. (I doubt that we few black women even rated a stereotype. We were the ultimate outsiders.) Black students, the whole atmosphere said, would not attend graduate or professional school because their grades must be poor. Women had no business in postgraduate education because they would waste their training by dropping out of careers when they married or became pregnant. No one said out loud that women and minorities were simply and naturally inferior to white men, but the assumptions were as clear as day: whites are better than blacks; men are better than women.

I am one of the few people I know who will admit to having been helped by affirmative action. To do so is usually tantamount to admitting deficiency. To hear people talk, affirmative action exists only to employ and promote the otherwise unqualified, but I don't see it that way at all. I'm black and I'm female, yet I was hired by two history departments that had no black members before the late 60's, never mind females. Affirmative action cleared the way.

Thirty-five years ago, John Hope Franklin, then a star student, now a giant in the field of American history, received a doctorate in history from Harvard. He went to teach in a black college. In those days, black men taught in black colleges. White women taught in white women's colleges. Black women taught in black women's colleges. None taught at the University of Pennsylvania or the University of North Carolina. It was the way things were.

Since then, the civil rights movement and the feminist movement have created a new climate that permitted affirmative action, which, in turn, opened areas previously reserved for white men. Skirts and dark skins appeared in new settings in the 1970's, but in significant numbers only after affirmative action mandated the changes and made them thinkable. Without affirmative action, it never would have occurred to any large, white research university to consider me for professional employment, despite my degree, languages, publications, charm, grace, *despite* my qualifications.

My Philadelphia white man and my Carolina black women would be surprised to discover the convergence of their views. I doubt that they know that their convictions are older than affirmative action. I wish I could take them back to the early 60's and let them see that they're reciting the same old white-male-superiority line, fixed up to fit conditions that include a policy called affirmative action. Actually, I will not have to take those people back in time at all, for the Reagan Administration's proposed dismantling of affirmative action fuses the future and the past. If they achieve their stated goals, we will have the same old discrimination, unneedful of new clothes.

CHAPTER FOURTEEN

BACK TO THE MOVEMENT (1979–MID-1980S)

Introduction by Vincent Harding

By the close of the 1980s the message was clearer than ever before: The powerful social struggle that had so often been identified in constricting terms as a "civil rights movement" for black people's rights was really much more than that. At its best the freedom movement was another stage in the continuing, often faltering, historic American quest for "a more perfect union." At its heights the epic contestation was a gift to the entire world, inspired and led by African-Americans, but shared at deep levels by many other persons who ardently believed in the expansion of democracy in the United States and who sought freedom and hope across the globe.

Back in Montgomery, Alabama, at the first boycott meeting in December 1955, the young Martin Luther King, Jr., had somehow sensed much of this larger, universal meaning. For on that night, inspired by the people's courageous determination, he proclaimed to the thousands who gathered in and around the church:

> When the history books are written in the future, somebody will have to say, "There lived a race of people, black people, fleecy locks and black complexion, of people who had the

moral courage to stand up for their rights." And thereby they injected a new meaning into the veins of history and of civilization. And we're gonna do that.

Then he paused and added, "God grant that we will do it before it's too late."

For many harsh and troubling reasons, King's expansive early vision did not return easily to the 1980s. Indeed, when that decade began many persons could only reflect on the portentous pause and hear again with sadness the last words of King's Montgomery statement. For they thought it was already "too late." By that time they had seen too much in America that looked like a terrible revival of the most recalcitrant and racially polarized elements of our past. And in a special way the events in Miami, Florida, seemed to present a bloody and frightening reenactment of all the ritual agonies of our black and white history. There, one night in December 1979, a well-respected member of the African-American community, Arthur McDuffie, had been brutally beaten by white policemen in connection with a traffic incident. Four days later, McDuffie was dead. A U.S. Marine Corps veteran, he had now become one more ironic black victim of white police brutality—"another man done gone."

In the spring of 1980, like so many others before them, the killers of Arthur McDuffie were exonerated by an all-white jury. Remembering our history, it was hard for anyone to be surprised when after the verdict of acquittal was announced an enraged and frustrated African-American community burst out with fire, bullets, and deadly force, seeking some satisfaction in vengeance against hapless whites who represented for them a system of hard, unfeeling injustice. Penned up in a place named Liberty City, set in a losing competition with the new immigrants from Latin America and the Caribbean, too many African-Americans heard words like *civil rights, human rights,* and *democracy* as nothing more than mocking echoes from a movement that had apparently passed them by. It all seemed so cruelly familiar (except for the deaths of seven white civilians, who were among the seventeen men and boys who paid the ultimate cost for the nation's unremitting resistance to infusions of King's "new meaning"). Then, when

America's dwindling white majority voted a conservative former movie star into the presidency that fall, the hour of hope appeared to be really long past.

But history is lived out in many layers and neither Miami nor Reagan was the last word for the eighties. For King had accurately envisioned "a people of moral courage," standing against all odds, standing up for their rights as citizens, for their identity as human beings, refusing to be defeated even by atavistic reversions to the worst elements of the nation's past. And before long, his faith was vindicated, his courageous spirit resurrected in the city where he had actually failed in life, Chicago. Indeed, in the course of the epic campaign to elect Harold Washington as the first black mayor of what had long been designated as the most segregated city in America and the most dominated by white machine politics—in that unlikely setting the meaning of the entire freedom movement was reopened, deepened, and expanded.

Of course, the black community of Chicago itself was an eloquent testimony to the multifaceted complexity of our racial history. For in spite of (and because of) the notorious segregation and white political domination in their city, there had always been a vibrant social, cultural, and political life surging beneath the surface of the "Black Metropolis." In the immediate post–World War II years Chicago's "Bronzeville" had helped to nourish such artists as Richard Wright, Gwendolyn Brooks, Charles White, Margaret Walker, St. Clair Drake, Mahalia Jackson, Muddy Waters, and dozens more. Then during the late 1960s, the streets, walls, and auditoriums of its African-American community reverberated to all the sounds, sights, and high energies of the Black Power/Black Arts/Black Education movement, nurturing powerful young cultural workers who became Haki Madhubuti, Abdul Alkalimat, Carolyn Rodgers, Herbie Hancock, Phil Koran, and the Black Arts Collective OBASI, to name only a few. Not accidentally the city was also home to Johnson Publishing Company, the world's largest black publishing organization (with its two gifted editorial bellwethers, Lerone Bennett, Jr., and Hoyt Fuller). And for a significant time it was the headquarters of the Honorable Elijah Muhammad and his Nation of Islam, as well as Jesse Jackson's Operation PUSH.

So neither King nor Washington had met a tabula rasa when

they launched their historic campaigns. That becomes very clear as we read the documents on the following pages, as we absorb images from the Washington election campaign in the *Eyes on the Prize* episode "Back to the Movement." Against such a rich background it is possible to enter Chicago in 1982–1983 and to re-vision what King had seen in Montgomery, what Washington had helped to call forth in his own hometown. We meet men, women, and young people who were determined to bring new meaning into their own lives and the life of their community. We are engaged by formerly marginalized citizens who insist—even for a brief moment in history—on participating fully in a struggle for the realization of our best humanity and our most responsive democracy, all the while sending a life-giving message to the world.

In fact, the video images are powerful, surging into our consciousness: the faces of older women, renewed by hope and struggle. Young men who at other times and places were often perceived as nothing more than wasted, threatening, dark integers, now seen fully, facing the friendly registrars, daring to dream, determined to be counted—including the twenty-two-year-old man who came to register for the first time with his young baby snuggled in a carrier, the infant resting against his strong, revitalized heart. The dark was light enough.

Images: Rosie Mars, the single mother in the housing project, remembering, knowing "We were making history," coming finally to her own most personal self-recognition—"I made it happen." Even images of Selma, Greenwood, Birmingham, and Nashville return when we hear the report that "everybody was organizing—barbers for Harold, beauticians for Harold, taxicab drivers for Harold," for themselves, for their grandchildren, making it happen.

The human images of the campaign for the expansion of democracy in Chicago were deeply moving, even when they were only imagined, as when we are told the story of the old man who struggles along with his walker on his way to the polls on election day. Sitting to rest, but refusing an automobile ride, he declares, "No, I want to go on my own and vote for that boy." Surely the old warrior was related to the faithful walking woman in Montgomery who had inspired Martin King a generation earlier as she sacrificed for her grandchildren and proudly announced, "My feets is tired, but my soul is rested."

Did the old man dance in the streets that glorious night in the Windy City when his surrogate son, "Harold," had won for everyone? We can probably be certain that if nothing else was shaking, his marvelous and stalwart soul was surely dancing. That was it: walking, dancing, resting courageous old souls. That was it: black business leaders like Soft Sheen's Ed Gardner and his family, recognizing their debt to the heroes of the past, sharing their resources to help create a new future. That was it: younger men and women, children, discovering new meaning for their own lives, offering new possibilities to the nation and the world. Yes, that was it: babies nurtured within the heart of the struggle for freedom. That's what King had seen. That's what inspired the man with the "wise eyes," the first black mayor of Chicago, to use his inaugural address to call the people of his city to healing beyond racial and political lines, to encourage them with words like these:

> Most of our problems can be solved. Most of them will take brains, and some of them will take patience, but all of them will have to be wrestled with like an alligator in the swamp.

What marvelous metaphors of struggle and renewal he brought to the people, assuring himself, assuring them, that "our creativity and energy are unequalled by any city anywhere in the world. We will not rest until the renewal of our city is done."

That was the moral courage King had seen rising among us, against all odds, faithful to the best traditions of our forebears. It did not mean that Miami and Ronald Reagan did not exist. It did not mean tragedies like the untimely death of Harold Washington could not occur, opening the door to temporary chaos in the politics of black Chicago. But there was always more, always resting, standing, dancing, wrestling folks who were determined to stand for freedom, to do the right thing. So we discovered that the 1980s were also Jesse Jackson and his courageous challenge to America to come closer to its best self, to break out of the straitjacket of race and continue exploring a more perfect union.

And the 1980s were Henry Cisneros and Vine Deloria responding, recognizing the common ground of Hispanics and Native Americans and African-Americans with all who believe in freedom.

This was the promised land that King had finally seen at the end. Not a place but a process, a movement toward our most humane possibilities. And before the decade was over we looked around the world and saw more clearly than ever before what King had meant in Montgomery, what Eleanor Holmes Norton was really saying as the surging democratic forces flung out their banners, announcing "We Shall Overcome." For King was right, and Norton was right when she declared, "What gives our movement its majesty is the example it set throughout the world. . . ."

In 1989 the images were formally returned to us, from Tiananmen Square, from Prague and Leipzig and the tumbling Berlin Wall, from Havel and Mandela and the millions they represent— all seeking for that "new meaning" which must fill "the veins of history and civilization" before it is too late. And when the new decade began we heard the words of Shen Tong, one of the honorable exiles from Beijing's powerful student pro-democracy movement, speaking to himself, speaking to us, testifying during King Week from the pulpit of Ebenezer Baptist Church in Atlanta, a long way from home, yet always coming home:

> Only after I escaped and had the time to reflect could I see that nonviolence is the only way for the future. . . . We must learn from each other. All our communities must learn peace from each other. And there is . . . so much I must learn from you and from Dr. King. Please teach me. Please help China and the Chinese find that crystal way which will lead to the crystal goal. And together, as one movement for human rights and peace world-wide, we will be able to look at the tyrants and oppressors of history and say to them, in Dr. King's words, "We have matched your capacity to inflict suffering with our capacity to endure suffering. We have met your physical force with soul force. We are free."

So when the 1980s had ended we discovered that the last word of that decade belonged neither to Reagan nor Miami, in spite of all the deep pain and loss they represent and still reflect all around us. Rather, it may be that the greatest discovery of the decade was the fact that there is no last word in the human struggle for freedom, justice, and democracy. Only the continuing word, lived out by men, women, and children who dance and rest, who wrestle with alligators and stand firm before tanks, and presidents, and drug lords and deep, deep fears. We learned again that the continuing word remains embedded in those who determine not to be moved, who know, against all odds, that they will overcome, will continue to create a more perfect union, a more compassionate world. The word remains with those who discover, in the midst of unremitting struggle, deep amazing powers within their own lives, power from, power for, the planet.

As Julian Bond, the *Eyes on the Prize* narrator, says—and he should know—as long as there are women, children, and men of every color and nationality who are willing to stand up, "the movement is not yet over."

As Fannie Lou Hamer said, "Go tell it on the mountain!" As Mrs. Hamer did, the call is issued again: Go *be* the mountain!—this time accompanied by Gwendolyn Brooks's wonderful words of homage to Harold Washington and encouragement to all the people of struggle: "What is minor and malnourished can be fed, can develop, can grow beyond the present fact."

So if there is anything resembling a formal last word, it must be something like this: "Go feed my swamp wrestlers, before it is too late." Those who believe in freedom cannot rest.

1. "A Historic Look at Our Neighborhoods"

The twenty-page local history journal from which these excerpts on the history of the black community in Miami are taken was published after a conference following the May 1980 riots in Miami. The 1981 conference was initiated and developed by the Black Archives, History and Research Foundation of South Florida, founded in 1977. One view expressed at the conference was "the need to provide opportunities for the various ethnic groups in Greater Miami to focus on the history, problems, customs, and values of black people in America as perceived by local black communities," and this journal (published in connection with Black History Month, February 1982) was an attempt to begin to meet that goal.

In the Beginning . . .

It started with a number of black families from the Bahamas who settled in Coconut Grove and began working at the Peacock Inn located at what is now known as Peacock Park. In 1896 Henry M. Flagler, builder of the Florida East Coast Railway System, extended the railroad from West Palm Beach to Miami. Anticipating a tourist city similar to Palm Beach, he sent the black work force to Miami to build hotels and cottages before completing the railroad.

Not only did this black work force stand for the incorporation of Miami, they comprised more than one-third of the number required by the State of Florida for the incorporation.

Later the opinion of the 1896 Supreme Court Case Plessy vs. Ferguson disenfranchised these same black incorporators. It was a disenfranchisement to last several decades for black people throughout the South. This attitude limited black people's lives.

Local and state segregation laws, supported by the decisions of the U.S. Supreme Court, continued into the 20th Century. As a result of such local laws and customs for public schools, businesses and other phases of life, Miami and Dade County developed two separate cultures—black and white. It was the beginning of the unique black community.

The area was first referred to as "Colored Town" or Central Negro District before residents named their community Washington Heights in honor of Booker T. Washington, the noted black educator. D. A. Dorsey, a black millionaire, Florence Gaskin, who started the Red Cross for the black community during World War I, R. E. S. Toomey, a black lawyer, H. E. S. Reeves, founder of The Miami Times newspaper and Kelsey L. Pharr, Sr., a mortician and consul for Liberia, are remembered as active pioneers.

Booker T. Washington, opened 31 years after Miami became a city, was the first school in South Florida to provide a 12th grade education for black children. Culture was transmitted through lodges, civic and social organizations such as sororities and fraternities. Such organizations fostered a sense of pride, civic understanding and a sense of belonging. They made the black community conscious of its emerging responsibilities—in education, in economics, and in its society.

Despite limitations "Colored Town" developed into a self-contained vibrant area. This community supported black-owned businesses and hosted numerous state and national conventions. Night life in the area flourished for residents and tourists alike. Second Avenue became the cradle of business and cultural successes for black people in South Florida. When world famous entertainers such as Billie Holiday, Nat "King" Cole, the Ink Spots, Cab Calloway, Count Basie and Ella Fitzgerald came to Miami, they stayed in [the] Overtown [section]. These superstars also performed at Overtown's Rockland Palace, the Mary Elizabeth Cabaret, Elks Club and the Harlem Square Club.

In the late 1940's discrimination continued into black life. Black people could not vote in primaries until 1944. Sam B. Solomon was an early activist to secure voter registration. He assisted Marie D. Roberts of the National Youth Council with this project.

A beach—Virginia Beach on Key Biscayne—was opened exclusively for black people in 1945. During the 1950's, black police, mail carriers and a municipal judge were provided to serve only the black community. Sit-ins and explosions in 1951 underlined the community's growing racial problems. In 1954, Brown vs.

Board of Education legally integrated schools throughout the United States. Almost a decade later, the first noticeable change in greater Miami began with the integration of teaching staff and admission of the first black children to white (county) schools.

Colored Town died of decay. The demise of the area west of downtown and across the railroad tracks had been predicted by government planners more than 25 years before. Slum clearance, construction and urban renewal eventually destroyed it. The Reverend John E. Culmer, a pioneer civic activist, initiated the first local slum clearance program through the Negro Civic League. As a result of this program, Liberty Square was built in 1935, and was the first low-income housing project in the state of Florida for blacks or whites. James E. Scott was the first administrator for the Liberty Square Projects. Colored Town was renamed Culmer-Overtown in 1967 in memory of Reverend Culmer.

During the 1960's black people in Dade County gained some political positions for the first time since Reconstruction. Joe Lang Kershaw was elected to the State Legislature followed by the late Gwen Cherry. In 1965, Athalie Range became a City Commissioner. In 1970, former Governor Ruben Askew appointed Mrs. Range to a State Cabinet post, Secretary of Community Affairs.

Others followed in various appointed and elected positions. After the 1968 riots, Dewey Knight was appointed to the County Manager's staff. Later he became Interim County Manager. Dr. Johnny Jones was appointed Superintendent of Dade County Schools at a time when the school system was the fifth largest in the United States. In 1978, Carrie Meek was elected to fill the state seat left by Gwen Cherry's untimely death. Marcia Saunders became the first director of Black Affairs. This department is under the auspices of the County Manager's Office. In 1979, Dr. Barbara Carey was appointed to the county commission. Howard Gary was appointed Manager for the City of Miami in 1981. Miller Dawkins gained wide support throughout the community-at-large by winning a seat on the City Commission, which was left vacant by Theodore Gibson.

During Miami's history—through its Boom and its Bust, its hurricanes, its share of the Depression and of recession, black workmen were a primary work force.

But culmination of political events overseas frustrated this employment picture. Fleeing refugees began arriving. Their numbers mounted. In the mid-sixties, Cuban refugees came; later Haitians arrived by the boatload. It presented employment and economic problems for Miami's blacks. Their frustrations ignited in 1979. They erupted in May 17–18, 1980, in what has been termed the McDuffie riots, named after the black whose death resulted with a protested court case decision. It was one of the nation's worst riots; fifteen lives were lost, more than $100 million damage done and more than 3,000 jobs lost.

REBUILDING OUR NEIGHBORHOODS

Today we are rebuilding—our neighborhoods, some of our lives, all of our futures. It is with the help of individuals, of organizations with the same vision that the earliest black pioneers held as they stepped into Miami, from the Bahamas, from other Southern states, from elsewhere in Florida. It was a time to begin. It is a time now to do the same. With vision. With direction. With purpose.

In addition to economic development, a revitalization can be successful when human issues are kept in mind. Issues such as:

—Heritage and values of black people in Greater Miami;
—Pride of rebuilding the riot area to incorporate its pioneer identity with its future potential;
—Future Opportunities for black people in Greater Miami.

No one builds a future alone. The entire community is needed.

2. "Death Watch"
Marvin Dunn

Dr. Marvin Dunn, a professor of community psychology at Florida International University, wrote this article on the May 1980 riots for a special issue of the Miami Herald's Sunday *magazine.*

Late in the afternoon of Saturday, May 17, I received a call from a wire-service reporter, asking if I had heard of a minor disturbance in Liberty City. He called, I imagine, because I had been quite outspoken about the Arthur McDuffie killing. I had written a long article for The Herald, expressing my outrage. After it appeared, the media made me a spokesman for "the black community."

I told the reporter that I knew the four officers on trial in Tampa had been acquitted earlier that day by an all-white jury. I knew the events surrounding McDuffie's death, as brought out in the case, had inflamed the city's black neighborhoods, which waited, tensely, for a verdict. But I knew nothing about a disturbance.

With the announcement of the acquittals, Miami exploded. The riots sent shock waves through a community that preferred not to believe the potential for such horror was still dwelling within its midst. I saw that horror close-up. I saw the brutal slaying of innocent people on a street named for Martin Luther King. The images of that day, the fiery scenes at the Metro Justice Building that night, the chaos and destruction I witnessed at the Scott-Carver housing project in July, haunt me.

If, in Miami and in America, we are to avoid a reliving of those fateful days and nights, we must first come to know them for what they were—an American tragedy that could have been predicted if only we had looked.

To the American public, Liberty City has replaced Watts as a symbol of interracial strife. Abroad, it is compared to Soweto as a symbol of the racial oppression of black people. Neither comparison is precisely accurate, yet Liberty City remains known across the country and around the world as the most racially volatile community in the nation.

The intense interest in the area now is, of course, based on the extensive violence that has occurred there and which many local blacks insist could resurface at any time. But Liberty City has been around for a long time and it has not always been a particularly violent place, even though the community itself was born as a result of racial conflict.

In 1951, when I was 11, my father, who had been a laborer in the orange groves of Central Florida, moved his wife and five small sons to the new black community called Bunche Park, 12 miles north of Liberty City. The little houses were available only to black veterans, and through the G.I. Bill my father had acquired one. To us, the small three-bedroom, one bath, cement-block house was a mansion. It contained the first bathtub I had ever seen. Bathing in the old tin washtubs was now a thing of the past.

For our family, the move to Miami represented a quantum economic leap forward, although we could only barely be considered even lower middle class. My father worked first as a truck driver, but eventually joined the longshoreman's union.

The essential difference between the blacks in housing projects—most of whom also worked as hard as my father—and those who were then buying up the little boxes called homes in Bunche Park, was ownership. As tenuous as it was, we had gained a small edge on survival. For us, that toe-hold had come through my father's veteran's benefits (he served a 2-year hitch in the Navy). The G.I. Bill had allowed him to buy a house with little or no down payment. This was a feat which, without federal help, he probably never would have achieved no matter how hard he worked, since the everyday needs of his large family consumed every penny he wrenched from the orange growers of Central Florida. Without the G.I. Bill, had we moved to Miami at all, it would have probably been to a housing project.

Even if we had narrowly escaped the necessity of living in public housing, starting in the fall of 1951 I came to know life in the projects—and life in Liberty City.

It is hard to believe that there was a time when Liberty City was considered to be out in the sticks, in a sea of palmetto bushes and swarming with rattlesnakes. Blacks from the Coconut Grove area about 6 miles to the south would take half a day to walk or ride their mules up a narrow, panther-infested trail which is now called 27th Avenue and is one of Miami's busiest thoroughfares.

The area was conceived in 1922 by Alonzo Kelly, and its center, now called "germ city," is located at NW 17th Avenue and 62nd

Street, which is known as Martin Luther King Boulevard. The land boom of the 1920s in Miami eventually resulted in a decision by local whites to evict or remove most, if not all, of the blacks who lived in several of the small enclaves around Miami, but particularly those who occupied an area known as "Railroad Shop Colored Addition," which was located a few blocks south of what is now Liberty City.

With the forced and sudden movement of so many blacks into the area, Liberty City became primarily a community of renters rather than black homeowners. By contrast, in the black sections of Coconut Grove and other areas, the blacks were left relatively unmolested. The large number of renters constituted the first strike against Liberty City. Huge sections of the community were never owned by blacks themselves.

As thousands of displaced blacks streamed there, principally in the late 1940s and early '50s, the shortage of rental housing—white-owned and black-occupied—became crucial. The housing crisis was met by the growth of public housing projects that came to be known simply as "the projects." One of the first and largest was the massive James E. Scott development, which was built in 1955. The sprawling development straddles NW 22nd Avenue in the vicinity of 75th Street. It was named after a successful black real estate man and civic activist.

The blacks who moved into these projects represented some of the most dispossessed and chronically unemployed of all blacks in Dade County. Although most people were happy initially to be given a unit in public housing, eventually many people came to feel trapped in an overcrowded, under supported, large community of poor people. With so many low-income people cramped together, the squalor was not long in setting in. With the advent in the 1940s of public welfare, the mold of despair was finally cast.

The fact that this ghetto was created by whites out of greed for land during and after the boom years is a historical fact which, in the heat of the present crisis, may be uncomfortable to restate. The truth remains, however, that ghettos in this country were not created by the blacks who live in them. Sometimes by design and often through neglect, they were brought into being by white people who, beginning in the 1960s and now again in the 1980s, are being made painfully aware of the terrible costs of their creation.

The enormous Liberty City ghetto would probably never have come into existence had blacks been allowed to remain in their smaller communities, which have disappeared. Today, only the old black people in and around Dade County can remember the names of the tiny black enclaves such as Knightsville, Bolestown, and Nazarene, which thrived in their time.

It may be tempting to view the history of Liberty City and of black-white relations in Miami in terms of an unending series of conflicts, confrontations, and the continuous spilling of blood. But such an account would be inaccurate. Certainly there have been moments of drama, ranging from the enormous parade and rally of the Ku Klux Klan on Palm Island in May of 1923, to the day in February, 1968, when two white police officers stripped Robert Quentin Owens, a 17-year-old black, and dangled him by his heels from an overpass, an event which, among others, led to Miami's racial explosion of that year.

There were other incidents, too, but essentially the history of blacks in Miami and in Liberty City is a history of being ignored, displaced, or quietly oppressed.

Reflecting on it today, it seems a paradox that in those days on 22nd Avenue, white students would throw rocks at our school bus. We jeered and the most brazen among us would curse, but we rarely returned the volleys. Retaliation against whites was almost unheard of in 1951.

Dade County's school system was still racially segregated then, and there were no schools yet for black children who lived in Bunche Park. We were bused 12 miles south down 22nd Avenue, now infamous for its violence, to Liberty City Elementary School.

As a boy I found life around Liberty City completely enthralling. Most of my schoolmates lived there, and I visited them in the housing projects and elsewhere before finally having to take the late school bus back north to Bunche Park.

I have easy memories of fresh, cold snow cones on a hot summer's day, and chasing my friends around the dusty ball field at school. Since integration had not yet surfaced as an issue, black schools were filled with bright, well-behaved students from families of all incomes. Expulsions were rare. Our black teachers often stayed hours after school working feverishly with us, pushing, even forcing, us to excel. The idea of a student striking a teacher was alien to our thinking.

Even so, there were signs that all was not well. It was in Liberty City that I first witnessed a brutal act of assault. Two girls from the projects, fighting over a boy, slashed each other with razor blades, laid neatly between their fingers. The cuts were so meticulously executed that neither knew that her flesh had been laid bare to the bone until the fight was over. For the first time, I wondered if the kids from the projects were somehow different from me and my friends from Bunche Park.

Dorsey Senior High School, which I eventually attended, was located in the heart of the community. It was considered to be one of the best black schools in the state, rivaled only by the massive Mathew W. Gilbert Senior High of Jacksonville. These two black schools, and others including Mays Senior High in South Dade and the venerable George Washington Carver High in black Coconut Grove, went into decline with the integration of public schools in the early 1960s. The black communities surrounding many of these schools also declined as middle-class families moved away, to newly integrated neighborhoods, leaving primarily the children of the poor to attend those schools. In leaving, we upwardly mobile blacks helped create the monster of the projects later to surface.

Between 1957 and 1970, a critical period in Dade County history, I did not live in Miami, having left the county to attend Morehouse College, in Atlanta, Ga., and for a 6-year stint as a naval officer—neither of which would have been likely but for the efforts of dedicated black teachers at Liberty City Elementary and Dorsey High. After graduate study in psychology at the University of Tennessee, I returned in 1970. Things have changed.

I had traveled around the world, gained a doctorate, and had lost contact with the black community of Dade County. Even as a community psychologist at the new Florida International University, I remained more a student of the black community than a member of it.

Between 1970 and 1979 I was often assigned the role of a black leader, but never fully welcomed the designation. I wrote grants at the university mostly relating to race relations in the community. I even ran for a seat in the Florida House of Representatives. Some black leaders and others accused me of being a dilettante, a dabbler in the black community, but not a real "soul brother." In the eyes of some, I was not one who "knew" the black community. The fact is, they were right.

The profound changes that had occurred in Liberty City since my boyhood days of roaming through the project courtyards were still not known to me. Although I had attended civic meetings in the area, my first real ventures back there were precipitated only last winter by my interest in a bizarre set of killings, which were reported in the media as "The North Bay Village Murders."

The killings occurred on February 17 in the white middle- and upper-income Dade community of North Bay Village, located 5.3 miles due east of Liberty City. Ray Anthony Mitchell, a 17-year-old black, was charged with the brutal slaying of two white couples. Police said the boy, using a knife and a screwdriver, first killed one couple, looted their home, stole their car, and left. Within a matter of hours, he returned to the same street, two houses down, and killed another couple, again leaving the island—heading for Liberty City and the James E. Scott housing project where he and his family lived. Having gotten high on drugs, he drove erratically and was chased and eventually halted by a policeman, who discovered the boy's hands were covered with blood and that the car was filled with looted goods. Although the state demanded the death penalty, a Circuit Court judge sentenced the youth to a total of 606 years in prison.

The murders shocked the entire community. They shocked me, too. I had grown up with kids from the James E. Scott projects, but I had never known anyone I thought would commit such a brutal crime.

Clearly I had lost touch. It was time to go back, really go back, to Liberty City, and to the James E. Scott dwellings. I did, weeks before the riots—which would also take me back again. I can only describe each visit as a journey into hell.

In March of this year I started visiting the James E. Scott project regularly. I sought out Ray Mitchell's mother and members of his family. I spent hours in the small dark pool room on 22nd Avenue where he spent most of his time. I talked at length with his friends and other youths who knew him.

What emerged was a chilling, sobering picture of a project youth who would not permit himself to be deprived; a respectful, even obedient boy, but one who stole practically anything he could get his hands on. Ray Mitchell is a boy who gave the appearance of great self-control, yet one whose mind was twisted by drugs and who was given to extended periods of mental instability.

His mother is on welfare, but she does not fit any stereotype of a welfare cheat. She *does* fit the classic picture of a working black woman, deserted by her man, with six children to rear alone in a public housing project. What happened to her and her family is occurring all over America: black children left on their own while their mothers eke out a living in a menial job; difficulties in school, suspensions, expulsions and an inevitable drop-out; trouble with the law—little things at first—but all too soon an escalation.

In the same housing block as the Mitchells, there are four other families with six teenage sons among them. Five of these boys have been implicated in murders. Ray Mitchell's older brother, Dennis, has already been convicted. The others were, at the time of this writing, in various stages in the prosecution process. Mrs. Mitchell believes the projects contributed. "I'll never get out of these projects," she told me once.

She said: "It's all stacked against you. I work every day as a switchboard operator over on the Beach. When my salary goes up $30 a month they raise my rent and they take away $60 worth of my food stamps. There ain't no way you can get ahead. When they come to bury me, I'll be right here in this project."

In early March and April, Mrs. Mitchell and others in the James E. Scott development project convinced me that I no longer knew the projects. The hours there did not prepare me for the riots but I knew things were different. The laughter of the '50s was gone. On the afternoon of May 17, when in response to the call from the wire-service reporter I returned to Liberty City, a different kind of laughter could be heard.

As I arrived, there were no police officers in the area. They stood behind barricades several blocks away. I parked a block from 62nd Street near 13th Avenue and walked the short distance to 62nd which by this time was rapidly filling up with people. There were hundreds in an area in the vicinity of an older project that fronted on the main thoroughfare. Some two blocks away, a small band of street gospel singers could be heard. There was laughter, shouting and then—shots.

Approaching Martin Luther King Boulevard, I thought at first the small figure lying motionless on the center line of the street was a bundle of discarded clothing. Moving closer, I was horrified to see that it was a young white boy of about 14 or 15. I thought, "Oh my God, they're killing people." He was dead.

The realization hit me with a sickening thud. I started backing away. A slow sense of panic made me dizzy for a moment. My eyes were still fixed on the boy lying so still on the street. For a second, I thought of my own daughter, who is 16. It was as if I saw her there, a crazed mob swirling about, no one paying attention as life oozed out of her body. A scream slapped me across the face.

I looked up. Twenty yards away, on the other side of the street, a mob of about 30 or 40 people, men—and boys in their late teens—was standing over two young white men lying in the gutter. One was still moving feebly, reaching up with his arms as if to fend off the short, sharp kicks that were still chopping at his body. The other youth was as motionless as the boy who lay bleeding in the street. Two or three men were firing pistols in the air.

Most of the people stood by, watching. A few drifted back into their apartments, heads bowed. (Days later, many came forward to tell the police what they had seen. Their reports after the riots led to the arrests of several black men who are now charged with the murders committed that day on 62nd Street.)

A young shirtless black man walked away from the melee towards me, his body streaming with sweat. "I know them Crackers got to be dead," he said. He laughed and held out his hand for a "soul shake." I stood transfixed, staring at his fingers. He looked puzzled, then glided away.

Someone shouted, "Kill the Uncle Tom niggers, too. They ain't done shit for us." The threat was not aimed directly at me, but I felt fear. For the first time in my life I feared my own people. I felt indicted. It was true. I really hadn't done anything for these people. I wanted to disappear on the spot.

A woman came up to me. She looked to be about 25 or 30 years old. She wore no shoes. Her breath reeked of beer. "I know who you are." A grin crept across her face. She was swaying. "I seen you on television. Ain't you Mr. Dunn?"

I said, "Yeah, that's me." My words seemed to be coming from someone else. My attention was still on the melee across the street. It seemed to be winding down.

"Hey, Sarah, this Dr. Dunn over here," she yelled. Some of the men across the street looked up from their victims, lying still against the curb. It was only a momentary glance. They weren't interested in me. In a second, they were looking down at the two men again. I could still hear the Gospel singers.

The woman leaned over and whispered in my ear. "They sho' is gettin' them, ain't they?"

I couldn't answer. I turned and left for the refuge of my car. If this murder of children was the "black rebellion," I was not going to make a good soldier. I drove, wildly, I think, several blocks south to the 46th Street station, where City of Miami police were massing in riot gear. Clarence Dickson, a black police major, was in command.

I followed him as he paced around the small parking lot where his officers milled about, awaiting orders. I said, "There are people—white people—trapped up there."

"Where?" he asked. "Do you know where exactly? On 62nd Street? I have to know exactly, so I can get my men in and out. Where on 62nd Street?"

An officer came up to the major and said a crowd was forming rapidly at the Metro Justice Building. They thought there might be trouble.

I looked at my watch. It was nearly 8, still daylight. Earlier in the afternoon, following the announcement of the verdicts, Joyce Knox, Dade's only black member of the school board, had asked me to attend a demonstration at the Metro Justice Building. Now I didn't know what to expect. I left the station and drove south along 17th Avenue, toward the Metro complex. At 36th Street, I stopped. And threw up.

My community was coming apart.

Riots erupted about an hour after I arrived at the Justice Building. In the gathering dusk, the crowd grew to 3,000, mostly black, but including many whites who had come to join in protest. After the first auto was set afire, the mood turned ugly. I had been dealing with guilt since the deaths on 62nd Street. This time I felt better about my actions. Whites came under attack, and several of us placed ourselves between the mob and people trapped in cars. Other blacks nearby were doing the same thing.

It was not heroism. It was a matter of doing what had to be done. Coming to the Justice Building, I told myself I'd arrived too late to save anyone at 62nd Street. But I knew, too, that I had been immobilized by fear.

Fear was not something I alone felt that night. Terror reigned throughout Coconut Grove and Liberty City. I saw the fires, heard the gunshots, felt the anger. It was a frenzy of violence, but nothing that night could exceed the horror I felt on Martin Luther King Boulevard, across from the project.

It was days before the irony of it hit me: blood flowing on Martin Luther King Boulevard.

The anger that is Liberty City, rooted deep in the dilapidated housing projects, would not be stilled. On the afternoon of July 15, I was recording commentaries at a radio station, when news flashed across the police radio that all news departments monitor: "Policeman shot at the James E. Scott project."

The nightmare was beginning anew.

That evening, with Georgia Jones Ayers, a well known black social worker, and two other black activists, I returned to Liberty City.

By then the facts were known: three county police officers were trying to apprehend three black youths who tried to rob a white motorist near the Scott project. The officers, chasing the youths into the project, were run off by residents. Someone fired a bullet into an officer's back, wounding him.

By nightfall, gangs of black youths, many not yet in their teens, had seized the incident as a signal to commandeer streets around the project. White motorists were stoned. Police were fired upon as they entered the area.

About 10 p.m., our group of four entered the vicinity of the Scott project. It was eerie. Order had completely collapsed. A 9-year-old was directing traffic, cursing. Bands of youths ebbed and flowed, rocks and bottles in hand, looking for whites to hurt.

We parked our car and walked among the youngsters, intoxicated with their power.

I spoke to a small group of older boys who stood watching the scene. "Why is this happening?"

"I was born here," one of them said. "Why should I have to learn Spanish to get a job? Next it'll be Haitian. This country ain't worth a damn. Let it all burn down."

At first I found the July riot more difficult to fathom than the McDuffie riots. The underlying poverty was the same, but the sparks that had set them off were very different. Or so it appeared.

In May, it had been the acquittals in the McDuffie case. In July, however, it was the legitimate effort of police to enforce the law. The public generally seemed to see only this distinction. But what was common to both was the involvement of police.

This is what must be understood: the legacy of the McDuffie killing was that for some blacks, police had lost their authority. In the refuge of the projects it was easy to make this point—with stones and bullets.

As we walked and tried to urge people to return to their homes, I saw a boy of about 14 or 15 standing on the median strip of 22nd Avenue near 75th Street, the heart of the Scott project. To the delight of the crowd, he began pouring gas from a milk carton onto the street. Unemotionally, he lighted a match, setting the gas ablaze. It was the first fire of the night.

The fire seemed to ignite the crowd. Some of them began attacking a service station across the street. It was owned by a black man. I had seen him earlier at the police barricades, four blocks away. Now the crowd was trying to get a fire going. Several attempts were unsuccessful. Then I saw small fires burning inside the office area. The station itself refused to burn, so the owner's tow truck was pushed out onto 22nd Avenue and set afire.

It was nearly an hour before the station finally began to blaze.

Once it caught, it belched forth a gust of wind from within itself, and finally lighted up the sky.

The young people of the project seemed pleased.

I talked to people, asking them to get off the streets. I expected the gas tanks to explode. Nobody left; there was too much excitement. Suddenly a great many people ran west down 75th Street into the darkness. I had no idea why.

Then, in the distance, surrounded by the mob, I saw two fire-rescue engines. The firemen were being pelted with rocks and bottles. Incredible. The station had been burning for nearly an hour by now. Surely they had not expected to save it. What were they doing in this most dangerous area without a police escort? Fire-rescue apparently was not in touch with the Police Department, which certainly would have told it to stay out.

Fleeing for their lives, the firemen gunned their trucks eastward on 75th Street toward us, away from the mass of attackers. At 22nd Avenue they swung south, wheels screeching, firemen clinging to the trucks. In a hail of rocks they disappeared down the avenue.

As the long night wore on, most of the curious retired to their apartments. A few dozen youths kept trying to lure police into an area between projects known as "the canyon." They sent word that people were trapped. The idea was to draw police into ambush. Twice, carloads of police entered darkened side streets, lights off. Both times police were subjected to heavy gunfire.

As things quieted down, we urged the youths to go home.

We said it was a dangerous situation for children and old people; that it was no way to make their point—that sooner or later the police would take over.

To no avail. These were not times for talking.

So after awhile we stopped. In the end we were mere spectators to the carnage.

As we started to leave, I saw the boy who had set the fire from the milk carton filled with gas. I thought he might be persuaded to leave the streets.

Looking into his wild, dark eyes, I asked him, "Do you want to get killed out here?"

He didn't look up. "We don't give a f---," he said. "It's time to die."

He sat down on the curb waiting for something else interesting to do.

We left.

Driving home, the boy's reply sliced through my consciousness like a cold, sharp knife.

"It's time to die."

The question kept haunting me: what would make a mere child say such a thing?

As we drove without talking past the now dark windows of the Scott project, the question answered itself. This is a place of human suffering. For the people here, one day is very much like the next. Life for many holds no hope of change. In those unlit rooms, cockroaches and rats hold sway.

In a place such as this, dying is no big thing.

Weeks later, in the middle of the night, I sat alone, nursing the ice cubes of a drink long gone, and I wondered about my people, especially those in the projects. These were not the projects I had known as a boy. I no longer understood. What has happened to us? How could we do the things we did during that long night of shame? For my part, what had I not done that I should have? And the whites—the power establishment of Miami—how could they let it come to this? Would they see the connection between the riots and the housing projects, those monstrously violent cesspools of human existence where killing is a way of life? What would, or *could*, be done?

That night I was certain more than ever that I am not a "black leader." I could never lead or follow a protest which invoked violence, and I wondered if I could really help lead my people out of the misery and frustrations which make violence inevitable. It was a time for soul searching.

What is the future of Liberty City? The area still has a share of working class and professional people who are far from the food-stamp lines. But it has its poor, and in Liberty City, public housing is the Achilles' heel. It produces youngsters for whom dying is no big thing.

How could it be so, this place of fond memories from my boyhood days? Tenured and ensconced in academia with a doctorate, it is easy for me to talk about how hard work and sweat delivered me and my family from the James E. Scott project. But it was not the same project. And it was not hard work and sweat—it was my dad's G.I. Bill and the fact that he didn't desert us. *Then* it was hard work and sweat.

The order of those things is extremely important, because without the help of the government, he just might have given up in frustration and left us.

Today nearly 40 per cent of the black women in this country who have children are rearing those children alone. In projects like the Scott homes, nearly 70 per cent of the black women living there do so without the fathers of their children. In 1951, had my mother with her five children, been deserted, I would probably not be on a university faculty. Those of us who appear to have "made it" should not be so easily convinced it was entirely through our own efforts, especially if at some time, someone or something— perhaps the government—gave assistance.

But what sort of help? Are welfare, food stamps, Medicaid, or rent subsidies really helping? Ask Ray Mitchell's mother.

Beyond the short run, these things do not help people. They consume people. Through the mazes of rules, regulations, policies and guidelines, they entrap. And it seems that they never let go. After a time people come to depend on these "programs" and not upon themselves.

In the telling of a story such as this, the logical place to end is with a plea for the elimination of "the projects" and a demand that we find alternatives to the way and the places where we now house poor people.

No such plea will be issued. I fully realize that the projects and their subculture of violence will not be eliminated. This story will not change that fact. Probably nothing will.

The North Bay Village murders in February did not move this community to deal with the environment that spat out Ray Anthony Mitchell.

The McDuffie riots in May did not move us, either, to look more closely at the housing projects around which much of the killing occurred. Indeed, as a result of the riots this community may receive more than $10 million to build *new* projects, most probably in Liberty City.

The violent spasm of the Scott project riot in July will not awaken us to the necessity to confront and solve the miseries of the poor and to find an answer once and for all for the hell that is the James E. Scott project.

Why? White people don't *need* the projects. They don't see them, of course, but then that's the point. They serve as the dumping grounds for America's dispossessed. This is as true today as it was with the eviction of blacks from "Railroad Shop Colored Addition." White people, and also middle class blacks who have escaped the ghettos, display little patience with, or tolerance for, poor people. We simply must have a place to put them other than in our own neighborhoods. "Projects" serve that purpose extremely well.

I still go to Liberty City. I visit the Mitchell family to help arrange a way for them to maintain contact with Ray and Dennis while they are in prison. There is work to be done with the people of the Scott project in order to determine how to change the public housing policies that have led to the entrapment of several generations of poor people.

If I am not a black "leader," I am at least a black "helper." I remain convinced that at least some of the laughter that I heard as a boy in the courtyards of the projects can be heard again.

But I have been unable to return to that hellish spot on Martin Luther King Boulevard where I saw the small, still figure late that Saturday afternoon.

There are no visible changes in Liberty City. The people of the projects, who so desperately need to own just a tiny piece of this rich community, are just as far away from that ownership as they were before the riots. That slim edge on survival that my father was able to deliver to us is no longer possible for the people of the James E. Scott development.

We can design and build more of the same if we must. We can continue to insist that those who live there do so as a result of their own lack of effort to get out. We can find all the comforting and reassuring rationales we need in order to convince ourselves that none of us is responsible for what is happening in America's black ghettos. But, in the end, many, many more of us, both white and black, may eventually become their victims in our homes and on other Martin Luther King Boulevards.

3. "Confronting Racial Isolation in Miami"

Following the May 1980 civil disturbances in Miami, the U.S. Commission on Civil Rights conducted hearings into the events and their causes. This is the summary of the commission's report.

SUMMARY

The black community in Miami is characterized chiefly by its isolation from the city as a whole. Blacks are in the city, but in a crucial sense, they are not part of Miami. They are not politically and economically powerful sectors that control community resources and make community policies. Their concerns have not been a priority for the city, the county, or for the private sector. Their frustration fed the violence that recently erupted in the wake of what was viewed as yet another in a long line of abuses suffered at the hands of an unresponsive and uncaring officialdom.

The isolation of Miami's black community results from a series of events that have contributed to the deterioration of what was once a vibrant and viable community. What Miami needs is a recognition of the causes for the alienation that has overtaken the black community and a commitment by responsible leaders at all levels in both the public and private sectors to provide the leadership and resources and exert the effort to turn this situation around.

One of the events that precipitated the isolation was the physical destruction of a large portion of the black community by the municipal government. Under the urban renewal program, the city tore down a massive amount of low-cost housing, forcing large numbers of blacks to leave their traditional neighborhoods and move into other areas that could not accommodate them. New units of low-cost housing were never built to replace all that had been demolished. In a city with a vacancy rate of less than one percent, the remaining low-cost housing has become severely deteriorated and overcrowded. The consequences are isolated and disparate ghettoes.

Neither the children who are transported to schools outside of these communities nor those who remain in neighborhood schools receive, in many respects, an education that addresses their needs. The city has not allocated enough resources and effort to provide adequate vocational-technical programs and well-trained guidance counselors or to address the myriad other needs of students from low-income families. When children exhibit inappropriate behavior, Dade County's school system often responds by shunting them into programs that do not respond to their needs rather than intervening with effective counseling. The public school system has many capable black employees, but they are concentrated in the elementary schools and low-level administrative posts. This practice not only undermines these employees' upward mobility but also deprives young blacks of positive role models, compounding the youths' sense of isolation within the schools.

Blacks are isolated in Miami's economy, as well. Although the local economy continues to grow at a rate higher than that for the Nation as a whole, there are few black entrepreneurs, and the black unemployment rate remains high. Stymied by their own lack of capital and their inability to obtain capital from commercial lenders, would-be black businesspeople fall through the cracks of unimaginative and nonaccommodating programs of the State, local and Federal government. Blacks with the education and talent to succeed in business often leave Miami for other parts of the country that appear to offer more opportunities for blacks. Those who remain and try to establish businesses in Miami run into many obstacles, such as insurance redlining, that increase the likelihood of failure.

Federal programs established to help the disadvantaged businessperson, including the Small Business Administration, have helped some persons. The fact remains, however, that in Miami, black entrepreneurs are receiving a disproportionately small number of the loans the Small Business Administration provides for disadvantaged businesspersons. Witnesses before this Commission questioned the degree to which other federally-funded economic development programs are benefitting blacks. Although it is clear programs like urban redevelopment are providing some assistance to some disadvantaged persons, federally-funded programs in Miami have not improved the quality of life within the black community as much as anticipated. Blacks continue to be largely excluded from many economic opportunities in Miami.

Blacks in Miami have limited employment opportunities. A few Federal agencies, such as the U.S. Postal Service and the Veterans Administration Medical Center, have significant numbers of black employees. But most Federal agencies in the city employ few blacks. Local public and private sector employers have a dismal record with regard to hiring blacks. Some employers go so far as to recruit workers from other States rather than provide on-the-job training to unskilled workers in Miami.

Compounding this situation is the fact that justice in Miami is administered in a way that excludes blacks and appears incapable of condemning official violence against them. Black complaints of police violence are common in the city. The incident that took the life of Mr. McDuffie was one of many confrontations between black residents and the system that is supposed to protect all of Miami's inhabitants. The underlying causes range from employment practices to inadequate police training and evaluation. The department screens applicants for the police force with an allegedly biased test. Dade County has established an Independent Review Panel to investigate complaints against the police, but the Panel lacks resources and has no subpoena power. A Governor's Commission found that local police internal review procedures were totally unsatisfactory.

The proportion of the youth in the Miami juvenile justice system who are black is more than three times as great as in the Dade County population. Counseling for such youth is inadequate, in part, because the system employs counselors who meet minimal educational and experience requirements. Services for rehabilitating juveniles are grossly inadequate.

Many of Miami's problems have answers—more and better-qualified teachers and counselors, better selection and training of police officers, rehabilitation of housing, and so on. But remedial steps cost money. The housing situation is a good example of the cost-benefit approach that appears to have taken hold in Miami. Because it is a seller's market, landlords can rent or sell any housing they choose to make available, no matter how deteriorated. As a result, they do not appear to view rehabilitating housing as being to their advantage. In the rare instances when they are brought before municipal authorities for violation of housing ordinances, landlords generally find it cheaper to pay the fine than to make the repairs. The question is whether one approach is indeed "cheaper" than another when the trade-off involves human suffering and frustration.

As indicated throughout the report, Miami suffers the range of urban problems that seem endemic to all major American cities today. The vast majority of the black community, regardless of economic status, feels powerless and frustrated. It is possible to identify and perhaps to ameliorate some of the sources of tension, but any long-term solution requires a coordinated attack on the underlying causes of racial isolation and exclusion.

Other reports, including those by the Kerner Commission and by this Commission, have indicated many specific remedial steps that officials at each level of government could take in areas such as education, employment and housing. To the extent that Miami has implemented any of these recommendations, however, it has not been a comprehensive effort. Consequently, racial isolation and exclusion have intensified.

A major question facing Miami is whether local leaders will see it in their community's interest to take the coordinated long-term concrete action that is necessary to turn Miami around. Other riots have occurred without generating such a commitment.

Many black Miamians are contributing to the progress of their communities and the city as a whole. Black support for a rapid transit system in a 1978 referendum made the project possible. The black Miami-Dade Chamber of Commerce, albeit with limited success, has coordinated efforts with the Greater Miami Chamber of Commerce in two projects designed to increase the number of black businesses in Dade County. But the black community in Miami has neither the size nor wealth that commands political power and accountability in Miami. Acting alone, it cannot control or improve the circumstances in which they live.

It is important to identify sectors of the community that have both the political influence and economic capacity to address problems of such magnitude. According to Miami's Mayor, the city suffers a power vacuum:

> Nobody runs Miami. . . . [T]here is no automobile industry; there is no steel industry; there is no tobacco industry; there is no company that permeates, that dominates. So we don't really have the typical power structure that you have in some American cities. In addition to which, unlike Atlanta and other cities that have deep roots, you don't have a social structure. Nobody has really been here for more than 50 years. . . . [E]verybody here came from somewhere else. Very few native Miamians are more than 30 years old. . . . Then who are the wealthy people? Who are the money interests here? For the most part, absentee corporations where the management is in New York. So, therefore, when you get to the Chamber of Commerce, what you see, with all due respect, are a bunch of lawyers that represent interests and corporations. They do a nice job, but this is not Atlanta . . . [where] you can get together a dozen people and something will happen. That cannot happen in Miami.[1]

Miami may not have the same power structure as some other American cities, but there is leadership in both the private and public sector that can get things done. Private sector involvement will be crucial to any successful remedial effort and is becoming increasingly important as Federal financial aid to cities is being cut back. The idea of organized private sector involvement is not new. "Metropolitan affairs non-profit corporations" (MANCs) and "community" foundations have improved the quality of urban life in a number of cities, including Detroit, Philadelphia, Pittsburgh, and Atlanta. These organizations, however, tend to limit their activities or developing downtown areas to sponsoring cultural affairs.

In Miami, one project that reflects private sector leadership is

---

1. Maurice Ferre, testimony, Hearing Transcript, pp. 1139–42.

the New World Center development. Working with community groups to rejuvenate the downtown area, the private sector put together a commercial package supplemented by Federal monies. Although this project emphasized physical construction, the elements of commitment, coordination, and monitoring are apparent.

The same groups, individuals, and units of government that worked together to rebuild downtown Miami can—if they want to—work together with the black community to bring about that community's participation in all aspects of growth and progress in Dade County. The knowledge and skills are available; the question is one of commitment. This report unmistakably demonstrates that without such a commitment, conditions will worsen, isolation will increase and violence will recur.

4. Interview with Edward Gardner

Edward Gardner, chairman of the board of Soft Sheen Products, Inc., was approached in the summer of 1982 for financial help in publicizing a massive voter registration campaign that would ultimately lead to the election of a black mayor of Chicago. This is an excerpt from a 1989 interview with Gardner by the Eyes on the Prize *production team.*

INTERVIEWER: You told me you were inspired when you started your business way back in 1964. And you were a schoolteacher then. Tell me that story. How did you get into that?
EDWARD GARDNER: Well, you know, when you got a wife and four kids, and you're making ten thousand dollars a year, you wonder how you're going to make it to send those kids through college and so forth. We just felt that we had to do something else. Not that it wasn't a good job as a teacher, assistant principal, but the dollars were not there. In addition to that, that was the time that Dr. Martin Luther King struck in the South. And we felt so inspired, particularly by those black youngsters who were giving up their lives in many cases, and whites, too, suffering so that we could probably have a better life for all Black Americans throughout the nation. So we just kind of felt that maybe we could do more than just being a schoolteacher. And we felt that our best chance was to go into business.

I was not a picketer. I was not a marcher, but I felt that I could build a major corporation supplying jobs for hundreds of people. I was just that naive, you know. And so I was selling hair care products out of the back of my car, up and down Forty-seventh Street, Sixty-third Street, making twenty-five percent profits on a part-time basis.

So I started going down the basement, stirring my pot there with some wax and some petroleum on a hot plate. And I got a product that looked pretty good. I said, "Gosh, this is a good product. I think I can sell it to the beautician." Talked to the beautician, she said, "Mr. Gardner, wherever you got that product from, don't ever bring it back here again." It was just that bad. But again, I wanted to build a major black business. I went back and started stirring the pot again. No chemistry background. No business training, but I wanted to be an entrepreneur and a businessperson. So we finally improved the product, took it back. She said, "That's great. Leave it just like it is. Don't change it." And from that point on we started building the present multi-million-dollar Soft Sheen Products Company. But it was all based upon the fact that we wanted to do more of what Dr. King was talking about. He says, "If you open those doors, who's going to walk through there?" Now, we had to have businesses to supply jobs, so we wanted to supply those jobs. And that's why Soft Sheen was built from the very beginning.

INT: Coming now to 1982. You're sitting in your office and you're called upon by Renault Robinson. What happened? What did you guys talk about?

E.G.: Renault Robinson called me. He was, as far as I was concerned, a very active person in politics and social movement, a former policeman. . . . And Renault called me, he says, "Ed, we need help with the voter campaign." So I said, "Well, come on by." And I thought it was a donation which we were probably going to do. And he came by and explained very clearly to us that our problem was voter registration. Blacks are not registered. And so my son Gary and my daughter, they were here. And they said, "Well, Dad, why don't we devote our last quarter of advertising budget—instead of using it to advertise Soft Sheen, use it to get blacks to register to vote." And that was a lot of money. That was about a quarter of a million dollars we allocated for advertising for that period of time. So we just decided that let's go with it.

What we did was to dedicate not only the dollars, but the time and the creativity of our marketing department, advertising department to really get involved behind voter registration. And Renault was surprised that we wanted to do this. But we knew things were not going to change in Chicago unless we got blacks registered. . . .

INT: . . . How did people, say, in the middle class and the other parts of the business community respond to this? This was like a first, wasn't it?

E.G.: My son said, look, let's not say that Soft Sheen is behind this. We ran radio commercials for two or three weeks. "Come alive October 5." Real sharp commercials that would alert and really get our black community behind it. And they kept saying, well, who's paying for all these? There were many spots, something like fourteen and fifteen spots a day. But also, once we advertised on a station, we had the station also match our spots. So we had a large number of spots running every day. But we had that power and the strength as a major advertiser to get them to do this. . . . Finally one of the disc jockeys said, look, this is going on long enough. We're going to say Soft Sheen is putting up the dollars for this commercial. We didn't mind it, but we felt that we didn't want people to say, well, here's Soft Sheen using it for some type of advertisement ploy to help them sell products. We wanted to be known as a company that's going to try to increase voter registration in this city of Chicago in the black community. There's no reason for us to be here and not take part in helping to run this city. And if you got a quarter of a million blacks not even registered, then don't tell me about Jane Byrne or Richard Daley or anybody else until we do our job. So, we felt that the registration job had to be done. We did it and we had not only the dollars but most important, most important, we had the minds. We had the sharp, creative black minds who came through black colleges because of what Dr. King did during that period of time, whose parents had the dollars to send them through school because of what Dr. King did. All this was made possible because of Dr. King, when we were just getting Soft Sheen started [in 1964]. . . .

INT: Tell me about the little people and how things were organized and rolling before that October 5.

E.G.: Well, keep in mind that Soft Sheen Products Company was the major corporation at that time involved in voter registration. But the work, the masses were done by the little people throughout the city of Chicago. Those were the ones who put up the streamers and stickers throughout the city. They passed out the buttons. They kept shouting, "Come alive October 5." I remember one time I walked into a gas station and I wanted some gas. I paid for my gas. And the fellow said—this fellow could hardly speak his name; he wasn't the sharpest fellow in the world—last thing he said, "Have you registered to vote?" Now, you know, to me, when I reached the person who you think is insignificant in this city and voting is important to him, we were extremely successful. And that's what you had happen. Now, certainly, the middle-class blacks and the smaller businesses, they got involved too. But they got involved after the momentum started going and the momentum was really done by the masses of Black Chicagoans who did not have those big dollars. They only had the numbers and desire to change things in this city. And that was so rewarding.

INT: Tell me that story about how you went to Operation PUSH.

E.G.: The theme of the voter registration campaign was "Come alive October 5." And that was the big date. If we could have registered those two hundred fifty thousand new black voters, [we'd have] a chance of having a black mayor for the first time. So, on that night, we had on 47th and King Drive an outlet where we have something like forty telephones. And those folks, the little people, now, were manning those phones all day long. I walked in and those phones were just ringing like the dickens. And I said, "Well, guys, looks like we're going to have a victory."

So that night I came back to see just how things were going. I went into Operation PUSH around ten o'clock at night. And they were surprised to see me. Here's Ed Gardner, this fellow owned this multimillion-dollar company. He's taking the time out at ten o'clock at night to come by and see how we're doing and to thank us. I walked in. I thanked them for all the support Operation PUSH had given us and all the people who supported the program at the very beginning. And they were just surprised first to see me. And they said, "Did you come by yourself?" I said, "Yeah, I drove." And they seemed to be apprehensive about me being there at that time of night by myself. So when I left they said, "Mr. Gardner, we're going to walk you back out to your car. Thanks for coming," but it showed how we were really together as a family and very much concerned about one another.

5. Harold Washington's Announcement of Candidacy for the Democratic Nomination for Mayor of Chicago

By October 5, 1982, the voter registration campaign conducted by a coalition of community organizations had resulted in the registration of more than 100,000 new black voters. The next month, U.S. Congressman Harold Washington agreed to run for the Democratic nomination for mayor of Chicago in the primary election the following February. He announced his intention in this speech, delivered at a press conference held on November 10.

Chicago is a divided city. Chicago is a city where citizens are treated unequally and unfairly. Chicago is a city in decline. Each year for the last decade, we have lost 11,500 jobs, 3,500 housing units and nearly 36,000 people.

Since 1955, women, Latinos, Blacks, youth and progressive whites have been left out of the Chicago government. Since 1979, the business, labor and intellectual communities have been allowed but token involvement in Chicago government.

Sadly, we have learned what happens when there is no governmental stability—and when the few rule over us. The results are that more people don't have jobs, more are out of food, out of their homes and out of hope.

Our businesses are failing at the highest rate since the Depression, in part from high interest rates, and the only answer the city government provides is fat consultant contracts for a few politically connected firms and jobs for a few patronage workers.

We have a school system which does not educate, in which students continue to lag far behind the rest of the country in tests of reading and math ability.

We have a continuing crime problem in the city. Despite a drop in crime statistics, it's still not safe to walk the streets or run a business. Even at home, Chicagoans are robbed, mugged and beaten.

We no longer have dependable housing in this city. There has been an epidemic of abandoned buildings and rents have sky-rocketed. Subsidized housing is no longer being built. And, with interest rates as they are, no one can afford to buy their own home anymore.

Finally, "the city that works" doesn't work anymore. City services cost more than in any other city in America, and yet they just aren't there—sewers are in disrepair, streets are marred with giant potholes. We have one of the highest infant mortality rates in the country, and traffic appears to be permanently snarled.

We have these terrible problems in Chicago, partly because leadership has not striven for unity and pointed boldly to the new directions. Instead, it has perpetuated outdated politics and pie-in-the-sky financing.

I have compassion for the terrible plight of [its] people and a vision for its future: I honestly believe that of those candidates mentioned, only I can rebuild Chicago by rallying Chicagoans to create a city in which every individual will receive his or her full measure of dignity. In the future, I see a Chicago of compassion; a city where no one has to live with rats, where the sick can be cured and where no one is overtaxed on property and burdened with other hidden taxes.

All the other candidates who have declared and who will be running for mayor would perpetuate politics as usual. Those candidates will continue the shell game of city financing at a time of crisis.

I would prefer not to run. But, there is a sense of urgency which moves me. Chicago can only be rebuilt if all the people of Chicago and her leaders work together. I was born, raised and educated in this city, and I have served it on three levels of government. I love representing Chicago in Washington, where we need courageous voices to speak out and act against [President Ronald] Reagan and Reaganomics. But I can't watch the city of Chicago be destroyed by petty politics and bad government.

I have heard the earnest pleas of thousands of people to enter the race. Therefore, I declare that I am a candidate for the mayor of Chicago. Not to do so would be a mockery of my longstanding dedication to public service.

I see a Chicago that runs well, in which services are provided as a right, not as a political favor.

I see a Chicago of educational excellence and equality of treatment in which all children can learn to function in this ever-more-complex society, in which jobs and contracts are dispensed fairly to those that want and qualify for them, and in which justice rains down like water.

I see a Chicago in which the neighborhoods are once again the center of our city, in which businesses boom and provide neighborhood jobs, in which neighbors join together to help govern their neighborhood and their city.

Some may say this is visionary—I say *they* lack vision.

Already, a new day is dawning. The unprecedented voter registration and voter turnout in Chicago in the last week [Washington had been reelected to Congress on November 2] is evidence of this. The people of Chicago who have been neglected by the political bosses have announced their willingness to become involved, to unify and to act. I invite them to join my campaign. If I'm to be mayor, it would be as the spokesperson of this new movement—not the mayor of just a political faction, but mayor of all Chicago. We devoutly search for unity.

As mayor of this city, I would open the doors of City Hall. I would dig into that untapped reservoir of talented whites, Latinos, women and Blacks and unleash that ability for the benefit of this city.

Fairness will be our standard. On my first day in office, I will sign a freedom of information order to open the secret files of City Hall to inspection by all citizens. We seek *accountability*. As mayor, I shall gather the best talent of the city to tackle the record of problems I have outlined. We shall strive for excellence.

Thousands of Chicagoans have beseeched me to undertake this task. Their faith is not misplaced.

6. "Harold Washington: Uniting Chicago for *All* People"

Harold Washington defeated his two opponents, Mayor Jane Byrne and Richard Daley, son of the late mayor, in the primary election on February 22, 1983. In the April 12 general election he faced Republican Bernard Epton. These are excerpts from one of Washington's campaign leaflets.

HAROLD WASHINGTON IN THE GREAT DEMOCRATIC TRADITION

The Democratic party has a great tradition reaching back over a half century of dedicated, compassionate, and strong leadership.

The tradition was established at the height of the Great Depression by Franklin Roosevelt. John F. Kennedy and others have carried it forward. Harold Washington represents the tradition today in Chicago.

Harold's record of strong leadership and excellence during three decades of public service testifies to the depth of his commitment.

The cornerstones of the Washington campaign—jobs, fairness, and sound, compassionate social programs—represent the fundamental ideals of the Democratic party.

Harold Washington is committed to reaching out and serving all of Chicago's citizens. Just as a nation must be united if it is to be strong, so too must Chicago.

With Harold Washington as Mayor, Chicago will be a strong and united city.

THE WASHINGTON RECORD

Harold Washington will be bringing thirty years of solid leadership and brilliant achievement to the Mayor's office. No candidate for the office has ever been better qualified.

Congressman Washington has experience at all levels of government. He began his career in 1954 as Assistant Corporation Counsel for Chicago. He went on to serve as Arbitrator for the Illinois Industrial Commission. He was elected to the Illinois House of Representatives in 1965 and then to the Illinois Senate in 1976. In 1980 Harold Washington was elected to the U.S. Congress. Last year he was re-elected by the largest plurality received by any congressman in the nation—a remarkable 97.4 percent.

The wide range of significant legislation successfully sponsored by Harold Washington indicates the quality and strength of leadership he will bring to Chicago. He has sponsored the Consumer Credit Reform Act, the Older Americans Act, the Child Nutrition Act, the Witness Protection Act, the Equal Employment Opportunity Act, the Human Rights Act, and the Currency Exchange Reform Act.

Harold Washington's leadership has been widely recognized. He received the Top Ten Legislators Award from Chicago Magazine. The IVI-IPO gave him its Best Legislator Award. He has received the highest honor given by Labor, The Legislative Excellence Award, given only to those with a long and consistent record of support. He has been endorsed by the Chicago Federation of Labor, AFL-CIO. Countless other organizations—the Cook County Bar Association, The National Lawyers Guild, and the Disabled American Veterans have honored Harold Washington. Harold Washington won the democratic party's nomination for Mayor of Chicago on February 22. With our support he will be elected Mayor on April 12.

THE HAROLD WASHINGTON PROGRAM FOR CHICAGO

Harold's First Priority: Jobs

- Establish a department of employment and economic development that will fulfill the first priority of the Washington administration: the creation and retention of jobs for Chicagoans.
- Work vigorously in Springfield and Washington for programs that will bring jobs to Chicago.

- Develop a public transportation system that links Chicagoans to the growing suburban job market.
- Retain and attract business and industry by using the community colleges, community organizations, and business and labor to deyelop effective employment and training programs for Chicago's work force.

Harold's Pledge: Fairness and Justice

- The Washington administration will demand no more of its employees than a full day's work for a full day's pay. The requirement to perform political work in order to keep one's job will be abolished.
- Hire, upgrade, and promote city employees on a merit basis.
- Establish a freedom-of-information ordinance that opens city government files to public examination.
- Conduct city business fairly and equitably.

Harold Will Restore Fiscal Stability

- The Washington administration will fight for passage of a state income-tax increase and the resumption of the state's mass transportation subsidy for Chicago.
- Appoint a blue-ribbon tax commission to review the city's over-all tax structure.
- Open and extend the budgetary process in order to provide for greater participation by citizens and city council alike.
- Establish stronger agency accountability in order to increase efficiency, modify or terminate unproductive programs, and eliminate the excessive use of outside consultants.

Harold Will Revitalize the Neighborhoods

- Adequately fund and decentralize Chicago's public schools and remove all political influence from their management.
- Reorganize the police department to provide for greater responsiveness to community needs, notably more protection for senior citizens, our schools, public commuters, and small businesses.

- Provide better balance between neighborhood and downtown developments so that neighborhood housing can be better maintained and rehabilitated and more affordable housing built.
- Expand the city's health care services, including reopening community clinics and better addressing our critical infant mortality problem.

THE CHOICE IS CLEAR. CHICAGOANS REJECTED REAGANOMICS IN NOVEMBER. WE MUST SPEAK OUT AGAIN ON APRIL 12.

Harold Washington, by virtue of experience and excellence, stands head and shoulders above his Republican opponent.

Harold Washington's Republican opponent is trying to run from, but he can not hide his support for the Reaganomic social and economic policies that are destroying Chicago and our nation.

The Republican Candidate Supports Reaganomics
The Republican Candidate Is No Friend of Consumers
- He voted against lowering the cost of utility bills for those on low and fixed incomes.
- He voted to eliminate interest rate ceilings on consumer loans and contracts.
- He voted to make it more difficult to redeem foreclosed property and to redeem goods repossessed by finance companies.

The Republican Candidate Is No Friend of Education
- He supplied the deciding vote to eliminate $6.5 million for handicapped students.
- He voted to eliminate over $1 million for free school books.
- He voted to take away funds from the free school lunch and breakfast program.

The Republican Candidate Is No Friend of Labor
- He voted in favor of the union busting right-to-work law for Illinois.
- He opposed granting collective bargaining rights to state employees.
- He voted to drastically cut workers' compensation benefits and to give fewer benefits to disabled and handicapped workers.

The Republican Candidate Is No Friend of Women's Rights
- He voted against removing the 3/5 rule for passage of the ERA.
- He voted to reduce funding for day care centers.
- He voted against an Act to fund rape crisis centers, domestic violence centers, and senior citizen assistance centers.

The Republican Candidate Is No Friend of the Needy
- He cast the deciding vote against reducing the sales tax by 1¢ on food and medicine.
- He voted against a 5% cost-of-living increase for those on welfare.
- He voted against lowering the cost of utility bills for needy senior citizens.

CHICAGO NEEDS WASHINGTON
WASHINGTON NEEDS US!

7. Harold Washington's Inaugural Speech

On April 12, 1983, Harold Washington was elected mayor of Chicago. He was inaugurated on April 29. This is a part of the speech he delivered that day to an audience of more than four thousand.

. . . My election was the result of the greatest grassroots effort in the history of the city of Chicago. It may have been equaled somewhere in this country, but I know not where.

My election was made possible by thousands and thousands of people who demanded that the burdens of mismanagement, unfairness and inequity be lifted so that the city might be saved.

One of the ideas that held us all together said that neighborhood involvement has to replace the ancient, decrepit and creaking machine. City government, for once in our lifetime, must be equitable and fair. The people of Chicago asked for more responsibility and more representation at every city level.

It's a good thing that philosophy prevailed, because otherwise I'm not sure the city could solve the financial crisis at hand.

Reluctantly, I must tell you that because of circumstances thrust upon us, each and every one of us, we must immediately cut back on how much money the city spends.

Monday, I will issue an order to freeze all city hiring and raises in order to reduce city expenses by millions of dollars. We will have no choice but to release several hundred new city employees who were added because of political considerations.

With malice toward none, but only in the interest of clarity and truth, we will continue.

Beginning Monday, executive salaries will be cut. Some members of my cabinet will be required to take salaries considerably less than their counterparts are making now. Holdover chiefs will be ordered to take salary cuts as well.

Unnecessary city programs must end, and the fat removed from all departments until they are sinew and bone. So that there is no confusion, these cuts will begin in the mayor's office.

But these measures are not enough to make up the enormous deficits we have inherited. Like other cities across the state, we simply cannot provide adequate public service without additional sources of revenue. During the election I said that there was no alternative to higher state income taxes.

Chicago is not an island unto itself. Other municipalities and municipal and state officials have joined us in the fight for more tax support. We must have new sources of income soon, and I have joined the governor of this great state in his quest for additional sources of income.

In the months ahead, we are going to be instituting some new fiscal methods and controls and I shall certainly keep you informed—if necessary, on a day-to-day basis—as to our progress.

But when it finally comes down to basic issues, I'm only going to be successful if you are involved. The neighborhoods and the people who reside in them are going to have to play an active, creative role in this administration. I am asking you now to join that team.

In the late hours last night, while contemplating the enormity of the challenge we face together, I remembered the great words of President John Fitzgerald Kennedy at his inaugural address in 1961, and I quote: "Ask not what your country can do for you," he said. "Ask what you can do for your country."

In that same spirit, today I am asking all of you—particularly those of you who have taken the oath with me today [a few members of the audience had raised their rights hands as Washington raised his while taking the oath of office]—to respond to a great challenge: help me institute reform and bring about renewal of this city while there is still time. Business as usual will not be accepted by the people of this city. Business as usual will not be accepted by any part of this city. Business as usual will not be accepted by this chief executive of this great city.

The only greater challenge in our history was 110 years ago when Mayor Joseph Medill looked over a city burned to the ground and called for an enormous outpouring of civic spirit and resources to make the city new.

I'm asking the people in the neighborhoods to take a direct role in the planning, development and city housekeeping so that our city becomes a finer place to live.

I'm calling for more leadership and more personal involvement in what goes on. We know the strength of grassroots leadership because our election was based on it. We want this powerful infrastructure to grow because the success of tomorrow's city depends on it, and the world and this country look for examples.

The city's books will be open to the public because we don't have a chance to institute fiscal reform unless we all know the hard facts. I believe in the process of collective bargaining when all the numbers are on the table and the city and its unions sit down and hammer out an agreement together. The only contracts that ever work are the ones that are essentially fair.

Having said all this, I want you to know that the situation is serious, but not desperate. I am optimistic about our future. I'm optimistic, not just because I have a positive view of life, but because there is so much about this city that promises achievement.

We are a multiethnic, multiracial, multilanguage city and that is a source of stability and strength.

Our minorities are ambitious, and that is a sign of a prosperous city on the move. Racial fears and divisiveness have hurt us in the past. But I believe that is a situation that will and must be overcome.

Our schools must be improved. They're going to get a lot better because we're calling on students, teachers and administrators to study longer and achieve more.

I'm going to set a personal example for what we all have to do by working harder and longer than you've ever seen a mayor work before.

Most of our problems can be solved. Some of them will take brains, and some of them will take patience, but all of them will have to be wrestled with like an alligator in the swamp.

But there is a fine new spirit that seems to be taking root. I call it the spirit of renewal. It's like spring coming here after a long winter, this renewal. It refreshes us and gives us a new faith that we can go on.

Last night I saw the dark problems and today I see the bright promise of where we stand. Chicago has all of the resources necessary for prosperity. We are at the crossroads of America—a vital transportation, economic and business center. We are the heartland.

We have a clear vision of what our people can become, and that vision goes beyond mere economic wealth, although that is part of our hopes and expectations.

In our ethnic and racial diversity, we are all brothers and sisters in a quest for greatness. Our creativity and energy are unequalled by any city anywhere in the world. We will not rest until the renewal of our city is done.

Today, I want to tell you how proud I am to be your mayor. There have been 41 mayors before me and when I was growing up in the city and attending its public schools I never dreamed the flame would be passed my way. But it has.

It makes me humble, but it also makes me glad and emboldened. I hope some day to be remembered by history as the mayor who cared about people and who was above all fair, a mayor who helped to heal our wounds, who stood the watch while the city and its people answered the greatest challenge in more than a century—and who saw that city renewed.

My good friends and neighbors, the oath of office that I have taken today before God binds us all together. I cannot be successful without you. But with you, we cannot fail.

I can reach out my hand, and ask for your help. With the same adventurous spirit of Jean Baptiste DuSable when he founded Chicago, we are going to do some great deeds here together.

In the beginning, there was the Word. Throughout this campaign, you have given me the word. The campaign is over. Let's go to work!

8. "Of Harold Washington"
Gwendolyn Brooks

Harold Washington died of a massive heart attack on November 25, 1987. The previous April he had won election to his second term as mayor of Chicago. This tribute to him by Illinois poet laureate Gwendolyn Brooks appeared in Chicago *magazine.*

"**I want to reach out my hand** in fellowship, and friendship —to every living soul in this city."

He looked us straight in the eye, and said that; exactly that.

Powerful was the honesty of that commitment, the will, the sweet social hunger. We feel cared for still. We are aware of a physical warming still, an echo-warmth from the gift of a fistful of years. Harold Washington the Mayor has left us a standard to try for, a standard of hardy integrity.

An integrity sounded and hounded and pounded.

Once, during a little ceremony in his office, at a time when he was *best* beleaguered, when council cruelties were at their height, when whispered doubts in the city were multiplying, when many of his now-inconsolable friends were joining his enemies, I said to him, "We are proud of you. We love and support you still. Hold on." I'll never forget the wealth of relief and gratitude that flooded his eyes as he grabbed my hand and said, "Thank you. *Thank* you."

To die is to stop. Somebody else goes on or begins. The big, the middle, the little jobs are through. One may or may not have worked the puzzle, seen the comet, minimized, mastered, established, or tamed. One may or may not have managed the Miracle. What was to be done to be done to be done is done or not done.

See the people! They come by the thousands, the hundred thousands. They come a million-and-more. They file past his bier at City Hall. They queue up outside City Hall. They queue up outside his funeral.

And after—they come running out of their houses, as Himself passes silently. They line the highways, the little avenues, to pay tribute. What can they Give him? this now still man, this man who indefatigably loved them. Only *presence*. Only body-presentation. They give that. They make a gift of that.

Harold Washington's last car cannot grace all the streets of Chicago. But the people are not petty. Even the unvisited get out of their houses, assemble. They form little groups, little congregations. They mourn, but mourn strangely. Their mourning is heavy, but *sunlit*. There is sun in their mourning. Because that is what Harold Washington was to them. Clean sun. Clean influence. Clarifier. Extender. The city's Best Friend.

Says a little black boy of nine or ten: "It *hurts*. I feel sad. And *mad*."

Says an old woman: "I happen to be white. I want to know: *Why* is it the *best* people go?"

Says a wet-eyed young Hispanic: "Until *he* came, we had no friend in government to *value* us."

Here's a little black lady in her wheelchair. Red tam, red blanket over her lap and legs. Erect in wordless tribute. She is a seated tree! The camera finishes with her rapidly but not before we have heard her silence saying: I am waiting for Harold. Nothing this day is more important than my sitting outdoors here to wait for my Harold.

See the people. On this funeral day, thick rows of them, thick live ribbons, lining each side of road after road. People. People standing for hours in the wet and cold.

All over the city, tears and a bewilderment of ache and loss.

And *now*. **Now the small jackals,** the insecure demonettes, wee scavenger-beasties—in New York, Chicago, Washington, D.C., Tattertown—feel free to nip and chip: free to plot and plan against all that was rich and radiant in a clean design. See the narrowing, tightened eyes. See the fear, that instinctive fear of strength, of magnificent strength, of recognizable quality, of direct integrity. The wee ones cannot understand. The wee ones are uneasy, are fearful. The wee ones pick up pebbles, are pelters.

Yes, the wee ones deal in pebbles, and throw them. They deal in bunches of pieces of silver, in packs of *pennies*.

Direct integrity dazzles and terrifies that which is wee among us.

Still! **Perhaps you believe** Harold Washington would want to tell us that what is minor and malnourished can be fed, can develop, can grow beyond the present fact. I can see the wise eye winking! Certainly Harold Washington knew that evil and good and impudence come in small and large packages—are to be recognized, labeled, managed. And I think he would say: Don't be afraid to be hot, if heat is what will heal. And I think he would endorse a variant of Mr. Murphy's law: If anything can go right, it Must.

9. "Address by the Reverend Jesse Jackson"

Democratic National Convention
San Francisco, July 17, 1984

Jesse Jackson's campaign for the Democratic presidential nomination in 1984 not only mobilized black communities but also attracted a considerable amount of white support. Jackson's experience in the southern struggle and in northern ghetto organizing, combined with his skills as an orator, gave him unique assets for his campaign. Although resented by many black leaders at the national level, Jackson was able to attract the support of many black voters. His efforts to bring nonblacks into his "rainbow coalition," which exceeded the predictions of most political experts, might have been more successful had he not alienated many Jewish voters by making a remark that was considered disparaging to Jews. Jackson's address to the Democratic National Convention provided an opportunity to try to heal those wounds as well as to summarize the themes of his campaign and set forth his vision of the future.

Our flag is red, white and blue, but our Nation is a rainbow— Red, Yellow, Brown, Black and White—we're all precious in God's sight.

America is not like a blanket—one piece of unbroken cloth, the same color, the same texture, the same size. America is more like a quilt—many patches, many pieces, many colors, many sizes, all woven and held together by a common thread. The White, the Hispanic, the Black, the Arab, the Jew, the woman, the Native American, the small farmer, the businessperson, the environmentalist, the peace activist, the young, the old, the lesbian, the gay and the disabled make up the American quilt.

Even in our fractured state, all of us count and fit somewhere. We have proven that we can survive without each other. But we have not proven that we can win and make progress without each other. We must come together.

From Fannie Lou Hamer in Atlantic City in 1964 to the Rainbow Coalition in San Francisco today; from the Atlantic to the Pacific, we have experienced pain but progress as we ended America's apartheid laws, we got public accommodations, we secured voting rights, we obtained open housing, as young people got the right to vote. We lost Malcolm, Martin, Medgar, Bobby and John and Viola. The team that got us here must be expanded, not abandoned.

Twenty years ago, tears welled up in our eyes as the bodies of Schwerner, Goodman, and Chaney were dredged from the depths of a river in Mississippi. Twenty years later, our communities, Black and Jewish, are in anguish, anger and in pain. Feelings have been hurt on both sides.

There is a crisis in communications. Confusion is in the air, but we cannot afford to lose our way. We may agree to agree or agree to disagree on issues; we must bring back civility to the tensions.

We are co-partners in a long and rich religious history—the Judeo-Christian traditions. Many Blacks and Jews have a shared passion for social justice at home and peace abroad. We must seek a revival of the spirit inspired by a new vision and new possibilities. We must return to higher ground.

We are bound by Moses and Jesus, but also connected with Islam and Mohammed. These three great religions—Judaism, Christianity, and Islam—were all born in the revered and Holy City of Jerusalem.

We are bound by Dr. Martin Luther King, Jr., and Rabbi Abraham Heschel, crying out from their graves for us to reach common ground. We are bound by shared blood and shared sacrifices. We are much too intelligent; much too bound by our Judeo-Christian heritage; much too victimized by racism, sexism, militarism, and anti-Semitism; much too threatened as historical scapegoats to go on divided one from another. We must turn from finger-pointing to clasped hands. We must share our burdens and our joys with each other once again. We must turn to each other and not on each other, and choose higher ground.

Twenty years later, we cannot be satisfied by just restoring the old coalition. Old wine skins must make room for new wine. We must heal and expand. The Rainbow Coalition is making room for Arab Americans. They, too, know the pain and hurt of racial and religious rejection. They must not continue to be made pariahs. The Rainbow Coalition is making room for Hispanic

Americans who this very night are living under the threat of the Simpson-Mazzoli bill. And [for] farm workers from Ohio who are fighting the Campbell Soup Company with a boycott to achieve legitimate workers' rights.

The Rainbow is making room for the Native American, the most exploited people of all, a people with the greatest moral claim amongst us. We support them as they seek the restoration of land and water rights, as they seek to preserve their ancestral homelands and the beauty of a land that was once all theirs. They can never receive a fair share for all they have given us. They must finally have a fair chance to develop their great resources and to preserve their people and their culture.

The Rainbow Coalition includes Asian Americans, now being killed in our streets, scapegoats for the failures of corporate, industrial and economic policies.

The Rainbow is making room for young Americans. . . .

The Rainbow includes disabled veterans. The color scheme fits in the Rainbow. The disabled have their handicap revealed and their genius concealed; while the able-bodied have their genius revealed and their disability concealed. But ultimately, we must judge people by their values and their contribution. Don't leave anybody out. I would rather have Roosevelt in a wheelchair than Reagan on a horse.

The Rainbow is making room for small farmers. . . .

The Rainbow includes lesbians and gays. No American citizen ought to be denied equal protection under the law.

We must be unusually committed and caring as we expand our family to include new members. All of us must be tolerant and understanding as the fears and anxieties of the rejected . . . express themselves in many different ways. Too often, what we call hate, as if it were some deeply rooted philosophy or strategy, is simply ignorance, anxiety, paranoia, fear and insecurity.

———————

In 1984, my heart is made to feel glad, because I know there is a way out—justice. The requirement for rebuilding America is justice. The linchpin of progressive politics in our Nation will not come from the North. . . . [It] in fact will come from the South.

That is why I argue over and over again. We look from Virginia around to Texas. There is only one Black Congressperson out of 115. Nineteen years later, we are locked out of the Congress, the Senate, and the Governor's Mansion.

What does this large black vote mean? Why do I fight to win second primaries and fight gerrymandering and annexation and at-large elections? Why do we fight over that? Because I tell you, you cannot hold someone in the ditch unless you linger there with them. . . .

If you want a change in this Nation, you enforce that Voting Rights Act. We will get 12 to 20 Black, Hispanic, female and progressive congresspersons from the South. We can save the cotton, but we have got to fight the boll weevils. We have got to make a judgment. . . .

It is not enough to hope ERA will pass. How can we pass ERA? If Blacks vote in great numbers, progressive Whites win. It is the only way progressive Whites win. If Blacks vote in great numbers, Hispanics win. When Blacks, Hispanics, and progressive Whites vote, women win. When women win, children win. When women and children win, workers win. We must all come together. We must come up together.

I have a message for our youth. I challenge them to put hope in their brains and not dope in their veins. I told them that like Jesus, I, too, was born in the slum, and just because you are born in the slum does not mean the slum is born in you, and you can rise above it if your mind is made up. I told them in every slum there are two sides. When I see a broken window, that is the slummy side. Train some youth to become a glazier; that is the sunny side. When I see a missing brick, that is the slummy side. Let that child in the union and become a brick mason and build; that is the sunny side. When I see a missing door, that is the slummy side. Train some youth to become a carpenter; that is the sunny side. And when I see the vulgar words and hieroglyphics of destitution on the walls, that's the slummy side. Train some youth to become a painter, an artist; that is the sunny side.

We leave this place looking for the sunny side because there is a brighter side somewhere. I am more convinced than ever that we can win. We will vault up the rough side of the mountain. We can win. I just want young America to do me one favor. . . .

Exercise the right to dream. You must face reality—that which is; but then dream of the reality that ought to be—that must be. Live beyond the pain of reality with the dream of a bright tomorrow. Use hope and imagination as weapons of survival and progress. Use love to motivate you and obligate you to serve the human family.

Young America, dream. Choose the human race over the nuclear race. Bury the weapons and don't burn the people. Dream—dream of a new value system.

Teachers who teach for life and not just for a living, teach because they can't help it. Dream of lawyers more concerned about justice than a judgeship. Dream of doctors more concerned about public health than personal wealth. Dream of preachers and priests who will prophesy and not just profiteer. Preach and dream! Our time has come. Our time has come.

Suffering breeds character, character breeds faith, and faith will not disappoint. Our time has come. Our faith, hopes and dreams will prevail. Our time has come. Weeping has endured for night, but now joy cometh in the morning.

Our time has come. No grave can hold our body down. Our time has come. No lie can live forever. Our time has come. We must leave the racial battleground and find the economic common ground and moral higher ground. America, our time has come.

We come from disgrace to Amazing Grace. Our time has come. Give me your tired, give me your poor, your huddled masses who yearn to breathe free, and come November there will be a change because our time has come.

Thank you and God bless you.

10. Interview with Unita Blackwell

In 1984 Unita Blackwell, mayor of Mayersville, Mississippi, spoke before the Democratic National Convention, the same body that had refused to seat her and fellow members of the Mississippi Freedom Democratic Party twenty years earlier. In this excerpt from a 1989 interview by the Eyes on the Prize production team she discusses how she felt on that occasion.

INTERVIEWER: It's 1984 and you're standing up at the podium at the Democratic National Convention. Having been an MFDP delegate before, fighting all these people before, how did you feel?

UNITA BLACKWELL: In 1964, I went to Atlantic City, New Jersey, challenging the regular Democratic party, and we couldn't get in. It was a long process there of trying to get people to know that we had been denied the democratic process within our state. By 19 and 84 I was asked to speak in the national Democratic convention in San Francisco. I felt, I don't know what I'm going to do, or what I'm going to say, and I tried not to get emotional about it, but that was a feeling that it was worth all of it that we had been through—that we made it thusly far.

I can remember a woman told me one time when I was running for justice of the peace, and . . . she said, "Well, the reason I won't vote for you is because they going to kill you." The whites had told her that they were going to kill me and she thought she was saving my life.

And when I stood on that podium twenty years later, that I was still living, that feeling that I was standing there for this woman, to understand that she had a right to register to vote for whomever she wanted to, and that we as a people was going to live. Jesse Jackson spoke before me—prime time of course—but on several stations in our area, people did see me late at night. And some of them that know me know that . . . I felt tears because Fannie Lou Hamer should have been standing there, she was standing there in us, in me, in Jesse, in all of us, because in 1964 she testified—Chaney, Schwerner, Goodman died in my state, Mississippi, for the right for me to stand there at the podium. That's what I felt, that I was standing there for all who had died, all who will live, for all the generations to come.

11. "Platform Presentation by Mayor Henry G. Cisneros"

Democratic National Convention
San Francisco, July 17, 1984

This is an excerpt from a speech by Henry Cisneros, mayor of San Antonio, Texas, delivered on the same evening as Jesse Jackson's address and Unita Blackwell's platform presentation.

My task this evening is to speak about justice. But it would be impossible to talk about justice without saying a word about what we have heard tonight and over the last six months from the Reverend Dr. Jesse Jackson. As a Hispanic American who has seen my city change for the better because of the Voting Rights Act, and who has seen children's futures brightened because of our national commitment to equal opportunity, I say sincerely to the Black leaders and the Black community of our Nation, thank you, thank you, thank you for the sacrifices and the leadership that have opened up our country for all the rest of us.

Dr. King used to say that all America would be better because of what he was trying to do. Today, we know that countless thousands of women, Hispanics, Asian Americans, disabled persons, Native Americans and working people . . . are better off because there was a civil rights movement, because the Black community set the course for 20 years of change and because Jesse Jackson ran for the Presidency of the United States in 1984.

Political change is always difficult to make, but it is made by those who are willing to push at the margins, step out into that territory where no one has been before. It is boggy, it is murky, it is swampy, it is not clear what is out there but those who are willing to take the step into that swampy territory often find that the ground is very solid indeed, and generally it is most solid when the ground has been based on solid truths—on simple, clear, understandable truths.

One of those truths is the idea of justice in our system, fairness in our lives. When I first became the Mayor of San Antonio in 1981, I remember a man about 80 years old who stopped me on the street one day. He had all the signs on his face of weathered wisdom, a gentleman who had worked hard, and he said to me, "Mr. Cisneros, we have had a troubled time. It has been difficult. We have suffered badly. But please, we are not asking for revenge, or hostility, or anger. Just do a good job, and be fair."

People understand fairness. People also understand unfairness, and they know which political Party in this country is more likely to be fair to average folks. It is the Democratic Party. . . .

12. Address to the National College and University Student Conference
Shen Tong

One of the highlights of the National College and University Student Conference, held during King Week 1990 and sponsored by the Martin Luther King, Jr., Center for Nonviolent Social Change, was this January 13 speech by Shen Tong, one of the student leaders of the prodemocracy movement in China. He escaped from China one week after the events in Tiananmen Square that electrified the world in 1989. At the time of this address, he was a student at Brandeis University and chairperson of the Democracy for China Fund. Shen spoke from the pulpit of the Ebenezer Baptist Church.

It is such a great honor to be speaking with you here today. I cannot begin to find the words which express how moved I am to be here surrounded by an atmosphere of Dr. King and his nonviolent teachings. And when I sat there I really feel you, you are the same age . . . as my friends who are still in China. And I do want to do my speech, you know, without any paper, just like what I did in China, but because of my poor English I should write down and read it.

To fight without fighting, that is the razor's edge of nonviolence.

This is what I believe happened in the American civil rights movement. I am here to learn as well as to inform, so you must teach me. But I know that this definitely happened during the spring of 1989 in Beijing's Tiananmen Square.

My first encounter with the concept of nonviolence was in high school when I read about Martin Luther King and Mahatma Gandhi. At the time this method of nonviolence seemed, to my superficial understanding, extremely logical and beautiful. Here was a method which would clearly win in the end, no matter how long the struggle may last. Although the process may take longer, you get the true result—a real and lasting change—not a fake result.

At the time, Dr. King's ideas seemed very idealistic to me from my simple understanding of his principles. Just like the sense of nonviolence which Albert Einstein gave to me, which Gandhi gave to me.

But that was the first step in my life, and that was the first step in the lives of many young Chinese seeking some beautiful way for China. We were exposed to the principles of nonviolence and it gave us inspiration. It was something very pure, very idealistic in our minds.

There is one thing you must know, however, to understand China's nonviolent movement and the principle of nonviolence within the Chinese individual: China has suffered through more than four thousand years of violence and revolution. The Chinese people have suffered oppression and tyranny for over four thousand years. One dynasty after another was established and then violently destroyed. And always the people suffered. The most recent dynasty, with its most recent set of emperors, is the Communist Party. I say this without bitterness or ill will. It is a statement of fact. The Communist Party leaders have followed in the footsteps of all other violent, oppressive dynasties in China. And soon they too will fall.

This is where we took the second step towards nonviolence as we moved closer to the spring demonstrations. In the universities, the student organizations and salons studied and discussed the future of China—the culture, history, and psychology of the Chinese people. And we realized quite clearly that China cannot suffer any more. China cannot possibly live through any more violent revolutions or any more "national salvation." This myth of "national salvation" plays into the circle of dynasty after dynasty. Those who carried out the revolt knew only what they wanted to destroy, not what they wanted to achieve or build up. "Destroy the empire," they said, "and we will be saved." But saved from what? To what goal? The end result is violence and tyranny again, perhaps more terrible than the tyranny which was destroyed. Just look at Mao and the so-called Cultural Revolution, a grand name for the national salvation which jailed, persecuted, and terrorized a generation.

The "universal truth" for Chinese people is that government comes from a barrel of a gun.

In the light of this Chinese reality, we had to find a good way for China, a good way to achieve true change. First of all, we came to the conclusion that individualism—the self-awareness which recognizes the value of every human life—this individualism was the only way for the Chinese to break out of the dynastic cycle. And I feel that these two are the same thing—nonviolence and individualism.

But this has also confused me. I'm still unclear. How can this nonviolence and this individualism come to some reality, to some practical skill or method in social revolution? It is still a question for the Chinese. Perhaps you can help me to understand this. So many nonviolent struggles succeed, like the civil rights movement and Eastern Europe. But the question still remains for the Chinese youth—How? It is a time for us to really learn and practice the principle, to learn from the examples of struggles like yours.

But personal learning, learning through experience, came to us through our third nonviolent step, the actual movement itself.

We knew that the one thing necessary to achieve real democracy and human rights in China was peace. China could suffer no more violence. Peaceful revolution was the only answer.

Early on, we leaders were approached by several high-ranking military generals. They stated that they would support us and stand with us against the other part of the army. We knew this would lead to civil war. We knew that. So we refused to even meet with them.

We did not want to give the government any excuse to crack down on the demonstrations. So we tried to prevent anything from confusing our principles or our goals. We prevented not only violence, but even people saying some bad slogans against the Communist Party. We tried to prevent this to keep our goals and principles very clear. Even if people wanted to support us and join us we said, "OK, you can stand beside us and support us and cheer and protect us, but you cannot join our march." We wanted to be sure that the people participating were those dedicated to our goals and nonviolent principle[s] with full understanding. And those people were primarily the students from Beijing.

And the more strict we were in this path the more support we received from the people, until, automatically, almost four million people supported us. And they began to have their own demonstrations—the workers, the intellectuals, the journalists, even the peasants, held their own demonstrations. It was beautiful and moving.

Also, we were dedicated to making this demonstration absolutely peaceful. We controlled the traffic, policed the Square and surrounding areas to be sure no violence or crime would happen. Actually, during those months, the crime rate in Beijing dropped tremendously because thieves declared something of a strike to support our movement. They didn't want to give the government any excuse to crack down either.

I would also like to talk about the reasons why our movement failed. There are many reasons. The primary one is that sight of our goals was lost. Our original plan was to return to the campuses, regroup, and continue our movement through the broadcasting stations, the newspapers, and the tremendous support we had gained from the people. But the movement got out of control. So-called conservative leaders, like me, lost power and so-called radical leaders gained it. Rather than moving to achieve something positive, the students started to merely react. If the government did nothing, the students remained in the Square doing nothing. If the government made some statement or did something the students proposed another hunger strike. Some students even proposed to immolate themselves in protest for no constructive reason. We prevented this.

But the new leadership chose reaction over creation and so lost sight of why they were there. Oddly enough, when this new leadership was voted into power, the Beijing students had been joined by many students from other cities. These students had not been "educated" in our goals and principles. And so more than seventy percent of those supporting the new leadership were from outside Beijing. And most of them left a few days after the vote.

Nevertheless, after all these experiences, we knew there was no way to use violence in this revolution. No radicalism ever took the students to that stage. And not only the students, but the people themselves realized that nonviolence was the most important skill for social change.

At the time, quite honestly, I did not see clearly how important this nonviolent principle was to the future of China. Only after I escaped and had time to reflect could I see that nonviolence is the only way for the future, for the real Chinese beautiful future. And one thing I truly believe now after all of these experiences is that beautiful goals can only be reached through pure and beautiful means. This is my lesson from Tiananmen Square.

And I still see in my heart all of the beautiful and heartbreaking examples of nonviolence displayed by the students. In the early part of June, when the martial law soldiers began to send their small groups into downtown, they [left] their weapons and some [of] their trucks and some soldiers on purpose in downtown streets. But the students, the students collect all of the weapons on the street and the weapons people give us to . . . and collect it and give it back to the authorities.

And during the small conflict before the massacre the students tried to persuade the citizens to hold back, to be peaceful. They shouted at the crowd, "Stop throwing stones, do not hurt the truck, do not hurt the soldiers."

And even during the night of the massacre, our students, the marshals, they tried to prevent people from hurting, from even killing the soldiers who shoot into the crowd, and protect the wounded soldiers and send them to the ambulance, send them to the hospital.

And at that time I was in the Chang An Avenue, one mile west of the Tiananmen Square, in the most brutal killing field, and now the people in Beijing they call that part of Chang An Avenue the Blood Alley. And, at that time me and the other students, we tried to organize a line to prevent Beijing's people to throw stones, bottles into the trucks rushing through the avenue, Chang An Avenue. I felt at that time really angry because the people lost— out of control, they lost their ideas, their original principle of nonviolence. They are too angry, they lost their brothers, lost their friends, lost their neighbors to shooting without any reason, and dead. So I understand they are angry, but the more they fight back the more they got hunted.

So at the end me and other students went to the middle of the road and talked with the soldiers in the trucks and said, "Do you know where you are? You are in the Chang An Avenue. This means 'Avenue for Peace Forever.' Even in 1949, the year the so-called People's Republic of China [was] founded, there's no fight, no fire in the downtown Beijing. And our movement is peaceful. You're the army of the people, so don't shoot us." But at that time the officer of that truck hold his pistol [pause] and two people beside me hold me back immediately but another student [pause], she's only nineteen years old [pause], stand beside me and keep talking with one soldier who had seemed moved by her. But the officer shoot on, on her face [pause] and she died immediately.

And the most moving picture I have in my mind is that one of my schoolmates he got a rifle [pause] that rifle some person got from another area, not from Tiananmen Square, and send it to the Square, give the rifle to the student. But he didn't want to use it, he just hold it and want to send it back to the soldiers. And he went to the first group of soldiers [pause] he held it in his hand and, above his head, but the soldiers didn't listen to him. They hold billy club, begin to beat him. But my schoolmate, he kneeled on the ground, still holding the gun above his head till the death.

[Long pause]

All this memory shows me that once you practice nonviolence it becomes rooted in your heart.

I do not fully understand the theory of this nonviolent principle. But I feel I know its spirit. I know that it is the only way for China and the only way for the world, if we are to survive. Our various communities struggle to achieve justice and equality, freedom and human rights. We must join our hands and stand as one. As Dr.

King once said, "Injustice anywhere is a threat to justice everywhere. Whatever affects one directly affects all indirectly."

We must learn from each other. All our communities must learn peace from each other. And there is much, so much, I must learn from you and from Dr. King. Please teach me. Please help China and the Chinese people find that crystal way which will lead to the crystal goal. And together, as one movement for human rights and peace worldwide, we will be able to look at the tyrants and oppressors of history and say to them, in Dr. King's words, "We have matched your capacity to inflict suffering with our capacity to endure suffering. We have matched your physical force with soul force. We are free." Thank you.

13. Address by Nelson Mandela

When African National Congress leader Nelson Mandela toured the United States in June 1990, three months after his release from prison, one of his stops was Atlanta, Georgia. This is the address he gave at a mass rally held at the Georgia Institute of Technology on the evening of June 27, preceded by the introduction by Coretta Scott King.

INTRODUCTION BY CORETTA SCOTT KING:

My friends thank you, thank you so much for that very warm welcome to Mr. Mandela and Mrs. Winnie Mandela. On behalf of the host committee I thank all of you for coming out tonight [to] this tribute to Mr. Mandela and the ANC. The man we are honoring tonight provides us with a luminous example of African manhood and dignity. [In] the African diaspora, the mere mention of his name awakens a glowing sense of pride, but Nelson Mandela is not only a great leader of the struggle against apartheid; everywhere he has gone he has lifted up the hopes of the oppressed people of all races in their struggles for justice and human dignity. A man of Nelson Mandela's background and brilliant intellect could have chosen a life of quiet comfort and prestige as an exile in another country, but like Martin Luther King, Jr., Nelson Mandela heard a different drummer and he chose instead a life of personal sacrifice for the freedom of his people and his nation. When the apartheid regime sent Nelson Mandela to prison for life back in 1962, they thought they had silenced a powerful voice for freedom. But how wrong they were. No chains, no iron bars could still the revolutionary spirit of Nelson Mandela and his courageous colleagues in the African National Congress. When he was sentenced to life imprisonment he concluded his speech to the Court with a soul-stirring vision that embodied the hopes of all Africans yearning for freedom and self-determination. And he said, "During my lifetime, I have cherished the ideal of a democratic and free society in which all persons live together in harmony and with equal opportunities. It is an ideal which I hope to live for and to achieve but if need be it is an ideal for which I am prepared to die." Mr. Mandela became a living legend during the 27 years of unearned suffering in prison in which he was separated from his colleagues in the struggle, from his children and beloved wife, Winnie, who has so courageously carried on in the struggle in the face of relentless adversity. But when he emerged from twenty-seven years of prison last February, Nelson Mandela captured the imagination of the world with his unyielding pride, his remarkable lack of bitterness, and most of all his uncompromising principles and vigorous commitment to the struggle against apartheid. He has challenged us to maintain strong sanctions against the racist apartheid government and, brothers and sisters, this we must do until a nonracial democracy based on one person, one vote, is firmly established in South Africa. With courage, incorruptible integrity, and unshakable dedication to the liberation of South Africa, Nelson Mandela has set the highest standard of leadership for freedom-loving people everywhere. Brothers and sisters, it is my great honor to present to you a man who provides a clear voice and a vision of the new South Africa to come. A man whose life and work burns as bright as a bright beacon of hope for the disadvantaged and downtrodden of every nation. Now, will you please welcome, with your warmest welcome, one of the greatest leaders of this twentieth century, Mr. Nelson Mandela, deputy president of the ANC! . . .

NELSON MANDELA:

Mrs. Coretta Scott King, Dr. John Crecini, Dr. Norman Johnson, Mayor Maynard Jackson, Mr. Andrew Young, Dr. Lowery, distinguished guests, sisters and brothers, ladies and gentlemen, I am happy to bring you warm and fraternal greetings from the ANC, the mass democratic movement, and the fighting people of South Africa. In particular, I bring you the very best wishes of our president, Comrade Oliver Tambo. We cannot forget that in 1982 Mayor Maynard Jackson received an ANC delegation led by Comrade Tambo. Since then Mayor Jackson has supported the ANC and our cause. On behalf of our president and myself I thank him for his unwavering support and solidarity.

I am doubly happy to be in Atlanta. Atlanta which is the hometown of Dr. Martin Luther King, Jr. And the scene of many civil rights battles. We are also conscious of the fact that in the southern part of this country you have experienced the degradation and inhumanity of slavery and racial discrimination as well as the lynchings and brutal intimidation from those men in white robes. We continue to be inspired by the knowledge that in the face of your own awesome difficulties you are in the forefront of the anti-apartheid movement in this country. Your principled stand demonstrates clearly to us that we are in the midst of fellow freedom fighters, that here we have powerful fighters against racism wherever and whenever it rears its evil head.

The extraordinary reception accorded to us by the people of New York, Boston, Washington, and Atlanta fills us with joy and gives us added strength for the coming battles. I am honored by your presence in the city that gave the world a Dr. Martin Luther King, a giant among giants. Dr. King lit up the firmament of struggle against racism, injustice, poverty, and war. In our prison cells, we felt a kinship and affinity with him and were inspired by his indomitable fighting spirit. Even now, twenty-seven years later, I am deeply moved by his outstanding speech at the mammoth march in Washington in 1963. With passion, sincerity, and brilliant eloquence he declared, I quote, "I have a dream that one day on the red hills of Georgia the sons of former slaves and the sons of former slave owners will be able to sit down together at the table of brotherhood. I have a dream that one day even the state of Mississippi, a state sweltering with the heat of injustice, sweltering with the heat of oppression, will be transformed into an oasis of freedom and justice," unquote. As the fervor and applause of the crowd reached a crescendo, Dr. King exclaimed, quote, "Let freedom ring," unquote. Let us all exclaim, Let freedom ring in South Africa. Let freedom ring wherever the people's human rights are trampled upon, let freedom ring.

Dr. King's dreams are now becoming the stuff of reality. At the time he began his anti-racist civil rights crusade there were only 300 elected black officials. Today it fills me with pride to know that there are nearly 6,000 black elected officials in this country. His dreams are suddenly going to see the light of day in our country as well. Dr. King also has the distinction of being the first black American to put the issue of apartheid racism into the middle of the American political agenda. Dr. King rightly deserved the Nobel Peace Prize. We are of course proud that two of our sons, Chief Albert Luthuli and Archbishop Desmond Tutu, were similarly honored. Chief Luthuli was a patient, humble, kind, warm, and compassionate person. He was a brilliant thinker and political strategist. Under his leadership the ANC emerged as a powerful, united, and disciplined mass organization. Both these great freedom fighters were men of honor and noble dignity. Of them we can say the man died but his memory lives. The man died but his fighting spirit imbues us all. The man died but his ideas and ideals live. Allow me to express our best wishes to Mrs. Coretta Scott King.

Brothers and sisters, as you know, apartheid South Africa is skilled in imparity. The unrelenting racist tyranny and the destructive fury of war unleashed on peoples of our region has led to the death of hundreds of thousands of people and the impoverishment of millions. But our people did not flinch from doing their duty. Prisons, torture, and even death could not and never will cow us into submission. We will never acquiesce in our own oppression. We will never surrender. We will pursue the struggle until we have transformed South Africa into a united, nonracial, nonsexist democratic country.

Our people who have shed the rivers of blood need democracy; all our people, black and white, need democracy. We are engaged in a life-and-death struggle to bring into being a future in which all shall, without regard to race, color, creed or sex have the right to vote and to be voted into all elected organs of the state.

Sisters and brothers, we are on the brink of major changes in South Africa. Victory is in sight. But before we reach that promised land we still have to travel a torturous road. Apartheid is still in place. Apartheid continues to imprison, brutalize, maim, and kill our people. Apartheid continues to destroy the future of our children. Apartheid remains a crime against humanity. In this context we say that sanctions must be maintained. We appeal to you, keep the pressure on apartheid. Keep the pressure on apartheid.

I am happy to report that we had warm, friendly, and fruitful meetings with President Bush and Secretary of State Mr. Baker. It was a meeting of minds on the most important issues determining the future of our country. It gives us great confidence to know that in your country there is developing a national anti-apartheid consensus. From the streets of New York, the institutions of learning in Boston, the churches of Atlanta, and the corridors of power in Washington, the message is clear and very unequivocal. Apartheid must go. It must go now!

This consensus was reached due to the hard and unceasing work of thousands of people, black and white. It is truly an anti-apartheid rainbow coalition. To all of you we say thank you. To all of you we say, we respect you, we admire you, and above all we love you. Thank you.

ABOUT THE
GENERAL EDITORS

CLAYBORNE CARSON is professor of history at Stanford University. He was active in the civil rights movement and has written extensively about modern black protest movements. His first book, *In Struggle: SNCC and the Black Awakening of the 1960s* (1981), won the Frederick Jackson Turner Prize of the Organization of American Historians. Carson is director of the Martin Luther King, Jr., Papers Project, which will edit and publish twelve volumes of King's letters, speeches, and other writings.

DAVID J. GARROW is professor of political science at City College of New York and the City University Graduate School. He is the author of *Bearing the Cross: Martin Luther King, Jr., and the Southern Christian Leadership Conference* (1986), for which he won the Pulitzer Prize and the Robert F. Kennedy Award in 1987; *The FBI and Martin Luther King, Jr.* (1981); and *Protest at Selma: Martin Luther King, Jr., and the Voting Rights Act of 1965* (1978). He is the editor of *The Montgomery Bus Boycott and the Women Who Started It: The Memoir of Jo Ann Gibson Robinson* (1987).

GERALD GILL is associate professor of history at Tufts University in Medford, Massachusetts. He is the author of *Meanness Mania: The Changed Mood* (1980) and co-author of *The Case for Affirmative Action* *for Blacks in Higher Education* (1978). He has been a fellow of the W. E. B. Du Bois Institute for Afro-American Research at Harvard University.

VINCENT HARDING is professor of religion and social transformation at the Iliff School of Theology in Denver, Colorado. Long an active participant in the black struggle for freedom, justice, and transformation, he has served as chairman of the department of history and sociology at Spelman College, as director of the Martin Luther King Memorial Center, and as director of the Institute of the Black World. His books include *Hope and History: Why We Must Share the Story of the Movement* (1990), *There Is a River: The Black Freedom Struggle in the United States* (1981), and *The Other American Revolution* (1980).

DARLENE CLARK HINE is John A. Hannah professor of American history at Michigan State University. She is the author of *Black Women in White: Racial Conflict and Cooperation in the Nursing Profession, 1890–1950* (1989), *When the Truth Is Told: A History of Black Women's Culture and Community in Indiana* (1981), and *Black Victory: The Rise and Fall of the White Primary in Texas* (1979), and the editor of *Black Women in United States History: From Colonial Times to the Present* (a sixteen-volume series published in 1990) and *The State of Afro-American History: Past, Present, and Future* (1986).

EYES ON THE PRIZE:
The Film and Publishing Project

The *Eyes on the Prize Civil Rights Reader* is part of a larger project encompassing the six-part series *Eyes on the Prize: America's Civil Rights Years, 1954 to 1965* and the eight-part continuation of the series, *Eyes on the Prize: America at the Racial Crossroads, 1965–1985;* an archive of oral history interviews and research material (administered by the Civil Rights Project, Inc.); and numerous publications. The entire project is the creation of Blackside, Inc., a Boston-based film and video production company whose president and executive producer is Henry Hampton.

Following are some of the *Eyes on the Prize*–related publications produced by The Publishing Project at Blackside, Inc.:

Eyes on the Prize: America's Civil Rights Years, 1954–1965, by Juan Williams and the **Eyes on the Prize** Production Team. New York: Viking Penguin, 1987; Penguin Books, 1988. Illustrated. 306 pages. $10.95 pbk. (The companion volume to Series I.)

Eyes on the Prize: America's Civil Rights Years, 1954–1965—A Sourcebook, edited by Steven Cohen. Boston: Blackside, Inc., 1987. 68 pages. $3.95 pbk. (An anthology of readings for secondary school use.)

Hope and History: Why We Must Share the Story of the Movement, by Vincent Harding. Maryknoll, N.Y.: Orbis Books, 1990. 250 pages. $9.95 pbk. (Inspiring essays on using *Eyes on the Prize*—for educators from all walks of life.)

Voices of Freedom: An Oral History of the Civil Rights Movement from the 1950s through the 1980s, by Henry Hampton and Steve Fayer with Sarah Flynn. New York: Bantam, 1990. 692 pages. $25.95; $15.95 pbk. (An oral history based on the one thousand interviews conducted for *Eyes on the Prize*, Series I and II.)

Eyes on the Prize: America's Civil Rights Years, 1954–1965 (Williams) and *Voices of Freedom* are available at bookstores everywhere. *Hope and History* is available at selected bookstores or from Orbis Books, Maryknoll, New York 10545 (phone: 800-258-5838). *Eyes on the Prize—A Sourcebook* (Cohen) is available from the Civil Rights Project, Inc., 486 Shawmut Avenue, Boston, Mass. 02118 (phone: 617-536-6900).

The entire fourteen-part *Eyes on the Prize* series is available for institutional use through PBS Video, 1320 Braddock Place, Alexandria, Virginia, 22314 (phone: 800-344-3337).

For information on the college telecourse, of which this book is the text, contact PBS Adult Learning Service, 1320 Braddock Place, Alexandria, Virginia 22314 (1-800-ALS-ALS8).

NOTES ON SOURCES

PROLOGUE: WE THE PEOPLE: The Long Journey Toward a More Perfect Union

[p. 25] "Let America Be America Again," by Langston Hughes. Copyright 1938 by Langston Hughes. Copyright renewed 1965 by Langston Hughes. Used by permission of Harold Ober Associates Incorporated.

CHAPTER ONE. AWAKENINGS (1954–1956)

1. "Articles on the Emmett Till Case." From the *Chicago Defender* (October 1, 1955). Used by permission of The *Chicago Defender*.

2. "Coming of Age in Mississippi." From *Coming of Age in Mississippi*, by Anne Moody (New York: Doubleday, 1968). Copyright © 1968 by Anne Moody. Used by permission of Doubleday, a division of Bantam Doubleday Dell Publishing Group, Inc.

3. "A Letter from the Women's Political Council to the Mayor of Montgomery, Alabama." From Jo Ann Gibson Robinson's *The Montgomery Bus Boycott and the Women Who Started It: The Memoir of Jo Ann Gibson Robinson*, edited, with a foreword, by David J. Garrow (Knoxville: University of Tennessee Press, 1987). Copyright © 1987 by The University of Tennessee Press. Used by permission of The University of Tennessee Press.

4. "Interview with Rosa Parks." From *My Soul Is Rested: Movement Days in the Deep South Remembered*, by Howell Raines (New York:

G. P. Putnam's Sons, 1977). Copyright © 1977 by Howell Raines. Used by permission of the Putnam Publishing Group.

5. "The Movement Gathers Momentum." From *Stride Toward Freedom: The Montgomery Story*, by Martin Luther King, Jr. (New York: Harper & Brothers, 1958). Copyright © 1958 by Martin Luther King, Jr., renewed 1986 by Coretta Scott King, Dexter King, Martin Luther King III, Yolanda King, and Bernice King. Used by permission of HarperCollins Publishers.

6. "Speech by Martin Luther King, Jr., at Holt Street Baptist Church," December 5, 1955. Copyright 1955, 1968 by Martin Luther King, Jr., and the Estate of Martin Luther King, Jr. Used by permission of Joan Daves for the King Estate.

7. "At Holt Street Baptist Church." From "At Holt Street Baptist Church, Deeply Stirred Throng of Colored Citizens Protests Bus Segregation," by Joe Azbell in *The Advertiser*, December 7, 1955. Used by permission of *The Advertiser*, Montgomery, Alabama.

8. "Resolution of the Citizens' Mass Meeting, December 5, 1955." From a copy of the document reprinted in the *Birmingham World*, December 13, 1955.

9. "The Violence of Desperate Men." From *Stride Toward Freedom: The Montgomery Story*, by Martin Luther King, Jr. (New York: Harper & Brothers, 1958). Copyright © 1958 by Martin Luther King, Jr., renewed 1986 by Coretta Scott King, Dexter King, Martin Luther King III, Yolanda King, and Bernice King. Used by permission of HarperCollins Publishers.

10. "Desegregation at Last." From *Stride Toward Freedom: The Montgomery Story*, by Martin Luther King, Jr., (New York: Harper & Brothers, 1958). Copyright © 1958 by Martin Luther King, Jr., renewed 1986 by Coretta Scott King, Dexter King, Martin Luther King III, Yolanda King, and Bernice King. Used by permission of HarperCollins Publishers.

CHAPTER TWO. FIGHTING BACK (1957–1962)
1. "*Brown et al.* v. *Board of Education of Topeka et al.*" Decided by the U.S. Supreme Court, May 17, 1954. 347 U.S. 483 (1954).

2. "How Children Learn About Race." From *Prejudice and Your Child*, by Kenneth B. Clark (Boston: Beacon Press, 1955). Copyright 1955 by Beacon Press, Inc., 1963 by Beacon Press. Used by permission of Beacon Press.

3. "The Atlanta Declaration." From *The Crisis* (the official organ of

the NAACP), Vol. 61 (June–July 1954). Used by permission of the NAACP.

4. "Black Monday: Segregation or Amalgamation . . . America Has Its Choice." From *Black Monday: Segregation or Amalgamation . . . America Has Its Choice*, by Tom P. Brady (Winona, Miss.: Association of Citizens' Councils, 1955).

5. *"Brown* v. *Board of Education*—The Implementation Decision." Decided by the U.S. Supreme Court May 31, 1955. 349 U.S. 294 (1955).

6. "The Long Shadow of Little Rock." From *The Long Shadow of Little Rock*, by Daisy Bates (New York: David McKay, 1962). Copyright 1962, 1986 by Daisy Bates. All rights reserved. Used by permission of Daisy Bates.

7. "A Roundtable Discussion." From "Transcript of Mrs. Jorunn Ricketts' Conversation," *The New York Times*, October 14, 1957. Copyright © 1957 by The New York Times Company. Used by permission.

CHAPTER THREE. AIN'T SCARED OF YOUR JAILS (1960–1961)

1. "Is Violence Necessary to Combat Injustice? For the Positive: Williams Says 'We Must Fight Back' " by Robert F. Williams. From *Liberation* magazine (September 1959). Used by permission of Robert F. Williams.

2. "The Social Organization of Nonviolence." From "The Social Organization of Nonviolence," by Martin Luther King, Jr., in *Liberation* magazine (October 1959). Copyright 1959 by Martin Luther King, Jr. Used by permission of Joan Daves for the King Estate.

3. "Interview with Franklin McCain." From *My Soul Is Rested: Movement Days in the Deep South Remembered*, by Howell Raines (New York: G. P. Putnam's Sons, 1977). Copyright © 1977 by Howell Raines. Used by permission of The Putnam Publishing Group.

4. "An Appeal for Human Rights." From "An Appeal for Human Rights," by the Atlanta Committee on Appeal for Human Rights, a paid advertisement in the *Atlanta Constitution*, March 9, 1960.

5. "Student Nonviolent Coordinating Committee Statement of Purpose." Courtesy of Clayborne Carson.

6. "Bigger than a Hamburger," by Ella J. Baker. From *The Southern Patriot*, a publication of the Southern Conference Educational Fund (June 1960). Used by permission of Anne Braden.

7. "A Conference on the Sit-Ins." From "A Conference on the Sit-Ins," by Ted Dienstfrey in *Commentary* (June 29, 1960). Used by permission of Ted Dienstfrey and *Commentary*. All rights reserved.

8. "In Pursuit of Freedom." From "In Pursuit of Freedom," by William Mahoney in *Liberation* (September 1961).

9. "Interview with Robert Zellner." From a September 19, 1978, interview with Robert Zellner by Clayborne Carson. Copyright 1978 by Robert Zellner. Used by permission of Robert Zellner.

10. "Eve of Nonviolent Revolution?" From "Eve of Nonviolent Revolution?" by James M. Lawson, Jr., in *The Southern Patriot,* a publication of the Southern Conference Educational Fund (November 1961). Used by permission of Anne Braden.

CHAPTER FOUR. NO EASY WALK (1961–1963)

1. "Organizing in Albany, Georgia." From an untitled work by Charles Sherrod. Used by permission of Charles Sherrod.

2. "Letter from the Albany Movement to the Albany City Commission," a public document prepared by the Albany Movement.

3. "Interview with Bernice Reagon." From a 1986 interview by the *Eyes on the Prize* production team. The *Eyes on the Prize* archives are administered by the Civil Rights Project, Inc., 486 Shawmut Avenue, Boston, Mass. 02118.

4. "Letter from Albany Merchant Leonard Gilberg to Albany Police Chief Laurie Pritchett, July 23, 1962." Used by permission of Leonard Gilberg.

5. "Birmingham: People in Motion." From "Birmingham: People in Motion" (Birmingham: Alabama Christian Movement for Human Rights in cooperation with the Southern Conference Educational Fund, 1966).

6. "Wiretap Transcript of Phone Conversation between Martin Luther King, Jr., and Coretta Scott King, April 5, 1963." Courtesy of the Martin Luther King, Jr., Center for Nonviolent Social Change, Atlanta, Georgia. Used by permission of Joan Daves for the King Estate.

7. "Letter from Birmingham City Jail." Copyright 1963, 1964 by Martin Luther King, Jr. Used by permission of Joan Daves for the King Estate.

8. "The Birmingham Truce Agreement, May 10, 1963." From the Burke Marshall Papers, John F. Kennedy Library, Boston, Massachusetts.

9. "President John F. Kennedy's Nationally Televised Speech, June 11, 1963." From the John F. Kennedy Library, Boston, Massachusetts.

10. "Original Text of Speech to Be Delivered at the Lincoln Memorial," August 28, 1963, by John Lewis, distributed as a leaflet at the March on Washington.

CHAPTER FIVE. MISSISSIPPI: IS THIS AMERICA? (1962–1964)

1. "Mississippi: 1961–1962." From "Mississippi 1961–1962," by Robert Moses in *Liberation* magazine (January 1970). Used by permission of Robert Moses.

2. "To Praise Our Bridges." From *To Praise Our Bridges: An Autobiography of Mrs. Fanny* [sic] *Lou Hamer* (Jackson, Miss.: KIPCO, 1967). Used by permission of Arybie Rose, Fannie Lou Hamer Living Memorial Charitable Trust Fund, and the Hamer family.

3. "Interim Report of the United States Commission on Civil Rights, April 16, 1963." Washington, D.C.: U.S. Commission on Civil Rights, 1963.

4. "Freedom Summer." From *Freedom Summer,* by Sally Belfrage (New York: Viking Press, 1965; and Charlottesville: University Press of Virginia, 1990). Copyright 1965, 1990 by Sally Belfrage. Used by permission of the University Press of Virginia and Sally Belfrage.

5. "Mississippi at Atlantic City." From "Mississippi at Atlantic City," by Charles M. Sherrod in *Grains of Salt,* Union Theological Seminary, Vol. 18, No. 3 (October 12, 1964). Used by permission of Charles Sherrod.

6. "Student Nonviolent Coordinating Committee Brief Report on Guinea," by James Forman. Courtesy of Clayborne Carson.

7. "The Trip," by John Lewis and Donald Harris. Courtesy of Clayborne Carson.

8. "To Mississippi Youth." From "To Mississippi Youth," by Malcolm X in *Malcolm X Speaks* (New York: Grove Press and Merit Publishers, 1965). Copyright 1965 by Merit Publishers. Used by permission of Pathfinder Press.

9. "From Protest to Politics: The Future of the Civil Rights Movement." From "From Protest to Politics: The Future of the Civil Rights Movement," by Bayard Rustin in *Commentary* 39 (February 1965). Copyright 1965 by Bayard Rustin. Used by permission of Bayard Rustin.

CHAPTER SIX. BRIDGE TO FREEDOM (1965)

1. "Early Attempts at Betterment." From *The Bridge Across Jordan: The Story of the Struggle for Civil Rights in Selma, Alabama,* by Amelia Platts Boynton (New York: Carlton Press, 1979). Copyright 1979 by Amelia P. Boynton Robinson. Used by permission of Amelia P. Boynton Robinson.

2. "Selma, Alabama." From "Selma, Alabama," by Bernard Lafayette, in *Freedom Is a Constant Struggle: Songs of the Freedom Movement,* compiled and edited by Guy and Candie Carawan (New York: Oak

Publications, 1968). Used by permission of Guy and Candie Carawan.

3. "A Letter from a Selma, Alabama, Jail," by Martin Luther King, Jr., originally appeared as a paid advertisement in the *New York Times*, February 5, 1965.

4. "Midnight Plane to Alabama: Journey of Conscience." From "Midnight Plane to Alabama: Journey of Conscience," by George Leonard in *The Nation* (May 10, 1965). Copyright 1965 by The Nation. Used by permission of *The Nation* magazine/The Nation Company, Inc.

5. "SNCC-SCLC Relations." From "The Toilet Revolution: First Day," a chapter in *Sammy Younge, Jr.: The First Black College Student to Die in the Black Liberation Movement*, by James Forman (New York: Grove Press, 1968; and Washington, D.C.: Open Hand Publishing, 1986). Copyright 1968, 1986 by James Forman. Used by permission of James Forman.

6. "Personal Letter from Muriel and Art Lewis to Her Mother, Selma, Alabama, March 19, 1965." Excerpts used by permission of Muriel N. Lewis.

7. "Our God Is Marching On," by Martin Luther King, Jr. From *A Testament of Hope: The Essential Writings of Martin Luther King, Jr.*, edited by James Melvin Washington (San Francisco: Harper & Row, 1986). Copyright © 1986 by Coretta Scott King, Executrix of the Estate of Martin Luther King, Jr. Used by permission of Joan Daves for the King Estate.

INTERLUDE: WE THE PEOPLE: THE STRUGGLE CONTINUES

[p. 242] From *The Other American Revolution*, by Vincent Harding (Los Angeles: UCLA Center for Afro-American Studies, 1980). Copyright 1980 by the Regents of the University of California and the Institute of the Black World. Used by permission.

[p. 243] From "Creation Spell," by Ed Bullins. Used by permission of Helen Merrill, Ltd.

CHAPTER SEVEN. THE TIME HAS COME (1964–1966)

1. "Message to the Grass Roots." From "Message to the Grass Roots," by Malcolm X in *Malcolm X Speaks* (New York: Grove Press and Merit Publishers, 1965). Copyright © 1965 by Betty Shabazz and Pathfinder Press. Used by permission of Pathfinder Press.

2. "Malcolm." From *Homecoming*, by Sonia Sanchez (Detroit: Broadside Press, 1969). Used by permission of Sonia Sanchez.

3. "Black Belt Election: New Day A'Coming." From *Black Power:*

The Politics of Liberation in America, by Stokely Carmichael and Charles V. Hamilton (New York: Vintage Books/Random House, 1967). Copyright © 1967 by Stokely Carmichael and Charles V. Hamilton. Used by permission of Random House, Inc.

4. "Lowndes County Freedom Organization Pamphlet." Courtesy of Robert Mants.

5. "How the Black Panther Party Was Organized." From "How the Black Panther Party Was Organized," by John Hulett in *The Black Panther Party* (New York: Merit Publishers, 1966). Copyright 1966 by John Hulett. Used by permission of John Hulett.

6. "From Black Consciousness to Black Power." From *The River of No Return: The Autobiography of a Black Militant and the Life and Death of SNCC,* by Cleveland Sellers with Robert Terrell (New York: William Morrow, 1973). Used by permission of Cleveland Sellars.

7. "What We Want." From "What We Want," by Stokely Carmichael in *The New York Review of Books* (September 22, 1966). Copyright 1966 NYREV, Inc. Used by permission.

8. "Black Power: A Voice Within." From "Black Power: A Voice Within," by Ruth Turner Perot in *Oberlin Alumni Magazine* LXIII (May 1967). Used by permission of *Oberlin Alumni Magazine.*

CHAPTER EIGHT. TWO SOCIETIES (1965–1968)

1. "A Proposal by the Southern Christian Leadership Conference for the Development of a Nonviolent Action Movement for the Greater Chicago Area." Courtesy of the King Library and Archives, Martin Luther King, Jr., Center for Nonviolent Social Change, Atlanta, Georgia.

2. "Demands Placed on the Door of Chicago City Hall by Martin Luther King, Jr., July 10, 1966." A condensed version from *Autobiography of Black Politics* (Vol. 1), by Dempsey J. Travis (Chicago: Urban Research Press, 1987).

3. "Agreement of the Subcommittee to the Conference on Fair Housing Convened by the Chicago Conference on Religion and Race." From *Confronting the Color Line: The Broken Promise of the Civil Rights Movement in Chicago,* by Alan B. Anderson and George W. Pickering (Athens: University of Georgia Press, 1986).

4. "Interview with Linda Bryant Hall." From a 1989 interview by the *Eyes on the Prize* production team.

5. "Profiles of Disorder . . . Detroit." From *Report of the National Advisory Commission on Civil Disorders* (Washington, D.C.: U.S. Government Printing Office, 1968).

6. "A Man's Life." From *"A Man's Life: An Autobiography*, by Roger Wilkins (New York: Simon and Schuster, 1982). Copyright 1982 by Roger Wilkins. Used by permission of Roger Wilkins.

CHAPTER NINE. POWER! (1966–1968)

1. "Taking Over." From chapter titled "Taking Over" in *Promises of Power: A Political Autobiography*, by Carl B. Stokes (New York: Simon and Schuster, 1973). Copyright 1973 by Carl B. Stokes. Used by permission of Carl B. Stokes.

2. "Interview with Thompson J. 'Mike' Gaines." From a 1988 interview by the *Eyes on the Prize* production team.

3. "Interview with Geraldine Williams." From a 1988 interview by the *Eyes on the Prize* production team.

4. "The Founding of the Black Panther Party" and "Patrolling." From *Revolutionary Suicide*, by Huey P. Newton with the assistance of J. Herman Blake (New York: Harcourt Brace Jovanovich, 1973). Copyright © 1973 by Stronghold Consolidated Productions, Inc. Used by permission of Harcourt Brace Jovanovich, Inc.

5. "Seize the Time." From *Seize the Time: The Story of the Black Panther Party and Huey P. Newton*, by Bobby Seale (New York: Random House, 1968). Copyright © 1968, 1969, 1970 by Bobby Seale. Used by permission of Random House, Inc.

6. "Interview with Dolores Torres." From a 1988 interview by the *Eyes on the Prize* production team.

7. "A JHS 271 Teacher Tells It Like He Sees It," by Charles S. Isaacs. From *The New York Times Magazine* (November 24, 1968). Copyright 1968 by Charles S. Isaacs. Used by permission of Charles S. Isaacs. "Ballad of the Landlord" by Langston Hughes (copyright 1951 by Langston Hughes, copyright renewed 1979 by George Houston Bass) is used by permission of Harold Ober Associates Incorporated.

8. "Interview with Karriema Jordan." From a 1989 interview by the *Eyes on the Prize* production team.

9. "Anti-Semitism?—A Statement by the Teachers of Ocean Hill-Brownsville to the People of New York." An advertisement in *The New York Times* (November 11, 1968) from *Confrontation at Ocean Hill-Brownsville: The New York School Strikes of 1968* edited by Maurice R. Berube and Marilyn Gittell (New York: Frederick A. Praeger, 1969).

CHAPTER TEN. THE PROMISED LAND (1967–1968)

1. "A Time to Break Silence." From "A Time to Break Silence," by Martin Luther King, Jr. Copyright 1967 by Martin Luther King, Jr. Used by permission of Joan Daves for the King Estate.

2. "Conversation with Martin Luther King." From "Conversation with Martin Luther King," in *Conservative Judaism* (published by the Rabbinical Assembly and the Jewish Theological Seminary of America), Vol. XXII, No. 3 (Spring 1968). Copyright 1968 by the Rabbinical Assembly. Used by permission of *Conservative Judaism*.

3. "I See the Promised Land," by Martin Luther King, Jr. From *A Testament of Hope: The Essential Writings of Martin Luther King, Jr.*, edited by James Melvin Washington (San Francisco: Harper & Row, 1986). Copyright 1986 by Coretta Scott King, Executrix of the Estate of Martin Luther King, Jr. Used by permission of Joan Daves for the King Estate.

4. "My Last Letter to Martin," by Ralph David Abernathy. From *And the Walls Came Tumbling Down,* by Ralph David Abernathy (New York: Harper & Row, 1989). Copyright © 1989 by Ralph David Abernathy. Used by permission of HarperCollins Publishers.

5. "On the Case in Resurrection City." From "On the Case in Resurrection City," by Charlayne A. Hunter in *Trans-Action* magazine (October 1968). Copyright © 1968 by Transaction Publishers. Used by permission of Transaction Publishers.

CHAPTER ELEVEN. AIN'T GONNA SHUFFLE NO MORE (1964–1972)

1. " '. . . I'm the Greatest,' a poem by Cassius Clay." From *Life* (February 15, 1963). Used by permission of Muhammad Ali.

2. "The Greatest." From *The Greatest: My Own Story,* by Muhammad Ali with Richard Durham (New York: Random House, 1975). Copyright 1975 by Muhammad Ali, Herbert Muhammad, and Richard Durham. Used by permission of Muhammad Ali.

3. "Muhammad Ali—The Measure of a Man." From *Freedomways* (Spring 1967).

4. "Interview with Paula Giddings." From a 1988 interview by the *Eyes on the Prize* production team.

5. "An Open Letter Sent to Howard President James M. Nabrit." From "The Spear and Shield," a newsletter published by the Howard University Ujamaa, Vol 1, No. 2 (February 1968).

6. "Interview with Tony Gittens." From a 1988 interview by the *Eyes on the Prize* production team.

7. "The Nature and Needs of the Black University," by Gerald

McWorter. From *Negro Digest* 17 (March 1968). Used by permission of Abdul Alkalimat (Gerald McWorter).

8. "It's Nation Time," by Amiri Baraka. From *It's Nation Time: Selected Poetry of Imamu Amiri Baraka* (Chicago: Third World Press, 1970). Copyright © 1970 by LeRoi Jones (Amiri Baraka). Used by permission of Sterling Lord Literistic, Inc.

9. "We Must Pave the Way: An Independent Black Political Thrust," by Richard Hatcher. A speech delivered at the National Black Political Convention, March 11, 1972. Used by permission of Richard Hatcher.

10. "National Black Political Agenda. The Gary Declaration: Black Politics at the Crossroads." Reviewed and ratified May 6, 1972; released to the public May 19, 1972.

CHAPTER TWELVE. A NATION OF LAW? (1968–1971)

1. "Fred Speaks." From *Fred Hampton 20th Commemoration* (Chicago: December 4th Committee, 1989). Copyright 1989 by December 4th Committee. Used by permission of Akua Njere.

2. "Interview with Akua Njere (Deborah Johnson)." From "Interview with Akua Njere (Deborah Johnson), Survivor of December 4, 1969 Chicago Police Raid & Murder of Fred Hampton & Mark Clark," a special supplement to *Burning Spear*, Vol. 17, No. 3 (June 1990). Copyright 1990 by the *Burning Spear* newspaper. Used by permission of the African People's Socialist Party.

3. "Search and Destroy: A Report by the Commission of Inquiry into the Black Panthers and the Police." From *Search and Destroy: A Report by the Commission of Inquiry into the Black Panthers and the Police*, by Roy Wilkins and Ramsey Clark (New York: Metropolitan Applied Research Center, 1973). Copyright © 1973 by the Metropolitan Applied Research Center and the National Association for the Advancement of Colored People. Used by permission of Harper-Collins Publishers.

4. "The FBI's Efforts to Disrupt and Neutralize the Black Panther Party." From *Final Report of the Senate Select Committee to Study Governmental Operations with Respect to Intelligence Activities, Supplementary Detailed Staff Reports on Intelligence Activities and the Rights of Americans,* Book III (Washington, D.C.: U.S. Government Printing Office, 1976).

5. "Angela Davis: An Autobiography." From *Angela Davis: An Autobiography* (New York: Random House, 1974; and New York: International Publishers, 1988). Copyright 1974, 1988 by Angela Davis. Used by permission of Angela Davis.

6. "Letter from George Jackson." From *Soledad Brother: The Prison*

Letters of George Jackson (New York: Bantam Books, 1970). Copyright © 1970 by World Entertainers. Used by permission of Bantam Books, a division of Bantam Doubleday Dell Publishing Group, Inc.

7. "Attica Prisoners' Demands." From *A Time to Die,* by Tom Wicker (New York: Quadrangle, New York Times Book Company, 1975).

8. "Negotiations and Failure." From *A Bill of No Rights: Attica and the American Prison System,* by Herman Badillo and Milton Haynes (New York: Outerbridge & Lazard, 1972). Copyright 1972 by Outerbridge & Lazard, Inc. Used by permission of David Outerbridge.

9. "The Brothers of Attica." From *The Brothers of Attica,* by Richard X. Clark, edited by Leonard Levitt (New York: Links Books, 1973). Copyright 1973 by Richard X. Clark and Leonard Levitt. Used by permission of Richard X. Clark.

CHAPTER THIRTEEN. THE KEYS TO THE KINGDOM (1974–1980)

1. "Statement to the Boston School Committee, June 11, 1963." Used by permission of Ruth Batson.

2. "Death at an Early Age." From *Death at an Early Age,* by Jonathan Kozol (Boston: Houghton Mifflin, 1967; and New York: New American Library, 1985). Copyright © 1967, 1985 by Jonathan Kozol. Used by permission of Jonathan Kozol.

3. *"Tallulah Morgan et al.* v. *James W. Hennigan et al."* Decided by the U.S. District Court, Massachusetts, June 21, 1974. 379 F. Supp. 410 (1974).

4. "Commencement Address at Howard University," by Lyndon B. Johnson, June 4, 1965. From *To Heal and to Build: The Programs of President Lyndon B. Johnson,* edited by James MacGregor Burns (New York: McGraw-Hill Book Company, 1968).

5. "Inaugural Address," by Mayor Maynard Jackson, January 7, 1974. Used by permission of Maynard Jackson.

6. "Can Atlanta Succeed Where America Has Failed? An Exclusive *Atlanta* Magazine Interview with Mayor Maynard Jackson as He Completes His First 500 Days in Office." From *Atlanta* magazine (June 1975). Copyright 1975 by *Atlanta* magazine. Used by permission of *Atlanta* magazine.

7. "Amicus Curiae Brief in *Regents of the University of California* v. *Allan Bakke."* From the amicus curiae brief of the National Medical Association, Inc., The National Bar Association, Inc., and the National Association for Equal Opportunity in Higher Education. Courtesy of J. Clay Smith, Howard University School of Law.

8. *"Regents of the University of California* v. *Allan Bakke."* From the Supreme Court judgment, June 28, 1978. F. Supp 438 U.S. 265 (1978).

9. *"Regents of the University of California* v. *Allan Bakke."* From Justice Marshall's dissent, June 28, 1978. F. Supp 438 U.S. 265 (1978).

10. "Whites Say I Must Be on Easy Street," by Nell Irvin Painter. From *The New York Times* (December 10, 1981). Used by permission of Nell Irvin Painter.

CHAPTER FOURTEEN. BACK TO THE MOVEMENT (1979–MID-1980S)

1. "A Historic Look at Our Neighborhoods." From . . . *without vision the people perish . . .* , by Dorothy Jenkins Fields (Miami: Black Archives, History & Research Foundation, 1982). Copyright 1982 by Dorothy Jenkins Fields. Used by permission of the Black Archives, History & Research Foundation of South Florida, Inc.

2. "Death Watch," by Marvin Dunn. From "Tropic," *The Miami Herald* (August 24, 1980). Copyright 1980 by Marvin Dunn. Used by permission of Marvin Dunn.

3. "Confronting Racial Isolation in Miami." From *Confronting Racial Isolation in Miami* (Washington, D.C.: United States Commission on Civil Rights, June 1982).

4. "Interview with Edward Gardner." From a 1989 interview by the *Eyes on the Prize* production team.

5. "Harold Washington's Announcement of Candidacy for the Democratic Nomination for Mayor of Chicago." From *Harold: The People's Mayor,* by Dempsey J. Travis (Chicago: Urban Research Press, 1989). Used by permission of Ramon Price for the Washington Estate.

6. "Harold Washington: Uniting People for *All* Chicago." Excerpts from a Washington campaign leaflet. Courtesy of Archie Motley, Chicago Historical Society.

7. "Harold Washington's Inaugural Speech." From *Harold: The People's Mayor,* by Dempsey J. Travis (Chicago: Urban Research Press, 1989). Used by permission of Ramon Price for the Washington Estate.

8. "Of Harold Washington," by Gwendolyn Brooks. From *Chicago* magazine (February 1988). Copyright 1988 by Gwendolyn Brooks and *Chicago* magazine. Used by permission of Gwendolyn Brooks.

9. "Address by the Reverend Jesse Jackson." From *Proceedings of the 1984 Democratic National Convention,* published by the Democratic National Committee. Copyright 1984 by the Reverend Jesse Jackson. Used by permission of Jesse Jackson.

10. "Interview with Unita Blackwell." From a 1989 interview by the *Eyes on the Prize* production team.

11. "Platform Presentation by Mayor Henry G. Cisneros." From *Proceedings of the 1984 Democratic National Convention,* published by the

Democratic National Committee. Copyright 1984 by Henry G. Cisneros. Used by permission of Henry G. Cisneros.

12. "Address to the National College and University Student Conference," by Shen Tong. Courtesy of the Martin Luther King, Jr., Center for Nonviolent Social Change, Atlanta, Georgia, and the Democracy for China Fund, Newton, Massachusetts. Copyright 1990 by Shen Tong. Used by permission of Shen Tong.

13. "Address by Nelson Mandela." From an address delivered on June 27, 1990, at the Georgia Institute of Technology. Courtesy of the Martin Luther King, Jr., Center for Nonviolent Social Change, Atlanta, Georgia. Used by permission of the African National Congress and the Mandela Freedom Fund.

INDEX

Abernathy, Juanita, 229
Abernathy, Rev. Ralph David, 206,
    219, 224, 229, 411; friends with
    MLK, 409, 419; letter to MLK
    from, 419–26; and Montgomery
    Improvement Association, 128–
    129; and Resurrection City, 427,
    429, 431, 433, 437
Abramowitz, Dr. Elizabeth, 629
Adams, C. J., and Dallas County Vot-
    ers' League, 208–9
Affirmative action, Lyndon Johnson
    on, 594, 611–13; and effects on
    black women, 652–53. *See also*
    Bakke, Allan; Jackson, Maynard;
    *Regents of the University of Califor-
    nia* v. *Allan Bakke*
Africa, Bandung Unity Conference
    and, 36, 249–50; black revolu-
    tions in, 253, 254, 279; emigra-
    tion of Afro-Americans to
    proposed, 11, 12, 14; European
    domination of, 18, 24, 495; inde-
    pendent aspirations of, 21–23,
    30, 31, 155, 201; SNCC tour of,
    169, 190–200, 246. *See also*
    South Africa

African-American Teachers Associa-
    tion (ATA), in New York City
    public schools, 367, 368
African National Congress (ANC),
    718, 719, 720, 721
African People's Socialist Party, 509
Alabama, "bloody Sunday" (March 7,
    1965) in, 213–14, 216; conflict
    between SNCC and SCLC in,
    217–20; and Democratic party,
    203, 217, 275, 276–77, 284;
    Freedom Riders in, 109; Ku
    Klux Klan in, 274; voting-rights
    struggles in, 163, 204, 205, 206.
    See also Birmingham; Lowndes
    County; Lowndes County Free-
    dom Organizaton; Montgomery;
    Selma; University of Alabama
Alabama Christian Movement for
    Human Rights (ACMHR), 135–
    136, 147–50, 154, 159
Albany City Commission, letter from
    Albany Movement to,
    140–42
Albany Movement (Ga.), boycott of
    white businesses by, 146; letter
    to Albany City Commission

Albany Movement (Ga.) (*cont.*) from, 140–42; organization of, 133, 134–35, 138–39; songs of, 143–45
Alford, Rev. W. F., 48
Algeria, revolution in, 253, 449
Ali, Muhammad (Cassius Clay), 439–441, 443–44; induction refusal of, 440, 444–59
Ali, Noble Drew (Timothy Drew), 17, 27
Alkalimat, Abdul (Gerald McWorter), 470–79, 658
Allen, Ivan, Jr., 621
Alpha, Diallo, and African impressions of U.S. civil rights, 190–92
American Medical Association, and black medical students, 630
Anderson, Blair, 523, 524
Anderson, David, 558
Anderson, Doc, 173–74
Anderson, W. G., 142
Angola, 250, 490, 507
Appalachia, 486
Arbenz, Jacobo, 489–90
Argentina, 489, 490
Arkansas, 63. *See also* Little Rock crisis
"Aryan Brotherhood," 540
Asia, 155, 249, 253, 254, 279. *See also* Southeast Asia
Askew, Ruben, 665
Association of American Law Schools, 627
Atlanta, 154, 594, 686, 718, 720; Maynard Jackson as mayor of, 614–24
Atlanta Committee on Appeal for Human Rights (statement), 117–118
Atlanta Declaration (of NAACP), 82
Attica prisoners, demands and proposals of, 557–59
Attica State Correctional Facility (N.Y.), 503, 519; negotiations, failure of, at, 560–86; prisoners' demands at, 557–59; violence at, 586–90
Ayers, Georgia Jones, at Liberty City (Fla.), 676

Ayers, Thomas G., and Chicago Freedom Movement, 303–10
Azbell, Joe, at Holt Street Baptist Church (Ala.), 51–53

Babylon, United States as, 504, 506
Bacon, Kay, 103, 105–6
Badillo, Herman, and Attica State Correctional Facility, 560–86
Baker, Ella J., 32, 108, 119, 166, 188; advises SNCC, 120–22
Bakke, Allan, 595, 631, 632–33, 650. *See also Regents of the University of California* v. *Allan Bakke*
Baldwin, James, 260
"Ballad of the Landlord" (Hughes), 363–64, 376, 603
Ballantyne, Erna, 602
Baltimore, 286, 287
Bandung (Indonesia) Unity Conference, 36, 249–50
Baraka, Amiri (LeRoi Jones), 239, 247; poem on racial solidarity by, 480–82
Barbee, William, 126
Barkley, Elliot James, 584
Barnett, Ross, 63, 165
Barrett, Ronnie, 510
Basie, Count, 664
Bass, Charlotta, 491
Bass, Rev. Harry, 100
Bates, Daisy, and Little Rock crisis, 97–103
Bates, L. C., 97–98, 100
Batista, Fulgencio, 489
Batson, Ruth, statement to Boston School Committee by, 596–602
Bay Area Soledad Committee (Calif), 545
Belafonte, Harry, 190, 192
Belfrage, Sally, and Mississippi Summer Project of 1964, 180–86
Belgium, 250, 295
Bell, James, 342
Bella, Ahmed Ben, 449
Bennett, Lerone, Jr., 658
Berea College v. *Kentucky*, 69n
Bevel, James, 177, 211, 295, 385
Bhutto, Zulfikar Ali, 449

Bill of Rights, 104
Billups, Rev. Charles, 149
Birmingham (Ala.), 127, 130, 162,
    225, 234, 257, 258, 403, 412,
    418, 424; AMCHR in, 135–37,
    147–51; MLK's letter from,
    153–58; SCLC campaign for so-
    cial change in, 135–37, 147–51,
    293–94; truce agreement be-
    tween protest leaders and white
    businesses of, 159–60
Black Archives History and Research
    Foundation of South Florida,
    663
Black Codes, 642
Black Consciousness, defined, 279
Black Muslims. See Nation of
    Islam
Black Panther Party (BPP) (for Self-
    Defense), 235, 335–36, 337, 503,
    506, 507, 556, 558, 565, 575; at-
    tacks against by police and FBI,
    516, 517, 518–38; Breakfast for
    Children Program, 505; Chicago
    branch of, 501–2, 504, 509–18,
    520–21, 523, 527–28, 529–38;
    founding of, 345–48; protest at
    California State Capitol by, 348–
    361. See also Cleaver, Eldridge;
    COINTELPRO; Hampton, Fred;
    Newton, Huey; Seale, Bobby
Black Panther Party (Ala.) (Lowndes
    County Freedom Organization),
    284–85; organization of, 273–78
Black Power, 238, 246, 247, 285,
    290, 384, 397; Black Conscious-
    ness, development from, 279–
    282; and CORE, 286–87, 312–
    313; MLK's views on, 398–400;
    and SNCC, 281–84
Black Power Conference (Newark,
    1967), 246–47, 442
Black Star Line, 22
Blackstone Rangers, 501; vs. Black
    Panther Party, 529, 531–37
Black university (model), 470–79
Blackwell, Unita, at 1984 Democratic
    National Convention, 710–11
Blair, Ezell, Jr., 114
Bloomfield, Steve, 370

Blossom, Virgil, 98–99, 101
Blyden, Herbert X., 565
Boggs, Grace, 32
Bolling v. Sharpe, 73n
Bond, Blond-Eva, 558
Bond, Julian, 190, 662
Borah, William E., 93
Boston (Mass.), school desegregation
    in, 592–93, 598, 600–03, 607,
    609, 611. See also Dorchester;
    Roxbury
Boston School Committee, 592–93;
    NAACP statement to, 596–602.
    See also Tallulah Morgan et al. v.
    James W. Hennigan et al.
Boynton, Amelia Platts, 204–5, 208–
    209, 210, 229
Boynton, Samuel William, 204, 208,
    209
Bradley, Mary (Amanda), 38
Brady, Tom P., 63; on Brown v.
    Board of Education, 83–94
Brandeis, Louis, 90
Breitman, George, 248
Brewer, Verlina, 524
Briggs, Harry, 32
Briggs et al. v. Elliott et al., 64n, 65n
Britt, Travis, 172–73
Brooklyn. See Ocean Hill–Brownsville
    experiment
Brooks, Gwendolyn, 658, 662; tribute
    to Harold Washington by, 702–4
Brooks, Lila Mae, 431–32
Brown, Ewart, 464
Brown, H. Rap, 451, 456
Brown, Minnijean, 97, 103, 105
Brown, Oliver, 32
Brown et al. v. Board of Education of
    Topeka et al., 28, 82, 107, 591,
    639, 645, 650, 651, 664; reac-
    tions to, 35–36, 62, 231; text of
    U.S. Supreme Court decision
    (May 17, 1954), 64–74
Brown v. Board of Education (Brown
    II), 62, 639; text of U.S. Su-
    preme Court decision (May 31,
    1955), 95–96
Brownell, Herbert, 88
Bryant, Roy, 40
Bryant, C. C., 170

Buckney, Edward, 507, 531n
Bullins, Ed, 243
Bunche, Ralph, 28, 229
Bureau of Refugees, Freedmen, and
    Abandoned Lands. *See* Freed-
    men's Bureau
Burma, 250
Bush, George, 722
Byrne, Jane, 689, 694

Califano v. *Goldfarb*, 648
Califano v. *Webster*, 648, 649
California, Black Panther Party in,
    235, 335, 348–61, 507. *See also*
    Jackson, George; *Regents of the
    University of California* v. *Allan
    Bakke*; San Quentin prison; Sole-
    dad prison; Watts
California State Supreme Court, 626
Calloway, Cab, 664
Campbell, Les, 369, 371
Campbell, Rev. Will, 100
Campbell Soup Company, boycott of,
    707
Carawan, Candie, 209
Carawan, Guy, 209
Carcione, Samuel, 464
Carey, Dr. Barbara, 665
Carmichael, Stokely. *See* Kwame
    Turé
Carter, Bunchy, 549, 556
Caston, Billy Jack, 171, 172
Catholic Archdiocese of Chicago, 308
Catholic Interracial Council, 297
Cavanagh, Jerome, 317, 318, 319,
    326, 327
CCCO. *See* Coordinating Council of
    Community Organizations
Central High School. *See* Little Rock
    crisis
Central Intelligence Agency (CIA),
    489
Champen, Roger, 565
Chaney, James, 168, 420, 706, 710
Charles, Robert, 11–12, 19
Charleston (S.C.), 484
Charlotte (N.C.), 593
Che-Lumumba Club, 539, 543, 548
Cherry, Gwen, 665

Chiang Kai-shek, 489
Chicago, 234, 235, 241, 290, 311–12,
    314, 315, 421, 425, 494, 507;
    African-American community in,
    history of, 658; branch of Black
    Panther Party, 501–2, 504, 509–
    518, 520–21, 523, 527–28, 529–
    538; and Chicago Freedom
    Movement, 303–10; City Hall,
    SCLC demands placed on door
    of, 300–3; Real Estate Board of,
    304, 305–6; and SCLC, 288–89;
    tribute to Harold Washington of,
    702–4; voter registration in,
    687–91; Washington announce-
    ment of mayoral candidacy in,
    691–93; Washington campaign
    in, 694–98; Washington inaugu-
    ral speech in, 698–702
Chicago Association of Commerce
    and Industry, 309
Chicago Board of Education, 302
Chicago Board of Rabbis, 308
Chicago Commission on Human Re-
    lations, 289, 304–5, 306, 307
Chicago Conference on Religion and
    Race, 289; and ten-point agree-
    ment between City of Chicago
    and Chicago Freedom Move-
    ment, 303–10
Chicago Dwelling Association, 301
Chicago Fair Housing Ordinance,
    303–5, 306
Chicago Federation of Labor and In-
    dustrial Union Council, 309
Chicago Freedom Movement, 289,
    383; and Chicago, 303–10
Chicago Housing Authority, 301, 306
Chicago Mortgage Bankers Associa-
    tion, 307, 309
Chicago Plan, and SCLC, 291–300
China, People's Republic of, 30, 31,
    32, 196, 388, 392, 413, 489, 495,
    661; prodemocracy movement
    in, 712–18; Tiananmen Square
    massacre in, 715–17
Chinese, 13, 529
Chinese Revolution, Malcolm X on,
    252

Chisholm, Shirley, 239
Christopher, Warren, 324, 325, 326, 331
Church Committee Report. *See* U.S. Senate's Select Committee to Study Governmental Operations
Church Federation of Greater Chicago, 308
Cicero (Ill.) march, 290, 313–15, 338, 340
Cisler, Walker, 330
Cisneros, Henry G., 661; speech at 1984 Democratic National Convention of, 711–12
Citizens' Councils, 49, 53, 62, 63, 83, 128, 156
Civil Rights Act of 1875, 87, 642
Civil Rights Act of 1957, 204
Civil Rights Act of 1960, 204
Civil Rights Act of 1964, 204, 212, 224, 245, 294, 418, 591, 595; Title I of, 302; Title VII of, 594
Civil Rights Act of 1965, 245
Civil Rights Act of 1966, 302
Civil Rights Acts, 5, 181, 184, 642, 643, 651
Civil Rights Cases, 642, 649–50, 651
Civil Rights Commission, 403
Civil Rights Statutes, 527
Civil War, 3, 37, 85, 86, 228, 484; blacks, status of following, 641–642. *See also* Reconstruction
Civil War Amendments, 642, 643, 647
Clark, Gregory, 541
Clark, James G., Jr., 205, 206, 212, 218, 222
Clark, Kenneth B., 28, 62; on racial prejudice, 74–81
Clark, Mamie, 75n
Clark, Mark, 502, 517, 518, 519, 521–22, 524
Clark, Ramsey, 323, 324, 325, 326, 517
Clark, Richard X., 566, 569–570, 571, 574, 575–76, 577; on Attica violence and aftermath, 586–90
Clay, Cassius Marcellus, Jr. *See* Ali, Muhammad

Cleage, Rev. Albert B., Jr., 248, 253–254, 256, 329–30
Cleaver, Eldridge, 349, 350, 355, 358, 500, 555, 556; arrest of, 360–61; writings of, 335–36
Clement, Kenneth, 339
Clergy and Laymen Concerned about Vietnam, 387
Cleveland (Ohio), 399, 482; Hough neighborhood, 334, 383; Stokes mayoralty campaign in, 338–41
Clifford, J., 90
Clutchette, John, 539, 540, 542, 543, 544, 556
COFO. *See* Council of Federated Organizations
Cohen, Wilbur J., 434, 435
COINTELPRO, 501, 530, 536. *See also* Black Panther Party
Cole, Nat "King," 664
Collins, Charles Wallace, 86
Collins, LeRoy "Too Tight," 38, 220
Colored Independent Party, 491
Comfort, Mark, 356
Commercial Club (Chicago), 309
Commission of Inquiry into the Black Panthers and the Police, report by, 517–28
Communist International, 24
Communist Party, in China, 713, 715
Communist party, in U.S., 23–25
Community Relations Service (CRS) (Justice Department), 323
Congo, Belgian (Zaire), 196, 250, 295, 490
Congress, U.S., 13, 18, 40, 83, 88, 89, 94, 118, 123, 137, 162, 163, 164, 206, 226, 258, 385, 386, 403, 404, 408, 432, 433, 434, 458, 531n, 612, 693, 708; and Civil Rights Acts, 591, 594, 642, 651; and Fourteenth Amendment, 67, 87, 643, 647; and Radical Republicans, 86; and Reconstruction Acts, 642; and voting rights, 207, 234. *See also* House of Representatives; Senate
Congress of African Peoples, 238

Congress of Industrial Organizations (CIO), 90

Congress of Racial Equality (CORE), 116, 176, 218, 235, 236, 246, 258, 261, 279, 280, 310, 312, 315; attacked by Roy Wilkins, Malcolm X on, 258; effects on MLK, 313; and Freedom Rides, 109, 124; internal problems of, 237; programs of, 286–87

Connor, Eugene "Bull," 136, 150, 339, 412, 413, 424, 425

Constitution, U.S., 50, 84, 86, 87, 89, 93, 94, 128, 266, 418, 564, 634, 648; and Black Panther Party, 346, 351; and freedom, 104, 141; ideals in, 142; Preamble to, 1, 232; and racial discrimination, 612, 635, 640, 641, 650; and U.S. Commission on Civil Rights, 179. *See also* Bill of Rights; Equal Protection Clause; Fifteenth Amendment; Fifth Amendment; First Amendment; Fourteenth Amendment; Fourth Amendment; Second Amendment; Thirteenth Amendment

Cook County (Ill.), 525, 527; circuit court of, 306

Cook County Board of Commissioners, 306

Cook County Council of Insured Savings Associations, 307

Cook County Department of Public Aid, 302, 306–7

Coolidge, Calvin, 485

Cooper, Henry, 447

Coordinating Council of Community Organizations (CCCO) (Chicago), 289, 291, 293, 297, 310, 311

CORE. *See* Congress of Racial Equality

Cosmopolitan Chamber of Commerce (Chicago), 309

Council of Federated Organizations (COFO), 166, 167, 168, 181, 183

Council for United Civil Rights Leadership, 259

Covington, Hayden, 450, 451, 456

"Creation-Spell" (Bullins), 243

Crecini, John, 720

Crenshaw, Rev. J. C., 99

CRS. *See* Community Relations Service

Cruikshank case, 87, 88

Cuba, 10, 196, 489

Cuban Revolution, 253

Culberson, George, 324

Culmer, Rev. John E., 665

Cultural Revolution (China), 714

Cumming v. *Richmond County Board of Education*, 70, 90

Cunningham, Edward, 574

Currier, Stephen, and Council for United Civil Rights Leadership, 259

Dade County (Fla.), 663–64, 665, 669, 670, 671, 672, 675, 683, 684, 685, 687

Daley, Richard, 235, 288, 289, 425, 486, 689, 694

Dallas County Voters' League (DCVL) (Ala.), 204, 205, 208–9

Daniels, Jonathan, 420

Danville (Va.), 425

Davis (study), 75n, 76n, 77

Davis, Angela, 483, 491, 556; and prisoners' rights movement, 539–48

Davis, Benjamin, 491

Davis et al. v. *County School Board of Prince Edward County, Virginia, et al.*, 64n, 65n

Davis Medical School. *See Regents of the University of California* v. *Allan Bakke*

Dawkins, Miller, 665

Dawson, Charles, 187

Dawson, Curtis, 171

DCVL. *See* Dallas County Voters' League

Deacons for Defense, 280, 281

Deadwilder, Leonard, 541

Dearmon, Cheryl, 546

Declaration of Independence, 83, 164, 418; slavery implicitly protected by, 640–41

Delaware, 64, 66n, 67, 70n, 72n, 83, 96
Deloria, Vine, 661
Democratic party, 10, 33, 205, 395, 396, 484, 711, 712; and Alabama 203, 217, 275, 276–77, 284; and Chicago, 691, 694; in Cleveland, 334, 340–41; and Declaration of Independence, violation of, 164; and Great Depression, 485; and Gary convention, 496–97; and "Great Society," 383; and Jesse Jackson address to, text of, 705–709; and LCFO, 245, 267, 272, 273; and Mississippi, 168, 178–179, 186–189, 201, 203, 491, 710; and NAACP, 88
Department of Health, Education, and Welfare, 434, 648n
Department of Justice. See Justice Department
Detroit, 27, 30, 236, 257, 260, 288, 290, 330, 385, 404, 686; disorders in, 316–22, 323–32
Detroit Council for Human Rights, 248
Devine, Annie, 187
Dickson, Clarence, 675
Diem, Ngo Dinh, 390, 391, 392, 489
Dienstfrey, Ted, on sit-in movement, 122–24
Diggs, Charles, Jr., 38–39, 239
Dirksen, Everett, 404
Divine, Father, and Peace Mission, 26
Dixiecrats, 203, 485
Doar, John, 173, 324, 325–26, 330, 331
Dominican Republic, 490
Dorchester (Mass.), 598, 601
Dorsey, D. A., 664
Douglass, Frederick, 5, 6, 421, 491
Douglass, Robert, 570
Drake, St. Clair, 658
Dred Scott v. Sandford, 641
Drew, Timothy. See Ali, Noble Drew
Driver, Rev. Z. Z., 100
Drumgo, Fleeta, 539, 540, 542, 543, 544, 556
Du Bois, W. E. B., 8, 9, 14, 15, 16, 21, 33, 192, 239, 477, 483, 491; on Democrats, 495–96; and Niagara Movement, 471–72; on Republican party, 484–85
Dunbar, Walter, 564, 569–70, 577, 581–82, 583, 584, 585
Dunkley, S. Steven, 452, 453
Dunn, Marvin, on Liberty City (Miami) riots, 666–82
Dunne, John, 568, 570, 573, 576, 582
Durham, Richard, 444
Durr, Clifford, 47
DuSable, Jean Baptiste, 702
Duvalier, François, 449
Dylan, Bob, 351
Dymally, Mervyn, and Soledad prison, 549
Dyson, Walter, 441

Eames, Ivan, 464
Eastland, James O., 164, 165, 431, 432, 437; on segregation, 92–93
East St. Louis (Ill.), 19
Eaves, Reginald, 623–24
Eckford, Elizabeth, 97, 100–03, 105, 107
Ecuador, 490
Edlund, John F., 584
Edmonds, Nathaniel, 320
Edwards, Cleveland, 541
Edwards, Dick, 575
Egypt, 18, 195, 196, 369, 410, 411, 449
Einstein, Albert, 713
Eisenhower, Dwight D., 63, 496; administration of, 40, 88, 593–594
Elam, Barbara, 602
Ellison, Ralph, 616
El Salvador, 490
El-Shabazz, El-Hajj Malik. See Malcolm X
Emancipation Proclamation, 36, 62, 410
Embree, Edwin, 31
Endicott (school), 608, 609
Enforcement Act of 1870, 87

Engels, Friedrich, 511
England, 29, 85, 250, 254, 640. *See also* Great Britain
Epton, Bernard, 694
Equal Employment Opportunity Commission (EEOC), 619
Equal Protection Clause (of Fourteenth Amendment), 633, 650
Equal Rights Amendment, 698, 708
Eskridge, Chauncey, 456
Ethiopia, 24, 195
Europe, 12, 20, 33, 369, 474; colonies, revolutions in, 21, 30–31; imperialism of, 17–18, 250
Evans, Rev. Clay, 297
Eve, Arthur O., 558, 560, 561, 562, 565–66, 568–69, 572, 573, 574, 582, 583, 584
Evers, Medgar, 32, 160, 167, 178, 420, 706
Executive Order 11246, 594, 611
Ex parte Virginia, 69n

Faisal Abdel Aziz, 449
Fanon, Frantz, 335, 556
Fard, W. D., 27
Farmer, James, 109, 188, 218, 219, 258, 260
Farrakhan, Louis, 240, 558
Faubus, Orval Eugene, 63, 97, 98, 104
Federal Bureau of Investigation (FBI), 151, 152, 451, 455; and Black Panther Party, 501–2, 518–38; investigates killings in Mississippi, 168; protects Montgomery-to-Selma march, 207; refuses protection to Summer Project volunteers, 182
Federal Deposit Insurance Corporation, 302, 308
Federal Savings and Loan Insurance Corporation, 308
Ferre, Maurice, 686n
Ferretti, Fred, 567
Fields, Rev., U. J., 48
Fifteenth Amendment, 86, 642
Fifth Amendment, 73n
First Amendment, 141, 413, 458, 636, 637

Fitzgerald, Ella, 664
Flagler, Henry M., 663
Florida, 433, 663, 664, 665, 666, 668, 672. *See also* Dade County; Miami; St. Augustine; Tampa
Folley, Zora, 449
Folsom prison, 539
Ford, Henry, 330
Ford, James W., 24
Ford Foundation, 336
Forman, James, 177, 188; on African trip of SNCC, 190–95; on SCLC vs. SNCC, 217–20
Fort, Jeff, 531–35, 536–37
Forte, Sherman, 360–61
Fortune Society, 558
Fourteenth Amendment, 66, 90, 94, 630, 642, 643, 646, 647, 649; and *Bakke* case, 595, 639; consideration of, 67–73; Equal Protection Clause of, 5, 633; ratification of, 86–87; segregation a violation of, 62, 88
Fourth Amendment, 527
Fox, Joseph, 103, 104, 105
France, 19, 29, 250, 253, 391, 414, 449. *See also* French Revolution
Franklin, Rev. C. L., 248
Franklin, John Hope, 640n, 654
Frazier, E. Franklin, 28, 477
Freedmen's Bureau, 642
Freedmen's Bureau Act, 647
Freedom Now Party, 248
Freedom Rides (Riders), 108, 124–127, 130, 134, 135, 138, 141, 166, 231, 424, 441; effects of, 109, 131, 132
Freedom School (Baltimore), 287
French Revoltuion, 251, 254
Fuller, Hoyt, 658

Gaines, Thompson J. "Mike," on Stokes mayoralty campaign, 341–342
Gaines v. *Canada*, 90
Gandhi, Mohandas K., 31, 113, 116, 184, 420, 713
Garcia, Rudy, 568, 575, 582
Gardner, Edward, 660; on voter registration in Chicago, 687–91

Garrity, W. Arthur, 593; on Boston school system, 609–11

Garvey, Marcus, 24, 27, 239, 421; emigration to Africa proposed by, 21–23

Gary, Howard, 665

Gary (Ind.), 334, 339, 399; conference at, 443, 482, 493–99

Gaskin, Florence, 664

Gayle, Addison, Jr., 247

Gayle, W. A., 44

Gebhart et al. v. Belton et al., 64n, 66n

Gendler, Rabbi Everett, 393, 395, 397, 402, 406, 408, 409

General Assembly, of United Nations, 198

Geneva Agreement, 392, 393

Georgia, 19, 45, 92, 133, 138, 140, 163, 164, 212, 384, 389, 408; inequalities in, 117–18. See also Albany Movement; Atlanta; Savannah

Germany, 20, 252. See also West Germany

Ghana, 195, 196, 410, 449, 473

Giap, Vo Nguyen, 555

Gibson, Theodore, 665

Giddings, Paula, on Black Power movement at Howard University, 460–62

Gilberg, Leonard, 146

Girardin, Ray, 317

Gittens, Anthony, 464; on Howard University demonstration, 465–470

GOAL. See Group on Advanced Leadership

Goldman Committee, 589

Goldwater, Barry, 164, 186, 203, 500

Gong Lum v. Rice, 70, 90

Goodman, Andrew, 167–68, 420, 706, 710

Goodman, Mary Ellen, 75n, 76n

Graetz, Robert, 60

Grauman, Lawrence, 450

Gray, Fred, 219

Great Britain, 84, 414. See also England

Greater Miami Chamber of Commerce, 685

"Great Society," 383, 384

Greece, 410, 489, 496

Green, Edith, 188

Green, Ernest, 97, 103, 104–6

Green v. County School Board, 648

Greene, Nathanael, 84

Greenich, Ben, 279

Greensboro (N.C.), 107–8, 424

Gregory, Robin, 441–42, 460–62

Group on Advanced Leadership (GOAL), 248

Guatemala, 489–90

Guevara, Che, 505, 555, 556

Guinea, 250; SNCC visit to, 190–95

Guyana, 241

Haiti, 449

Hall, Linda Bryant, 289–90; on MLK's efforts in Chicago, 310–315

Hall, Prathia, 190

Hall v. Decuir, 90

Hamer, Fannie Lou, 2, 190, 191, 192, 242, 662, 705, 710; on struggle for equal rights, 176–79

Hamilton, Charles V., 262

Hammond, David, 464

Hampton, Fred, 501, 502, 515, 519, 529, 532, 533, 534, 535, 536, 556; murder of, 509, 516, 517, 518, 524–25, 538; organizing ability of, 510–12; speeches of, 504–9

Hampton, Fred, Jr., 509, 515

Hancock, Herbie, 658

Hanrahan, Edward V., 527

Hansen, Bill, 190

Hanson, Warren, 564, 581n

Hardy, John, 172, 173

Hare, Nathan, 464

Harlan, John Marshall, 643–44, 650

Harlem, 26–27, 30, 234, 284, 300, 389, 486, 494

Harrington, Michael, 616

Harris, Abram, 28

Harris, Brenda, 522, 524

Harris, Donald, 190, 246; African trip of, 195–200

Harris, Rutha, 144

Harrison, Hubert, 18, 30

Hartley, Eugene, study by, 77
Harvard College, 637
Hatcher, Richard C., 239, 334, 337, 339, 399; address to 1972 National Black Political Convention, text of, 482–92
Hayes, Curtis, 171, 175
Hayes, Rutherford B., 484
Haynes, Milton, 560
Henderson, John, 590
Henkin, Dan, 325
Hennigan, James W. *See Tallulah Morgan et al.* v. *James W. Hennigan et al.*
Henry, Aaron, 188
Herndon, Angelo, 23
Hershey, Lewis B., 442, 450
Heschel, Rabbi Dr. Abraham Joshua, 408, 409, 709; on moral religious leadership, 393–94
Hicks, Louise Day, 592
Hiroshima, 3, 358n
Hitler, Adolf, 24, 29, 252
Ho Chi Minh, 392, 555
Hodges, Luther, 111
Holiday, Billie, 664
Holmes, Oliver Wendell, 90
Honduras, 490
Hooks, Benjamin, 415
Hoover, Herbert, 485
Hoover, J. Edgar, 501, 502, 529, 535
Hope, John, 6, 9, 28, 29, 31
Horne, Lena, 33
Horowitz, Eugene, 75n
Horowitz, Ruth, 75n, 76n
Hough rebellion (Cleveland), 334, 383
Houlihan, Gerald, 576, 582n
House of Representatives, U.S., 92. *See also* Select House Committee on Crime
Houston, Charles Hamilton, 29, 32, 61, 628, 629
Houston (Tex.), 19
Howard, Charles, 491
Howard University, 28–29, 229, 429, 441–42, 443, 630; *Bakke* case, Law School brief on, text of, 625–30; Gregory, Robin, as homecoming queen of, 460–62;

LBJ's address at, text of, 611–13; students' letter to university president, text of, 462–64; student takeover at, 465–70
Howe, Harold II, 434
Huehn, Elmer, 581
Huff, William Henry, 38
Hughes, Langston, 25, 31, 292, 363–364, 376, 603, 614
Huitt, Ralph K., 434, 435
Hulett, John, 265, 268; on Black Panther Party (Ala.), 273–78
Hull, Lawrence, 85
Human Rights Charter, U.S. violation of, 198
Humphrey, Hubert, 187, 491
Hunt, Frank, 125
Hunter (Hunter-Gault), Charlayne A., on Resurrection City, 426–438
Hurst, E. H., 173, 174
Hutton, Bobby, 352, 353, 355, 356, 357

ICC. *See* Interstate Commerce Commission
Illinois, 514, 516, 518, 527. *See also* Chicago; Cicero march; Cook County; East St. Louis
Illinois Public Aid Commission, 302
India, 18, 30, 31, 113, 250
Indochina, 489, 519
Indonesia, 36
Ingram, Jim, 558
Ink Spots, 664
Interracial Ministerial Alliance (Ark.), 99
Interstate Commerce Commission (ICC), 134, 139, 140, 141, 143
Iran, 489
Ireland, 22, 449
Isaacs, Charles S., on Ocean Hill–Brownsville schools, 362–76
Islam, 27
Israel, 394, 482
Italy, 24

Jackson, Alexander Stephens, 616
Jackson, Frances, 540
Jackson, George, 502, 519, 539, 540,

542–43, 544, 545, 546–48; letter from Soledad prison by, 548–57
Jackson, Georgia, 540, 542, 545, 546
Jackson, Harry, 436, 437
Jackson, Jesse, 239, 241, 297, 385, 414, 428, 658, 660, 710, 711; address to 1984 Democratic convention, text of, 705–9
Jackson, Jimmy Lee, 206, 420
Jackson, Jonathan, 547, 548
Jackson, Mahalia, 658
Jackson, Maynard, 594, 720; inaugural address, text of, 614–18; interview with, 618–24
Jackson, Penny, 540
Jackson, Rev. Ralph, 413
Jackson State College (Miss.), 519
James, C. L. R., 32
Japan, 29, 252, 391
Japanese Americans, internment of, 357
Javits, Jacob, 164
Johns, Ralph, 116
Johns, Vernon, 423
Johnson, Bernice. See Reagon, Bernice
Johnson, Deborah. See Njere, Akua
Johnson, Frank, 219, 220
Johnson, Jack, 449
Johnson, Lyndon B. (L.B.J.), 168, 225, 383, 386, 395, 501; administration of, 384, 490; and affirmative action, 594; black dissatisfaction with, 485, 491, 496; and 1964 Democratic convention, 186, 187; on Detroit riots, 324–25; Howard University address, text of, 611–13; and National Advisory Commission on Civil Disorders, 291, 316; and voting rights legislation, 206, 207
Johnson, Rev. Mordecai, 28, 29
Johnson, Muriel, 432
Johnson, Norman, 720
Johnson Publishing Co., 658
Jones, Charles, 133, 143, 144
Jones, Clarence, 558, 561, 565–66, 570, 571
Jones, Cody, 446
Jones, James, 241

Jones, Johnny, 665
Jones, LeRoi. See Baraka, Amiri
Jones, Mathew, 190
Jones, Mutt, 40
Jordan, Karriema (Theresa) (interview), 376–77
Justice Department, 38, 39, 111, 164, 173, 206, 275, 276, 327, 328, 530n; Community Relations Service (CRS), 323. See also Federal Bureau of Investigation

Kansas, 12, 64, 65n, 70n, 72, 83
Karenga, Maulana Ron, 247
Katzenbach, Nicholas, 206, 220
Kelley, Asa, 145
Kellock, Alan, 370
Kelly, Alonzo, 668
Kennedy, John F., 159, 694, 700, 706; Abernathy praises, 421; administration of, 63, 135, 136, 137, 163, 490, 593–94; assassination of, 186, 248; Birmingham protests supported by, 160–62; black dissatisfaction with, 484, 485, 496; and civil rights legislation, 136–37, 163, 404; elected president, 108–09; Malcolm X critical of, 258–60; and MLK arrest, 136, 151–52; troops used in South by, 63, 160
Kennedy, Robert, 136, 152, 159, 395, 396, 706
Kent State incident (1970), 518, 519, 586
Kentucky, 439, 449–50, 459. See also Louisville
Kenya, 169, 195, 197–98, 250, 253, 410
Kenyatta, Jomo, 197
Kerner, Otto, 291, 316
Kerner Commission, 316, 402, 404, 406, 685. See also National Advisory Commission on Civil Disorders
Kerner Report, 402. See also Report of the National Advisory Commission on Civil Disorders
Kerriem, Elijah. See Muhammad, Elijah

Kershaw, Joe Lang, 665
Keyes case, 609–11
Khrushchev, Nikita, 254
King, A. D., 153, 218–19
King, C. B., 164
King, Coretta Scott, 56, 108, 136, 151–53, 229, 239, 416, 422, 720, 721; introduction to speech by Nelson Mandela, 718–19
King, Rev. Edwin, 188
King, Rev. Dr. Martin Luther, Jr., 2, 37, 108, 119, 122, 123, 128, 151–53, 188, 191, 192, 204, 240, 242, 246, 259, 260, 280, 281, 283, 383, 430, 433, 616, 667, 687, 688, 689, 706, 711, 712; Abernathy on, 419–26; and Albany Movement, 134, 135; assassination of, 237, 238, 386; and Birmingham, 136, 150, 153–58, 404; on Black Power, 397–401; and Chicago, 235, 289–90, 300–303, 311–12, 315; and Cicero march, 313–14; and Cleveland, 338, 339–41; criticized by Adam Clayton Powell, 395–96; and Detroit, 257; "I Have a Dream" speech of, 138, 425, 720–21; "I See the Promised Land" speech of, 409–19; on justice, 717–18; "Letter from Birmingham City Jail," 153–58; on March on Washington, 138, 407, 408, 720; and Memphis, 386; and Montgomery, 48–51, 224, 225, 229, 233, 244, 263; on movement's momentum, 47–48; and NAACP, 384; on nonviolence, 56–60, 112–14, 713; "Our God Is Marching On!" speech of, 224–27; pessimism of, 383–387; and Poor People's Campaign, 237, 385, 386, 402–03; on 1968 presidential election, 395; and radical reconstruction, 236–37, 241; on role of non-blacks in civil rights movement, 406–09; and Selma, 205, 206–7, 211–12, 217, 218, 219, 220, 222, 224–26, 265; on "soul of America," 13; as spiritual leader, 116, 394; "Time to Break Silence" speech of, 387–93; and Vietnam, 236, 384, 387–93, 405; vision of, 656–57, 658–59, 660, 661; and Watts, 345; vs. Roy Wilkins, 257–58
King, Melvin, 602
King, Slater, 144, 164
KKK. *See* Ku Klux Klan
Kluger, Richard, 640n
Knight, Dewey, 665
Knox, Joyce, 675
Knox, Preacher, 171
Koran, Phil, 658
Korea, 32, 104, 182, 252. *See also* South Korea
Kozlowski, Ronald, 581n
Kozol, Jonathan, 364; on teaching in Boston, 603–9
Ku Klux Act of 1871, 87
Ku Klux Klan (KKK), 4, 13, 20, 49, 111, 127, 128, 130, 133, 149, 156, 208, 263, 274, 286, 485, 540, 554, 670
Kunstler, William M., 558, 561, 566, 567, 573, 574, 575, 578
Kyles, Billy, 413

Lafayette, Bernard, and voter registration in Selma, 209–11
Lafayette, Colia Liddell, 209
Lancaster, Burt, 260
Laos, 393
Lasker, Bruno, 75n
Latin America, 253, 279, 490
Lawrence, Brother, 90
Lawrence, James, 85
Lawson, Rev. James M., Jr., 108, 123, 280, 386, 413; nonviolent revolution proposed by, 130–32; statement of SNCC purpose drafted by, 119–20
LCFO. *See* Lowndes County Freedom Organization
Lee, Bernard, 219
Lee, Don L. *See* Madhubuti, Haki
Lee, Rev. George, 40, 170, 420
Lee, Herbert, 167, 173–74
Lefcowitz, Alan, 464
Lenin, V.I., 505, 555, 556

Leonard, George B., on "bloody Sunday," 213–17
Lesher, Steve, 51
Lester, Julius, 176
"Let America Be America Again" (Hughes), 25
Lewis, Art. *See* Lewis, Muriel
Lewis, John, 190, 206, 218, 229, 246; on African trip of SNCC, 195–200; on Kennedy administration position, 137–38, 163–65
Lewis, Muriel, on white sympathizers in Selma, 221–23
Liberia, 195
Liberty City (Miami), 657; 1980 riots in, 667–82
Liberty Party, 495
Lincoln, Abraham, 15, 94, 161, 324, 410, 421, 462, 484, 495, 496
Lindsay, John, 336, 570
Liston, Sonny, 440, 444, 456
Little Rock (Ark.) desegregation crisis, 63, 97–103, 107; roundtable discussion on, 103–6
Liuzzo, Viola, 208, 231, 263, 420, 706
Locher, Ralph, 334
Loeb, Henry, 412, 415
Loggins, Henry Lee, 38
Long, Worth, 210
Long Island City (N.Y.), 577
Loomis, John, 331
Loomis, Suane, 331
Los Angeles, 234, 329, 335, 383; "Committee to Defend the Bill of Rights," 540. *See also* Watts
Louisiana, 87, 170, 212, 227, 280, 287, 421, 643. *See also* Opelousas
Louisiana Purchase, 85, 641
Louisville (Ky.), 459, 593
Love, James, 210
Lowe, Keith, 464
Lowenstein, Allard, 167
Lowndes County (Ala.), 245, 283, 335; SNCC campaign in, 262–68
Lowndes County Christian Movement for Human Rights, 265
Lowndes County Freedom Organization (LCFO), 169, 245, 264, 265, 267, 268, 284, 345, 491; organi-

zation of, 273–78; political pamphlet, text of, 269–72
Lucas, Bob, 315
Lumumba, Patrice, 490
Luthuli, Chief Albert, 721
Lynch, Jack, 449

McCain, Franklin, on sit-in movement, 114–16
McCarthy, Eugene, 395, 396
McCarthy, Joseph, 192, 379
McComb (Miss.), 133, 134, 166, 185; voter registration campaign in, 170–76
McCoy, Rhody, 336–37, 381
McDaniel v. *Barresi*, 647, 648
McDew, Charles, 175, 180
McDuffie, Arthur, 657, 666, 667, 677, 680, 684
McGhee, Jake, 181, 183
McGhee, Silas, 181
McGhee brothers, 182–83, 184
McKissick, Floyd, 246, 280, 281
McLaurin v. *Oklahoma State Regents*, 70, 71
McNamara, Robert, 324
McNeil, Joseph, 114, 115
McReynolds, James, 90
McWorter, Gerald. *See* Alkalimat, Abdul
Maddox, Lester, 384
Madhubuti, Haki (Don L. Lee), 247, 658
Madison, Jim, 323
Mahoney, George P., 286
Mahoney, William, on Freedom Rides, 124–27
Maiorana, Ronald, 577–78
Malcolm X, 191, 229, 234, 237, 242, 335, 421, 440, 485, 493, 500; 1964 African trip of, 169, 196, 197–98; and black nationalism, 244, 245, 246; on international identity of man, 474; "Message to the Grass Roots," text of, 248–61; "To Mississippi Youth," excerpts from, 200–01; tribute to by Sonia Sanchez, 261–62
Mandela, Nelson, 661; background

Mandela, Nelson (*cont.*)
of, 718–19; speech in Atlanta, text of, 720–22
Mandela, Winnie, 718, 719
Mandracchia, John, 367–68
Manns, Adrienne, 464
Manuei, Hoss, 425
Mao Tse-tung, 254, 335, 486, 505, 529, 555, 714
March Against Fear (Miss.), 234, 282
March on Washington, 32, 163, 201, 485, 593; and MLK's "I Have a Dream" speech, 138, 425, 720–721; John Lewis's speech at Lincoln Memorial, excerpts from, 163–65; objectives of, 403–8; organizing of, 258–60
Marks (Miss.), 407
Mars, Rosie, 659
Marshall, Burke, 159
Marshall, John, 85
Marshall, Thurgood, 29, 90; dissent in *Regents of the University of California* v. *Allan Bakke*, text of, 639–51
Martin Luther King, Jr., Center for Nonviolent Social Change, 712
Marx, Karl, 505, 511, 555
Marxist-Leninists, 506, 529
Maryland, 257
Massachusetts. *See* Boston; Dorchester; Roxbury
Massachusetts Commission Against Discrimination, 592, 596
Mau Maus, 253, 537
Maxwell, Doris, 540
Mayer, Steve, 364, 371
Medill, Joseph, 700
Meek, Carrie, 665
Meharry Medical College, 630
Memphis (Tenn.), 7, 385–86, 409–415, 418
Meredith, James, 63, 246; and March Against Fear, 234–35, 282; shooting of, 235, 279–80
Metropolitan Council for Educational Opportunity (METCO) (Boston), 593

Metropolitan Housing and Planning Council (Chicago), 309
MFDP. *See* Mississippi Freedom Democratic Party
MIA. *See* Montgomery Improvement Association
Miami (Fla.), 657–58, 660, 661, 667, 668, 669, 670, 675, 679; history of black community in, 663–66; racial isolation in, 682–87. *See also* Liberty City
Miami-Dade Chamber of Commerce, 685
Michigan, 290, 324, 327–28, 330. *See also* Detroit
Middle East, 284
Milam, J. W., 38, 40
Milam, Leslie, 38
Miller, Alvin, 541
Miller, O. G., 541
Mississippi, 2, 7, 18, 35, 63, 83, 91, 109, 124, 125, 126, 127, 131, 133, 134, 138, 163, 191, 212, 218, 227, 246, 252, 262, 279, 280, 282, 284, 285, 287, 291, 292, 385, 398, 407, 420, 421, 424, 486, 491, 519, 706, 710, 721; brutality in, 37–40, 41–43; Democratic party and, 168, 178–179, 186–89, 201, 203, 491, 710; interracialism in, 180–86; March Against Fear in, 234–35; racial repression in, 179–80; struggle in, 166–69, 200–03; voter registration in, 170–79. *See also* McComb; Marks; Sunflower County; University of Mississippi
Mississippi Freedom Democratic Party (MFDP), 168, 178, 183, 186–89, 203, 491, 710
Mississippi Summer Project, 167–69, 180–81, 245
Missouri, 641
Missouri Compromise, 641
Missouri ex rel. Gaines v. *Canada*, 70
Mitchell, Dennis, 673, 681
Mitchell, Ray Anthony, 672–73, 680, 681
Monterey County (Calif.), 541, 545

Montgomery (Ala.), 37, 59, 130, 234, 424, 657, 659; bus boycott in, 44, 45–47, 48, 49, 50–51, 53, 54–56, 112, 116, 148, 231, 263, 384, 656; civil rights movement in, 127–28; Freedom Riders harassed in, 124–25; march from Selma to, 206, 207–08, 217–20, 224, 225; meaning of movement in, 228–29, 232–33; and Supreme Court, 57, 58, 148
Montgomery Improvement Association (MIA), 58, 128
Moody, Anne, on Emmett Till murder, 41–43
Moore, Amzie, 32, 170
Moore, William, 420
Moors, 17
Morgan, Carl, 221
Morgan, Daniel, 84
Morocco, 17
Morris, Ruth, 216
Morse, Wayne, 188
Moses, Robert, 166, 167, 177, 180, 188, 190, 191, 201; on voter registration campaign in Mississippi, 170–76
Mossadegh, Mohammed, 489
Mothershed, Thelma, 97
Mozambique, 490, 507
Muhammad, Elijah (Elijah Kerriem; Elijah Poole), 27–28, 157, 240, 244, 245, 246, 248, 440, 658
Mulford Act, 358n
Muslims, 157, 440, 457, 474. See also Black Muslims
Mylai massacre (1968), 574, 586

NAACP. See National Association for the Advancement of Colored People
Nabrit, James M., 465; Howard students' letter to, 462–64
N.A.G. See Non-Violent Action Group
Nairobi (Kenya), 494
Nash, Diane, 109, 244–45
Nashville (Tenn.), 6, 109, 117
Nasser, Gamal Abdel, 449

National Advisory Commission on Civil Disorders, 291. See also Kerner Commission
National Association for the Advancement of Colored People 4(NAACP), 29, 32, 33, 35, 89, 90, 99, 108, 110, 111, 114, 116, 120, 123, 143, 147, 148, 160, 167, 170, 229, 246, 258, 384, 592, 593; in Alabama, 135–36; and Albany Movement, 134; "Atlanta Declaration," text of, 82; in Boston, 592; history of, 87–88; leadership of, 16–17; and March on Washington, 137; statement to Boston School Committee by, 596–602; strategy of, 61–62, 107
National Association for Equal Opportunity in Higher Education, 625
National Bar Association, 625
National Black Political Convention (Gary, Ind.), 239, 443, 482, 493–499
National College and University Student Conference, 712
National Guard, 160, 352, 570; and Attica prisoners' uprising, 576, 580–81, 586; and Cicero march, 314–15; and Detroit riots, 319, 320, 321, 322, 326, 327; and Freedom Rides, 125; and Little Rock crisis, 63, 98, 100, 105; and Selma to Montgomery march, 207
National Medical Association, 625
National Urban Coalition, 330
National Urban League (NUL), 137
Nation of Islam, 28, 33, 240, 244, 246, 248, 440, 450, 564, 658. See also Malcolm X; Muhammad, Elijah
Neal, Larry, 247
Neal, Patrice, 540
Newark (N.J.), 236, 321, 323, 385, 442
New Detroit Committee, 330
New Jersey, 321. See also Newark

New Rochelle (N.Y.), 592
Newton, Huey P., 335, 353, 357, 358, 507, 508, 555, 556, 565; on Black Panther patrols, 347–48; and Executive Mandate Number One of Black Panther Party, 349–50, 356; on founding of Black Panther Party, 345–47; legal knowledge of, 351, 355; strategy of, 352
New York City, 336, 338, 368, 373, 385, 421, 429, 564, 570, 686; anti–Vietnam War demonstrations in, 458; Board of Education, 361–62. See also Harlem; Long Island City; Ocean Hill–Brownsville experiment
New York Civil Liberties Union, 379
New York State, 559; Attica Correctional Facility in, 503, 519, 560, 577, 589. See also New Rochelle
New York State Suffrage Association, 491
Niagara Movement, 14–15, 16, 472, 483
Niebuhr, Reinhold, 155
Nixon, E. D., 47, 423
Nixon, Richard M., 108, 395, 486, 496, 500, 554
Njere, Akua (Deborah Johnson), on Black Panther Party, 509–17
Nkrumah, Kwame, 449, 471, 475, 555
Nolen, W. L., 541
Non-Allied Nations conference, 196
Nonviolence, affirmed by Temporary Student Nonviolent Coordinating Committee, 119–20; James Lawson on, 130–32; MLK on, 49–50, 56–60, 112–14; Montgomery bus boycott, 54–56; SCLC economic campaign in Birmingham, 135–37, 149–57, 293–94; student sit-ins, 114–123. See also Alabama Christian Movement for Human Rights; Albany Movement; Chicago Freedom Movement; March on Washington; Selma to Montgomery march; Southern Christian Leadership Conference; Student Nonviolent Coordinating Committee
Non-Violent Action Group (N.A.G.), 124
Norman, Silas, 218
"North Bay Village Murders, The," 672, 680
North Carolina, 23; affirmative action in, 652–53. See also Charlotte; Greensboro; Raleigh Conference
Northeast Regional Conference of the Ladies of Charity, 582n
Northern Negro Grass Roots Leadership Conference, 248
Northern Negro Leadership Conference, 248
Norton, Eleanor Holmes, 661
Norway, 212
NUL. See National Urban League
Nystrom, Sandy, 370

Oakland (Calif.), 335, 337, 350, 353
O.A.A.U. See Organization of Afro-American Unity
OBASI, 658
Ocean Hill–Brownsville experiment (Brooklyn), 336–38, 361, 362–376, 377–82
Office of Economic Opportunity, 302
Ogden, David, 100
Ogden, Rev. Dunbar, Jr., 99, 100
Ohio, 707. See also Cleveland
Oklahoma, 12
Oliver, Rev. C. Herbert, 373
O'Neal, William, 502, 536n
Opelousas (La.), 287
Operation Bootstraps, 287
Operation Breadbasket, 399
Operation Exodus, 593
Operation PUSH, 658, 690
Opportunities Industrialization Centers, 300
Organization of Afro-American Unity (O.A.A.U.), 198, 201
Ortiz, G. I., 569
Oswald, Russell G., and Attica prisoners' uprising, 560, 563, 564, 566, 569, 570, 575, 578, 582, 583, 585, 590; and twenty-eight

points, 567–68; ultimatums presented by, 571–72, 573–74, 576–577
Owens, Robert Quentin, 670

Pack, Nannie, 320
Page, M. S., 142
Paine, Thomas, 84
Painter, Nell Irvin, on affirmative action, 651–55
Pakistan, 250, 449
Pan-Africanist Congress, 197
Paris, Jose, 569, 574
Parker, Mack, 110
Parker, Sammy Dean, 103, 104–6
Parks, Paul, 598, 602
Parks, Rosa L., 49, 51, 52, 229, 423; interview with, 45–47
Patterson, Bill, 491
Pattillo, Melba, 97
Peace Mission, 26
Penn, Barbara, 464
Pennsylvania, 491. See also Philadelphia; Pittsburgh
People's Republic of China. See China
Pepper, Claude, 569
Perón, Juan, 489
Perot, Ruth Turner, 286–87
Peru, 490
Petersen Committee, 530n
Pharr, Kelsey L., Sr., 664
Philadelphia, 234, 300, 385, 686
Philippines, 10
Pittsburgh, 686
Plessy v. Ferguson, 5–6, 29, 69, 71, 90, 643–44, 650, 651, 663; reversed by Brown v. Board of Education, 62, 67, 70, 72
PNAC. See Positive Neighborhood Action Committee
Policy brutality, against Black Panther Party, 516, 517, 518–538. See also Attica State Correctional Facility; COINTELPRO; Detroit; Liberty City
Pollard, Sister, 224
Poole, Elijah. See Muhammad, Elijah
Poor People's Campaign, 237, 385,

386, 387, 402, 403; Charlayne Hunter-Gault on, 426–38
Porter, Albert S., 340
Portugal, 250, 490
Positive Neighborhood Action Committee (Detroit), 319–20
Poverty Program, 388
Powell, Adam Clayton, Jr., 31, 36, 246, 248, 259, 287, 458; confrontational leadership style of, 26–27; criticisms of MLK, 395, 396–97
Powell, Lewis, 631
Power, Joseph, 526–27
Pratt, Jack, 188
President's Commission on Technology, Automation and Economic Progress, 403
Price, Elizabeth, 602
Pritchett, Laurie, 134, 135, 136, 145, 146, 424

Queen, Jesse, 326
Quinn, William, 564

Raby, Al, 311
Racial Imbalance Act, 592
Radical Republicans, 86
Radke, Marian J., study by, 75n, 76n, 77, 78
Railway Mail Association v. Corsi, 647
Rainbow Coalition, 512, 705, 706–7
Raleigh Conference (N.C.), 119, 120–22
Randolph, A. Philip, 19, 30, 32, 84, 137, 229, 258, 259, 260
Range, Athalie, 665
Ray, Gloria, 97
Reagan, Ronald, 351–52, 543, 550, 554, 555, 655, 658, 660, 661, 692, 707
Reaganomics, 692, 697
Reagon, Bernice (Bernice Johnson), on importance of music in Albany movement, 143–45
Reagon, Cordell, 133, 138, 143, 144
Reconstruction, 4, 5, 12, 85, 92, 238, 287, 483, 484, 642
Reconstruction Acts, 642
Red Summer of 1919, 21

Reeb, James, 420
Reed, Andrew, 144
Reed, Willie, 38
Reese, F. D., 205
Reese, Rev. Fred, 229
Reese, George, 173
Reeves, H. E. S., 664
Regents of the University of California v. *Allan Bakke*, amicus curiae brief in, 625–30; Justice Marshall's dissent, 639–51; Supreme Court judgment on, 595, 631–39. *See also Bakke* case
Report of the National Advisory Commission on Civil Disorders, 316–22. *See also* Kerner Report
Republican party, 9, 10, 491, 495, 497; and blacks, 484–85; and Chicago, 697; and Cleveland, 334; and Declaration of Independence, 164; and "Great Society," 383; and LCFO, 272; and Mississippi, 189; and Reconstruction, 483–84
Resurrection City, 386; Charlayne Hunter-Gault on, 426–38
Reuther, Walter, 260
Rhee, Syngman, 489
Rhodesia, 490
Richards, Dona, 190
Richardson, Gloria, 257
Richardson, Judy, 183
Richmond, David, 114
Ricketts, Mrs. Jorunn, 103, 105, 106
Ricks, Willie, 281–82
Rivers, L. Mendel, 450
Roberts, Marie D., 664
Roberts, Terrance, 97
Roberts v. *City of Boston*, 69n
Robeson, Paul, 33, 192, 239, 491
Robinson, Clarence, 181–82, 183–85
Robinson, Jo Ann, on proposed bus reforms in Montgomery, 44–45
Robinson, Reggie, 177
Robinson, Renault, 531n, 688, 689
Robinson, Ruby Doris, 190
Rockefeller, Nelson, 503, 560, 563, 567, 568, 569, 570, 571, 574, 575, 577, 580; statement on Attica prisoners' uprising, 572–73

Rodgers, Carolyn, 658
Roman Empire, 410
Rome, 496
Romney, George, 319, 324, 325, 326
Roosevelt, Franklin, 29, 32, 484, 485, 496, 616, 694, 707
Roosevelt, Teddy, 484
Ross, Emory, 265
Roth, Richard, 558
Roxbury (Mass.), 494, 592, 598, 601, 608
Rush, Bobby, 532, 533, 535, 536
Russell, Bertrand, 447, 448, 457
Russell, Richard, 92, 404
Russell, Stu, 370
Russell Sage Foundation, 426
Russia, 24, 32, 36, 388, 413, 414, 606
Russian Revolution, 251, 254
Rustin, Bayard, 32, 188, 229, 335; on future of civil rights movement, 201–3

Salinger, Pierre, 190
Sanchez, Sonia, 247; tribute to Malcolm X, 261–62
Sanford (associate justice), 90
San Francisco, 458
San Quentin prison (Calif.), 539, 542, 548, 550
Santo Domingo, 473
Sargent Report, 598, 601
Satchel, Ronald, 523, 524
Saudi Arabia, 449
Saunders, Marcia, 665
Savannah (Ga.), 424
School desegregation, in Boston, 592–93, 598, 600–03, 607, 609, 611; in Little Rock, 63, 97–107. *See also Brown* v. *Board of Education*; *Brown II*; Meredith, James; University of Mississippi
Schwartz, Herman, 590
Schwerner, Michael, 167–68, 420, 706, 710
SCLC. *See* Southern Christian Leadership Conference
Scott, James E., 665, 669
Scottsboro Boys, 24
Seale, Bobby, 335, 337, 345, 483, 507, 555, 556, 565, 566; at At-

tica, 567–68; on California State Capitol protest, 348–61
Sears, Barnabas, 526–27
Seay, Rev. Solomon, Jr., 128, 219
Second Amendment, 351
Select House Committee on Crime, 569
Sellers, Cleveland, on Black Power, 279–82
Selma (Ala.), 214–17, 226, 231, 234, 246, 403, 418, 425; march to Montgomery from, 206, 207–8, 217–20, 224, 225; MLK arrested in, 211–12; role of white liberals in, 221–23; struggle in, 204–5, 208–11; violence in, 213–14
Senate, U.S., 92, 93, 258, 612, 708. *See also* U.S. Senate's Select Committee to Study Governmental Operations
Shanker, Albert, 378, 379, 380, 381
Shen Tong, 661; on prodemocracy movement in China, 712–18
Sherman, William Tecumseh, 86, 165
Sherrod, Charles M., 133, 143, 144; and Albany Movement, 138–39; on MFDP, 186–89
Shipper, Harold, 464
Shuman, Jerome, 628–29
Shuttlesworth, Rev. Fred L., 135–36, 147, 148–49, 150, 151, 154
Simpson, Euvester, 178
Simpson-Mazzoli bill, 707
Sipuel v. Oklahoma, 70
Sit-in movement, by students in South, 114–23
Six Claims, The, 13–14
Slaughter-House Cases, 69n, 641–42, 647
Slave Codes, 641, 642
Small Business Administration, 683–84
Smiley, Rev. Glenn, 58
Smith, LaMarr, 40
Smith, Lillian, 433
Smith, Michael, 583
Smitherman, Joe, 221
SNCC. *See* Student Nonviolent Coordinating Committee
Snowden, Frank, 463

Soft Sheen Products Company, Inc., 687–90
Soledad Brothers, 539–40, 541–45, 546
Soledad Brothers Defense Committee, 543
Soledad Brothers Defense Fund, 545
Soledad prison (Calif.), 502, 539, 540, 541, 544, 549, 551, 552, 553
Solidarity Committee, 558
Solomon, Sam B., 664
Sons of the American Revolution, 83
Soto, Tom, 569, 573
South Africa, 2, 3, 167, 197, 250, 285, 295, 410, 473, 490, 719, 720; struggle against apartheid in, 721–22
South America, 284
South Carolina, 64, 65n, 66n, 70n, 83, 212, 287. *See also* Charleston
Southeast Asia, 30, 389, 393, 489
Southern Christian Leadership Conference (SCLC), 108, 112, 119, 120, 125, 134, 147, 204, 279, 290, 310, 395, 396, 415, 419; and Albany, 257; and Birmingham, 135–36, 150–51, 153–54, 159; and Chicago, 288–89, 383; and Chicago Plan, 291–300; and Cleveland, 340, 341; and Mississippi, 235; motto of, 389–90; and nonviolence, 131–32; and Operation Breadbasket, 399; and Poor People's Campaign, 385, 386, 403; and Resurrection City, 428, 431–33, 437; and Selma, 205–6, 208, 211, 212; and Selma to Montgomery march, 207; vs. SNCC, 217–20
Southern Rhodesia, 250
South Korea, 489
South Vietnam, 393, 489
Southwide Student Leadership Conference, 108
Soweto (South Africa), 667
Stalin, Joseph, 24
St. Augustine (Fla.), 425
Stender, Fay, 540, 541–42; George Jackson letter to, 548–57

Stokes, Carl B., 334, 337, 342, 399, 482; and MLK visit to Cleveland, 338–41; mayoralty campaign of, 343–44

Stone, Harlan Fiske, 90

Strauder v. *West Virginia*, 69n

Strider, H. C., 37–38

Student Nonviolent Coordinating Committee (SNCC), 108, 109, 119, 120, 127, 129, 137, 163, 237, 441; African trips of, 190–200; and Albany Movement, 133, 134, 135, 138–39; and Black Panther Party, 235; and Black Power, 235, 281–85; in Lowndes County, 262–63, 265, 266–67; and Mississippi, 133, 166–70, 176, 177, 180, 181, 182, 184–86, 279; position paper on black militancy, 245–46; vs. SCLC, 217–20; and Selma, 205, 206, 207, 208, 209–11; and Vietnam, 236

Subcommittee to the Conference on Fair Housing, 289; agreement between Chicago Freedom Movement and city of Chicago, text of, 303–10

Sugarman, Jule, 616

Sullens, Frederick, on *Brown* v. *Board of Education*, 91–92

Sullivan Act, 185

Summer Project. *See* Mississippi Summer Project

Sunflower County (Miss.), 431

Supreme Court, U.S., 6, 40, 50, 92, 93, 94, 110, 124, 209, 230, 457, 598, 663; amicus curiae brief received in *Regents of the University of California* v. *Allan Bakke*, 625–630; and *Brown et al.* v. *Board of Education of Topeka et al.*, 35, 62, 64–74, 83, 107, 591–92; and *Brown* v. *Board of Education (Brown II)*, 95–96; dissent on *Regents of the University of California* v. *Allan Bakke*, 639–51; and Fourteenth Amendment, 87; judgment on *Regents of the University of California* v. *Allan Bakke*,

595, 631–39; and Montgomery, 57, 58, 148; and *Plessy* v. *Ferguson*, 90; power of, 88–89; and Reconstruction, 5

Sussman, Morton, 455

Sutherland, Bill, 32

Swann v. *Charlotte-Mecklenberg Board of Education*, 647–48

Sweatt v. *Painter*, 70, 71

Taft, Seth, 334, 344

Taft, William Howard, 90, 484

Taiwan, 489

Talbort, Bobby, 175

Tallulah Morgan et al. v. *James W. Hennigan et al.*, 609–11

Tambo, Oliver, 720

Tampa (Fla.), 593

Tamu, 540

Tanzania, 197

Taylor, Andress, 464

Temporary Student Nonviolent Coordinating Committee, statement of purpose, text of, 119–20

Tennessee, 86, 279, 285, 291. *See also* Memphis; Nashville

Tepper, Julian, 580

Terrell, Ernie "The Octopus," 445

Terrell, Robert, 279

Texas, 85, 450, 708. *See also* Houston

Thailand, 393

Third World, 279, 471, 489, 490, 495, 499

Thirteenth Amendment, 86, 642

Thomas, Mattie, 320

Thompson, Louise, 24

Thorne, John, 547

Throckmorton, John L., 320, 321

Thurmond, Strom, 165

Tianammen Square massacre (Beijing, China), 712, 713, 715–17

Tilden, Samuel, 484

Till, Emmett Louis, 107, 176, 239; editorial on, 39–41; murder of, 37–39, 41–43

Tójó, Hideki, 252

Toomey, R. E. S., 664

Torres, Dolores, on Ocean Hill–Brownsville experiment, 361–62

Touré, Sékou, 192–95

Trager, Helen G., study by, 75n, 76n, 77
Travis, Brenda, 173, 174–75
Trotter, William Monroe, 14, 15, 16, 17
Truman, Harry, 32, 88, 496, 644; administration of, 593–94
Tucker, Warren, 352, 353, 355, 359
Turé, Kwame (Stokely Carmichael), 218, 229, 235, 280; and Black Power as slogan, 246, 281–82, 312, 398; on Black Power, meaning of, 282–86; and SNCC voting struggle in Lowndes County, 262–68
Turner, Henry McNeal, 11
Turner, Nat, 421
Tutu, Archbishop Desmond, 721

UFT. See United Federation of Teachers
Ujamaa, 465
UJO. See United Jewish Organizations v. Carey
UNIA. See Universal Negro Improvement Association
Union of American Hebrew Congregations, 308
United Federation of Teachers (UFT), 336, 337, 368, 369, 371, 372–75, 377, 378, 379, 381
United Fruit Company, 490
United Jewish Organizations v. Carey, 648
United Nations (U.N.), 196, 200, 346, 490; General Assembly of, 198
United Pastors, 340
United States, in "cold war," 36; Communist Party in, 23–25; doctors in, 629–30; exports of, 414; and Guinea, 190; and Human Rights Charter, 198; in Korea, 32; lawyers in, 627–29; Malcolm X on violence in, 252; racial backlash in, 500; structure of injustice in, 194; unequal treatment of blacks in, statistics on, 645–46; urban warfare in, 385; in Vietnam, 234, 284, 357n,
358n, 384, 385, 387–93, 440, 458; violence in, 252. See also Congress, U.S.; Constitution, U.S.; Supreme Court
United States Code, 527
Universal Negro Improvement Association (UNIA), 21, 239
University of Alabama, 160
University of California at Davis, 595
University of Californina at Los Angeles, 626
University of Mississippi, 63, 180, 234–35
Urban Coalition, 404
Urban League, 246
Urban Renewal program, 307
U.S. Commission on Civil Rights (reports), 179–80, 682–87
U.S. v. Cruikshank. See Cruikshank case
U.S. Postal Service, 684
U.S. Senate's Select Committee to Study Governmental Operations, excerpts from report by, 529–38

Vance, Cyrus, 325, 326, 327, 329–30
Vance, Gay, 327
Vann, Albert, 367, 368
Varela, Maria, 176
Veterans Administration Medical Center, 684
Veterans of Foreign Wars, 450
Vietnam, 196, 220, 236, 237, 273, 316, 402, 405, 444, 445, 447, 448, 456, 459, 465, 473, 489, 519, 537, 553; U.S. in, 234, 284, 357n, 358n, 384, 385, 387–93, 440, 458. See also South Vietnam
Virginia, 64, 65n, 66n, 70n, 83, 124–125, 257, 429, 491, 707. See also Danville
Virginia v. Rives, 69n
Voter registration, in Alabama, 163, 204, 205, 206; in Chicago, 687–691; in Lowndes County, 262–268; in Mississippi, 170–79; in Selma, 209–11. See also Dallas County Voters League; Lowndes County Freedom Organization
Voting Rights Act, 708, 711

Voting Rights Act of 1965, 208, 234, 266, 383, 591

Walker, Margaret, 658
Walker, Rosa, 147, 148–49
Walker, W. O., 339
Walker, Wyatt T., 151, 152
Wallace, George C., 165, 225, 226, 277, 425, 500; attempts to defy court-ordered desegregation, 63, 137, 160
Walls, Carlotta, 97
Warren, Earl, 64, 95
Washington, Booker T., 5, 14–15, 90–91, 472, 484, 664
Washington, George, 84
Washington, Harold, 241, 658–59, 660, 662; announces Chicago mayoral candidacy, 691–93; campaign leaflet, excerpts from, 694–98; inaugural speech of, 698–702; tribute to by Gwendolyn Brooks, 702–4
Washington, D.C., 350. See also March on Washington
Waters, Muddy, 658
Watkins, Hollis, 171, 175
Watts (Calif.), 234, 287, 335, 345, 383, 494, 667
Wells-Barnett, Ida B., 7, 9, 11, 16, 17, 239
West Germany, 414
Weusi, Nabowiah. See Jordan, Karriema
White, Charles, 658
White, Robert, 191
White House Conference on Civil Rights, 404
Whither Solid South (Collins), 86–87
Wicker, Tom, 558, 567, 570, 571, 573, 575, 578, 579–80
Wilkins, Roger, 290, 308; on Detroit riots, 323–32
Wilkins, Roy, 137, 229, 246, 259,

280, 281, 462–63, 517; vs. MLK, 257–58
Williams, Geraldine, on Cleveland mayoralty campaign of Carl Stokes, 343–44
Williams, Henry, 578, 579
Williams, Hosea, 206, 219, 424, 428, 433–35
Williams, Inez, 540
Williams, John Bell, 83
Williams, Mary Lucy, 56
Williams, Robert F., 35–36, 107, 130; on violence, 110–12
Wilson, Lionel, 337
Wilson, Woodrow, 18, 484, 644
Wise, Stanley, 280
Women's Political Council (Ala.), 44–45
Woods, Robin, 103, 104–5
Woodward, C. Vann, 640n
World War I, 17–18, 19–20, 21, 30
World War II, 29–30, 32, 36, 104, 333, 357n
Wormley, Stanton, 463
Worthy, William, 248
Wright, Mose, 40
Wright, Richard, 23–24, 658

Young, Andrew, 219, 720
Young, Whitney, 137, 246, 259, 280, 281, 462–63
Younge, Sammy, 441
Young Lords, 512, 558, 574, 575
Young Negroes' Cooperative League, 120
Young Patriots, 512
Youth March for Integration, 122–23

Zaire. See Congo, Belgian
Zambia, 195, 197
Zellner, Robert, 175, 183–86; on white involvement in SNCC, 127–30